Flying in the Land of Sand and Sun

Flying in the Land of Sand and Sun

The Land of Mystery and Intrigue

by **James D. Fox**
CFII/ATP JETSTAR, G-I, G-II, G-III

COPYRIGHT © 2013 BY JAMES D. FOX.

LIBRARY OF CONGRESS CONTROL NUMBER:		2013901486
ISBN:	HARDCOVER	978-1-4797-8507-0
	SOFTCOVER	978-1-4797-8506-3
	EBOOK	978-1-4797-8508-7

This book was printed in the United States of America.

To order additional copies of this book, contact:
Xlibris Corporation
1-888-795-4274
www.Xlibris.com
Orders@Xlibris.com
85114

DEDICATION

To my family and friends that pushed until this manuscript was finished.

CONTENTS

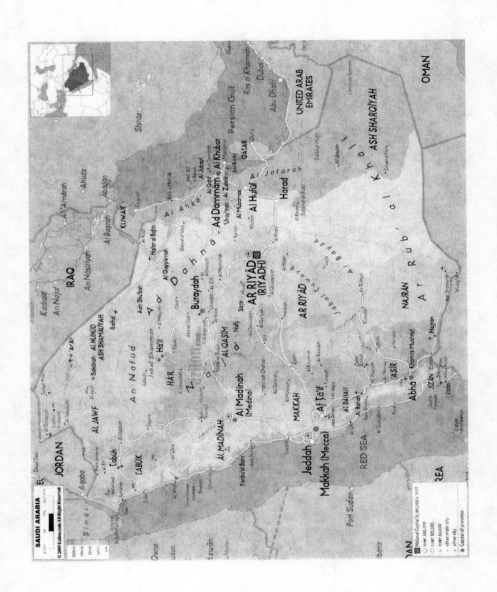

Preface

The year of 1986 was a big year for me. I started a new hobby (golf), chose to retire early from my corporate aviation job, married my childhood sweetheart, and accepted a new job in Saudi Arabia. I started golf lessons in January, decided to take early retirement in June, accepted a job offer in Saudi Arabia in July, got married on August 16, retired on the last Friday in August, and reported for duty in Riyadh the following Monday. I stopped on Saturday in London to play a round of golf.

Getting a job was something new for me. I had worked for one company for thirty-eight years, so my experience at searching for a job was lacking. One day, I came back to the pilots' office on the second floor after visiting with the mechanics down on the first floor. Someone had placed a clipping from a magazine in my inbox. It was an advertisement for a Gulfstream pilot!

I guess some of my discomfort with my present boss had gotten to someone's ear, and that person decided to help me out with another job. It wasn't altogether my boss that I wanted to get away from, but just a change in direction. In less than three years, I would be forced to retire anyway—the old sixty-year-old rule for pilots. I was in the mood to look over into that other green pasture.

The ad was from a company in Saudi Arabia! Wow, that certainly sounded like an adventure. I had never been across the Atlantic in my travels, and to go all the way, deep into the Middle East, was certainly more than just changing jobs. At the same time, Exxon was offering yet again the "golden parachute" for those that wanted to retire early, and that was a temptation. They were offering me a twenty-five-thousand-dollar bonus and the same benefits that I would accrue when I became sixty years old. The bonus was not such a huge amount, but with my retirement, it meant that I really wouldn't have to work anymore if I didn't want to.

Well, I wasn't ready to quit flying, so why not take the retirement and keep flying? My buddy Brent Crabe was shocked when he saw that I was going to answer the ad.

"Hey, Fox, you're not really serious, are you?"

"Yeah, why not? I'm about to get married, and if my new bride agrees, then why not?"

The conversation was longer, but the end result was a phone call to the headhunter in Portland, Oregon, that placed the ad. They were very anxious to get my resume. *Hmm, I wonder if that's a good sign.*

Brent had been trying to talk me out of my idea of early retirement since I first started showing signs of leaving. Brent was twenty years my junior, but we were having a lot of fun together. I was living alone and able to play golf any day that I wasn't flying. At that time in my flying career, trips came up only about once a week for two days, so there was a lot of time for golf. I guess he hated to lose his golfing partner.

Since the Portland people showed such interest, I thought maybe I should check around and see what I might be getting into. The company used Universal Weather for some of the services that they performed all over the world, so I called John Adell for possible information.

"Hello, John, this is Jim Fox. How ya' doin'?"

"I'm doing fine, Jim. What can I do for you?"

John was near the top of Universal Weather, had been for several years. We were not close friends, but he knew me and my company for a long time. Universal Weather did more than just provide weather information. They made flight plans, over flight permits in foreign countries, arranged hotel accommodations, and provided fueling, catering, and anything else that an aircraft crew might need.

"Say, John, do you happen to know anything about a company in Saudi Arabia called GAMA?"

"Well, I guess so. We do a lot of business with them. Why do you ask?"

"Well, they're advertising for a Gulfstream pilot, and I might be interested."

"Jim, the chief pilot over there is a fellow named Mohammed Hanno, and he's a good friend of mine. So if you want the job, then just let me know, and I'll call him, and you will get the job, okay?"

"Hey, that's great."

"Jim, does that mean you're leaving the company?"

"Yeah, John, it's time for me to be moving on."

"What's the problem, Jim, you having *personal* problems?"

"Yeah, you know the guy, and life is too short to put up with the jerk."

"Yeah, I know. Now if you want this job, then just let me know, okay?"

"Okay, John, that's a deal. When I make up my mind, I'll call you."

I told the people in Portland that I would take the job, and they sent me to the doctors for a medical exam and all kinds of shots. It looks like I'm on the way. The medical tests were all satisfactory, and I'm waiting on a date and airline tickets. Not so fast. I got a call from someone called Newbiggen, and he told me that I was not acceptable! He said he was in charge of hiring new pilots, and he deemed that I was not acceptable.

This was after all the medical tests and shots. I called John.

"John, this is Jim Fox."

"Hi, Jim, what can I do for you?

"John, I accepted that job in Saudi Arabia, and now I get a call from some guy named Newbiggen, and he says I'm not acceptable. I don't know what his objection is. I have all the qualifications they listed."

"Oh, Jim, I know that guy Newbiggen, he's a jerk. Now do you want the job?"

"Well, yeah, that's what I signed up for."

"Okay, just stand by, I'll call Mohammed Hanno, and we'll get this straightened out."

Within an hour, I received a call from Mohammed Hanno. He wanted me over there on the next flight. I told him that I couldn't leave until my retirement was approved, and that meant the first of September. He was disappointed, but he agreed. He seemed real upset about the Newbiggen thing. I found out later it was just another underhanded way that many things were done in the Land of Sand and Sun. Newbiggen was a Brit, and he was still looking for another Brit to apply for the job—either that, or he was not getting his *baksheesh* (under-the-table pay).

And that's the way it happened. GAMA was very short of pilots, and they were about to lose another that had been caught bringing in a case of booze. I found out later that Mohammed wanted me there in a hurry because he was getting married and wanted to leave on his honeymoon!

My idea of what to expect when I arrived in Riyadh was something like you might remember from an old Bob Hope and Bing Crosby movie. I expected there to be open bazaars and camel caravans moving slowly through the dusty streets. I had heard that it was very hot and there was a lot of sand; beyond that, I didn't have the slightest idea what to expect. Perhaps I was like most of my American contemporaries who knew little or nothing of that mysterious land.

In preparation to making the big change in my life, I had tried to prepare for what I was going to find there by talking to everyone that I could find that had lived in Saudi Arabia. Oddly enough, the story related by all I talked to was remarkably the same except for one. My advisors were almost unanimous that it was a great place to work, save money, and travel, and they all left the Kingdom for the same reason. Westerners are encouraged to remove their children by the age of fifteen years of age[1] or about the ninth grade of school. Everyone, except one, told me they left when they had to face the decision of staying without their children. They came home to keep from breaking up their family.

---

[1] It's more than just an encouragement. No schooling is provided or allowed in the Kingdom for the ninth grade and beyond for the children of foreigners. If an individual, for the sake of discussion, wanted to keep his children in the Kingdom without sending them to school, then I'm quite sure that a "new" excuse would be invented to make sure the children didn't stay. It is generally assumed that the underlying reason for this is that the *Mataween* (religious police) don't want their young people fraternizing with that age of foreigners. If the foreigners accept Islam, then these rules don't apply.

The one exception to all of the above was a pilot working for FlightSafety as a simulator instructor in Savannah. I learned he had *misrepresented* himself to the Saudis as a flight instructor with much experience. Once he was in the Kingdom, it was soon discovered that he wasn't what he claimed to be, and so he was issued papers to leave. He was just one of the several examples of pilots that I met while working in Saudi Arabia. The simulator instructor had his own reasons to lie when sending his resume. One of his reasons was to get away from a bad marriage. Another reason was to almost triple his salary. The Saudis, his employers, found him out and sent him home. After his return, he bad-mouthed the country, the people he lied to, and the people he worked with. After all, he had to have a story for anyone that asked to justify his short stay in the Kingdom. I saw this same story repeated several times while I was there. For many, it was a place to hide, to replace a job that had disappeared in another part of the world, to run away from a bad love affair, or perhaps just a chance to improve on what they were leaving behind.

Please don't think of this as a blanket indictment of all those that work overseas, but rather think of this: there are many good reasons for taking overseas employment. The adventurous spirit is just below the surface of many like me, and once the veil of mystery has been pierced, then the prospect of working overseas in an unknown land becomes a viable option. In most cases, not all, the individual can save a good deal of money. A worker can actually work for a smaller salary and still save more money in a couple of years overseas than he can save in several years back at home wherever home is. The reason is taxes. Expatriates pay no taxes to Saudi Arabia, and their home countries offer some measure of relief from the taxes back home. In the case of USA, the first seventy-thousand-dollar foreign pay is tax exempt!

The Kingdom of Saudi Arabia is a foreign country that has recently become very wealthy and wants to spend a part of its wealth to come forward into the ode modern world. Saudi Arabia didn't exist as a country until 1932. Theirs was a country to be taken advantage of by the more sophisticated countries of the world. The Saudis were tribes of Bedouins (Bed-oh-wins) that were the nomadic rulers of the very harsh environment. They were traders that did very well with very little to trade.

The story of the Saudis' wealth goes like this. Old King Saud contracted with the British to drill for water. After the Brits had drilled a few water wells, suddenly, they wanted to make a long-term exclusive drilling contract with the Saudis. The king got suspicious and contacted the Americans to do some drilling. The Americans discovered what the Brits had found but had kept secret oil. So the king made the exclusive drilling contract with the Americans (Standard Oil or Exxon).

The Saudis have their problems, just as every other country or groups of people. My stories of the time I spent in the Kingdom are personal experiences that are recounted here because of the general interest shown by people I have met that want to know more about, the Land of Sand and Sun, where there are no tourists, and is the seat of many mysteries!

This book is my effort to pass along part of what I learned about the people there. It is compiled from writings, which I did while living there, in the form of so-called dispatches sent back to friends and family in America. In some cases, the dispatches needed to be explained or expanded later, which I did by adding "afterthoughts" to the end. There are also letters from my wife that helped to explain her point of view. Newspaper clippings, Medevac memos, and magazine clippings have been included as well. I have tried to give the reader as complete a picture as possible of what I learned in the land of mystery.

You should keep in mind that my remarks about the Islamic religion state what I learned from talking to believers and reading the daily newspaper, *The Arab News*, which carried a full page every day on the Quran (Koran).

Whatever, it's all true . . . well, from my point of view.

Resume of James D. Fox

Date: —July 3, 1986

Address: —22715 Imperial Valley Drive, Apartment 1415
                  Houston, Texas 77073
                  —713-821-7535 (Home)
                  —713-443-0700 (Bus)

Date of Birth: —January 3, 1929

Certificates: —Airline Transport Pilot #1005120
                  —Type Ratings: G159, G1159, L1329
                  —Flight Instructor (CFII): SEL, MEL
                  —Commercial Privileges SEL
                  —First Class Medical, May 5, 1986 (No Waivers)
                  —PIC (24 month) Check completed, April 24, 1986

Flying Exp: —Total flying: Thirty-nine years
                  —Multi-Engine Turbo-Jet: Twenty years
                  —G159: PIC 1.5 years, 1,000 hrs
                  —L1329: PIC sixteen years, 7,000 hrs
                  —G1159: PIC six years 3,000 hrs

Employment

History: —June 6, 1948 to present time with the same company

Original company name, Humble Oil & Refining Co. Present company name, Exxon Company USA. The first eighteen years, I was employed in the production department, civil engineering division. The last twenty years, I have been employed in the aviation division, located in Houston, Texas. My experience within the aviation division has been the transportation of corporate executives in domestic and international travel. My flying career has been accident free. My departure from this company is by voluntary early retirement.

Education: Civilian: High School, graduated 1946, Corona, New Mexico.
130 Hours college credits in civil engineering and electronics. No degree was taken.

— Military: Artillery familiarization course, artillery career course, command and general staff college, University of Armed Forces Institute, logistics and management career course. Graduated from all the above plus others of only short duration.

Military: —   Career spanned thirty-eight years, including US Army, Texas, National Guard and US Army Reserve. My branch was the artillery, with specialties in communications and survey. My last rank was lieutenant colonel.

My Mentors

At forty-five thousand feet, the outside air temperature is—37°C, and when you are traveling at .82 Mach, the temperature rise of the aircraft skin is +28°C. What does that mean? Well, it means that the air outside is very cold, but the object passing through that very cold air heats up more and more as the speed increases.

But so what? We learned that early in ground school about flying jets into the stratosphere, and in those days, long ago, it was startling information. Now flying high and fast has lost a lot of its mystery, and such little tidbits of information are no longer considered even interesting.

Numbers, irrelevant information, characters from the past, humorous incidents, and even the meaning of life are just some of the things that can pass though your mind in random order while staring out the pilot's DV window at cruise altitude.

On a clear night, it's easy to get the feeling that you can see forever. The sky is black but freckled with tiny points of light. What are they really? The ground is black but also speckled with tiny points of light. That's something peculiar about flying at night, the different view from high altitudes compared to the view from low altitudes.

Below ten thousand feet, the earth can be ominously black, a void, dark nothing. What lights that are down there are not seen until you are fairly nearby. But at the higher altitudes, it seems that the ground below is thick with lights. Even in parts of the country where you think the habitation is scarce, there are pinpoints of light everywhere. Isn't that interesting? Of course the higher your viewpoint, the greater your viewing area. Maybe it's just an illusion, an optical illusion, a trick on the pilot that has little to do but look out the window and wonder about such things.

Is it boring, you ask? Oh no, far from it, not for me at least. On an eight-and-a-half-hour flight from Riyadh to Bangkok, there are seven hours that the captain will find himself with little to do. First, you climb to cruise altitude, level off, and that takes about twenty-one minutes. Hours later, you push the nose over and descend to land, and that takes about twenty minutes. So what does a guy do for the time in between? The answer won't be found in Hollywood. I can assure you.

The copilot handles the communication and navigation. The autopilot flies the aircraft, so what is left for the captain to do but look out the window and ponder the small and large things of life.

Flying, what a joy, what a pleasure, what a wonderful way for a man to spend his time! And just think he gets paid for it as well. How could all this be? How could this happen to a kid with such humble beginnings? Perhaps it depends on the viewing area of the person with the vision.

FLASHBACK: LATE SPRING OF 1947

"Jimmie, I want you to think seriously about going on with your flying," Lt. T. E. Kane, my flight instructor, was saying.

"Aw, Mr. Kane, there are thousands of pilots coming out of the military with thousands of hours of flying time, and I'm having a hard time just getting thirty-five hours for my private license. I wouldn't have a chance against those guys, and besides, they have multiengine time. I could never get a job flying airplanes with that kind of competition.

"Sure, you could, Jimmie, you just have to keep trying. It'll happen, just don't quit trying," Mr. Kane insisted.

But it was no use; in 1947, I was eighteen years old, and my viewpoint was from low on the totem pole. I couldn't see what my flight instructor could see.

Lt. T. E. Kane had been a barnstormer in the years preceding World War II and then became an instructor for the US Army Air Corps when the war came nearer. He was a great pilot and friend, but I couldn't see what he saw.

Working at the airport when I wasn't in class at Hardin Junior College was slowly moving me toward my goal of a pilot's license. But it didn't leave me any time for making any money. I was broke and tired of being broke.

Colonel Gilchrist, the owner of the little airport with grass runways and a flying school, had been willing to give me one and a half hours of flying time in a J3 Cub airplane in exchange for my servicing his fleet of aircraft. I worked from sunup till dark on Saturday and Sunday and from noon till dark on Monday, Wednesday, and Friday.

I had agreed to the deal back in February when I first started, but in my enthusiasm, I didn't reserve enough time to make any money. A fellow needs some money sometimes. It didn't take much then for a fellow to survive, but having just a little was hard to come by.

I lived with my folks, was attending college, and had no car. We lived about five miles out of town, and I rode the high school bus to college on Tuesdays and Thursdays. Those were the days that I went to class all day long. On Mondays, Wednesday, and Friday, I borrowed the family car, a '39 Chevy. When you don't have money and there are things that you want to do, then you must become inventive.

Learning to fly was what I wanted to do, but in my youth, there was no long-range plan. It was just something that *I really wanted to do.* There had been no plan, and there was no money. I had to get inventive again.

This situation led me to tell Mr. Kane that I was leaving my no-pay job for something that would put some cash in by pocket (I always called him Mr. Kane even though he still wore the leather jacket with the name tag that said Lt. Kane. Since I had never been in the military, I just felt a little uncomfortable calling him anything but mister.).

Lieutenant Kane could not have known my situation. My father was in poor health, and I felt guilty about not being able to help at home. My mother and older sisters had insisted on my going to college, and as the second semester drew to an end, the well was running dry.

Mr. Kane saw a great number of young men trying to learn to fly airplanes. It was his business before the war, during the war, and now on the GI Bill. There will soon be pilots numbered in the thousands. The FAA must have thought that every young man in the country was going to be a pilot because they issued pilot certificate numbers in blocks instead of individually. When I finally received my license, it had a number of more than one million, even though they had not actually issued half that number.

Yes, Mr. Kane had watched the wanabes reach for the brass ring. Some missed it, some grabbed it and then dropped it, but only a few were able and willing to go all the way. He thought he saw in me one that could go all the way.

Wouldn't I like to be able to see Mr. (Lieutenant) Kane tonight and show him his vision was true? I had made it all the way, but my mentor never got to see it happen. Is there a son, who, after arriving at some level of accomplishment, likes to show his father what had been done? As fathers, we know how we long for our sons to do well. I don't mean money; I mean happiness, and doing what you love to do is not work at all.

Mr. Kane might say, "Well, Jimmie, isn't this something? You know I never got to fly a jet. Tell me what it feels like."

"Mr. Kane, it's really great. You know the first jet that I ever flew was back in the 1960s, and you should have been there. My instructor was Art Hanson, the Lockheed test pilot that had flown the FAA certification on the Lockheed JetStar which we were in."

"We lined up on runway 12 at Hobby Airport there in Houston, and he told me to push the throttles up all the way to the firewall. I wasn't nervous at all, just excited as I took the four power levers in my right hand and moved them all the way to the stops."

"You know, Mr. Kane, jets don't accelerate as fast as a prop plane, but they don't ever seem to quit. Before we had used a quarter mile of runway, I was being pushed back into my seat, and we hadn't even got started good. It was like being a kid in a runaway wagon going down a steep hill. I couldn't hold on, and I couldn't turn loose."

"Rotate!" Art called out.

"I pulled back on the yoke, and the nose came up smooth and easy. At five degrees on the flight director, I stopped the nose and held it there. Mr. Kane, that JetStar just kept on accelerating."

"I wasn't fifty feet in the air on my first takeoff in a jet, and Art, the instructor, reached over and pulled the number 1 engine back to idle. The jet yawed to the dead engine, and I reacted with right rudder to hold it straight."

"Well, Jimmie, how does that feel?" Art smiled as he spoke.

"Not too bad," I replied. "I got three more [engines]!" said the excited and smiling kid.

With that reply, my instructor reached up and pulled back number 2 engine back to idle, and there was a hard lurch to the left, harder than before. My right leg was fully extended trying to hold the JetStar straight. Art just watched as I struggled with the four-engine jet. We had two dead engines on the left and two good engines on the right developing full power. Iwas on the edge of a maneuver, which the FAA stopped using about that time because of the fatal consequences. If I let that left wing get down just a little bit more, the result would be on the six o'clock news.

Art was no longer smiling as he spoke. "Well, Jimmie, how does it feel now?" There must have been a strain in my voice as I answered. "It's okay, Art, but don't pull any more back!"

"Art watched me a moment longer and saw that I was rolling in right aileron and the right wing was going down. The aircraft was stable, and it was still accelerating!"

"Okay, Jimmie, let that be a lesson to you. You got in this bird, set yourself down, and you never adjusted your seat or your rudder pedals. If you weren't such a long-legged peckerwood, you wouldn't have been able to hold it. Now next time, get your seat and rudders adjusted before you ever move the aircraft."

"Art was a little guy, probably about five foot nine or ten, and he let me learn a good lesson the first time out. There were a lot more things that I learned from Art before our short time together was over. He was like you, Mr. Kane; he seemed to enjoy showing me how to do my job better. I think it must be what any good pilot would like to do, that is, pass along what he has learned to the new guy.

"You know, Mr. Kane, it was you, Bill Wheeler, Art Hanson, Ken Brace, and others that put me in this seat. You guys have saved my life many times over, and I have tried to pass it along just as you did for me."

At this point I think, Mr. (Lieutenant) Kane would give me one of Smilin' Jack smiles with a wink and a nod of his head.

1986

THE DESERT FOX LEAVES FOR SAUDI ARABIA

Just as promised, here is the first newsletter from the Middle East. Hopefully, it will not be my last.

One of my first observations is that pilots here don't seem to enjoy longevity. One of the Gulfstream[2] pilots is in serious jeopardy as I speak. He will be going home the October 13. He was caught trying to smuggle in a case of whiskey.

Well, let us not start in the middle, but rather the beginning. Of course, the adventure began upon my arrival in England. I will not bore you with what you already know about England, but rather just my first impressions of a new world. To begin with, the airport at Gatwick was at first glance very "suburban" in its appearance out the side window of the DC-10. That is, it seemed more country than city. Perhaps *unsophisticated* would be a better word. Of course, Gatwick is a large, ode modern, and busy airport. It just seemed to give me the impression from the passenger window that it was just a little country airport such as you might find in the USA in Virginia, for example. I was to find out later that it is because space is at a premium in the UK, and many things appear to be small and quaint.

We traveled by bus from the aircraft to the arrival gate. The buses were similar to the ones they operated at IAD (Dulles) at one time. I don't know why they weren't a good idea at Dulles, seemed to work well at Gatwick.

I walked into a line at Immigration and after a medium wait delivered my passport to a female agent. She asked my profession, and when I replied that I was a pilot, she said, "Oh, you must be here for the air show at Farnborough. Have a good flight." The next step was to find my bags. After a short search for signs, I found them and was pleased to see the carts were free. Recovering them was simple, just like the baggage handlers that beat up my new 36" Samsonite Pullman. Another search for signs and directions with a short walk, and I was in front of Customs. A double labyrinth gave me a choice of Declarations or No Declarations. A sign warned that

---

[2]   Gulfstream: The aircraft referred to is a transport category type jet with two engines and is considered to be the queen of all business jets. The aircraft is produced by Gulfstream Aerospace of Savannah, Georgia. In business aircraft, Gulfstream has always been the pacesetter. They produced the G-1 turbo-prop in the early 1960s, the G-2 pure jet, in the 1970s, the G-3 pure jet in the early 1980s, and the G-4 pure jet in the late 1980s. The company is now about to produce the G-5, and again, there is nothing in the business class of jets that can touch it for speed, range, and overall desirability. The Saudis had two G-2s and one G-3 at the time I was flying for them.

there would be severe penalties for those that tried to slip through with contraband. The list of articles showed that only two hundred cigarettes were allowed. Knowing that I had brought four cartons for David, my Jaguar mechanic friend, a decision had to be made. Well, what the heck, I could always plead ignorance. That I could prove. I chose the one marked No Declarations. After negotiating the maze, I found there was no one there, so I just walked through. I'd rather be lucky than smart or rich any day.

David was waiting for me in the lobby, and with his help, we were able to negotiate our way to where he had illegally parked his Ford Thunderbird (still wearing Texas plates). Too bad, a Bobby was in the midst of giving him a parking ticket. No one seemed to be bothered, either by the illegal park or the receiving of the ticket. The Bobby was interested in the car, and David told me later, "No one pays the bloody things anyway."

David was a young man that I had met in Houston. Our meeting was by chance just after a serious disappointment that I had received at the hands of one of the local Jaguar repair centers. The cost for a simple tune-up on an American-made car in Houston, at the time, was about $75. The Jaguar dealer wanted $750 for a tune-up on the car I was driving.

David happened to be walking across the parking lot when I drove through in a 1974 XKE[3], and he heard the V12 engine not running just right. He came over and introduced himself and complimented me on my Jag but added that it sounded not well. As I soon discovered, he was a Jaguar mechanic looking for work. He had been trained in the UK at the Jaguar factory and had been living in Texas for a short while. David loved Texas, and he was a genius under the "bonnet" of a Jaguar. Through adverse conditions, to be revealed later, David had to leave his adopted Texas home and return to the UK "between the suns" as my grandmother used to say. We continued to communicate after his departure, and now we are reunited.

---

[3]   XKE Jaguar: For uninitiated, it is a classic automobile made in England. The car is attractive to many because of its design, but it is equally appealing to those who like speed. The US version is always a little slower than the UK domestic model because the Brits downsize the rear axle ratio for the colonists—that's us. Unlike the US-built sports cars like the Corvette, the V12 engine in the XKE will run all day and night on the engine red line (max RPM). The Corvette may beat the Jag in short race for a mile or so, but you Corvette owners shouldn't try it for the long distance because you'll just burn up your pride and joy while trying.

"My XKE Jaguar when in Texas"

We left the airport at breakneck speed, down the wrong side of the road. The Brits claim that the left side of the road is the right side of the road. They can even justify their claim by reminding you that in the beginning, the driver of a wagon sat on the right side so that he could press on the foot brake located on the side of a wagon with his right foot. Therefore, when they started to build automobiles, it was natural to put the driver on the right side and drive down the left side. The reasoning for this is British all the way. They don't bother to explain why they didn't build aircraft by the same reasoning. They build aircraft with the pilot's seat on the left, and they must fly aircraft according to the rules of foreigners. That must gall them to no end.

Although the roads were wider than I had imagined, the thrill was still there. There seemed to be more open country than I would have thought. However, once we were among the dwellings, it was one small community after another. After something like twenty minutes, we arrived at Cobham in Surrey. For those who don't know, Cobham is the city, and Surrey is the county. That's so you don't confuse this Cobham with two others around London. The village was small, very small, and picturesque. But first, we had to stop on the way at the auto parts store and buy a battery and ask about some other items on order. All inside seemed glad to see David, the owner and chief mechanic of Lone Star Mobile Auto Repair. They were also glad to share his new stock of American cigarettes.

Next, we had to stop by the Bear, David's favorite pub, for a spot of lunch, buffet style. I chose the sour kraut and wieners, a poor choice. Everyone was introduced to "my friend from Texas" by David. They were very friendly and relieved to find that I *did* wear Western boots, I *did* have a large belt buckle, and I *was not* nine feet tall. Of course, we had to conduct a little business before we left. A car that David had sold to Carlos, a friend just over from Columbia, South America, would not start. David gave him the battery we had just picked up, and the friend installed it himself. It started, and everything was fine. Of course, we saw this fellow several more times with the same problem before I left two days later.

After another short drive, we arrived at David's mother's home. It was a small house, two-story and probably 1,500 square feet. The house was small for a two-story house gauged against two-story houses in Texas. That is, the lot was probably fifty by eighty feet with some fruit trees in the back. However, if it were compared to houses of our own northeast USA, then it would be very much the same.

Mrs. Groves was trying to dig up an old rosebush as we pulled into the driveway. She was pleasant to me but fussed at David because of the excessive number of cars in the drive. Besides three customer cars and his Thunderbird, there was his mobile unit. The mobile unit was a Datsun pickup truck with four-wheel drive, a mobile phone, and some very professional sign work on the truck consisting of a large red star and a sign, which read in three colors "Lone Star Mobile Auto Repair, 24-hour Service."

The single stall garage was very small, hardly large enough for a small car. Of course, it was filled with an assortment of equipment, air compressor, paint gun, paint, and much more. What I learned later was that David had an agreement with his mother not to work on cars in the driveway. This agreement was in constant violation. For mother and son, it was a Mexican standoff. They both knew and understood that neither would ever change nor would the rules.

After the introductions and howdys, we took my bags in the house. Mrs. Groves had given me her bedroom. I tried to decline, but to no avail. The tea was ready, and she was twice surprised—one that I liked hot tea and two that I drank it without cream or sugar. Her eyes said that Americans were indeed strange people. By the way, in the UK, the United States is called America, mostly, and sometimes, the States.

David had not scheduled any work for the time of my visit, but there were a couple of jobs that just had to be finished straight away. He had a Jaguar XJ6 that he was doing a tune-up on, and he was just about finished. I watched as he set the CO_2 level on the Jaguar with his new test instrument. The car was a right-hand drive model, of course, and after the tune-up, I was elected to deliver it to the customer. It was with mixed emotions that I agreed, never having driven a right-hand drive before or on the left side of the street. Driving down the left side of narrow and bending streets took some mental adjustment on my part.

The worst part is at the corners. You catch yourself looking the wrong way for traffic. Never mind the mix-up between turn signals and windshield wipers. The horn in the middle of the steering wheel is the only thing that's in the right place.

The rest of the day was spent finishing up a few other jobs, which were on the verge of completion, including painting and installing a door on a small English Ford. That evening, we had to go back to the Bear and meet all the chaps. David and the chaps drank ale, and I drank a Coke. I was forced to tell a few jokes. Some laughed, some smiled, and some wondered what the others were laughing and smiling about.

Soon it was time for several of us to return to the Grove's home to watch some UK tele. The TV room or den was about ten by ten, and there was about six of us there. It was very friendly; it had to be. We were up till three in the morning. After my trip, once I got into bed I just collapsed. It was noon the next day when I awoke.

The following two days were spent mostly working on cars. Carlos (from Columbia) came back several times with his starting problem. Intermittently, the little mini just would not start. Each time David fixed it, but somehow the little car wouldn't stay fixed. It's an example of a typical problem in the service business when you are trying to solve an intermittent problem. How can the serviceman be sure that his latest fix is not going to be final, when the problem doesn't reappear? The answer is, of course, he can't—an age-old problem when you're in the service business. I know the feeling well.

My friend David was an excellent mechanic but impatient with the small mundane jobs. I had a feeling that what was wrong with the car he sold Carlos was probably an intermittent ignition problem—hard to find unless you just change out the ignition switch. They probably didn't have one at the auto parts store, and David just didn't want to fool with it. Knowing David, he probably sold the car too cheap in the first place and just wanted it to disappear.

David had a friend that played golf, so Saturday afternoon, we got a tee time, and the three of us went to the links. David didn't play; he just acted as my caddie. I had borrowed his father's clubs, and let me tell you they were old and battered. However, I got in the grove right away. No, I didn't misspell the word. I mean, I got in the grove. Out of bounds was too dense for Tarzan. After a couple of holes, then I got into the groove and didn't do too bad.

Starting the game was very informal. After paying the green fees, we just went to the first tee and began at the previously appointed time. There was not a starter as you might have expected. The course was long, rustic, and the greens were large and rolling. Grass on the greens was very short and very fast. To me they were plenty tough. There were hardly any water hazards until we arrived at the seventeenth. It was 158 yards and all water. No way around the left or right; you just had to make it across it one shot.

There were two Oriental men in front of us, and we watched while one put four balls into the water before he gave up. He and his partner just picked up and walked around the cart path. Too bad I didn't have one of my special water balls[4] with me. I could have offered it to him. Perhaps it's better that I didn't. It might have set back our relations with Japan several years.

There was not a single golf cart on the course that I could see. That fact alone made the English golf course considerably different from those in the United States. David confessed that he was happy to see the eighteenth hole even though he claimed to have enjoyed his part of the golf game. It was a lot of fun.

The weather was beautiful for the three days of my visit. They said they had ninety-five inches of rain in the last forty-five days. It didn't look like it. David's mother took me for a walk downtown to pick up the paper on Sunday morning. She may be seventy, but I was pressed to keep up. After we got downtown, she decided to take the scenic route back. I was glad to get back to the cottage and have a cup of tea. Mrs. Groves was a very nice widow lady, and it was easy for me to sit with her for a chat. We discussed the neighbors, local politics, international polices, and the type of vegetables she was preparing for lunch.

All too soon, it was time for me to go. Heathrow is about forty-five minutes from Cobham, so the trip was not long. An interesting point for the traveler to remember is that most times when you stop in London at one airport, you will leave from another airport. I had come in at Gatwick, and I was leaving from Heathrow. There are some other points of international travel that I learned later, but I had to learn the hard way, so I don't want to give all the secrets away at one time.

The terminals at Heathrow were marked as A, B, and C without a clue as to which airlines were located at each. So we had a time finding the proper one for Saudi Airlines. On a subsequent pass, we made it, and after a good search inside, we arrived at the counter to check my bags. The airline hit me with a surcharge of $150 for the extra weight of my bags without mercy.

David, his golfing friend, and I had a last cup of coffee, said our good-byes, then I was off to the SV (Saudi Airlines designation, you figure the SV) gate. I soon got the first evidence of the Saudi dress. At the gate, all the Saudi women were wearing their black outer covering and black veils over their faces. The first impression was nothing more than very interesting. A deeper thought would develop later.

The Jumbo jet was very comfortable, even in the cheap seats. The food was absolutely the best that I have ever had on an airline, very excellent. I was able to sleep most of the time. We left Heathrow at roughly 2030 (8:30 p.m.) and arrived in Riyadh at 0445 Monday morning. My retirement after thirty-eight years was effective on Friday, and I was at my new job location on Monday. I had the weekend off in the UK.

---

4   Water balls: It's an inside joke. In golf, the term is used to denote old, cut, or throwaway balls destined to be sacrificed to the "water gods" that live in the water hazards on golf courses. A good friend of mine put two new golf balls into a water hazard in Houston one day. I gave him one of my water balls to waste. In reality, it was an exploding golf ball in disguise. When my friend hit the ball, it exploded into a cloud of talcum powder. His facial expressions after the explosion put the rest of us on the ground and rolling around.

Dispatch:
Riyadh, Saudi Arabia
September 1, 1986

A NEW COUNTRY

We'll, here I am in a new country, with new people, and new procedures to learn. My advisors in the States warned me of culture shock. I had no idea what that meant. But the lessons began with my arrival at 4:45 in the morning.

I've spent a lifetime of traveling, but nothing prepared me fully for my arrival into the Kingdom of Saudi Arabia.

Saudia at King Khaled International Airport, Riyadh

saudia
SAUDI ARABIAN AIRLINES

"This is the airport for the commoners. A separate airport for royalty is across the road to the east."

AIRPORT IMPRESSIONS

The passenger terminal at King Khalid International Airport is beautiful. Marble floors, marble walls, massive marble columns, and flowing fountains are more than a mere traveler could imagine. Nowhere in the world have I seen anything to compare. Sometime in the past, someone described his desires to an architect and added, "Money is no object." The architect must have taken him at his word.

Even at such an early hour, I caught myself looking from side to side like a country boy on his first visit to town. *Awesome* comes to mind. My mind was pulled back to reality as I noticed the other people moving quickly to the queues (British for lines) in front of the several little booths for the Immigration agents.

The booths are manned by men in army-type uniform, and each booth is for a different group. It seemed that everyone knew where they were going but me. The end result was for me to be near the end of the line that I finally joined.

Just like back home when you're number 58 in a line waiting to get a car title, you wait for what seems like forever, and as you near the booth, you find that you're in the wrong line. Or some extra help comes in and opens another booth. All the people behind see the new booth open before you do and move over into the new line, which puts them in front of you. That part is just like back home.

The part that is not like at home is the way the locals stand in line. They don't. All Saudis wear traditional clothing in the Kingdom with no exceptions that I have knowledge of, and they don't stand in lines. Maybe it's their dress that gives them priority, but whatever, they don't stand in lines. Twenty or more Saudis will crowd an opening in the booth window as all try to shove their passports or whatever into the agent. Without a word, the agent takes them one at a time while the line behind waits with patience. He doesn't seem to care and proceeds to wait on them just like they were supposed to be there. It happens everywhere—at the money changers, at the bank, at the computer store, everywhere. No, that part is different from the United States. Come to think of it, they don't do that at the supermarket. Wonder why!

Once at the booth, the military agent takes my passport, checks for the required visa, enters something into a green-screened computer off to his side, stamps the visa, enters some numbers on top of the visa, closes passport, and hands it back to me—all this done without a word or a smile. His eyes hardly take note of me as he reaches for the next passport.

Okay, I'm past the Immigration checkpoint and onto the baggage pickup area. The bags are coming up and onto a carousel in the center of a huge open space that is bounded on one side by Immigration and on the other side by Customs. It was every man for himself on the bags. There were plenty of trolleys (British for carts) available, and all free. It was just beginning to dawn on me; the United States is the only place in the world where I have been that charges a fee for baggage carts. It just occurred to me, the Saudis did the routine just the opposite of the way the Brits did it. That is, here we went through Customs first and then through Immigration. Don't know why.

All those knowledgeable people that got in front of me in the line a few minutes before are still waiting for their bags. I guess it all evens out.

After all the warnings I had about contraband, the Customs check was a big disappointment. The agent made a very casual look at my open suitcases. He didn't even bother to check in the pockets. I had the feeling that he wasn't interested in me or what I might have in any hidden pockets. I was wrong.

As I moved past him to close my bags, he reached around and touched me on the shoulder. He indicated he wanted me to turn and face him. When I did so, he pointed to my waist. It was my money belt. I had forgotten all about the money belt. It was stuffed with several thousand dollars worth of American Express travelers' checks.

I opened my shirt and opened the belt. The agent nodded okay and motioned me on. He never spoke a word, and I only learned half the lesson. Bringing money into Saudi Arabia is not a problem, but in some other countries, it is very serious. In Kenya, you must declare the money you bring in, the money you leave with, and have receipts for the difference.

With my bags still on the trolley, I moved a few feet past the Custom agent through an L-shaped exit. There were at least a hundred people waiting just beyond a rope barrier. Many carried signs with people's names on them. No one had my name. Suddenly it occurred to me. I don't know where I'm going. All the paperwork I had, showed post office box numbers and phone numbers. There were no street addresses.

Well, that couldn't be too much of a problem. I'll just call one of the phone numbers and ask directions. The next effort was to find a pay phone. I found one, but it required coins that I didn't have. Okay, then how about money changers to get the right kind of money? No, I can't do that. The money changers are not open at 0500 hours in the morning. Come to think of it, if I had the right change and made the phone call, who would be there to answer at such an hour?

I made a pile of my bags and sat down on them to wait. The arrival crowd thinned out then disappeared, and I was left alone. I mean alone. There was not a soul in sight or hearing. The cabs were all gone. It was as if everyone had just vanished. I can never remember being in any terminal, train, bus, or airline when there was no one present. It reminded me of a *Twilight Zone* episode.

My patience paid off for in about a half hour, a dark-complexioned man arrived with a sign that read Captain Fox. He didn't need the sign because I was the only one left in the terminal. And even if I weren't the fellow he was looking for, I was all set to go with him.

The sign holder was the chief driver for Medevac, Jyantha. The driver was very pleasant and helpful, but just a little late. I learned that Jyantha was responsible and usually very punctual, but he sometimes had conflicting assignments that made his timing on the job very difficult.

"Medevac symbol"

This is a good time to stop for a statement of facts. In the first place, my spelling has never been worth a spit in the ocean. In the second place, no one can spell these names over here because the Saudis are continually changing the way they spell them. Yesterday, Captain Hardy received his papers for a base pass at last. A Saudi copilot noticed they had spelled his name s-h-a-r-d-y in Arabic. Before you know it, there were six copilots in an argument. The final result was all same-same, that's close enough. So never mind criticizing my spelling. Here you can spell any way you want to, or you can just change the name. That seems to happen often. Well, why not? We do it in the States, don't we? Streets, airports, etc.

Jyantha was my first contact with a TCN. *Third country national* is the term used here for workers imported to do the work for the Saudis. No, I'm not a TCN because of my country of origin and my profession. People like me are called expats, short for expatriates, of course. The TCNs may be from Sri Lanka, Pakistan, Thailand, Korea, the Philippines, or any other small country that desire to send their workers out of the country. If you don't know, then I'll explain.

Saudi Arabia has labor contracts with other countries that have a need to export workers. The country with the workers sponsors labor agents that advertise for workers. Say a young man or woman in the Philippines sees an advertisement in their paper regarding jobs in Saudi Arabia with the promise of easy work and big wages.

The hopeful worker makes contact with the labor agent and learns that he or she must pay a fee to apply. "It is required for the paperwork, you see." The fee is nonrefundable. The fee is paid, and the worker may or may not get the job. The agent pays a fee to his own government for each worker that he places. He doesn't have to pay a fee for those that apply and are not placed.

If the worker is successful and receives a job, then the contract is written and the worker's government receives income tax from the worker. The average contract is for twelve months of pay for eleven months of work, i.e., the worker gets a month's paid vacation at the end of the year. Transportation to and from the point of hire is included.

While the worker is in Kingdom, his local employer is responsible for his room and board, his medical, and his transportation. If the worker gets in trouble while in country, his employer shares his responsibility.

There are five million Saudis in the Kingdom. There are over one million foreign nationals in the Kingdom. It is a serious business, and the Saudis run a tight ship.

Anyway, Jyantha (from Sri Lanka) helped load my things in the Buick with a GAMA sticker on the side, and away we went. Did I explain the GAMA stands for General Arab Medical Association? I think.

As I settled back into the seat of GAMA company car, Jyantha pulled away from the curb. I noted that the outside of the terminal was equal to the inside in attractive design. The access road was wide with large sweeping turns. No thrift in construction or space came into view. We left the curb in a northerly direction and slowly turned to the south. As we completed the turn and emerged from under an overpass, I caught sight of another terminal, larger and grander than the one we had just left. The new terminal was just opposite and across the road from the one where I had been.

"Jyantha, what's that?" I had to ask.

"Ah, Captain, that is the royal terminal. It is only used for the royal family," my driver answered.

It was my first lesson in the local royalty. I had many more lessons in store.

We drove south toward Riyadh forty kilometers (twenty-five miles) away. I noted the vast expanse of nothing but dirt—not sand, just dirt. West Texas, New Mexico, Arizona, and parts of California have bare land and even deserts, but none have anything like what I saw that morning. I expected sand dunes, perhaps, but there were none, just dirt. We were near the geographic center of the Kingdom at an elevation of two thousand feet above sea level. As far as you can see, it's as flat as a bookkeeper's stool. The air is dry and hot even at six in the morning. It's not real hot, but you can tell that it is going to get much hotter before long.

About ten miles north of Riyadh, we passed near a large complex under construction. Jyantha offered that it was the new university. The casual observer could see it would be a compliment to the airport that we had just left.

Along the road near the construction site, I saw the first evidence of something growing. Workers were planting and watering small trees planted alongside the road. I couldn't tell what kind of trees they were, but I wondered how they were going to keep them alive. I would learn the answers to both questions later.

Past the university, I caught my first sight of the skyline of Riyadh. The first thing I noted was the great number of construction cranes. There must have been at least a hundred in sight. It looked like they were just building the city as we approached.

"Jyantha, who is doing all the construction?" I asked.

"Oh, it is the Koreans. They have all the construction contracts," the driver answered.

I had asked the wrong question. I asked who, but I didn't mean who was doing the work, but who was having the work done. Was it companies or the government or who? Jyantha thought on a different level. He told me who the construction workers were. It left the question in my mind. That also would be answered later.

We turned east before actually getting into the city and passed by the air base where I would soon be working. Another ten kilometers, and we turned off the six-lane freeway at an exit marked NASSEEM in English and Arabic. I didn't note until later that there were three exits for the little community where I would be living. Each exit was spelled differently. I would learn more about the Arabic ideas on spelling later.

After explaining about the spelling here, perhaps I should pause for conversion factors: one kilometer = 0.62 statute mile, one liter = 1.06 quart, and one kilogram = 2.2 pounds. It is very important that I learn to think in these terms because just the other day, I bought a watermelon (from Cypress). It was marked SR 7.5, and my mental calculations figured about $2. Wrong. It cost me $17. The SR 7.5 was per kilo. I ate everything except the green part. So I'm working diligently to convert my thinking so that I won't make that mistake again. Got to get it right before I buy a car.

I might add that Jyantha is a good driver. All the Medevac drivers are good drivers. They have to be very careful because they are held responsible for traffic tickets, etc. They treasure their jobs. No one can come into this country without a work sponsor. The sponsor is required to provide him with housing, insurance, and the sponsor is responsible for his behavior while he is in this country. Therefore, there ain't no messing around. The individual gets in trouble, the sponsor is in trouble. Retribution is swift; there are no jobless TCNs. Might not be such a bad idea in the States, eh?

I have never seen so much construction under way. There are cranes everywhere. The buildings, in general, are constructed with reinforced concrete for floors and piers with cinder block walls. Many are reinforced concrete complete. They could withstand a nuclear attack. Maybe that's the idea. Most of the large construction is done by the Koreans. A local joke here is, if the Saudis ever go to war, the Koreans will probably get the contract. I lived long enough to see that when war really came, the Saudis got a better deal than the Koreans. The Americans did it for free.

Highways in and around the city are very new and clean. They have four to six lanes in each direction, even parts of downtown. You see very little roadwork. It's mostly done. Maybe the road workers have all been scared off by the local drivers. They drive fast and just where they want to. Not unusual to see one come across several lanes of traffic to make an exit just in front of you. Watch out!

Just a block off the freeway, we arrived at the GAMA compound. I saw solid walls of cinder block ten feet high with another six feet of chain-link fencing on top of the cinder block. Parking was outside the compound. Two large steel doors opened to the compound, and we were inside. Immediately on the left after entering was the guard shack. The guard is another TCN. He has no uniform and isn't really a guard, but more of a receptionist. He just takes the names of visitors and who they are going to see.

Jyantha introduced me as the new captain, and a large smile with friendly hand gestures welcomed me into the compound. GAMA's Nasseem compound covers the entire city block. My apartment was on the opposite side from the entry gate, so I got a tour on the way. We passed several lines of duplexes called the A villas, an open playground for children, and another walled area located in the center of the compound. The second walled area surrounded an Olympic-sized swimming pool, library, assembly hall, video library, and radio room. The swimming pool was featured in the brochures I received prior to signing the contract for this adventure.

Jyantha guided me past the inner compound wall of the pool to a line of two-story rooms that looked much like a motel back home. My apartment was about halfway down on the second floor. I hate climbing stairs, especially with a heavy load of bags. I had already suffered the first lesson for having more bags than your class of ticket allowed. In London, Saudi Airlines charged me an additional $185 for excess baggage. The second penalty is carrying them upstairs.

After entering the C unit, I set the bags down, shook hands, and Jyantha departed, leaving me alone once again. The GAMA compound had five classes of living units. The A units were three bedrooms with two baths and were called villas. The B units were two bedrooms with one bath. Both the A and B units had living room-dining room combinations and a separate kitchen. The C unit had the living room, dining-room-and-kitchen combination, one bath, and a separate bedroom. The D units were like efficiency apartments with everything except the bath in the same room.

The A units or villas are all on the ground floor. The rest of the units are formed just like a motel back home with first and second floor units.

My new home was clean, neat, and very acceptable. An air conditioner was roaring away near the front door. It was not in a window but mounted in the wall. There was a second unit in the wall of the bedroom. I checked the refrigerator and found a few days' supply of food. Well, that's thoughtful, but I didn't feel like eating. All I wanted was to use the bathroom and go to bed.

The bathroom had a tub/shower combination, lavatory, commode, and a ten-gallon hot water heater mounted on the wall near the ceiling. I noticed the commode looked like the kind you see in public restrooms. There was no water closet; it was flushed by a valve action, which could deliver enough volume to do the job. Well, no problem there until it was time to flush. I was a little apprehensive of things we take for granted in the States, like electrical outlet voltages. But I was not prepared for the flushing toilet. *Ka Wooosh*, and I thought the whole thing had blown up. I fell back from the blast to the opposite wall as a cloud of steam rose from the ode commode.

What happened? I checked myself, then the ode commode, then the bathroom, but there was no sign of damage. *Could this be normal?* I thought. *No, of course not.* It was shocking, but I was too tired to investigate further. I headed for the bed, clothes and all, for the nap that would not wait. The fifty-seven-year-old man had enough.

The phone woke me about noon. It was the chief pilot for GAMA, not Medevac, Captain Newbigin, a Brit. We had a short chat. He welcomed me to Saudi and promptly left the country. There were two pilots that flew for GAMA—Capt. Eric Newbigin and his copilot a Mr. Cox. I never found out what his first name was because during all the time that I was in the Kingdom, I only spoke to him a couple of times.

To explain a little, GAMA, General Arabia Medical and Allied Medical Services Ltd., is a contractor to the Ministry of Defense and Aviation, MODA. Medevac, Medical Evacuation, is a division of GAMA. Since Prince Sultan is the head of MODA, anything we do backs up all the way to Prince Sultan. That explains why we are located on an air force base.

"Prince Sultan"

A little later, I got a call from Capt. Walt Schmitz. Walt seemed to be a nice fellow about my age with a mop of silver hair and wanted to show me around a bit. We went to a photo shop and had 8 IDs made. I had to borrow the money from Walt. So our next stop was to the money changers. I cashed a thousand dollar worth of American Express. Now I had a lot of money. The exchange rate was 3.751 Saudi riyals to one American dollar. The exchange was set and did not float or change. The paper money is in color and a different size for each denomination. I had a double pocket full of the funny money. It makes you feel rich.

The Saudi money changers were another sight completely new to me. Outside it was just another building, and inside it looked something like a bank, you know, with several windows with bars for the men with the money to sit behind. But everything was made of wood. There was no marble. I went to an open window and gave the man a thousand dollar worth of American Express checks. He in turn wrote out something on a piece of paper and motioned for me to take it down to the end of the counter where another man sat behind an open window—no bars. That man took the piece of paper, read it, and then opened a large drawer just in front of his lap. The drawer had to be two feet wide and about twelve inches deep. It was full of Saudi riyals of all denominations. The money was not organized in stacks according to denominations or any kind of organization, but just strewn around, but a drawerful. Regardless, the man fished around through the bills and came up with a stack of money that would choke a horse and gave them to me. I counted it, and the money changing was complete.

It looked like a chancy operation, but I guess it works for them. They have some funny practices over here, but they don't take chances with money. You can depend on that. The banks here don't charge interest nor do they pay interest. It's against their law. Any interest is considered usury, and that's against the law. I'm going to ask someone with knowledge to how do the banks make money. You and I know they do, but how?

Walt and Pat, his wife, live in B13 (upstairs). They invited me in for a spaghetti supper. It was much appreciated. After a visit and some preliminary advice for the new pilot, I left for my apartment to finish what the phone call at noon had interrupted.

Author's Note: I am too trusting according to my wife, Charlotte. Walt Schmitz turned out to be quite a bit different from my first impression.

Yes, he was a tall, charming, silver-haired American, but he had a world-class aversion to the truth!

Like most of the pilots, Walt claimed to be from Texas. His real home could never be determined. Someone said he was really from Washington State.

He liked to tell about his past accomplishments as a US Air Force pilot. There were many entertaining stories about his early days in cadet training. One day, Walt was riding with me after I bought a white 1985 XJS Jaguar when we passed a C-54 air force plane parked on the ramp.

"Hey, look at that! I used to be a crew chief on one like that!" exclaimed Walt.

"A crew chief? I thought you were a pilot, but the crew chiefs were all enlisted men," I noted.

"Uh, oh yeah, well, you see, the colonel used to say, 'Hey, Walt, come up here to the cockpit and show this lieutenant how to fly an airplane.'"

In February and March of 1987, I left for thirty days on an around-the-world trip, and since Walt's old worn-out Mercedes was not running, I let him keep my new Jaguar to drive. While I was gone, Medevac was visited by a couple of representatives from Universal Weather, our handlers from Houston, Texas.

The reps like to visit their customers around the world about once a year. You know, public relations. Walt, with his charm, was chosen to be their contact, and he furnished them with transportation while they were in Riyadh.

A year later, the same reps came by, and I was chosen to be their contact. Walt Schmitz had already become a "runner" (Left the Kingdom without permission. My grandmother used to call it "leaving between the suns.") by then and was no longer around. I picked the gentlemen up at the Marriott, and their first remark was that my car was just like Walt Schmitz's car they rode in last year!

Walt's other accomplishments included being chief pilot for the Southland Corp. in Dallas, flying a Saberliner as a chase plane for the air force's new F-111 (that's the one with the wings that moved in flight). I wonder why he left the chief pilot's job. Walt is also the one that on occasion would roll the Gulfstreams, with crew members walking down the aisle or nurses sitting on the floor.

I flew MSD (GII) into Basel, Switzerland, for maintenance and left it to return later. A week later, I had to take MS3 into Basel on an emergency (I'll explain that later). While there, the maintenance chief told me he had something to show me on MSD.

They had the seats and most of the flooring removed in the cabin. We went back to the galley in the aft starboard side, and he pointed down to an area just adjoining the galley where the flooring should have been. The box frame is made of twelve I beams, which is the foundation for the rest of the airframe. In that corner, the I beam was twisted and deformed so that it protruded upward about two inches from its normal position.

"That's how we found them," the chief told me. "We noticed a bulge in the carpet right there at the corner of the galley. It was almost hidden by the overhang of the galley, but one of the men saw it and called me. When we took the carpet up, we could see that the floor paneling was bent and distorted. Then we pulled up the panel and saw the box beam was bent. Man, no one has ever seen anything like this before. That's when we called the factory at Savannah. The engineers said we must be mistaken. It couldn't happen. Well, you can see. It surely did happen. So we insisted, and they sent a couple of engineers over, and they just left yesterday."

"Well, what did they say caused it? Could it have been a rough landing?" I asked, knowing the Gulfstreams had been exposed to some of those. Walt Schmitz had not long before landed short of the pavement on an unlighted runway, and the crew told me they thought he might have had some serious damage that night.

"No, they said they didn't think so. They said it was more than likely an incident in the air due to extreme turbulence with the weight of those full-size oxygen tanks mounted on the floor in that area."

Oh yeah, well, no one reported any such "extreme turbulence." It came to my mind, what would happen if a guy tried to do a barrel roll while in a cloud, lost the horizon, and fell out of the maneuver? He might experience some "extreme turbulence" while recovering. Yeah, that might have been it, but who can tell. The Gulfstream engineers claimed that what they saw on floor of MSD was a one of a kind and that they had never seen or heard of such a thing before.

I was just glad that the wings didn't come off while I was flying the thing into Bazel.

It wasn't too long after that Walt took his wife back to the States on his annual leave and didn't bring her back. While his wife was gone, he invited one of the nurses up to his apartment for dinner with some of the mechanics. The truth of what happened may never be known, but the chief mechanic ended up with a black eye, and the nurse came by our apartment for some "counseling."

Walt quietly got rid of his old Mercedes, and on the day of his next paycheck did a "runner." He left the Kingdom for good. (See chapter on "Runners.")

Dispatch:
Riyadh, Saudi Arabia
September 2, 1986

FIRST DAY AT THE AIRPORT

The next day, I got a call from Captain Schmitz. We are commonly called as Captain so and so, but man to man, it's just Walt or Phil. He took me to the King Fahd Air Base where our hangar is located. It's only about fifteen minutes' drive from the compound, but depending on the mood of the gate guards, it can take a lot longer.

There they stand, with an automatic weapon in their hands, no socks on their feet, and no shoelaces in their shoes. They look as if last week they were probably milking goats.

Walt had a letter authorizing me to get on the base, but it was not satisfactory, so we had to wait while one of the Medevac directors made another with an official seal. That worked for the main gate, but then the guard at the gate to the flight line was not happy with it and had to get a second letter for him. Typical. Anything official should have a seal. The guards can't even read their native tongue, so they depend on the seal to make any piece of paper mean something.

"USAF AWACS"

The air base looks quite a lot like those in the States. Even the aircraft are the same. Many have US markings. Most of them are flown by US crews. Several AWACS (Airborne Warning and Control Systems) are here, and I hear maybe even more coming. They fly missions around the Arab Gulf constantly, I suppose. They have the old KC135 (Boeing 707) tankers and the new KC10 (DC-10) tankers as well. In fact, they are in the next hanger to ours. Our hangar is just large enough to hold one G2, a Lear, and a helicopter, with offices on the front, upstairs, and down. Our flight operations office is on the second floor, overlooking the hangar floor. We also have a little coffee corner on the second floor. New offices in front of the hangar are almost finished.

The administration offices are downstairs, and the flight crews are upstairs. It can get pretty crowded at times. There are about sixty-eight people involved. I don't have it all sorted out yet, but besides the fixed wing group of two G2s, one G3, one Lear 35, ten C130s, and there are about six helicopters (two Bell 212s and four French Dauphin 2s).

"Gulfstream II"

"C-130s"

"Bell 212 Helicopter"

After some introductions and a few "how ya' doing?" remarks, we left the airport. No one in particular caught my attention, and I can't remember names anyway. But I did remember the national guard (the Saudi name for their army), Major Shablan, who was in charge, and Bruce, the dispatcher. All the pilots were missing.

"Dauphin Helicopter, French, with crew"

It was time to go shopping. That is the big thing here, going shopping. Well, consider this, there are no movies, no theaters, no radio, nor any other form of regular mass entertainment, except TV, and there are only two channels—one in English, part time. So shopping becomes a big deal.

I made some purchases in the supermarket, Hassim's, just to get me started. The apartment was prestocked with a small amount of food, just enough to get by for a couple of days. This is happening on Tuesday, which is like Thursday at home. Their first day of the week is Saturday, and they work until noon Thursday with their Sabbath on Friday. Gets real confusing.

Dispatch:
Riyadh, Saudi Arabia
September 3, 1986

FIRST FLIGHT

Today was Wednesday, September 3, and I was assigned to go on a mission with Capt. Odie Pond. It is supposed to be my check ride. Odie is from the Dallas area, I believe, the same as Walt. I found out later that everyone claimed to be from Texas. As far as foreigners are concerned, there are only two places to be from in America, Texas and California. They know all about our cowboys and that the movies are made in California. All important people either come from Texas or California—in that order.

We received the mission via the handheld radio. The radio operator's call sign is Romeo Base. His physical location is the King Khalid Hospital. We have a relay antenna here in the compound so we can stay in touch with our handheld handy talkies or, as they are referred to here, talking bricks. It doesn't take long to get to know Romeo very well. Each handy talkie is equipped with selective calling or SELCAL. Each radio receives all calls from Romeo, but each one has an individual ring so we can know when the trip being called is for us. We can set our units on SELCAL at night and not be bothered by missions other than our own that are called.

This first mission called was to Ta'if (Tah-eef) to pick up a patient and transfer him back to Riyadh. We left late in the afternoon, expecting an uneventful 1:10 trip to the southwest. Of course, I can't understand half what is being said on the radio, but it's okay. *This thing don't fly backward, does it?* I thought. Not a cloud in the sky. The haze[5] level here goes up to fifteen to eighteen thousand, so it's bumpy up to there. I noticed that Odie turned the radar on for takeoff; he was in the right seat. Then he turned it off on the climb out (Some pilots take off with the radar on because they think it might keep the birds out of the way.). I asked, "Why?" He said, "Well, there is nothing to look at anyway." I said, "Well, let's turn it back on anyway. It's what I'm accustomed to, and I'd like to play with it." After a few adjustments, I said, "Hey, Odie, that looks just like a thunderstorm right over our destination." He said, "Yeah, I think you're right."

---

[5] Haze level: Refers to the top of the haze. Haze is the part of sky from the ground up to the bottom on the clouds, if any. Clouds form at the very top of the haze level. It is the area of sky that is bumpy from convected heat waves from the ground. The top varies with the temperature. Once above the haze level, the air can be expected to be smooth. In the USA, the haze level is usually below ten thousand feet.

"Odie"

As it turned out, we were both right. Heck of a deal, my first leg for a check ride in Saudi Arabia, the Land of Sand and Sun, and I am in the middle of a thunderstorm. Well, it wasn't a large one by our standards in the States, but it had plenty of wind and rain and more lighting per pound than we usually see. Not to worry, the Desert Fox got it on the ground with a nice landing and surprised everyone onboard. "Hey, Odie, I thought you told me that you never had any weather over here." "Well," he said, "we don't, except sometimes at Ta'if."

The ambulance was waiting as planned. We loaded the patient without incident, and after the nurse secured him, we were on our way. Waleed Zahed took the right seat for the return trip. Waleed was one of the Saudi copilots and the favorite storyteller, but on this leg, he was just another dumb Saudi.

Odie was on his case constantly. He didn't do anything to please the captain. As I watched from the jump seat, it seemed to me that he was doing a satisfactory job, at least for the pressure that he was under. I didn't know if the situation was the fault of the copilot or the captain.

There is much more radio work here than in the States. Even though we are under radar surveillance most of the time, we are required to give position reports. Their radar works much better than their communications, not unusual to have to get a relay or give one from another aircraft. In addition, we must keep Romeo informed of our ETA at the next stop and requirements for the patient, if any.

The nurse fills out a form on the patient needs as soon as possible after takeoff. The form has number codes for each item. So the first contact with Romeo will be on HF, and if the communications are poor, we can usually get the numbers through. If you say "say again" more than two or three times, there will probably be an American voice come on the air with instructions and requests that I can understand. I'll probably get the hang of it in a year or two.

The Gulfstreams are modified extensively for the Medevac missions, including the bulkhead area just aft of the entrance door. As you come up the stairs, just to your right, all that area has been removed so a stretcher can be maneuvered with little difficulty. There is no cabin door. They have four chairs in the front and a couch in the rear, opposite the hospital bed. There is quite a bit of medical equipment installed, more that can be brought along for a particular patient's needs. The galley is on the starboard (right) side like normal Gulfstreams, but opposite, on the left is solid with medical equipment.

We have the same facilities for food catering, just not for so many people. There is a small refrigerator on the right, plenty of 115 volts, 60 Hz (unusual for aircraft). The couch can be removed and a second hospital bed installed. Two full-sized oxygen bottles are stored beneath the couches or beds in the rear.

"One of a kind, a Gulfstream with a cargo door."

The G3 has a large cargo door installed just aft of the radio rack. There is a crane and winch, just aft of the cargo door, for loading stretchers horizontally on to the aircraft. The G3 has facilities for three stretchers. The aircraft are serial numbered

103, 256, and 385. The flight directors are Sperry, the radars are Bendix, the INS[6]s are Litton with the CRT (cathode ray tube) read out and Vandling database, and the GNS500A series IIIc (they share the data base with the INSs). Just like at home, we usually have only one of INSs working and maybe the GNS500a.

Let me take a moment to explain the work schedule here. All pilots are carried on the schedule as:

1 = On duty from 0600 until 1800. He is first priority for the day.
2 = On duty from 1800 until 0600. He is first priority for the night.
3 = On duty from 0600 until 0600. He is a backup for number 1
    and number 2.
0 = Days off

The rest are either on vacation or on an extended flight out of the Kingdom. When the number 1 pilot is out of the country, the schedule becomes a little squirrelly, so number 3 becomes the first one called. If a second mission is called, then number 2 may be called or maybe even a pilot that is shown on day off. In other words, it's much like working for Exxon.

Reviewed by _____ Project Administrator   Approved by _____ Director of Medevac

SUBJECT TO CHANGE AT SHORT NOTICE

SCHEDULE FOR FIXED WING PILOTS

MONTH APRIL 1988

NO CHANGES ARE TO BE MADE WITHOUT COMPLYING WITH CURRENT APPROVED PROCEDURES

DATE	1	2	3	4	5	6	7	8	9	10	11	12	13	14	15	16	17	18	19	20	21	22	23	24	25	26	27	28	29	30	31
DAY	F	S	S	M	T	W	T	F	S	S	M	T	W	T	F	S	S	M	T	W	T	F	S	S	M	T	W	T	F	S	S
01 ALGHORAIBI	1	3	2				1	3	2		2	2		3	2		2	2	2	2		2	2	2	2			2			2	2
68 FOX		1	3	2			1	3	2			3	2			1	3	2		1	3			1	3	2						
67 GILL			1	3	2			1	3		1	1	1	3		—			LEAVE												1
69 WALKER				1	3	2			1	3		1	3		1	3	2		1	3			1	3							
21 BORMAN	2			1	3	2			1	3	2		1	3		1	3		1	3			1	3							
66 LONG	3	2			1	3	2		1	3	2		1	3		1	3		1	3	2		1	3							
06 ALROUDHAN	1	3	2		1	3	2		1	3	2		1	3	2		1	3	2		1	3	2						1		
14 DAGHSTANI	1	3	2		1	3	2		1	3	2		1	3	2		1	3	2		1	3	2						1	3	2
09 ALGHAMMASH	2		1	3	2		1	3	2		1	3	2		1	3	2		1	3	2		1	3	2				1	3	2
10 ALJOHANI	3		1	3	2		1	3	2		1	3	2		1	3	2		1	3	2		1	3	2				1	3	2
11 ALSOHAIBI	2		1	3	2		1	3	2		1	3	2		1	3	2		1	3	2		1	3	2				1	3
22 OLSON		LR		LR	LR		LR		LR		LR	LR		LR	LR		LR	LR		LR	LR		LR	LR		LR	LR		LR		
23 GASPAROTTO	LR		LR		LR		LR		LR	LR		LR	LR		LR	LA		LR	LR		LR	LR		LR	LR		LR	LR		LR	LR
07 ZAHED	LR		LR		LA		LR		LR		LR	LR		LR		LR		LR		LR		LR		LA		LR		LR			
08 BASHIR		LR		LR		LR		LR		LR		LR		LR LR		LR		LR		LR		LR		LR		LR		LR			LR
18 ALHOGBANI						LR LR			LR	LR		LR LR		LR LR		LR LR		LR LR		LR		LR			

"Our Monthly Schedule"

---

6   INS: Inertial Navigation System, GNS: Global Navigation Systems. Technical information for the pilot types. INS costs $150,000 each. GNS costs $50,000 each. The Vandling database is a listing of navigation points used by the navigation systems. Don't worry about it.

Dispatch:
Riyadh, Saudi Arabia
September 4, 1986

THE COMPUTER

After looking at several computer stores, I decided on one that sold nothing but the IBM PC clones. They are identical to the original, except the name, MYCOM. The one I selected has a 9088-V2 (8088-2) chip and speed selectable for 4.77 MHz or 7.33 MHz. These people are so busy, it's almost impossible to get waited on—ten people side by side at the counter and three deep. The people behind the counter are pleasant enough when they get to you, but you need to know what you want because they really don't have the time to explain much. Besides, they don't always understand exactly what you are saying. My personal opinion is that many times that is an excuse to ignore.

As I was saying, the computer I picked out was a clone of the IBM PC-XT, from Japan, assembled in Taiwan. However, the case and keyboard are the PC-AT. The PC-ATs are not available yet. They say in October, they will have a plug-in board for this computer that will make it AT compatible, i.e., a plug-in board with a 80286 chip! The conversion board will be priced about SR1500 or $400. If indeed, that is true, then it sounds like a heck of a deal.

After some, not much haggling, I ended up with 640k of RAM, 20MB hard disk, an IO board with clock, game port, two serial and two parallel ports, a color monitor, and printer (Epson type) for about the same money that I sold my Compaq and printer for in Houston.

Software is so cheap that it is a joke, about $30 for most anything you want. I had some that they didn't have, so I traded a copy of *Manage Your Money* (1986 ver) for a copy of WordStar 2000. It is seven disks and very versatile. I bought a copy of 3.2 Dos for SR20 or $5. The documentation for 3.2 Dos was SR30, but I got him to throw that in for a good deal.

Phil Hardy had a radio shack back in the States but couldn't live any longer without one just like mine, so now we have twins. That has worked out just fine because we trade ideas and information. The dealer promised us each an extra ten programs of software with the purchase of computers. As yet, we haven't collected. We can't make up our minds as to what we want.

We are having a lot of fun with these things, and it passes the time. So far, I haven't bought a TV or stereo, so it really helps to pass the time away, which reminds me, the TVs and VCRs are a little more expensive than in the States. The reason is, they have to play several different systems (PAL, SEACAM, etc.). I've seen them on display, advertising fourteen different systems in the same set. They are automatic, so any station or system you tune in on is received.

Here is a copy of the roster that was given to me soon after my arrival with Medevac. Of course, my name and Phil Hardy had not yet been added. We started the same day. Phil became GS 67, and I became GS 68.

Armed Forces Medical Services
Flight Department

قدمات الطبية للقوات المسلحة
رئة خلاة الطبي الجوي

13 August 1986

Ref. Mev/Irm 86-104

TO : Radio Room
      Flight Crews

FROM: Major M.Y. Al-Shablan
      Director, Medevac

SUBJ: Updated Call Signs, Phone & Apt Numbers

Call Sign	Name	Phone Numbers	Apt/Villa
A30	AL-SHABLAN, Mohammed	478-9479	MODA Bldg. No. 6 Apt # 4
GS01	HANNO, Mohammed	464-1615	Al Khalij Towers
03	YAGHMOUR, Abdulatif		Al Khalij Towers
04	GHANIM, Ali		
05	BALAWANI, Abdullah	477-1094	Near RKH
06	AL-ROUDHAN, Eid	465-5289	
07	ZAHED, Walead	478-8012	
08	BASHIR, Betim	465-6774	Al Khalij Towers
09	YAHYA, Tariq	465-6910	
10	KAKA, Samir	465-6764	Al Khalij Towers
11	AL-GHORAEBI, Khalid	231-1040	
12	AL-HAIDAR, Abdullah		Al Khalij Tower
13	FAGEEH, Issam		Al Khalij Tower
14	DAGHISTANI, Mohammed		
15	AL-SEHRI, Abdulrahman		
16	AL-WOSAIEBA, Mohanna	Ext.4035	Apt D-24
17	AL-DARWETI, Khalid	477-8871	
18	AL-SHAHRANI, Mohammed	477/2295	
19	SUTHERLAND, Bruce	Ext.1111	Villa A-5
20	IAINTHBURY, Allan	Ext.1132	Villa A-14
21	SCHMITZ, Walter	Ext.2018	Apt B-11
22	FOND, Ody	Ext.1011	Apt A-1
23	McKAY, George	Ext.3045	Apt C-29
23	OLSON, Jerry	Ext.4017	Apt D-6
24	HALL, Robert	Ext.3016	Apt C-15
25	NEELY, Gary		
26			
27	MARTIN, Lloyd		
28	LANDRON, Gerard		
28	RICHARD, Armand		
28	ENBATIER, Jean-Joseph		
29	LUDVIGSEN, James		
29	CHING, Virgilio	478-4116	
29	EL HAQ, Ashar		
31	CHESHIRE, Martin		
	BALLSON, Bon		
	BORKDALE, Stephan		
	MARINAS, Virgilio	478-4116	
	ZIMMER, Rogel	478-4116	
	KOBRA, Roberto	478-4116	
34	BALLICE, Albert		
34	KASTANO, Pierre		
35	BOKER, Douglas III	Ext.1121	Villa A-13
36	PADOVA, Jerry	Ext.2043	Apt D-27

"Roster-01"

Call Sign	Name	Phone Numbers	Apt./Villa
GS38	TSCHIDA, Kevin	Ext.2031	Apt B-15
39	ZAMAKHSHARI, Hashim	463-3286	Back of GAMF.
40			
41	PILLI, Hans	Ext.3046	Apt C-28
42			
43	de VERENNE, Chris	Ext.1152	Apt A-25
44	IDEN, Dave	Ext.1091	Villa A-15
45	EINFIELD, Gordon	Ext.3015	Apt C-16
46	WYLES, Ian	Ext.4042	Apt D-26
?	GANNAWAY, Gerard	Ext.3021	Apt C-1
47	ABDULRAHMAN, Jamal	Ext.6048	Cabin P-8
48			
49			
50	ZARD, Chuchrallah	Ext.3028	Apt C-29
	GRIM, Rodney	Ext.4025	Apt D-16
	KERSH, Douglas	Ext.4047	Apt D-30
51	PETRAVICIUS, Tina	Ext.3038	Apt C-21
52	DURHAM Stephanie	Ext.3037	Apt C-22
53	BAUD Lindda	Ext.3035	Apt C-24
54	~~Elizabeth~~	Ext.4054	Apt D-3
55	LOGAN, Mary	Ext.4053	Apt D-3
56	CHISTE Merit	Ext.4058	Apt D-3
57	NORMAN ELSA	EXT.4056	
58	MADILL Jenny	Ext.4052	Apt D-3
59	TYLER Andrea	Ext.4051	Apt D-3
60	FARMER Sally	Ext.4044	Apt D-28
61	STILINGER Cherene	Ext.4046	Apt D-3
	~~Elso~~	~~Ext.4056~~	~~Apt D-3~~

GAMA COMPOUND 232-0878

"Roster-02"

Dispatch:
Riyadh, Saudi Arabia
September 8, 1986

THE WRITTEN TEST

Well, I have lost track of a couple of days here. Sometimes, in the last couple of days, Phil and I went to Jeddah (some spell it j-i-d-d-a-h) and took a written test for our Saudi pilot license. It's time to stop and explain about Saudi standards for spelling. They don't have any!

Now you may know that I am no expert on spelling in any language, but over here, they don't have any standards, and they seem proud of it. There are three highway signs that show the get-offs to our compound. They are labeled, Nasseem, Nahseem, and Nassim in that order. Now how did that happen? Did they have three different guys making the signs? Did they make them at three different times? Did they make them at three different locations? Or did one guy make them all and just got tired of doing the same thing over and over? I don't know anyone to ask for the answer, but personally, I favor the last choice.

Maybe you didn't know it, but a pilot has to have a license to fly an aircraft that agrees with the aircraft's registration number or tail number. A US-licensed pilot can fly a US-registered plane into France, for example, but he can't fly French registered plane while he's there. Just thought you might like to know things like that. No telling when the subject might come up, and you could amaze the coffee crowd!

We went over to Jeddah by commercial air and were picked up by an American representing the PCA, the equivalent of the FAA. Guess what? He was retired from the US FAA. Another double dipper. His office building was on the airport, so after a short drive, we were in his office. I have to tell you, it was just like in the States. You know, all the desks were of the gray steel type and looked like they had been picked up at an army surplus store for a bargain.

We had a short get-acquainted session and then came the written test. It was an open-book exam. I was given a copy of the Saudi AIP (I could guess Airman's Information Publication, but I'd probably be wrong), similar to the US AIM (Airman's Information Manual). Phil was given the inspector's copy, and we were sent to opposite ends of the hall so we wouldn't cheat.

After about thirty minutes, the inspector came in asked, "How ya' doing?" I had answered all but two of the questions, so I just told him that I couldn't find the answers. He said, "Well, let's just go down to the office with Phil and see how he's doing." Phil had been unable to answer the same two questions. The inspector took his manual back and looked them up for us, that is, he tried. After a while, he said, "Well, this test is out-of-date anyway. The guy that made it up is no longer here, so

I'm going to have to make it over." With that, he threw our test papers in the trash and gave us our licenses, just like in the States.

The license is valid for one year and then has to be reissued. The inspector tried to charge us SR500 each for the license but then found that we were exempt since we worked for the government. At least, we are now legal and can fly anywhere we want to as long as it's within the Kingdom. You have to have an *iqama* (work permit), a multiple exit visa, and passport to leave the country. We have no passport because they had to send it off to get the iqama from Immigration. When it gets back, then it's sent off again to get the multiple exit visa. Then we start getting our other papers, but that's another story.

Author's Note: The Saudis are computerized. They have the means and the intellect to handle the paperwork involved with such things as just described. So why does it seem to take forever to get anything done? It is my belief that a large part of the problem is that they don't trust anyone, not even each other. It's built-in. A Saudi told me that they have an old proverb that says: "A father puts his hand on his son's shoulder and says, 'Son, it is you and I against all of them.'" Well, that's paraphrased a bit, but the idea is expanded to include the family, the tribe, and the country.

They have to make sure, so all the "facts" have to be checked and rechecked. I wonder if that's not a takeoff the old joke: A father is explaining the way of life to his very young son as he sets him high on the mantelpiece above the fireplace and says, "Jump, son, Daddy will catch you." The son says, "No, Papa, I'm afraid." "Don't be afraid, son, jump, Papa will catch you." The son is still afraid, but the father continues to reassure the young son, so finally the boy jumps to the outstretched arms of his daddy. The father steps back and lets the boy fall to the floor. As the father stoops to pick up the crying child, he says, "First lesson, son, don't trust nobody!"

Dispatch:
Riyadh, Saudi Arabia
September 10, 1986

ANOTHER CHECK RIDE?

Odie's last day. He leaves tomorrow for fifty-two days in the States. He has been saving his leave and is borrowing some from the future. They say you can do that. Also, he's going to FlightSafety in Savannah for the G3 refresher. His wife is a semi-invalid, and since there is a Medevac trip to New Haven, she is going on the company plane. I think that permission is given for dependents to travel on the company plane from time to time. Many of the rules have not been exposed to me yet, but I will certainly find out soon.

In the last few days, there was a trip to Zimbabwe (Rhodesia), and within the next two weeks, there are two trips to London: one to Cologne, Bohnn, Athens; one to Hanover, Geneva, and Athens. I can't go on any of them. No iqama, no passport, no exit visa. So what's new?

In the afternoon, Odie, Phil, and I went on a mission together. It was the last chance Odie would have to fly with us before he left. Walt was on his way to London, so there was no one left to check us out. We went from Riyadh to Najran, Ta'if, Khamis, and return. I flew the first leg, Phil the next two, and Odie the last. Pilots are bad, you know. The deal is, we're supposed to be getting checked out, and Odie just can't help it, he has to fly a leg. Oh well, we had to see how he did it, didn't we? What? Was that all there was to a check ride? Well, of course. All Odie needed to see was if we could get into the air and back on the ground without hurting anyone. What else was he going to report? A negative report meant he would miss his vacation.

We had flown MS4 on the mission, which means, I had flown one leg on MS4 and one leg on MSD, both the G2s, and now I'm checked out and ready to go. Heck of a deal! This afternoon, Odie leaves, which leaves me and Phil to cover one G2 and the G3. Phil has always flown G2Bs and G3s. He has had a couple of more missions here than I because he arrived three days before me. He is not at all that familiar with the straight G2, and I have never been in a G3.

Phil quit Mobil after seven years. He was in Nigeria for five years and has good experience flying in this part of the world—a real nice fellow, about thirty-seven, from Vernal, Utah. So what do ya think? Right, the first solo mission is the G3 for me and the G2 for Phil. That's another story.

Author's Note: Time for musing. Why would a pilot flying great airplanes for a great company leave after only seven years. Well, he had spent five of them in Nigeria, and that's known to be less than an ideal spot for a family. He left before

55

he could be vested in any of Mobil's benefit programs, for less money, and for an unknown company with an unknown future. Phil left Riyadh a little over a year later before he had another job. He went back home to Utah, took his family on a great vacation to Disneyland, and spent all his money. Then he came back to Saudi Arabia, broke, and flew for another company. It was not his personality nor his flying talent. Phil was a super nice guy, and everyone liked him, so the mystery. I think Phil had wife problems, but that's just my guess.

Did I tell you about my wife? Well, we were married just two weeks before I came over to this great adventure. Charlotte Anne was working for a food broker in the Los Angeles area as an operations manager. No small job. Part of her job was hiring certain employees and managing them. This is to explain the background for my wife, who knows that I am too trusting of strangers. She's probably right. It takes a while for me to catch on to some of the people I meet.

I trust everyone I meet until they prove otherwise. It's an expensive habit, but that's just the way I am. Three years with the group in Medevac taught me some new lessons about people. But I'll get into that a little later.

Dispatch:
Riyadh, Saudi Arabia
September 11, 1986

THE FIRST MISSION

Very early this morning, I was awakened by the phone. Romeo Base had been ringing the phone off the wall. The window air conditioner in the bedroom kept me from hearing the phone, which was in the living room next to the front door and right under another air conditioner. We had an ASAP mission. Romeo's real name depends on which shift you get the call. I've never met the fellows that man the radio, but they are both Brits. One is known as Big John, and the other is Little John. One of the Johns was giving me the mission over the phone so fast that I had to ask him to repeat it several times.

I finally got it written down, threw on a white shirt and my Exxon pants. The uniforms I don't have yet are dark blue pants, so dark they look black to me, and a white shirt with flap pockets and epaulets. Should have borrowed a few from Crabe. Brent Crabe was a flying buddy back at Exxon and had prior experience with the airline, so he had shirts with epaulets. The only shirts that I had with epaulets were for the army.

The mission was to Jubail and return with a baby that was only three hours old. I think he said a blue baby. I didn't know where Jubail was and couldn't find it on the dadgum map. Well, not to worry. My copilot, Samir Kaka (I'm not kidding), knew all about it. The nurse was Mary Logan from Ireland, whom I had not met before. No problem.

Well, not much. We were going on the G3, which I had never been in before. I barely had time to get in the cockpit for the preflight. Man, they had really messed up the G2 panel. "Well, it don't fly back'ard, does it?" Away we go. The G3 handles better than the G2, I think. It's much heavier than what I've been accustomed to but pulls much less fuel for the same speeds and altitude. Without a hitch, and about forty minutes later, Kaka identified the airport from about ten miles out, and with no tower, no landing system, and no radio, it was just a left turn in and set her down. Jubail is a naval base just a few kilometers north of Dhahran on the east coast. I got to see the Persian Gulf for the first time.

No ambulance to meet us, but no one seemed to be concerned. Kaka said not to worry for it happened all the time. The man in the terminal was very nice. He came out to bring us coffee in china cups and saucers on a silver tray. Heck of a deal. After about fifteen minutes, we got a phone call from the doctor with the baby. He was more than a little upset. "What are you doing at the royal airport? You are supposed to be at the navy airport!" We were at the wrong airport—the shortest career in Saudi Arabia. Surely, I'll get fired for this. Never did it before, but I've

57

done it now. Okay, fire 'em up and let us be gone. Ten minutes later, we are at the other airport just a few miles of sand to the east, and the ambulance was waiting. I apologized to the doctor for not knowing there were two airports. He was very nice and assured me that no harm was done. The baby was stable, and he was quite sure she would be okay.

Just as soon as I got back, I reported the incident to whoever was in charge. Major Shablan was not there. I wasn't too sure about who that was either. Anyway, I told him that Romeo just told me to go to Jubail, and I went to the only one on the map. He said, "Didn't Kaka tell you that we always go to navy Jubail, not royal Jubail?" "No," I said, "he's the one that filed the flight plan and first identified the airport when we got there." The boss in this case was Mohammed Al-Shahrani, nice fellow (see, didn't I tell you, they are all nice guys, at first). He was very nice to me. Told me not to worry about a thing for it was not my fault. Then he went into the next room with Samir Kaka and had some heated words in Arabic. Little doubt from the tone what he was saying. Perhaps he was "samearing some kaka." (I shouldn't have said that.) I have no idea why the guy sat there in the right seat and said nothing. Perhaps he just wanted to start out by putting me in my place. He didn't expect me to report my own screwup. Well, it covers the old six o'clock, right?

Later in the afternoon, another mission. This time up north to Tabuk, another air force base. Lots of F-15s and T-38s. You can bet that I knew exactly where we were going this time. For one thing, Tabuk is just south of the Syrian border. That's where the Israeli fighters made touch-and-go landings. Maybe I've already told that story.

This is a good time to fill in with some afterthoughts about the Saudi copilots I was flying with. They became my primary example, not the only but the primary example of the Saudi people. As a group, they were very friendly, helpful, and a pleasure to fly with. Of course there were exceptions. As a group, they are very suspicious! Kaka told me of a friend that could do "magic."

We were driving down the road one time, and I told my friend we ought to stop for a hamburger. He said, "We don't have to stop, here you go." With that, he opened his window and reached out and just picked a hamburger out of the air and handed it to me! Now that's real magic, right?

Part of what I know of the Islamic religion is from asking questions of the copilots. They believe in the Old Testament, they say, but they don't believe that Jesus was the son of God.

"But you know what?" one asked me. "When Jesus was born, he had a full set of teeth and could speak like a grown-up!"

Well, such statements won't be of universal interest, but they help to understand some of the people that I was flying with.

JDF Letter:
Riyadh, Saudi Arabia
September 21, 1986

A LETTER TO THE WIFE

My Dearest Charlotte,

Don't faint, but here is the letter I promised. It takes so long to do anything here it is unbelievable. My trip to the American Embassy has not happened yet. The local phrase "tomorrow or maybe next week" certainly applies. The reasons are numerous. There is a mission to fly, or there are no drivers available, or there are no vehicles available or all three. Of course, the common one is that "We are closed that day."

I made a trip to Madinah on the fourteenth with a copilot named Kaka. No, I'm not making that up. There is much more to tell about that character, but I'll wait until I see you to explain. Madinah is one of their holy cities, and I can fly into the airport but am not allowed to leave the airport. I just stayed in the airplane while we waited for the ambulance to show up.

I tried to go to the embassy yesterday, but the driver had to be back to pick up the school kids and didn't have time for the trip. None of the other pilots were required to have their licenses stamped anyway[7]. Perhaps a rule that someone just thought might be a good one. Don't be dismayed. I'll do it yet.

You'll find the signed card enclosed. Perhaps it will allow you to deposit the checks you spoke of. If not, then just mail them to me, and I'll get them cashed here. The only reason I didn't ask you to do that anyway is, it's best to keep all the money in American denominations if possible. There is always a loss in the exchange rate going each way. The possible exception is, we may need cash here to do something with before we have saved enough in SRs to do the trick. An automobile is an example or perhaps a holiday. I'm sure you will find many things here that you will want to buy. The city is filled with a myriad of shops and stores. We'll see.

The houseboy, Mohammed, is doing very well. He comes in on Saturday at six and cleans the whole apartment in a couple of hours, including the laundry. Well, there is not really that much to clean I suppose, but it's nice to have it done anyway.

Phil and I got a ride at last with Joseph, a driver, and made a couple of stops including one at the Euromarchie, which is a large shopping center. The chain franchise is owned by the French, I think, and they really have a large selection

---

[7]   Someone decided that Phil Hardy and I, the new guys, had to have our US pilot's license
        stamped at the US Embassy there in Riyadh. No one before had that requirement.

59

of goods. There is one shop devoted to nothing but nuts. The last time I was there, I bought a half kilo of pinion nuts and the same amount of almonds. Last night, I found a shop there that had white shirts with epaulets. They had three with neck size 17 1/2; however, they agreed to make them short sleeve at no extra charge. They were priced at SR50 each. The automatic discount brought the price for the three down to SR113. They also agreed to shorten my other long sleeve (Exxon) shirts and use the material to make and install epaulets for SR40. However, the number of shirts was not clear. We'll have to iron that out when I take the shirts in.

Let me take a moment to explain the work schedule here. All pilots are carried on the schedule as:

1 = On duty from 0600 until 1800. He is first priority for any mission that is called for his type of aircraft.

2 = On duty from 1800 until 0600. He is first priority for the night missions.

3 = On duty from 0600 until 0600 the following day. He is a back up for number 1 and number 2.

0 = Days off

The rest are either on vacation or on an extended flight out of the Kingdom. When one pilot is out of the country, the schedule becomes a little squirrely. He may be shown as a number 1, so number 3 becomes the first one called. If a second mission is called, then number 2 may be called or may be even a pilot that is shown as off. In other words, it's much like working for Exxon.

Night before last I was a number 3. At 2200 hours, just as I was preparing to go to bed, the radio squawked with a mission to pick up a patient at Ar'ar. Ar'ar is only forty miles from the Iraq border. The area is under Baghdad control, and you are required to call them at least ten minutes prior to entering Baghdad's airspace. We were never able to contact them either on VHF (very high frequency) or HF (high frequency). We were very near the border, and I'm looking for boggers in the dark that were going to get us. Finally, a Jordanian flight gave us a relay, and Baghdad control gave us permission to land from FL390. There is no tower there, and we were told that we had to call on the phone for permission to take off. Our pickup was a road traffic accident victim that needed immediate surgery. To explain a little bit, the mission had been called as an ASAP, which is very common so far. They are not all that way of course, but each mission has to be approved by the Medevac commander. Sometimes a crew is called to the airport to stand by while the approval is coming back via radio. Well, anyway, the copilot made the call to Baghdad and was told we had a ten-minute slot to get airborne. We made the slot, and the trip back to Riyadh was uneventful. The worst part was getting in at 0400 after being up all day and night. It makes a fellow not know when to take a nap—a whole lot like flying for Exxon.

I just got a call from Phil Hardy. Jyantha, the driver's coordinator, says that he is going to try to get us a ride to the American Embassy just after lunch. Shops open here at 0900 and close at 1200. They open at 1600 and then close at 2200. In the meantime, they close for all prayer times, which can be twenty to forty-five minutes. So just after lunch will be fine, if it happens. That means that traffic will be light because all the shops will be closed. It will also give me a chance to post this letter. There is no good way to post a letter. There are no mailboxes. Well, what can you expect in a city of almost two million people that doesn't have any phone books?

This should be enough to give you an idea how things are going here. Of course, once you are here, we can get down to more important things. I sure do miss you. Thinking of you makes me homesick for you. When you arrive, all will be okay. By the way, I'm trying to find out how you can be routed directly into Riyadh. The first thing is to not have you change airports on the way. If you do not, then your bags can be routed straight through to here, and that will save you a lot of hassle and bother. Also, you would miss the extra tariff for baggage if you stop in London. I'll get it figured out. I love you, sweetheart. See you soon.

Love,
Jim

PS I couldn't get this dumb thing off the computer to the printer in time for my ride to the embassy, so mailed the letter without it. Guess what? It's a thirty-minute ride to the embassy, way on the other side of town. When we got there, at 1400, they were closed. Sorry, eight to one Saturday through Wednesday. I told them that they had told me on the phone they were open eight to five Saturday through Wednesday. Well, never mind that. We have to go back tomorrow, if we can get a ride. That's the way it goes. I still love you.

Dispatch:
Riyadh, Saudi Arabia
September 22, 1986

A DARK AIRPLANE

Stayed in the apartment today, just working on the computer. Phil called and said he had us a ride to go shopping, which meant with one of the Medevac drivers. He needed to pick up some things at the supermarket. One of the nurses, Andrea, was going along; she needed to stop at the travel agency. She's going home in a couple of weeks for a vacation. We went to the travel agency first, and after that, I was outvoted. They wanted to go to the gold souk. *Souk* is what they call a market here. Well, it's getting close to Charlotte's birthday, so why not?

More contrasts. The gold suqs (sooks) are located in the old sections of Riyadh. The *batha* (baat-ha), a part that I had not seen before. The buildings are old, the streets are narrow, and the area is solid gold! I've never seen anything to compare. Now I know why so few women are seen around town. They are all down at the gold suq.

"My friend, Phil Hardy"

Some of the shops were literally no more than a hole in the wall—eight feet wide and six feet deep with a pull-down steel gate across the front. The walls were lined with solid 18-karat items of gold! There were some larger shops, of course, but there were many as I just described.

It was in and out, in and out, in and out of these little holes in the wall shops until the nurse, Andrea, found just what she was looking for. It was a gold necklace with a herringbone design, about fifteen inches long. The gold here is normally 18 karat, so the first price was SR1,975. Remember, there are 3.75 SRs to the dollar. So the man was asking $526 for the necklace. He weighed it of course, and it weighed 30.6 grams (A28.35 grams equal one ounce by weight). We had already got a price per gram from several dealers, so it was easy to see he was way too high. The other dealers were dealing for SR47 or SR48 per gram. This guy was trying to get SR65.

About this time, right in the middle of the deal, there was a big flurry in the street. We were unceremoniously pushed into the street. It was prayer time, and all stores must close or face the wrath of the *Mataween* (religious police). Don't be deceived, the stores close, but they don't necessarily pray. Some lock the doors, pull the blinds, and continue to do business. That is the case in Western stores anyway. At the computer store, we were pushed into the back at prayer time while they locked the doors and pulled the drapes. We continued to do business out the back door.

After milling around for a while in the street, I was accosted by the police. The "street" we were standing in was not one for automobiles, but rather one that you might see in an old Bob Hope and Bing Crosby movie *The Road to Morocco*. I noticed this uniformed policeman pass by me slowly, and he was giving my handy talkie radio a very close and lingering look.

You see, civilians, in general, are not allowed to have transmitters here. So they are suspicious of anyone in civilian clothes with what looks like a two-way radio. Well, he circled me and disappeared in the direction he had come.

I told Phil and Andrea, "We are just about to have some trouble." They didn't believe it, but sure enough, in a couple of minutes, here came the same fellow with two of his buddies. His buddies had guns while he had none. They approached very slowly and cautiously while smiling and gesturing. Finally, they were within touching distance, and they began to point at my radio.

Andrea, the nurse, had a radio as well, but hers was out of sight in her handbag. It was at that time I remembered that I had left my puff bag at home. That was a real dumb thing for me to do! I had no iqama, no radio license, no ID, nothing. We were all three talking English and gesturing, but to no avail. Andrea pulled her radio out of her handbag. It had her licenses, IDs, etc., attached to the antenna. All such items have your photo attached under plastic. So they can see that she is the person to which they are made out to. After only a short inspection, we were released with many smiles and hand waving. Boy, was I lucky! They would have taken me to jail sure as the world. Shouldn't leave home without your IDs.

Well, by now, the stores and shops are opening again. The evening prayer only lasts about an hour. You know, they pray six times a day with the first one starting at about 4:00 a.m. and the last one at about 8:00 p.m. Before any other piece of authority came by, I gave my radio to Phil to carry. He had his puff bag with him. What is a puff bag, sometimes called a fag bag? Well, it's a little leather purse that men carry over here. It has a pocket for your radio and other pockets for IDs and money.

Most of the pilots that I have met carry around six or seven thousand dollars worth or SRs in them. That's a lot of money, I know, but you never know when you might have to make an overseas trip and need a lot, or if you are stopped for a traffic violation you are required to pay on the spot or go to jail. The puff bag is safe enough, nothing like in Houston. Not to worry. There is no such thing as muggings here.

Okay, times up, the praying time is over, and it's back into the shops. Andrea had to look in a couple of other stores, but Phil convinced her that the other necklace was by far superior, and if she didn't move fast, someone else would surely get it. We returned to the shop that had "her" necklace. Andrea was in her midtwenties and was going home for her first visit since coming over here four months ago. She told us that she had paid all her debts, bought both her sisters presents, and wanted to get something for herself. She wanted to buy something for her mom but thought she would just wait till she got home and get her a nice outfit.

Andrea was English as many of the nurses are, I think, and was from somewhere about ninety kilometers north of London. She was a pushover for the salesman, but with the help of Phil and I, we got him to come down to SR1,600 ($426) as a final price. We both felt that we could have gotten it cheaper if Andrea wasn't so anxious to have it.

By this time, it was 1830 and time to meet the driver for our return to the compound. We all needed to stop for a few groceries, so Hussam's was on the way. The drivers are on an eight-hour shift, and these shopping trips are overtime. They have mixed emotions about the overtime. The money is good, but they put in so much overtime, it becomes a burden.

While we were in Hussam's, Romeo called a mission. Number 1 was out on a mission. I was number 2, so that was me. Andrea was a number 3, so she would be the backup nurse. The number 2 nurse was Cherene, and by the time we got back to the compound, she was ready to go. Most missions are called with a captain, first officer, flight nurse, and engineer. The exception would be for a VIP mission, and then they might or might not call a flight nurse.

Most captains, first officers, and engineers have their own cars, so they seldom ride with the compound driver. Since the nurses cannot drive in this country, they have to have transportation to the hangar. The engineers are supposed to do the walk-around inspection, pull the engine covers, etc.

The first officer, or copilot, does the cockpit preflight and programs the inertial navigation system or INS. The captain files the flight plan and requests an ADC number. The ADC number is for all airports except Jeddah and Riyadh. That's the way they keep up with all aircraft and try not to let any unknown types into the Kingdom. A short time before my arrival, they had two Israeli jets penetrate the border and made a couple of touch-and-go landings at the Saudi Air Force Base at Tabuk. They tell me that there were two Saudi fighters in the traffic pattern at the time. One of the Saudi pilots punched out, and the other crash-landed in the desert. So, I guess, that the Israelis claimed to have shot down two Saudi fighters without firing a bullet. That's what they tell me anyway.

The mission was for the transfer of two babies in incubators and an old man, a cancer patient. One baby was to get off in Ta'if. The old man and the other baby were to get off in Khamis. We were assigned to HZ-MSD, a G2. No big problem so far. As far as flying goes, the trips are very simple and easy. Our basic fuel load is 18,000 pounds. That will take us most anywhere in the Kingdom and return. Sometimes with multiple stops, we put on more or buy more on the way. It seems that most of our missions are to air force bases anyway, so if we buy fuel from them, it sort of keeps the money in the family.

We had a delay on the ambulances arriving from RKH (Royal Khalid Hospital), the hospital that does most of our business, so we didn't launch until 2045. That was about an hour and a half after the mission was called. We are supposed to be ready to launch in one hour on the ASAP missions, and usually we do. However, waiting on ambulances gets to be a way of life.

The trip to Ta'if was uneventful. The ambulance was waiting, the baby was transferred, and away we went. So far, so good. Khamis is a high altitude airport 6480 feet, I believe. There was a 16-knot crosswind, so I had a good crosswind landing. Well, guess what? No ambulance. We were expecting two. After about thirty minutes, one ambulance with no equipment for the baby's trip to hospital finally arrived. Since the baby was critical, the nurse decided to take the baby in our incubator to the hospital and then return for the old man.

All scheduling of the ambulances with the necessary equipment is handled by Romeo back in Riyadh. Romeo does a good job, but as in the States, there is always someone that doesn't get the word.

About the time the transfer of the baby to ambulance is completed, we get the word that the other ambulance is on the way and will be here in just a few moments. The trip to the hospital is about forty-five minutes. The nurse didn't want to be gone that long unless necessary. Besides, the second ambulance was the one for the baby. She didn't want to bring the baby back onto the airplane because of its tender condition. So she decided to wait off the airplane with the baby in the ambulance. She was being aided in these decisions by the doctor and male nurse who had accompanied us from Riyadh. It was their first trip on a Medevac mission. I think that was their primary reason for coming.

An hour passed and no second ambulance. The captain is supposed to help in these times if able, and I was running around like an Exxon captain without his business card. It'd been so long, and now we had another crisis. The portable incubator was running out of oxygen. Someone had to make a decision—transfer the baby back to the airplane or wait.

Finally, we heard that the second ambulance was on the airport, but lost. While all this was going on, the copilot was in the cockpit in contact with Romeo by HF radio. Romeo was working the landline to try to get the ambulance to the airplane. The second ambulance arrived, and by now, it was well after dark. The baby was transferred, and then we could put the old man into the first ambulance.

Suddenly, I saw the lights going dim in the airplane. I ran for the cockpit, but too late, the battery voltage was already going down through 16 volts. The copilot, Bashir, said the T/R switch was not on. He said that he had just turned it on, but nothing happened. Well, we know why nothing happened. After the voltage gets below about 18 volts, the relays start relaxing, and even though you put a switch to the on position, nothing happens because the batteries are below the minimum operating voltage for the relays involved.

Okay, now we got a black airplane, and the old man, a doctor, a male nurse, and all the rest of us were setting there in the dark like a bunch of dummies. Bashir was just finishing taking fuel, and the fire trucks were still there. So I asked the chief to call on his radio to see if we could get a power cart. He made the call, and in about ten minutes, down the flight line we see the flashing yellow light. The GPU, ground power unit, was on the way. We were on an air force base, right? They only had an AC unit, no DC. Well, I got the power cart plug in the right hole, got an indication on the AC meter on the airplane, but no way to charge the batteries. I couldn't get the relays to close.

Yes, I know what the book says, but the relays won't close, remember. The AC from the power cart is incoming. The relays have to be powered on the inside going out, and the batteries are so flat that they can't energize the relays to let the AC come into the batteries.

Then was the time to say dadgum it. The only thing I could think of was to wait for a while for the batteries to internally build themselves up till the relays might see enough voltage to close. Knowing that batteries will build up a slight voltage if left to rest has saved my bacon more than once.

In the meantime, the doctor, male nurse, flight nurse, firemen, and several other well-wishers were moving the old man to the ambulance—in the dark. It took about thirty minutes, and sure enough, I checked the batteries; they showed 18 volts. I put the battery switch to emergency, the T/R switch to emergency, and the external DC switch to on, and guess what? They latched, and we were in business. Shortly thereafter, we were able to start the APU and get a good charge on the batteries. Saved again.

The batteries took a high rate of charge on the way back to Riyadh and kept kicking off-line (they get too hot when charging at such a hight rate), but I let one battery at a time rest a while and then reconnected. By alternately charging the batteries one at a time, we arrived back at the hangar at about three thirty in the morning. We keep in almost constant touch with Romeo. He made sure there was an engineer to meet us.

The engineer had the DC GPU ready to plug in when we nose into the hangar. He called for a fuel truck and brought it up to the basic 18,000 pounds. He checked the logbook and worked off all the squawks that he could. The aircraft must be ready to go immediately, if it's not grounded. Never know when the next ASAP mission will be called. Remember the outfit is 24/7. The flight nurse, meanwhile, was removing the drugs and any other lockup items from the plane. The copilot and captain were filling out the paperwork.

We completed a flight report, which was also a part of the squawk list. We also made a report out for the hospital showing patient's name and details for the charges for time of the aircraft and crew. We also made out a per diem report for the time after 1800 hours and before 0800 hours. The captain made SR29/hour ($7.75), the copilot made SR27/hour, and the flight nurse made SR25/hour. Not too bad. The per diem was rated different for out of the Kingdom trips, long maintenance trips, etc., but it was not bad.

We don't keep a detailed expense account here because there are no taxes; therefore, the government is not interested, and the company can pay any way they want to. The driver showed up to take Andrea and me back to the compound, and now it was four thirty. With a little luck, I could be in bed by five thirty.

"Well, it's the twenty-third now, and I'll take a nap, and that'll be it, right? Wrong, but I'm going to put that story under a new heading!" I decided.

Dispatch:
Riyadh, Saudi Arabia
September 23, 1986

THE DESERT FOX GETS A JUMP-START!

The night before was a hard night, in bed at 0530 hours, so the idea was to sleep in. That's a good plan, but as good plans go, it didn't work out. The phone rang about 1000 hours to tell me that Medevac had an appointment for me to get my base pass. That usually happens the first day when you arrive at a new military base in the States, right? Not here. It has been three weeks, and it's just now happening. If I had needed to get a sticker for my car, if I had owned a car, then I'd need another appointment. Getting passes and permits here is just not easy.

There were four of us from Medevac that had the same appointment time: me, Linda Baud, and two other nurses. We were driven to the area near the main gate by our driver, Kingsley. We wandered around a cluster of small buildings nearby, looking for the right one. The way to find the right building over here is to just keep going to different buildings, opening the door of each, and saying hello. If anyone there understands English, ask him where the right building is; if they don't understand, then you show them your letter. For these occasions, you always have a letter from the director of operations explaining what you need and with an official seal. The seal is what makes the letter work because chances are they can't read. An attached black-and-white photo of passport size is also good. It's best if the photo is made on paper, not plastic.

"Linda Baud. The sergeant said she should be married."

Phil tells a story of when he was in Nigeria; there was a guard that kept giving them a hard time because their letter had no seal. It would have taken a long time to get another letter with a seal, so American ingenuity came through. They stamped it with the bottom of a Coke bottle, and the guard was very happy with the letter and its new "seal."

The most senior one in the room is identified immediately. His demands to see the letter left no doubt in our minds or in any others in the room that he was the man in charge. His reading of the letter would take some time. Even if he can't read English, he would read it several times. Even if it was in Arabic, he would read it several times. The letter could get quite worn quickly. The senior man would then motion you to the next building. The buildings on this air force base have no numbers. That's okay because the streets have no names either. Working this system only as a bunch of *kawajees* (white faces) could, we finally arrived at the correct building. There were two GIs inside, and neither spoke English. We gave the sergeant our letter, which was written in Arabic. The sergeant read the letter several times, but there was still something wrong. Even the hand waving part didn't help. Well, we gave up and backtracked to our driver. He followed us to the sergeant for an attempt at translation.

We shouldn't have expected too much in any case because the driver was from Sri Lanka, and his Arabic wasn't so hot either. With much hand waving, he eventually got the message. The sergeant needed film for the Polaroid ID camera. We were supposed to bring our own film. We never even thought about furnishing the Saudi Air Force with film so they could make our pictures for a base pass to get on to their air force base. They may be one of richest nations of the world, but we're going to pay for the film, or we don't get the passes. So we chipped in and sent the driver for film. That meant he would be gone for some time.

Our little group waited in the room for about forty-five minutes and was completely ignored. Abruptly, the sergeant got up and waved for us all to follow him. He backtracked through the same buildings we had been through. He took us into the latrine. He shouted a few commands at all there, and we left. I couldn't help thinking he was just putting on a show for us. He wanted to be sure that we all understood that he was in charge of this particular part of the air force base.

After finally arriving at a building that we hadn't seen before, we were surprised to find it was the right one. Inside there was a Samsonite suitcase with a Polaroid camera mounted on one side and a laminating device on the other. In a matter of ten minutes, at the most, the base passes were made for all of us. We were not through. The sergeant had placed one of the nurse's photo on my base pass, so they had to be made over. Then we had to return to the first building and wait for the driver.

Suddenly, the sergeant started speaking to the nurses in Arabic. Linda told me later that he said to her, "Why don't you wear a veil? Are you not married?" When she told him that she was not married, then he said, "Well, you ought to wear one anyway, but those other two don't need to!" He had just admired Linda's looks and insulted the other two nurses.

When the driver came back with the film, we were allowed to sign the roster and receive our passes. The sergeant kept the film. You see, the system works, but it just doesn't work the way we think it should.

I have a theory about the system over here. The Saudis have visited other nations of the world. They have educations from the finest universities and have brought back to their home country the best ideas of the USA, UK, West Germany, France, etc. The Kingdom has enough financial strength to implement many of the best procedures from abroad. The drawback or the reason that the procedures don't work as well here as they do in the countries that they were borrowed from is that they are carried out with Saudi customs, traditions, and the *Mataween* (religious police). In addition, the customs from the different countries are all mixed together. It is a difficult trio to deal with. Many of our procedures only work because of the total network of politics, law, voter acceptance, and general acceptance of the local public. Remove these background factors from our country, and I feel sure that many of the day-to-day goings-on in the USA would simply disappear.

Consider this, the United Kingdom operated as a monarchy with power shared by the Roman Catholic Church for several hundred years. It took a revolution and many more years before the present form of democracy in the UK to emerge. Don't forget all the trouble the common people had with this combination. Before it was all sorted out, the United States was formed from people that wanted to escape the tyranny of that system.

Before the people here are criticized too severely for their inability to perform well under our system, then we must remember that they didn't even have a country as such until 1932. Perhaps, the next time we see *Lawrence of Arabia* on TV, we'll watch a little closer and realize that these people have made the jump from camels to jets in only a couple of generations. I'm sure that even Lawrence never dreamed of the development and advancement of these nomadic people in a mere fifty-four years.

Enough of the sympathetic remarks about the local society. Recently, an airline captain was relieved because he announced to the passengers just prior to landing in Riyadh, "Welcome back to the fifteenth century."

One is constantly reminded of the vast amount of funds that are spent for the betterment of the people here. There are no elections coming up that require those in power to spend and promise their way successfully through those same elections. I can remember returning to New Mexico several years ago for a visit with my mother. After the greetings, I had to ask, "Mama, when is the election?" She would say, "In about two weeks, why?" "Well, I noticed that the Grand Quivera road has just been graded." It was common knowledge that the politicians in power always graded the roads just before election time to remind the voters what fine fellows they were. The voters knew that it would be two years before they were graded again.

Well, that little story is not limited to New Mexico by any means. Once in a while, I think the American people should stop and consider how things are really accomplished in our own country before we criticize the way they are accomplished in other countries.

All of this must be viewed with the realization that my opinions are formed through the eyes of a newcomer. Perhaps after a longer observation, my views will have to be modified. We will see. I am reminded of the classic remark often made when the Exxon pilots were holding one of their high-level meetings in a hotel room after a flight, "Well, this next year is really going to be interesting!"

$$*\quad*\quad*$$

At a quarter to 10:00 p.m., Romeo called a mission; it was to Jeddah with three doctors. They were going over to make an evaluation of a patient. The old fellow had a very serious heart problem with several other complications, and the experts in Riyadh were not that sure that he should be moved or that they could help him if he was transferred.

It was not uncommon here to have conflicting decisions concerning the patient. Sometimes it finally comes down to the captain. When the doctor in charge says the patient shouldn't be moved, the nurse says the patient shouldn't be moved, but the relatives insist on moving the patient to what they perceive to be better conditions, then the captain must make the final decision. We are provided with release forms that all the relatives present must sign, then I can go ahead and move the patient with no fault to myself (or Medevac). That is another trick that they probably learned from us. Cover the old six o'clock, eh? Don't get me wrong.

It never was the intention to make the aircraft commander responsible for a medical decision. It's more like at a certain time and place, there is always someone that has to make the final decision. The first time I saw the "hold faultless" form, I refused to sign it. The original was in Arabic, and the English translation made it sound like the captain was making the decision over the heads of the doctors and relatives. I told them that I wouldn't sign the form, and I didn't think any of the other captains would either. They wanted to know why not, so I told them that the way it was written, the captains were being held responsible not being released from responsibility. Oh, they didn't mean it to be that way, so they changed it to my suggestion. Who said my law training would never pay off? Twenty-three episodes of Perry Mason came in handy one more time.

The mission was called on MS3, which has the large cargo door for loading the patient. That's good because loading and unloading critical patients can be a struggle up and down the stairs. At any rate, as soon as the doctors arrive, we launch and are on the way. It is about one hour and ten minutes to Jeddah from Old Riyadh; not a whole lot can happen in at hour ten, so we arrived in a very normal fashion. The ambulance from the hospital was waiting at the security gate, and the doctors

71

left in it with the word that they may be delayed in returning. You know, they have to see the patient and then do all that doctor stuff, where they stand around and stroke their chins and say "hmm" a lot.

I think that I might like to be doctor one of these days. I've watched them over the years, and it looks real easy. First rule, don't ever give anyone a straight answer (that would work if I wanted to go into politics also). Second rule, if you are forced to be more specific, then use Latin words. Third rule, if they understand Latin, then fall back on the first rule. It's easy to be a doctor; all I need is some knife time. Now that's the tough part, getting the knife time. I almost got some knife time while in the army, but the MPs broke it up before I was able to do any good; besides, it was the other guy that had the knife. But that's a whole different story and doesn't have a thing to do with picking up the patient in Jeddah.

Well, we settled in for a long wait. The consensus was it would take two hours before the doctors got back. It was over three hours by actual count. We ordered some sandwiches from Saudi Airlines. They were club sandwiches without the ham, of course. We had sandwiches, soft drinks, and plenty of time for conversation. The copilot, Tarak Yahya, told me he was saving his money in aviation to move back to the desert. He was going to raise camels and sheep. He had always wanted to be just a plain Bedouin. Well, that's a switch. I would have thought that it would be the other way around. Save your money and leave the desert is the way I would have figured it. Just goes to show you, how can you ever be successful in deciding what someone else wants? The fact is you can't. Seems to me we spend an awful lot of our time doing just that, however.

We were in the middle of finding out the origin of the Arab people when the doctors returned with the patient. Okay, just load him up and leave, right? Wrong. We have to get him through the security gate. The FBO at Jeddah is Arabasco. They are the only general aviation dealers on the field and are as competent as you will find here. They have a little building for their operations, which include a lounge for waiting crew members. The next building north is a building marked Arrivals. The second building north is marked Departures. The one marked Departures has several guards and the necessary equipment for checking bags, personnel, etc., for those that are departing by private aircraft.

Access from the rest of the airport is controlled through a chain-link sliding gate. The gate is kept locked at all times. To gain access, you must request the key from airport security. The key is kept at the main terminal, and the security people will not honor any request for the key until they have checked with Customs and Immigration, even for domestic flights. They will not leave the key with their own guards that are stationed right next to the gate. It makes no difference how critical the patient is. You may as well get ready for a thirty-minute delay for the gate being opened. It took me five months to come to this realization.

Calling ahead on the radio and telling them you have a critical patient onboard and will be landing in fifteen minutes is just a complete waste of time. Airport security will do nothing until they see you arrive with their own eyes, and then it takes about thirty minutes. Don't trust nobody, remember?

The crew uses those thirty minutes to open the cargo door, get the flight plan "on request," and any other last-minute details. The key finally arrives, and the ambulance is allowed to enter the ramp area and approach the aircraft. It was a good operation that night, and the patient was loaded with no problem, and as soon as the doctors and nurse were ready, we started engines. Well, we started one engine. Pilots always start engines from right to left. Never mind why we do it that way. We just do. Anyway, the right or number 2 engine starts fine, but no go on the left or number 1.

Oh man, what a mess! The patient in the back is just barely hanging on by his IVs, and I can't get the number 1 started. No, we can't go on just one, so don't ask.

It was quickly determined that the problem was with the start valve; it wouldn't open. These engines are started by air delivered by the APU to the starters that are air driven. If the start valve doesn't open, then you can't make the start. Maybe, if we could get a wrench on that sucker, we could open the valve manually and get it started. Well, that's a two-man job, and I got to stay in the cockpit to make the start. I can't expect the copilot to open that valve because I'm not that sure how to do it myself. We needed some help, and it's now way after midnight. The circus was back in town. After nearly forty-five minutes, we found a mechanic from Saudi Special Flights that agreed to come down and give us a hand.

In the meantime, the doctors were getting real antsy (see nervous). One of the younger ones was following me around like a shadow while I was trying to find a mechanic. He was asking a lot of questions that I hadn't got time to think about yet. Finally, he had me cornered, and I had to give him my attention. He wanted to know what we were going to do. I tried to explain that we were trying to get the aircraft fixed and that I should have an answer within about thirty minutes. If at that time I had determined that we couldn't get it fixed right away, then I would have to call for another aircraft to relieve us. I assured him that just as soon as I had an answer, I would let him know.

This didn't satisfy him at all. You see, I thought he was concerned with the health of the patient. Well, he wasn't concerned with the patient at all. He was afraid of flying on this aircraft. Was it going to be airworthy? Would it be safe? Should it be trusted? and What were our chances? By that time, I felt like I was the doctor and he was a relative of the patient. So I just fell back on rule number 1 and told him, "Oh, no problem, don't worry, we are just going to make a jump-start." That was all he needed. He understood jump-start for he had a couple of those himself, so he relaxed and got back on the aircraft.

We got it started okay, and the doctor never knew that I had used his own rule number 1 on him.

Dispatch:
Riyadh, Saudi Arabia
September 30, 1986

FLIGHT LOG FOR SEPTEMBER 1986

Hey, guys, just to show you that we stay busy over here. Not every trip is worthy of a story.

Date	Aircraft	Route	Note
September 03, 1986	HZ-MSD	OERY-OETF	first flight to Ta'if, thunderstorm
September 03, 1986		OETF-OERY	return to Riyadh
September 10, 1986	HZ-MS4	OERY-OENJ	Check ride w/ Odie Pond and Phil Hardy
September 10, 1986		OENJ-OETF	to Ta'if
September 10, 1986		OETF-OEKM	to Khamis
September 10, 1986		OEKM-OERY	return to Riyadh
September 11, 1986	HZ-MS3	OERY-ORJB	first mission, to Royal Jubail,
September 11, 1986		ORJB-OEJB	then Jubail, pu baby, at wrong airport
September 11, 1986		OEJB-OERY	return Riyadh
September 11, 1986	HZ-MS4	OERY-OETB	second mission same day to Tabuk
September 11, 1986		OETB-OERY	return Riyadh
September 14, 1986	HZ-MS4	OERY-OEMA	to Medina and return
September 15, 1986		OEMA-OERY	return Riyadh
September 15, 1986	HZ-MSD	OERY-OEJN	to Jeddah
September 15, 1986		OEJN-OERY	return Riyadh

September 19, 1986	HZ-MSD	OERY-OEJN	to Jeddah
September 19, 1986		OEJN-OEDR	to Dhahran
September 19, 1986		OEDR-OERY	return to Riyadh
September 19, 1986	HZ-MS3	OERY-OERR	to Ar'ar
September 20, 1986		OERR-OERY	return Riyadh
September 22, 1986	HZ-MSD	OERY-OETF	to Ta'if
September 22, 1986		OETF-OEKM	to Khamis, dark airplane, no DC power cart on air base
September 22, 1986		OEKM-OERY	return Riyadh
September 23, 1986	HZ-MS3	OERY-OEJN	to Jeddah, jump start no. 1
September 24, 1986		OEJN-OERY	return Riyadh
September 29, 1986	HZ-MS4	OERY-OEBA	to Al Baha
September 29, 1986		OEBA-OERY	return Riyadh

Dispatch:
Riyadh, Saudi Arabia
October 3, 1986

THE DESERT FOX GOES TO AFRICA

For all I know, you may have never been to Africa, so maybe you would like to hear about my first trip. Memorable experiences can come from first impressions, and this was no exception.

Just about the time you think everything is calm, look out. The day is Friday, which means the Sabbath here. I haven't gotten used to that yet, but I'm faking it. Today I'm a number 1 (we call it F1), but Romeo has been quiet, so nothing is going on. You can tell sometimes, in advance, when something is up. Romeo will call "Alpha 3-0" (pronounced, Alpha three zero), which is the call sign of the project manager, for permission to lay on a mission. We can't hear the replies to Romeo, but if the mission receives a go, you will hear the SELCAL go off four times. If you're a captain, and it's your day to be it, then the first one will be yours, the second will be for the copilot, the third for the engineer, and the fourth for the flight nurse. If the call is for you, then you might just as well head for the airport.

If the mission is iffy or is of some private nature so that Romeo is not sure, he may ask Alpha 3-0 to call him on the *lima, lima* (landline) or the telephone, to those of the unknowing. But as I said, the day is calm, nothing is happening, so when Phil calls to ask me to go for a ride in a little rice burner car that he and I or we might be interested in buying, I'm ready to go. Anyway, we need to go to Hussam's or the Panda store and buy something for the big party tonight at the compound swimming pool.

Didn't tell you about that? Well, don't worry. It didn't happen for me anyway. We had just returned from the store in the little Mazda 626; in fact, I was still at Phil's place when Romeo started the radio calls. He called for Alpha 3-0 to call him on the landline. We knew then that it was going to happen.

Sure enough, a couple of minutes later, I heard my SELCAL go off. You see, each of our radios has an individual identity for the SELCAL, so when Romeo punches in the tone codes for a station, each one can be called separately. If we have our radios set on SELCAL, then we hear only our own call. If we have our radios set on NORMAL, then we can hear all stations called. For each station called, you hear two tones: sort of a *boop . . . beep*; if the call is for you, it does a sort of a *boop . . . beeee . . . leep*. The second tone sounds like it has been split. Sure enough, here comes the *boop . . . beeee . . . leep* on my radio, and the show is about to start.

Now I've been over here a little more than a month, and so far, nothing has been uninteresting. When the SELCAL goes off, everything stops. Sort of like the TV advertisement. You know, "When E. F. Hutton speaks, everyone listens." A very good analogy. Picture a group of people on the compound sidewalk, just chatting, when the tones start: all conversations stop—man, woman, and child. After the four calls, we will hear something like, "Gulfstream 68, 08, 53, and 42, this is a mission for Gulfstream MS3 from Riyadh, to Khartoum, to Riyadh. Transfer a patient from Khartoum to Riyadh. Gulfstream 68, acknowledge please." After I acknowledge, then he calls each of the other four in turn for their acknowledgments.

It's as simple as that. I've just been called for a trip to Khartoum. Phil and I wondered about the location. Phil thought it might be in Africa! No, it couldn't be there. Surely, I wouldn't get called out for a trip to Africa without some kind of prior notice. I told Phil, "Catch ya later" and was gone. Now I've got to get dressed and head for the airport.

There was no need to run, but I walked fast to my apartment. As I walked in the door, the phone rang. It was the nurse, calling to see if it was an overnight stay. "Have to call you back," I said. "I don't know anything yet." While I'm peeling off my clothes, the phone rings again. Now it's Romeo. "Forty wants to know about the fuel load." The engineer was already at the hangar; in fact, he was just putting the aircraft to bed from its last trip. Dadgum, I haven't even had a chance to find out for sure where Khartoum is, let alone how far it is or how much fuel I'll need. I told him I'd call him back.

I had a uniform shirt but no uniform pants, so I put on the uniform shirt with my black Wranglers. I know, they are not part of the uniform, but they are black, and they look pretty close. Before I could get them on good, the phone rang again. It was Phil. "Hey, I was right, Khartoum is in Africa." He had guessed right. Well, close enough, so I called Romeo and told him to tell 40 to top off the tanks. Phil said it was in Sudan. That didn't help a lot, but it seemed that I remembered, vaguely, reading about the "Charge of the Light Brigade," and maybe that was in the Sudan. You know, "Cannons to the right of me, and Cannons to left of me, and not a drop to drink," or something like that. No, maybe that was in the Crimea.

Anyway, by then, others are getting into the act. Walt Schmitz calls to give a few points of advice because he heard the mission called and knows it's my first international trip for Medevac. Well, it's not my first international trip, but it is the first one from here, and there is considerable difference. In fact, back in the States, I had spent two or three weeks preparing the aircraft and paperwork for an international trip other than Canada. Sometimes it can take several weeks just to get landing or over flight permits.

I found out later after arriving at the airport and looking up the numbers in the Jeppesen that the Sudanese government requires seven days notice for giving a landing permit in their country. So when Walt told me that Bruce, the dispatcher, was on his way to the airport, it made me feel a lot better.

I was there the night that Odie and Walt were called on a mission to Africa, and that was a circus. Bruce was on leave, and there must have been ten people present, all involved, trying to get landing permits, over flight permits, determine routes, get weather, and all the rest. It was a mess, but they got it done. Now it's my turn, and any constructive help will be appreciated. Advice from Walt accepted; I called the nurse and told her, "It's an out and back, no overnight." I think.

Phil had lived and flown in Africa for five years when he worked for Mobil, so I called him and asked if he would like to go with me to the airport. Of course, he was glad to help, and I would do the same for him. We met the nurse at the front gate, where Jyantha, the Medevac driver, was waiting for us, and away we went.

The nurse, Linda Baud, had some additional information on the patient, which she shared with me. That is one of the nice things about sharing a ride to the airport with the nurse on these missions. They have information having to do with the patient that the rest of the crew doesn't get. There is just not enough time for Romeo to tell everything to everyone that's involved. Linda was from the UK, a very capable nurse. I learned later that she was ICU qualified.

She said that the patient was a RTA, i.e., a road traffic accident victim with a head and neck injury. What a coincidence. I just finished reading *Patton's Last Days* about the way General Patton died—a traffic accident with head and neck injuries.

The injured man was a member of the Sudanese government, perhaps a brother to the headman and would have some people with him. How many, we did not know. It turned out there were four, which meant that the nurse might not have a place to sit on the return trip.

Bruce was at work when we arrived. Bruce was a white man from South Africa. He's a good man to have. He was making inquires about handling at Khartoum and on the route we would take. In aviation, handling means arrangements for fuel, catering, permits, whatever. In this case, he was using Nile Valley, which is a large FBO (fixed base operator) in Egypt and other parts of Africa.

Phil and I started searching the Jeppesen charts and maps for information on a route and airport facilities while the nurse was loading the aircraft with the medical supplies needed for this particular patient. The engineer had finished fueling before we arrived, so he started the APU (auxiliary power unit on the plane) for the nurse to check out her equipment.

The first call came in at 1430 hours, and all this was happening just forty-five minutes later. The copilot, Hatim Bashir, arrived about that time and started helping Bruce with any information that he could. Hatim was a Saudi, about my height, with dark black hair and eyes to match. He became one of my favorites to fly with—always in a good mood, great sense of humor, and competent help as a copilot.

Once the route was established, the copilot would load data into the navigation equipment (INS and Global VLF). Everyone was there, and everyone was busy.

Bruce had requested a flight plan from Universal Weather in Houston just as a matter of routine. We were having a difficult time getting Africa weather information from the local source, and we knew that Universal could be counted on for a good weather report along with the flight plan. Universal does handling also in many parts of the world, but not at Khartoum. (Hmm, I wonder why not Khartoum?) All the telex messages had been sent, so then the crew was free to do the preflight on the aircraft while waiting on the answers.

While we were doing all this rushing around, there was a lot of high-level maneuvering going on at high levels (where else?). What goes on at the high-level meetings is over most people's heads. That is why they call them high levels, you see. Back in the States, the flight crews almost always had a high-level meeting after a flight. In fact, we just called them high levels, and what went on in those meetings was usually over the heads of all present.

But in this case, the needs of protocol had to be attended to. You might think that the needs of the patient would be paramount. Well, they are, but only after the bureaucrats get the protocol straight. Expecting some delays because of it being an international trip, I had taken time to gather up my camera equipment and bring it with me. As it turned out, the only pictures that I made were on our ramp of our aircraft, which is a definite no-no.

We are not allowed to have a camera on the air force base. It takes special permission and a lot of paperwork before we can photograph our own aircraft on our own ramp, so if you want to take a camera with you on a trip, you have to sneak it in. The security police are on constant vigilance for such naughty goings-on and have been known to confiscate both the film and the camera. The security police are watching for anything suspicious. Anything that they don't understand comes under the heading of something suspicious.

For example, I recently bought a dash compass for my car. It has compensating magnets built-in so that it can be swung like the compass in an aircraft. The problem is finding a place with known directions to swing it. For those that are wondering what "winging a compass is, then a brief description might help. A compass, being a magnet, likes to point to magnetic north. It also likes to point to other magnets, ferrous metals, and sources of electromagnetic influence (electric motors, radios, television, soldering irons, etc.).

To compensate for these external influences and distractions, small magnets are mounted on the north-south and east-west axis of the compass needle, and by turning the little compensators slightly, the compass needle can be fooled into pointing in the correct direction and not be distracted by the other influences. This is usually done by pointing the vehicle, with the compass mounted, in each of the four cardinal directions, while adjusting the compensators. This usually takes a half hour of turning, twisting the compensators, turning some more, and fine-tuning the compensators. The big problem is where to find the points of known direction.

In this country, you can forget using the streets. They don't run in any particular direction. Well, at the airport, the streets by the hangar are oriented in relation to the runway, which is laid out on a magnetic heading, so why not use the streets near the hangar?

On the given afternoon, I was leaving the hangar after a trip; it was a weekend, and no one was around to use the streets or roads, and it should be a good time to swing the compass. There was an intersection a couple of hundred meters in front of the hanger, so I began to drive back and forth in the intersection, alternately pointing the car north, east, south, and west. I never finished the exercise. The security police grabbed me and very nearly took me to jail. They didn't know whether this kawajee was up to something no good or had just gone crazy; either way they were taking me out of action.

They didn't speak English, so I fell back on the tried and true—hand signals, pointing, and waving. They were finally convinced that I was up to no harm, and after I promised to leave right away, they figured I would be out of their hair. They probably still think I've been out in the sun too long.

Okay, back to the mission to Khartoum. I was successful in smuggling the camera on to the airport and into the aircraft. While awaiting our final departure clearance, I snuck (remember, over here you can spell any way you want to) the camera out and took a couple of pictures of the aircraft and crew. It wasn't because of bravery. The truth is, I didn't realize what a chance I was taking at the time. All the ramps are considered high-security areas regardless of what they have on them. The first ramp south of the Medevac ramp is filled with air force tankers.

Some of the old-type tankers were built on the Boeing 707 frame. Some of the new ones are built on the Douglas DC-10 frame. The next ramp south of that is filled with the AWACS. That's the spy in the sky, 707 with all the electronics equipment built inside and the big mushroom-type radar antenna mounted on top of the fuselage. They are shown on US television now and then and have been for years. Here they are very secret. They are in daily flight training here. Every afternoon, they are practicing touch-and-go landings on runway 19. They are within two hundred feet of the ground when they pass over the highway, so anyone could take a picture of them if they so desired. Still, they are a big secret. The US Air Force has a training detachment here trying to teach the Saudis how to fly the AWACS planes. So far, no checkouts.

McDonald Douglas has a hanger just north of ours. They have a Lear. Lockheed has a hangar farther down the ramp also, and I understand they are flying a Gulfstream III. The Saudi Air Force Intelligence has a couple of Lockheed JetStars. One is a Dash 8, and the other is a 731. So far they haven't asked me for any advice on flying the JetStars.

When I was a small boy in the early 1940s, we lived just outside of town near Sheppard Air Force Base in North Texas. I was about thirteen years old and had been building ode model airplanes since I was about eight. One day about noon, I saw a convoy of three military vehicles coming down the road, and they were going to pass right in front of our house. The center vehicle was a flatbed truck carrying a real honest to goodness fighter plane. It was a P38. I had been dreaming of flying something like that when I grew up.

Building ode models, drawing pictures, seeing them in the movies for years. Wow, what a thrill for a kid! My skin crawled just to think of being that close to a real P38. I ran in the house and got my little box camera and rushed back out to the road and got ready to get a real close-up. Not a chance, the air police jumped on me like a hen on a June bug. I thought I was going to go to jail for sure. I can't remember all the things that they charged me with or all the things that they threatened me with.

They tried to make me feel that I and my box camera would cause the United States to lose the war. Even for a thirteen-year-old boy, it all seemed absolutely ridiculous. So I just waited till they passed and took a picture as they were going away. Then I ran and hid in the storm cellar. I still had the picture the last time I looked. So much for national security!

Part of our getting ready was to get our passports stamped for exiting the country. The Immigration people can be very contrary; that day was one of those days. They were watching a soccer game. It was a very important game. They were busy and didn't want to be bothered. Our normal procedure is to send the passports by company driver to the Immigration office there on the field and get them stamped. The driver tells me they wouldn't do it now, later. Now if I wanted to wait for a couple of hours, then maybe they would. Well, I couldn't wait; too many arrangements had been made that were to be coordinated on my arrival time in Khartoum.

The captain had to make a decision, and the captain is as green as a peach tree limb. So we left without the stamp. This would be no problem if we came back to Riyadh, but if we landed at any other airport on arrival back in Saudi Arabia, we would be in the deep stuff because the agents there would not know when we left. Just another one of those decisions that has to be made. There is no good choice, but at least you have a choice. As it turned out, it would have been nice to stop in Jeddah on the return trip. Of course, we didn't know that at the time.

We were finally in the air and on the way. I had the fuel tanks topped off because this would be a maximum effort on range and fuel economy. The leg to Khartoum is a little less than three hours with head winds. The return leg will be a little less than two and a half hours with tailwinds, maybe. The idea is to make the round trip without refueling in Africa or running out before we get back. The mission aircraft was a Gulfstream GIII. It is the longest-range aircraft that we have and has been *the* long-range business jet since its introduction into service a few years back. It is powered by two Rolls Royce (Spey) engines that are real fuel guzzlers at low altitudes but deliver a lot of power and do pretty good on fuel economy at altitudes above thirty-five thousand feet. It is certified to forty-five thousand feet.

Our direction of flight was to the southwest, so that meant we could file for thirty-nine thousand feet initially and expect to go to forty-three thousand feet after burning off some fuel. We could climb directly to forty-five thousand feet on the return trip.

The reason I planned it as a round trip without refueling was to keep from buying fuel in Africa. They have had some trouble on the Dark Continent, and I didn't want to take on a load of fuel that some bad guys may have been piddling with. Besides, they charge about three times more for the jet fuel there than we pay for it here, and the boss likes to save the money.

Our route would take us southwest over Jeddah, across the Red Sea, and then turn more southwest to Khartoum. Jeddah was not quite halfway, so we were expecting about two hours and forty-five minutes in route. The critical point in this trip was to establish two-way radio communications with Port Sudan on the coast of Africa ten minutes prior to entering their airspace over the Red Sea. That sounds easy, but if you call and they don't answer, then what do you do? Besides, we only had *verbal permission* from some African politician to enter their country.

Not having the formal conformation from their minister of aviation is what had caused the delay in our departure from Riyadh. That adds to the tension in the cockpit. As I said before, the normal channels can take a week or a month depending on the country. Yes, that's right; we were going down there on a mercy mission for one of their diplomats that was in dire need of the hospital care available in Saudi Arabia—the hospital care that was not available in his own country. Yet they dillydallied around and would not give us permission until our king talked to their imperial potentate (or whatever).

We started trying to make contact a half hour early on the HF (high frequency, long range) radio. Lots of calls, no good. As we got closer, we tried on VHF (very high frequency, short range) radio. Lots of calls, no good. We finally had to relay through Jeddah control via landline (telephone). Once Jeddah talked to them on the phone, then they decided to talk to us on the radio. They had been hearing us all the time. The Sudanese rebels shot down a jet with a Russian-made SAM about a year and a half ago, and I didn't want to make anyone angry on that night.

The communications were established, so now we could relax. It was dark before we got to the Red Sea, and I was bemoaning the fact that I would not be able to get any pictures. Then Hatim displayed his sense of humor and mused that the night was dark, the continent was dark, the people were dark, and if the airport were also dark, we would be lucky if we didn't miss the whole thing. That was good for a nervous laugh. Perhaps you understand the feeling of getting on an airplane to go to a strange country. Well, how would you feel if it was dark with thunderstorms, and then you found out that it was the captain's first trip also?

Maybe it wasn't quite as bad as it sounds; the thunderstorms were not so thick that we couldn't find our way around them, and the airport did have lights, so it didn't turn out so bad after all. I will say that flying over at night without a moon is all you will need to convince you that Africa is a dark continent. Those campfires are not all that noticeable.

Hatim was flying the leg into Africa. It is customary to let him fly the empty legs, i.e., the ones with no passengers or patients. When the copilot is flying the airplane, then it is my turn to handle the radios. I'll have to say that if I had not had a good idea what they meant to say, then I would have been hard-pressed to understand what they were saying. You know, I'm a long way from where the people talk right. Pilots always get a laugh from the movies that show the captain doing all the flying, talking on the radio, and anything else that happens in the cockpit. If they show a flight engineer, he is always busy with the dials and gauges from his turnaround seat. They would have you think that the copilot or first officer has nothing to do.

Oftentimes, the copilot is the hardest working one of the group. True, the captain must have the skill and knowledge to handle the aircraft, but the copilot has to physically handle the radio communications and navigation. On approaches, he monitors the captain's actions and calls out critical points of altitude and speeds while reading the checklist. I hope none of our copilots read this for it would certainly have a bad effect on their attitudes.

Copilots in fixed-wing aircraft normally sit in the right seat. In some corporate flight departments, they are allowed to fly the aircraft from the left seat. I have never flown with the air carriers, but they tell me that in most cases their copilots are not allowed in the left seat. We fly under the same rules here. The copilot is not allowed to fly from the left seat. There are mixed opinions about the wisdom of this procedure.

There are a few things, like control of the aircraft on the ground, that can only be done from the left seat, so how can a copilot ever gain the experience and confidence he needs if he never has full control? Oh well, not to worry. Regardless of whose hands are on the wheel, the captain is still responsible.

We landed without incident. That means no one was hurt. As I taxied in to the terminal, the view was a lot like I had expected. Just like in the movies, the adobe-type buildings were rundown, guards everywhere with automatic weapons, and a general atmosphere like nothing exciting had happened there in a long time. Little did they realize that we were about to create some excitement of our own. We didn't mean to, really.

Just as soon as we could open the door, we were confronted with official-looking people with official-looking papers in their official-looking hands. In the English-speaking countries, it is usually the Customs and or Immigration officials that greet you first. In fact, it is a super no-no to open the door before they arrive. I have learned to expect the unexpected here.

The first fellow up the stairs was an airport official. I had to sign the papers he had so we could be charged for the landing. (They learned to do that from the Westerners.) The next couple of fellows were just interested and curious bystanders, maybe kinsfolk of the first fellow. By that time, I was all the way back in the cabin, and there were still more people trying to get on the aircraft. "Hold it, hold it, everyone off, everyone off," said I in my best captain's commanding voice. It is more effective if you wave your hands a lot. They began to leave the aircraft reluctantly. We never saw the Customs or Immigration officials at any time.

One of the last on the aircraft identified himself as working for Saudi. Saudi can stand for Saudi Airlines or Saudi Special Flights. This can get confusing. The Saudi Special Flights is relatively new outfit that was created to place all the various business jets, owned by individual princes, under government control. They have control of several GIIs and GIIIs like we in Medevac fly, plus a lot more types. The idea was to save the government money because they were all being charged to government expense in one way or another. So the government figured that if they were being charged with the use of these aircraft, then they might just as well own them, not unlike the thinking of the bureaucrats in our country.

The first thing the new organization did to cut costs was to cut the salaries of the pilots 40 percent. Well, everyone knows that pilots are paid too much, and they don't have to work very hard either. I think cutting salaries is all they ever did to cut costs. Saudi Special Flights have been trying, through political maneuvering, to get control of Medevac. So far, they have not been successful. You know, our prince is bigger than their prince.

So when this big fellow announces that he is from Saudi and wants to know what our needs are, then I have to stop and think. Besides, where was the Nile Valley rep? I told him, "Yes, we would like to have some catering for our return trip." In a demanding voice, he asked, "You don't want any fuel?" You see, that is where the real money is. I told him that we were supposed to buy fuel from Nile Valley. This really made him hot. The hand waving got much wilder.

"Hey, hold it, don't get all excited, I'm just a new guy," I said. "We're not going to buy any fuel anyway." That helped to calm him down a little, and he took our order for catering. We often get catering from Saudi Airline, and their food is excellent. On my first trip into the Kingdom, it was on a Saudi 747, and the food was by far the best that I have ever had on any airline. They are well known for the food they serve.

What we received from them that night in Africa was not worth bragging about. They gave us fried egg sandwiches and cheese sandwiches made from camel's milk or something. We were told we would have chicken and cheese sandwiches. It was fried eggs that turned out to be the chicken in the chicken sandwiches. It was much later that night before anyone got hungry enough to try them.

I didn't realize until over a month later what had really happened to Nile Valley that night. Competition in the area of aircraft fueling is always very evident. It's not unusual when taxiing onto a ramp to have more than one "follow me" buggies trying to woo you over to their ramp. Some have girls in short shorts while others give steaks and wine to the members of the crew. Those inducements are mostly in the USA. Well, it is not out of the ordinary at all to sell one business jet three to six thousand dollars worth of fuel. Even the small Lear can easily buy a thousand dollars worth of fuel and be gone in fifteen minutes. So the profits are in the fueling, and competition is fierce—no, very fierce.

The Saudi man at Khartoum had probably faked out the Nile Valley man by convincing him that Saudi had the contract for our flight. It can happen like this; we had to get a Saudi flight number to make the flight appear to be a commercial air carrier. We can sometimes cut through red tape that way, so almost always, we cross international borders as Saudi flight number so and so. The local man will use this number to intimidate his competition into thinking they have been misinformed that this is really a Saudi flight.

The competition leaves the scene, and Saudi has the fueling. This happened to me for the second time about a month later in Frankfurt. That time, I caught them at it and traced it back to the roots. Like how does Saudi know when we are coming so they know when to start the subterfuge? They have an inside man in Medevac back at Riyadh. But that's a different story under a different heading, and I'll have to get to that later.

Hatim went off to the tower to file our return flight plan. The nurse and I waited for the ambulance to arrive. We had several offers of tea or refreshment from some affluent-looking locals, but I had to decline. We had to have one of the cockpit crew remain with the aircraft. The nurse had no interest in going off by herself. So we waited. After half an hour, Hatim returned.

Since there was no way of knowing how long the delay would be, the nurse and I decided to go into the terminal and buy a souvenir. The terminal was only about two hundred feet away, so we moved off in that direction. We made our way past the first guard on our uniforms alone. Once inside the terminal, we could tell it was quite dingy and rundown. It reminded me of parts of Mexico. You could tell that it had been new and maybe even grand at one time, but that must have been a long time ago. It was beginning to look just like I expected it to look. Who says Hollywood never gets it right?

There was a little rundown gift shop on the far left side of the entrance. Only one person on duty and they had little or nothing to interest us. The clerk did tell us that there was another gift shop on the other side of the partition. She pointed more to the left, but there was no obvious way to go where she was pointing. The clerk's English ran out about that time, so we were on our own.

We wandered on through the terminal main room, looking for a door to our left. Just as we saw one coming into view, we found ourselves being hailed from a room on our right. Turning, we saw several guards with guns, and one wanted us to stop and show papers. We had no papers, so I showed him my passport. My passport is US of course, but it has a large white sticker on the outside with large Arabic writing on it. The guard took it, handed it back, and in English said, "This is no good, you cannot leave, you cannot go to town, you must go back."

Well, we didn't want to go to town; we only needed to go ten feet farther to turn left down the corridor to what we thought must be the other gift shop. I tried to explain that we were not trying to leave; we just wanted to go down that hall or corridor. He wanted to know why. We just wanted to buy gifts to take with us when we left Africa, but his English had already run out; besides, one of the other guards said that there was no such place down there anyway.

Finally, we were permitted to go that way. The guards were tired of the game, and we were allowed to go and see for ourselves what was down the hall. We found another waiting room with a large gift shop and many choices of gifts to choose from. It finally dawned on me what had gone wrong. I had been calling the gift shop a duty free shop all the time, and they didn't know what I was talking about. It's a good lesson. Many times these people will not understand what you are saying, but they never will tell you that they don't understand. You must learn to know when they don't understand all by yourself.

We found several unusual gifts. Some black bracelets that looked unique and were adjustable. We found out later they were made from the hair of an elephant's tail. There were several articles made from the skin of the boa constrictor (snake), handbags, belts, etc., and several items made from ivory, even some made from the crocodile, but I couldn't feel it easy to do much shopping. We had been gone longer than I had intended, so we really needed to get back to the ship. We made some purchases, and while we were paying for them, a man came and told us that the ambulance had arrived. The nurse left with the messenger back the way we came.

I stayed long enough to complete payment for the gifts, then I left. I was in a different terminal from the one we had entered, so I thought I'd shortcut out the nearest door and down the ramp. Good idea, but as some good ideas go, this one didn't go very far. The first guard gate was locked. I could see several hundred people on the ramp, and they were all around the Medevac plane. Something was going on there, and I didn't have time to go back the way I came, so this old man just put one hand on the fence and vaulted over. Felt pretty good. I hadn't done that in several years. Fortunately, the guards nearby were all looking at the commotion down the ramp, and none of them even noticed my arrival on the ramp. I am not a jogger, but I moved along at a pretty good clip back to the ship.

It was necessary for me to force my way through the crowd and up the stairs. The stairs were full, the vestibule was full, and the cabin was full. The vestibule will hold maybe three people if they stand straight up and real close together. That night we had three people in the vestibule and each one had two large suitcases, not in their hands but stacked on the floor, and their bodies were contorted and pressed around their suitcases.

Hatim had been forced all the way back into the baggage compartment. He told me later that the suitcases were what caused him to lose control. He told everyone to take their bags around to the rear of aircraft to load their bags through the baggage door. That's the way it's supposed to be done. There was something lost between his Arabic or their Arabic, or maybe they thought that was too much trouble, or maybe they just didn't want to.

It's always about that time when you start having language problems. I think it's for their convenience. Now it's time for some serious hand waving. I didn't have any idea who these people were, friend or foe. I knew the patient was a diplomat of some sort, but that can mean political enemies, and in those countries, they can get real serious about their enemies.

I had to get them off the airplane before I could start worrying about bombs or incendiary devices planted on the plane. After a short while, I got them off the plane, the bags sorted out, the copilot recovered, and the patient loaded. Once all the people were off the airplane and the patient was loaded, I posted Hatim at the top of the stairs and with a flashlight made a walk around exterior inspection of the plane.

After the passengers were counted and entered on the manifest, we shut the door and made an interior check of the aircraft. We couldn't open any of the bags but felt comfortable with the thought that no one was too likely to blow himself up. Yeah, I know, you can never be that sure over here.

I mentioned loading the patient as if there was nothing to it. Almost every time it is a problem, and that night was no exception. The GIII has a special cargo-type door on the right side of the fuselage just in front of the wing. It is about eight feet long and opens from the floor to the ceiling. We have a winch mounted on the floor of the aircraft and attached to the ceiling. It has a boom that we can swing out of the aircraft to lift and lower a special stretcher. The normal routine is for the captain to stay on board while loading or unloading, and the copilot and nurse go down to ground level to handle loading or unloading the patient.

The patient arrives by ambulance with a minimum of two drivers and a nurse. Often, there is a relative, maybe several relatives, a doctor, another nurse, and they all want to help. That night in Khartoum, there were several hundred that wanted to help. It looked like a scene from one of Cecil B. DeMille's movies. A dark night, lots of natives surrounding the ambulance, eerie shadows, noise from the APU (auxiliary power unit) on the aircraft, a badly injured patient that must be removed to the hospital right away, and political intrigue—yes, it was all there. Well, on second thought, DeMille would probably have opted for the natives all holding flickering torches instead of the electric lights of the airport. But everything else was there for a great scene from a great movie.

The crowd was so thick that the crew could hardly get the man out of the ambulance on the mobile stretcher he came in on. Then they had to move him about twenty feet to our stretcher lying on the ground and attached to the hoist. There were enough people to lift the aircraft and turn it around, but they were less than useless in helping to transfer the patient on to the hoist. At this point, the hand waving part doesn't do much good.

I am happy to report, however, that the Medevac crew prevailed over all adversities, to the relief of the patient, I'm sure.

It turned out that all the people were political supporters of the patient and our passengers. They meant no harm, just wanted to show their respect and well-wishes.

It's a wonder he didn't expire (I learned that from a doctor) while they were in the middle of their wishing the patient well.

I climbed into the cockpit and started flashing all the outside lights that I could. There was still a large crowd milling around near the plane. They got the idea when I started the engines. Fortunately, we didn't suck any turbans into our turbines, and away we went.

The rest of the trip was uneventful, except when one of the passengers announced that he had permission from the King of Saudi Arabia to land in Jeddah. Dadgumit, I knew we should have insisted on those passports being stamped. Well, I wasn't going to stop till I checked this story out. By the time we had his story verified, we had passed Jeddah on the way to Riyadh. Then we decided it would not be in the best interest of the patient to stop on the way, so we took him to Riyadh, refueled, and then took the VIP back to Jeddah.

Turned out, he had an appointment with His Royal Highness at 1000 hours the next morning. It was nearly 0400 hours by the time we got him to Jeddah, so I told him my name was Capt. Roy Strangefellow and to please give my regards to the king. It must have worked for I haven't heard a word about it since.

First Printing 1987, copyright in Saudi Arabia, the Land of the Sand and the Sun. (They don't have copyright or patent laws in this country among other things, like maple flavoring, pectin, or fresh cornmeal.)

Author's Note: I should say a few words here about my crew, Hatim Bashir and Linda Baud. Hatim was soon to become a favorite to fly with. He was good at his job and always in an agreeable mood with a great sense of humor. Hatim was about six feet tall and of course black wavy hair, black eyes, and I'm sure would be considered handsome by the ladies. I was always amused by his efforts to learn the local language of whatever country we were in at the time by riding up front with the cab driver on the way to the hotel. Hatim and I always had a good time together on our adventures. You will read more about him a little later.

Linda Baud was an attractive nurse from the UK with dark hair and eyes to match. She was also the intended of Jerry Padova, the mechanic from New York. Linda and I became good friends as well. We had many discussions regarding the US versus the UK. They were friendly, of course, well, sort of. One time, she said, "Jim Fox, your English is atrocious!"

"Oh yeah?" I replied. "I thought it was pretty good for a second language." Linda said, "A second language! What is your primary language?"

"American," I replied.

You, the reader, must remember that most everyone that I worked with spoke at least two languages, and many spoke several. I know that Linda also spoke French. You'll read more about Linda later also.

JDF Letter:
Riyadh, Saudi Arabia
October 5, 1986

LETTER TO CHARLOTTE

Hello, Sweetheart,

I was just told by the nurse, Mary Logan, that she is leaving this evening for a holiday in London, Ireland, and Mexico. That means that if I hurry, she will be able to mail this for me outside the Kingdom. That's always a bonus. Mail is very slow in the Kingdom, and sometimes even gets lost. So if we have a chance to have it mailed on the outside, we take it.

Did I tell you about Mary? Well, she's from Ireland, friendly, happy, but she never looks you in the eye. While talking, she will look past you, over your shoulder, or up at the ceiling. Very weird. Maybe after you get over here, you can find out why.

It's very easy for me to stay busy. Never had a problem with boredom anyway, but it seems that I just don't have enough time here to get it all done. The fact that I don't have a car is quite an imposition—the first time I've been in that condition since I was twenty years old. It seems that I am waiting on a driver for most anything I need to do. The company, GAMA, claims to furnish a car and a driver for all our needs. However, there are only four drivers, and they have to cover the airport twenty-four hours a day. They have to take the children to school and pick them up, make shopping trips for all that don't have a car, and run errands for GAMA. That doesn't leave much to spread around.

I've enclosed a small trinket, nothing exotic, except where it came from. So don't think you have to wear it. It's just sort of a keepsake. I picked it up night before last in Khartoum, Sudan, Africa. Since it was my first time there, I just had to buy something. Didn't have time to go shopping but found this in the gift shop at the terminal. Maybe next time, I'll have longer to look around and can do better. This is just to let you know that I was thinking of you at the time.

Perhaps my next out-of-Kingdom trip will be somewhere glamorous, but no telling. I'm trying to make a deal on a car that I found at the local Jaguar dealer. It's an '85 model that belonged to the general manager, a four-door sedan, white, with very nice appointments. The price is less than half its cost in the States. Well, you wouldn't want me to ride around in some old piece of junk, would you? The project director has a black one just like it, so perhaps he will be flattered that I have such good taste.

Of course, my last boss was not flattered that I bought a V12 Jaguar in the States at the same time that he bought a Corvette. They are not even in the same class. The truth is that I'm past the stage in life that I need to do anything to impress someone else. My motives are strictly selfish. I tried some of the little Japanese and even the German Mercedes, but the Jaguar is what turned on my key.

The weather here is still very warm in the middle of the day, but the nights are beautiful. They are not too cool, just comfortable, about 75°F. Of course, the sky is always clear here. Cities like Riyadh have something like pollution that hangs over the city. It's really dust, but you can't see it very well in the daytime, just at night. Coming in at night from a distance, it looks very much Houston—that is, a dull glow of city lights reflecting on particles in the air. However, when nearer, you can see that it is dust hanging above the city more than in the city. It's not so bad really, makes me sneeze, but no worse. At any rate, the heat is not bothersome at all. It still gets to about 104°F as a maximum, but there is practically no sweating. And if you pass into the shade, it's comfortable enough.

Well, I can't stay with this long as I don't want to miss the "post" as the English say. You need to know that, so far, I am enjoying the work here very much. It is a great adventure. Wouldn't want to have missed it. Besides that, what we in the Medevac do is very worthwhile.

I do appreciate the mail, so if you have the time, inclinations, and forty-four cents, drop me a line.

This was a formal letter that I made up real quick to make a copy for you, Louise, Babe, Mary, Colleen, and whoever else that I might think of at the last minute. Just had to tell you that I really do long for you and miss the good times we had in the past, how be it short. I love you and want you to be here just as soon as possible. The idea of meeting you in London for a few days on your way over sounds better all the time. Just as soon as I know when you can come, then I'll set up the arrangements. I'm still working on my Africa story, so will have to mail that later. Shook hands on the Jaguar deal last night, so am just waiting on the money. This is Sunday night, so maybe it will be here tomorrow. Till later, I love you.

Always yours,
Capt. James D. Fox
GAMA Compound
PO box 41728
Riyadh, 11098
Saudi Arabia

*   *   *

Author's Note: This is a good place to explain about the car and the money. As stated in the letter above, I found a white 1985 Jaguar XJ6. The price agreed upon with the Jaguar dealer was $14,000 USD. The same car new in the USA is about $35,000! What's the difference? Well, it's second hand, though barely, and there are *no taxes here. The "no tax" thing makes everything unbelievable. You can buy a brand-new Jaguar here for less than you can buy it in the UK! No UK taxes and no Saudi taxes. Wow, what a difference taxes make!*

Now the money thing. The GAMA people let me have $8,000 as a no-interest loan, so I needed another $6,000 to close the deal. I called Charlotte and asked her to wire me the money. It took eight days for the money to arrive. Another lesson learned. When money is being transferred through several hands, it seems that each one (hand) may keep control of the sum for long enough to count it as an asset before passing it through. You didn't know that? Well, check it out.

All the folks here were amazed with my purchase.

"Hey, Fox, are you crazy? You bought a new Jaguar!" they ask.

"Well, what's the matter with that?" I ask.

"Man, don't you know what you've done? You bought a better car than Major Shablan, now you'll really be on his list."

"Well, who cares, they don't give raises or bonuses here anyway, do they?"

You see, all the other captains were either driving the cheap rice rockets or real old junker Mercedes. I was riding with Odie one day in his Mercedes the other day, and as we turned a corner at a moderate rate of speed, the right rear tire rolled off the rim!

"Dadgum, Odie, what are you doing running around with a tire like that? Now we got to change a tire in 120-degree heat."

Odie seemed unconcerned and opened the trunk to get a jack. I saw three other old, worn-out tires in there, aired up and ready to put on the ground. They drive around with air conditioners that didn't work and tires that roll off the rims. Why? It all came clear later when I found that some of them intended to leave in the middle of the night without notification and leave everything behind! I learned later that those types were called midnight runners.

Well, I didn't intend any such thing, and further, I didn't want to drive my wife around in that harsh environment in a car that is less than untrustworthy. Besides, I had a Jaguar XKE back in the States, and I loved it.

"How can you afford to buy a new car, Fox? You just got here," they asked. I hadn't stopped to figure it out yet. I was the only captain there that came because I wanted to. All the rest had come to get away from something or had been out of work broke and couldn't find a job flying.

"Oh, you mean the money? Well, see, I don't have to worry about the money. I just married a rich widow woman from California! She has money that she hasn't counted yet."

It was an outlandish lie, and no one was expected to believe it, but it seems they all did. So I never attempted to correct them. I didn't tell Charlotte about her being a rich widow woman for a long time. She may have wondered about the unusual amount of respect that she received.

It was about this time that I gave Major Shablan an ultimatum! Before coming over, they told me that my wife could follow in two weeks. Well, six weeks and still no wife.

Charlotte had gone back to her home in California when I left Houston for Saudi Arabia. She had sold her house in anticipation of leaving soon to follow me. The soon part didn't happen, so she was camping out with her girlfriend waiting on her visa.

"Major Shablan, I was told that my wife could come over here in two weeks after I arrived. It will soon be six weeks, and every time I ask about the status of her visa, all I hear is that it will be soon. That is no longer good enough. Now, she's sold her home, has no place to live, and is sitting on a curb in Los Angeles. So I'm giving you notice, either get my wife over here or I'm leaving!"

Charlotte got her visa and was in London in about two weeks.

Earlier, the major had called me in for a heart-to-heart talk. He said the he had complaints from the copilots that flew with me that I didn't let them fly on empty legs of our missions.

"Captain, we are like a large family here, and we try to help those who are less fortunate than ourselves. It is our custom for the captains to allow the copilots to fly the legs of a mission when there are no passengers. From the right seat, of course. Don't you agree?"

"Major Shablan, no one told me of your custom. Certainly, I'll be glad to let the copilots fly from the right seat when we're empty. You see, how can I be expected to follow rules that have not been explained to me? Here is my position: I came over fully intending to fly your airplanes and to comply with and live within the laws and regulations of your country. It is your obligation to explain your rules to me. I can't be expected to follow customs that I don't know about. Now, you tell me what you want me to do, and if I agree, then I'll do them. If I don't agree, then I'll just go home! You see, I'm not here because I'm broke and can't find another flying job. I'm here because I want to be. So tell me the rules, and I'll tell you what I'm going to do, okay?"

There was an instant of shock on the major's face. I suppose he was not accustomed to such a speech. The first look was quickly replaced by a big smile and hand gestures and offers of goodwill and understanding.

The major never called me into his office again.

Dispatch:
Riyadh, Saudi Arabia
October 6, 1987

CONFRONTATION WITH MAJOR SHABLAN

Enough is enough. They told me that I could bring my wife over here within two weeks after my arrival. It's been six weeks, and I'm fed up with their stalling. I went in today and had a sit-down with Major Shablan.

I think he has been dreading to see me coming to his office. It's because he knows what is on my mind. The other day while riding down the street with my friend Phil Hardy, I suddenly yelled at the top of my voice, *"I want my wife!"* Phil nearly wrecked his little Nissan, and after a couple of seconds, he laughed and said he felt the same way.

We were promised before we came over here that our wives or families, as in Phil's case, would be allowed to join us within two weeks. Now it's more like six weeks, and they are still not here. Every time we ask why the delay, we are given a new excuse. The most used excuse is that they still have not received the visas for our wives or families. I had decided to make a move toward settling the delay.

"Ah, good morning, Captain Fox. It is so good to see you this morning," said Major Shablan with a large smile as he stood up from behind his desk with his right hand extended.

"Well, you might not feel the same when you hear why I'm here."

"Why, what could be the problem?" Major Shablan was much practiced in this condition, that is, pretending to be surprised.

"Major, it's time for you to make a decision. Either get my wife over here *now*, or I'm going home."

"But, Captain Fox, we must receive her visa first, you understand?"

"No, Major Shablan, I don't understand, and further, I don't even intend to try to understand. Visa or no visa, I want my wife here, and that's the end of the story."

"But, Captain Fox, we can't bring her here without a visa."

"Look, Major, here is what you should understand. Before I came over here, I was told that my wife would be able to join me in two weeks. From talking to other captains here, I've found that is a story that is told to all new hires. Well, I agreed to come over here based on what was told me before I came. My wife has sold her home in California based on what we were promised, and now she has no place to live. That's right, my wife is homeless in California. She is sitting on the curb with no place to sleep, and I'm not going to stand for it anymore. You can either have her here in the two weeks that was originally promised, or I'm leaving."

It was not an idle threat. I don't make such things. The conversation continued for a couple of more exchanges without a change in my determination, and the major seemed to get the message.

Three days later, I was called in to see the major, and he reported that a "breakthrough" had occurred in the visa paperwork, and the approval for my wife and Phil's family had been received and that they would be allowed to be here within two weeks.

"Well, that's good news, Major. Now I'd like a week off to go to London and meet my wife there. Also, I need to move into a larger apartment."

"Oh yes, of course, all that will be approved, *mafi Mesculah*." (The last phrase meant "no problem.")

And that's how I got to go to London for a week's leave to meet Charlotte. Phil was glad to hear that his family would be arriving at about the same time.

Author's Note: I found out later that it was common procedure to wait for at least ninety days to approve a new hire, therefore bringing wives or families was delayed until the new guy had been approved. It was time needed to see if the new hire was going to be approved for the full contract. It is not an unusual requirement, but they just refuse to tell the prospect the truth. They need pilots, and they don't want to say anything that might be considered to be negative.

Dispatch:
Riyadh, Saudi Arabia
October 15, 1986

THE DESERT FOX . . . BUYS A CAR

Well, Charlotte will soon be here, and I bought a car to bring her to our new home . . . in the compound . . . in Riyadh . . . in Saudi Arabia.

The major has finally approved the visas for our wives, Phil Hardy and mine, that is. What a great announcement! So it's time to go on with prior plans.

I've been bumming rides with Phil Hardy in his little Nissan, and he doesn't mind, but he is expecting his family soon, so it's time for me to get my own transportation. Phil helped me look through the car souk until they all started to run together and look the same. I was having a hard time making my mind up until I saw the Jag. It was love at first sight. It was a dealer demo and last year's model, a 1985 white XJ6. Maybe I have soft spot for the Jaguar because I have a 1969 XKE back home in Houston. Perhaps I'll have better luck with the XJ6 than I've had with the XKE.

"Me and the Jag ready for Charlotte"

I bought the XKE in Alexandria, Los Angeles, from the retired head of the Louisiana highway patrol. If you don't know, the Jaguar XKE is a sport coupe with a V12 cylinder engine. The American version has a slightly different gear ratio than the continental version but will still do over a 150 miles per hour without getting in a strain.

95

Now, I am not a fast-car driver. I'm not in the habit of getting speeding tickets, but I just love the sound of that twelve-cylinder engine. There is nothing else like it! You don't believe the part about not being a speeder? Well, let me tell you why it's true.

In 1960, I was serving time in the US Army at Fort Sill, Oklahoma. Fort Sill is seventy miles north of my home in Wichita Falls, Texas. My wife and two sons were living in Wichita Falls, and I was staying in the BOQ (bachelor officers' quarters). My roommate was a lawyer who had taken a Jaguar in as fee from a client, and he hated to drive the thing. I don't know why he didn't like it, but he gave me the keys and told me to drive it when and where I wanted. It was a perfect deal for me to go home on the weekends to see my family.

This was the same Jaguar (XK 140) that had won the Le Mans road race in France in 1958! It was the straight six model but was built for speed. Boy, was that a fun car to drive! I had never even ridden in a car like that before. Now, my father had warned me about fast driving when he was first teaching me to drive. He said, "James, it is expensive. It's hard on the engine, hard on the brakes, uses more gasoline, and speed kills!" My father always gave me good advice, and at that point in my life, I had never had a speeding ticket. I was a good boy . . . well, about speeding anyway.

But now, I was driving a real racing car, and it was fun. This part you won't believe, but I was driving that Jag back and forth to Wichita Falls each weekend and never broke the speed limit. At sixty miles per hour in fourth gear, the Jag was only turning 2,500 revolutions per minute. It was just loafing. That all changed on a Sunday afternoon when I was just loafing along on the way back north to Fort Sill. It was a two-lane US highway and hilly and crooked. I was slowly overtaking a brand-new Ford with three young boys in the front seat. As I pulled out to pass without even changing gears, the Ford suddenly speeded up. At the same time, oncoming traffic forced me to drop back behind the Ford.

It was a silly and dangerous thing for the kid driving the Ford to do, and as I dropped back into place behind them, I could see all three of them laughing at keeping me from passing. I'll have to admit the sudden surprise of the danger they had forced on me made me a little hot.

I pulled up real close on their rear bumper and gave them a beep, beep on the horn. The Jag's horn button is not on the wheel, but on the dash left of the wheel, and makes the most irritating little noise. The race was on! The kid in the Ford accelerated quickly, and I shifted down to third. It was not my intention to pass but to stay on the Ford's bumper and honk to irritate the driver in front.

The Ford topped out at 120 miles per hour and was dancing on the pavement. The Jag seemed to just settle down closer to the road and seemed to be in no strain at that speed. I stayed on the Ford's rear bumper for what must have been no more than just a few minutes while still beep, beeping.

Suddenly, the Ford seemed to explode just in front of me! The hood was hinged in the front and blew open. Black smoke billowed over the windshield, roof, and under the car. The Ford's motor was gone, and the driver began to leave the road. Fortunately, there was a sort of scenic turn out there, and that's where he came to a stop.

I pulled over next to them and rolled the passenger window down. "You boys need some help?" The driver, with eyes as big as saucers, said, "Uh, no, sir, she just got a little hot, that's all." I pulled back onto the pavement and continued on to Fort Sill. I had to smile a little when I thought of what Daddy was going to say when those boys finally got home with that Ford that got a little too hot.

Now I had a taste of speed, and it didn't hurt at all. It was kind of good, you know. But that is not the end of this little confession.

Not long afterward, I was going south on the same road, and it was Friday night, and I was sort of anxious to get home to my family. The night was dark, and with some Friday night going-home traffic, I was cruising along about ninety miles per hour. The traffic offered me no hindrance. As I came to the car in front of me that was doing about sixty miles per hour, I just leisurely swung to left a little then just as leisurely swung back to right without ever braking my stride.

In my driving career, I've been hit in the rear a couple of times, and it had made me keep a close eye on my rearview mirror. A glance at the mirror, and I saw a pair of headlights, way behind me doing the same thing I was doing. Bingo, I got a cop on my tail! My first thought was, *Well, it's not that far to the Texas bridge. I'll just run off and leave that sucker.*

Honest, that was my first thought. Never mind my father's advice, never mind the other traffic, never mind the danger, I downshifted and punched it. I can't remember looking at the speedometer because that first thought was soon followed by reality. Yeah, I can outrun him to Texas, but I can't outrun his radio!

What was the matter with me? I had never done anything like that before in my life. What had come over me? Well, the judge wouldn't care how my past had been. He would throw the book at me, so I just slowed down, dropped back into traffic, and waited for the ticket.

In 1960 Oklahoma, that US highway came to a T intersection with a stop sign. Most of the traffic was turning right after the stop on the way to the Texas Bridge. The cop was still coming in my rear view, but after my turn to stop at the sign, I made the right with the other traffic. My Jag had not gone a hundred yards when the cop pulled up beside me, and I saw the big shield on the door, but he went right on by me and stopped the guy in front of me! I just continued on to Texas.

Wait, that's not the end of the lesson. I didn't tell you, but the Jag had an electrical problem that made it not want to start some time. It seemed like a loose battery connection to me, so that weekend was a good time for me to check it out. I stopped to get fuel on Saturday and decided to check the battery cables. I raised the hood or, as the Brits say, the bonnet, and I looked all over the engine compartment and then all over that car, but I couldn't find the battery. I looked in the trunk, under the seats, but no battery. After several trips around the outside, I finally found the battery or, as it turned out, the batteries. There were two huge six-volt batteries, one behind each front wheel. Inside the wheel well, there was a removable panel, which hid the battery.

Well, the battery cables seemed to be okay, but during the search, I found the key to life and death on that Jag. The steering column from the steering wheel to the rack and pinion steering was connected through a rubber universal joint. I had never seen one made of rubber before, and this one was cracked nearly into. It was just hanging by a thread. If that thread had broken, the steering wheel would have just come loose in my hands! I had a visual picture of what might have happened during my high-speed runs.

I replaced the universal joint that day, and never, ever was tempted again.

Well, to make a long story longer, I made a deal with the dealer for the just like new white Jag for $14,000. A new one in the States would be over $35,000. I paid far less than the car would have cost in the UK. The difference was in taxes. No taxes in Saudi Arabia! You see the results everywhere.

Now, all of a sudden, I'm the subject of controversy.

"Hey, Fox, are you crazy? You bought a better car than Major Shablan!" My answer was a little heated, "What difference does that make? Nobody here gets a raise or bonus anyway."

"Yeah, but now you'll get all the worst trips."

I let them have their fun with me and reminded them, "Well, fellows, see money doesn't mean anything to me since I married a rich widow woman." It was supposed to be a joke, but they all seemed to believe my little white lie about the rich widow woman that no one had seen. I didn't bother to ever tell them different. In the final analysis, I didn't want to be driving my wife around in that harsh environment in an old junk car. Besides, I wanted it.

Dispatch:
Riyadh, Saudi Arabia
October 16, 1986

CONFRONTATION WITH MAJOR SHABLAN (#2)

A few things have been happening that were not included in my dispatches or letters. Major Shablan called me into his office.

"Captain Fox, come in, have a seat. Would you like some coffee?"

"Yes, thank you."

"Som, bring coffee." Som was a foot boxer from Thailand, always nearby, and the busiest TCN of all. He seemed overly anxious to be my friend, but I had to be there a few more days before I found out why.

"Well, Captain Fox, how are things going for you?"

"Just fine, Major," I replied, still wondering why he called me in.

"Captain, we are like a big family here, and we like to think of our captains as part of that family."

Uh-oh, that sounds like the beginning of something bad.

"And, uh, I have been told by some of the copilots that you don't let them fly the empty legs on your missions. Is that true?"

"Well, yes, Major, it is true. I didn't know I was supposed to let them fly. No one told me that they were supposed to fly. In fact, I didn't know that they could fly."

"Oh well, you see, as I said, we are like a big family here, and we want to be sure that all have their chance to improve themselves. You know, copilots would like to become captains someday. Don't you agree?"

"Of course, I agree, but, Major, you must understand where I stand. I didn't know you wanted me to help these young men to learn to be captains. From what I've heard, some of them have been flying as copilots for seven years. It was my assumption that being captains was not part of your plan, or they would already be captains.

"Now let me explain something else while I'm here. I didn't come over here into your country to change any rules. It was and still is my plan to abide by your rules, regulations, and laws as far as I know them. You see, it is up to you to tell me what the rules are before you can expect me to abide by them.

"Now here's the deal, you tell me what you want me to do, and I'll consider it. If it is something that I think is right, then I'll do it, if not, then I'll just go back to my country, and you won't be bothered with me any longer. Okay?"

"Oh, uh, well, Captain, as I said, we are like a big family here, and we want to make you happy while you are here. So, of course, I'm sure if you can see your way clear to let the copilots fly some time on the empty legs from the right seat of course, then everything else will be okay.

"Now, is there anything that we can do for you?"

"Well, yes, there is. I'd like to learn some of you language if possible."

"Oh, that will be no problem. I'll find out about some language programs and let you know. How will that be?"

"That'll be fine. Is there anything else?"

"No, Captain, that is all, and many thanks for coming in."

I started letting the copilots fly the empty legs from the right seat—that is, the ones that could fly—but there were never any language lessons. It was just the beginning of my learning what dealing with the Saudis was all about. They are traders, they are dealers, and they don't need to tell the truth to make a better deal. But I never got called back into the major's office after that.

I learned that I was going back to the States for retraining near the end of February. It was about the same time someone told me that I could borrow toward my annual leave time of thirty days. There began to form an idea in my mind that if I was going west halfway around the world, then why not just keep going west on the return and make it an around the world trip? Yeah, why not?

While Major Shablan was in a good mood, I got it approved! The Foxes were going on a great adventure!

JDF Letter:
Riyadh, Saudi Arabia
October 29, 1986

Date: October 29, 1986
To: Project Director Medevac
From: James D. Fox, Captain, GII/GIII Medevac
Reference: Copilot/FO Eid Al-Roudhan

This report is meant to bring to your attention the behavior and actions of the above-named individual on the occasion of his assignment as copilot/FO on my trip to Jeddah and Frankfurt, Germany, which began on October 26, 1986, and ended on October 27, 1986.

Copilot/FO Eid, on at least three separate occasions, refused to obey a lawful order by his Captain. This is ground for immediate dismissal for most countries of the world. Because I am newcomer to this country and unfamiliar with its customs and traditions, I am not familiar with how a situation like this should be handled. For that reason, this report is being written to you, my senior officer.

The details of Eid's insubordination are as follows:

The trip was called as a late-night departure for the transfer of a patient from the hospital at Jeddah to another hospital in Frankfurt, Germany. The patient was an elderly gentleman that was to be accompanied by his son to Germany. The crew was ordered out as a captain, two copilots, two flight nurses, and a doctor. As a new captain in Medevac, it was my plan to share the flying duties with the copilot/FOs. The trip was planned to fly from Riyadh to Jeddah to Frankfurt to Riyadh.

Due to the length of the trip to Germany, it was predetermined for the crew to have rest before returning to Riyadh. There were to be three legs to the trip, so I decided to give one leg to each of the copilot/FOs, and the final leg I would fly myself. This would give each of the flight crew a takeoff and landing. Further, I requested that the copilot that was not flying, sit in the third seat or jump seat for the experience and to help the captain and the other copilot when we got into the congested areas over Europe. This plan was explained to both of the copilot/FOs prior to departure in Riyadh, and they agreed.

At the same time, I assigned the first leg to Eid and the second leg to the other copilot/FO. The first leg was fairly uneventful—that is, nothing unusual happened. I noted that Eid needed my attention to the details of his flying, but as I say, this was not, in my opinion, out of the ordinary; after all, he was a copilot/FO, and I considered it part of my duty to help him learn to do his job better. We prepared to depart Jeddah after loading the patient and his son. The time was after midnight. The leg to Frankfurt was to be flown by the next copilot. When I was ready to start engines, I noticed that Eid had not come forward to sit in the third seat as I had requested and he had agreed to. At the time, I thought he was helping in the back and would come up as soon as he could, so rather than delay the flight, I started without him. Later in the flight, I asked one of the nurses if Eid was helping in the back, and she told me no and that he was asleep and had never helped them at all.

Had I known of his intention to sleep while we worked, I would have left him in Jeddah. Because I was so new to the job, I decided to let it pass and see what happened next. All the work and details on the ground in Frankfurt after landing and before departure was done by myself and the other copilot/FO. Eid offered no assistance; in fact, he stayed out of touch and out of reach most of the time. I did not have time to find out what his problem was for it was more important to me to attend the details at hand.

The morning of our departure from Frankfort, I made the decision to let the other copilot/FO ride in the right seat on the departure from Frankfurt, and after we were at cruise altitude, he would change seats with Eid. That meant that each of the copilot/FO would have two legs in the right seat. This was explained to the crew prior to departure. It was my desire to have the other copilot/FO in the right seat for the departure from Frankfurt because it is a difficult departure to make without breaking some rules, and I wanted to have the best help that was available.

Eid had already demonstrated his lack of ability as well as unwillingness to follow orders; however, I was offering him another chance to be a part of the crew after we got out of the congested area around Frankfurt airport. He refused to sit in the third seat again. After we were en route, I sent the other copilot/FO to the rear to see why he refused to come to the cockpit. I was told that Eid said that he didn't need to watch, and if he couldn't do the flying, he would rather sleep. That is exactly what he did. Later, I went to the rear to talk to Eid. When I asked him to do something, he just ignored me as if I had no authority to ask him to do anything.

All of these facts can be vouched for by the other copilot/FO as well as the nurses and doctor that were on the trip. I made a verbal report to my immediate senior officer the following day in which I said that I was willing to fly with any of his crew members and help them to learn in any way that I could; however, there was a minimum requirement for a copilot/FO, and that is, he must be willing to at least try to do what I ask him to do. If he is unwilling or refuses to try, then I cannot be expected to help him, and for the safety of flight, he should be removed from flight status until his attitude changes toward what his job is all about. It is my understanding that Medevac is actually a part of the military. I wonder how the army here would handle one of their own if he behaved in such a fashion. Aside from all that, it is my opinion that this young man does not treasure his job; he does not recognize the authority of those assigned over him, and he does not have the moral strength to face his assignments directly but rather tries in an "underhand" fashion to dodge his duties by just not showing up where the work is.

Finally, Eid's flying ability is poor. Medevac would be safer with him on the ground. The first part of this report is based on the facts as I saw them. This second part is based on my opinion, and I stand ready to defend both. If there is any doubt about Eid's action in the cockpit, ask for any qualified check pilot to fly with this individual for confirmation.

Sincerely,

Author's Note: Eid did not get fired until much later. You know, "we are like a large family here."

Charlotte's Journal

October-November 1986

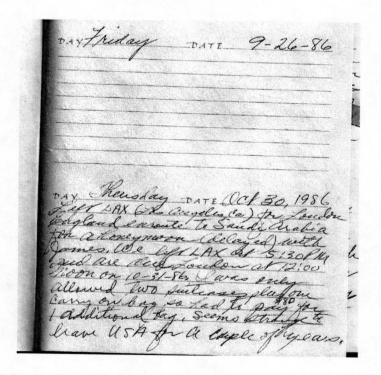

Thursday, October 30, 1986:

Left LAX (Los Angeles, California) for London, England, en route to Saudi Arabia for a honeymoon (delayed) with James. We left LAX at 5:30 p.m. and are due in London at 12:00 noon on October 31, 1986. I was allowed only two suitcases plus one carry-on so had to pay $80 for one additional bag. Seems strange to leave USA for a couple of years.

Friday, October 31, 1986:

We had a good tailwind and arrived ahead of schedule in London Gatwick Airport. James was there—all smiles and better than I have ever seen him. We went immediately next door to the Hilton Hotel where we had reservations. After freshening up, we went to dinner at the hotel.

Dispatch:
Riyadh, Saudi Arabia
November 30, 1986

FLIGHT LOG NOVEMBER 1986

10-Nov-86	HZ-MS4	OERY	OEJN to Jeddah
10-Nov-86		OEJN	OERY return to Riyadh
10-Nov-86	HZ-MS4	OERY	OEJB to Jubail
11-Nov-86		OEJB	OERY return to Riyadh
15-Nov-86	HZ-MS3	OERY	OEMA to Madina
15-Nov-86		OEMA	OERY return to Riyadh
16-Nov-86	HZ-MS3	OERY	OETB to Tabuk
16-Nov-86		OETB	OERY return to Riyadh
20-Nov-86	HZ-MS3	OERY	OETF to Ta'if
20-Nov-86		OETF	OEJN to Jeddah
20-Nov-86		OEJN	OERY return to Riyadh
25-Nov-86	HZ-MS3	OERY	OEJN to Jeddah
25-Nov-86		OEJN	OERY return to Riyadh
26-Nov-86	HZ-MS4	OERY	OEJN to Jeddah
26-Nov-86		OEJN	OERY return to Riyadh

Riyadh, Saudi Arabia
November 11, 1986

THE DESERT FOX GOES TO LONDON

The day has finally arrived. It's time for me to go to London to meet my wife. Well, it's been two months since I've seen her, and that's a long time when you're in the Land of the Sand and the Sun. Can it only have been two months? It seems like much longer than that. After all the excitement of the last two weeks of August, and now to find myself here, in this land halfway around the world, it's enough to make a fellow wonder about reality.

Let me see, in the last thirteen days of August, I married my high school sweetheart, whom I hadn't seen or heard of in almost forty years. I retired from my job of thirty-eight years and took a new job in a new country on the other side of the world. And it wasn't just another job in another country; the job was flying medical evacuations for Prince Sultan in Saudi Arabia. Now you have to admit, that's real woo-woo stuff for most Westerners.

In the first place, not all that many people know about medical evacuation, and there are a whole lot less that knows anything about Saudi Arabia. Well, I can tell you this, there is something new every day. It is exciting. In many ways, it's like being young again with a new job, a new career, a new place to live. There is a lot for me to learn again, it's a challenge, it's fresh, and at the same time, you feel needed. Of course, in time, all of this will change and become humdrum, okay; then when it becomes routine and boring, I can think about my next adventure, but right now, it's the day to meet my wife in London.

A person can get very lonely over here. It seems to be exaggerated by the area or the cost of the long distance phone calls ($3 per minute) or something, but I can assure you that it does creep up on a fellow. There are plenty of the female types here, and I'm sure they are available. For one thing, there is a whole dormitory full of nurses, and they are all single. I don't believe GAMA will hire married nurses. But that's not my style, and besides, I have a better one back in the States, and I'm crazy about her.

I knew that my time was nearly up the other day when, as Phil and I were driving through the *batha*, my safety valve popped. It was hot, and we had the windows rolled up with the AC going, and without warning, I just yelled at the top of my lungs, "*I want my wife.*" Phil nearly wrecked his car. Less than two seconds later, he was laughing hard. "I have been wanting to do the same thing," he said. Then we both laughed. Well, this is serious stuff.

Didn't I tell you? Phil bought a car! GAMA gives the captains an interest free loan of $8,000 if they want to buy their own transportation. Phil got a little four-door rice rocket as they are called, and it seems to be doing okay.

Trying to break the loneliness with a phone call is not all that easy. In the first place, there is the time difference. Saudi Arabia is a minus three hours from Greenwich. California is a plus eight hours from Greenwich, so that's a total of eleven hours time difference. That's without considering daylight saving time. They don't use daylight saving time here in the Kingdom. They already have too much of it as it is. They have so much saved up now, they may never use it all up. So they don't even think of participating in daylight saving time. For those of the unknowing, Greenwich, England, is the zero point of world time reference.

That's the way those of us that cross time zones frequently keep up with the real time. Almost all aviation matters are referred to in Greenwich time or Z time or Zulu time. Time for another short lesson. Time zones are named alphabetically. By the time you get to Texas, you are in the Sierra (Central) time zone. Don't bother to try counting them because whoever laid them out missed one or two.

Crossing time zones can be very confusing; in fact, the direction you cross them can even add to the confusion. I seem to handle crossing them to the east better than to the west, but that may very well depend on the person. Anyway, when man started to cross them on a regular basis with navigation and later communications, it was easy to see the need to have a central reference point or a starting point. You see, basic navigation by the stars depends on an accurate time reference.

The ephemeris is sort of an almanac that tells where the sun, and Polaris (north star) will be at absolute times of the day and night. As far as that goes, we also have an ending point, and that's known as the International Date Line, but that's way out in the Pacific Ocean, and no one ever bothers with that unless you're the one crossing it. Don't you remember studying about that in elementary school geography? You know, the world is divided up east to west by meridians, lines of longitude (the ones that run through the north and south poles).

The mathematicians, in their wisdom, used three hundred and sixty of them. Just like the number of degrees in a circle, right? They made the 0-360° point to run through Greenwich, England, and the 180° point just naturally ran down through the Pacific Ocean. Since it takes the earth approximately twenty-four hours to rotate once, they called that a full day, and that meant that the 180° mark was at the midnight place when the date change takes place, so they just called it the International Date Line. When you cross it east to west, you lose a day, and when you cross it west to east, you gain a day. If you run right down it, you don't do either one. Now wasn't that easy?

Sounds very reasonable to folks on this side of the world, but how about that old boy that only lives a block from the date line? His wife wants to know why it takes him two days to go to the grocery store. Where did Z or Zulu time come from? Well, there was a corporal in the army signal corps that was handling messages from all around the world when he decided it would be nice to have a universal way of referring to the time zones.

Not everyone in Europe knew about Eastern or Pacific time, so, starting at the 0-360° meridian, they called it Zulu, the phonetic equivalent of Z as I mentioned earlier. Then they gave a letter to each of the time zones around the world from east to west, backward. Now, don't ask me why start at the beginning with the last letter and then count backward. There is probably some real good reason for it. It probably made a lot of sense to the army. In the USA, starting in New York, it's Romeo time. In Houston, it's Sierra time, then Tango time, and on the West Coast, it's Uniform time. Now, see there, Romeo in New York, Uniform in California is not backward. It's forward!

Well, this is getting awfully complicated, and all I was trying to do was explain why it's so hard to coordinate phone calls. Wait until I explain why there is only two hours of one day in a week over here to conduct business with the rest of the world. You don't believe it? Okay, here it is. In the first place, their (S/A) weekend is Thursday and Friday. Most of the rest of the world uses Saturday and Sunday. There are four days out of the seven gone already and were not even started good.

That only leaves Monday, Tuesday, and Wednesday to do business, right? Wrong. You have to remember the time change. When it is Monday morning in New York, it's Monday night over here (S/A), so you lost that day. Well, Wednesday has the same problem at the end of the week that Monday has at the beginning, so that only leaves Tuesday. Now were down to one day. Even on that day, opening time of 0900 hours, there is 1700 hours here, and the businesses close here (S/A) about 2000 hours, so that only leaves three hours. Wrong. There are two prayer times after 1700 hours, and they take thirty minutes each. That only leaves two hours once a week to conduct business. If you get a busy or a don't answer a couple of times, you can lose the whole week.

Today is Thursday, and I'm riding on British Caledonian airlines, BCal, for short. I'm leaving Riyadh just after lunch, but due to the time change, I'll arrive at Gatwick a little before 5:00 p.m. Charlotte is due in tomorrow just before lunch, so I'll have time to get a room and maybe give my friend David a call.

The trip to Gatwick was an easy trip. There were two families onboard that were making their termination trip out of the Kingdom. One was a young couple that were expecting and had decided they would rather start their children off back home. The other family was leaving by request, but that is another story, and I'll have to tell that all on it's own. At least, traveling with some people you know can make the time pass even more swiftly.

The best part of the trip came from the fact that I was wearing my uniform. Now, feature this, when a captain or four stripper of any kind boards an aircraft, the treatment is different. It doesn't seem to make any difference what airline or whether you're riding coach or first class, they make sure that you are taken care of. A week later on the return with Charlotte, we arrived at the ticket counter with several bags and at least a hundred pounds overweight. I was in uniform, and they didn't say a word about extra weight charges. Two months ago, traveling alone and not in uniform, they charged me $150 for excess weight. They have given me seats in the first-class section when I was holding only a coach ticket. They have asked me to come and visit in the cockpit. Probably wanted me to be close just in case, you know. No doubt about it the uniform makes a difference.

David wasn't at home when I called, but I left a message on his machine and went to dinner alone. Shortly after dinner, David called and came straight over in his Thunderbird. He is very proud of that car, wouldn't trade it even for a really fine automobile. He still wears the Texas plates, even though they are way out-of-date. The UK plates are in the window, if the Bobbies are interested. We had a nice visit.

David is still operating his Lone Star Mobile Auto Service. The longevity of this business is noteworthy, for David anyway. Of course, he wanted me to stay at his house, but of course it would not be appropriate, not with this sort of being our honeymoon. We didn't have one after the wedding last August, you know.

Lone Star-David Groves

Well, the next best thing was to loan me a car. He had a Volvo that was up for sale, and it would be just what we needed to see jolly old England. I begged off that by saying that after my wife got in tomorrow, we would probably like to just visit and be alone until Saturday lunch. In fact, I suggested, "Why don't we get together Saturday afternoon, and you can drive us on a sightseeing tour of London." That sounded great to him, so it was all set.

David would enjoy driving us around and showing us the sights, and I wouldn't have to drive. The taste I had before of driving from the wrong side of the car on the wrong side of the road had been quite enough for me. It's hair-raising! We sat up until 0100 hours drinking coffee, and David was telling me all about whose doing what just as if his old chums were my old chums. One of these days, I'm going to take a few days off and try to figure out why so many of my close friends are young enough to be my children. It's a thought.

I watched the tele (or tely for English TV) until late so that when I got up, I wouldn't have so long to wait. It worked, woke up about 9:30 a.m., had breakfast, and was over at the terminal an hour early. The hotel is connected to the terminal, so you can just walk over. Makes it easy to push the baggage carts back and forth also. I won't forget soon how she looked as she came into view. Tall, blonde, with the California shades, dressed in a red suit, impossible to miss. Now there is a real classy lady. It's good that I met her there in England because what we did there in the terminal is against the law in Saudi Arabia.

What a great time we had. Laughing like a couple of kids, I even told her about the episode in the car with Phil when I just had to scream out, "*I want my wife.*" It was when I repeated it at the top of my lungs there in the hotel that she was embarrassed. She has told me since that she is quite sure that I was heard three floors away.

Enough of this trivia. On to the meat. We had the drive through London the next afternoon and even stopped in for a visit at Westminster Abbey. They were having a service, and Charlotte made a recording on her little hand tape recorder of the choir.

I've got to tell this. Just to the left as you enter the Abbey, there is a statue of white marble, which is slightly larger than life size. The statue is of a man reclining on a couch with a handmaiden seated on the floor near his side and a servant with a large fan standing behind him. The caption said, Charles James Fox. History says he was the man that convinced King George III to release all the slaves. If you would like to assume that he was one of my ancestors, then I can't prove otherwise.

We bought some souvenirs at the bookstore just in front of the Abbey, and on to the next sight. Well, we saw the palace and the towers with the associated picture taking, and it started to rain. Great, this is the first time I've seen it rain in London. David was a good tour guide, and we were soon on our way to his home in Cobham of Surrey. We had decided to take David and his mother out to dinner, and our request was that it be a real English pub.

David's mother was very glad to see us and gave Charlotte a very nice welcome and was somewhat dismayed that we had not given her some notice, for she would most certainly have wanted us to stay with her. She was a very nice lady, and I am quite sure that she was sincere. She failed to tell us that she had already prepared our supper. We insisted that they should all go to dinner with us. It was a short fight. I'm sure that Mrs. Groves has not all that many invitations to turn down.

By the time we had all the details straightened out, we had acquired another couple. Richard, the young man that I played golf with last August, and a young lady would accompany us to the pub. It was the Prince of Wales and only a few minutes' drive from David's home. The choice was excellent. The pub was several hundred years old and had lots of atmosphere. It was much as you might expect, but with a few extras for a bonus. In the center of the dining room was a huge copper boiler. The boiler was about seven feet tall and at least six feet in diameter. Apparently, it was used to heat water and the premises. Very interesting, and the food was excellent as well.

After an evening of good food and interesting people to talk with, it was too soon time to find our way to the inn. We had made reservations earlier at the Thatchers Hotel (inn). It was very picturesque just as we had hoped it would be. The inn was only a short drive from David's home. Come to think of it, everything else is just a short drive from David's home as well. Actually, its address is at East Horsley, or was it Leatherhead. Well, no matter, you don't know the difference anyway, right?

The inn had several smaller buildings surrounding the main building. We were given a room in one of the smaller buildings. Our room was upstairs and very comfortable. It was very old, but had just been freshly decorated with wallpaper, paint, etc. The bed was great, and the night went very well.

Some time during the night, David brought over the Volvo for me to use the next day. He insisted that I not have to stand the expense of a rented car. Now I wish I had.

Thatchers Hotel

We were up at nine-ish, and the first thing that I noted was, we had no hot water for the bath or anything else. When I stepped into the shower and turned on the hot water, all I got was one little dribble, and that was it. I tried everything that I knew

111

of, but to no avail. There was little to none on the chances that I was going to take a cold shower in the UK in November, forget it. Charlotte had no more desire than I, so we went to breakfast. We would report the problem to the desk clerk and bathe after we got back.

Sounded like a good plan, and we did almost exactly that, all except the part about taking a shower when we got back to the room. After breakfast, we returned to our room to find it filled with steam. While we were out, the hot water came on, and I had left the tap on. The steam was so thick we could hardly see. We could see well enough to see the fresh hung wallpaper hanging down all around the room and in the bath. It turned loose at the top and had peeled itself about halfway down the wall and was just hanging there. What a disaster. Quickly, we opened the windows after turning off the hot water tap of course.

While the steam and vapor was dissipating, we were running around the room trying to press the wallpaper back on to the walls and ceilings. Might just as well forget that, so I went down to the desk clerk and reported the incident. She didn't seem anymore interested the second time than she had been the first time, so we decided to let it drop—the report, that is, not the wallpaper. We did get to take a shower after that, however. All in all, it was a nice stay at the Thatchers Hotel. I wonder if Margaret has anything to do with that inn?

It's time for me to get on the road with the Volvo. As I said earlier, my first taste of driving in England was enough to give me bad feelings about the whole thing. But what the heck, I've been driving for well over forty years and have never been in a wreck judged to be my fault. What could happen?

David had brought us over to East Horsley in the dark, so I had to ask for directions on how to return to Cobham. Sure enough, the guy told me just the opposite directions that I needed. He had me turn left on leaving the inn, and it was fifteen miles. Had I turned right, it was less than five miles, and I would have missed a lot of trouble. Hey, listen, this is no kidding. It's bad enough to drive on the wrong side of the road and from the wrong side of the car, but the stick shift being on the left just put the cap on it. I'm as nervous as that long-tailed cat in a room full of rocking chairs.

Don't talk to me; just keep looking to see where the other cars are coming from. Some of them look as nervous as I feel. Down the straightaway is not too bad. It's the corners that really tear me up. After years of doing it by memory without thinking, now it takes extreme concentration just to remember which way to look for the traffic. After what seemed a very long time, we came to our first real chance to screw up. The roundabout got me.

We call them circles in the States, but they are called roundabouts here. I have seen a few in my travels around the States, but not many, and you may agree that at best they are a hazard. The only reason for them in the first place is to save money on traffic lights and to be more convenient than a four-way stop. Well, they are bad enough when you circle to the right, but when you circle to the left, look out.

The first roundabout was just ahead, and there was no way to miss it. If I could, I would gladly have detoured twenty-five miles to miss it. No luck. I approached it with great caution. Okay, no sweat, I'll just take my time and wait for the traffic to thin out. It doesn't thin out. The horns start, and one fellow yells, "Hey, mate, the bloody sign says Yield, it doesn't say you have to surrender." Well, I just jumped out in it and let them dodge me.

After four times around, I got off on the wrong road. Somehow, we were on the freeway to London. Pretty soon, I found a place to park on the side of the road (wrong side, that is) while we sorted out the maps. The consensus was that if we took the left just ahead and then looped back on the flyover, we would be on the way to Leatherhead, and surely we could get back on course there. They call an overpass a flyover.

The plan worked as far as Leatherhead, but while trying to navigate through the small town, I ended up in a dead-end parking lot. One way in and no way out. That's it. I've had it. I'm parking this thing and getting some proper directions. Well, fortunately, I was in a parking lot, and just in front of me was a lady pulling out, so there was a parking space just for us. With great relief, we got out and walked around the corner to a photo shop. We bought some film, and the fellow drew us a map on how to get from where we were all the way to Cobham.

We returned to the car to find a female Bobby writing a ticket for the Volvo. "What have I done, officer?" I asked. She said, "You've parked in a handicap zone." "Of course, I parked in a handicap zone, and if you had seen me drive in, you would have thought that's exactly where I needed to park." The reasoning was lost, and I got the ticket. I asked what was I to do with it. She said that in a fortnight or so, I could go to somewhere and pay the fine. I told her we were leaving the country in a few days, and she said that in that case, we just forget the whole thing. Well, I liked her reasoning better than mine, so we left.

Now we have a hand drawn map, and it's only a little farther to Cobham than when we first started, so that's got to be considered progress. After some careful negotiating, we got out of town and once again was on our way. Turning right from an intersection is tough. You must look to the right for your head-on traffic, and when you go around the corner, be sure and swing out to the left. Sounds easy? Of course it's easy until you add the pressure of heavy traffic. Sure enough, we arrived in Cobham, and as I drove carefully along, I could see the street ahead where I needed to turn to the right. The traffic was fierce, and besides, it looked like that might make me turn into the wrong way on a one-way street, so I passed on that corner.

It was my intention to go on down a couple of blocks and find an easier place to turn. There was a grocery store and just passed it looked like a place to turn. When I got there, I could see there was construction and where I had started my turn was hatched in yellow. I had already completed half my right turn when I saw that I was turning into the yellow-hatched area. I stopped momentarily to think.

That was my downfall. As I looked to the left, a Volkswagen was bearing down on me. I stomped the accelerator to try to get out of the way. Too late, I couldn't quite make it.

The VW hit me in the left rear quarter panel. The wing, it's called here. I got out to see the damage. The Volvo had stood up pretty well. The panel was caved in, but I could pull it off the wheel with my hands, no problem. The driver of the VW was a middle-aged woman of about twenty. She was very nervous about what was not that easy to see. Her VW was hardly scratched. The contact with the Volvo was a square blow to her bumper. I could replace the whole bumper in Houston for twenty dollars at the wrecking yard.

But we are not in Houston, and I don't know where the wrecking yard is. I asked if she was hurt. She said that she was not. I asked if she could drive. She said that she could. I told her who I was and where I was staying, and that the Volvo had insurance, and that I would be glad to repair her car. I also told her that I was unacquainted with the local law and asked if we needed to contact the police. She said that would not be necessary and that she would call me later after she found out what the damage would cost to repair. She also gave me her phone number, and then we both left.

To be involved in such a silly little accident really bugged me, but I noticed that my nervousness was largely gone. It was like, I had the accident in me and just had to get it out. Now it's better.

Reporting to David that I had wrecked his car was difficult, but what else to do? He said the bad part was that a chap was coming over that evening to buy it. We took it over to a couple of fellows that he knew that were in the body business. They agreed to get right on the fender and would put it right for fifty quid (about $70). The problem was, could they do it before 1700 hours? Well, they would try. They did try and let me tell you when David picked it up a 1630 hours, you couldn't tell it had ever been hit.

The young lady had followed me to David's home, and we both explained that we would be glad to fix her car; in fact, I told her that I would pay to have it repaired, or if she wanted to leave it, we would do it right then. Her real concern was that her father was going to come down on her real hard. The whole left side of the car was caved in from a wreck she had the previous week. Her bent front bumper was the best-looking part of her car. She had to go to work, and I had to go down and rent a car. I rented a brand-new VW Rabbit for about $26 per day and drove it the rest of our stay in the UK without even a close call.

In the meantime, the young lady had some second thoughts about the accident and was afraid that maybe I'd run out of the country, and she would be left with a bent bumper and an irate father. So she went to the police and reported the accident, and when we got to the inn that evening, we had a message to call PC McCloud. I was so dumb, I thought that PC was his fist two initials. They stand for police constable. This was embarrassing. I had wondered aloud all over the lobby, "I don't know any PC McCloud, who could that be? I wonder." After I made the call, I had something new to wonder about. It didn't seem like something that they would throw me in jail for. Maybe I could just leave Charlotte for hostage.

The next day was a busy day; we had an appointment with David's banker to talk about opening an account. The interest rate is very good in the UK, and we needed a bank to put my paycheck in (the banks in Saudi Arabia don't pay interest). Now I also had an appointment with the police. The banker was first, and he turned out to be a nice fellow. He welcomed our business—what banker would do otherwise?—and said that it had been his pleasure to meet us. He further stated that he didn't know that David had any reputable friends.

We drove straight to the police station. It was a small red brick building, very quaint, very neat, and just past the outer limits of downtown. We went in the front door and made an immediate left turn into a small office. There were three officers there, two without their coats or tunics and one with his coat on. I announced in a moderate voice from the counter, "My name is Fox, and I have an appointment to see PC McCloud."

One of the officers in his shirtsleeves said, "With a voice like that, you must be from Texas."

I said, "Yes, I am and proud of it."

He returned with, "John Wayne was the greatest American that ever lived."

I came back with, "Yes, that's true, and he was a close personal friend of mine."

He said, "I have an 8" x 10" picture of John Wayne."

"Is that so?" I said, "Would you like to have me sign it for you, and if so, just tell me the front or the back."

We both laughed at the exchange as I signed the photo, and the younger of the group identified himself as McCloud, then invited me into the next office. We spent a little time discussing the accident. He was surprised to find out that I had offered to pay for the damages and that the girl had refused. After that, it was all downhill. He said that he would file the report, and I could just forget about it. I asked if I was being charged with anything, and he said yes, with careless driving. "But don't worry about it," he said. "We'll just file it, and in five years, we will throw it away, don't worry." After he told me to not worry the third time, I thought it was time I did just that.

We went back into the main room, and the officer, which spoke of John Wayne, identified himself as Tom Holloway and stated the fact that he was particularly proud to meet a Texan like myself and wanted to know what I thought of his station. I told him that I was impressed and that if he wanted to have an in-depth analysis, then I'd be glad to compare it with those we have in Texas because I have been in lots of them and was considered to be knowledgeable in that area.

We had another laugh, and he said, "Here, I have something I want you to have." He removed a pin from his tie, brought it over, and proceeded to pin it on my shirt. It was miniature of the emblem on his hat, an official seal. He said he was making me an honorary PC. I don't know if that is anything like being an honorary deputy, but I imagine that the pay is about the same. Regardless, I was honored.

After the pinning, Tom insisted that we go out front of the station and have our pictures made. They put on their tunics and hats with all buttons buttoned, and we marched out the front door for the photographs. The camera had to be readied, so Tom took advantage of the time to point some historical points on the outside of the station. The light on the gate, for example, was over two hundred years old. He found out that we played golf and wanted us to be sure and give him a chance to invite us to play golf on our next visit. The pictures were finally completed after everybody posed with everybody.

After the pinning, with my new best friends. From left to right,
Sgt. Tom Holloway, me, PC McCloud.

We promised to send copies, which we did, and took our reluctant farewell. Well, golly, it's not every day that a fellow goes to the police station to pay a fine and comes out an honorary PC in Her Majesty's forces.

I couldn't leave this story without telling about our stay at the Woodland Park Hotel. As we drove up on the wrong side of the road, we thought we were approaching the home of a duke or baron or one of those extremely rich English lords. It looked like it was right out of a Hollywood movie.

Woodland Park Hotel. Once an English lord's mansion.

Well, you know, we were on our honeymoon, right? The lobby was just like the entrance to a fine home, and we were quietly ushered up to our room on the second floor. It was the King Edward VII room. The *room* was not just a room but a *suite* and nothing like anything we had seen in England for a hotel room. It had a private foyer, a king-size canopy bed, a marble fireplace, walls and ceilings done in white and wedgwood blue, a crystal chandelier, a bath with a shower, a raised bath with Jacuzzi that would have made the Romans happy. It was all carpeted and very elegant. It had a large bay window overlooking something like twenty acres or several city blocks of a green pasture surrounded by manicured shrubs. Wow! We felt like royalty.

After a good night's sleep in the fine bed, I laid there just a moment to survey the room in the morning light. The sun was shining through the picture window in just the right angle to make me notice a panel in wall extending out from the door. That wall came out from the entrance door about ten feet, then made a corner and extended another ten feet to the bay window. The sunlight drew my attention to a panel between the door and the inside corner of the wall. Somehow it didn't seem to fit just right.

I got out of bed and went over to examine said panel. Curiosity you know. A close examination made me think the panel just didn't quite fit. It was standing out at least an eighth of an inch. You say that's not much, and you are right, but the sunbeam made it noticeable. So I pushed on the panel as if to make it recede. It did and then sprang open revealing a two-inch crack! Enough room to reach over and pull on the panel. It opened up to reveal a hall leading to a set of stairs.

I had just discovered a *secret panel in the wall!* It had been open all night into our bedroom!

"Charlotte, come look what I have found." She's not going to believe this unless I show it to her. Well, to make a long story shorter, we just stood there together and stared at the open panel. It was just like in the movies.

We never reported what we had found to the management. Surely they knew. It was just another *panel* in our honeymoon to remember about our few days in merry ole England.

Dispatch:
Riyadh, Saudi Arabia
November 15, 1986

THE BRIT AIR CAPTAIN

The trip back from London with Charlotte was a new experience. It was one of those all night jobs where we leave London late at night and arrive in Riyadh early in the morning. We rode on a British Airways 747 and didn't get the outstanding meal as I had received on Saudi Airlines a couple of months before.

We had not been at altitude very long and had a nice meal when the hostess came to me and said the captain would like for me to come to the cockpit. Who me?

The captain that had sent for me was a senior captain riding in the right seat with a junior captain in the left seat. He welcomed me into the cockpit and offered me to sit in the jump seat behind the junior captain in the left seat. This made it easier for him to turn and talk to me. We talked a little about the 747, but he seemed to be more interested in me and what I was doing in the Kingdom.

I spent quite a long time in the cockpit and found that my host would be laying over in Riyadh for three nights before returning to London. With that information, I asked how would he like to come out and have dinner with Charlotte and me. He seemed anxious to accept, and I didn't think to offer the same invitation to the other captain. Well, he hadn't much to say while I was in the cockpit anyway.

It never occurred to me that Charlotte might object to my inviting a stranger to dinner, and she had no idea what she was going to find when she got to our home. But she was a good sport, and she would have a couple of days to get ready.

(From Charlotte's journal: Saturday, November 8, 1986. The captain of British Caledonian airlines had invited James into the cockpit we were en route from London to Riyadh, so we in turn picked them up at their hotel and drove them downtown so they could see the gold souks. Unbelievable the amount of 18-karat gold. Then we had dinner (lamb) with them at the Sheraton Hotel. Yum yum.)

We did have the dinner at our apartment, and the British Airways captain got a home-cooked meal. The captain revealed that he alternated routes between London to Riyadh, and London to Houston. Hey, maybe he wouldn't mind bringing a little loot from my son in Houston for me? He was agreeable, and so I laid the burden on for his next trip to Houston.

So here I am two weeks later with my video camera that I had left behind! Too bad, Greg forgot to include the battery charger, so I can't take many videos until I can make a battery charger. But since I have this free transportation service between here and Houston, I'll get Greg to send the charger on the next shipment.

Dispatch:
Riyadh, Saudi Arabia
November 16, 1986

THE EMBASSY BOOK

Well, we finally got to the embassy, and they stamped our licenses. Big deal. What does their stamping our licenses mean? It makes them official. I guess. The embassy doesn't know if they are real or not. They don't have any way of verifying them, but I guess the Saudis have been lied to and cheated so often in the past that they just wanted one more chance at verification.

But the trip was not wasted. They gave us a booklet called "Welcome to Riyadh." It has all kinds of interesting information that can be useful to the newcomer. For example:

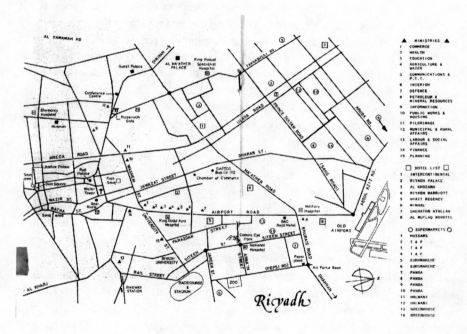

Riyadh City Street Map

The map would even be better if the streets were actually named at street level. There are *no, I say, no street signs.* If you look at the map near the bottom just above the map name of Riyadh, there is a street named Pepsi. It is so named because the Pepsi Cola plant is located there, but there are no street signs. We find our way around town by referring to the names of places that have been previously pointed out to us. The French Corner refers to the corner where the French restaurant and bakery is located. The Ruptured Rocket refers to an abstract culture of a rocket. We are shown by others where things are located, and then it is up to you to remember where they are located and how you get to them. Yes, the map would have been much more helpful if they had street signs.

Another thing they don't have is stop signs in their residential areas. A typical street is lined with walls eight feet high surrounding each residence. I have seen no residence without the wall. These walls run the entire length of the block from street corner to street corner. If you are driving down the street, then it is imperative that you stop and look at each corner because you can't see around the corner for on coming traffic, and they may be coming at break-neck speed because that's the way they drive, and they don't stop and look at the corner.

Since they don't have street signs, then you might like to know that neither do they have a phone book. Oh yes, they have telephones everywhere, but there is no such thing as a city phone book. We must remember these folks are very private. They don't want their phone number spread all over town. The only phone numbers listed are by each group such as GAMA or Medevac, and that's just for the convenience of the group. The embassy help book lists a few numbers on one page for such things as in case of a traffic accident. I'll bet that's the busiest one on the list.

Gold Suq (store or market)

Sorry, folks, the black-and-white picture does not give credit to the gold suq shown here. In reality, they are bright, shining, glittering, awesome, hundreds of them. They go for blocks and blocks on both sides of the streets in the area on the map called the *batha*.

Did I tell you that the men do all the shopping here? Well, not all the shopping, but nearly everything. I thought there were no women here at first. They are not seen in the grocery market, computer store, or electronics stores because that's where I do my shopping. Then I went to the gold suqs, and there they were. Ninety-eight percent of all the people there were women. They were buying gold, or they were selling gold. Who could tell? But there they were, and it looked like serious business to me. They seemed to prefer bangles, and even though they all have to wear a covering for the complete arm, you could see they had bangles out of sight up toward their elbow.

The embassy book told me that they are allowed to keep their personal possessions if they lose their husband, one way or another. I guess they are at the gold suqs stocking up on insurance.

Before we leave here, we are going to visit the rug suq. Someone told me to be careful; the price range was considerable.

The Rug Suq

I am enclosing here some excerpts from the booklet from the embassy:

HISTORY AND GOVERNMENT

The Arabian Peninsula has a rich history which dates from the latter stages of the Nile and Mesopotamian civilizations. The southern part of Arabia developed into a commercial center specializing in the production of frankincense and myrr, both highly prized by the Romans. This area became a trade center for silks, spices, and jewelry which were brought in from the Indies and East Africa for the eastern Mediterranean market. Gold and copper were mined in Arabia and transported to northern civilizations. A network of caravan routes emanated from Arabia to Egypt and Babylonia.

With the coming of the prophet Mohammed in the 7th century, Islam was founded, matured, and expanded. To this day, Arabia remains the center of the Islamic world with Makkah (Mecca)—as the holy shrine.

The modern history of Saudi Arabia dates from 1932 when King Abdul Aziz bin Abdul Rahman Al-Saud succeeded in uniting the three major territories of the Arabian Peninsula, A!-Nejd (Central Province), Al-Hasa (Eastern Province), and Al-Hijaz (Western Province).

In the following year, the first oil concession was granted to the California-Arabian Oil Company, the forerunner of ARAMCO. With the discovery of oil in commercial quantities in 1938, Saudi Arabia stood on the threshold of wealth and had the opportunity to modernize its governmental and economic life.

Abdul Aziz died in 1953, to be succeeded by King Saud bin Abdul Aziz, his son, with Crown Prince FAIA! first as Deputy Prime Minister and then as Prime Minister. Faisal ultimately assumed control of affairs and started a program of modernization within a program of austerity which averted an imminent financial crisis. He was proclaimed King on 2 November 1964 with Prince Khaled as Crown Prince and First Deputy Premier. King Faisal was assassinated in 1975 and was succeeded by Crown Prince Khaled.

King Khaled died in June 1982 and Crown Prince Fahd was proclaimed King. The Kingdom of Saudi Arabia is superficially an absolute monarchy, but a decisive legislative and executive role is played by the Council of Ministers in which the King occupies the position of Prime Minister.

There is no constitution in the conventional Western sense—it has recently been re-stated by a responsible Minister that the constitution of the Kingdom is the Qur' an (Koran). The affairs of the Kingdom and its citizens are regulated in accordance with the Islamic "Sharia" (literally, "The Path") which governs the religious, political, social, economic and private lives of those that profess Islam. Non-Muslims are naturally expected to abide by these, the laws of the Kingdom.

The King is also the "Imam"—the acknowledged leader in religious matters of his people. This position makes him the ultimate appellate authority in judicial matters and enables him to issue executive instructions, within the framework and spirit of the Sharia, to meet particular contemporary circumstances. The King *is advised where appropriate by a body of religious authorities (The "Ulema") particularly when dealing with religious, judicial and social matters. Justice is administered by "Qadhis," often characterized as "religious" judges, but, in practice, given the all-embracing nature of the Sharia, they are the civil and criminal judiciary. Standing arbitration tribunals have been created by regulation to deal with disputes in specific areas—such as labor cases or commercial disputes.*

THE PEOPLE

The population of Saudi Arabia is estimated at about eight million.

Contrary to popular Western conceptions, settled mercantile and farming communities have existed in Arabia for centuries, although it is true that until recently a high proportion of the population of Saudi Arabia was a nomadic or semi-nomadic. King Abdul Aziz pursued a policy of encouraging the nomads to settle and the trend which he started has accelerated more recently because of the economic attractions of settlement. As the populations of the major cities have increased and new settlement. As the populations have sprung up elsewhere, so the nomad population has decreased; it is now estimated to be between 10% and 20% of the total.

This is all interesting stuff, and I wish it could have been available to me earlier. But after reading the whole booklet, it's easy to see why you need to live here awhile before you can understand it. Yes, it's written in English and probably by some American, but it reads like a Saudi propaganda pamphlet. There is a section on Travel. It recommends places to visit as if this was a tourist center. As far as I have been able to find out there is no such thing as a tourist in the Kingdom. In the first place, you can't get into the country without a visa, and you can't get a visa unless you have a sponsor. Well, maybe it's possible, but you'll have to agree it is highly unlikely. In a word, the Saudis are a very, very private group. As I have said elsewhere, they don't like for anyone to write about them, true or not. They don't trust anyone, and they frown on anyone just snooping around.

Once you are here, you can't go beyond the forty—or fifty-mile limit without a special travel permit from your sponsor defining where you are going, for how long, and why you are going in the first place. No, I think we can forget the tourist thing.

It was late that I found out they don't allow video or pictures to go out of the country without first passing the censors, and no one ever seems to get any pictures of videos returned from the censors. Not knowing this, I had Charlotte standing up in the front seat of our Jag and sticking up through the sunroof while taking videos while I drove through the car suq. The locals were running out and waving to the camera like they were going to be on the six o'clock news. Providence must have been smiling on us that day. My friends stood with their mouths open when I told them what we had been doing.

"Fox, are you crazy? It's a wonder they didn't throw you both in jail before shipping you back home."

"Why, what did we do wrong?"

"You were taking pictures and videos. Don't you know that is forbidden?"

"No, nobody told me."

"Well, you guys were just lucky, believe me."

The Saudis took the videos from our luggage when we left the country the first time, and they didn't give them back. I fooled them though. I had made copies, so we left them in the apartment. I brought them with me later on a Medevac trip to the States.

So the embassy booklet was nice and interesting, but you still have a lot to learn here that's not in the book.

I wonder if the Saudi censors had to approve the booklet.

CAF Letter:
Riyadh, Saudi Arabia
November 29, 1986

CAF LETTER TO SAM DUNCAN

November 29, 1986

Dear Rev. and Mrs. Sam Duncan,

James has finally found time to teach me a little about his computer, so now I can write letters easier. This will be a general letter so that I can send it to different ones and try to cover everybody by Xmas time.

It seems that no matter how hard we try to get letters written to everyone, there is always something to do that interferes.

I will tell you a little about our apartment and compound quarters. Imagine going west on a street and making a left turn into an alley. As you start down the alley, to your left are high walls that are around a tennis court. To your right is another high wall with a fence on top of it.

This wall extends around a long city block. As you pass the tennis courts on the left, there is a parking area, which is partially covered as a carport, and the rest is open parking space, paved of course. To the right in the middle of the wall, there is a gate. As you pass through the gate, immediately to your left is a guardhouse with a guard twenty-four hours a day.

No one can enter the compound without an ID or as an authorized guest. There are always shopping carts at the gate that you can use to transport groceries, etc., to the apartment. Our apartment is situated to the rear of this block, so we have a pretty good hike from the gate.

Once inside our apartment, you step directly into the living room/dining room area, looking directly ahead into the bathroom and laundry area. There is a door, but whoever keeps it closed?

If you go to the extreme right, you enter the small bedroom, and if you go a little to the right of the bathroom door, there is a door to the master bedroom.

The master bedroom has a king-sized bed that has a bedspread that matches the headboard, draperies, and lampshades on the nightstands. The room is tastefully decorated with pastel blues and beige, which is easy to live with. Thank goodness.

The bathroom and laundry area has light green tile with a floral pattern. James just had an inspiration because he thinks that his computer can do anything, so he is going to work out the floor plan for me. There is so much that I don't know. Well, anyway, everybody knows that I never had any ambition to become a computer expert.

Since we have the apartment as a subject, I need to tell you that I am having a little problem with the Italian oven. First, I thought it was because I couldn't understand Italian, but it is more than that. I have baked two batches of light bread, and the bottom portion never browns nor does it bake properly. Actually, that wasn't all my problem with the first batch.

Please understand that I didn't sacrifice space in my luggage for my *Betty Crocker's Cookbook*, and I have wished ever since that I had brought it. All the cookbooks over here are very different.

Well, anyway, one of the ladies, Mrs. Sharon Hardy, gave me a bread recipe. We found dry yeast in the market, but it was in a quantity in a can (small), but since it was written in Arabic, I wasn't sure how many ounces were in it. The recipe called for two packages of dry yeast (American), so I put what I thought would be two packages.

It turned out to be excessive yeast, but the rising was excellent; however, the taste of yeast was overwhelming, so I had to dump all but the cinnamon rolls. The raisins, cinnamon, and icing canceled out the strong yeast taste. Poor James, he suffers in silence. In the second batch, I cut the portion of yeast too much, so my yield wasn't as great.

One of these days, I will figure out the right portion of yeast, but I wish I had a different recipe, one like Mama used to make. On Thanksgiving, there was a large dinner being made in the Schmitz apartment, which we were invited to, and one of the nurses asked me to bake off her two pumpkin pies and a raisin pie.

I cooked the pumpkin pies two hours and the raisin pie one hour, and the crust on the raisin pie was soggy on the bottom. The little man is here working on the oven now. Practically every thing is imported, and the instructions are not always written in English, but a lot of the time, it is or is partially English.

All the workers here on the compound are what everyone refers to as TCN, third country nationals, all men. Some are from India, Africa, but mostly from Sri Lanka. There are many Koreans in the city, and maybe there are some here on the compound.

When we were at Thanksgiving dinner, Mohammed Hanno came by to visit, and for those of you who do not know, he was the man who gave James acceptance to his job as captain for GAMA's Medevac. Mo. Hanno came in his Arabic attire of long robe and the guttra headdress, but James says Hanno doesn't wear this garb when he flies (he is also a captain) but wears the uniform that all of the captains wear.

I bought some walnuts and thought because they were sealed in a plastic bag they would not be stale, but I was wrong. I want to make some date bars for the holidays and need the nuts. James suggested that I soak them in water, and it has helped to relieve the rancid taste, so I think they will be edible.

When we want to get out of the apartment/compound, James will take me shopping, and then we will stop at the Hyatt or Marriott hotel to eat. The hotels here have the best chefs, and their food is excellent. There are shopping malls all over town, and they have many products that we have at home.

Someone must have had a big contract with Hoover for vacuums because that is the only type I have seen over here. We are going to buy one because even though they furnish one at the compound office, it is not always available when we want to use it. James's houseboy has been on vacation, and the substitute really doesn't want to work much, and when it comes to running the vacuum, there are too many excuses not to.

I think my time is running out, and everyone around here is getting hungry, so had better stop and scare up some food. James bought a BBQ grill, and we haven't used it yet, so maybe today is the day. We send our love and let us hear from you soon. Have a Merry Christmas and a Happy New Year.

Charlotte and James
Captain and Mrs. James D. Fox
GAMA Compound
PO box 41726
Riyadh 11531
Saudi Arabia

FROM CHARLOTTE'S JOURNAL

Saturday, November 1, 1986:

James's friend David Groves came to pick us up and drive us into London where we visited Westminster Abbey, had lunch in a little hamburger place below the street level. We then drove past Buckingham Palace and the Towers of London. We also saw Big Ben. It was raining most of the day.

Sunday, November 2, 1986:

David G. picked us up at the Hilton Gatwick and drove us to Cobham in Surrey County to meet his mother, Beryl Groves. He then took us to East Horsley where we obtained a room in the Thatchers Hotel. The hotel was very English with a knight's armor standing in the lobby. We took numerous pictures. David loaned James a Volvo to drive.

Monday, November 3, 1986:

We tried to shower, but it wouldn't work, so we had to use the bath. Anyway, after breakfast, we left for Cobham so James could keep in touch with David. We got lost and ended up in Leatherhead where James got a ticket for parking in a handicap zone. A fellow drew a map for us, and we found our way to Cobham. On a right turn, we were hit by a girl in a Volkswagen.

Tuesday, November 4, 1986:

We had appointment with banker at 12:00 noon and 1:00 p.m. with Police Constable (PC) McCloud. James opened a saving account with the bank and reported to PC (M). He was not fined and was given an honorary badge to wear that has Queen Elizabeth Regena's initials ER beneath the crown. Presented by Tom Holloway. We checked in to the Woodland Park Hotel.

Wednesday, November 5, 1986:

The Woodland Park Hotel gave us the King Edward VII suite that was spectacular. Private foyer, canopy bed. Marble fireplace, walls and ceiling done in white and wedgwood blue, crystal chandelier, badette, elevated Jacuzzi. All carpeted and very elegant. Large bay window overlooking the countryside. Left for Saudi Arabia.

Thursday, November 6, 1986:

Arrive in Riyadh, Saudi Arabia, on British Caledonian airlines. Airport was beautiful and terrain similar to Las Vegas, Nevada, or Albuquerque, New Mexico. We were met by Walt Schmidt who was driving James's Jaguar, which is beautiful and impressed me. We arrived at the GAMA Compound, and I saw my new home for next year or so.

Friday, November 7, 1986:

James was still not on call, so we had an opportunity to meet some of his friends and drive to the Panda Market for food as the cupboard was bare. I was impressed with the store, comparable to our small supermarket in the USA. The dairy, eggs, and produce were exceptionally good.

Saturday, November 8, 1986:

The captain of British Caledonian airlines had invited James into the cockpit when we were en route from London to Riyadh, so we in turn picked him up and his copilot (actually his cocaptain) and drove them downtown to the gold souks. Unbelievable the amount of 18-karat gold. Then we had dinner (lamb) with them at the Sheraton Hotel. Yum yum.

Sunday, November 9, 1986:

The highlight of today was shopping at the produce souk. Excellent fruit and vegetables, but they only sell in wholesale quantities, so the best way is to share with another couple. Cost is much less than the Panda, so it was very worthwhile. One of James's Saudi copilots paid us a visit.

Monday, November 10, 1986:

We stayed home today and rearranged furniture, and James got a call for a trip from Riyadh to Jeddah to Riyadh. I have unpacked everything but haven't caught up on ironing yet. Just finished the last load of laundry. Maybe I can finally catch up tomorrow.

Tuesday, November 11, 1986:

We were supposed to take the laundry to the office but got there too late and will have to wait until next Tuesday for a pickup.

Wednesday, November 12, 1986:

We were invited to the Hardy's to celebrate their daughter Windy's thirteen birthday. She is now a bona fide teenager.

Thursday, November 13, 1986:

We went grocery shopping at what used to be the Safeway and is now T&P. Mary, one of the nurses, went with us. She is from Dublin, Ireland, but has lived in London prior to SA about nine years. Bought some mums (yellow) and a plant. A rarity here. James bought a Betamax VCR.

Friday, November 14, 1986:

Barney came to clean at 10:00 a.m., so James took me to the Marriott for breakfast.

Saturday, November 15, 1986:

James was called out on mission to Mecca (Charlotte made a mistake here. We, kawajees, were not allowed to even fly over Mecca. It must have been to Madinah.) around 9:30 a.m. Just called to get water delivery service. Have to buy a coupon book for two hundred riyals. That is approximately fifty US dollars.

Thursday, November 27, 1986:

Thanksgiving Day in Riyadh, Saudi Arabia, was at Walt Schmitz's house. Nurse Stephanie asked me to bake her pies off and had trouble with my oven. Took two hours for the pumpkin and one hour for the raisin, which had soggy crust when served.

Dispatch:
Riyadh, Saudi Arabia
November 30, 1986

FLIGHT LOG NOVEMBER 1986

Date	Aircraft	From	Route
10-Nov-86	HZ-MS4	OERY	OEJN to Jeddah
10-Nov-86		OEJN	OERY return to Riyadh
10-Nov-86	HZ-MS4	OERY	OEJB to Jubail
11-Nov-86		OEJB	OERY return to Riyadh
15-Nov-86	HZ-MS3	OERY	OEMA to Madina
15-Nov-86		OEMA	OERY return to Riyadh
16-Nov-86	HZ-MS3	OERY	OETB to Tabuk
16-Nov-86		OETB	OERY return to Riyadh
20-Nov-86	HZ-MS3	OERY	OETF to Ta'if
20-Nov-86		OETF	OEJN to Jeddah
20-Nov-86		OEJN	OERY return to Riyadh
25-Nov-86	HZ-MS3	OERY	OEJN to Jeddah
25-Nov-86		OEJN	OERY return to Riyadh
26-Nov-86	HZ-MS4	OERY	OEJN to Jeddah
26-Nov-86		OEJN	OERY return to Riyadh

JDF Letter:
Riyadh, Saudi Arabia
December 2, 1986

JDF LETTER TO FAMILY IN HOUSTON

Dear Kids,

That ought to cover it. Kids, grandkids, the whole works. Even includes those that are not kin. You know, when you get to that certain age, everyone else is just a kid.

Charlotte has been at the computer writing letters and has made me feel guilty for not writing. So thought that I might add a few thoughts of my own for this season of the year. I hadn't planned this to be an annual Christmas letter, but why not? A few moments to reflect on the past have gotten to be a worthwhile endeavor.

This past year has brought great good fortune to me, so it is appropriate that I pass along good tidings and well-wishes to those that I love and that care for me. Since my arrival here in the Land of the Sand and Sun, there has been one question that keeps coming to me from almost every contact that I have with those left behind. "Are you happy over there?" Well, the answer is an emphatic yes. Of course, you must understand that I would like very much to see you and visit with you, but for every great joy, there must be a sacrifice or price to be paid. A prudent man always must count the cost of his decisions. The great experience that is happening to me at the present time is not without cost. Missing you kids is a great one, but I'm sure that you all understand.

Many years ago, as a young man, it was my ambition to travel and see the world. I was associating daily with soldiers returning from the great world war. Listening to their stories of overseas happenings made me yearn to see those places that they described so easily and casually as if they were describing a second home. They had spent long periods of time in strange countries with strange people learning strange customs. It all sounded so exciting. I really wanted to go. Deep in my heart, I dared not even to hope. You see, the time for me was always wrong. Life's schedule for me was always screwed up. Too late for World War II, too broke for college, too married for the Korean War, too late for the Viet Nam War—my life schedule has always been a mess. Before this letter is through, however, you will understand how a fellow with such a fouled-up schedule can turn out at the age of fifty-eight years to be the happiest one in class.

Don't misunderstand me, not since a very young age have I wished to go and kill the enemy. I can remember in August of 1942 when we received the telegram

133

that my brother was missing in action off the coast of Guadalcanal. I was only thirteen and felt that time was just moving too slow for me to get into war and kill all those Japs. It seemed to me that the Japs were particularly bad and needed killing. The Germans were bad also, but only the Nazis needed killing. That was the thoughts of a thirteen-year-old in 1942.

One of the things that was impressed on me in those days was that the wrong ones were going to war and getting hurt. It was some years later, kids, that I learned one of the great truths. Nowhere is it promised that there would be justice in this life. That all comes later. Man keeps trying to make it seem that we deserve justice, and he can provide it if we will just place him in a position of power. They never do and never will. God alone will do that, and even he said not to expect it in this life. So I missed the wars, never got shot at. Wished for the adventure and didn't have it. Sometimes I think of those that had the adventure and would gladly trade it for a loss of the memory.

Regardless of the feelings of a teenager, a man can grow up, raise a family, and gradually see his early dreams become very, very dim. As they dim, they seem to become less and less important. Dreams of travel and adventure have no place of importance in the mind of a man that is struggling to feed, clothe, and educate his children. They don't have to disappear; they can just get to be very unimportant. Besides, a man can get awfully busy with his chores, and dreams are for tomorrow anyway. Many hours were spent in my early days with Humble Oil & Refining Company listening to Sherfesee, Dan Bader, LeRoy Foerster, Nate Baurer, Homer Weeks, and others that passed through my office remembering their adventures during the "big war." LeRoy was in the army and could never understand though he crossed the ocean twice in a troop ship why every so often the navy would blow that funny whistle and call over the PA. "Clean sweep down four and a half," or what it meant. It took Dan, who was in the navy, to explain that they were actually saying, "Clean sweep down fore and aft."

Of course, C. M. Sherfesee was the ranking (US Army, lieutenant colonel) veteran and could always be counted on to have the final say in discussions of military adventures that required a final say. Come to think of it, Sherf had the final say whether the subject required one or not.

Ah yes, Sherf had a profound effect on my dreams of adventure and faraway places. Not just from his war experience, but continuing on until the present day, he has continued to travel and visit exotic places of the world. For your information, Charlotte and I plan to meet Sherf and Lola in Rome sometime in March of '87. The last twenty years of my career with Exxon certainly did add to the miles of travel I have seen, but the adventure of that finally disappeared, and something new was needed.

I have often said to my friends and others that might inquire that I could do better accidentally than I could ever do on purpose. If you think this is a light remark, of course it is, but nonetheless true. I remember the endless times that C. L. Andrus would ask me as we cruised along at Mach .80, "Fox, what are your goals?" My reply was that I had none. He appeared never to believe this even though I explained that I had already run past where I thought the goal line was and was still going. I even shared with him my thought of doing better accidentally than on purpose, but CLA was busy in those days measuring everyone for the size of their obstruction to his goals. He would never believe that what he wanted so badly would not be just what anyone and everyone else would want also. It seems to me that a lot of people have that problem. They assume that what they want must be what everyone else wants also. Not so, not so, not so. One man's meat is another man's poison, yes?

Perhaps that is why some find it hard to understand why I can be having such a great time over here. Well, you see, one of the things that gives me great pleasure is talking to people. "Ah," you say, "I knew that all the time." But perhaps what you didn't know was that I also love to listen, especially if the other guy has something to say. Now don't be offended, but you know that there are a lot of people around talking but are not saying anything. It is really a lot of fun for me to talk to the natives. We talk about every sort of thing including religion. Perhaps, in another letter I'll tell about a three-hour discussion I had with a Saudi on Islam, Judaism, and Christianity.

In England, I didn't see the changing of the guard, but I did discuss with an old lady local politics, the fruit she grew in the backyard, and relative value of parsnips and pole beans. Who else do you know that would answer a call to go to the local police station to discuss a minor traffic violation and come out with a badge and title of Honorary Police Constable of Her Majesty's Forces, Elizabeth Regina II? Well, you need to take a little time to visit. My good friend James Keegan knows what I'm talking about because next to me, he's the best.

I've just been reminded that post time is near. We had to set a deadline, or we would never get the mail out. So as a final effort of this year to communicate with those of my kin and what is left of my friends, let me say that all is well here in the Land of the Sand and Sun not to be confused with those adds from Florida and California that say Land of Sun and Fun.

Don't worry about us. We'll be back your way one of these days for a good visit.

My philosophy has been to believe in God, Jesus Christ, and the Holy Spirit and to treat my fellow man fairly. That last part is the hardest. This philosophy is not copyrighted or patented, please feel free to duplicate it with your fellow man.

The return address below is accurate, and the box is large enough to hold any letters that come this way. No packages please. They are not accepted by regulation. However, if you have the overpowering urge to write or phone, please feel free to do so. Our time zone is—3 hours Zulu, Greenwich, CUMT, or whatever time standard you might recognize. They don't use daylight saving here; they have plenty. The present time is nine hours ahead of Houston, if that helps. The best time to find us at home is after 2230 or 10:30 p.m., if you wish to call.

The best of season's greetings to you all.

Sincerely,
Capt. James D. Fox and Charlotte
PO box 41726
Riyadh 11531
Saudi Arabia
Ph. country code: 966
city code: 1
232-0878, ext. 2014

JDF Letter:
Riyadh, Saudi Arabia
December 2, 1986

Dear Rev. Sam and Wife,

Hello from Saudi Arabia. Sorry about the "and wife" part, but cannot recall her name. Seems like it should be Shirley, but I just can't remember.

Charlotte and I wanted to remember you and your church at this time of the year. Our thoughts are of you often, so it is only fitting that we write this letter and enclose something for you, your family, the church, and what I assume to be a cause that is close to the hearts of Baptists. I have been a Baptist since my baptism in 1948. The Lottie Moon offering was always remembered at this time of year. The meaning has never been as clear as it is now.

To live in a country that does not allow the Holy Bible or even a simple crucifix on a necklace is an experience hard to describe. The rules here are very strict about such things, and punishment is swift and harsh. We were told in government publications to bring nothing connected with the Christian religion. There were several ideas that came to mind to try and bring in a Bible. Frankly, I was afraid to try to smuggle something in that was expressly forbidden. Well, to my surprise, Charlotte brought my brief case with her and didn't bother to check its contents. When I met her in London, I didn't bother to check its contents either because it was just my regular old brief case that I had carried for years in the States. Well, guess what, after arriving in the Kingdom, I found that my little New Testament was in the case and had made it through Customs with no problems. Do you suppose that was just luck?

Best wishes to you and yours on this season of cheer, and remembering that it is the occasion of celebration of the birthday of Jesus Christ, the Son of God, we wish you and yours well in his name.

Sincerely,
Capt. James D. Fox and Charlotte
PO box 41726
Riyadh 11531
Saudi Arabia

JDF Letter:
Riyadh, Saudi Arabia
December 20, 1986

C. M. Sherfesee
2402 Hampstead Lane
Wichita Falls, Texas 76308

Dear Charles and Lola,

We received your letter on the sixteenth. It was postmarked in Wichita Falls on the first and in Dammam on the thirteenth. All incoming mail must go to Dammam first because they have a new sorting machine there. It's the only one in the Kingdom. After Dammam, it is distributed around the Kingdom by truck, so if it arrives on Thursday or Friday, then it will not be sorted until the first work day, which is Saturday (Yom as'sabt) Insha'allah.

The distribution by truck takes from one to two days at least, and then final distribution in the city of destination takes another day or so, and then we finally receive it from the compound distribution. Looks like they have been taking notes from the US system.

We were glad to hear from you. As you can imagine, most any contact with the folks back home is appreciated. We are anxious to learn more of your plans for Rome. If you can let us know the name and time of your tour, then I'm sure we can join you with no difficulty. The tour, as you explained it, sounds interesting. Also, you might let us know if others could join the tour.

My sister Margarete has mentioned in the past that she would like to see Rome, and although we have not mentioned the trip yet to anyone, I'm sure that she would like to be there if possible. Anyway, I would not like to add to any burden on yourself, but if this is a regular guided tour, then perhaps she could join us there. At any rate, I will make no mention until your plans are more complete.

I just learned today that I may be coming to the States in February or March for training. The schedule is not for sure, but the dates of the training will be set by me after the training has been approved. As you may know, we are required by the FAA to have recurrent training each twelve months with an extra requirement each twenty-four months. Most corporations send their pilots to simulator training each six months so that these requirements can be met, and also any other requirements such as minimum instrument time and approaches can be met.

More emergency situations can be done in the simulator and much cheaper, so away we go. At one time, I attended simulator and ground school classes four times a year—two for the Lockheed JetStar and two for the Gulfstream. The Saudis use FAA regulations as their own, so now they are going to initiate the school requirement for us, and we will go each six months.

It is a good idea for crew training, and it will give me a chance to get back to the States for a few days. We are going to plan the training around the end of our contract, which in my case is September 1. That means that I could make the next period in February or March. I'll make sure that the date doesn't conflict with the tour dates.

Our first winter in the Middle East has been very interesting. Two nights ago, it snowed just about 150 miles north of here. The weather here has been cool, but not below 35°F. A lot of wind today, but mostly very, very nice. Florida and California would love to have such weather. I have never seen such a long period of good weather without a break.

The long periods of mild days and cool nights will have a brief interruption of one or two days of overcast sky and then back to absolutely beautiful days. Skies are clear, and the air is fresh. I presume you know that we are about the same latitude as the Florida Keys and with 2,000 feet elevation here. It's about 275 statue miles to the Persian Gulf (Arabian Gulf), the nearest body of water, so it's very dry here even in the wintertime. Reminds me a lot of the fall and spring in New Mexico.

Flying here is very simple, but interesting. I'm just about to get accustomed to the strange sounding names and instructions on the radio. That is, I'm doing a little better. The flying is very easy after a career of fighting thunderstorms along the East Coast, Gulf Coast, West Coast, High Plains, the Southwest, and the Southeast USA. The legs are about one hour duration and then return home. Sometimes there is more than one leg, but not often. Very easy. I've had a quick trip to Khartoum, Africa, and a overnight to Frankfurt, Germany. A friend is leaving in a few minutes for New York, so am going to let him mail this for me. Merry Christmas and Happy New Year.

Sincerely,
Capt. James D. Fox and Charlotte

Dispatch:
Riyadh, Saudi Arabia
December 22, 1986

THE DESERT FOX HAS LUNCH WITH THE KING

Romeo base called the mission for early the next morning. It was another run to Jubail, my old nemesis. That's the place with two airports. One is navy Jubail, and the other is royal Jubail. Navy Jubail is not on the maps, has no approach facilities, not even a little beacon or a unicom radio, but that's the one that we must use. Anytime we have a mission called out that is not an ASAP (as soon as possible) mission, then it must be a VIP (I'm not going to explain that one). Well, this trip was neither! Now that's interesting. Next, they call out a helicopter for the same place. Hey, something is going on that I don't know anything about. We are told to be in position at navy Jubail tomorrow morning at 0800.

After a discreet phone call, I found the answer. King Fahd ibn Abdul Aziz Al Saud (referred to on television and in the papers as the Custodian of the Two Holy Mosques) will be dedicating the opening of something or other at the navy base at Jubail tomorrow. He will be accompanied by Prince Sultan, the second in line for the throne.

His Majesty King Fahd Bin Abdul Aziz Al Saud, King of Saudi Arabia
and Defender of the Three Holy Mosques

They always have hospital planes or Medevac standing by in case they are needed by the king. He has a Boeing 747 outfitted as a hospital, including a surgical room with all the attending personnel. Since the 747 cannot land at the tiny strip at navy Jubail, they called on the next best thing. A helicopter to take the patient from the location of his accident or injury to the nearest hospital, or if his needs are more severe, he can be evacuated by jet to the big boys in Riyadh.

His Royal Highness Prince Sultan Bin Abdul Aziz Al Saud, Second Deputy Premier and Minister of Defense and Aviation and Inspector General

Jubail is only about ninety kilometers north, up the coast, from Dhahran. So it's only about forty to forty five minutes from Old Riyadh. The military base that I fly from was at one time the municipal airport. Since opening the new airport forty kilometers north of the city, we are now known as Old Riyadh, and a military air base.

We left in the Gulfstream III at 0645. They wanted me to be in place by 0800, so we arrived at 0725. They got thirty-five minutes change. We were met by some people from the local hospital who wanted to make us comfortable and welcome. They offered to take us to the hospital for breakfast. I declined for the crew, feeling that if anything happened and we were needed, we should be in place to do our thing, not at the hospital eating breakfast. Besides, we are only going to be there a couple of hours and return home. I knew that because Romeo had told me. He also told the helicopter crew to prepare to spend the night. I figured that was because it took so long for them to get back and forth to Riyadh. I should have known better.

The welcome wagon left, and we settled in for what all flight crews do when they are faced with a wait aboard the airplane for any length of time. We took naps. The copilot slept on a stretcher, and the nurse and I sat up in the chairs. We hardly had a chance to get the nap started before the welcome wagon returned with a pasteboard box of food. There was a thermos of coffee and fried egg sandwiches and another invitation to go to the hospital. We took the food but declined the offer to visit. Before we finished the food, they returned and insisted that we go to the hospital. I had been given the hospital administrator's name as the man who was in charge of our mission there, so when the welcome group used his name with the request for the visit, we went.

It was a short ride from the airstrip to the hospital, all within the confines of the base fence. The ride was short, but interesting. I suddenly realized that I had never ridden with a Saudi driver before. That probably puts the wrong idea in your mind right away. The Saudis are not *really* bad drivers, in my opinion, even though they do tend to drive with certain ricochet tendencies. I dare say that a great percentage of them are first generation drivers. I know of no other country in the world where they had roads before they had automobiles.

In this country, they tell me that the road systems have been developed in the last two five-year plans. The beautiful concrete (I don't think they use asphalt because of the extreme heat) freeways and road systems here are far from complete, but there was nothing here but trails ten years ago. What would it be like in our country if they first built the roads and then issued the autos? Well, everyone starts even that way. It's a combination of bumper cars, demolition derby, and Saturday night stock car races all together. To survive, you must learn to drive the same way that everyone else drives. Some of the worst offenders of good driving techniques are expatriates. In learning to survive, they become more aggressive and more offensive.

The temperament of the local drivers are aggressive, impatient, and with no hint of fear. They obviously believe they are in the care of Allah for the fear of death or injury is nowhere seen. Their Nomadic background of *wandering* the desert has survived until today. The efforts of civilization to change this wandering has not succeeded. Living in houses, sleeping in beds, cooking inside, bathing inside, none of these things have removed or replaced the wandering heritage deep in their nature. It is all too evident in their driving habits. They never like to stay in one lane. They change lanes as the desire strikes them. They "wander" back and forth. The only exception is when they have taken homestead rights to the fast lane. They may have picked that up from a visit to Texas.

Another exception to the wandering from lane to lane is when they elect to straddle the stripe. This more than likely comes from another part of their heritage, i.e., straddling camels, horses, etc. I'm quite sure that when I return from this country, I will need to have a driving debriefing. The driver taking us to the hospital was very nice and courteous, but as soon as he got on the straightaway, he straddled the stripe and wound up the spring. I have never seen one of the local drivers stop for a stop sign. They are absolutely and perfectly ignored. This driver was no exception.

The short trip was completed without incident or accident. He never stopped for a single sign on the way, nothing happened, no one was excited, and no one even noticed but me. You see, they know what to expect from each other. You come over here and start changing up things, and someone is going to get hurt. That is the reason why you must drive the same way to survive. Start stopping for stop signs, and you're going to get hit in the rear!

It is still a little difficult for me to fully realize and understand my status here. I am a foreigner, but I am also a captain of a government aircraft. My uniform is my credentials in most places. Of course, those of us that have been in the military know the feeling of what a uniform means, but here in a foreign country, it is still new and strange to me. There are guards everywhere on the military base, many more, I think, than at home on military installations. One must remember also that we are not that far from the guns and their firing. Perhaps it's just me, but I have not quite become accustomed to the attention that I receive here. The hospital guards want to salute, but are not sure. The uniform is not navy nor is it army, but it's definitely something, and you should do something. If you don't salute, then at least stand at attention and wait for it to do something.

We were ushered down a long hall to the administrator's office. He was an army captain. Just a little on the chubby side, but very nice, very neat, and eager to make us feel comfortable. He ordered us coffee and tea, and by now, we had been joined by the helicopter crew. I knew better than to order Arabic coffee. It is very dark and thick with some sort of herbs floating on top that gets in my teeth. I have never favored coffee that sticks between your teeth like you've been eating popcorn. So I have learned to order my coffee as American, black-black, no cream, no sukar (sugar).

American means "without the herbs," *black* means "no cream with sugar," so you must say "black-black no sukar" to make sure you don't get the sugar. Even then, to order such an item causes some following conversation. They can't believe anyone would drink it that way. I made the mistake of drinking tea with some Arabs at the car souk when I was in the market for a car. It was served in a small glass not much larger than a shot glass maybe three ounces. It is very hot and very sweet. In fact, it is so sweet it's almost a syrup. A little of that goes a long way.

The helicopter crew consisted of a Saudi captain and copilot, with a Brit flight engineer. The six of us visited with the hospital administrator for a couple of hours. He was an administrator for GAMA before his present job, so he was well known by the others there. We talked of many things including the Saudi economy, OPEC, President Reagan and the Iran incident, and much more. You might be surprised to find that many Saudis believe from what they read in the papers, that the American people should be more appreciative of their president. Most have a lot of respect for President Reagan. Of course, the papers here and in Europe make everything seem bigger than Watergate, and if you believed what you read, you'd think the American public is about ready to lynch the president.

I find that the people here are eager and willing to talk about their country and their religion in addition to other things. So I never miss an opportunity to ask them their feelings and opinions on almost any subject. For example, the reason that they treat their women in the fashion they do is scriptural. That's right, they quote the Bible. You see, the first woman was made from Adam's rib, right? Well, the rib used was a crooked rib, and women have never been straight. If you try to straighten her, she will break. So it is Allah's will (Insha'allah). When I hear such things, I laugh, and they laugh. It is a funny thing, not to be taken too seriously. These people have a good sense of humor and enjoy storytelling very much.

When you can converse even a little, they are very anxious to talk and laugh with you. They don't understand Aggie jokes here, but if you just change the subject to Egyptian or Pakistan, they think it's hilarious. I have been stopped on the street by a complete (I'm talking complete) stranger, and he says, "Hello, I went to school two years in Bloomington, Indiana. Are you from Texas?" The hat and boots give me away. He wants to tell me about how good it was in the States. There is a lot of smiling and waving. We part and go our separate ways. I don't really know who he is or what he does.

Of course, not all Saudis are that way, but I've seen them when they were in a group and very somber and serious looking until one spoke to me in decent English, and when I responded, they all got up from their tea and began smiling and listening to the two of us converse. They held back initially because they could not speak English. With an interpreter, they are ready to go.

Perhaps you are wandering, if we are at a navy base, why is an army captain in charge? Well, it's because the army has medical responsibility for all branches of the military and the royal family. The top man in the Medevac program is an army major. Everyone else in the organization is a civilian, like myself. The captain asks us if we would like to attend the dedication ceremony and the luncheon. The helicopter crew opted for both. I declined the dedication ceremony, but I was intrigued by the prospect of the luncheon, so I accepted the captain's gracious invitation. My copilot agreed to go also; however, the nurse had to have other arrangements. No women allowed, you know. The luncheon was scheduled for about 1345 hours.

In the meantime, we had a couple of hours to kill, so a tour of the hospital facilities was arranged. All of us, including the nurse, were given the grand tour. The hospital was relatively new, being only about two or three years old, I believe. It was immaculate in every detail. Of course, there are two of everything. On the left is for the female and on the right is for the male. Each section is segregated, and as we passed by, our guide repeated the same description, "Over here on the left is for the women, and over here on the right is for the men."

When we arrived at the maternity ward and were told, "This is the maternity ward for the women," I asked the captain, "Where is the maternity ward for the men?" The captain jerked his head around and looked at me with great concern on his face as if they had forgotten to build this hospital correctly. In a few seconds, they all laughed, and we continued the tour. They had many impressive-looking pieces of equipment. I have some knowledge of electronics and computers, but I have little idea what is the latest and greatest in the medical field. The computerized blood analyzing machine was an item they were very proud of. It was white and about the size of an extra large washing machine. It could fit in the utility room of most homes in the States.

The captain told me they could completely analyze a blood sample in five minutes. I asked, "Do you mean that if you took my blood right now that the result would be ready in five minutes?"

"Oh no," he said, "it would not be ready until Tuesday."

"Why Tuesday, that's several days from now?"

"Oh, that's because we only operate the machine on Tuesdays."

So it still takes up to a week to get back the results of a blood test. Now don't laugh. It works the same way in our army. You see, they probably only have one medical technician that knows how to operate the blood machine, and Tuesday is the day that he comes to Jubail! He has other blood machines to operate in other parts of the Kingdom. The medical tech is probably from Syria.

The time finally arrived to go to the luncheon. We were all loaded into a big Buick, and away we go. They don't have Fords over here; they are forbidden as is Coca Cola. The reason, I am told, is that Ford and Coca Cola have factories in Israel, and the Saudis don't do business with companies that have factories in Israel. How would it look if they bought an order of Coca Cola and found that on the bottom of the bottle it said, "Made in Israel"?

It's not far to the building where the luncheon is to be held. We were released in the parking lot and left free to mill around until something happened. There were military personnel present of all sizes, shapes, and descriptions. We got your army, we got your navy, we got your marines, and I'm talking about from several countries. What an array of uniforms. We could recognize those from the US, Britain, France, and Saudi. The rest were a guess.

The whole thing reminded me of when I was in the National Guard. Lots of ruffles and flourishes, and everyone with any rank at all was in charge of something. There were about three hundred people in the parking lot, loosely assembled. There were at least twenty of the group that were running around and appeared to be in charge of something or somebody. I noticed there were two Saudi marine guards posted in front of an adjoining building. A third marine obviously was giving them drill in the manual of arms. "Pooooooort ahhhhhhhhms, right shoulderrrrrrrr ahms, preseeeeent ahms." Of course it was all in Arabic, but I didn't need an interpreter to know the commands. I thought, *Man, if they don't know it now, how do you expect them to learn it while the king is on his way?* The troops were formed, they were dressed to the right, they were inspected, they were called to attention, then at ease, then at rest, then attention. Yes, it really did remind me of the National Guard that I was in. A bunch of civilians that was willing, but not quite up to speed with the regular army. Well, that's not really fair; even the regular army here will post a guard at the main gate without socks or laces in his shoes.

We finally went into the foyer of the building where the luncheon was to be held. Many guards were there armed with automatic weapons. They were not practicing the manual of arms. A lot of milling around with several false starts toward the door was made by many. The false starts were made when a rumor was passed around that "The king is coming!" I was the only one there of some three hundred guests that had it figured out.

I told the rest of the guys with me how to know when the king really arrived. You couldn't tell by the armed bodyguards because they were in and out almost continuously. If you really want to know when he's coming, then watch the TV camera men. They were all casually lounging around, leaning on vehicles, or sitting on the grass. When the main man shows up, they will come to attention.

About this time, I smell something that makes me think the dinner is ruined. Glancing around the room, I see the smoke, and then the little guy in a white thobe comes into sight carrying a metal device holding charcoals and smoking with a real funny smell. I have seen these things for sale in the souks but had no idea what they were for. If you can imagine two pyramids joined at the tops so that you have square base on the bottom and a square base on the top and pinched in in the middle. They are made of heavy metal to hold the charcoals and can be used for cooking in the tents. Being portable, they are also good for smelling up large areas with incense. The little guy's job was to get the air ready. Well, it's a false alarm.

We decided to go into the next room and sit down. There are forty to fifty large sofa-type pieces of furniture in the next room, so I went in and found a place down at the far end and had a seat. In fact, all five of us did. I sat next to a couple of old Arabs that were talking to each other, so they ignored me even though I was sitting next to them. After a few minutes, I saw a better seat only a few feet away, so I got up and moved. We were sitting in a sort of U seating arrangement. I moved from the bottom of the U to one side. The sides of this U were like seventy-five feet long. I had hardly been seated when there was a big commotion back out front, and the royal entourage entered the room. Well, we all stood up, and guess what, the main man entered the door with his thobe flowing in the breeze. Just like in the movies. Much to my surprise he came in, separated himself from his bodyguards, and came over and sat down directly across from me, not ten feet away. When he sat down, then I sat down. Everyone sat down.

A couple of minutes later, the helicopter captain came and got me. We left the room. It seems that I had crossed my legs, and he was afraid that I might show the sole of my foot. This is extremely rude and in poor taste. Well, okay, as it turned out, it wasn't the king anyway, just a prince. There are about five or six thousand princes in the kingdom. We went back out to the foyer. Just in time because here comes the real one. The TV men are alert, and when the camera work starts, *you know, this is no kidding*. He passed within a few feet of me and, with much smiling and nodding, went directly into the dinning room. He didn't stop to shake anyone's hand, not even mine.

After a short delay, you know, get in line, it's the navy, isn't it? I passed into the dining room also. It was random seating, i.e., sit anywhere you want to. The royalty was sitting at a long table across the north end of the room. All the other tables were arranged perpendicular in several rows. I told my copilot to stay close because I needed someone to show me what to do. He assured me that I would have no problem, but we sat together anyway.

There were no speeches, no announcements, nothing. We sat down and began to fill our plates. Those already seated were already eating. I don't think anyone said a blessing. Each place was set in the Western fashion, with plate, silverware, glasses, cups, etc. The food was family style, so you had to pass your plate to someone near the platter for serving. I had no idea what was on the platter. It was a carcass of some kind on a bed of rice and surrounded by vegetables. There were several of these platters on each table, and you could tell by the number of platters versus the numbers of guests that there was plenty to go around. Each platter was at least thirty-six inches in diameter. It would have been a full load for a man to carry. In fact, I think they were being distributed by two men for each platter. The meat on the carcass was not a shape that I could recognize. No matter, if it's the least bit palatable, I'm going to eat it anyway. The fellow that helped my plate was very generous, and as it was passed back to me, I couldn't help but wonder how it would taste.

It was delicious. I said nothing but ate it all. Desert was white cake with icing just like back home. All the time I was enjoying the food, I was trying to figure out what the meat was. It wasn't beef, though you couldn't be sure from the taste the carcass was wrong. I finally decided it was camel. Wrong. It was lamb. It tasted nothing like any lamb I have tasted before. Delicious. I would enter that meat in a contest against the best roast beef that I have ever eaten. Fit for a king.

By the time I finished eating, I noticed that many had already finished and left. As they finished, they just got up and left. The front table was mostly empty. It was apparent by this time that no one was going to call on me to say a few words about Texas, so I got up and left also. As I was leaving the dining room, I noticed two guards at the back of the room were eating directly off one of the platters. They were eating the rice in a traditional fashion. They reached into the platter with their right hand and took a large handful of rice and squeezed it several times until it compacted into a football shape, then they ate it. It looked messy, but they weren't eating out of my platter, so guess it was okay. Their left hand was clutched in a fist behind their backs.

On the way out of the building, I noticed a line had formed behind the little incense burner. The Arabs were taking turns stooping over with their faces in the smoke and, with both hands, were first capturing the smoke, and then rubbing it into their beards. Can't tell you the significance of this, except they do like to smell good. Maybe they wanted an extra dose. There seems to be quite a difference of opinion between the East and the West about what smells good.

We drifted in ones and twos back out to the Buick. Once we were all back to the car, we were driven back to the hospital. I expected to be released at any time. No such luck. We went back to the airplane to wait for a release that never came. About 1900, they came and said the king had decided to spend the night and dedicate something else tomorrow. We had to spend the night.

Another new experience. None of my crew was prepared for spending the night, but we were going to anyway. We were taken back to the hospital for dinner, and while there, arrangements were being made for us to spend the night. The nurse was taken away separately and housed with other nurses in some sort of a dormitory. We were taken to a housing unit much like one on a military post at home. It had three bedrooms and a bath and a half. There was fruit and juice in the refrigerator, coffee, tea, and sugar in the cabinets. Sheets and pillows on the beds, everything had been thought of, except for soap and towels or toilet paper. There were some napkins in the refrigerator with the fruit. They worked. Two of the bedrooms had two single beds each. One bed room had a double bed. Seniority prevailed, and I got the double bed.

After the usual bathroom exercises, we began to gather in the living room. Pretty soon the cards came out, and the game was on. It was called *baloot*. The Brit and myself were merely bystanders, even though I sat on the floor just as they did, and they tried to explain the game. It was no use; I couldn't keep up with it. No gambling, but the losers are expected to have to do anything the winners tell them to. They play with four, partners opposite each other. They remove about half of the cards from the deck and have to follow suit and capture tricks, but that's as far as I could get. They didn't pick out the cards they separated from the deck. They just split the deck into two stacks and played with one stack. The hands are played too fast and with too much yelling and hand waving for me to keep up. There was an argument after each trick. It's all in Arabic, so I can only guess what they are saying.

After a while, someone decides to make some tea. This is how it's done. They got the coffee pot, took out the center part, and just used it to heat the water. They used about ten tea bags in this one pot, so I know it's going to be strong tea. I was planning on having a cup; in fact, I was trying to say no *sukar* when they added the sugar to the pot itself. There was a pint-sized fruit jar in the kitchen that was a little over half full of sugar. They put all of that in the coffee pot and started looking for more sugar. This stuff is going to be so thick it may not pour. That's the way they like it, and that's the way they drink it. That did it for me, so off to bed, and we'll see what happens with the king tomorrow.

Well, nothing happened to the king neither that night nor the next morning, and at 1445, we returned empty to Riyadh. I called it an interesting adventure.

FROM CHARLOTTE'S JOURNAL

Wednesday, December 3, 1986:

We just received a letter from Muriel (Charlotte's sister). It is great to get letters from home. Have readied packages for Walt Schmitz to take to Dallas on December 14 to be mailed in the States to Riley Killian (flying buddy in Houston) and Austin (Charlotte's son). James had to fly two missions today. I baked chicken and sweet potatoes ala Harriett Browne.

Thursday, December 4, 1986:

Today is Muriel's birthday. Believe it is her seventy-fifth. James and I haven't done much today. We had waffles made from my new waffle iron. They were great. We watched a couple of movies and didn't go anywhere except the Hardy's on our nightly walk.

Friday, December 5, 1986:

Couldn't sleep in, so got up at 5:00 a.m. and put on a pot of beans. James is on call today, and if he isn't on a trip, we will go with Hardy's to the gold souk and batha souks (local description of downtown).

Dispatch:
Riyadh, Saudi Arabia
December 31, 1986

FLIGHT LOG DECEMBER 1986

Date	Aircraft	From	Route
04-Dec-86	HZ-MS3	OERY	OEPA to Hafr Al-batin
04-Dec-86			OERY
04-Dec-86	HZ-MS4	OERY	OEMA to Madinah
04-Dec-86		OEMA	OERY
16-Dec-86	HZ-MS4	OERY	OETF to Ta'if
16-Dec-86		OETF	OERY
18-Dec-86	HZ-MS4	OERY	OEDR to Dhahran
18-Dec-86		OEDR	OERY
22-Dec-86	HZ-MS3	OERY	OEJB to Jubail, had lunch with king, Yahya, Tina
23-Dec-86		OEJB	OERY
25-Dec-86	HZ-MS4	OERY	HSSS 2nd to Khartoum, Yahya, Logan
25-Dec-86		HSSS	OERY
30-Dec-86	HZ-MSD	OERY	OETB to Tabuk
30-Dec-86		OETB	OEJN to Jeddah
30-Dec-86		OEJN	OERY
30-Dec-86		OERY	OEDH to Dhahran
30-Dec-86		OEDH	OERY

You notice they had me out on Christmas Day? All the Saudis take off on Christmas Day and the expats have to do all the trips. They tell me it happens every year.

Happy New Year anyway.

1987

Dear Mrs. Parker,

I just had to add a note to the letter that Charlotte has written to make sure you understand how thrilled we were to hear from you. The pleasure was increased when we were able to share the clippings with friends from Sweden, Ireland, United Kingdom, Canada, South Africa, and the United States. When Charlotte gives a party, it's international in scope.

The people in Hatch have a loss, and those in Raton have a gain. Wana Beth lived in Raton for a few years, and I had the pleasure to visit her there on a couple of occasions. It seemed like a very nice town and very picturesque. Perhaps in your new surroundings, you will have some spare time while becoming adjusted. If so, we would certainly appreciate a letter now and then. Besides, the pleasure of hearing from you, I have a selfish motive for asking.

Let me explain. Since the time you were my teacher in Corona, I have been to many places and have done many things. I have worked for one company for thirty-eight years, but while doing that, there were several other things going on in my life. Mr. L. Parker, your husband, gave me the suggestion to study engineering in college. This I did and went to work for an oil company after two years of college. I worked in their civil engineering division for eighteen years.

At first, I was a junior draftsman, mail boy, but later, after becoming a senior draftsman and getting transferred to Houston, Dallas, and Tyler, they promoted me to party chief in land boundary surveys. For a brief period, I wrote technical reports for the legal department. During these years, I served my time in the US Army (started as an enlisted man and finished as a lieutenant colonel). Also, I found the time to finish 140 hours of college credit in residence, made the academic honor society before finishing. Among other efforts, I have done the following things as a profession or for hire:

1. Manufacture of sporting goods
2. Stage performer
3. Hypnotist for the medical profession
4. Performed live on TV as an archer5. Corporate pilot for one of world's largest corporations
6. Owned and operated an electronics retail and service store
7. Owned and operated a computer dealership
8. Owned and operated a computer bookkeeping service
9. Medical evacuation pilot for Prince Sultan of Saudi Arabia

I have been on the ground within six hundred miles of the North Pole, halfway around the world. I have been to the coldest spot on earth, and now I'm in the hottest. Before much longer, I hope to finish the trip around the other half of this world. The one thing that I really would like to do is be able to write it all down so that it would be interesting enough for someone to read.

Mrs. Parker, you were an inspiration to me many years ago. Do you recall teaching vocabulary to us from words in the *Reader's Digest*? Do you recall acting as an Algebra teacher for a while when they couldn't hire one? You were the one that made it understandable to me. By the way, years later, I made straight As in calculus. My poorest subject was English and still is. I never could spell and still can't.

So here is the proposition for you. Do you think, if I sent you my writing efforts, you might read them over and give me a critique? The understanding is that I know that I'll never be a serious writer, and I know that I can "tell" a story and would like to be able to write it in somewhat the same manner. Believe it or not, I still remember some rules of what a good paragraph should be like. However, doing it is something else. If this sounds like too much of a burden for you, then I will certainly understand.

It was just an idea that came to me when I read your letter. I'll never be good at spelling or grammar, but I do intend to write. We'll just have to wait to see if it can be of interest to anyone else. At any rate, we will be very interested in hearing from you.

Sincerely,
Capt. James D. Fox

Author's Note: Mrs. Parker was the wife of the principal and our teacher in Corona, New Mexico. She and her husband were world-class examples of what a teacher should be. They encouraged the students and could not be forgotten over the years.

Charlotte and I visited Mrs. Parker just before coming to Saudi Arabia. She was still driving herself around and was ninety-two years old. She told us that she kept busy with the folks down at the old folks' home even though she didn't live there. She still lived alone.

"I lead the singing down there, you know," Mrs. Parker told us.

"Oh well, I guess you must be in charge there, considering your age."

"Oh no, the older ladies are in charge" was her reply.

Mrs. Parker still had a lively and active mind. That's why I could and did mail her six of my stories and ask for credit as if I was still in high school.

Because of the censorship particularly of mail leaving the Kingdom, I was careful to mail my stories from another country. To my astonishment, Mrs. Parker mailed them back with her comments! I couldn't believe they got through the censors, but they did. Mrs. Parker didn't make any red marks on my papers, but she added the comment:

"James, I am so proud of your literary efforts. However, I might say that if you expect them to have commercial appeal, then I suggest that you might consider adding a love interest."

Mrs. Parker's only son lived in Raton, New Mexico, and decided that his mother should not be living alone there in Hatch so many miles away. He moved her to Raton to live with him and his family. I'm sorry to say that Mrs. Parker didn't last long there. I didn't hear from her again.

CAF Letter:
Riyadh, Saudi Arabia
January 8, 1987

Dear Bessie,

You are the recipient of my first attempt at writing letters on James's new computer, so I will have to see how it goes.

James has gone on a mission to the border of Kuwait to a town called Al Khafjiy and left me a note as I was having afternoon tea in unit B-15 with the Medevac ladies. Some have just returned from Christmas vacations, so there was a lot of catching up to do. Anyway, James left the computer on for me so I could attempt writing this letter.

Well, now that I did a few little things to get into the program I am writing, but printing it will be a task in itself. I had just learned the old computer he had enough to write letters, and he sold it to upgrade. Well, so much for computers. Thank goodness, James has it to play with, or he would go bananas. (So would I!)

Received your very nice and interesting letter and want to thank you for writing. I know how busy you are, so I really appreciate you taking your time to think of me. You have probably already surmised that mail as the highlight of our day. I spoke to Jean today but forgot to tell her that we had a long letter from our old high school teacher, Mrs. Parker, who is now ninety-one years old. She wrote a beautiful letter and sent us a check for a wedding present. Maybe you can mention this to Jean for me. She will probably be on her Far East trip, and I will probably forget to tell her by the time she returns.

Mohammed just arrived to clean my house. He is the houseboy James had before I arrived, so I have kept him. There isn't much for him to do, but it gives him extra money. He is from a family of ten, the father is dead, so why not. The price is right, and it is a help to me on some things I don't care about doing, at least one day out of the week.

Tonight is ladies' night out. We will group up at the gate, and the compound bus will drive us to one of the big hotels for dinner. The hotels are the best places to eat. Most of the time, we go to the Marriott, but this time we are going to a hotel that has a Saudi name, and I don't know how to spell it or pronounce it. There is also a Hyatt Regency downtown that is very nice. They have an Italian restaurant that serves very good food.

Most of the ladies associated with Medevac are British. There are several from Sweden and Canada but none from the States or as they say America. As in all women's groups, there are one or two rabble-rousers that keep the gossip line stirred up. I wish I could hear better because I could eavesdrop better.

Today one of the nurses said to another, "Have you heard the latest?" and all I heard were two names mentioned, one nurse and one male name, so naturally I wanted to know what the gossip was, but I couldn't hear. The British accent throws me off also. Well, anyway, if the single women are caught with a male, there is immediate dismissal, and they are exported.

No value is placed on the job because there is a waiting list for employment. We may be coming up short in the nurse crew soon. Never thought I would see the day when I would relish a good piece of gossip, but there isn't much else for excitement.

I gave James a birthday party the evening of January 3, 1987, and that was fun. We took video pictures, and each person stated their name and where they were from so we will have this for future times. Bessie, when you go bowling, be sure to say hello to all my friends. Do you and Jean still see Helen? Jean hasn't mentioned Helen in any of her letters, so I don't know if she is still bowling.

Helen had to move her business, so I imagine she has been very busy and tired. If you see her, say hello for me. I wrote to her, so maybe she will find a little time to answer.

Sounds like Marie Callander's has gone downhill since Ramada Inn took them over. It was going down when I left because they had changed the corn bread, which was a big part of their menu. It seems to be hard to keep a good thing going.

Mohammed just told me that I received a thick letter today because he distributed the mail and he remembered. There are no secrets around here. Jean told me this morning that she sent me three packets of yeast in her last letter. The letter had been opened, and the yeast was removed. No one bothered to seal the letter back up, so I am lucky there was anything in it at all. So it goes.

Would have liked to have the yeast. I have some, but it is not the same as we have, and I haven't quite figured out how to use it yet. James's sister, Louise, sent me a good recipe, and I am going to make it the first day James is gone early in the day. It has to rise and be kneaded, so I will need daytime. Maybe I should explain.

We have crazy hours because he is on standby at different times. One day, we may sleep until 10:30 or 11:00 a.m., and the next day get up at 6:00 a.m. On Christmas morning, James had to fly to Khartoum, Africa, leaving our house at 2:30 a.m. for a departure from the air base at 4:00 a.m. He got home shortly after 12:00 noon but had to go to bed to sleep. I called him at 6:00 p.m. as I had a turkey dinner ready for him. You just have to hang loose and sleep when you can.

Most of the time, we do not go to bed until 1:30 or 2:00 a.m. Depends on the schedule. Also, we can check out video movies, such as they are, from the switchboard room, and this is our total recreation. Sometimes we go for a brisk walk around the compound at midnight or anywhere from sundown to midnight. We try to find the shopping carts that are scattered throughout the compound and take them back to the gate where they should be. When you come in from shopping with a load of groceries, it is bad if the carts have not been returned to the gate. Usually, you are dying to get home to the bathroom, and if you have to go hunt carts, that is "el bad-oh." (Tex-Mex)

Bessie, a belated Happy Birthday wish! It is too bad you have to combine it with Christmas, but I guess you have worked that out over the years. Sounds like you had a nice Christmas. I hope this new year will be good to you and will be all you want it to be, yes, prosperous too. Thank you so much for the nice letter. James says he wants some credit also because he read it. He is always looking for "his" credit.

We send our love.

JDF Letter:
Riyadh, Saudi Arabia
January 12, 1987

Dear Greg, Mary, David, Sandy, John, Gail,

That's just about a page full. Finally, I got the charger for the video camera this morning. Guess what? It has a polarized plug, and there is nothing in the house that will take a polarized plug. Well, that just means a little more rooky-doo, but you know me, I'll get it yet. I have made a list of things, to the best of my memory, of the things that were moved from the garage to storage.

This is not supposed to be everything or even absolutely accurate. It's just the best that I could do at the time. You know that I will never be able to remember all the different tools that I have bought over the years, and even if they were to be replaced by insurance, I would have to replace them as they were needed. Charlotte had the foresight to take out insurance with USAA before she left California for our goods left in storage.

I intend to tell USAA today, being Monday, to contact you for any details. I don't know if they will send an agent out to see the warehouse or not. If so, then I would appreciate it if you would cooperate with them. There isn't a lot that they can do now, but we will just have to wait and see.

It seems that I took some pictures and videotape of the apartment, which may not be in with the stuff that I left with you. They may be in the warehouse. If so, they would show the bookcases and other items that were in the apartment. You didn't say if they took any of the electronics.

Need to know that. That amateur equipment is hard to replace and is expensive. I'm glad that I'm not there right now. The old feelings came back quick about wanting to do something ugly to someone that breaks in and steals. I'll always believe that it was the Lord that kept me from ever catching the thieves at Fox Electronics. I still feel that some of those burglars involved Gary or friends of his. No proof.

The weather is still great here. No one would ever believe it, but it's so. The temperature is just right. You can wear sleeves or a light jacket, your choice. They say the summer won't start for two or three months yet. We can handle that.

Got a letter yesterday from Sherfesee. He said that he and Lola enjoyed reading my dispatch but asked me to look in the dictionary for the meaning of Ahab. It says that he was a wicked king of Israel, whose wife was Jezebel. Well, I'm no king. See you later. Love.

Dispatch:
Riyadh, Saudi Arabia
January 14, 1987

ODIE

Odie and Gazelle live in an A villa just down the walk and facing our direction. Their front faces west, and our front faces north. The situation makes it possible for Odie and Gazelle to look out their front and see the coming and going from our B unit. Well, so what you ask? The "so what" is that my fellow captain and his wife seem to be overly curious about our comings and goings and when we do it.

When Romeo base calls out a mission, all stations are able to hear the call if their handsets were set on Normal. If the handsets are set on Sel (for Select), they will only hear the calls that are intended for them. The idea is that if it is late at night and you didn't want to be bothered by calls that are not meant for you, then you will not hear them. All the captains keep their sets on normal because if the mission isn't for them, then by deduction, you might know that a quick change might make the next call for you.

Odie and Gazelle at his birthday party

Odie seems to pay particular attention to how long it takes me to respond to a call for a mission. Romeo Base seems to make all his calls as ASAP missions (as soon as possible). He has even made calls for us to stand by for an ASAP mission.

When I found out that Odie was playing as monitor for Medevac, I had to think up something to entertain him.

I usually wear my uniform when I am an F1. You could never expect to get away without a trip when it was your duty day. One day, I was in my apartment when the mission was called. I answered the call, kissed my wife good-bye, and left through the back door, proceeding to leave the compound. Odie can't see our back door.

On my return, Charlotte told me that about fifteen minutes after I left, she got a call from Odie wanting to know if something was wrong as he hadn't seen me leave the apartment. Charlotte told him, "Oh no, Odie, James left sometime ago." Now Odie was in a quandary. How had I gotten past his sentry post? When he asked me about it, I feigned ignorance, just to agitate my monitor a little more.

I probably should not have treated Odie in such a fashion, but he had this junior high school attitude, and he was so easy to predict. We were walking down the compound walk together one day, and I purposely stepped on one of the huge red ants that were racing across the sidewalk in front of me. (I called them thirty-knot ants because that's about how fast they ran across the concrete sidewalk. Well, you would too if you were barefooted.)

"Oh, Captain Fox, don't do that."

"Don't do what?" I asked.

"Don't step on those ants like that," Odie replied seriously.

"Oh yeah, how should I step on them?"

"Well, you shouldn't step on them at all."

"Why not?" I asked.

"Well, you see, we have an agreement with them, that is, if we don't bother them, then they won't bother us."

I didn't bother saying what I thought, but as I glanced at Odie, it was obvious that he was serious. Oh well, he and Gazelle were just a little different I guess. Gazelle is from Canada and a leftover from the hippy generation. When she flew on the airline, she had to lie down on the floor. She couldn't be comfortable sitting up in the seat. Car seats were okay, but airline seats wouldn't do. Oh yes, Gazelle was also a vegetarian. When we went out to dinner with the couple, Gazelle would order a salad only but then ate all the meat off Odie's plate while he complained. Yes, a strange couple.

Early in our relationship, I asked Odie for advice on where to keep my salary. The local banks paid no interest.

"Oh, that's easy. You need to talk to Gazelle. She's a financial genius, you see."

"Well, we would like to come by sometime soon and talk to Gazelle then."

"Sure thing, why don't you all come over this afternoon for some tea?"

Well, we made the trip, and when the subject came up, Gazelle said, "We keep our money in the Canary Island Banks. You know they are very safe."

"Well, yes, I've heard that, and that they were like the Swiss banks, very protective of their investors."

"Oh yes, very protective."

"Well, I don't know about the Canary Island Banks, but the Swiss banks pay a very low percentage of interest. Is that true?"

"No, I believe they pay a reasonable rate."

"Well, I have a friend in England that has suggested the Westminster Bank there. They seem to pay a rather large percentage. My friend said they paid 11 percent. Could that be true?"

"Well, that may be true, but you see that's in pounds!"

"I don't understand, Gazelle. What difference does it make? A percentage is a percentage whether it's pounds or dollars. Isn't it?"

There was no answer from the financial genius.

Odie didn't stay very long after I started flying for Medevac. He took a job flying for a sheikh over in Jeddah. That meant he was then chief pilot. Well, hey now, that looks important on your resume. It happened that Odie and I were in Basel, Switzerland, for maintenance at the same time when the G-2 that Odie was responsible for was involved in an accident within the workshop. It was a freak accident. Somehow, a paint gun was over pressurized and blew off the airline. It sailed across the workshop and hit Odie's Gulfstream on the leading edge of the starboard wing just about six feet out from the root. It left a quite noticeable dent in the wing. Odie was beside himself.

"What am I going to tell the sheikh? He's going to have a spasm when he sees that damage."

"Well, Odie, it's not that bad. It can be easily patched. The shop can just cut out that section and replace it."

"Yeah, but he may see the patch, then what will I say?"

"Odie, just tell him the truth. Tell him what happened, and then you don't have to worry about him seeing it. Besides, it wasn't your fault."

"Oh, I know, but you don't know the sheikh. He'll probably fire me."

"Well, my advice is to tell the truth and right away. Get it over with, or you're going to be a nervous wreck."

Odie chose not to say anything. Just let it ride. I don't know if the sheikh ever saw the patch, but Odie was not about to tell him what happened.

Oh, one last thing. Odie always had copilot problems. They could never please him. One that he hired after arriving in Jeddah was arrested! Yes, that's right. He was put in jail over letters he was writing back home. He was writing about the Saudis, and they didn't like it. So they put him in jail for sixty-days, then sent him home. That's the reason I mail my stuff from out of country.

Dispatch:
Riyadh, Saudi Arabia
January 15, 1987

BAD NEWS FROM HOME

Bad news from home. Thieves broke into my storage locker in Houston and stole or trashed all inside! Keepsakes and treasure alike were gone. Greg called me with the news. I had left him with a key and with the instructions to go by now and then to check on things. He did this a few times since my departure, but this last time he found that his key didn't fit.

It is common for the owners to lock out renters who have not paid their bill. Greg went to the office to see if that was the case but found that no, the bill was paid and in advance. So what could be the trouble? The thieves had cut off my lock and helped themselves to the contents, perhaps several times, and then replaced my lock with theirs when the left. They may have been going in and out for some time.

Greg's description was of a big mess. This was going to be several tens of thousands dollars loss besides the treasures of sentimental value which could not be replaced. To me, it was just the icing on the cake—with thieves. While operating Fox Electronics in Houston, thieves had given me more than a share of break-ins. Perhaps I'll write that as a separate story, but frustration is hardly the word for it.

THIEVES IN HOUSTON

I've been threatening to write this story up for some time, and now may the best time to do it. Perhaps it will help to get my feelings about some things smoothed out.

A few years ago in the late 1970s, I opened a TV repair shop. My son Greg and I had finished several semesters together at the San Jacinto Jr. College on electronics. The idea of the TV repair shop grew out of the idea that Greg needed extra money to help pay the medical expenses for his first child. We had been repairing TVs in my garage, and the demand was beginning to be too much for the garage.

Of course, Greg and I both had full-time jobs, but there was enough time for garage work. I was flying airplanes for Exxon, and Greg was a firefighter with the Houston Fire Department. We lived on FM1960 twenty-five miles north of Houston center, which at the time was the fastest growing part of Houston, and Houston was the fastest growing city in the USA. The area was without a TV repair service. I figured it was the perfect spot and the perfect time for Fox Electronics to be born.

"My business card for Fox Electronics. The little fox was my own creation."

The first fiscal year in our new shop was six months long, and we grossed $35,000. Just the two of us, and we couldn't keep up. The second year was a full twelve months; we moved into the above address, took on retail sales, and grossed $70,000. We now had three full-time employees and again doubled our gross to $140,000. The next year, we grossed $350,000 and added three more full-time employees.

We were now big enough to attract more than customers—thieves. They loved the video recorders and cameras. The first color camera was an RCA and retailed at $1,000. It was small enough to carry in one hand—perfect for the thieves. The recorders were also small enough to handle easily and expensive. The thieves loved them. I had burglar bars on the outside of my show window and over the front door. Greg and I installed a perimeter alarm system that covered all windows, doors, and called my home phone number when tripped. It didn't call the police because they were twenty-five miles away, and the quickest response time was twenty minutes. That was sixteen minutes too late.

The thieves were educated by a couple of old cons that had a burglar school on the west side of Houston in an old barn, where the young students, less than eight years old, were taught to be in and out of their mark in five minutes or less. When my phone rang at two or three in the morning, I didn't even bother to answer it. I knew it was another break-in. I jumped from my bed into a housecoat, grabbed my .45 pistol, and down the stairs, out the front door, and into my little 65 Mustang. It was only six blocks to the shop from my house, and I could be there six to seven minutes. It was never soon enough.

One night, I got there just a little too late, but the puddle of water made by the air conditioner of their waiting vehicle was still rippling from the last drop that fell in it. My shop backed up to a six-foot cedar fence with residences on the other side. That same night, a resident just across the fence met me in the parking lot with a double-barrel shotgun. He heard my alarm go off, grabbed his gun, and climbed over the fence. He ran around the building. Too late they were gone.

My alarm was a siren from a fire truck—plenty loud. It was situated in the attic of the shop and powered by a truck battery, which was kept charged by a trickle charger that was always connected. The thinking was that even if they killed the phone lines and electricity, that siren was going to go off when the alarm system was tripped. It was a good idea, but no alarm was going to be able to beat the thieves' five-minute rule. I learned about the burglary school and the five-minute rule from the sheriff's department. They called the cons that were teachers Fagens from Charles Dickens's stories. They had broken that ring but suspected there were more than one still in operation somewhere nearby.

The drawing shown is a sketch showing the layout of my shop. Please note a few things that are important to this story.

1—The glass front door ($700 to replace), the show windows in front.

2—All outside walls are of concrete blocks or bricks.

3—The side door made of steel.

4—On the back wall, there is space four feet wide. The only spot on the outside wall that is unprotected by either heavy-duty shelving, burglar bars, or the alarm system!

"Floor Plan of Fox Electronics"

In the beginning, all break-ins were through the front door. The door was covered in steel bars, but that was not a deterrent to young educated thieves. Sometimes they would just drive a corner of their vehicle bumper through the bars and glass. Or they would use a car jack horizontally between the doorjambs and just jack the frame until the door fell out. The door seemed to be no problem, and the alarm didn't go off until the door was smashed or fell out of place. Then they were in and grabbed what was handy, and then they were gone. It was as simple as that. But they were getting smarter. I think they may have seen that angry neighbor coming over the back fence with a shotgun and decided that five minutes might not be enough the next time. So a new approach.

How about that spot on the back wall that was not obstructed? They could take a sledgehammer and knock a hole in the back wall, and it wouldn't set off the alarm. There was no alarm system there! Yeah, that would work, and they wouldn't have to hurray. They could loot the store all night long if they wanted.

The sheriff also believed they used lookouts with handheld radios to warn of traffic on the road in front of the store. All the modern conveniences, and that is just what they did. One weekend, my family and I were out of town, and that's when they broke through the back wall. The hole they left was centered between the filing cabinets and the shelving. Are you wondering how they knew where to break through? That blank space cannot be seen from anywhere the customers might be. It looked like an inside job. Or was it?

Toward the end of the burglaries, and there was an end to them, I noted that two or three days before a break-in, we had an alarm system salesman drop by to make a survey and try to sell me his latest and greatest alarm system. Either the alarm salesman or someone in my shop was telling the bad boys all the information they needed for the break-in. Well, almost everything. Now it was time for me to get smarter.

I called my old friend in Dallas, Bob McNeme, that had once worked with me when we were in the civil engineering department of Humble Oil & Refining Co. Bob was now in the alarm system business and had a new smart system that might be just what I needed for the guy with the sledgehammer. It was a sensitive microphone or microphones that could be set in the ceiling and could tell the difference between footsteps and telephone rings!

Bob sent one down, and the next day, I installed the same. That weekend, the guy with the sledgehammer was back. The second time he swung that sledgehammer, the alarm went off, and I was down there in six minutes. When I arrived, the shop was still locked up, but the alarm was still going off. I went inside and turned off the alarm, looked throughout the shop, and all was intact. But when I went outside and around to the rear, I found where the sledgehammer had broken a hole in the external side of one cinder block but had not penetrated all the way through. The thief had been thwarted, but I knew it was not the end.

My next step was to sleep down at the shop. Another TV shop down on the west side of Houston was in the news. The owner had surprised two of the kids in the process of robbing his store. He shot one of them, and the bullet passed through without killing one kid but went on and killed the second kid. He got two with one bullet! Well, it was my turn, and I was determined to break up the cycle of *my* break-ins.

An army cot, my M1 carbine, a S&W .357 magnum, and I camped out on a Saturday night at Fox Electronics. About 10:30 p.m., the sheriff's deputies began to show up in my parking lot. Even the desk sergeant was there. We were discussing my problem while I was standing next to the phone. It rang, and without thinking, I picked it up on the first ring and said, "Fox Electronics." Immediately, I knew

I had made a mistake. There was no on at the other end of the phone line. The sergeant said, "That was the thieves, checking to see if anyone is here!" I knew he was right.

The sergeant turned to the group of deputies and said, "They intend to hit here tonight! Okay, all you guys spread out and let's catch them tonight."

There were six cars there at that time, and they all did double-time back to their cars and left in a cloud of dust. I didn't think the thieves would show after my foolishly answering the phone, but I was going to play it out anyway. So I turned out the lights and sat down to wait and see. There was no need to try and sleep, not yet anyway.

It must have been about 2:00 a.m. when I saw lights turn into my parking lot and then go out. It was only a few steps to that $700 glass door that I had left unlocked. My insurance had refused to replace it again, and I didn't want some kid to crash through it. I had the .357 in my right hand and my back against the wall. The muzzle of the pistol was close to the door and about waist high. *If you break that door, I'm going to kill you where you stand.* It went through my mind clearly but not across my lips. It seemed an eternity as I waited for what I knew was about to happen.

And then it happened. A face slowly came into view, and it was looking right down the barrel of that .357. For just a moment, time stood still, and the face froze in place. Slowly, I lowered the pistol, and the face withdrew. I had recognized the face; it was the sheriff's deputy!

After lowering the pistol, I stepped to the door and pushed it open and took another step partly outside and said, "Come on in, officer, and have a cup of coffee." He didn't reply but just nodded, stepped inside, and followed me into the work area and the coffeepot. I poured us both a cup, and he took his, still without saying a word.

I laid the pistol down, and after about thirty seconds and two sips of coffee, the young rookie spoke for the first time, "Can I see your piece?"

"Sure, go ahead," I replied.

He examined the S&W and without a word replaced it on the table.

"Officer, don't ever do that again."

The rookie replied, "You can count on it."

I think he had learned a lesson he wouldn't soon forget. How did he think he was going to slip up on some crooks if he drove up to the front of my store with his lights on? Then come peeping around the corner like he expected to see them inside picking up their loot. Now really.

Well, the Lord never allowed me to catch the thieves, and I guess it's just as well. I might have done something to be sorry for later.

But I had to do something. I had to outsmart those bad guys. The alarm system was not going to do it because they could get away too quick, and I couldn't sleep down at the shop every night. But wait a minute, maybe that's the answer. I had to do something about the time thing. It was for sure that I couldn't get to the store any sooner, but what about slowing them up?

I had already had an idea about pasting a map on the showroom window giving directions down the road three miles to another TV shop that didn't have a burglar alarm. But I think the thieves had already fallen in love with my location.

I got on the phone and called the same people that had installed the burglar bars for me and told them to come and install a set of bars on hinges like a gate that would be installed outside of my precious glass door.

My front door was hinged on the right as you stood outside and looked in. I wanted the new gate to hinge on the left with a steel plate about six inches square to cover the lock and handle of the glass door behind. The new gate was made of flimsy wrought iron and was secured to the building with a simple hasp like you might put on a chicken house. The lock I used to secure the hasp was a $2 combination lock—the cheapest I could find. And that was my design. To enter the shop, you had to first open the wrought iron gate and then open the glass door.

The small steel plate over the glass door meant that it was protected from the outside. Even a key couldn't get to the lock. The simple hasp and cheap lock was strictly a bluff. The would-be thief could not be sure there wasn't something there to set off the alarm before he could even begin to break in to the store. That would be eating into his five minutes.

A few nights later, the alarm went off, and again I was down there in six minutes, but no break-in. The wannabe robber was so frustrated when he finished examining the "gate," he just took a sledgehammer and broke my showroom window. It was probably the same hammer he intended to use on my door. That was the end of my break-ins. Those last six weeks I had suffered through seven break-ins, and that was enough. My insurance was gone, and so was my will to continue.

On a Saturday morning, I went down to open the store, and while the key was still in the lock, I said to myself, "What the heck!" Then I relocked the front door. The Closed sign was still displayed, and that was the end of Fox Electronics.

I might add as an additional thought. Three of the thieves were caught, not by the police, not by the sheriff, but by the Constables.

In Texas, we have a law enforcement group called Constables. They are at the bottom of the totem pole, so to speak, and supposedly under the control of the Justice of the Peace, an elected official. The Constables are police wannabes. They would much rather be playing cops and robbers than doing the boring and mundane things that they are responsible for. Like many law enforcement officers, they are underpaid and are commonly found doing security work to fill in the slack at the bank. They get to have patrol cars with sirens, they get uniforms, they get guns to wear, and they get to arrest the suspected wrongdoers.

On a sunny afternoon, a Constable patrol car saw a car failing to stop at a stop sign. It was time for the siren and flashing lights. On observation, they found the automobile in violation was driven by a teenager accompanied by two other teenagers all in the front seat of the sedan. On closer observation, the Constable noted that the backseat was covered in briefcases. The alert Constable quickly decided that something was just not right. After conferring with his partner, they decided to take these suspects *in*.

Once down to the place where evildoers are interrogated, the suspects began to tell on each other, and the next thing they knew, the Constables had through ingenious detective work, hand uncovered a *burglary ring*. The young evildoers led the Constables to an abandoned house in the country, filled with the results of their efforts.

Of course, the local weekly paper was notified, and photographers were dispatched to photograph the proud Constables standing with their arms resting on a stack of 19" color TV sets. That picture showed me on of my missing TV sets. I had a police report for the TV set and one microwave set that were stolen a few weeks earlier from my shop. The ink was hardly dry on the newspaper when I showed up at the Constables' office.

"Can I help you?" the lady asked.

"Yes, I hope so. My name is Fox, and I own Fox Electronics. I saw a picture in the paper where the Constables had recovered some of my property. I would like to recover that property please."

About that time, a uniform showed up. He had heard my request for my property.

"Uh, Mr. Fox, we can't return your property just yet. You see, it has to be held for *evidence*."

"Well, when can I expect my property to be returned?"

"Oh, that will have to be after the trial, you see."

"Okay, how long will that take?"

"Oh, probably six months or a year."

My effort was hopeless. To make this story shorter, I called the office later when I read the case had been settled. The thieves had been convicted but released. Two of the offenders were sixteen, and the third was seventeen years old. The seventeen slashed the tires of a Constables' patrol car when he left the courthouse and was seen by another Constable. The judge decided to revoke his probation and put him behind bars. The other two were sentenced to repay me for damages to my shop. They never did. A phone call to the Constables' office told me that I would have to talk to the district attorney of Harris County to find out the disposition of my property.

I called the district attorney's office and got the beginning of a runaround but was finally told that they didn't have the authority to release my property. I needed to contact the judge. Now I have to find the judge.

A later phone call to the judge's office—I never got to talk to the judge—revealed that they had never had the so-called *evidence*, which was still in possession of the Constables' office.

Okay, now to retrieve my property. You think? Now it is a trip back to the Constables' office—in person.

"Officer, my name is Fox, and—"

"Oh yes, Mr. Fox, what can I do for you?"

"Well, the judge says that you still have my property, and his office has no claim on it any longer, and I'd like to get it back. There is a 19" RCA color TV and a Quasar microwave, and here are their serial numbers with the police report."

The officer made a casual glance at the paperwork without really reading anything.

"Oh, uhm, Mr. Fox, hasn't your insurance taken care of this claim a long time ago?

"No, officer, they have not. I cannot get insurance anymore. I've had too many break-ins. Now I would just like to get my property back. If you please."

"Well, you see, Mr. Fox, that's been a long time, and I don't know where your property is just right now, you see?"

"What do you mean you don't know where it is? Don't you have a property room? Don't you keep track of such things?"

"Now, Mr. Fox, don't get upset. I tell you what, what do you want for the TV and microwave?"

It was plain to me that my property was already in some Constables' home.

"You mean, someone has already *liberated* the property, and now they are willing to pay for it."

"Well, I don't know exactly, but we don't want you to get all upset," replied the Constable.

At this point, I knew I was on the verge of make an enemy of the law enforcement branch of the Justice of the Peace. Not a good idea. How do you tell the burglars from the cops? One wears a uniform.

So now, I am twelve thousand miles away, and they have got me again. I guess the thieves got the last word after all.

JDF Letter:
Riyadh, Saudi Arabia
January 21, 1987

Dear Louise and Gerald, (my sister and husband)

Mohammed came over this afternoon to deliver a letter from you that for some reason was not in the regular mail. That is not his job, to deliver mail; he just likes us. The letter turned out to be my birthday card. A very nice surprise. We love to receive mail, and consider this, we are both writing a *lot* of letters. Charlotte tries to answer her mail just as soon as she receives it, usually the same day. So since I would like to look good to her, I'm going to answer your letter right now, the same day.

The young fellow that brought our mail, Mohammed, is from Sri Lanka. If you are not familiar, Sri Lanka is an island country just off the southeast tip of India. It was known when we were studying geography as Ceylon. There are many Sri Lankans that work here in the Kingdom. It's not that far from here, and their home country is very poor.

Saudi has a work policy that is worth commenting on. If an employer wants to hire someone for his business here that is not a native of the country, then he must do it with the government's blessing. That is he must get them a visa and transport them to the place of work. He must then get them a work permit, which is known as an *iqama*. The *Iqama* becomes his ID. He must carry it at all times. If he loses it, it costs SR3,000 ($800) to replace (SR3.75 equals $1).

The employer is also responsible for the employee's place to live and transport back and forth to work. The employee is limited to a radius of travel of fifty miles. To go beyond that, he must have a letter of release from his employer. That rule includes Charlotte and myself. If we want to go to Dhahran, about like going to Dallas from Houston, we will have to get a letter from our employer. It's no problem to get the letter, but if you get stopped by the police and don't have permission, then straight to jail. When the job is finished, the employer must furnish airfare back to the place of origin for the worker.

Often, there are notices in the paper showing a man's picture, iqama number, and the date that he is leaving the job and the Kingdom. Notice is given that any debts that the worker has must be presented for payment by a certain date before he leaves the Kingdom. The reasoning here is that the employer is ultimately responsible for his employees completely. When the worker is no longer needed, then he is not just let go, he must be returned to his home country. There are no out-of-work foreigners here, and they can't run out of the country leaving debts nor can they be grossly mistreated by their bosses. Seems like a pretty good system

171

to me. Since my arrival here six months ago, I have seen one person that *might* be considered a beggar. Not too bad in a city of 1.5 million people.

Charlotte just brought in some bread that she made with your recipe, Louise. She wanted me to tell you that it worked out fine. The Italian oven has been partly subdued. She said the trick with the bread was to cook it the first ten minutes with the lower element only and the last ten minutes with the top and bottom elements both. The smell is great, and it looks just like what the big girls do.

We got interrupted to go to a party here at the compound. One of the mechanics has returned from leave, so it's time to have a party. We had a party when he left also. No offense to him, but it doesn't take much of an excuse to pitch a party here. We got there a little late, and the regular drinkers were already, as the Brits say, feeling quite merry. Most everyone knows by now that we don't drink, so the coffee is on and ready. So after a few cups of coffee, a couple of pieces of cake, and a few stories, we are released for the evening. It will probably be two or three days before the next party.

Louise, your wine making might fit in very well here. I can't say for sure the number of those that make wine and beer here, but the percentage is certainly high. They buy apple juice in bottles that look just like wine bottles. It's not unusual to see several cases of this juice being carted in by one individual. That's for the wine. Most everyone that makes wine also makes beer. I don't know how they make that, but there is always plenty around. Everyone knows it, even the Saudis, but nothing is done. It's sort of like back in Wichita Falls when the guys would go to the parties with a bottle in a brown paper sack with the sack twisted uptight around the neck of the bottle. It looked just like a bottle in sack. Even after it wasn't against the law, they still did it. No one really cared as long as they behaved themselves.

Well, the weather here is just unbelievably good. Temperatures are just right for sleeves, and the air is dry. If we just had some grass, it would be perfect for golf. We found the golf course here a few weeks ago but have not ventured back to try it out. Maybe so later. They told us they had a waiting list for membership. Unbelievable.

The big news from Houston is that the thieves broke into our warehouse and helped themselves to everything, even took my saddle and audiocassettes. Charlotte had the foresight to get insurance on all our stored goods. The insurance will help, but you know that it can't be replaced with money. Just another price to pay, I suppose. All the old feelings came back from the days and nights that I was battling the thieves at Fox Electronics. The urge to kill is overpowering. I believe that God kept me from ever catching them in the act because I already knew what I was going to do if I did catch them. I told Charlotte that I was glad that I wasn't in Houston just now. They took the bookcases that were in my apartment, all my mechanic tools, electronics, even the kitchen utensils. Our golf clubs were not spared either. Greg is running an inventory for me to work with the insurance people. Well, we will see.

The good news is that we are coming back to the States in February for about ten days. We will leave here on February 20 for Savannah, Georgia, for training. We will be in Houston on February 27 and probably leave Houston around the March 3 for Los Angeles. After a couple of nights there, we will continue on to Hawaii, Tokyo, Hong Kong, Bangkok, and finally for four or five nights in Singapore. That's right, we're going around the world in something like thirty-two days. We just decided a couple of nights ago when it was established that I was for certain going back for training. We will send more information when the dates and reservations are firmed up. What do you think? A couple of country kids from Texas and New Mexico are going to see the world. Now, never mind telling me that it is a long trip in a short time. Think of it this way. When we are already halfway around, then to keep going the same direction to complete the trip is not all that big a deal. Right? We'll let you know more later.

We will be videotaping the whole thing, so stand by for some movies if you think you might be interested. We have about three hours already made here in Riyadh and will be adding more to that before we come back in February. We will probably leave the tapes with Greg and Mary, so if you want to see them, they will be able to send them along.

Oh yes, you wanted to know how the divorce finally ended. Sorry, didn't mean to not finish that story. I wrote Exxon an ugly letter about the December 12 to complain about not hearing from them about what was going on. Their attitude was if nothing was happening, then they had nothing to report. Their letter was back here in about a week, so I think our letters passed each other. At any rate, Jennie and or her lawyer delayed sending in the divorce decree to Exxon. Exxon processed the claim within six weeks after receiving the instrument.

I finally received my annuity check the first week of January. In the meantime, the check for 1985 IRS refund came, and Jennie had to endorse it for it to be cashed. I sent the check to my lawyer with my endorsement and my personal check for half the amount of the IRS check. His instructions were to have her endorse the IRS check, then he could give her my personal check for her half. This worked pretty well except when he took the check to my bank for deposit; they wouldn't deposit it without Jennie being present. Had to do with it being a check from IRS. So now my lawyer is trying to run it through his bank. If that doesn't work, then I'll have to go back on the IRS to issue a new check to me.

The latest development is that my lawyer received a letter from Jennie's lawyer demanding $4,500 in alimony payments for October, November, and December. You see, the way the papers were written, I was supposed to pay $1,500 per month until she *received* her first check from Exxon. I reasoned that had she and her lawyer returned the papers to Exxon promptly, then she would have received her first payment back in September. I told the lawyer to tell them I wasn't paying it and that they could just come and get me. The last I heard, her lawyer had charged her nearly $8,000 to handle her case. The kids say that she is *very* upset with him. So what's new?

I think that's about it. Don't know that I've left out any of the juicy details. It's all settling down now, so I'll let it die.

That's about enough for this time. Louise, I have enclosed a short story for you to read. Please note no names were used. I wonder if you remember the incident with Mama that is mentioned.

Love you both,
Jim D. Fox

CAF Letter:
Riyadh, Saudi Arabia
January 27, 1987

Dear Muriel,

Received your letter yesterday with the Mary Fox clipping and thank you very much. Sounds like there is vandalism existing in good old New Mexico as well as the rest of the world, or at least it sounds like that is what the man had in mind.

Have a bit of good news for you, I hope. At least I will tell you about it, and if it doesn't come to pass, I hope you won't be too disappointed. James has FlightSafety school in Savannah, Georgia, on February 23 to February 27. He wants me to come with him (already have my exit visa), and if we can make the proper arrangements with the time we have, we will come to Albuquerque for one night if we can. The way things look now, that night would be either Tuesday, March 3, or Wednesday, March 4. We plan on leaving Savannah for Houston, Houston to Albuquerque, and Albuquerque to Los Angeles. I have some business that I would like to take care of there and visit with Jeanie.

The travel agent said it would be cheaper airfare if we travel around the world in lieu of Riyadh to Savannah to Riyadh. The idea sounds good, but we haven't completed the details yet. Anyway, if we do this, we will leave Los Angeles to Honolulu, Honolulu to Tokyo, Tokyo to Hong Kong, Hong Kong to Bangkok to Singapore and on in to Riyadh. We have R & R time plus GAMA has granted James extra time. We have to be back here by March 21 or 22. If we do the Far East this time, next time we will go to Europe.

Sis, this has been the greatest experience we could have in a lifetime, and we have been very happy in this great adventure. Unless there are unforeseen problems in the future, the way things look to us now, we will stay here until James reaches sixty years old—that is, if GAMA renews his contract after September 1 this year. I don't remember if I told you or not, but at the end of this contract, they pay both of our ways back to the United States, and of course if they renewed his contract, they would have to pay our way back to Saudi. There are a lot of variables here, but there is a possibility that we may come home then for a visit, or if they pay us the airfare in cash in lieu of tickets, we may take a trip to somewhere in Europe. It takes a long time to get to the United States flying straight. We were smart coming over to stop in London and rest up.

Going to Savannah, we don't have the stopover privilege as this is strictly business. There will also be a Saudi copilot going at the same time. The king stipulates that we have to leave the country via Saudi Airlines and reenter the country via same. This is the only way GAMA can receive reimbursement from the government for the tickets. GAMA is a contractor with the air force to supply civilian pilots, nurses, and doctors for the Medevac program, and as you probably

175

have already gathered from previous correspondence, James flies from the air force base to other air force bases over the Kingdom, transporting patients to and from the hospitals. He can tell you all about it when we see you. We are looking forward to a change in the weather and hope it doesn't give us a cold.

James has gone downtown to the computer store where he bought his new computer. The man that owns the business is not as knowledgeable as he should be, so he is drawing on James for information. They are negotiating a deal with one of James's friends in Houston to buy some discs, and the first thing I know James will be involved in computer business over here. He already sees a potential for being a US broker for the software. You just think Tom was the best horse trader you have ever known; James comes in a close second. He is at his best when he is wheeling and dealing.

I am looking forward to being able to buying some things that we can't get over here, for example, maple flavoring, bran, pectin, and a timer. While James is in school in Savannah, I will go shopping. We are going to take an empty suitcase just for items we buy. I would like to bring back some dry yeast, but Jeanie Shelton tried to send me some, and it was removed from her letter. People over here use it to make wine and beer, which is illegal.

Did I tell you that we joined the US military club here, hoping that we could get an APO Box (James still has US Army Reserve status), and because he is not active military, they would not give it to us except for official mail only. They said that when he is sixty years old, he can have it then. That will be too late for our purpose. Well, we tried anyway.

One of these days, we are going down to see the American Embassy. We really are supposed to register with them, so I guess we will do that. James didn't want to open the door for his ex-wife to hassle him, so that is primarily why we haven't done it yet. The terms on his divorce were that he was supposed to pay her alimony until she received her first annuity payment, which should have been September 1.

She and her attorney would not sign the necessary release papers for Exxon to pay her, so James refused to pay her any more alimony. They must have reasoned that as long as she didn't sign the papers, James would just have to keep sending her alimony forever. She finally signed, and she didn't receive her share from his Exxon savings in December. She saw the loophole in the divorce and was taking advantage of it. Now she claims that James owes her three months' alimony and is going to try to collect it. He says she will have to sue him first. Because she wouldn't sign the Exxon papers that held his retirement money up for three months and he lost interest on his money plus numerous expensive phone calls from here, so he now feels stubborn about paying her more money. At least he forced her to sign the papers by cutting her off on alimony. That could have gone on for a long time. James had signed up with Exxon for me to receive the surviving espousal benefit; however, the Federal Government law that was passed a few years ago says that Jennie was entitled to it, so the Exxon attorneys gave that to her. She also was made beneficiary to the existing life insurance policy Exxon holds.

James made out his will to cover me with the income derived from his Exxon stock, which was granted to him through divorce, so she cannot touch that. On my death then, his stock will be divided equally between his sons. Also, any income from other investments will go to me until my death. Having my own investments plus social security at age sixty-two, I think my future will be okay financially without having to work again. Don't ever let anybody tell you they just don't know what they would do if they didn't work. I am so busy that I wonder how I ever had time to work. It is so nice to take a nap if I feel like it or not get up early if I want to sleep in. Seems like that is all I can remember about working is that I was tired most of the time and wished I could sleep.

When I was younger, the kids kept me busy, so I was tired then. Oh well, I certainly do count my blessings now. One nice advantage we have being over here is that if we are here three hundred days, we are allowed exemption on $70,000 before paying US Federal income taxes. We will be stuck for 1986 taxes, but the above will help in 1987.

Just received a letter from Jeanie Shelton, which I must answer, so will say bye for now and thank you for your many letters. I really look forward to them. James asked me this morning if you had a VCR yet. He wants to cut you a film of our doings here in Saudi. We have about three hours, which can be edited. Guess you could still see them at Jamasene's, so I told him to go ahead and make you a film. Don't think we would have a problem bringing it with us.

We send our love and hope the family is all well and over their flu and tell Milton to take care of himself. He is one of the nice guys, so we want to keep him around for a long time. Give Tom a hello for us and tell him if we come to Albuquerque, we will stop in to see him if he isn't asleep. When I receive more firm info, I will write you, and if it is the last minute, I will call you from Savannah or Houston.

Love,
Charlotte

JDF Letter:
Riyadh, Saudi Arabia
January 31, 1987

To: Project Manager
          GAMA, Medevac
Subject: Place of Residence
From: James D. Fox
          Captain, Fixed Wing GII/GIII

Dear Sir,

This letter is to request a change in my place of residence. My present residence is unit B-10 in the GAMA Nasseem Compound. The apartment is located next to a sewer receptacle that has a constant and very disagreeable odor. It is impossible to open the windows or sit on the patio due to the foul smell. Within the last four weeks, the sewer has backed up into my apartment four times. Three of these incidents were reported by work order; one incident was not reported due to its late-night occurrence. The compound manager has responded in each case and has assured me that the problem has been taken care of, and indeed, at the present time, the floors in the bath and kitchen are dry. The smell, however, is still with us.

There are other vacant units in the compound. I request one of these units that are presently available, one that is on the ground floor, far away from the sewer smell, and commensurate with my age, rank, and station.

It is not my intention to cause anyone any discomfort or embarrassment, but it is my intention to move away from this disagreeable situation.

Sincerely,
Capt. James D. Fox

(Author's Note: This is the beginning of a running gun battle between me and GAMA for a different place to live. Since I was new, I had not learned of the many manipulations that the GAMA people went through in regard to our housing. I was to learn that my rank deserved an A unit, which was a three-bedroom apartment, or as they called it a villa. It was GAMA's habit to place a new guy in the smallest unit that was available and that they could get by with. Doctors and captain pilots were the privileged class, and sometimes the living accommodations were used as bargaining chips to woo a new employee. I didn't have sense enough to suspect that I was being misused and mistreated. Charlotte always says I'm too trusting. This letter was just the beginning of my awakening!

Dispatch:
Riyadh, Saudi Arabia
January 31, 1987

FLIGHT LOG JANUARY 1987

1/8/1987	HZ-MS4	OERY	OEKM	1:30	to Khamis
1/8/1987		OEKM	OERY	1:15	return to Riyadh
1/14/1987	HZ-MSD	OERY	OEKM	1:30	to Khamis, ambulance fight, military won, patient each way
1/14/1987		OEKM	OERY	1:20	return to Riyadh
1/20/1987	HZ-MSD	OERY	OEHA	0:45	
1/20/1987		OEHA	OERY	0:40	
1/20/1987	HZ-MSD	OERY	OETK	1:55	to Tabuk
1/20/1987		OETK	OEJN	1:25	to Jeddah
1/20/1987		OEJN	OERY	1:25	return Riyadh
1/26/1987	HZ-MS3	OERY	OEKM	1:30	to Khamis
1/26/1987		OEKM	OERY	1:25	return Riyadh
1/27/1987	HZ-MS3	OERY	OEDR	0:45	to Dhahran
1/27/1987		OEDR	OERY	1:30	return Riyadh

Thought that you might like to see what my notes on a day might look like. Nothing to write a story about.

January 08, 1987

I got a call from Romeo to ask about a small airport at Al-Hafjiy. 1,500 meters. Could we get in there with a Gulfstream? I checked it over and said that we could. Later, he called and gave me a mission to OEKM Kahmis. Pick up two patients for return to Riyadh. Crew, 68, 10, 60. 10 was an F3 today, 14 called him for relief, 14 had to take his wife to airport. Took doctor. Call came at 1440, in the air at 1535. Trip no incident. Met the fire chief again. He was on duty the night that the batteries ran down on MS3. Doug Holt from Saturday. Uncle has ranch at Corona, New Mexico, Tommy Tarry. Mother lives there. Her name is Mogford, maiden name of Criders. Return trip no incident. Wrote up left engine start, stalled at 40 percent when fuel moved to open. Selected start and engine continued to spool slowly to 52 percent. engine two days out of overhaul. Charlotte had night out with the girls.

JDF Letter:
Riyadh, Saudi Arabia
February 3, 1987

Sgt. Tom Holloway
Police Station,
Cobham, Surrey
UK

Hello Tom,

It certainly doesn't seem that it's been four months since my wife and I were last there. You and your friends were very nice to the two of us and made us feel comfortable so far from Texas. In fact, it was much of a Texas welcome we received the day we came into your station.

Both the Saudis and the Brits here can't believe that I returned from the UK with a PC pin for my tie. They have never seen one except when worn by the proper constable. Of course, I wear it every chance I get and when asked how I received it, then I tell everyone a different version of the story. It's been a lot of fun, but I want you to know that I cherish that little pin.

My wife and I are going on vacation (holiday as you chaps say) in a few days, and we will be spending some time in Texas. It is my intention to pick up some memento for you and will have it on my next trip to Cobham. I don't know yet what it may be. May have to wait and see what inspires me. I'll never be able to match the pin that you gave to me.

Say hello to PC McCloud for us and the other gentleman at the station that day. I never got his name. We send you all our best wishes.

Sincerely,
James D. Fox
Captain GII/GIII
Medevac for Ministry of
Defense and Aviation
Box 41726
Riyadh 11531
Saudi Arabia

Dispatch:
Riyadh, Saudi Arabia
February 3, 1987

ANOTHER OF LIFE'S CHECK RIDES

Living in Riyadh, Saudi Arabia, is not so bad. It's different, but not so bad. I can tell you one thing. It's nothing like I expected. After five months of working, living, and surviving in this strange land, perhaps it is time for me to reflect a bit.

*   *   *

The whole thing started back in June 1986 as a joke back on me. I was fifty-seven years old and completely fed up with the man I worked under. It was coincidental that the world's largest oil company was once again downsizing, and the offer to me was very tempting. After thirty-eight years with the same company, maybe it was time for me to move into new circumstances.

I loved my job. Flying executive jets for a large company is a job that most pilots would give body parts for. But it's difficult for a job to be better than the man in charge. I didn't have a college degree, but I had ratings on executive transports that were still in demand. So there were options on my horizon. I just had to find them.

One day, I returned to my desk to find a clipping from an international aviation magazine. It lay right out in the center of my desk, not in my inbox, right out in the center. Someone didn't want me to miss it.

"Wanted: Pilot rated in GII and or GIII type aircraft to fly for General Arab Medical Association . . . in Saudi Arabia. Contact . . . etc.

Something came to my mind. An adventure, it had the looks of an adventure. I was instantly interested. In fact, I said so out loud. As I read the advertisement, all eyes in the office were watching me. When I voiced interest, the jokester couldn't believe me.

"Hey, Fox, you're not serious, are you?"

"Well, I don't know. I think it might be interesting, and besides, I can see some things I've never seen before."

"You got to be kidding. You wouldn't really consider living over there, would you?"

"Well, why not? I think I'll give them a call. They have a 1-800 number."

And that's it. A phone call, then some more phone calls, then more questions, and here I am. After all that, it's not at all what I expected.

Where are all the camels? Where is Bob Hope, Bing Crosby, and Dorothy L'amour? That's what I expected. So far, I have seen none of the above.

Before leaving the comforts of the United States in August 1986 for a country I knew nothing about, I asked questions. About to retire from an oil company, the world's largest, I could ask some company people I knew that had worked and lived in Saudi Arabia. The answers to my questions came like they were played from a tape recorder. I talked to over thirty people on the phone, and a few I visited with in person. With a single exception, they all told me, "Well, it wasn't so bad. I can tell you this, I have never had so much money in my pocket before or since, and I'd go back in a minute if I had a chance."

That response was universal, and it prompted me to ask, "Well, if that's so, why did you leave?"

The answer to that question was also common to all the parties that I talked to.

"Well, you see it comes down to the family. If you stay, your kids are going to miss growing up in the United States, so we left to keep the family together." That answer was taken as stated. I didn't know enough to ask more. Only after living in country for a while did I come to know why foreign teenagers are not allowed to stay in the country. The expatriates boys and girls are forced to leave on or before their sixteenth birthday. The Saudis don't want the fraternization problem. Children were not a problem with my wife and me. Ours were all grown.

The single exception to all the positive responses I had was from a simulator instructor working for FlightSafety International in Savannah, Georgia. Oddly, everything he had to say was negative. He didn't like anything about the time he spent there. He had not one good thing to say. "I didn't like the country, and I don't like the people, so I left the first chance I got."

Since he was the only negative response, I just remembered what he had to say and decided there was more to his story than he was telling. It was another question left in my mind that was answered once I was here for a short time. The simulator instructor didn't leave voluntarily; he was fired and forced to leave. He had lied about his experience on the Gulfstream aircraft he was supposed to fly, and the Saudis caught on to him right away.

None of the positive answers were what I expected. No one mentioned the temperature.

What about the so-called 140°F? No one even mentioned that, good or bad. Hmm, interesting.

* * *

On arrival in the Kingdom, everyone appeared to be friendly and helpful. The longer I'm here, the more emphasis I put on the word *appeared*. It didn't take me long to figure out that I'm something of a unique character. No, it's not my looks; it's the reasons that brought me here. It seems that I'm the only person here with a choice.

The foreign pilots here are all Americans, and they are here as their last chance to hang on to aviation. They all report leaving better jobs than the one they have here, but then they tell a story that doesn't fit. Their stated reasons for leaving that better job don't always make sense. One pilot told me that he left his last job because his wife didn't like for him to be gone all the time. Well, he didn't help himself much by coming here.

Another American reported having been chief pilot for at least three other companies. My first thought was, *Then why are you here*? The answers never fit. They come, and they go, sometimes willingly and sometimes not. Within the first few days of my arrival, an American was sent home for smuggling whiskey into the Kingdom. Every day, this place reminds me more of the old movies about the French Foreign Legion.

The organization has two GIIs, a GIII, a Lear 35, eight helicopters, and ten C-130s.

The aircraft are all American except for six of the helicopters that are French. The C-130s are seldom ever flown, and I don't think they could get more than two in the air at the same time. Parts, pilots, and mechanics are in serious short supply.

Getting aircraft into the air is the Saudis' big problem. They only have two Saudi captains for the fixed wing jets. So they have to rely on Americans to crew the American aircraft. Maybe I should explain. The United States of America is the world's largest supplier of aircraft. France is probably second, and the UK is third. France and the UK are distant rivals of the United States.

The United States easily has the largest supply of pilots in world. The pilot supply comes from several things, but you can say with certainty that the cost of training is one of the largest factors. In France, an Airline Transport Rating takes two years of ground school and costs over hundred thousand dollars. In the UK, it's almost as bad. That doesn't include the experience requirement. In the United States, ground school can be accomplished in a matter of days, and the cost is more on the order five to ten thousand dollars (1987 dollars).

With few exceptions, the country of origin for a given aircraft will have a far greater pool of pilots for the aircraft they produce. The Gulfstream line of jets began with the Grumman Aircraft Company of New York and are now produced by Gulfstream of Savannah, Georgia. They are considered by their owners, and most others to be finest business jets available. In 1987 dollars, their cost is pushing twenty million dollars a copy. They are expensive to buy, to operate, and to crew.

The lay person would need more of an explanation for the large discrepancy. Two words will explain: labor unions. The pilots' union in Air France has almost total control of the Directorate General of Aviation. The Air France pilots, in effect, pick their own replacements and the number of those replacements. Their claim is that their effort is to maintain the quality of French Airline Transport pilots. Well, that's their claim. There are no pilots' unions in Saudi Arabia. Neither are there any other kinds of union. Unions are not allowed. The Kingdom of Saudi Arabia is a real

Kingdom with a real king and five thousand princes. There is no telling how many princesses because they are literally not counted. That's because they don't count, not in the royal order of things, that is. The Kingdom didn't even exist until 1932, and the original king's crown passed to his oldest son, and that was it. That's right, King Fahd the present king has no successor because no rules were written down about what to do when the original king's eldest son passed on. I guess the original king thought that it would be every man for himself once his son was gone.

One of my Saudi copilots told me that they have an Arabic saying, which translates to mean, "We don't recognize a problem at a distance, only when it is close enough to touch us on the shoulder." Once I learned that, many questions in my mind were answered.

One thing the old king figured out was to split the power between his descendants. Since the oldest son was going to inherit the crown, he made the next son in charge of the army (they call it the National Guard), the next son in charge of the air force, and so forth. Their navy is hard to find, so I haven't heard who's in charge there, but since the first king had thirty-eight sons, there were plenty available for governorships, etc.

Prince Sultan is in charge of the air force, and he insists that his air force has all the airplanes. Prince Abdullah (generally expected to be the next successor to the crown) is in charge of the army, and he thinks he should have some aircraft just like the American Army has. Prince Sultan said no.

Well, the army doesn't have airplanes, but they have the responsibility for the medical service for all the military services plus the royal family. That means the hospital at the navy base in Jubail is built and operated by the army. The army types had an idea. Since they are responsible for all medical service, they needed a medical evacuation service that could cover the whole Kingdom. The natural answer was aircraft. The army's argument was persuasive, so the king allowed the army to build its own air force.

Prince Sultan had to have a last word, so he had the operation placed under his Ministry of Defense (MODA). It meant that the aircraft was his, not the National Guard (army). The trade-off was to let the National Guard provide operational control. The result was an air force operation operated by National Guard officers that didn't know airplanes from sailboats. The operation was supposed to serve the medical transportation needs of the military and the royal family, but in reality, it was also to be used for National Guard VIPs. It's called Medevac, and that's who I work for.

Dispatch:
Riyadh, Saudi Arabia
February 8, 1987

THE BARCELONA BODY

"It was the best of times, it was the worst of times," Dickens said. I would have added, "It was all the time." A guy can love to fly, but there are those who would keep you in the air all the time if you'd let them. After you've flown missions all day, they would ask you to take another one that would take another twenty hours of duty time.

Our radio dispatcher, Romeo Base, was given to frequent attacks of drama. He loved to call us out on Medevac ASAP (as soon as possible) missions. One of our biggest laughs came when Riyadh made a call, "Stand by for an ASAP mission!" Ninety-nine point forty-four percent of the missions he called were routine. They were transfer cases—transferring a patient from one hospital to another. But to Riyadh (our most dramatic radio dispatcher had a first name that was the same as the Capitol City), they were all a matter of life and death.

We all had radio call signs. Mine was Gulfstream 68. We had several radio dispatchers because the job was covered twenty-four hours a day, seven days a week. But all the dispatchers used the same call sign, which was Romeo or Romeo Base. My nickname for Riyadh was Romeo ASAP Riyadh.

No one could forget the Friday afternoon late when Riyadh called an ASAP mission for every person in the unit. Captains, copilots, nurses, engineers, and operations personnel for three Gulfstreams, a Lear, eight helicopters, and ten C-130s were all sent to their respective positions for a most urgent ASAP mission. It was like the beginning of World War III. The first aircraft was fifteen minutes in the air when it was discovered that the alert was based on an unconfirmed rumor. Riyadh had been notified that there were some Saudi casualties in Jubail as a result of some sort of Iranian bomb. Before he verified anything, he assumed the much-dreaded Iranian-Saudi war had begun, and it was going to be bloody. He didn't wait to find out there were only five Saudis involved, and the worst injury was a broken arm. You might say Riyadh was excitable.

One time, at about ten in the evening, Romeo called me on the phone. When Romeo calls on the phone, you know there is a problem. When the Romeo calling is Riyadh, he usually starts out by apologizing.

"Ahhhh, Captain . . . I hate to bother you at this late hour, but we a have a most urgent mission for you. You are needed to pick up a body in Barcelona."

"Riyadh, what is *urgent* about picking up a body? He's already dead, isn't he?"

"Ah yes, Captain, but you see, he is a general!"

"Look, Riyadh, I've been up all day, and you're talking about a mission of at least fourteen duty hours. The general is dead, and if you want me to take the mission, I'll leave tomorrow morning at 0800 hours, so set it up that way, okay?"

Riyadh didn't like the rebuff, but when you are the only captain left on the roster, you have a better chance of standing up for what's right. Besides, I knew all he really wanted was for me to get in the air as soon as possible. He could then report to the higher powers that the mission was launched, and they would quit calling and pestering him. The sooner he could get us in the air, the sooner everyone in the chain of command both operational and political could relax.

Riyadh said he would have to check with the major and let me know. About fifteen minutes later, my handheld radio went off with its distinctive *booooooop—bullleeeep*! The captain was always the first crew member called, and the selective calling feature of our little handheld radios let me know by its tone that the call was for me. If it wasn't for me, the tone would just be a *boop—beeeeep*.

My crew would include my friend Hatim Bashir as copilot, Phil Thorpe as engineer, and Jenny Madill as flight nurse—an American, a Saudi, and two Brits. It was an integrated flight crew. The mission was called for 0800 the next morning.

There were always a few clues in the callout. Our normal domestic crew was a captain, a copilot, and a nurse for transferring patients. For an international trip, the engineer was added. Why schedule a nurse to pick up a body? The answer had to be that there would be women on the return trip. Women meant family, so the mission would be to pick up an air force general that had died in Barcelona while they're on vacation with his family. The code is simple when you learn to read the cracks between the lines.

The next morning was a beautiful day for a flight as most days are in Saudi Arabia. It was in September 1988, and the day was going to be hot later, but we were in the air by 8:30 a.m., and the temperature was still very nice. The trip was six hours and thirty-eight minutes, and we made it nonstop in the GIII (HZ-MS3). With the two hours gained by going westbound, we arrived in Barcelona, Spain, by early in the afternoon. The Spanish handler was very glad to see us and greeted us literally with open arms.

"Ah, Captain, it is so good to see you arrive! When do you want to load the body?"

"Oh, I guess tomorrow morning at about 1000 hours will be all right."

"But, Captain, are you not leaving right away?"

"No, we will be leaving tomorrow at 1200 hours." That's noontime.

The man was now showing much distress.

"But, Captain, what shall I do with the body?"

"Where is it now?" I asked.

"It is in my office."

"Well, if I were you, I'd look for a large refrigerator."

His pain was real, but he could see I was not about to relieve his distress.

"Please, Captain, you must call the family! They are expecting to leave for Riyadh right away!"

I knew what was happening because it had happened to me so many times before on international missions. Someone in the political loop back in Riyadh had told the family that a Medevac mission would be launched immediately, and the crew would arrive and be ready to leave as soon as they could refuel. That made everyone at both ends of the loop happy, at least until the flight arrived. Then it would be the American captain who delivered the bad news. The Medevac people had rules regarding crew rest requirements, but they just didn't pay any attention to the rules when it interfered with what they wanted to happen. Many times, I and other captains did violate the crew rest rules voluntarily because we knew there was a real medical emergency involved.

I took the business card the handler gave me, turned, and gave it to Hatim.

"Here, Hatim, how about taking care of this?"

Hatim knew I meant it when I said we wouldn't leave until around twenty hours later. We needed some rest before we started back, and he agreed with me that we should have it. He also knew that calling the family and telling them of the delay would not be easy, but he took the card. We both knew the family had some political pull or we wouldn't be there. It would be a long night. But it was better that Hatim, who was in his early thirties, lose a little sleep so that the old captain would be sharp for the next day.

*   *   *

Soon we had the aircraft closed up and were in a cab on the way to the hotel. I hadn't spent a lot of time in Spain and had forgotten that Spaniards take the afternoon off. It was their siesta time. After checking in and dropping our suitcases in our rooms, we met in the bar. It was the only place we could meet. It wasn't open, but it wasn't locked up either, so we got drinks from the Coke machine and sat on the bar stools and started to wind down after the flight.

Spaniards really do take the afternoon off. We were accustomed to businesses being closed from noon until about 4:00 p.m. in Saudi Arabia, but at least the restaurants would remain open, particularly in the hotels. The other businesses would just lock up and the owners would leave. But in Barcelona, they didn't bother to lock up. They just are not there.

It was only about five thirty in the afternoon, and I knew better than to go to sleep, and besides, I was hungry. My body thinks when I lie down for a nap, it's the real thing, and it goes the whole way. So not wanting to wake up at two or three in the morning, I knew I had to stay up until bedtime.

Someone suggested we get out of there and go for a walk and maybe find something to eat. We found that the city was something like Riyadh in the afternoon. No wonder the shops were closed: everyone was on the street in an automobile. The traffic was heavy. After crossing the street a few times and narrowly missing death, we decided we were not going to find a restaurant open. We had gone into several nice-looking places, but there was no one there. The restaurants were open, but no one was home.

At that point, the crew split up. Hatim and Phil wanted to do a little exploring, and Jenny and I decided to return to the hotel. The flight nurse and I had not gone more than a block on our return when we spotted a place to eat that was open and serving! It was a Colonel Sanders Kentucky Fried Chicken! It was just exactly like back home: people were sitting around those little bitty tables eating fried chicken and french fries with lots of ketchup. No one behind the counter was over fifteen years old or paying any attention to business. The only thing was, no one spoke English or even American. Oh well, it was time to break out a little of my Tex-Mex and order some chicken.

I can remember some vocabulary in a few foreign languages, but putting the words together into a sentence is another problem. One more problem was my preference for white meat over dark. It's no big deal, but that's my preference. Well, I could figure that out easy enough. Chicken is *pollo,* three is *tres,* and white is *blanco.* It would be easy. All I had to say was, "Buenos noches. Tres pollo blanco, por favor." That would be, "Good evening, three pieces of white chicken, please." I know it's not exactly right, but they could fill in the cracks, right?

Wrong. The kid behind the counter looked at me as if I were speaking Mandarin Chinese. After repeating my statement several times, all I was getting back was an incredulous look from the boy behind the counter and giggles from the chicken-eating crowd. To complicate matters, Jenny, my British flight nurse, was trying to help. She didn't have a hint of what Spanish was all about, but she had traveled through many foreign counties and knew the value of hand signals.

She knew what I wanted, and she could see that my "three pieces of white meat" wasn't getting across, so she approached the problem from a different direction. In her mind, the white meat was breast meat, so she made a cup of each of her hands and held them about three inches in front of her breasts and repeated, "Blanco, blanco, blanco!" with great enthusiasm.

You need to know that Jenny Madill was amply endowed, and her hand signals were completely misunderstood. The Spaniards could not understand why this British lady in an airline uniform was insisting that everyone know she had "white breasts." To them it was taken for granted that her breasts were probably white.

We got our chicken, but it wasn't white, and it wasn't three pieces, but what the heck, we got enough attention to last a stage performer a week. I found out much later that the Spanish don't refer to chicken as having white and dark meat. Oh well.

*   *   *

I don't know what time Hatim and Phil returned, but my phone rang about 2:00 a.m. It was Hatim, and he had a problem. He had received several calls from the son-in-law representing the family. Hatim had handled the calls very well, but the last call had stumped him. The son-in-law had been negotiating with some political contact in the Kingdom. He, in turn, had been in contact with someone at Medevac. Whoever it was didn't want the grief and knew I wasn't going to change my mind with political pressure, so he hadn't even tried to call me. Instead, he just told the son-in-law that the reason we were staying was engine trouble. The son-in-law was not sure the family wanted to ride on an airplane that had engine trouble. This was a new development, and Hatim was not sure what his answer should be, so he called the captain.

I put on a few clothes and padded down to Hatim's room. I had told the desk clerk that I didn't want any phone calls nor did I want anyone to know my number. Hence I decided to call the son-in-law from Hatim's room. We got the son-in-law on the line, and he first told me of his concerns about the aircraft. I told him simply there was nothing wrong with the plane.

"They lied," I said. He was taken aback for a moment, then he went to a completely different approach.

"Captain, we must leave right away."

"Why? Don't you know that we need to have some rest?"

"Yes, Captain, but you see the general has been dead for . . . four days."

"Yes, I understand, and he is as dead as he will ever be. Now we are going to try once more to get some sleep. If you continue to call and disturb our rest, we will just have to delay the departure until even later. Good night."

I found out later that the family had negotiated with a company called Jet Aviation in Switzerland to charter a Gulfstream to take the general back to Riyadh. They were shocked by the cost of such a trip—it was probably over a hundred thousand dollar. So the family had decided to try to get the free ride through Saudi political contacts. That's why it had been four days.

No one else called that night, and we were at the airport by 10:00 a.m. Then it got worse.

*   *   *

The family arrived at the airport terminal right after the crew and wanted to load right then. I told them emphatically that we would first take on fuel, then catering, then the body, and last the family.

"Captain, where will the body be carried?" the son-in-law asked again.

"The body will be placed on a bed in the cabin," I replied.

"Oh no, not in the cabin, we can't have it in the cabin, not with the family! Don't you have a cargo place or something?"

"Not for a body. We only have storage for bags and suitcases. It's not large enough for a body."

"Well then, can't we strap it on the outside somewhere?"

"What do you mean 'strap it outside'?"

"Well, you know, like on top of the cabin or on the wing."

"No, we're not putting it outside, on the top of the cabin or under the cabin, or on top of the wing or under the wing, or in the engine. We are putting it in the cabin where I said, and that is that!"

It took a little time for the concerns of these people to soak in on me. Slowly, it came to me. They were simply afraid of the body. It wasn't reverence for the departed—they were just plain scared. I had noticed earlier the reluctance of locals to help in the loading of patients sometimes when we were at remote sites and without enough help. Another copilot (not on this flight), Dhagistani, had told me that Bedouins were afraid of dead people and even those who were very sick. I felt that perhaps it was because they were afraid of catching some bad disease, but it was more than that. I don't know just why, but they have a deep aversion to having anything to do with the dead or those seriously ill. I have been told they don't attempt to embalm the bodies of those who die. That was why the general being dead for four days was important. He was probably getting a little ripe by now. Our time of departure meant we would not arrive back in Riyadh before dark, so it would be another day before he could be interred.

Regardless, my decision was easily supported by the physical restraints of the aircraft. The body would have to be placed on the bed. There was no other choice. At this point, I had not seen the body, but I expected it to be in a rubber body bag like so many I had transferred before. I wasn't prepared for the way it came packaged.

*   *   *

We got the fuel onboard and were working on the catering when the family began boarding. I had to order them off the airplane so we would have a place to walk back and forth. They were not happy with having to wait in a couple of vans on the ramp while the crew finished the chores.

The mission was being flown on HZ-MS3, a Gulfstream III with a specially modified interior for Medevac purposes. We had three hospital-type beds and six litters. All the beds and litters could be replaced with couches and chairs for VIP missions. On the Barcelona mission, we had one bed in the front, opposite two chairs, and two couches in the back next to the galley.

MS3 also had a cargo door, which is very unusual for a Gulfstream of any type. The large door was located on the right side of the aircraft just in front of the wing. The door was hinged at the top and measured about seven feet wide by five feet high. There was an electric hoist that was mounted on a four-foot pedestal at the aft end of the door just inside on the cabin floor. The hoist or wench had a four-foot arm that could swing outside of the open door for lifting purposes. The hoist was equipped with a length of stainless steel cable that was attached to sling made to hold a stretcher or litter. With this apparatus, we could open the huge cargo door and swing the arm outside and lower the sling to the ground. The patient would be transferred from by litter to the sling, then lifted by the hoist up to just above floor level of the aircraft, swing the arm or boom inside, and lower the sling and litter to the floor. From that point, the pilot and copilot would lift the litter and then place it in one of the beds. That was the usual way. This was not going to be the usual way.

Someone announced, "Here comes the body." We all looked out the open cargo door and dropped our jaws in unison.

The body arrived on a forklift in a box made of three-fourth-inch fir plywood. The box was over seven feet long, about three and a half feet tall and three feet wide. The weight was stamped on the outside of the box as 200 kilos—approximately 440 pounds. The body must have been in a casket inside the plywood box. It was obvious to all that the box was not going to be loaded in any normal manner. Further, it was wrapped with a wire cord like a present, with Spanish Customs seals affixed to the cord in several critical places. We weren't supposed to open it.

Phil Thorpe, the engineer, and I decided to take out the pedestal and arm that the hoist was on and see if the box would come in the door. About twenty minutes later, we had the pedestal removed, and the forklift was able to place the box on the floor inside the aircraft. We had four very large locals lift the box and set it on the hospital bed. The box was too long, too wide, and too tall. It hung over both ends of the bed, so it rested on the frame, not the mattress. We pushed the box as close to the side of the aircraft as possible, but because of its height, it touched at the top of the box while it was still six or eight inches from the wall at the bottom, the inside of the aircraft being oval. That meant it would extend out into the aisle and would only leave about ten or twelve inches between the box and seats for anyone to squeeze by.

Phil and I thought we had really accomplished something by getting the box in and strapped down. The son-in-law said it would not do. He wanted to put a curtain around it.

"How can we put a curtain around it?" I asked.

"You could hang it from the ceiling," he said.

"How can we hang it from the ceiling?" I returned while I passed my hand over the texture of the headliner.

"We could nail it," he suggested.

With great control, I stated that we would not be nailing anything to the ceiling.

Jenny came to the rescue with a suggestion that we cover the box with bedsheets. It sounded okay to me. It took three sheets to cover the box, and they extended down within six inches of the floor. The son-in-law said it wouldn't do.

Jenny had another plan. The cabin was separated fore and aft by a metal rack that circled from the floor across the ceiling to the floor on other side. It was wide enough to hold certain pieces of medical test equipment (standard 19"). Jenny said she could make a curtain out of bedsheets and stretch it across the cabin on the rack. It would separate the front section of the cabin—with the box—from the aft section of the cabin with two couches. The family could sit on the couches and not have to see the box. That sounded good to me. The son-in-law agreed, and the contract was signed.

With all other details settled, the family members were finally permitted to board. They filed by the box with their eyes shielded by their left hands. They weren't going to even look at that box.

There were seven family members and a maid. The two couches held three each, which left two over. I suggested the maid sit on the toilet and the son-in-law sit in the front section. The toilet was a legal seat with a seat belt, so we now had everyone seated and quiet. It was time for me to get back to my "flying the airplane" duties.

* * *

Hatim called for our clearance, and we were told there would be a one-hour delay due to traffic over Italy. From Barcelona, our route would take us over the Mediterranean, across the center of Italy, and then south to cross Lebanon, Syria, and Jordan. You can't fly direct in that region if the route takes you within the disputed airspace north of Libya. The return flight would take a little over seven hours; we would arrive in Riyadh after 11:00 p.m.

Once in the air and established at our altitude of forty-one thousand feet, I made radio contact with Romeo Base in Riyadh. I passed along our arrival time and requirements. I told Romeo that we needed to be met at the VIP gate with a forklift and four very large locals to lift a box weighing two hundred kilos. Romeo "rogered" my message, and I was able to sit back and relax for a while.

About an hour after departure, Jenny came to the cockpit.

"What's the problem, Jenny?"

"It's the catering. The family won't let me back there to prepare the meals. They want their maid to do it."

The catering is always stored in aft section of the aircraft near the galley. There is a certain amount of preparation to be done even in the best of cases. The food is *never* ready to serve as it arrives from the caterer, and it is best done by someone who knows what needs to be done. The maid might be willing, but she would just make a big mess.

"Jenny, I don't know what to tell you. Why don't you just see what you can work out on your own?"

"Okay," she said with a shrug and went to the rear.

About half an hour later when I turned and looked down the aisle over my right shoulder to see what was going on in the back, what I saw gave me a real laugh.

"Hey, Hatim, have a look at that."

Hatim leaned over and looked over his left shoulder.

"Oh my god," he said and quickly returned to an upright position. He stared straight ahead and repeated, "Oh my god!"

Jenny had all the catering spread out on the box and was preparing trays for the maid to serve the family. She was using the box for a kitchen table. The son-in-law sat rigid in his seat with his eyes closed. He didn't want to see what was happening next to him.

About an hour later, Hatim began slowly to rock in his seat.

"What's the matter, Hatim?"

"I need to go to the toilet—bad!" The toilet is in aft section of the airplane.

"Well, why don't you go?"

"Uh uh. Not me. I can't walk by the family!"

"Well, it's another four or five hours to Riyadh. Can you wait that long?"

"I don't think so."

"Hey, Jenny," I called down the aisle, "come here a minute."

"Yes, what's the matter?"

"Jenny, do you have any of those large water bottles left?"

"Why yes, I think so, why?"

"Well, bring one up for Hatim. He's in need."

A moment later, Jenny returned with a liter of bottled water. She didn't get my meaning that Hatim needed an empty one.

Hatim took the bottle, and when Jenny retired to the rear, he said, "What am I supposed to do with this?"

"Well, Hatim, I guess you'll have to drink enough of that bottle to have room for what you need to do."

It was a little after 11:00 p.m. when we parked at the VIP gate in Riyadh. There were at least two hundred people on the ramp waiting to meet the airplane. We're talking about wall-to-wall Mercedes. As was the custom, they were all trying to get on the aircraft at the same time to comfort the family. I had learned a long time before to just sit in my seat and let happen what was going to happen. There was always a certain amount of weeping, wailing, hugging, and kissing that had to be done before anything else could be accomplished, so I just let it happen.

But the Customs and Immigration agents wanted to get onboard the aircraft immediately and do their thing. They did this with no problem when it was just the crew, but high-ranking political figures were accustomed to having their way regardless of the desires of some lowly fellows wearing one or two stripes on their blue uniforms.

The man on the forklift was Doug Acker, the chief of maintenance. Doug was one of the four very large locals I had requested. He was about six foot two and weighed around 250 pounds. He and his men were mixing in with the family, the mourners, and the agents. It was a big mess. Right in the middle of this melee, Hatim came back to the cockpit.

"Captain, we have a problem."

"What's the problem, Hatim?"

"The Immigration man says we have to have a passport for the body!"

"A passport for the body! Good grief! We don't have a passport for the body! Did you give him the paperwork we got in Barcelona? There were about twenty sheets of death certificates. Didn't you give him that stuff?"

"Yes, I gave all that to him, but he insists that we must have a passport for the general."

That was the last straw. My patience was at an end, but it was time for me to act wisely. It is not wise to cross the young men in the blue suits. I thought for about five seconds.

"Hatim, tell the man the passport is in the box!"

Hatim paused for a moment as he considered what I had said. It looked like he was thinking, "How did the captain know the general's passport was inside the box? No one told us that." Then his face burst into a giant grin.

"All *right!*" he said.

He left immediately and went to the rear. In a moment, he returned with the grin still in place and reported.

"The man said it would be all right—he won't need the passport after all!"

Dispatch:
Riyadh, Saudi Arabia
February 12, 1987

To: Mr. Wahid Tarifi,
          Compound Manager
From: James D. Fox
          Captain Fixed Wing
          Medevac Program, GAMA
Subject: Appropriate Dress
Copies: Mr. Hamad Al-Assaf,
          Assistant Vice President, GAMA
          Mr. Eric Newbigin
          Project Director, Medevac

Within the last two days, I have read two separate dispatches regarding the dress code here in the Kingdom. One was posted on the cafeteria bulletin board and had to do with the dress code for males and females, in general, while in the Kingdom. The second one was delivered to my door today and had to do with the dress code as applied here within the compound walls.

These requirements may be very clear in your mind, but to the Westerner, they are very confusing. Perhaps, if you desire, strict compliance to your rules, then you need to be more specific for those that don't understand. May I remind you, that people's understanding of rules in general come from their cultural upbringing. For those of us that do not have the same cultural upbringing as yourself, then you must be more specific. We do not have the years of training that you have had, and therefore, we need more detailed instructions.

For example, your letter speaks of the "public areas" of the compound. My question is: where are the public areas exactly? Are these areas limited to anywhere there is common access between those peoples of different cultures? If the problem is that some people dress in a way that is offensive to other people, then we need to know where these areas are.

You speak of wearing "modest dress" over the sportswear on the way to the squash areas. Does this apply to both male and female? If so, what is modest dress for a male to wear over his sportswear or for a female? How about the swimming pool? What is the dress code for the swimming pool?

People of different cultures freely pass in and out of the swimming pool when it is filled with both males and females in sportswear. What are the rules here?

Before I agreed to come to the Kingdom on contract, I was given some idea from those that hired me, what the rules were, so that I could realize what to expect in this foreign country. You see, this country and its rules are not well known to the rest of the world. No offense is intended, but that's just the way it is. This statement, in no way, means to say that your ways are right or wrong, just that they are "your" ways, and as such, they are generally unknown in many parts of the world.

After reading these rules and conditions presented to me before hiring, I freely signed the contract. It was my intention to come over here and obey all the rules to the best of my ability. After all, I have done no less in my own country. The problem is, it is difficult to find out what *all* the rules are regarding the dress and behavior of my wife and me. How can we be expected to honor the requirements if we don't know what they are? A brief letter now and then won't do it. The letters are too vague for this foreigner to comprehend.

You see, the recruiters led me to believe that the GAMA compound was a Western compound and that we would mostly be left alone inside the walls. It has taken a while for me to find out this is not true, and if it ever was, I'm not sure. We were told right away that my wife should wear certain forms of dress when we left the compound. Male dress was never ever mentioned. The instructions were so unclear, she decided to always wear the abaya just to be sure. Most of the other females do the same, not all, but most do. Just to be sure. We don't want any trouble.

Now it sounds like she must wear the abaya inside the compound walls. Could this be true? What do we wear if we are jogging? What do we wear at the swimming pool?

If the problem is that you and your people are offended by the way we dress, then perhaps the best way to solve the problem is segregation. I didn't say the easiest way, but the best way. I thought that the reason for the Arab custom of building walls around their place of residence was for security and privacy. If we are allowed no more liberties within the walls than without, then why do we need the walls at all? Certainly not for security.

The Kingdom's reputation for lawful conduct would seem to say that we do not need the security. Of course, you should know more about that than me.

Perhaps you should consider making the swimming pool off-limits to anyone without the proper attire. Guards could be posted at the gates to make sure there were no violations. Or perhaps the guards would just keep out those that might be offended. Of course, the guards would have to be posted on the outside of swimming pool so they themselves would not be offended.

Maybe the solution in the long run is to move all those that are being offensive into a different compound from those that are being offended. That would make enforcement unnecessary or at least a lot less bothersome. It seems that those in authority are most offended by what they see. The reasoning follows that if they don't see, then how can they be offended?

Please keep in mind that the undersigned wants to comply with the rules as far as they are known. Living here in the Kingdom means to me obeying the rules. If and when I cannot comply with those rules as they are explained to me, then I will leave. The statement here is if you want me to comply, then you must tell me what the rules are *in a way that I can understand.*

Your reply will be appreciated.

James D. Fox
Captain Fixed Wing
Medevac Program
GAMA

Dispatch:
Riyadh, Saudi Arabia
February 16, 1987

SHOT IN THE FOOT

Very seldom, if you are an F1, will you miss a trip. Well, today I was an F1, and at 1236 hours, Romeo called the mission.

"Boop—bleeeep, boop—beep, boob—beep, boob—beep. "Gulfstream 68, 10, 46, and 53, a VIP mission Riyadh, to Madinah to Riyadh. Pick up VIPs at Madinah for transfer to Riyadh, 68, acknowledge please."

That's the way a mission is called. This time Romeo requested that I call him on the phone. The request to call him on the phone meant that he didn't want to put the details on the air. That added a little mystery to the mission. The voice on the radio acting as Romeo was brand-new, and that added more mystery. I made the call not knowing what to expect.

The new Romeo told me that I needed to be in Madinah by 1530 hours and that when I arrived I should call the hotel and ask for room 309. The party answering should be told that General Monsuer's aircraft and crew were "there" and ready to go. I was also supposed to tell the party on the phone where "there" was. We were further instructed to be ready to depart by 1600 hours. This all sounded a little less than routine, but not necessarily mysterious, but Charlotte said, "Oh boy, this sounds like the basis for another story."

My crew was going to be Shamir Kaka (10), Jerry Padova (46), and Linda Baud (53). Of course with Kaka as the copilot, there was no telling what might develop. Since we would be empty going over, Kaka was supposed to fly the trip, but maintenance wanted me to check out the autopilot on the way over, so Kaka didn't get to do the flying in cruise. He did get to make the approach and landing. The landing was the most exciting part of the trip, but not out of the ordinary for Kaka.

On the ground, I sent Kaka with the details to make the phone call to the general's room at the hotel. I assumed that it would need to be made in Arabic. After a short period, Kaka returned with the regret written on his face.

"Ah, Captain, I am sorry, but something is wrong with the telephone."

"What do you mean there is something wrong with the telephone?"

"It doesn't talk to the general's room at the hotel."

"Kaka, did you call the number I gave you?"

"Oh yes, Captain, just as you said, but it didn't talk to the hotel."

"Well, who did it talk to?"

"Well, when I called the number, a man answered, and I gave him the message just as you told me, and he told me that it was a family house, and we people were bothering him, so we should not call anymore."

Wrong number, so I got on the radio and reported to Romeo Base that we got a wrong number, and I was not able to call the hotel or get in touch with the general. Romeo just said "never mind" and that he would make the call himself.

General Monsuer arrived; we departed, then arrived in Riyadh without further incident. I should report that after arriving at the VIP gate, the general left the airplane and the vicinity without his driver that was waiting for him. I didn't miss him until the driver came on the aircraft and asked for his passenger. To this day, I don't know what happened to him. I wouldn't be surprised that Kaka had something to do with it.

Later at the apartment, Charlotte wanted all the details. I had to report there was nothing to tell and that it was just another routine Medevac mission.

* * *

You don't always have to be on mission to see the fun develop. Last night, the F2, Captain Schmitz, was called on a mission for early this morning. The mission was to depart Riyadh at 0430 hours to be exact. I was listening closely because when Romeo started talking about a mission early the next morning that meant me. I was due to go on duty as F1 at 0600 hours officially, but unofficially, they will call me for anything that comes up after 0500 hours. Never mind figuring that out. I don't think I can explain it right now. Anyway, everyone listens to the radio calls because they never know who may get hit with the splatter.

It seemed that all was going well with the call, i.e., the mission was called at 1830 hours so the crew would have time to get to bed and get some rest before that early-morning get up. The crew knew that they would have to get up around 0230 hours for a 0430 hours takeoff. It sounded like Romeo was doing things right.

Thirty minutes later, about the time everyone had settled down after the last callout, a second mission was called, and it was an ASAP. Romeo gave that mission to backup crew, the F3s. Sounded like a reasonable thing to me. Like I said, everyone knew and understood the F2 crew needed some rest for the early-morning mission. Well, the F3, Captain Yaghmour, got out the rule book and reminded Romeo that the F3 crew should not be called on the ASAP mission unless the F2 captain was unable to make the trip, and since this was not the case, then he reasoned that the F2 should have to fly the ASAP mission.

There is one in every bunch, right? Yaghmour was trying to get Schmitz hung with both trips. Romeo, the new guy, is not sure what he should do, so he has to call the big guns to find out what he should do. The big guns don't appreciate being bothered after hours by a problem that should not even have been brought up, but to placate the piqued F3, they told Romeo how to handle the problem.

Remember, we only hear from Romeo; we don't hear the calls made to him. Neither can we hear the phone calls being made. By this time, everyone is listening to find out what is going to happen. They all know that the F3, Yaghmour, is out of line; he is the only captain that would pull the rule book on another captain in a case like that. The rest of us would have been glad to help.

Within a few minutes, the radio calls start again, and everything is change. The F2 crew is now changed to take the ASAP mission. This causes a delay because Captain Schmitz has already gone to bed anticipating the 0230 hours getup. The nurse had not gone to bed, so she was the first to call for transport to the airport. Women can't drive, you know, so they must always be provided transport to and from the airport. Neither are they allowed to ride with the captains in the captain's car, but that's another long story.

Everyone forgot that Captain Schmitz had sold his car and was afoot. He had to have transport as well. The driver left with the nurse while the Schmitz was running down the walk to the gate. Now when the captain catches on that he has been left, his only hope is to call Romeo on his radio and have Romeo call the nurse on her radio and tell her to get the driver to return to the compound and pick him up.

Delay on an ASAP mission, and all involved have their temperatures rising. It was at this time that Romeo dropped the other shoe. He called out Yaghmour, the F3, for the early-morning mission, the one he would have to get up at 0230 hours for! Before Yaghmour could object, the reason was given that there was no way to know for sure when Captain Schmitz might return from his ASAP mission. So, just to be sure, Yaghmour and his crew were laid on for the early-morning getup. You could almost hear the cheers go up from around the compound. Old Yaghmour had shot himself in the foot this time.

*   *   *

Maybe I haven't told you about Captain Yaghmour. Captain Yaghmour is a Saudi with a colorful background, which extends into the present. I was told that he was suspected of being a conspirator in the attempted assassination of the king and barely escaped beheading by stealing an aircraft and flying him and some of this fellow suspects to Egypt for safety. He was in exile for eleven years, then forgiven and allowed to return to the Kingdom.

Well, that's the story I was told and have no reason to disbelieve it. What I know from firsthand makes me tend to believe whatever I hear about Captain Yaghmour. I have only flown with him once, and that was enough to convince me that as a pilot he is barely. The trip I was assigned to fly as cocaptain with Yaghmour was from Riyadh to Gassim to Dhahran to Riyadh. The timing was such that we would make the first two legs in the daylight and the last one in Riyadh after nightfall. As customary, Yaghmour flew the first leg to Gassim, which was only about thirty minutes to the northwest of Riyadh and had an eleven thousand foot runway. That's over two miles long, folks, and Captain Yaghmour used *all* of it! He was still on the brakes and reversers at the end of the pavement. There was just enough room left for him to make the turnaround. Did he just make a misjudgment and landed too long on the runway and too fast? I'm still trying to understand why.

I flew the leg to Dhahran without incident or comment from the other captain. Later, we returned to Riyadh, and Captain Yaghmour, once again, at his home airport landed too long and too fast and used all eleven thousand feet to get stopped. Whew, what a guy! It looks like it doesn't make any difference how much runway he's got; he's going to use all of it.

On the taxi checklist for the Gulfstream, there is an item for checking the thrust reversers. It is one of the first items on the taxi checklist. It is common for maintenance people to pull the circuit breaks on the bulkhead just behind the captain's seat to deactivate those thrust reversers while they are working near them. It's a safety precaution. If the reversers were accidentally activated while a mechanic was in the way, he would likely lose whatever part of him was in the way of them closing. Therefore, checking the thrust reverser's circuit breakers is on the pilot's checklist to make sure they are returned to their active position.

Now what happens if a negligent captain doesn't use the checklist either the one before taxi or after taxi? Well, many things perhaps, but in Captain Yaghmour's case, he made a normal takeoff, but his landing was hair-raising. He came in fast and long and reached up for the reverser throttles and pulled them full on. The reverser doors didn't close, and Yaghmour had just given himself a burst of 85 percent full forward thrust! He squirted himself right back into the air. Now he was in the air with full landing flaps, gear down, and flying on the thrust reverser throttles. Well, he got the airplane cleaned up, and with the circuit breakers restored to their rightful positions, he came back around and landed the airplane. The report that I got didn't mention whether or not he used all the runway the second time. Captain Yaghmour didn't mention the incident, but his crew was never the same after that.

Captain Yaghmour in addition to his quirky flying habits had a beard and a sour personality. He was the only one of the pilots that didn't speak or act at all friendly. In addition to all of the above, he had a very irregular work schedule. I could never figure out when he was going to be on the schedule. I'm sure it had to do with something political, and in this country, you just don't ask too many questions.

Maybe this helps to understand why Captain Yaghmour was not looked on with any degree of respect by his fellow workers.

Dispatch:
Riyadh, Saudi Arabia
February 15, 1987

Houston Amateur Autopatch
113 Phanturn
Bellaire, Texas 77401

Dear Fellows,

I just received your note asking for a $6 donation. The check is enclosed. Sorry to be so late, but there is a great gulf separating us. No pun intended. My mail is being forwarded by a friend. If you have already dropped me from the roles for one reason or other, then do what you wish with the check. It would be nice to retain my membership on your roster if and when I return to Houston. Please note the new address below.

I am over here on a one-year contract with a renewal option to fly for the Ministry of Defense and Aviation. It will be a while before I return to Houston as a resident.

The Westerner is not allowed to operate as an amateur radio here. There are only two amateurs licensed in the Kingdom I've been told, and they are both princes. I met the young man that worked on the construction of their rigs. They were custom-made and run about 20K watts. Who's going to check? Best wishes from the Land of the Sand and the Sun.

> Sincerely,
> James D. Fox K5CNP
> Box 41726
> Riyadh 11531
> Saudi Arabia

Dateline:
Riyadh, Saudi Arabia,
February 18, 1987

PREPARATION FOR THE GREAT ADVENTURE

Have you ever known someone who made a trip around the world? If they went just halfway around then came back, it doesn't count as an around-the-world trip for they have to complete the circle. T ell the truth, you've always had a desire to have the great adventure, but there was never the right time, or if the time was right, then perhaps there were two or three other things that weren't ready. I wonder if you have done what I have always done. You've kept all your desires beneath the surface. Secretly, you placed the globe circlers you've known in a place of special distinction. Perhaps you don't think of them equal to Marco Polo, Magellan, or David Niven[8], but at least you have put then in the same loose-fitting category. Well, it should be worth the money and effort to make that grand trip just to be associated with such an illustrious group, especially David Niven.

As a young man, raised in Texas (not reared, that's what a horse does when he stands on his hind legs), it was exciting just to talk to someone who had been all the way to California and returned. I guess you couldn't talk to them if they hadn't returned. My uncle Roy Gamble made the round-trip to California several times, but we didn't visit with his family very much, so I didn't hear much from him. But on my mother's side of the family, I had an Uncle Dave Cathey who made the trip, once I believe, and he was a fountain of information about the Golden State. It was the land of milk and honey. Uncle Dave said it was mentioned in the Bible! I could never get enough of his stories of this wondrous land. He knew so much and had seen so much with his *own eyes*!

The grown-ups said that Uncle Dave was a little *windy,* especially when he was telling us kids about the *personal* conversations that he had with *real life* movie stars. He met "lots of them and they were nothing like you see them in the movies." Uncle Dave could be very convincing with these revelations. In those days, we had barely arrived at the point of understanding that movies may not be true to life. What he had to say was shocking!

You need to know that Uncle Dave was from Oklahoma, and I'm sure that the Okies were not out in California just visiting with the movie stars in 1935. What can you expect from a kid whose only out-of-state travel was to Oklahoma? And we lived only fifteen miles from the Red River. A kid from Texas doesn't broaden his horizons much by going to Oklahoma.

---

[8]   David Niven was an actor who starred in the movie *Around the World In 80 Days*. The movie was an adaptation of the book by the same name written by Jules Verne.

It's easy to listen and believe when you are hearing a firsthand account of how Tom Mix mistreated his horses, even if he is your very most favorite cowboy star. Tom Mix was top billing in the mid-1930s. Why, I even had copies of his *real* leather chaps and Western vest with real simulated silver conchos and leather thongs. They had the *real* Tom Mix brand on them, *really branded* right there in the leather. They also had a little advertising from Purina, the Checkerboard company, because Purina sponsored his radio show.

The chaps and Western vest you got from sending in coupons from the tops of Purina products. I had my dad buying Purina feed for the livestock and chickens, and the whole family had to eat Tom Mix cereal every morning (Ralston, remember). The family was happy to cooperate because they knew how important that cowboy *outfit* was to me. After all, he was the original *square shooter*, wasn't he?

Now, after hearing the straight "skinny" from Uncle Dave, someone that had actually been there, the evidence was irrefutable. There was only one thing to do: I had to drop Tom Mix. Who could worship a cowboy that mistreated his horse? I had to find a new cowboy hero. Well, Buck Jones was easy to pick as a replacement; besides, he rode a white horse and always wore a white hat. It was a very tight-fitting hat, I think, because I saw him many times in the movies, fighting as many as six men at a time, and the hat never came off once. I noted that the hat came off only when he took it off, and that was at the very end of the movie when he was saying good-bye to the girl. Then he would hold it in front of himself, just in case the heroine got emotionally carried away and maybe tried something silly like *kissing* him because of his eminent departure. Yes, Buck Jones was a good pick. He never lost a fight nor did he ever kiss a girl. He was probably the perfect cowboy.

It was a terrible shock for me to learn that my hero, Buck Jones, was dead! He died in a terrible nightclub fire in Boston. I couldn't understand what my cowboy hero was doing in Boston, let alone at a nightclub. Things are just not like they appear in the movies, and people don't always tell the truth about faraway lands and people.

The answer, of course, is you must go and see for yourself. If you had been raised in Texas (no, not reared), you need to go a little farther than Oklahoma to see new things. I'll have to admit, however, that if we had gone to Louisiana, I would have seen some things that wouldn't have made sense to me until I was at least twenty-one. Now, with a career of traveling, I've seen plenty of *sights*, but *seeing the sights* alone has lost its flavor to me. You can take pictures of the Pyramids when you visit Egypt, but the magazines are full of the same pictures you just took, and they were made by professionals. What else is there, you may ask? Allow me to explain.

The real thrill of travel, for me, is visiting with the locals. This is much easier than it may sound because the *dollar* has taught people to speak in American all over the world. A surprising large number of people are willing to visit with you if you give them a chance. When you get the chance, then talk about the things that are important to them. It can give you a whole new outlook on the world.

About the time when you have become impressed with the great differences in the cultures of the world, you may become impressed with the great sameness of its peoples. Besides, sooner or later, they are going to ask you about Texas! Don't laugh, there are two spots in the United States (the US is usually called America or sometimes just the States) that are well known to foreigners. The two spots are Texas and California, in that order.

Sure, maybe they have heard of New York, but it is Texas and California they want to hear about. California means Hollywood, movie stars, and dark glasses. Texas means cowboys, wild Indians, wild horses, shootouts, the Cavalry, and everything else in the Wild West. It is universally believed that John Wayne was a Texan and is a typical example of what all men from Texas are like. In the United Kingdom, John's popularity has been split with that of JR[9]. If you wear a Western hat and boots in England, they are most likely to call you JR, regardless of what you look like.

Well, the Foxes are going to make the trip around the world, and I invite you to come along with us for one the great adventure!

---

[9] You remember JR, don't you? He was the main character in *Dallas*, the long-running soap opera on Friday night TV. If you don't remember, then I'm sorry, but there is not enough room here to explain it. Just ask some old friend. They'll tell you all about JR.

Dateline:
Riyadh, Saudi Arabia,
February 19, 1987

TRAVEL MAY BE BROADENING,
BUT IT WON'T MAKE YOU FAT

Travel is not easy. Never mind what you may hear from the business travelers who have secretaries to get their tickets and reservations and wives to pack their bags. With hardly a noticeable effort, these businessmen can go anywhere in the world on a moment's notice.

No, the travel that is *tough* is the kind where a man takes his wife out of town, overnight, on some form of public conveyance! My wife, Charlotte, was once the secretary who got the tickets, hotel reservations, and all other arrangements that the boss needed when he went on his business trips, so she should be above and beyond the average housewife in those areas of travel knowledge.

Of course, the wives in question may have packed a thousand bags for their husband's trips, but when it's time for them to pack their own bag, then all previous knowledge they may have acquired departs their precious heads. They can't handle the possibility of travel without their complete wardrobe. The prospect of such a condition in itself induces great stress. It is unthinkable.

The one thing that gets them all is packing their own clothes in a suitcase! Logic and reason have no part in the proceedings. A husband's pleas may only help in a very few isolated cases. Absolute demands are a waste of your time and the medication you may need to return you to normal health. *Save your breath.*

This advice is especially for those husbands who are subject to periods of hypertension and associated symptoms.

The logic that I used in preparing my wife for this extended trip of more than seven days was based on practicality. Dialogue associated with that logic follows:

"Sweetheart, I know you have little experience packing for long trips on the road, especially by airline, so may I suggest that you should take just enough clothes to last seven days? At the end of, say five days, you can have them laundered or cleaned, then they will be ready for the next seven days. We won't be in any of the places we are staying for more than five days, so we can put the clothes in the laundry the first day we arrive at a new place, and we will be sure to have them ready at the time of our departure. In that way, we will have clean clothes to travel in and to wear for the first few days at our next stop. Doesn't that make sense?" I asked.

Her reply was, "Yes, but we can't do that, we're going to be gone for thirty days!"

"Certainly," I claimed. "If we were going to be gone for two years, you wouldn't want to pack twenty-four times as much, would you?"

I'm going to leave her answer to your imagination. Besides, every husband should already know that his logic and reason will not work when he is talking to his wife about packing *her* clothes. He may know all about traveling, but it doesn't mean he will know zip about women's thought process about packing her clothes. The woman's only accepted teacher in this case must be named *experience*.

My last effort was to remind her of the airline rules regarding baggage.

"You will be allowed two bags to check and one to carry on. The two bags to check can be no larger than the three dimensions stipulated, and together can weigh no more than twenty kilos. The carry-ons weight is unspecified, but its dimensions must be such that it can be stowed inside the plane, under the seat, or in the overhead baggage compartment," I explained.

Explanation was wasted breath. When a woman is packing her clothes, the airline baggage restrictions, in her mind, are totally unfair and therefore irrelevant. Women view the logical rules of travel as a point to vary from. A man's effort at explaining those rules is, without question, the most contradictory, confusing, misunderstood, and baffling mystery of anything short of Einstein's unified field theory.

"Well, how much is twenty kilos anyway?" she inquired.

"I think it's roughly forty-four pounds," I stated.

"Is that for each bag?" she questioned.

"No, it is for the total of bags checked," I returned.

"Well, what about the carry-on?" she replied.

"What about the carry-on?" I rejoined.

"How much can it weigh?" she continued.

"As much as you can carry on and stuff under the seat" was my answer.

Now it's time for some different strategy on the wife's part.

"That forty-four pounds is that all we can check for both of us?" she queried.

"No, it is for each ticket," I responded.

"You mean twenty kilos for each suitcase," she went on.

"No, I mean twenty kilos for each ticket, whether it's one or two suitcases," I pronounced.

"You mean we can take more than one suitcase?" she requested.

"Yes, we can each check no more than two suitcases, and together, they must weigh no more than twenty kilos or forty-four pounds," I uttered.

"Well, what if we had a child, would it get forty-four pounds as well?" she solicited.

"If it had a full ticket, I suppose it would," I reasoned.

"That doesn't seem fair," she declared.

"No one said that it had to be fair," I maintained.

"Well, it doesn't make sense that you can have so little in a check-in bag, but you can carry on all you like. It just doesn't make any sense," she alleged.

She had me there. Okay, now it's time to play my final card—*the cost of excess baggage.*

"Well, honey, you know if we are over on our baggage, they can charge us 1 percent of a first-class ticket for each ten pounds of excess baggage," I added.

"That doesn't make any sense either. The allowance is in kilos, and the excess charge is for pounds," she rejoined.

Well, she had me again. With each additional explanation, I'm getting further behind. Okay, let's get serious. Out with the bathroom scales, I was determined to carry this to the end.

We don't have any bathroom scales.

The borrowed scales showed that my two check-in bags, as they were packed and ready to load, totaled only twelve kilos. Charlotte's two bags totaled fifteen kilos, well within the weight restrictions. My carry-on bag was the video camera, and Charlotte's was her overnight case. I had seen it to the end and had won! We were ready to go.

Before you get the idea that we had seen the end of the baggage problem, then let me set you straight. On our journey from Bangkok to Singapore, we had ten bags. We paid $130 in excess baggage charges. The last leg from Singapore to Riyadh, we paid another $375 for excess baggage. So much for me winning!

Our itinerary would take us from Riyadh to Geneva, Frankfurt, London, Boston, Memphis, Atlanta, Charleston, Savannah, Memphis, Houston, Albuquerque, Honolulu, Tokyo, Honk Kong, Bangkok, Singapore, and back to Riyadh. That's seventeen legs, and all the way around. Yes, we could have made some changes, and it might have been a little better, but that's hindsight and mine is just as good as yours. It's foresight that we all have trouble with, right?

Dateline:
Riyadh, KSA, Frankfurt, Germany
February 19-20, 1987

Leaving Saudi Arabia—An Experience

The trip to the airport when leaving Riyadh is usually planned through a man named Jyantha, the supervisor for the company drivers. You can hire a limousine, but the company provides free transportation, so why not use it? Jyantha is from Sri Lanka and is very conscientious, but something didn't click that night. We were ready at the guard gate at midnight as planned, and there was no driver. Our departure was for 2:30 a.m., and we were planning to be at the airport two hours before our departure time.

We called the barracks, woke the drivers, and Jyantha was at the gate in less than ten minutes. The drivers are accustomed to being awakened in the middle of the night for urgent missions.

I was flying jet transports (medical evacuation, VIP, and members of the royal family) for the Saudi military at the time of this story. All government hospitals are operated by the Saudi Army, but all the aircraft are controlled by the Saudi Air Force. The arrangement is a little complicated to explain fully, but I'll try an abbreviated version.

Foreigners must have a sponsor to be able to work in the Kingdom. The sponsor is responsible for all needs of that worker and liable for everything that worker does—good or bad. Housing, utilities, uniforms, medical, and transportation needs are all provided by the sponsor. Each worker is also provided at least thirty days of vacation once a year with a paid airline ticket, round-trip, back to the worker's point of hiring in his or her home country. There are many other provisions of Saudi Labor Law, but I will not try to enumerate them here. The Saudis hire their work to be done by foreigners, and they are very organized in the manner in which it is accomplished. The Saudis do not have *any* illegal immigrants, but they have a workforce of three million workers for five million Saudis. There is much we could learn from the Saudis if we want to hire people from south of the border to work in the United States. It's just a thought.

I was hired and paid by GAMA (General Arab Medical Association) as my sponsor. GAMA was funded by the Saudi Air Force under Prince Sultan, the second in line for the throne. My immediate supervisor was a Saudi Army major because, as I said, all government hospitals are operated by the army. So that is why I was flying Saudi Air Force airplanes, but they were operated by the army. If it seems confusing, then you may be getting close to the idea. The Saudis do things that make sense to them but are a mystery to the Western mind. From time to time, I try to justify and explain their reasoning. Often I fall short.

Our Medevac missions were likely to be called at any and all times of the day and night, and the drivers were required to provide transportation for each mission. Each of our flights will have at least a captain, a copilot, and a nurse. If the flight was not a Medevac flight, then the nurse became a hostess, but she was almost always a part of each mission. Sometimes there were also doctors, and on international trips, a flight engineer was added, and at other times, for various reasons, all crew positions may be doubled.

Most of the men I flew with had their own cars. Our sponsor, the company that hired us, provided interest-free loans if you wanted to buy your own car. I suppose their motivation for such an altruistic move was to take part of the load off the company-operated transportation. Regardless, it was common for the captain to drive his own car so he could arrive sooner at the airport and leave sooner to come home. I learned that it was against the law to charge interest on a loan.

Our missions were flown from the military airport in Riyadh, which was just on the northern side of the city, and nearby. But waiting for company transportation was always a hassle of some sort, and it was much more convenient to drive yourself.

Since women are not allowed to drive in the Kingdom, the nurses must *always* have transportation provided. A woman can only ride in a car with her husband or in a public vehicle with an assigned driver, and then she must ride in the back. The nurses are not allowed to ride in a private vehicle with the captains or the engineers that they fly with. If that doesn't make sense, then you may need more explanation, but that will have to come at a later time. Besides, it doesn't have to make sense to a Westerner (a Westerner is referred to as a Kawajee); it's just the rule.

Jyantha was apologetic for oversleeping, but we still had plenty of time, so the bags were loaded, and away we went. The night was another beautiful night. Except for blowing dust once in a while, the fall, winter, and spring seasons in Saudi Arabia are the most beautiful you could imagine. Every day and every night is near to perfection. Florida and California should have it so good. It is perfect weather for golfing, tennis, etc., especially the etc. That night was no different.

Along the forty-kilometer road (twenty-five miles) to the new airport were many parked cars. The occupants were out picnicking, playing soccer (at midnight?), or watching TV in their tents. The men sat in groups on rugs talking, drinking their super sweet tea, or perhaps playing *baloot* (an Arab card game that defies my description). It was Thursday night and time for the weekend outing.

All of this takes place in the desert, but it's not like the desert you see in the movies made in Hollywood. There is very little sand; it is mostly dirt and rocks. Vegetation is so scarce the animals have to graze at a full gallop. That must be why camels have such long legs.

Saudis that live in the cities like to go back to the desert on the weekend, and Thursday and Friday is their weekend. They seem to prefer the nights to the days for their outings. Thousands of years in the desert sun have produced nocturnal habits, I suppose.

Trips out of the Kingdom, for most places in Europe, depart in the middle of the night so that they will arrive at their destinations just after curfew is over in most of the large airports in Europe.

The airport curfew in Europe generally is for arriving and departing aircraft between the hours of 10:00 p.m. and 7:00 a.m. Our flight that night was planned for a stop in Geneva, Switzerland, with one hour and fifteen minutes on the ground to make our arrival time in Frankfurt, Germany, at just after 7:00 a.m. If I had taken the trouble to calculate our departure time against the known speed of travel and distance to Frankfurt, then I would have known that we had to stop somewhere, or we would arrive too early into Frankfurt. But again, that's hindsight.

Departing Saudi Arabia by commercial flight is quite an experience. The first time is terrible, and it never gets any better. I had made several international trips as a flight captain on Saudi Armed Forces aircraft, but my wife, Charlotte, and I were not ready for the security checks we received as departing civilian passengers. The Customs checks they do in Riyadh for departing passengers are stricter than the Customs checks associated with arriving passengers in other countries. All bags are X-rayed before checking them.

If they see something suspicious in the checked bags, then they will open them after you leave the area. On that night, I had two videotapes in my checked baggage. The tapes were of the local area, which we wanted to show friends back home. They confiscated the two tapes and never said a word to us. They were just gone when we got to Frankfurt. As a precaution, I had copied the tapes and left the copies in the apartment. The copies had to be taken out of the Kingdom later on a flight of my own.

Your carry-on bags are X-rayed and then opened, *always*. Yes, they S-ray them first, and then you must open them. They take long looks at picture albums. They give women's purses and makeup cases a very close inspection. Some folks say they are looking for drugs, but my own feeling is that most times they are just curious.

Charlotte had a problem. Custom agents, armed soldiers, took her away, and she had to do a strip search. *She had a wire in her bra.* They are not letting anything pass. The strip search was in front of Saudi women, of course, but if you think a strip search conducted by a person of your own gender will preserve your modesty, then you have a free think coming. I know about that firsthand!

It's easy for us to know what they are looking for when you enter the country because the items are posted. But what are they looking for when you leave? Oddly, I think they are looking for the same things. You can suffer the same penalties for being caught with contraband when leaving as you can when entering. They don't want booze, pornography, Christian articles (crosses or Bibles), or photographs of their country. Dope carries the death penalty, and that means a one-way ticket at high noon on Friday at Chop-A-Block Square!

You don't know about Friday noon at Chop-A-Block Square? A simple explanation is that the guest of honor will lose his or her head in the process. Do they really cut people's heads off? Do they still do such things in this day and time? The answer to both questions is an emphatic *yes*. Justice for the bad guys is swift and certain. For the good guys, it takes a little longer, but that's another story.

Once through the Customs check, we were free to sit or roam the isolation area provided for departing passengers that have already cleared the Customs checks. It is the same in almost any large airport in any country of the first order, but in Saudi Arabia, the area is huge. Of course, the terminal itself is huge, and the isolation part is larger than entire terminals in most other countries.

There are places to eat in the isolation area, but there are no duty-free shops there as in other countries. Can you guess why? The fellow way back there in the back guessed right. They don't have duty-free shops because there is no duty or taxes to pay in Saudi Arabia. There is no need of duty-free shops at the airport because the whole country is duty free.

The building itself contains much glass, marble, fountains, and curved arches. Did I say marble? I'm talking about acres of beautiful marble on the floors and walls as far as the eye can see. When the traveler approaches the King Khalid Airport terminal from the road, the first impression is of beauty. Night or day, you can't deny the impression. In the daytime, the view is of a structure of quiet beauty sitting in the desert surrounded by oasis-type greenery.

The nighttime view of the same airport is of a thousand lights in the pitch darkness of the desert. It looks like the beginning of a Disney movie on TV.

The Saudis plant the greenery and then water them every day with large water trucks and a four-inch hose. There is nothing growing that is not planted and watered. Not a tree, not a weed, not a blade of grass is natural.

The water truck and hose is worthy of an explanation because everything green gets watered every day, except on Friday of course, and large or small the water is gushed upon the green plant from a four-inch hose attached to the back of a water truck. The water truck is manned by two TCNs (third country nationals). When the gush of water from the four-inch hose washes out a small plant, they stop and replant it. Then they go on to the next plant and gush it in the same manner. The water boys are not sophisticated in the delivery of their water, but they are diligent.

King Khalid Airport is similar to the two other major airports in Saudi Arabia in that it has two separate sets of runways, with two separate terminals, separated by a single control tower. Does that seem strange? Well, the terminal on the west side is known as the royal terminal, and it has its own runways. As you might suppose, it is for the use of royalty. When I flew members of the royal family, I used those runways and stopped at the royal terminal; otherwise, they were forbidden. It's good to know such rules when you are living in a foreign country.

There is always a long wait in the isolation area before departure. The ticket office or the place where you get your boarding pass opens approximately two hours before each flight and closes one hour before each flight. That meant that if you weren't there at least an hour before your flight, then you weren't getting on. That's right; the aircraft could still be there, but your gate is closed, and you're not getting on the bus.

Oh, the bus, yes, they use the big buses like the ones in use at Dulles Airport in the USA. If you have never used them, then let me describe the buses. They are large like a city bus but with one major difference. The cab or cabins are attached to the chassis with hydraulic pistons that can raise them to the level of the 747 entrance door. Passengers load on the buses at the terminal gate with the cabs extended upward. Once the passengers are loaded, the driver then lowers the cab down to the bus chassis and drives out to the waiting aircraft. The aircraft is already positioned so that they don't need pushbacks.

At almost every airport in the world, an aircraft arrives at its point of disembarkation under its own power. Then, when ready to depart, it leaves under its own power or is towed by a tow tug to a place free of obstructions so it can then maneuver on its own. Since turning in a tight area is difficult and moving backward is more so for an aircraft, the moving back operation of the tug is simply referred to as the pushback. There are only a handful of airports in the world that uses buses to take passengers to the aircraft.

When the bus arrives at the waiting aircraft, the driver begins the lift of the cab until it is even with door of the aircraft. The driver may have to make several trips to fill a 747, but that's the way it is done. It may require a little mechanical monkey motion, but there is very little walking required and no running between gates to make connection flights. There are some definite advantages to the system.

Runways with lengths of eleven to fourteen thousand feet are common in Saudi Arabia. The taxiways to serve such runways must be just as long or longer, so extended periods of taxiing on the ground gives plenty of time for the Traveler's Prayer.

Every departure on Saudi Airlines is preceded by a reading of a travel prayer over the aircraft intercom from the Moslem holy book, the Koran. The reader is always the same voice on every aircraft and on every flight, day or night, early or late. A deep baritone male voice in a slow unemotional monotone asks for blessings to be bestowed on the enclosed travelers. Arabic is a beautiful language and lends itself to poetry, I am told. The departure prayer is one that is easily remembered by many, even if you don't understand the language. I don't remember it, but then I have trouble with my phone number as well.

The 747 is a comfortable ride, especially if you are fortunate enough to ride in business class. I had been advised to wear my uniform when traveling in and out of the Kingdom because professional courtesy by the airline would often upgrade me to business or even first class if space permitted. Of course, the upgrade included my wife. That night, it got us an upgrade from economy to business, and it was worth the effort. Saudi Airline gave us eyeshades and slippers for sleeping, very nice. The service and food on Saudi were always the best we had anywhere in the world. They were first class in all respects.

The stop we made in Geneva at 4:30 a.m. was unexpected. As I said before, if I had been paying attention, it wouldn't have been a surprise. No one told us there would be a stop. We thought the flight was a nonstop flight to Frankfurt.

Another lesson: read the fine print on the tickets, take nothing for granted, and ask many questions. Well, it was an hour and fifteen minutes in Switzerland for the stop that we hadn't counted on. At least we could tell everyone that we had been to Switzerland. The temperature was—01°C (30°F), the wind was about 10 knots (11.5 mph), and the night was dark. Charlotte, my wife, needed all the time we had for her duty-free shopping. She bought perfume for friends and barely had time to get back on the plane before departure.

I had never flown into Geneva myself, so I didn't have any technical information on runway length or elevation. Charlotte was convinced that we were not going to get into the air. There was a long run on the ground, probably due to the altitude and weight. We had filled every seat for the departure from Geneva, and we looked heavy even if we were not. So Charlotte mentioned three times about her fears of us not being able to get off. It's always funny to me that people seem to think that aircrews just load their aircraft up with fuel, bags, and people then get on the runway and start the takeoff just to see what will happen. Hmmmm, come to think of it, I think there have been some that did just that. I found later that Geneva, like many airports in Europe, have serious noise abatement restrictions. Our captain was probably using reduced power for takeoff. That would make the ground run extra long.

Dateline:
Frankfurt, Germany,
February 20-21, 1987

How to See West Germany in Thirty Hours

We arrived at the Frankfurt Flughafen (airport) at 8:30 a.m. There was a cold wind blowing with some snow. This was quite a change from the mild "picnicking" weather we had left only a few hours before in Riyadh. Frankfurt is seven hours by jet transport and almost due north of our home in Saudi Arabia. Charlotte observed that the black forest was white. I wish I'd thought of that.

We passed through German Immigration with no comment. Our six bags were passed with equal ease by the custom agents. Perhaps you have heard of German efficiency? The airports I have visited in Germany either as a crew member or as a passenger are impressive in the way they work. Perhaps it is an illusion, but you don't seem to notice construction problems. Everything is completed, and it works. In other countries, including the United States, there seems to be constant construction with the attendant inconveniences. This is not a statistical evaluation, but just an impression.

The Sheraton Hotel is a part of the Frankfurt Airport Terminal, so we found a *free* trolley and transported our own bags to the hotel lobby. The only place in the world that we had to pay for baggage carts was in the United States. Well, whatever works, I guess.

Clerks at the hotel desk spoke English well, and in a matter of moments, we were escorted to our rooms by a mature bellboy. It is my belief that he had been mature for something like the last forty years.

We had made no currency exchange, so I tipped the bellboy $2. He was unimpressed with my generosity. Much steam has gone out of the American dollar in many places of the world as we were to discover.

It is most helpful for the traveler to make his or her first stop at the money changers when arriving in a strange country. In most cases, there will be money changers at the airport. They are most convenient, of course, but don't change much of your currency until you have been in country for a day or so. The money changers are not all offering the same exchange rate, and sometimes those that are more convenient are also the worst bargain. The rules change if you're not leaving the airport, you know, like a layover for a plane change. As long as you are shopping in the duty-free shops, they can usually handle the currency that you brought with you.

The currency exchange is a lesson we soon learned and then had to modify slightly what we had learned from our earlier lessons. Perhaps that's because each country has a slightly different lesson to teach. The one thing you can count on is

216

the fact that it is *always* better to deal in local money if you can. You must be wary about all the funny money that passes through your hands, however. It is difficult sometimes to keep in mind just how much you are spending. When you change an American hundred-dollar bill into a large handful of local paper, you may feel like you suddenly got rich. Fight the feeling. It will pass soon enough.

The trip had been smooth, but we felt the need for a nap. Since we were only going to be in Frankfurt one night, we wanted to see the city right away. But the need for a little rest was overpowering, and besides, it would be a pleasure to sleep in a bed that didn't have a crack down the center. All the beds in our Riyadh compound that are called king-size beds have a crack down the middle. They are actually two small mattresses on a single frame. No box springs underneath either, just slats and a couple of small mattresses. If they are king size, then they had a small king in mind when they were built.

Oh yes, a little one-hour nap in a real bed without a crack would be a treat. But no, it was a trick! The bed had no crack, but the only covering was two *twin-sized* down-filled comforters. Now we had a crack that was above, not below. Our one-hour nap took four hours.

The trip to town was about forty kilometers (twenty-five miles). I had been to town before from the airport by taxi, and it was hair-raising. We agreed to try the train just for the adventure. Neither of us had ridden a train in Europe, so why not? It might be fun.

The train terminal (*baunhof*) was underground, across from the hotel, but still attached to the airport terminal. We could make our way there without leaving the building. We arrived at the train station to find it much like a clean subway. Everything very clean, very neat, and very German. There was no ticket agent, just machines that delivered a ticket if you primed it with the correct change. There were little or no directions in English. Just like the freeway markings in the States, you better have a map, be a local, or forget it.

We walked around a couple of the signs showing trains and their routes without gaining enough knowledge to make a choice. We couldn't even tell which direction the train should be going in order to get downtown. It was then we noticed a very native-looking fellow with a mustache, curved pipe, backpack, Swiss-type mountaineer's climbing boots, short knee pants (remember it was snowing outside), and one of those funny little hats with a feather on the side. I asked him, "Schpreckin Zee English?" He answered, "Yeah, a little." He was an American from Tucson, Arizona, who had just finished a five-year contract as a Lear mechanic. After a short holiday, he would be returning to his home in Tucson. What luck, he could tell us which train to take to town and which direction it would be going.

He first congratulated us on finding the train station; he said it took him two years to find it. His directions were simple: get on the first train that comes by going in *that* direction, pointing to the right. "Very good," I said, "and which one do we catch to get back?" We might just as well cover that base while we had someone tied down that we could speak to. "It will be the same train," he said. "Whatever the number is on the train you get on here, then just catch the same one coming back." That sounded easy, maybe too easy. We discovered later *why* it took him two years to find the train station.

Our new acquaintance had added "You can't miss it," an almost certain assurance that you will. The train to town was number 21, that is, on track number 21. The train back was on track number 3. That's the trick. Don't get the train number and track number confused.

The train was very neat, very fast, and no graffiti. Our arrival into the main station at Frankfurt was impressive. It was a huge structure, reminiscent of the grand structures you see in the movies. I expected to see some sort of spy operation happening at any moment. It was large and had a high ceiling, maybe three stories. There were a lot of people, but we didn't feel uncomfortable in the crowd like you would in New York. The trains don't go through the station; they begin and end there, simple. Perhaps there is another "through" station that we didn't see. We spent some time just looking around the station. There was a great deal for a couple of newcomers to see—little shops everywhere, selling books, videos, music tapes, whatever.

The entry to a small shopping area inside that train station was dwarfed by a huge poster of nearly nude women in a nearly pornographic pose. I don't know what the poster was selling. Just the sight of it being there was almost too much. What a shock for a couple that had been living in a society where women were completely covered (Kingdom of Saudi Arabia, not USA) when appearing in public! There are *no* large public posters of women in the Kingdom of Saudi Arabia.

We found out later there were several levels of tracks into the station. It was even larger than we had first guessed. We had arrived into the station on a set of tracks that were at ground level. I am guessing, but I think the trains that continued through Frankfurt were on one of the underground tracks.

We ventured out onto the street in front of the station and quickly ventured back inside. It was much colder than it looked. The wind must have been blowing 30 knots, and the snow was still falling. We had to reconsider this. Peering through the glass, we didn't see very many people on the street. The few we did see were disappearing from sight down to the left. It became evident that there was a walkway under the main street in front of the station. A couple of words of encouragement were exchanged between the two of us, and out through the front doors, we went into the cold night.

The stairs down were escalators. They were the first escalators I ever remember seeing outside. I wondered how they handled snow and rain on their tender mechanisms. It seemed to me that department stores back home had plenty of trouble with their indoor escalators. Then I remembered that we were in Germany, and the locals often have a few mechanical surprises for the Americans.

"Charlotte at escalator in Frankfurt"

At the bottom of escalators, we found what seemed to be another city beneath the streets. There were more stores and many more people. That's the reason we didn't see many people on the street above. They were all down below. After a short tour, we remembered there was only this one night for us to see Frankfurt, so we decided to brave the elements of the outside world.

Dateline:
Frankfurt, Germany
February 20-21, 1987

A NEAR TRAGEDY AT THE TRAIN STATION

We rode the up escalator and found ourselves on the far side of the street from the train station. Hey, we made it all on our own. The wind was just as cold as before we went underground. The snow was still coming down in a light, swirling motion and was still night. Only tourists and someone that really needed something would be out on a night like that. Maybe we fit in both categories.

We walked to our left, no idea of direction, and soon found we were running out of anything worth viewing or visiting. It didn't take long in that weather to decide that you needed to go inside for something or anything. Reversing our direction, we walked past the escalator, and on the corner was a little shop that sold knickknacks—a perfect place to shop for a few moments and warm our cold bodies.

Charlotte found some little clocks she was interested in but couldn't imagine one of them making the trip around the world. The idea of shipping it to Riyadh was as chancy as carrying it in a suitcase for twenty-four thousand miles. We didn't think they looked like they could "take the licking and still keep ticking." We did find some nail clippers, the finest I have ever seen regardless of the price. In the States, they make some fingernail or toenail clippers that sell for about $2.50, which do a decent job for a while. If the makers want to sell them for more money, they will add a gold tone finish. They are the same quality, but you have to pay $5 for them. Add a leather pouch to carry them in, and they will cost $7.50. These German clippers were plain Jane and stainless steel. There was no leather carrying case, and they cost 11 DM or about $6. They were great, far superior to any I have ever seen before or since.

There is only so much time one can shop in a store while buying just one pair of nail clippers, so it was out into the weather again. We crossed the street, turned left, and walked a block. Before we finished the block, the neighborhood had noticeably changed. By the time we got to the corner, we knew we had penetrated the red-light district, so across the street, a quick turnaround and back up the street.

We noticed a sign, which reminded me of the place back home, called Beef and Brew, Steak and Ale, or something like that. The German sign said "something & something" Steak Haus. Once inside, we found it was covered in what looked like Western artifacts. As it turned out, they were Argentinean. The bartender was friendly but spoke only a little English. Even a little English can understand "coffee," and in no time, we had two of the worst cups of coffee that either of us could remember. Never mind refills, the original cups were bad enough, so we ordered a couple of glasses of German wine. It was great and did a fine job of removing the chill that had overtaken our bones.

The bartender got into a big discussion with one of the waiters on the opposite side of the bar from where we were sitting. The bartender was getting a little huffy with the waiter's order. The waiter must have brought an order that was very complicated or distasteful to the bartender because suddenly, the bartender started filling the order with more gusto than normal. He was putting a little of everything in sight into one drink. The more ingredients he added, the more he smiled. Soon, even without understanding the language, you could tell he was very pleased with himself. He and the waiter began to giggle, and when they caught me laughing as well, it was even better. They were about to play a trick on one of their customers.

The bartender spoke something that sounded like Spanish and was so tickled that Charlotte and I understood and even replied in Spanish that he offered to make another of his "concoctions" for us. We declined with grace.

The waiter served the drink and came back to report that the customer enjoyed it very much. The bartender couldn't believe it but was in such a great mood by that time, he decided to make a duplicate drink for him and the waiter to try. When it was finished, they both tried a sip. It was so bad they had to spit it out. In whatever their native language was, they must have thought, *There is no accounting for some people's taste*. We all had a big laugh together. We laughed in American, however.

Soon we were back onto the street and didn't slow down until we were back inside the train station. It was getting late, so perhaps, we had seen enough of downtown Frankfurt for the time. Now it was time to test the Lear mechanic's instructions.

After some study and searching for more information, it was obvious that the return trip was not going to happen on track number 21. We bought some nuts from a vendor while we were breaking the German code. He had one of those stands that he can serve customers on all four sides. They were fresh, tasty nuts, but this was not getting us back to the hotel.

We finally gathered enough information to buy our tickets from a vending machine. While we were studying the vending machine, we noticed the approach of a small tug pulling a train of baggage carts behind. He was bearing down on us, and it seemed he was going to pass too close to the vending machines to miss us.

We stepped away from the vending machines to give the unconcerned tug driver room to pass between us and the ticket vending machines. In stepping back, we were stopped by another train of parked baggage carts. As the driver came closer, it became more obvious that there was not going to be room for him to miss us. The only problem was, there was no place for us to go. You can imagine our situation. At first we saw no problem, then yes, maybe there is going to be a problem; then, "Hey, it's a definite problem," and then panic because there was no obvious solution.

The tug driver gave no indication that he even saw us and therefore no reason to swerve or stop. At the last instant, we stepped between two of the halted baggage carts. The crack was small, but we forced our way into the crack between two of the parked carts to keep from getting crushed by the determined driver of the tug. The beds of those carts were about waist high, so they are not something you can step over or crawl under. The driver passed almost close enough to touch, his countenance never changing. We were squirming for safety when he passed us, and he looked as if he never saw, noticed, or cared.

Charlotte and I were being wedged between two halted carts, and there was no room for Charlotte's purse. One of the moving carts came so close it hooked her purse, and the purse strap was pulling her out into the small four-inch crack between the moving carts and the halted carts. It happened in a fraction of a second. The purse was on her shoulder, and as the force pulled her into the moving carts, she screamed, and I grabbed her. I was not going to let her get pulled into the crack. It would have meant many broken bones and maybe a German funeral.

Something had to give. The driver was, by that time, several carts down the line and made no move to show he had heard Charlotte scream. I was on one side pulling, and the purse, hooked solidly on a cart, was on the other side pulling. Charlotte was in the middle, and something had to give. The purse surrendered.

The whole episode had not lasted more than a few seconds. It was enough to make you want to sit down to get your breath and wonder if it actually happened. My thoughts later included what I would have done to that doltish driver if he had hurt my wife with his cavalier attitude. It might have meant the reopening of World War II.

Within a short while we had recovered sufficiently from our brush (no pun intended) with the baggage carts and their driver to once again approach the ticket vending machine. Further study revealed that our retun train would be in about thirty minutes on track number 3. Track number 3 was down in the subterranean bowls of the train station. I hoped the Lear mechanic from Tucson was better at repairing aircraft than he was at giving directions in train stations.

You know, it's amazing, but if you use just a little imagination and a little effort, you can get some understanding of German text. Take my word for it. It's easier than you might think. There are many words in German that are very similar to English words, and if you look for root words and their meanings, you may be able to get a rough meaning of what you are reading. Well, it works sometimes, especially if there are pictures.

We had another fast ride, and in a short time, we were back in the hotel and ready to settle in for the night between the comforters with a crack in the middle. Nobody got hurt on the train ride back from downtown.

The night passed quickly in the German bed with split comforters. We had a four-hour nap earlier in the day, but the effects of the earlier nap were not noticeable as we assumed the horizontal position for our night's rest.

Dateline:
Frankfurt, Germany—Boston, Massachusetts, USA
February 21, 1987

LEAVING GERMANY

We had a 10:00 a.m. departure time for Saturday morning, so we set the alarm for 7:30 a.m. That ought to do it. As it turned out, it was plenty as our Northwest Orient flight was two hours late.

The breakfast was another treat. We had both bacon and German sausage with our eggs. There are no pork items on the menu back in the Kingdom. I can't say that we had a biological craving for breakfast bacon; no, it's more like deprivation. When someone tells you can't have something, then you are deprived, and we had been deprived of our breakfast bacon for a few months. It seemed like we hadn't had any for years.

The walk from the hotel across the terminal to our airline connection took us by some very interesting items being advertised for sale in Germany. Here is an item of interest to my friends in electronics. In the terminal, there was a display of "spy" stuff. All the classic "goodies" were there, but the new stuff caught my eye. They had FM transmitters built into a fountain pen, tie clips, and some very interesting-looking telephone bugs for tapping phones from long distances. All the above are very *illegal* in the United States since Watergate. They are also much more sophisticated than what was available during the events that led to the Watergate scandal. I learned later that there are many things that are legal in Germany that are not legal in the United States.

Some of my friends will remember when I was involved in a debugging operation with a detective on the Houston Police force. We were supposed to be finding electronic bugs that the bad guys had hidden. That story could be the basis for a separate book. Maybe I'll write those experiences down someday.

To my other friends that didn't know of my involvement in the anti-spy business (ECM, electronic counter measures), don't worry, I never did anything illegal, but I ran into several that did! Some I had contact with but refused to do business with later went to the federal penitentiary. Their number included the chief of police of Houston, one of the brothers of a wealthy family, internationally known, that very nearly cornered the world's silver market, and more. Yes, that will certainly have to be another story. That display in the Frankfurt terminal brought back an avalanche of memories.

Don't you hate to stand in a long line? Everyone does, I suppose, but what I hate most is standing in a long line, and then just before you get to the counter, something happens that makes the time you have just spent in the line a complete waste. Usually, it turns out to be the wrong line, they open other windows that have been closed, or they close the window in front of you.

The worst case is after standing a long time, waiting to buy license plates for your car with all the discomfort of a courthouse without air-conditioning, they tell you it's the next window over. There have been only a couple of people waiting there all the while you have been standing in the wrong line. Just as you make a move in that direction, there are thirty-five people that beat you into the line. They each want to get two sets of licenses for autos, one trailer without a title, and an out-of-state motorcycle to register. I wonder how many mass murders there have been in courthouses' license plates lines.

After standing in a long line to the Northwest Orient counter for almost an hour, they announced that there would be a two-hour delay. Everybody in front of me left; they couldn't make their connections with a two-hour delay. Rats, I hadn't needed to wait in line at all.

THE UGLY AMERICAN

It was in the Frankfurt terminal, where we had our first taste of the traveling tourist from America. The examples we saw were of young people from the United States that were returning from their skiing holidays in Europe. They were loud, obnoxious, and embarrassing. They seemed intent on drawing as much attention to themselves as possible. Their efforts were successful. However, they were regarded with aversion by all around them.

There are many ways to be obnoxious, I suppose, but Americans seem to need volume to accompany their particular acts. We may not be the most obnoxious of travelers, but my experience has been that we are by far the loudest. Some Americans pick the wrong way to draw attention to the United States. Yes, I mean to say that when you are in a foreign country, anything you do out of the ordinary to draw attention to yourself is also drawing attention to the United States. In some cases, credit, good or bad, is assigned all the way down to the state of one's origin.

We thought it would be a pleasant flight on the Northwest Orient 747 to Boston. We were only half full when we left Frankfurt, and that is an excellent sign. About thirty minutes after departure, we began a descent into Gatwick Airport in London. The second time, in as many legs, we were making an unscheduled stop. There were to be several more such surprises before our journey was completed. The stops were not actually unscheduled, but they were not shown on our tickets, so we didn't know about them. Travel agents in Riyadh don't say anything about these stops unless you are swift enough to ask, "How many stops, and where are they?" Of course, most travel agents will provide an itinerary, but sometimes they do not. Oh well, live a little, learn a lot. (The Germans say, "Too soon oldt, too late schmart.")

224

Our stop in Gatwick had completely filled the 747. There was not an empty seat anywhere. That is not a pleasant way to travel. We were served an overabundance of peanuts, but the hostesses were so busy we couldn't get anything to drink. Yes, I know you can get up and get a drink for yourself, but when the seat belt sign is turned off, then you know the aisles are full, the toilets are full, and there are lines for drinks, magazines, or anything else you can think of.

We were two hours late leaving Frankfurt but not unhappy because if we missed our connection in Boston, then the next flight would be a better connection for our destination of Savannah, Georgia. Would you believe it, we made up the two hours over the Atlantic and arrived only a few minutes late in Boston?

Dateline:
Savannah, Georgia, USA
February 22, 1987

NEXT TIME WE SPEND MORE TIME PLANNING THE ITINERARY, OKAY?

The connection in Boston only allowed forty-five minutes, so we still figured there was no way we could make it. Subconsciously, we hoped to miss the connection because the next flight out would get us to Savannah with fewer legs. It never occurred to me to just dillydally and miss the next flight on purpose. I think the great airline person in charge somehow would know, and we would lose our reservation or something. I hate to change plans or planes en route.

—A POOR PLAN IS BETTER THAN NO PLAN AT ALL

When you need a long line, there is never one around. We went through Customs and Immigration, slick as could be. Even Charlotte's gold didn't slow us down. The Customs agent said, "You're not going to leave that gold here when you leave the States, are you?" I said, "Are you kidding, after what it cost?" I forced a laugh that may have seemed a little too much, and he forced just a trace of a smile. The smile said, "Oh yeah, who do you think you're kidding, cowboy?"

We were running to make our connection. It was a Northwest Orient DC 9-80 to Memphis, and it wasn't worth running to catch. Your connecting gate is always at the opposite end of the terminal, right? Do you know why this is true? If the airport has more than one terminal, then your connecting gate will be at the furthest end of the most inaccessible terminal. That's a standard airport rule. I think it has something to do with the "gozinta" and the "gozouta" rule.

This was Saturday afternoon, and it was a real "cattle car." Again, there was not an empty seat. The aircraft was filled with construction or oil field workers that were returning home for the weekend. They didn't go home every weekend, only now and then. We had picked either the now or the then for our trip.

I have encountered oil field crews more than once in my travels. One such was staying in the Sofitel Hotel in Paris waiting for the next day's flight out to the oil fields in Africa. They had been on leave in the United States and were returning to work. Another group flies out of Houston, several times a week, to the oil fields in Mexico. It seems that air transportation has made the oil field crews much more mobile in these modern days. I had no idea that such a practice was so common.

We were ready for some good luck in Memphis. It didn't happen. Forget about the good luck. It was another run to the other end of the terminal to get on another

226

DC-9, and we just barely made it. I hate DC-9s, don't you? They are too narrow, and they are always full. I've already told you what I think about traveling with a full load, and you know, it doesn't make any difference what type of a conveyance you happen to be on. If it's your family car, a train, cruise ship, or whatever, full is the poorest way to travel.

In Atlanta, the schedule showed we had a little more time to change planes. The problem was, we arrived on Northwest Orient at terminal D and had to change to eastern. Terminal D is the most easterly located terminal of all at the Atlanta airport. With our best efforts, we couldn't find out whether our next flight was leaving from terminal B or C.

We checked at each terminal, still carrying our hand baggage, first at C and then at B. We were finally sent to the main terminal, which was A. They told us we would have to go back to terminal D and find out from Northwest Orient what the gate and terminal was for the connecting flight. It seemed the computer and telephone lines were not working right, so that they couldn't call or check for us. It was the computer glitch that had kept us from finding out our proper terminal and gate in the first place.

It's time for a recommendation to the beginner at this point. When you arrive at a gate with a transfer in mind, then don't leave that gate until you are satisfied with the information on your connecting flight. Don't guess. It will just wear your back and patience out. If the video display doesn't have your flight, then you have the first indication of trouble. Insist that someone with authority makes a phone call or radio call to find out. Don't ever be afraid to be a bother. Sometimes you must assert yourself to make things work correctly. When it gets real bad, my wife can pitch a hissy fit. It always works.

We went to terminal D and started over. By this time, we were just about to miss our flight wherever it was. It was half past eleven at night, and we had been up since seven thirty that morning plus a six-hour time change. That's twenty-one and a half hours, I think. That's no record, but it's enough to wear everything thin. The trauma of the experience has left me with no memory of which terminal we left on, but I do recall that we were running to make it.

Now that you are armed with that knowledge, let me tell you that many travelers will tell you that if you have a proper travel agenda printed up before you leave, then you won't have the problem just described. Not true, a preprinted itinerary is very nice, and to be desired, but it doesn't control changes that are made by the airlines as you travel. You better use my advice and get your next gate settled before you leave the last one.

We were airborne and on the way to our final destination for that day before we were told there would be a stop in Charleston, South Carolina. I have been going to Savannah twice a year for several years for ground school and simulator training at the Gulfstream factory. This was the first flight that I ever had to stop in Charleston.

By the time we got to Savannah, there were two things we had learned for certain—one, we knew how to get on and off airplanes, and two, our bags were lost.

It was 2:20 a.m. on Sunday morning when we were finally checking into the Hyatt Regency in downtown Savannah. We had to spend some time at the airport—first waiting and looking for our bags, then next, filling out forms for them to be traced. With all the plane changing and close connections, we were not surprised that our bags did not arrive with us, but we didn't expect them to be lost. The good news is, if the bags are not with your arrive flight, then they are treated as lost by the airline agent where you happen to be at the time. The bags may be only one flight away, but they are treated as lost, and all the associated paperwork must be done.

I've had my bags lost many times by the airlines, but I must report that it was always just a temporary condition. Once in Orange County airport in California, I had to make a physical search of the storage area after the airlines gave up on finding my bags. My search was successful. I found my hang-up bag thrown on top of some lockers like workers use to change clothes. All ID had been removed from the garment bag. Maybe I found it just before some worker changed clothes. Whatever, it kept my record complete. I have yet to suffer a loss of bags with the airline that was permanent.

No, I can't leave airline bags on such a positive note. It just wouldn't be the right thing to do to my readers. You see, losing bags is not all the airline can do to you and your bags to ruin your day. They can mangle them, and they can remove items from your bags. The wary traveler must *try* to protect his interests against both happenstances.

How do you do that? First, don't check your expensive bags; you'll be sorry. The Humble Oil Company issued certain of its pilots Halliburton suitcases. The Halliburton is known as an expensive aluminum suitcase. What you may not know is that it is also very tough, sturdy, well-built, and waterproof. We were issued the bags because those of us that crewed the Lockheed JetStar in the early days were forced to put our bags in the aft equipment or machinery area of the airplane. The area was unpressurized and subject to oil and hydraulic leaks. The Halliburton protected our clothes against such torture. The first time that I checked that bag on the way to Savannah, the airlines knocked a dent in one end that would hide a baseball. Cuts and gouges are very common. Give them a cheap bag to tear up is my advice to you.

The second thing you must guard against is theft. Always lock your bag. I know, you don't have to tell me. They can get in if they want to do so, but do it anyway. The small deterrent of a little cheap lock will often make the thief go on to the next bag that is not locked. If you, my reader, does this, then just think, since there will be more people that don't read this advice than there will be that do, then you will be in the minority, and therefore there will always be more bags unlocked than there are locked. Join the minority and save your bag.

All those details took their toll in time and stress. It was no wonder that after checking in at the Hyatt front desk, we went to the fourth floor and found they had assigned us a room for the handicapped. We must have looked like that's what we needed. Well, a long day, a lot of stressful travel, peanuts and no water, lost bags, obnoxious fellow Americans, a cab ride from the airport that cost $18.20 but was worth no more than $7, and now a handicapped room. It was time to call it a day.

Not yet, think again. About the time we got into bed, someone turned on a stereo in the next room, and the party began. It was three in the morning. After a few minutes, it became obvious they were not going to turn it down, so I called the desk. That's right, I called the desk. I know that Clint Eastwood would have gone next door and "handled" it, regardless of whether the disturbance was being caused by four big men or four good-looking women. He would have just gone over there and handled it. Well, I called the desk.

The manager at that time of the night on Saturday, or Sunday morning, has to be the only person on the hotel staff duty roster that couldn't get off for the weekend. The voice sounded female and young. She said she had tried several times to quiet them down before we arrived but with no success. She was sorry, but the best she could do was to move us into a different part of the hotel the next day. It seemed the hotel was full due to the Black Hairdressers' Convention. That was the hotel spokesperson's description, not mine. Besides, it wasn't the color, but the noise that kept us awake. Finally, I had to go out into the hall and check.

From the sounds of it, the hotel was not going to last until tomorrow. My worst suspicions were confirmed; the hall was full of hair dressing people, and they were having a great time at three in the morning. It was no use. Go back to bed and make the best of it. We were so tired that the noise only awakened us a few times before morning.

Our hotel rates are usually discounted the same as airline crews, but we had noticed that when checking in, the rates were even better. The last time I stayed in the same hotel less than a year before, the airline rate was $74, and last night it was an even $40. I found out later they had given us the military rate because we were booked under the Saudi Armed Forces. I hadn't thought of that before. We welcomed the cheap rates, but the first night was not worth it. Don't forget these are 1987 prices.

CHEAP AIRLINE FARES

A few words to the reader regarding airline fares. When you start a transoceanic flight from overseas as a nonresident of the United States, the fares can be unbelievably inexpensive. The actual price will vary during the year, of course, depending on the peak season, but you need to know about the coupons. With a round-trip ticket out of Riyadh, we could buy coupons for $25 each. A coupon is the same as one airline ticket. You can buy a coupon for $25 and fly from New York to Los Angeles, Houston to Portland or whatever. Sounds too good to be true? The actual price of the coupon may vary a few dollars. The lowest I ever saw a coupon price was $25, and the highest was $35, I think. Now you know how all those foreigners can afford to see the United States.

The airlines negotiate the price of the coupons to encourage the sale of their transoceanic flights. One other thing, to change a coupon can be expensive, so if you make a mistake in planning, then live with it or pay the big price.

Dateline:
Savannah, Georgia, USA,
February 22-26, 1987

ALL YOU NEED TO KNOW ABOUT JET LAG

We couldn't believe it. We were up and showering in the handicap shower by eight thirty the next morning. There was no reason for us get up early. We could just have well slept in until noon. Savannah is a beautiful city on the river and near the Atlantic Ocean, but I had seen it many times before. So there was no desire to get up and see the sights. My simulator and ground school classes didn't start until Monday, and there was nothing in particular to get up for. It's just my policy to try and keep on a regular schedule wherever I happen to be at the time.

Our bags didn't arrive until four in the afternoon anyway. Perhaps the change in time zones would account for our early rising. It is a practice of mine in changing time zones to ignore their effects. Never mind the so-called jet lag. It's a popular idea that is supposed to explain the fatigue you feel after a long trip in a jet aircraft that perhaps crosses several time zones.

Sometime ago, it became popular to speak of how you would be wiped out after traveling from the United States to Europe.

"Girl, we lost eight hours on the way to Paris, and we were just wiped out for two days. It was the jet lag, you know."

The drama is increased considerably by adding the term *jet lag* to the story. If the jet-setters are having jet lag, then it can be widely acceptable as fashionable.

The next phase of the fashion fad begins when the PhDs publish articles in magazines on the effects of jet lag changing bodily biochemistry, biorhythms, and functions due to the "rapid crossing of time zones." The third phase begins with the diet faddists. They publish diet books to combat the effects of jet lag. Phase four is known to begin when the exercise nuts publish their books on special aerobics for combating the well-known effects of jet lag. Each phase capitalizes on the "well-known effects of jet lag" established by the proceeding phase. Soon the effects of this mysterious malady need no explanation because they are so well known. Once a mystery is established, then it is free game for every nut that wants to jump in and explain it. Well, maybe it's my turn.

First consider this. If you get jet lag from traveling west to east against the time zones, then what do you call the effect of traveling east to west with the time zones, jet gain? Shouldn't one reverse the effects of the other? Hmm, and what happens if you travel the same number of hours but north and south instead of east and west, or west to east? Perhaps that should be called jet null (look it up). What we are talking about, ladies and gentlemen, is fatigue, pure and simple, and it comes from traveling east to west, west to east, north to south, south to north, or in circles. It comes from traveling whether it's in a jet or a covered wagon. A little travel can be exhilarating, but past a certain point, it can become very tiring.

How do you suppose aircrews stand up to the mysterious effects of jet lag? Primarily, they ignore the mystery and get what rest they can. I'm *not* talking about the airline crews whose collective bargaining agencies have negotiated rest periods for them only. No, I'm talking about the great number of general aviation pilots like myself that have never had a bargaining agency to speak for them and are required to fly across many time zones as daily requirements.

Twenty-hour days are not uncommon for the general aviation pilots. We don't have the luxury of jet lag or a note from our mother to be excused from its effects. So just ignore all the books written about the mystery of it, the books on dieting for it, or the books on exercising to beat it. Follow my advice, and you can reduce the effects of travel fatigue sometimes known as jet lag. You will also find some relief for the fatigue that is associated with any long trip regardless of the type of conveyance or the direction of its travel. As a bonus, with all your new and little known knowledge, you can become a know-it-all at your next social gathering.

My advice is to nap as you travel if you can, and keep your watch set for whatever time zone you happen to be in at the time. When you arrive, then go to bed at your normal bedtime in your present time zone. Remember, what you feel is fatigue, and all you need is rest to beat it. Don't give into it. Going to bed and getting up at your regular time will help to quickly adapt your bodily functions to the new time zones. Sorry, to all you authors that were about to publish new books, but that's the way it is.

SAVANNAH IS A NICE PLACE TO VISIT

My refresher course at Savannah consisted of fifteen hours of classroom, or ground school, and twelve hours of simulator time. The ground school is mandatory, but the simulator time is not; however, captains normally select a pilot in command twenty-four-month check, which is done in the simulator. The twenty-four-month PIC check in the simulator fulfills the FAA requirements for a captain to act as pilot in command of a certain aircraft without being tested in the aircraft. It saves wear and tear on the aircraft plus a lot of money.

Pilots, who fly aircraft that weigh over 12,500 pounds, are required by the FAA to take a check ride each twelve months. It is called a PIC check (pilot in command). If a pilot is rated in more than one transport category aircraft, i.e., over 12,500 pounds, then he can be checked on alternate types if he took a twenty-four-month check previously in each type.

Simple math will tell you that if a pilot is rated in more than two types of aircraft, then he will have to have more than one check ride on certain years just to keep current in each type. You are not supposed to understand all that. It's just a little government gobbledygook. We normally take a twenty-four-month check every twelve months, just to be sure.

The simulator is very busy, and if your company doesn't act with alacrity and make your training schedule months or a year in advance, the unfortunate crew will receive simulator times that are the pits. From 3:00 to 6:00 a.m. is a particularly bad one. This year, I had 6:00 to 9:00 a.m. Not the worst, but a definite sign that the schedule was not prepared far enough in advance as it might have been. That meant that I would have to arise at four in the morning and leave the simulator directly into the classroom for the 9:00 a.m. to 12:00 p.m. (noon) class. Of course, that meant I would be off from noon until 6:00 the next morning.

We only have three hours of class and three hours of simulator each day after the first day. Of course, I could never get to sleep before midnight, regardless. The simulator week always wears me out. Maybe it's just jet lag.

Well, while my time was being occupied with classroom and simulated aircraft emergencies, Charlotte had time to visit the points of attraction in Old Savannah. She could make the River Walk, which ran under part of our hotel or see the Pirate House or other attractions, all within walking distance. She also had the rent car, so she could drive around and practice the skills that had been withheld from her while in Saudi Arabia. Remember, women don't drive in Saudi Arabia. The afternoons were filled with shopping trips for us both. The shopping skill is not withheld in Saudi Arabia because there are many fine places to shop there. American goods are what you yearn for and miss.

There is an abundance of good places to eat in Savannah, and that is another of the items we were anxious to catch up on. One evening, our hotel had a desert buffet that would have knocked your hat in the creek and rolled your socks down. They had pecan pie, bread pudding, chocolate cake, carrot cake, and so forth. I hurt myself. To be away from the kind of food that you have spent a lifetime developing a taste for can be devitalizing. We thoroughly enjoyed being returned to good ol' American food, especially the Southern variety. There is no food in the world at any price that can compare to USA Southern cooking.

Dateline:
Houston, Texas, USA
February 27-March 2, 1987

A Stop in Houston for Family, Taxes, and Dentist

Well, onward and upward. The week of training was soon over, and we were on our way to Houston through Atlanta of course. There is a saying that when a man dies, he will have to change planes in Atlanta regardless of his final destination. In Texas, we always thought it was Dallas.

Our time in Houston had to be divided between visiting friends, my three sons and their families, and the tax accountant. Yes, it was that time of the year again, and it was time to ante up for Uncle Sam. The time for tax consulting and advice was extended somewhat because our tax people were more interested in hearing about life in the Land of Sand and Sun than they were in discussing our tax problem.

People in the States have little knowledge about the tax problems of people that work overseas. Nonresident citizens of the United States must pay taxes as well as residents, but there is a slight difference. There is a dollar amount of all earnings from outside of the United States that is exempted from taxes! The amount hovers about the $70,000 mark. So a nonresident pays regular taxes on his income made in the United States and pays an additional tax on all income over $70,000 made overseas. If the individual doesn't make more than the exempted amount, then he pays no taxes on his overseas income. He still must file a return however!

I must say that if you have never lived in a condition where there are no taxes, then you will have a difficult time in understanding what I have to say. No sales tax means you pay only the sales price and no more. No income tax, no social security tax, no medical deductions means that on payday, you get the total amount that you know as your salary!

Living in a place with no taxes makes you feel rich. Maybe it is just a feeling, but it seems that the money is just not ever going to stop coming. I'm sure that given enough time an individual can get accustomed to a pocket full of money, but believe me, it's not easy.

In the least, an individual will forever change his attitude about the amount of taxes that we pay in the United States. I'm not against paying taxes, but I'm more interested in where the money goes now that I've seen another way of life.

We had to find time to pay a visit to the dentist. Our bravery for living in a foreign land did not extend or include the testing of their local dental facilities, so we needed time to see our familiar dentist while in Houston. Dental care was free in Saudi Arabia, but we were happy to pay for it in Houston. What does that tell you?

Of all the places we have lived or visited that had free medical treatment, there were always two things you could be assured of: First, the free medical treatment was not really free, and it was always overcrowded and of inferior quality. Second, the people with money never used the free facilities. It is my opinion that many people will willingly accept inferior quality in anything if they think it is free. I will admit, as well, that some people think if an item is expensive, then it must be better. The thinking person will find their group not listed with the above.

I worked in Houston, Texas, for twenty years. Family and friends reside there, and it is always a pleasure for me to visit with them. But it is difficult for me to fall in love with a city the size of Houston. It was a favorite pastime of mine to say, "I moved to Houston when the paycheck moved to Houston, and I left as soon as the paycheck stopped."

Lum and Abner was heard and loved by many people of the day. When the show was retired, Lum was hired by an oil company, Mobil I think, to be their public relations man. Lum could make a great speech, and I'll always remember what he said about the state that was his home and the center of his very successful radio show.

"Well, I don't think folks ought to criticize me for being from Arkansas. After all, I left there as soon as I knew there was some place else to go."

I love the United States, and I love Texas, both for the same reasons. There are other states to love, I'm sure, but I know about my state, and I know about the original thirteen colonies that made the United States. Both were founded by great men with character, bravery, and dedication. The more you know about either the country or the state, the more you have to love.

I've seen many countries that I know much less about, but the successful countries always have their own heroes. Great countries, states, or cities have their own founders that can be admired by strangers, if you just take the time to look for them.

The world knows about our Texas heroes. They may not have it just right, but they can't help but be impressed by the idea of the Alamo. Sure, some think that John Wayne was there, but it's the idea that sticks in their mind. Friends, be assured of this: If the foreigner speaks English, then he will talk to you about the States, Texas, California, and the Alamo. If they perceive that you are from Texas, then the order of the list I just gave you is changed. Texas and the Alamo become first on their interest list.

A traveler can use this information for an advantage at times. One cold rainy day in Paris a few years later, Charlotte and I needed a special form of transportation from Le Bourget Airport to Charles de Gaulle Airport. We had about eighteen bags, and you can imagine our transportation needs.

I called for two cabs and tried to explain why only two passengers needed two cabs. My French wasn't good enough for that chore. The occasion was on our movement back to Saudi Arabia after living on the French Riviera. That's right; we were leaving the Mediterranean coast for the Land of the Sand and Sun. Once more, our baggage was a millstone around our necks.

We had arrived at Le Bourget in a company aircraft that I was flying, so the bags, which were always a problem, became a much larger problem that day.

The cab arrived. It was a Mercedes station wagon, and it was alone. It was still cold; it was still raining, and the driver came with a foul mood. He didn't like our baggage load, he didn't like the rain, and he didn't expect to be properly compensated for his extra burden, and he didn't like us for bringing him this extra problem.

After loading the bags in the back of the station wagon, because of the rain, we attempted to put the rest in the seats of the wagon. Charlotte sat in the backseat with bags all around her, and I sat up front with the driver. I had bags under my feet, behind my legs, and in my lap. The driver's mood had become more sullen as we pulled away from curb. He mumbled something about the safety of such a load as he was carrying. He grumbled more about not being able to see out or steer his vehicle properly.

After a few moments of grousing, he fell silent. It was at that time that I attempted to cheer up the mood within the heavily laden wagon.

"You don't appear to be from around here. Where are you from?" I asked.

Paris is no different from Washington DC. The cab drivers are from all over the world. A local doesn't drive cabs in either of those cities.

"I am Bosque," the driver stated with a scowl, and then after a pause for effect, he looked my way and said, "You know about Bosque?"

"Sure," I said with more confidence than my education could support. "The Bosque are people that live in the Pyrenees Mountains. They live between France and Spain but are not French and are not Spanish; they are Bosque."

The driver smiled and nodded his head as he looked straight down the road. He was pleased that I had spoken correctly about his country. No, he was more than pleased. He was also proud. His mood changed immediately, and he asked,

"Where are you from, the States?"

"No, not the States, from Texas, you understand Texas?" I said Texas with the same tone he used when he spoke of his home.

"Oh yes, Texas, yes, Texas. Very good, Texas, yes, I understand Texas. You okay, mister!"

Then there were smiles and laughter and a generous tip at the destination. I noted that Charlotte sat in the back without mentioning California.

People like to be proud of their heritage whether it is family or location. A man needs to be proud of something!

A reunion with my sons and their children when I passed through Houston is usually accomplished at a place to eat. "Champs" is a common place for us to meet, and Dad always gets the check. My sons have grown to the point that they now make attempts to pay, but I always remind them that I'll pay now, and later when I am old, then they can feed me mush in the old folks' home. This is always followed by "Aw, Dad." Then we laugh, and I pay the check. It's best that way.

The pilots that I flew with when in Houston arranged for a dinner party at the Texas Tumbleweed, a Western-style steak house in Houston. The steak house has all the hired help dressed in costumes of the Old West. The men wear pistols, and the girls wear short dance hall skirts. They have shootouts with the bad guys, and the dance floor is filled with the old and young alike. It's a fun place, but the reason the locals go there is the great steaks they serve.

Enough of the free commercials. It was good to visit, but we had to move on to our next leg if we are to beat David Niven's record.

Dateline:
Albuquerque, New Mexico, and San Marino, California
March 2-4, 1987

THE NEW MEXICO GOLD RUSH

Too soon it was time to move on, and our next stop was in Albuquerque. Charlotte's sister, Muriel, and niece, Maxine, were there to meet us. We found that they had misunderstood our arrival time by twenty-four hours, so they had been waiting in Albuquerque since the day before. Their ranches are slightly more than a hundred miles southeast of the city, so waiting was judged to be better than an extra round-trip.

They took us from the airport to the Hilton, and we agreed that we would like to have more conversation over coffee before calling it a night. It was after 11:00 p.m., and the Hilton's dinning room was closed. It was cold, and Muriel insisted on wearing the abaya that Charlotte brought from Saudi Arabia. The abaya is nothing more than a black piece of silk that is floor length and is worn over the shoulders with full-length sleeves. I suppose the mystery of it is attractive, but that notion soon leaves a person when they are exposed to its use on a daily basis. Muriel liked it.

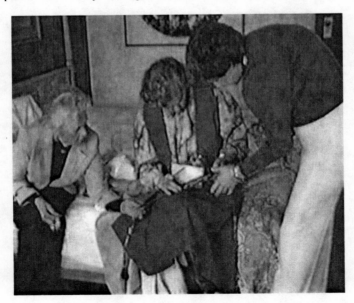

"Muriel, Maxine, and Charlotte checking out the gold!"

Early the next morning, the girls were deep into the gold. Charlotte had been purchasing gold jewelry on a regular basis since her arrival in Riyadh back in November. So she had four months to stock up on bracelets, necklaces, rings, earrings, and such. The Customs man in Boston wanted to make sure that we weren't going to leave any of that gold behind, and I assured him that after what I had paid, it would most certainly not be left behind. Well, it was true when I told him that story. The joke was on me and the bank.

A word about Saudi gold. The Saudis craft jewelry from 18-24 karat gold, nothing less! Gold is a very important part of the Saudi woman's life. It is their dowry, their security, and much of it they wear because they don't trust banks. One of my first impressions of Saudi Arabia was that there were no women there. They don't do grocery shopping, and they don't drive cars, so at a casual glance, you never see them, except at the gold souks, that is. The black abayas worn by the Saudi women literally fill the gold souks (markets). Now when American women return from a stay in Saudi Arabia, they *all* have a hoard of gold. Trust me on this, I said *all*. They tell their husbands that it is an investment, but when they first see the 18-24 karat gold, they are *hooked*, and there is little that a man can do about that.

No woman can resist gold. Many of them try to act unconcerned or above all that adulation. Don't be deceived. They are only waiting for the right opportunity to spring. Perhaps there are a few ladies that truly try to resist, but in the end, they succumb as well to the subtle odors of the golden metal. None can resist for any extended period.

Muriel and Maxine both own ranches of importance near Cedarvale, New Mexico. Their reaction to Charlotte's gold the night before was hardly more than "Well isn't that nice," but after a few restless hours of sleep that night, they experienced a mood change.

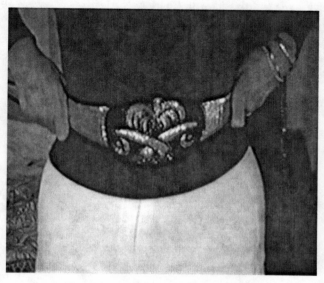

"Charlotte's prize . . . the Saudi belt!"

They were staying in Muriel's apartment, which was more than three miles away, but they could not rid themselves of the lingering odor of all that gold that had permeated their clothing in the brief time they were near the yellow metal. They were back in our room by sunup, and the gold was now spread all over the bed. The ooooooohing and aaaaaaaaahing was rising to a fever pitch. Within a brief span of thirty minutes, it was all over. The gold was gone. It was finished. Charlotte had nothing to show for her four months of shopping. Those female New Mexico ranchers had hit us like outlaws hitting a stagecoach. There was not a trace of gold left.

The episode with the ladies and the gold reminded me of a trait that exists in Saudi Arabia. I'm thinking of the one, whereby, if you admire something that belongs to someone else, then he may very well give it to you. That trait is probably disappearing somewhat with the advancement of modern times, but I have experienced this myself. If you say to an acquaintance, "Say, that's a fine pen you have there," then he very likely will insist that you take it. I do mean insist. I have seen someone ask for a light for his cigarette, and many times he is given the lighter. I've seen this happen when a clerk was asked for a light in a store or souk where they were selling the lighters! It works both ways. You must be prepared to reciprocate. It is a form of displaying your affluence. The more generous you can appear, the greater your personal wealth. A fellow needs to be careful playing that game, or he could end up losing his car and wife.

We hated to leave New Mexico after so short a visit, but the trip was primarily for our "around the world" experience, so on to Los Angeles. We could only stay there a short time as well. The little time there gave us a chance to eat more good food and have some short visits with Charlotte's friends. They were all interested to hear more of the exotic Middle East. I'm not sure about the exotic part. A few months ago, I couldn't have given an accurate definition of the term *Middle East*, but we gave them some personal stories, which had become well rehearsed. It is always good to visit friends, but we must push on to Hawaii.

Dateline:
Honolulu, Hawaii, USA
March 5-7, 1987

THE ISLANDS

Once again to the international terminal. We're becoming very good at this. The flight to Honolulu was fine. The service and food were good, but the kids are still a pain in the neck. Airline travel has degenerated to a point which is worse than bus travel was when I was a kid. You remember, the worst part of bus travel was the crowded terminals and the foul-smelling restrooms? Well, the airlines have outdone the buses on both counts. At least on a bus, you could stop and get off now and then even on a long ride. If you happened to get stuck with an irritating neighbor, you had an opportunity to change seats after a short while. On the airline, you can't get off, and the crying kid in the seat just behind never quits. We should never forgive the federal government for subsidizing airlines to the point of putting the trains and buses out of competition for the travelers' dollar.

We arrived in Honolulu on March 6 and found that the Hotel Illaki had our reservations. Don't laugh, you never know for sure until the man behind the desk says yes. We had room 1360, and it was overlooking a marina. I asked Charlotte if she had ever seen a picture of lots of money. She said that she had not, so I took a picture of the boats in the marina. If that's not a lot of money, then it will have to do.

"Picture of Lots of Money"

We had a comfortable room and a fine bed without a crack in the mattress or the cover. The TV was able to produce the current news in our native tongue. I noted, in the current news, that Linda Lovelace just had a liver transplant. I always suspected that show business was bad for a person's liver. Well, it was news anyway, and it was the first time on this trip that we had a few moments to sit and watch the news. We don't have a chance to see much news from the States while in Riyadh. How about none?

As luck would have it, Charlotte picked up a head cold. Well, no way was she going to let that slow her down. She had been telling me the virtues of the islands for quite sometime, so we were determined to have a good look in the four days we had scheduled there. You see, she had been there before, but it was my first visit.

Next morning, we walked down the beach road a couple of blocks and had breakfast in the Hale Koa Hotel, which is the military's R & R (rest & relaxation) hotel. It was a fine hotel, considering the reduced prices for those of us with military connections. We recorded it in memory for the next time, we come I should be retired military, and we will be able to partake of their reduced rates for rooms, golf course, and all the rest. They tell me the green fee is $1 for the military. Does that sound good or what?

Who says it's not a small world? We met a salesman and a sales manager with wife that had worked for Charlotte's old food brokerage company in Los Angeles. The salesman had quit the company the same day as Charlotte's retirement. He was from Albuquerque, now living in Newport Beach and representing a company from Fort Worth, Texas. The sales manager still worked for the food broker and was head of the island branch. We had a visit and chat with the Newport Beach salesman in the W. C. Fields ice cream store. For sometime, I have worked as an undercover agent assigned to checking the quality of various brands and flavors of ice cream all over the world. It is a difficult job without public rewards, but then it's a job that has to be done. You might be surprised to learn of how many inferior quality ice cream stores there are around the world. Well, they can't just sell anything, call it ice cream, and get away with it. They have to be checked, all of them. It's a thankless task, but it's my job.

The W. C. Fields ice cream store in Honolulu is okay.

WHY DON'T WE GO ON A REAL HAWAIIAN LUAU?

Where was I? Oh yes, well, after walking around a little in the rain, we began to look for what we were going to do next. Yes, it rained on us the first morning there. Charlotte's cold and a little rain weren't going to stop us, so we signed up for a couple of tours. The first tour was a *lou-ow* (the Saudi spelling for *luau*) tonight and tour around the island tomorrow, and we would leave for Tokyo the next day. That should about do it. This was to be our first effort at a tour. It was not to be our last.

Take a break, and I'll explain about Saudi spellings. The Saudis are not very diligent when it comes to spelling words with the foreigner's alphabet. The names of cities in Saudi Arabia are the best example of their varied ways of spelling the same name. The city of Jeddah on the Red Sea is well known, but they spell it in several different ways. We live on the northeast side of Riyadh in a little village known as Nasseem. The off-ramp of the freeway has it spelled three different ways on consecutive signs. My friend Phil Hardy from Provo, Utah, had his ID card examined by a half-dozen Saudi copilots one morning, and they got in a huge argument about the spelling of his name as it was written in Arabic. Some said it was spelled s-h-a-r-d-y, and some said it was spelled h-a-r-d-y. They all agreed that whatever, it was close enough!

The *lou-ow* tour was to be a real experience. We were to be guests at a real, honest-to-goodness Hawaiian *lou-ow*. The pig was going to be roasted in a pit in the ground under palm leaves, the fishermen were going to cast out their nets in the native fashion, the native women were going to dance in grass skirts, and the native men would dance with the knives! It was all just as advertised; however, there were a few things that were not advertised.

"Native fishing party . . . on the beach"

The fishermen threw out the nets for the tourists' amusement, but they didn't go out just right. I think they knew in advance that the nets might not go as hoped for because there were a couple of scuba divers there with their air tanks on and ready. The scuba divers took the nets out the proper distance so all the tourist pictures would come out right.

243

They did have a pig cooking in a pit, but we didn't get to eat it. They didn't have enough beach to cook all the pigs needed to feed the bunch that showed up there. We didn't know there were going to be over five hundred guests at this little get-together. The pork was catered on paper plates, and we ate at picnic tables a little way down the beach from where the pig was cooking. We could still smell pig roasting. The girls did their dance and so did the men, but not among us like in the movies. They were on a stage at the other end of the island.

"Just a small native lou-ow"

Well, a good time was had by all. The sponsors served pitchers of *my-ties* (Saudi spelling), and after a few of those *my-ties*, many of the guests didn't care much what they had just eaten or had just seen. It was a happy bunch! My wife and I didn't partake, stayed sober, and thereby created a small problem. We were likely to remember the truth of what had just happened. Because of this, we were required a special ceremony for any sober members of the group. We were required to participate in the custom of taking oaths after a "real" lou-ow, whereby we promised to never tell the truth about what happened there that night.

It was called the Tourists' *Hypocritical* Oath, I believe, and we all agreed to tell only exciting stories to their friends back home about the Hawaiian lou-ow. In exchange, they would be allowed to ride the tour bus the twenty-five miles back to the hotel. I refused to take the oath even though the pressure was intense, but because of the large number of people involved, I was able to sneak on to the bus for the ride back. I'm sure they will be greatly distressed to find that I told the truth about their *lou-ow* after being free of the trance of the islands.

Dateline:
Honolulu, Hawaii, USA
March 8, 1987

OUR FIRST TOUR OF THE ISLAND

The next day was the eighth and a beautiful day. It was to be our tour-around-the-island day. When we signed up for the tour, I mistakenly got the idea that we would be going by boat. What a surprise when we got into a Chevy van. I must start paying more attention to some of these details.

Some of you folks may be getting the idea that I'm not too swift when it comes to planning out the details of being a tourist. Well, I want you to know that it has nothing to do with intellect at all. It has to do with interest. I don't like planning out a trip in fine detail because it seems like there are nothing but changes. I know that's not a good excuse, but it is the only one I have. I will further admit that in many other things, I plan very well, but as a tourist, I'm something less than great. Maybe I've spent too many years being paid to travel. I'm just not very impressive as an amateur.

The driver of the van was Danny, our guide from the night before. He was a big jolly young man, and he remembered me. As Charlotte and I were getting on the van, he said, "Oh, hi there, how did you get back to the hotel last night?" I just told him, "On the tide," and let it drop. There was no use going into detail about slipping on to the bus. It might get someone in trouble, you know.

The only good picture I have of Danny, our tour guide, as he made some proclamation to the group. The picture catches my reflective mood as I ponder the overall scheme of things.

245

He was an entertaining guide, and he liked to tell jokes as he pointed out where the stars lived. He showed us the homes of Tom Selleck, Jim Neighbors, *Book 'em, Danno* from *Hawaii Five-O*, Frank Sinatra, and others. It was the first time I had ever been on a tour of stars' homes, and it was nothing like I thought it might be. If the guide hadn't told me, I would never have guessed that in "that house right there is where Frank Sinatra lives, when he's here."

There was nothing that would give you a hint about the identity of the famous person just out of sight behind those curtains of wood, brick, and plaster. The house just stood there, content to hold its secrets. Oh, what stories it must hold, and to think I passed right out in front of where Tom Selleck has his breakfast. The houses certainly were good at keeping those secrets all right because thirty minutes later, I would not have been able to point out a single one of those houses. They looked somewhat normal, you might say.

It occurred to me later, how do you suppose the guide keeps up with them? How can he tell them apart? Well, what if he didn't keep track of them? What if he got them mixed up and told us that the house *of Book 'em, Danno* house was really Jim Neighbors' house? I was discussing that problem with one of the other tourists, and she said, "You shouldn't be such a cynic. Of course, the guide kept them straight. He was paid to know such things." Her logic was untouchable, so I might just as well let the matter drop. But I still wonder, if you were to see all the pictures made by tourists of Tom Selleck's house in Hawaii, how many of them would be of the same house?

The drive was scenic, and Danny told us we were going down into an old inactive volcano. That statement may not be too clear. I meant to say we saw volcanoes that had been inactive for many years. I don't suppose there are any new volcanoes, and some that might look inactive to the tourist are still considered active by those that are experts in such things. But then what do I know? Volcanoes are pretty much a sideline with me.

Actually, I was never down in a volcano before, so I was exposed to much new information. I knew that there was an active volcano on Maui, but I didn't want to make any remarks out loud about an active volcano on the next island. I was already in enough trouble over my observations regarding the stars' homes.

It was after we left the inside of the volcano that I noticed Mesquite trees growing everywhere. With the trees and rolling terrain, it would have passed for San Angelo, Texas, and how much money could be saved by people that would just visit there instead of Hawaii? But I didn't say anything. Everyone would probably have thought I was just being a smart aleck.

As we passed by several good-looking restaurants, Danny, the driver, mentioned that he suspected that we as tourists had seen too much of such excellent places to eat. He had a "special" place in mind for our lunch stop. He said it was not like one of these places that we were passing on the main road. It was instead out of the way and off the beaten path. It was a place that the locals used. He said that tourists would never find "his" restaurant in a thousand years. We arrived at the secluded lunch stop about forty-five minutes later, and it was everything he said it was and more. Danny's favorite place to eat was certainly out of the way, and a tourist would never find it unless his or her guide took them there. The food wasn't too bad, and I noticed that Danny didn't have to pay for his. That was a nice gesture for the little out-of-the-way lunch stop restaurant to make. Danny said he stopped in there often.

I noticed the lady that ran the place had a striking resemblance to Danny. She looked like she could have been his mother. She even hugged him and kissed him before he left and told him to hurry home.

The proprietor was very friendly, but then the island people have a reputation of being friendly. I also noticed that she didn't offer to hug and kiss me or any of the other tourists. Probably she was just busy.

Anyway, I didn't say anything to the other van riders. They looked at me funny every time I tried to add a few of my observations to those of the guide. It's better to try and get along.

We saw the famous North Beach where there is so much activity. Or am I thinking of San Francisco? No, it's the North Beach on Oahu, all right. Danny says they have their biggest waves there, and many times it is too dangerous for surfing. Well, I've seen some of the waves that those TV surfers ride, and when the surf gets too big for the surfers, then I'd just as soon not be on the north side of the island. We had what is known in the tour guide circles as a photo stop, and I must confess waves are impressive.

"North Beach Surf"

After the stop at the beach, we were off to see the botanical gardens. Danny said we would spend an hour there, so we left the van and took a sub-tour around the gardens. Our vehicle was one of those trolley-like vehicles but with open sides, so the passengers could get off and on with ease.

"Native Hut"

We were able to see recreations of the original huts and lifestyles of the local inhabitants before the white men came. We could even get off the trolley and practice spear throwing. I declined saying that spear throwing always made my arm sore, and at my age, I've got to be careful of such activities.

It is often a matter of puzzlement to me when people that have been brought up in a society such as we have in the United States are so enthralled at the prospect of living the way the natives did back in those days. In my youth, we lived in central New Mexico without electricity, telephone, or indoor plumbing. Our running water was when the person carrying the bucket ran.

There is little glamour in such life. We didn't have to throw sharpened sticks for our food, and I believe because of that we were far ahead of the natives back in their good ole days before the white man brought them our version of civilization. Go back to the good ole days if you like, but it's not for me, thank you.

Isn't it interesting that when people describe the grandeur of the days of kings, queens, knights, and their fair ladies, they add that they would like to have lived then? They always picture themselves as one of the four groups just mentioned. If they lived in those days, they would have been more likely to have found themselves living in a hut under most undesirable circumstances.

Even the wealthiest of the good ole days didn't have what is common to most people in the United States today. For me it is to say no, thank you.

I must add, however, the videos we made of the gardens were filled with color and exotic flowers and plants.

As we buzzed along through the center of the island, on our return trip, we passed through the pineapple fields. The guide told us that there are three harvests of the pineapple. The fruit plant bears three times a year. Their first and second harvest produces the largest fruit, and they are used for export. The third harvest produces the smaller fruit, and it is used for local consumption. He also told us that sugar cane is the number one export, with pineapple the second. He said that other countries with cheaper labor were developing their own pineapple fields and the educated guess that in a few years the pineapple fields of Hawaii would be no more than a tourist attraction and for local consumption. That's what he said.

As a note, perhaps you noticed that I said in the beginning that this tour was to circle the island, and just now I said that we were returning through the center of the island. Well, it's all true. It was advertised to circle the island, but the road doesn't go around the northwest portion of the island. We were told that the dopers don't allow anyone through that area even to build a road. The guide was talking about the growers of marijuana. I couldn't believe that it was true, but that's what he said.

The guide asked us if anyone knew why there were no seashells on Waikiki Beach. No one knew the answer. I didn't even know there weren't any there. His answer was, Waikiki was not a natural beach and that it was man-made. The men who built it only imported sand, no seashells.

Well, what a rip off! The whole thing was moved in for the tourists. Now where do you go if you need beach sand? We're not talking about a couple of dump truckloads; we're talking much sand. Where could they get that much sand without it leaving a big hole in the ground? Your first thought might be, "Well, why not get it from some uninhabited island somewhere?" I don't know how easy it is to find uninhabited islands with a beach full of sand. And what about the seashells? Wouldn't all natural beaches have seashells?

It came to me in a flash—Saudi Arabia! That's where all the sand came from to make Waikiki Beach. Not only would it not leave a big hole in the ground, but there would be plenty more where it came from. While everybody else was buying oil from the Saudis, someone was buying sand and putting it all over the oceanfront at Waikiki when no one was looking. Maybe this whole island scene should be investigated by the Congress.

Come to think of it, they may have been in the middle of an investigation even now. There are so many congressmen on the island much of the time, maybe it's the sand scam that they are looking into. It'll be interesting to see the results of their efforts when they are finished. They could be near to completion because they have been working on it a long time. Remember the congressman that was lost on

December 7, 1941? He was on a yacht west of the islands, and it was thought to have been sunk by the Japanese before they attacked Pearl Harbor.

Chances are, the congressman was gathering data on the big Waikiki Sand Gate when his boat was sunk. Who knows, maybe the Japs were mixed up in the deal? He may have been getting too close to the answer. They had to sink his boat to keep him quiet. We may never know the real answer. You know how tough it is to figure out one of those conspiracies.

Danny delivered us back to ground zero in a safe and orderly fashion. He was a very entertaining guide, and I told him so. We had joked back and forth for the entire trip, and he told me it was a lot of fun for him as well. That's what I like to do is have fun with people. Our first tour was a great success. I can recommend it to you without hesitation.

Dateline:
Tokyo, Japan
March 9, 1987

Bye, Bye, Hawaii

The island was beautiful, and the van tour was interesting. Before we were through, we saw the pass that the Japanese flew through on their way to bomb Pearl Harbor.

We drove past Hickam Field and photographed a plaque In Memoriam To. I wonder how many generations it will take before the lump fails to form in your throat as your thoughts go back. Many more, I hope. The tear for the brave, honorable, and the innocent does not conceal any hate for the enemy. I personally got over that a long time ago. The memory of those that died and were injured on December 7, 1941, will be with me forever. I cannot, after many attempts, pass though the Alamo in Texas with a dry eye. Those brave men that chose to die for what they believed must stand as tall as any act of heroism recorded in history. The hate that was necessary to ultimately defeat an enemy should long be gone, but the memory of our heroes' valor should never die. As this is written, there is an attempt here and abroad to rewrite the history that I have lived through. Let it never happen. Regardless of all else, sentiment has no place when recording what really happened. For you, my readers, that didn't live the experience. Be skeptical of those who would like to ignore the part of history that they don't agree with.

It is my feeling that men who choose to wage war for selfish purposes are godless and should be regarded without sympathy. It is very difficult for those that have never studied such things to understand, but it is a matter of logic. War is about terrible things being done by one group of people to another group of people. You shouldn't be surprised to hear of atrocities being perpetrated by those that have to fight for their lives. Neither should you expect only one side to abide by rules set by nonparticipants.

What man would hesitate to save the life of a friend because the rules of war said that combat had to stop at sunset? What group of people would consider not doing whatever was necessary to save the lives of loved ones if it meant taking the lives of the enemy?

Today, there are those that would make the United States guilty of greater sin than the Japanese in World War II. There is enough guilt to go around for all, but you must remember who wanted war and who did not. Remember, it was the Japanese who made a sneak attack on every country they wanted to control. The people of China, Burma, Indo-China, and the Philippines will remember the facts.

Remember, it was the Japanese that not only bombed the innocents and defenseless, but also remember they were well known for their inhuman treatment

251

of civilians on a personal basis. There are many men who could find it possible to drop a bomb large or small from high altitude on the people below, but there are fewer men that could bayonet a baby in its mother's arms.

Those that waged war in the 1930s and 1940s did so during my lifetime. I remember their deeds before what they were doing in Europe, Africa, Asia, and China was a product of the propaganda from our side. Propaganda, of course, is the exaggeration and distortion of the truth to justify the acts of the propagandist. Of course, we were taught to hate. Don't you have to hate to kill? The first thing a soldier must learn to do if he hopes to survive in combat is that he must be better at killing than those he faces in combat. Does that seem cruel? If so, then consider what you would want your son to do to survive.

Remember, war is about killing people and breaking things. If you want your side to win, then you must be willing to destroy the enemies' *will* and *ability* to fight. The end of war for the United States has always been decided by the enemy. We have never declined to stop our war making when the enemy wanted, *unconditionally*, to quit.

All hate for our enemies of the past should be buried with those that transgressed. I don't believe passing hate down through offspring. It is therefore no problem for me to visit the countries of the enemies of my youth. Let us consider others for what they do today, not what their ancestors did in the past.

After all that being said, consider the irony of this: What a strong, dedicated, and aggressive enemy could not do in 1940s, the "dopers" have been able to do in the 1980s. The Japanese would have loved to occupy those islands in the 1940s, but with all their guns, ships, planes, and fanatical dedication they could not. Yet less than two generations later, a few men raising marijuana for no grander purpose than to make money have done what the enemy of the 1940s could not—that is, occupy and control a portion of the Hawaiian Islands. All the power of our federal, state, and local governments are unable or *unwilling* to enforce the law in our own land. The lesson to us may be our need to recognize the unbelievable power that money can influence on the human spirit. If nobody buys, then nobody sells.

Good ol' Northwest Orient got us out of town while we still were able to carry our bags. The real shopping by my better half would start later. A perceived bargain is an opportunity that cannot be denied.

The ride across the large part of the Pacific is always long and tiring even at jet speeds. But there are ways to make it even more tiring than usual. The outstanding irritation for us during that particular long leg was the aggravation of a group of young people onboard who were returning to their homeland. They sat in the nonsmoking area of the airplane and insisted on smoking. Nearby passengers complained several times to the hostess or host and the offenders were admonished to put out their cigarettes. They complied only as long as the warning continued to hang in the air. They promptly lighted new smokes before the person with the warning had disappeared from sight.

Earlier, I spoke of the ugly American. Well, in this case, it was the ugly Japanese. I must say that we never saw a repeat of that type of activity from the Japanese when on the ground. An analysis of such an incident is worthy of consideration regardless what the transgression is or who the transgressors are.

In my opinion, an investigation would find that many of the same factors are present in similar situations. First, the offenders represent affluence. Second, they knowingly flout the authority of the place where their action is observed. Third, they want an audience for their actions. Fourth, they are mostly young people. And fifth, their group represents a country of considerable consequence. You never see such rudeness from the members of third world countries or by individuals who are poor.

It seems that lawlessness has become an international pastime for the youth of many of the established countries in our world. It almost seems a form of national arrogance. Football players (soccer) and their fans have gotten so unruly that games in several parts of the world have had to be dropped from the schedule.

The question is larger than I can address here, but lawlessness can only grow when it is tolerated. However, it is fair to say that the term *ugly foreigners* is not limited to Americans.

Sometimes those long legs on public transportation can be broken up by meeting and chatting with strangers. We met a businessman from Chicago that was a computer expert and salesman for Zenith. I never fully understood why he was going to the Orient, but he very nearly convinced us to skip Tokyo and go directly to Hong Kong.

Our new and friendly expert on Japan told horror stories about the exchange rate, and he had me convinced that it was going to cost us $300 American to ride from the Narita airport to our hotel in Tokyo. Well, he didn't miss it much, just a zero; it was $30. Another expert bites the dust.

I should have been suspicious of that guy when he told me he was a computer expert. Experts shouldn't need to announce themselves. In the early 1970s, I was running a television sales and service store in Houston. It was the beginning of the computer revolution for small business, and I became part of the rush.

Yes, I believed what I heard advertised on TV and rushed right down and bought the biggest and best that radio shack had to offer. Oh yes, the best, why it even had a double disk drive for storage. No hard disks in those days for less than $10,000, remember?

The dealer didn't have a proper printer, so I paid $1,700 for a TI-810 printer. It was a seven-pin dot matrix for you computer types. Now the hardware was crude by today's standards, but it never failed me. No, it was the software that got me,. or didn't get me because there wasn't any software to do the job that I bought the computer to do.

It was a difficult lesson and expensive. All I wanted was an inventory program to track the parts inventory of my TV shop. I got lots of promises, and everyone that I met with a computer considered himself a programmer. It's true, "computer experts" were a dime a dozen in those days and not worth the price.

No one bothered to tell me that an inventory program was one of the most difficult pieces of software to write in those days, and that's the reason there weren't any inventory programs for me to buy. Yes, I should have been suspicious when the Zenith man said he was a computer expert. Come to think of it, he was the perfect picture of a self-proclaimed expert—overdressed, loud, expensive shoes, and too friendly.

It's a good lesson for the reader to remember. I'm just glad he wasn't selling anything because I would have probably bought some.

I had been misled in several other cases regarding our around-the-world trip. To this day, I have not been able to determine the why part. Charlotte says I'm easy.

People give incorrect advice like directions to a place they have never been. Two doctors (Americans by the way) in Riyadh had Charlotte and I convinced that we would miss the best part of our trip if we flew from Bangkok to Singapore.

"By all means, you must ride the train. It is a fabulous experience," said the first doctor.

"That's true, it is breathtaking. You'll be sorry if you miss it," said the second doctor.

"Well, how long a train trip is it anyway? I asked.

"Oh, it's only a couple of hours if I remember correctly. Wouldn't you say so, Doctor?"

"Yes, that's about right. It well seem even less because of the scenery of course," said the second doctor.

That's what the doctors told us. One lied, and the other swore to it. We were so convinced we didn't make airline reservations for that part of the trip.

While in Honk Kong, we found the train trip would take two and half days. The cars were open like the ones you have seen in the movies where the natives ride free on top and hang from the sides of the cars. No, thank you; not for me and my wife. We got airline reservations.

Now why do you suppose those doctors told us such a big windy? I never found them to be out of the ordinary in any other way, but their train ride recommendations stood in need of close examination. The affair did make me wonder about their skills in the medical field.

Our first big shock in Japan came while still in the Narita airport as we were clearing the Immigration agent. He said we had no visa! Well, of course, we didn't have a Japanese visa because our handling agent (Universal Weather in Houston) said we didn't need one.

The Japanese Immigration agent seemed to be better informed than our handling agent on the requirement of the Japanese government for Americans when visiting in Japan. We were informed that without a visa, our visit to Japan would be limited to seventy-two hours. It was pretty easy for me to see how our handler made the mistake. He looked at the date of our arrival and the date of our departure and decided three days equaled seventy-two hours. He got the dates right but the hours wrong.

We had to report back to the airport four hours before our flight, check in, and remain in isolation until our flight left. Our departure time was seventy-six hours after our arrival time. Well, it's no big deal, but it's something you might want to check on when you make your trip.

Now don't laugh, but I didn't know the Japanese drove on the wrong side of the road. The first clue is the way that the bus is facing when you get on it. It should be pointed to your right, but if it's pointing to the left, then you know they are going to drive funny. As far as I'm concerned, there are only two sides to a road—the right side and the wrong side.

It's not a large item, I guess, and not worthy of international mediation, but it looks like that somewhere in my travels I would have been alerted to the driving habits in Japan. No wonder they ship so many cars to the States. We are getting all their factory defects. If a car comes out with the steering wheel on the wrong side, they don't scrap it; they send it to the States!

Of course, it could be worse. A friend of mine that was in Nigeria for five years said that they decided to change the direction of travel on their nation's roads. You know, right lane or left lane. It seems an admirable thing to do, but my friend didn't tell me which way they were changing from. I never did find out because it wasn't what they did but how they decided to do it that became the point of his story.

It seems that the government of Nigeria recognized that to change the primary lane of travel and its direction was going to be a major thing, so that felt the need to work out a plan. The plan was to start commercial or truck traffic going in the new direction on the first of the month, and the rest of the vehicles would start their lane change two weeks later!

The drive from Narita Airport was about an hour, and there was nothing that caught your eye as strange. After all, we were on the other side of the world, right? Where are all the strange sights? If I hadn't known where I was, then I wouldn't even have wondered where I was.

The weather was cold, and it was "spitting" snow. There was little or no wind, so the comfort factor was within our range. It seemed the temperature was just above freezing.

A person shouldn't expect to go on an extended trip and have beautiful weather every day. A little weather adds character to a strange place. Whether it looked it or not, we were in a strange place.

Japan is very Westernized, they say. I don't know who "they" are or exactly what *Westernized* means. It may mean that these strange and foreign people have learned to speak our language and have "seen the light," so they are adopting our manner of living. Yes, it's true they are learning our language and adopting many of our pastimes and customs. But we are east of Japan, so why isn't what they are becoming called Easternized?

Don't be fooled, they are still well rooted in their own heritage. We must not be so vain as to think that our ways are the best. More properly stated, our ways may be the best for us, but our ways may not be the best for other cultures.

If the Japanese continue to do as they have been known to do in the past, then they will soon be marketing books on correcting the English language and on the amended rules of baseball.

We had a room at the Hilton in downtown Tokyo. It was comfortable and without surprises. Before it got too late, we started making preparations for the three days and nights that we had allotted for Tokyo. There was the standard tour service located in the lobby. So after a brief study of the brochures in the little pigeon holes, we chose two tours that looked interesting and might give us an overall look at Japan and Tokyo.

We signed for the evening tour of Tokyo and an all-day tour of the Nikko Shrines. The evening tour combined a Japanese traditional dinner, a visit to the national theater, and a brief stay at a geisha house. The Nikko Shrine tour included a ride on the high-speed train as well as a bus ride, and it looked interesting.

Our evening tour would be on the evening of our first full day in Japan, Wednesday, March 11, 1987. If you are wondering what happened to the tenth, well, we lost it when we crossed the International Date Line halfway across the Pacific Ocean. We hadn't been gone from home three weeks yet, and we were already doing Tokyo.

Dateline:
Tokyo, Japan
March 11, 1987

HELLO, TOKYO

After a good night's rest, we were ready for a breakfast at Hilton's coffee shop on the mezzanine. Everything was neat and clean. The hotel was neat and clean. The city was neat and clean. The country was neat and clean. You want a short description of Japan? It is neat and clean. A more complete description might include words like efficient, polite, picturesque, and busy. Observations past that would include quiet, mannerly, and diligent.

I hate to mention this again, but one of the most memorable events at breakfast, once more, was the loud-mouthed Americans. I have eaten in all types of restaurants, large and small, fancy and plain, expensive and cheap, city and country, domestic and international, and in many years of traveling, there have been very few times that I was embarrassed by people at the next table. That morning in Tokyo, four of my fellow countrymen were acting like they needed to be seen and heard by all in the restaurant.

If I were the employer of such men, I don't think I would want them to represent my company at home or abroad. Boisterous behavior is a sign of poor upbringing in any country. I can't help but try to point out such poor conduct in hope that my readers will know that regardless where you are, someone is always watching.

A short walk out of the hotel just to see a small part of the city was shocking. The slushy snow of the night before was gone, and so was all the evidence on the automobiles passing. They were all clean. There was not a single muddy car in all the traffic that we watched pass. It was like every driver in Tokyo had risen early that morning and washed his car. Either that or there was a giant car wash on the other side of the hotel, and all the traffic was routed through before they passed our way.

I don't believe the part about the car wash, but then it's hard to believe that all the cars were so clean. A little later, I began to note that taxi drivers, when not under hire, would get out and clean their cabs. No wonder they look so nice. A driver must wipe his cab down several times a day. I wonder what would happen if that habit came to the United States?

By the way, we didn't see any old junker cars either. They were all new or nearly new and shinny as well. The taxis had white lace dollies on the back of the seats front and back. All the taxi drivers wore white gloves and caps. It was as if the entire city was on dress review. How did they know we were coming?

Another point of interest was the little mirrors that many of the vehicles wore on the very front of their front fenders. Perhaps you have seen those little mirrors in some of the British movies with the old Jaguars. You know the ones with the long hoods, remember? Well, I don't know if their cars come out of the factory with the mirrors or if the owners add them later. Perhaps they are a fad like the bumper feelers in our own country a few years back. I can't testify to local fads because of the short time I was in Tokyo. I'll have to check out the mirrors on a subsequent visit and let you know.

Our walking tour of downtown Tokyo gave me a chance to check the prices of electronic items. I like to do that in a strange country because it gives me a feeling of the economy. A few years back, I was in the electronic retail business, and I sort of like to stay in touch, you see.

One of the items that I was looking for was a small battery-operated color TV with a three-inch screen. I'm speaking of the LCD or liquid crystal display. I bought one for Charlotte shortly before leaving Houston, and the price at Sam's Club was $169 plus tax. Guess what? I priced that same little Casio TV all over world including Germany, England, Tokyo, Hong Kong, Bangkok, and Singapore, and the best price was at Sam's Club in Houston, Texas. Yes, that's correct. You can say it's because of trade agreements, import duties, export duties, sanctions, or whatever; the result is that we can buy at least some Japanese products cheaper in our country than the Japanese can buy them in their country. Figure that.

A NIGHTTIME TOUR OF TOKYO

Soon it was time to assemble in the lobby of the hotel to go on our nighttime tour. There were fifteen in our group, which surprised me. Somehow I expected there to be an even number. You know, like we would just be couples. Not true, a lone guy was in our little group. Before the tour was over, the reason he was alone became clear. I don't think that guy could have hired someone to go with him, especially if they had been with him before.

Our guide was a very nice Japanese lady of middle age whose voice was soft and her English vocabulary extensive. I assumed it was extensive because she often used words that were not in an American's everyday stock. She used them in an unusual way, enough so as to bring a smile to my face when she described things for the group. A smile still comes when I hear some of the words she used. When it was time for us to "board" the bus, our guide politely asked us to "assemble" on the bus. Well, it worked better for her than if I had tried to say the same thing in Japanese.

TRADITIONAL JAPANESE DINNER

Tour group, not ours, eating raw fish and other things unknown

Our bus ride was not long, and soon we found ourselves parking in front of the place we were to dine. We always parked in front of wherever we were going. It was handy and all arranged.

The traditional dinner at a traditional Japanese restaurant was on the second floor of what seemed to be a very old building. Everything was traditional Japanese, I suppose. It was something just a little less than gaudy.

Charlotte was being a good sport regarding the prospects of what we might be served, but there was a question growing in her mind. I had not given it much thought.

"What if they give us raw fish or something like that?" Charlotte asked.

"Well, you've eaten raw fish before, haven't you?" I replied.

"Yes, but it was in Los Angles, and we knew the reputation of the restaurant, so we knew it was properly prepared."

"Well, the locals here eat it all the time, and they look pretty healthy to me. Don't worry about it, everything will be okay. Besides, how much difference can there be between good and bad preparation of raw fish?"

At a later time, I found the answer to that question when we were living on the French Rivera. The French have their own method of preparing raw fish, but that's another story, and I'll tell you about it sometime when it's not so close to mealtime.

Anyway, I don't think we had raw fish. We had sukiyaki, for one thing. Sukiyaki is sliced meat (beef?), bean curd (?), and other vegetables all stir-fried together. It tasted pretty good.

259

There was so much activity going on among the guests that there was little chance to ask "What is this?" So we mostly tasted first, then ate, if it was palatable. Maybe not knowing was a help.

What we ate was not as memorable as what we didn't eat. My taste in food is quite broad, but there are a few things I don't care for, especially if they seem to move while on the plate.

The *sake* was served in tiny little thimble-like ceramic-looking containers. It was just a taste, but it wasn't something that I thought would catch on. Of course, there was one in our group that demanded the whole bottle. He tried to make a case for his drinking prowess and wanted to show that he could drink the whole bottle and show no ill effects. The management resisted, and our tour member got loud and abusive until he got a bottle, then he decided to have it packaged so he could drink it later.

Charlotte and I have been on several tours after our around-the-world odyssey, and it seems there is always at least one member of a tour group that has to be seen and heard above the rest. This is particularly offensive to me, being a natural-born leader and entertainer.

As far as I could tell, the meal was accepted fair for the group as a whole. I saw no signs of undue discomfort during or after the meal. A pleasant-enough experience, but I don't think the sitting on the floor part will ever catch on, you think?

Visit to a Traditional Japanese Theater

"Kabuki Theater . . . They are all men!"

Now here is something you don't want to miss. The traditional Japanese theater is not like anything you're likely to see in the USA. *ka·bu·ki* also *Ka·bu·ki (k...-b›"* n. "A type of popular Japanese drama, evolved from the older no theater, in which elaborately costumed performers, nowadays men only, use stylized movements, dances, and songs in order to enact tragedies and comedies."

"They are still all men!"

Charlotte was thrilled with the theater. She loves to go to plays anyway, and the National Theatre in Japan was a special treat. She had none of the qualms for the theater as she had shown for the dinner, so we entered the lobby with quiet enthusiasm.

The building might be as you would expect. It was large and ornate—gaudy, perhaps. Bright colors, relief carvings on the wall, with gargoyle-type busts protruding from on high let us know that we were definitely in a Japanese theater.

We were offered headsets or earphones that allowed us to hear the dialogue in English. We accepted them of course. Japanese dialect is not one of my accomplishments. I'm not even very good at interpreting Oriental gestures.

I found, for example, that many Orientals shake their heads no when they mean yes and nod yes when they mean no. This can be a difficult gesture for an American to interpret.The program booklets we received explained in English that all actors on the stage were males. The female parts were played by men dressed as women. It seems an ancient custom forbade women to do "such things" in public places.

Of course, women were allowed to do other things in less than public places. The difference may be too subtle for the uninitiated to understand.

The headsets let us understand the dialogue of all that was being accomplished on the stage, and the music didn't need to be translated. That's an interesting thought, isn't it? Words are used to communicate feelings from one person to another, right? So to communicate feelings with words from one culture to another, they must be translated. Music also communicates feelings between cultures but without translation. Just a thought.

A VISIT TO THE GEISHA HOUSE

The ladies claim to entertain within the bounds of wholesomeness. Well, that's what they said. Now I don't know if you have any preconceived notions of geisha houses. Nothing I say here, I think, should change your present ideas. I say this because we felt that our visit was very much a staged and contrived affair.

I have been told for years the geisha girls were not what everyone in the Western world thought they were. As a sophisticated traveler, an intelligent person endowed with higher than average insight, I have always desired to look past the obvious for the truth, the truth often being hidden from the average observer. I must confess that there was nothing presented to me in our visit to the geisha House that added to my knowledge or understanding of the subject.

"Geisha Girls (?)"

The entrance to the geisha house was tastefully Oriental. We were ushered into a room adequate for our small group of less than twenty people.

Our entry to the room was alongside of a slightly elevated stage. I say slightly because it was only about twelve inches above the floor level of the rest of the room.

The audience was offered folding chairs to rest in, and the chairs were arranged to face the stage. Somehow, I got the idea that we were about to experience a period of low-budget show business.

Three females (?) stepped on to the stage after entering a door from the opposite side of the room where we had entered. As you can gather, there was no curtain like a real stage, only the raised platform in front of us. The entertainers circled on the platform in their short step, hobbled like walk. After the national play, who could be sure about the sex of those on the stage?

Music played, and those on the stage continued to circle. Every now and then, the circling would be interrupted by those on stage exchanging places with others on the stage. It was all done to music of course.

The dancing stopped when one of the dancers began to sing. The other dancers didn't help with the singing, but they stopped their dancing while one of their members did sing. The song was sung in a very quiet and timid manner. I don't have any idea what the words meant because we didn't have the little electronic translators like we had been issued at the National Theatre. However, I feel that if I had been Japanese, or at least been able to understand the words, they would have made me feel warm and tingly inside.

Singing and dancing was what we saw that night. The only conversation we received was from the tour guide. His description of the three small women (?) on the stage in front of us was right out of the dictionary: g**ei·sha** *(g³"sh..., g-) n., pl.* **geisha** *or* **gei·shas**. *"One of a class of professional women in Japan trained from girlhood in conversation, dancing, and singing in order to lend an atmosphere of chic and gaiety to professional or social gatherings of men."*

I'm sorry, but I left the geisha house with the feeling that there was something there that no one told us about. The word *whitewash* comes to mind.

THE NIGHT STREETS OF TOKYO

We left the geisha house and walked back to our van. I would like to report on an overpowering impression that came upon me as we walked.

There were many bicycles and small motorcycles or motorbikes parked on the sidewalk. The word *many* is not the best indicator of just how many bikes and cycles that were parked there. I should have said thousands, and none of them were locked! We didn't see a single chain or lock on the parked vehicles! I'm still impressed by the thought of what we saw that night.

Thieves would have been running over each other if those bikes and cycles were parked on the downtown streets of a large city in the United States. Well, wait a minute. Let me think this through. I remember when our local thieves would steal an old junker of a car if it had an eight-track tape deck inside. It was the same for CB radios; they just weren't safe on the street, day or night.

But have you noticed the practice of stealing CBs and eight tracks have trickled off to nothing? And do you know when thieves stopped stealing CB radios and eight track tapes? It was after everyone had one, and there were no customers left for the stolen property.

The first thing that happens in our country to break the cycle of stealing is when the market goes away. The pawnshops are the first in the chain. When they quit buying, then the thieves lose interest in the product. That very well may be the secret in Tokyo. Cycles and bikes are safe on the streets overnight without locks because everyone has one and no one can ride two. Well, it's the only thing I could come up with. You're free to try one for yourself.

Dateline:
Nikko, Japan
March, 13, 1987

THE NIKKO SHRINE DAY TOUR

The day tour of Nikko Shrines included a high-speed train trip to and from Nikko, which was about seventy-five miles north of Tokyo, lunch at a famous hotel in the mountains, and a bus trip to some lake-side shrines high up in the mountains. We felt that would give us a little variety of sights. We were to find later that it was one of the best decisions of our trip.

Early the next morning, we were making our way to the train station. It was there that we were introduced to the alter egos of those that inhabit the island of Japan. A word of warning, they may seem quiet, courteous, shy, and gentle, but don't get in front of them when they are loading onto a public conveyance of any sort. In a word, they are ruthless. Their method of getting on to a train is as if they had a real bad guy chasing them. Charlotte and I were taller than the group, and we could see where we were being pushed. But if you don't want to go with the group, then you stand well clear before the door opens on the said public conveyance.

You remember from the movies what happened to the Indians when the cowboys stampeded the cattle into them, don't you? I felt I was in a stampede while getting on or off a train in Japan. Fortunately, my wife and I were raised among livestock, so we knew how to take care of ourselves. Those of you without such experience to guide you should be extra careful.

Once onboard and located in our car, the atmosphere was completely changed back to quiet and serene. It was all calm and courteous as before the stampede. Apparently, it's the loading and unloading that created the group's panic mentality.

I noticed there was no graffiti! That's right, none outside or inside the train or station. Don't you wonder why? Maybe there is not enough room. You know, an artist needs a little elbow room, right? He or she needs to be able to at least stand back and admire what they have just created or covered up. There is no room for that in the Japanese train station.

Well, it could be the time. Perhaps they don't have time for graffiti. There was no one just loitering around. NO ONE. Everyone was busy doing something or going somewhere. That's probably it. No one has the time or space for graffiti.

Our seats were comfortable, clean, and spacious, nothing like airline seating. The hostesses were dressed in black with little white aprons and were ready with coffee, tea, or whatever. We were treated with first class service, but as far as I know, there was no such thing as coach class.

The trained moved gently forward as we pulled away from the station. We were on an elevated railway and were able to view the buildings, streets, and traffic

265

without difficulty. My wife and I could talk without discomfort or distraction. It was on the whole relaxing.

Tokyo is a modern city when compared to other large cities of Europe. In my view, the cities of America are modern. The cities of Europe are old, and they look that way. Tokyo does not look old. Change the billboards, and you could be passing through anyone of many cites in the US.

Can I take a moment to comment on train travel in general? I have spent a lifetime in the air, and I love it. I thoroughly dislike driving down the highway mainly because of the other traffic. The driver of an automobile must be constantly on the alert and vigilant for the danger of sudden death that is passing just six feet, or less, off his left elbow when on the open highway. When in cities, he can't relax, or his directions are lost. While his passengers are oohing and aahhing over some sight, he must attend to his driving.

As a pilot, my concentration and close attention to the flying of the aircraft is only required during takeoff and landing. The rest of the trip is mostly spent in enjoying where I am and what I am doing. There is always plenty of time to enjoy the landscape below. It is a very pleasant experience for me. And it is quick. Even in my own small twin-engine aircraft, I'm traveling at three to four times of ground transportation, and besides that, I'm taking the shortcut. It seems to me traveling in an automobile cross-country takes forever.

"A Japanese High-Speed Train"

But a train, ah yes, a train, a modern train that is quiet, air-conditioned, and fast, now that is very nice way to see the sights. In my view, travel on that sort of conveyance, except for the time, is much preferable to any other mode of travel.

Okay, I think I may have lost a few of you on that last comment, so I'll have to add that trains are not good for transoceanic travel. But, if you haven't traveled by modern rail, then you may have missed something worthwhile. Try it, you'll like it. But allow plenty of time, okay?

Time. That reminds me. The Japanese trains are on time, period. If the schedule says departure is 8:05, then the train is going to be pulling out at 8:05. Maybe that's the reason for the stampede. They don't fool around. Be there or be left.

I can't help but make the comparison to the trains in England. In England, the trains run on their own schedule. Never mind what the station schedule says. They come and go on schedule that is not printed down anywhere the passenger can see. If English schedule says 8:05, then the train can be expected to come at any other time but 8:05.

The story goes that once upon a time an English train scheduled for a certain time of arrival actually showed up at that time. An investigation held later determined that in fact the train did arrive at the scheduled time; however, it was due the preceding day.

It is my regret that Charlotte and I never got to ride the trains in France or Germany, but it is still on my list of want-to-do items.

The Japanese countryside was different. The great majority of the land was cultivated. The furrows were straight, precise, ready, and bare. A few traces of snow in the shadows, but none where the sun was shining.

In the US, we are accustomed to seeing broad expanses of green pastures and cultivation now and then. From my train window, I watched mile after mile of very organized farmland pass by. There were open plowed fields with nothing growing. It was March, remember? However, there were many plastic-covered portions of the fields, which appeared to me as hot houses. I haven't seen such a thing in the US, at least not on the same scale.

Our tour guide told us that the hot houses were for the rice seedlings. They would be removed from the controlled environment in April and planted in the ready furrows. The rice harvest would be in the following October. One crop each year.

Yes, rice fields everywhere, and they still have to buy rice from the farmers near Houston, Texas. They really like their bowl of rice, I suppose.

We saw no one working. Perhaps I expected to see workers in the fields, but there were none. It was March, remember? I wonder what all the workers do in the wintertime when there is no fieldwork to be done? Probably, they go to town and practice getting on and off trains.

We arrived at the Nikko station on train number 5 fast, quiet, first class. It was very pleasant experience. The tour bus was waiting, and we met our tour guide—a small Japanese lady with a friendly smile, and an interesting

"Train number 5 at Nikko Station"

267

handle on the English language. "Very well, please now we will all *assemble* on the bus." Still it was better than any attempt that I might make at her language.

It was a short ride later when we arrived at the Nikko Shrines. We "disassembled" off the bus. I say, shrines, because there were many. That's right they represented several of the Oriental or Asian religions. The tour guide remarked that they would appear to be new because they had just been refinished by workers from the country of origin for the religion.

"The Lady Tour Guide"

There were several "billboard" style of hanging shingles of contributors or supporters of the shrines. We were not told of the size of amount of support that was necessary to have a shingle hung there in your honor, but I couldn't help but notice that the shingles came in different sizes.

"Board of Contributors"

More of what I called billboards. There were a lot of contributors, I guess. I wonder how long those shingles will remain on display there? Do you suppose they may have to refresh their contributions? I wonder about such things.

"Another Billboard"

I never did find out what all these "birdhouses" were for. It's a mistake for a person from Texas to try and describe the use of such things in the Orient. Texas logic doesn't fit To describe the shrine tour in a few words would have to include ornate, awesome, and very interesting.

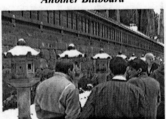

"Birdhouses?"

"A Birdhouse?"

Much ornate sculpture was seen everywhere. The pictures here are an effort to show some of the many different results of the Oriental artists' work. I am afraid my words fall far short.

"Ornate Sculpture"

"More Ornate Sculpture"

"Charlotte leaving one more shrine."
"Your guess is as good as mine."
"Hear No Evil, etc."

Well, enough of the shrine tour. It was well worth the effort. I was able to see something I had never seen before and not likely to see again. The shrines are certainly a testament to the faith of their supporters.

Once again, we assembled on the bus, and after a brief drive through the countryside, we disassembled for lunch at the picturesque hotel in the country. There were few guests that I saw, and none of them had lunch with our bus group. The stop there was hardly more time than that needed for the lunch and a tour of the gift shop. I did note that choral jewelry seemed to be very popular. Of course, I am no authority on such things. It's just that I had noticed that kind of jewelry before. If you look for jewelry in New Mexico, you should expect to see lots of turquoise.

"Hotel for Lunch"
Photo Credit: JDF

After lunch, we once again assembled on the bus and started the ride up the mountain to see the lake on top of the mountain, monkeys along the way, and the dance of the three virgins.

The road itself was of interest to me. We were told that it had eighteen turns going up and twenty-eight turns coming down. The engineering and mathematics of a road that had more turns going one-way than the other seemed incongruous to me. I was later to learn that we would be coming down a different road than the one we had ascended.

"The Road"

Our tour guide assured us that once on top of the mountain, we would be able to see where the lake "emanated"! I was able to control myself at this point, but the urge to help our tour guide was strong. Instead of correcting her, I kept mentioning the need to see this lake emanating.

When I visited Crater Lake in Oregon, I was told that the lake was formed on top on an ancient volcano, and the lake had no outlet. Nothing was ever said about Crater Lake emanating.

Of course, I was spending a lot of time with the video camera trying to catch the monkeys alongside of the road. I found no monkeys or any evidence of monkeys. Maybe early March is not monkey season in Japan.

There was still a lot of snow on top of the mountain, and the lake was a beautiful sight, but the dance of the three virgins was the main feature, and I was ready with the video camera for this chance in a lifetime. Perhaps I was too ready. We had to wait for the dancers to appear on stage, and I had the video camera on standby but not recording. Perhaps I became distracted by the stage supervisor that was seated stage right and front of the empty stage. He couldn't stay awake. His lack of excitement for what we were about to witness had some dampening effect. Maybe I was the only one that noticed, or maybe it was all part of the act. I must remind the reader that all is not as it may appear while in the Orient.

"Excitement Contained"

"An empty stage was all I got on video"

To make a long story longer, I forgot to push the record button on the video camera so the dance of the three virgins was not caught on tape. Fortunately, Charlotte was not distracted, and her still camera caught the dance. You may note, however, that there are only two dancers shown on stage even though all the advertisement was for three.

"Charlotte's still camera caught the virgins"

I was never ever able to find out what happened to the third dancer. None of my fellow passengers seemed to notice or even care. I did notice that after the two young ladies finished their dance and left the stage, they went outside and continued shoveling snow off the walk. Perhaps the third dancer had caught a cold and was unable to dance for us today. There were a couple of other ideas that occurred to me, but no

"Back to shoveling snow"

one seemed to share in my conjectures, so I just let it drop. No one was going to offer a refund or anything like that anyway.

On the way down from the mountain, we stopped at an observation point, and once off the bus, we turned and looked back to see a waterfall. I couldn't help myself but remember, "Look, everybody, the lake is emanating!" Well, I thought it was funny.

"The lake is emanating."

The next day, we had to go to the airport three hours too early because our visas ran out. Perhaps the authorities wouldn't have cared if we overstayed just three hours, but when in a foreign country, I don't want to take any chances.

Dateline:
Nikko, Japan
March 12, 1987

FINAL THOUGHT ON JAPAN

The final point to describe Japan has nothing to do with its aesthetic values, but values certainly. If you plan to travel to Japan or any other foreign country, then you must understand the value of the yen and take plenty of money! Our visit was only a year after the value of the yen was 300 to $1. At the time of our visit, the rate was 158 to $1. The effect is to make the dollar worth only half its value of the year before. You see, the home country's inflation rate can stay at 0 percent, yet to the traveler with foreign currency, the rate appears to be the same as the fluctuation rate of his currency to that of the host country. It can be 200 percent plus or minus. If your budget is limited, then you better pay attention.

Please excuse my simplistic approach at explaining the currency exchange problems of the world, but if you are like myself, then although you have read the papers, the cold hard facts can be a shock to your system if you have never been there and personally exposed to the real value of your money.

Or, if you happen to be rich, then just forget this page.

Dateline:
Hong, Kong
March, 15-17, 1987

A Few Days In Hong Kong

After a pleasant afternoon waiting in the isolation area part of the Narita airport, good ol' Northwest Airlines had us airborne once again. There was time for me to explain to Charlotte my latest plan regarding the money changers. It seems that each one has his own idea about what the exchange rate is at the exact time you want to change your American dollars into the local currency. It may not seem like a large item, but if you spend very much, then the exchange rate can become very important. Besides, I resent being taken advantage of, so we needed a new plan.

"One of the dreaded money changers. After a few dealings with these folks,
you will gain a better understanding of why Christ drove the
money changes from the temple back in biblical times."

We arrived on the little island just off the coast of China, and soon we were passing through the baggage pickup area. I noted the money changer. As soon as we cleared Customs and Immigration, it would be time to put my new plan into effect.

It seemed to me that the best idea was to decide approximately how much we were going to spend and then get it converted at the airport when we first landed. What you did not want to do was to have your money changed by the merchant you were dealing with. The temptation for them to cheat was too great because the likelihood of them being caught was very small. My logic was that probably the airport would be much more under the watchful eye of the government and therefore more honest. In addition, it would simplify not being able to find a money changer if you needed one. Yes, that sounded like a good plan based on sound logic, and it was quickly accepted by my executive vice president.

Passing through Customs and Immigration was simple enough that is we had no problem. Hong Kong was a place where they did not seem interested in how much cash we had with us. Many countries make that an important part of our declaration. The little declaration cards that are handed out by the hostess onboard the aircraft before landing has a place to write down how much cash you have with you. As a nonresident of a foreign country, the United States wants to know why if you carrying more than $10,000 with you when entering the country. They don't care how much you leave with; they just want to know if you are carrying a large sum of cash and why. On this trip, I had to carry a check to pay FlightSafety International for our simulator training, which was $18,000. To protect myself, I requested a letter from the Saudis explaining what the check was for. Of course, I didn't have the check with me since I left it in Georgia with FlightSafety.

In Kenya, Africa, they wanted to know how much money you came in with, and when you left, they wanted to know how much you were leaving with, *and then* they wanted to see receipts for the difference! When I asked the agent for a reason, he pleasantly replied, "Gun runners."

Once clear of the after landing agents, we headed straight for the money changers, and there were several to choose from. "Hey, Charlotte, why don't we go ahead and get our dollars changed into whatever they are using here before we even leave the airport? That will make it easier for tipping, cabs, etc., and we want have to look for one when we get to the hotel?"

Our transaction was quick and simple. It left me with the feeling like I had accomplished something out-of-the-ordinary. Of course, I didn't know at the time the government was going to run them out of the terminal the next day with a knotted rope. They were caught with their exchange rates down or up, as the case may be. We got ripped off again. Not the first and probably not the last. Well, it was my idea, and it did work out for the taxi fare and tipping, etc.

The cab ride to the hotel was straightforward, and even with heavy traffic, we were soon checking into our hotel. It was the Sheraton Hong Kong. We had a corner room on the twelfth floor, and we were ready for the next part of our great adventure. The room was small by US (our standards) but comfortable, and there was no crack in the mattress or covers.

We didn't feel the need for the excitement of the nightlife, so we ate dinner in the hotel coffee shop and retired to our room early.

The excitement for me began the next morning when I looked out our window and saw the construction going on at the building just across the street. The pictures I made with the video camera do not do justice to what I saw. The building across the street was taller than our twelfth floor. Laborers were working on scaffolding that was from the bottom to the top of the building without any safety equipment, and the scaffolding was being constructed of bamboo!

I could not see any means that was used to attach the bamboo to the building. It looked like it was free standing. Even with the zoom lens on camcorder did not reveal its secret. A later examination from the ground showed me that the scaffolding covered three sides of the building at that point of its construction and did have a few connections to the top of the building.

"Just the idea of scaffolding at this height was fascinating to me."

"Workman, up ten floors and no safety equipment."

"He's still hanging on, and guess what he uses to hold the bamboo in place? Plastic ties! And that's it."

"The sidewalk below. Notice, no spots."

To me, the view was interesting from an engineering point of view, but for Charlotte, it was frightening. She said it made her ill to look at those men climbing around the bamboo like Tarzan without any safety equipment. I took a view of the sidewalk below the workers to show her that there were no spots, so everything must be going well. She didn't think that was funny.

I bought a newspaper to go with my bacon and eggs in the hotel coffee shop. On the front page, we read where the authorities had raided the money changer at the airport. The charge was for using exorbitant exchange rates. Oh well, at least we had a plan. The lesson here is that even the best-laid plans sometimes go awry. At the time of our travel, credit cards had not become as universal as they are today. By far, the best way to handle the money changers is to use a credit card. The merchant gets the sales price of an item, less small percent for the company that issued the card, and the buyer gets the exchange rate that is posted by the government for that moment of sale. It's the best way.

If you have never been to Hong Kong, then there may be several things that you would expect to do when you arrive. Seeing the sights in Hong Kong amounts to shopping. Well, what else is there to see? We had heard of the tailor-made clothes, shoes, and etc., so the first thing we did was go down for the fittings.

You have to be much wiser than me if you are to look for name brands in Hong Kong. I'm sure they have some, but I didn't know them, so it was just take a guess and dive in for us. First, we went for the shoes. I got fitted for a pair of handmade loafers of eel skin, Charlotte was fitted for some special snake skin shoes for females, and we were told that they would be ready before our departure. We paid a deposit against a no-show, then proceeded to the next fitting. I needed a pair of prescription sunshades, and Charlotte was fitted as well. The get-ready time for the glasses also coincided with the day before our departure.

Charlotte topped out her shopping with eel skin purses (black and maroon), matching wallets (black and maroon), and matching key cases. Then to top off my shopping, I bought Charlotte a pearl and a gold earring set. No, that wasn't all we bought, but a fellow has to make sure that his wife is taken care of, right?

I did find a very nice Seiko Chronograph, black face, wristwatch for $150, which about a third the price that I had seen the same watch in Riyadh, Frankfurt, and the USA. Oh yes, I got Charlotte a pair of real pearl earrings. Well, how do I know if they were real pearls? The answer is, If you can't tell the difference, then what difference does it make? Besides, Charlotte thinks they are real pearls, and that's all that I care about. There were a few black boxes that I picked up, but those will have to be described in a later writing.

"The local authority. Looks like they come in pairs."

Of course, I should have been suspicious about everything—shoes, bags, and glasses, all taking the same length of time to deliver. As it turned out, we spent one day choosing and getting fitted, and then we would have to spend one day taking delivery on all we had ordered. In the meantime, Charlotte wanted to find a nice Chinese restaurant to try their Peking duck, a favorite of hers.

Now I'm not a fan of duck, regardless of where it came from, but Charlotte insisted that it was something fantastic back home, and therefore it would have to be something beyond description when prepared in its home country. I don't want to sound like a know-it-all, but you see, being just a country boy from Texas, I don't think the best Mexican food is in Mexico nor is the best Italian food in Italy. There are a few things that you can learn even if you're not paying attention. Even back in the States, you should know better than to try ethnic dishes in a cafeteria. Stick with simple stuff there, and you'll be much better off.

That's all that it took for me, so I looked in the yellow pages for a real fine Chinese restaurant. What luck there was one only a couple of blocks away, and no reservations needed. Maybe the no-reservations part should have given me some kind of warning.

Just down the street from the hotel, the Golden Dragon featured Peking duck. We arrived at the restaurant just in time for dinner. Dinnertime is when we get there. There was no problem in ordering the Peking duck dinner for Charlotte. I had something not worth remembering. I have never had a craving for duck dinners, having had one sometime earlier. It was less than impressive. Give me chicken, turkey, dove, or quail for a fowl lunch.

Charlotte's dinner arrived, and she would best describe it as a foul fowl choice for dinner. It was not what Charlotte expected, but it did defy description. She couldn't eat it, and I couldn't look at it. The simple order I made was okay. My wife said that her duck smelled like feathers, and we asked that it be removed from the table. I've seen better-looking birds at an oil spill. A couple of bites, and she was through. As usual, she wanted me to try it. I can never understand why when someone has a distasteful experience, then they want you to try it as well. Do they just want you to be nauseated as well, or do they not trust their own senses? We may never know, but it always happens, doesn't it? Oh well, maybe her dinner was *Hong Kong duck* anyway.

Charlotte has had this experience before and probably will again. Sometime after this trip and while living in France near Marseilles, she told me that she would surely like to try one of her favorite fish dinners that originated in Marseilles. It was called bouillabaisse. That was enough for me. If that is what she wanted, then it was off to Marseilles. It was only about twenty miles east down the Riviera (coast) from our apartment.

You may not believe this, but we drove into the horseshoe-shaped port with all the boats anchored there that is used in *all* the movies of the Riviera. The port is not only lined with anchored boats, large and small, but sports open-air restaurants side by side around the entire port. We walked three-quarters around the dock and chose one that looked like it might be the nicest one we had passed.

It was my choice to eat inside, even though the entire restaurant was open to the outside. The fish dinner was ordered, and again I ordered something less memorable. When Charlotte's fish arrived, it was at least eighteen inches long and stretched over each end of the biggest oval-shaped dinner plate that I have ever seen! It had its mouth open and one eye looking up at you. The fish was afloat in some kind of thin-looking liquid that I didn't recognize and bounded on the north by some miscellaneous vegetables.

Charlotte had cooked one of these fish dinners for me once before, and though not bad, it was not a close second to most any other fish dinner that I have had. Perhaps my opinion is biased because of the saffron used in its perpetration. She sent me to the market to get some saffron for the dinner. What saffron I was sold for the dinner came in a little plastic bag and was the smallest amount of any kind of spice that I had ever seen. It looked something less than a quarter ounce and cost $8. Doubt ran through my mind that the dopers don't get that much for what they sell.

Once again, there in Marseilles a couple of bites, and Charlotte wanted me to try it. Fat chance. I had lived in France for less than a week when they cured me of eating fish in France. Mine came out on the plate looking at me the same as Charlotte's, but mine looked *blue*. I had never eaten a fish that when cooked, looked *blue*. With temerity, I scrapped along the side of the fish with my fork. It still had the scales on it. Then I pushed on the middle of the fish with the same fork, and something squirted out the bottom!

The fish on my plate had not been cleaned, scaled, or cooked. That's why it looked blue. Well, I learned my lesson, and now Charlotte has learned another one.

I have a few photos that were extracted from the camcorder, showing the streets of Hong Kong. Perhaps you might find them interesting, especially the one of Carol Burnet. Did I talk to her? No, but if it's not the one of TV fame, then you tell me.

"Is this really Carol Burnet?"

"Or is this just another look-a-like? But that is a real gold Rolls-Royce convertible in the background."

"A Chinese gold souk could not compare to those we saw in Riyadh, KSA."

"A lot of people on the streets of Hong Kong. I wonder if they were all doing the same thing that we were doing?"

One morning for breakfast in the Sheraton's coffee shop, we sat in a little booth next to a young couple that turned out to be from Baton Rouge, LA. The booths there were not like the ones in the USA. They were more like little cubicles, and the tops were not quite shirt-pocket high. The partitions only reached halfway between your elbow and shoulder, so conversations were easily passed across from one to another.

The young couple was missionaries from the interior of China. They were in Hong Kong for, guess what, shopping. They seemed very excited about running into someone from back home, and our breakfast time became extended. Our new friends wondered why we hadn't planned to visit the Mainland. The simple answer was we didn't speak the language and really had no idea what we wanted to see. It was then we were invited to return, and they would be glad to act as our guides. The idea was very appealing to us, and we promised that we would go home (Riyadh) and give some serious thought to return to see them on the Mainland. We did just that, and the time was going to be at the end of our contract with the Saudis. Alas, it was not to be. You know, circumstances change, and our planed return to the USA via an easterly route was not to be. We wanted to visit friends we had met from Australia as well, but it was not to be. We would still like to go to Australia sometime.

The last day before our departure, we busied ourselves with picking up all that we had paid deposits on. Except for the pearl earrings, our handmade this and that was another disaster. The shoes fit all right, but they started coming undone before we got out of China. After you walked in them a while, they started to turn up on each end. The instep broke down, and you found that you were walking on your instep. The shoes were impossible. The eyeglasses were as bad as the shoes. Charlotte has astigmatism and is a difficult fit. Her glasses were unacceptable at the start. My glasses didn't start to make me cross-eyed until the next week. So when you go to Hong Kong, don't order handmade anything if you're not going to be there long enough to judge the quality!

I guess the high point of our visit to Hong Kong was the last night before leaving. At breakfast Charlotte said,

"Why don't we go to some nice restaurant for dinner this evening? Surely we can find something better than the Golden Dragon."

"Well, there is restaurant in the observation deck of this hotel, I think it would probably be okay. I think they even have entertainment as well as dinner."

My wife agreed to the sound of it, and after breakfast, I went back to the room and made a reservation for dinner for two at 8:00 p.m., next to the window overlooking the bay.

Just before 8:00 p.m., we left our room for the dinner and entertainment on the observation deck of the Hong Kong Sheraton. We were greeted by the maître d' as we entered, and since our reservation was intact, we were ushered directly to our table, which was in a dark comer behind a potted palm!

"Hey, this is no good. I promised this lady a view of the bay and island. We can hardly see the bandstand from here!"

"But, sir, this is all we have at the present time."

"I don't care if this is all you have. My reservation called for a table next to the window with a view. This table is entirely unsatisfactory. Now what are you going to do about it?"

An extra folding bill would do no good because I could see that all the tables were occupied.

281

"Sir, I'm very sorry, but if you would care to wait in the bar, then I am sure that I can have you a satisfactory table in about fifteen minutes. Will that be all right?"

A quick glance at Charlotte told me that she didn't mind the wait, so I agreed to wait in the bar. The maître d' escorted us into the bar and seated us near the door to the dining room. He then said something to the barkeep, turned with a giant smile, bowed, and departed.

Just a short while later, a server arrived at our table, and, we gave him an order for two glasses of white wine, brand and type unspecified. Soon after our order was made, the same young man returned with the wine and two saucers with something that looked like a small crustless sandwich with a toothpick through an olive on top. I say "looked like" because it was too dark in the bar to tell exactly what was on the plates.

As I described to you before, I am naturally suspicious when it comes to food in a strange country. Not being sure about what looked like a small sandwich with a toothpick through an olive on top, I toyed with the toothpick. It seemed to be loose in the olive. It shouldn't be loose if it was truly an olive. About that time I heard a *crunch, crunch* from Charlotte.

"Sweetheart, I don't think that is an olive you are eating. I think t is a raw pigeon egg!"

I didn't get the sentence completed before my sweetheart said, "Uuuhhkk" and grabbed for her napkin. I thought that would be the end of our dinner date, but she was a good sport with a lesson learned; and the cleanup was hardly done when the maître d' returned to escort us to our table by the window.

Now, if you can visualize the room, it would help with the rest of the story. As you entered the door, you would be facing the bandstand with a small dance floor in front. Between the front door and the dance floor were tables for guests that extended to your left to the far wall. To your right was the huge observation window overlooking the Kowloon bay of Hong Kong. There were booths along the window, and there was an aisle that separated the booths from the other tables and the bandstand. The booths were placed along the entire length of the window, all the way to the back wall. Our table was alongside and a little behind the front of the bandstand. The view was great, and we were happy to be there.

Our dinner was ordered, but before it could be served, the entertainment began. On this evening, we were to enjoy the singing of an American young lady that claimed to have just finished a gig in Vegas. She didn't say whether the gig was in Nevada or New Mexico, but she did a satisfactory job with a traveling mic and songs in front of the band on the dance floor. As she sang, she walked by the tables and paid personal attention to the patrons seated there.

But soon, she added a new feature to the act. After each song, she stopped and interviewed the individuals seated at the tables. I saw that she was working her way around the dance floor, and she was moving in our direction.

"Charlotte, you better get ready, that girl is going to be at our table any moment."

The words were hardly out of my mouth when the young singer started over to our table. As she moved in our direction, the spotlight from the front of the room near the entrance stayed with the entertainer. As she drew near, the spotlight was to her back and shining tight in my face. It happened very quickly. With a lovely smiling face, she leaned over the edge of our table and said,

"And you, sir, where are you from?" As she completed her sentence, she quickly poked the mic right into my face. I didn't answer her question, but instead I placed my hand up to shield my eyes from the spotlight and said with an angry voice,

"Get out of here with that thing, I'm out with another man's wife!"

Like I say; it happened quickly. That girl sucked that mic back so fast it left a hole in the air. The smile disappeared, and she was gone. Charlotte and I got a round of applause from the other tables, but the young lady didn't interview any other table that night.

Now, fellows, I do not recommend this for you to try. It might not go over so well with your wife or date as it did with mine. Charlotte was a great sport with the pigeon egg, and she was a great sport with my announcement on the mike. We are still having a laugh when we think of that night—our last in Hong Kong.

Dispatch:
Bangkok, Thailand
March 17-19, 1987

THREE DAYS IN BANGKOK

We're getting the hang of this thing now, but our bags are growing. Our carry-on bags are now five, and I cannot estimate their weight because when I lift them, my brain quits working and doesn't start again until I set them down. After that, my vision is blurred for another hour and forty-five minutes.

Coming out of the baggage area, there stands a young man holding up a sign Oriental Hotel.

"Hey, Charlotte, they are expecting us." The smiling young man gladly helped with the bags, and soon we were in his cab and on the way.

We had been hijacked. That's right, the young man was an independent cabby. I thought he was a driver for the hotel shuttle bus. As it turned out, he was a very enterprising young man, jovial, smiling, and he talking all the way to the hotel. He found out that we wanted to see some of the city's high points that afternoon, and he just happened to have a sister that was a tour guide.

No, no, we didn't need or want a tour guide, but we would use his cab for our afternoon look at the city. At the appointed time of 1430 hours, he was waiting at the curb. His sister Di was with him.

"Welcome to Orient Hotel"

Oh well, whatever, on with the tour.

Looks like the current fad here is to wear stereo headphones and walk around with your mouth open and a real stupid look on your face. Wonder if it's like in the fifties when it was a real sign of affluence if you had a two-way radio in your car? People that couldn't afford the radio but wanted the look just installed the whip antenna with nothing attached to it. Well, who could tell? Or maybe like earlier when you couldn't afford the air conditioner for your car but drove around with the windows up in the summertime. That idea didn't last long in Texas. Maybe there is nothing connected to the headphones at all?

If they do have them hooked up to a Walkman and if they listen as loud as they do without the headphones, then they must be getting a Walkman brain massage. Wonder how long a person can survive that kind of torture without permanent damage? Look on the bright side. We may be raising a generation of young people that can resist our enemies' attempt at brainwashing. The trouble is, I think they may become resistive to everything else as well. A recent scientific study has shown that it takes an IQ of at least fifty-two to keep one's mouth closed when not talking. Watch the Walkman Brigade. Count the number with their mouths open—over 90 percent. Can they recover? Can they be rehabilitated? Only time will tell, and then it will be too late I'm afraid.

Oh, and belt purses are becoming very popular. Everyone is wearing them, young and old. They seem to be good protection against pickpockets.

Charlotte made the mistake of mentioning that she wanted to buy a ring here with the native sapphire stone loud enough for the driver to hear. No problem, he had a "mother" that had a sapphire factory and could take care of all of Charlotte's desires in that category.

As it turned out, "mother's" sapphire factory was actually a government-controlled facility since the government has control of the sale of all native stones. No matter, we were soon inside and shown a vast array of stones in all kinds of settings. We were given complementary refreshments and treated like we were important guests. We never saw "mother," and after *two hours of deliberation,* we left with a token purchase of sapphire jewelry and silk. The jewelry was for Charlotte, and the silk was for me. A doctor friend of mine in Riyadh had a Thai wife that was going to make me some silk shirts if I brought back the silk.

I would have a photo of the jewelry displays inside the factory, but when we stopped to get out of the cab, my foot was caught in my camera strap. When I stepped out of the cab, my foot flung the camera out like a whip and banged it on the pavement. It was broken, so no pictures here. Too bad, it was a building full of blue sapphires.

Returning to the hotel, we passed the royal mansion. We didn't go in. I don't think the king was home anyway, but to our great surprise, we saw a windmill operating in the front yard of the royal mansion. It was not a phony either. It was really operating. The name on the tail was Samson, just like the ones we had back in New Mexico. A beautiful building with beautiful grounds, beautiful shrubbery, and a windmill. I looked for the livestock, but didn't see any.

One of the sights that I found interesting while staying at the Oriental was the dining area overlooking the river. Those little boats that tear up and down that river. What interests me is the motor on rear end. I guess all boat motors are on the rear end, but those on that river have the propeller on the end of a shaft that looks to be ten feet long. Why does those prop shafts have to be so long? Maybe some Thai reader will see this and send me the answer.

"Open-air Restaurant"

"Bangkok Traffic"

The traffic is just as it appears in the picture, but not without a humorous side. It was the little three-wheeled conveyance or taxi, I guess, called the To-To. We were told they were named that because of the sound they made when they started up, i.e., *to-to-to-to-to*. They had seating for a driver and two passengers with a small luggage rack in the back. It is not unusual to see ten people riding the To-To.

"The To-To Taxi"

We had allowed forty minutes to get to the airport, and it took an hour and a half. Traffic was unbelievable, far worse than any we had seen before anywhere on our trip. The terminal was just as bad, wall-to-wall people. Maybe that wasn't so bad after all. Due to overselling or something else, our tickets were upgraded to first class for the trip to Singapore.

Now, first class, that's the way to travel. The seats were so large on the airbus that you need extra pillows to keep from flopping around. Constant hostess attention, yeah, that's the way to travel. But it was with mixed emotions. By this time, we had accumulated ten bags, and they charged us $130 for excess baggage! It was not the sapphires or silk that we bought in Bangkok, but all the junk we had picked up in Hong Kong.

We had fallen for the advertising that made you think that anything you got in Hong Kong was going to be very cheap. Well, it was . . . cheap. We bought shoes, eyeglasses, etc. The shoes came apart in thirty days, the sunglasses almost made me cross-eyed, and the etc. just didn't last at all. The only good deal was the Seiko watch.

287

Dateline:
Singapore
March, 19-21, 1987

SINGAPORE IN THE RAIN

The flight from Bangkok was only two hours and ten minutes, but it was all very fine. First class on the airline is easy to get used to.

It was easy to tell we had left the cold temperatures and had arrived in the tropics. Lots of palm trees, and they are still driving on the wrong side of the road. Regardless of the side of the road we were on, we had to note the cleanliness of the countryside, the road, everything was clean—neat. The only other place that I have been that impressed me in such a way was Salt Lake City, Utah. That's a very clean city also.

Did you know that Singapore in only eighty-five miles north of the Equator? A little further information from the encyclopedia will tell you that Singapore is a city-state made up of sixty-three islands, was controlled by the British until WW II, and then occupied by the Japanese. It became self-controlled in 1965 and since becoming independent has become the fourth leading financial center of the world!

Our transportation from the airport was nonremarkable, but our hotel was. The Shangri-La Hotel, Singapore is a five-star hotel because they don't have such things as a ten star!

There's not a lot for me to tell about Singapore except the beautiful hotel, the camera shop, and the rain. That's right, for three days we mostly watched it rain.

I had broken my still-picture camera in Bangkok, and the video camera was beginning to show signs of less-than-satisfactory operation as well. Well, it was the end of a long trip, so just might as well sit back and enjoy watching it rain. We would see little of that on our return to the Kingdom.

The first day, I noticed a camera shop on the ground floor of the hotel.

"Hello there. I wonder if you could help me. I have a Pentax camera that has been dropped and doesn't seem to work anymore. Do you have a repair center that could perhaps help me?"

That's the way the conversation started, and before it was over, I was assured that their repair facility could make my camera like new or better.

"Oh yes, but it must be done by Friday," I added.

"If you can't have it finished by Friday, then I won't leave it because we are leaving on Saturday."

Again, I was assured that would be no problem. Well, I would certainly keep my eye on them to make sure. It's a little chancy leaving something in strange hands when you are in a foreign country. I didn't think the camera was bad broke. The big problem for me would have been to get the thing open. Also, I felt that if it could be repaired locally, it would save a lot of hassle with the mail.

I wasn't the only one making discoveries. Charlotte had found a jewelry shop not far from the camera shop.

Friday morning, I was back in the camera shop asking about my camera. They assured me it would be in at most any moment. At lunchtime I made another inquiry with the same results. That afternoon, while it was still raining, I made another trip into the camera shop. This time I made it clear that tomorrow morning I expected to have my camera returned repaired or not, but I wanted that camera back! Their assurances were overflowing accompanied by much bowing. I was getting a bad feeling about those little guys working in the camera shop.

Charlotte was still able to resist the jewelry shop, but I wasn't too sure how long she would be able to hold out. Our tickets were for early afternoon Saturday, and they couldn't be changed. In addition, it was the weekend, and any delay would carry us over until Monday, and the camera was not worth all that.

Scrambled eggs, toast, coffee, and orange juice the next morning, and soon the camera shop would be open. I gave them an extra hour for deliveries to be made and then made my entrance.

"Good morning, I am here to pick up my Pentax camera."

"Oh, I am so sorry, sir, please, but we have not received our delivery yet this morning. I am sure it will be arriving soon."

"I don't believe a word you are telling me. Here is what I believe. The camera has been repaired, and you are holding it back so that I will have to leave, and you will have free camera, or it has not been repaired, and you have been lying to me all along. Now here is what's going to happen. I am going upstairs and get my gun, and when I come back, I'm going to have my camera, or someone is going to be real sorry. Do you get me?"

The reader should understand that I was dressed in jeans, cowboy shirt, and a Stetson hat. Maybe I looked a little like an actor from a Hollywood Western, but when I returned at lunchtime, the camera shop had my camera with an insignificant bill attached. My daddy told me to never bluff, and I can't remember another time in my life that I did. Maybe it was the atmosphere. Maybe it was the way the little guys looked at me when I had my steam up, but I didn't have a gun upstairs or anywhere short of Houston, so I guess it was a bluff. I still don't know what I would have done if they had not returned my camera. I guess they didn't know either.

"Hmm, very tempting (photo was made after camera repair."

The trip to the airport was a nonevent, but once more, we had a problem with the airlines. Our scheduled final leg from Singapore to Riyadh was canceled! What? Now what are we going to do? I made such a scene when they told me that we would be going Jeddah instead of Riyadh that they upgraded us again to first class! I thought that we had just scored another coup until I found out that we would arrive in Jeddah at about 10:00 p.m. and couldn't get out to Riyadh until 6:30 the next morning! Before we got out of sight, they charged me another $375 for excess baggage. Have you ever set up from 10:00 p.m. to 6:30 a.m. in an airport?

What an end to the great adventure.

CAF Letter:
Riyadh, Saudi Arabia
May 5, 1987

Dear Henryetta,

Thank you for the nice long letter. It is always so interesting to read one of your letters. James commented that Henryetta must have been a secretary, and I told him you were for many years.

I had forgotten about your trip to the Orient until you mentioned it in your letter, then I remembered. We covered much of the same territory. It was such a fast trip seemingly because we were not in one place longer than four days at a time. As you know that your arrival day and departure day is pretty much lost as you don't do much shopping or sightseeing on those days. We may never have another around-the-world trip, but it was fun to do once. When we were in Hong Kong, we met two young missionaries, and they spoke the Chinese language well enough that they said if we ever came back, then look them up, and they would take us through China. That is something that James wants to do someday. It is strange how we met. We were having Sunday brunch, and there were no tables left, so this couple asked us if they could share our table, and of course, we were delighted to have someone from the States that could speak English. They were from Louisiana, so naturally that made it easy for us to talk to them, especially James because he knew of their hometown.

This has been a great experience for us to travel and live in a foreign country, especially Saudi Arabia where the dress and customs are so very different from the Western world. For once in a lifetime, it is like reversing places, and now we are looked upon as the foreigner. That in itself is a strange feeling. Your employer has complete control over where you go and what you do, almost. They are required to provide a place to live with complete accommodations, transportation, and they control your exit from the country. We are required to have an exit and reentry visa if we leave the country. James has a multiple exit and reentry visa all the time for any trip he is flying, but I have to make a special request for an exit visa. Then if I do not use it within sixty days, I have to pay a fine, which is quite a high figure. Can't remember offhand how much it is, but it is enough to discourage people from applying for it unless they are serious about leaving. We were shocked to find out that just less than half of the population of S A is expatriates. There is a large number of Koreans that handle construction, British who staff the schools and hospitals, and Americans that are associated with the oil industry, airlines, and some are involved with agriculture, water purification, etc. We have a Jordanian compound manager, and the dispatcher at the hangar is a South African that comes from British ancestors. Most of the cleanup crew here at the compound that also do housework, laundry, and ironing are Sri Lankans (men only). Women are not allowed to work over here unless they are associated with the medical field or education.

Living here is not unlike living in apartments at home. This is a regular Peyton place. Maybe the book originated here. I think James could write a best seller based on the characters we have here at this compound. Hans (Hans Pelie, a mechanic with Medevac) is involved with a Thai woman in Bangkok who is married to someone else, and she wants Hans to help her get a divorce and marry her. He is older than I am, and she is about twenty-five years old. That is just one small incident to what really goes on around here.

It is good to hear that you are back in good health now. I'll bet you feel much better now that you have recovered from you operation, and thank goodness, you have escaped any further malignancy. Apparently, you had a competent surgeon and good postoperative care.

CAF Letter:
Riyadh, Saudi Arabia
May 5, 1987

Dear Judie,

Jeanie Shelton sent me your letter of March 8, and congratulations on your ownership of the Brandon Inn. Sounds like an excellent idea for you and Bill.

You no doubt have knowledge that after James and I were married, we came to Saudi Arabia. James retired after thirty-eight years with Exxon USA, and since he is a jet pilot, he was offered a job flying over here for the Saudi Government Medevac program. His immediate superior is a Saudi Army major who reports to Prince Sultan. Most of his missions are transferring very sick people; however, sometimes he will fly a VIP mission. Occasionally, he will fly an international trip. He has had several trips to Africa, one to Frankfurt, Germany, one to Morocco, and a few days ago, he flew to London. It is amazing to me, as I have done very little traveling, that one's perspective can change so much when exposed to different cultures and conditions.

I have enjoyed so much being out of the Los Angeles rat race, and obviously, you and Bill must be enjoying the same. When I go back for a visit, I am all excited to see my friends and family, but the smog and tension start giving me a headache that doesn't leave until my departure from there. When James and I married, I left Bromar, sold my house, put my personal possessions in storage, and changed my entire way of life by coming with James to Riyadh, Saudi Arabia.

We came back to the States in February and came through Boston customs en route to Savannah, Georgia where James was going for FlightSafety school. We thought about you and Bill and talked about how we wish we had time to stop and see you. I would like to have you and Bill meet James and have him meet you. I showed him where you used to live on Monterey Road when we were in San Marino, but I am sure that he will not be able to put everything together that I have told him until you meet.

It is so interesting to us that you should choose to become involved in the inn business. We have been negotiating with a young man, who is the executive chef here at the Riyadh Marriott Hotel, to be partners with him in a restaurant venture in Barcelona, Spain, once our tour of duty is over in SA. James would like to have a business interest to keep him occupied since he doesn't know how to retire otherwise. About all he would have to offer to running the business would be to computerize the portions and print the daily specials. The chef is from Boston originally and grew up with parents that owned a restaurant. The reason for us talking about going to Barcelona is because this fellow is married to a girl from there. In her background, her mother has been manager of Cartier in Barcelona for fifteen years, and she feels that her mother will use her influence to send her clientele to the restaurant. The chef says that the town much needs a restaurant with atmosphere, which is what he wants to create, and we can vouch for his food, which is quality cooking. We will just have to wait and see if we will actually get involved with this venture. Probably if someone offered James a flying job, he would rather take it. Once a pilot always a pilot.

Saudi is the same as Exxon was on age. When a pilot reached sixty years, he can no longer fly for them, and James will be sixty on January 3, 1989. The reason he left Exxon early was because they offered early retirement the same as it would be at age sixty, plus a bonus if he took it. The deal was too good to turn down. As long as a pilot keeps current with his rating, he can fly after age sixty if anyone is willing to hire him. Some private individuals do hire older pilots, especially if they are jet pilots rated on their type of aircraft. Experience in that business is worth considerable.

Well, Judie, I won't bore you with anymore of this. We certainly would love to hear from you and would like to know what prompted you to choose the Brandon Inn over the other ninety-nine inspected. You obviously like New England, and being from California, what is it you like in preference to California? Are you enjoying the winter sports? I have known several people that went to New England to settle there. I used to have an uncle and aunt in Ridgefield, Connecticut, and still have cousins in Westchester County, New York. You see, my father was from Brooklyn, and all of his family remained in the east.

He was a Princeton alumni, year 1904, and several years after he left Princeton, he went west on the railroad to Texas. He met my mother there, married, and remained in the Southwest thereafter. They lived a short time in Texas and then went to New Mexico. My father taught school there for thirty-five years and was a real pioneer. His first schoolroom was one room with student ages ranging from first grade through eighth grade. So much for that. It makes me think about that part of the family when I think of New England and wonder if I would have liked it if my parents had settled there instead of what they did.

Judie, I know you will not have much time for letter writing now that you are so involved with a new project, but when you have time, we certainly would love to hear from you. Don't be surprised if we drop by one of these days.

Love,
Charlotte

Dispatch:
Riyadh, Saudi Arabia
May 25, 1987

THE DESERT FOX DISCOVERS RAMADAN!

I've been hearing of Ramadan ever since I arrived in the Kingdom, but to me, it was just another funny-sounding Arabic word. I had no idea of its meaning or the effect that it would have on me and others around me. After living through the experience, I just had to set down my impressions. Please don't expect the following to be a technically exact, but rather just a kawajee's opinions of what is happening around him. To the Moslem, Ramadan is the holy month. According to those that study the Quran, this is the month that God has used in the past to speak to his prophets. They believe that during this month, God spoke to Abraham on the mountain when he was about to sacrifice his son, and to Moses when he was about to cross into the Promised Land, and to Jesus after his forty days of fasting in the desert, and then again to Mohammed (peace be upon him). Yes, their Quran contains elements of the Old Testament. It is very difficult to verify all this because I have seen no English translations of the Quran, but we listen to some of the radio broadcasts that tell of such things.

The month of Ramadan is the tenth month of the Arabic year, which is now in the year 1407. It was almost the same as our month of May this year. Each month of their calendar begins on the first day of the full or new moon. The exact time and day of the beginning and ending is set by the holy men. The exact day is not known until only one or two days before when the public notice is made by the holy men. Let me assure you that this is a very serious matter. The exact time of beginning and ending is very important. One of the rules for observing Ramadan calls for fasting during the daylight hours. This includes anything that passes through the mouth. No water, cigarettes, chewing gum, nothing is allowed from sunup until sundown. For the purposes of convenience (?), a specific time is set for sunup and sundown for the whole month, even though the exact time of their occurrence varies. The time for sunup is 0600, I think, and the time for sundown is 1830. The specific times become very important for enforcement of the rules. Actual sundown as seen by the eye is too flexible; they need an exact time if they are going to "nail" you. Prayers are still scheduled for six times a day as usual.

There are other rules that are associated with the observance of Ramadan, and I won't pretend to be familiar with all of them. Some of the customs that we have heard or read about should not be confused with the observance of Ramadan. One that is generally known in the Western world is the annual pilgrimage to Mecca. To Moslems, the pilgrimage to Mecca is approximately the same as baptism for the Christian, and I don't know what for the Jew. It is sort of the public profession of

295

faith. All Moslems are expected to make at least one trip to Mecca. If they can go each year, then that's okay, but they need to go at least once. If they are poor and cannot make the trip, then that is okay also, but the pressure is there to do it at least once. Many Moslems make a pilgrimage to Mecca during Ramadan, but the real time for the pilgrimage is during Haj (sounds like the word *hodge*, without the *d*), which is during the last part of July this year. At that time, the Kingdom's population increases by more than 20 percent. The Saudis have a great problem getting them all to leave, but that's another story, and I'll know more about that later.

Prior to our first experience with Ramadan, we heard a few remarks and references made, but we didn't attach much significance to them. Now that we have seen firsthand what really happens, we understand why so many wish to leave the Kingdom during that month. For a Westerner or non-Moslem, to break the rules of fasting, for example, it can mean immediate expulsion from the Kingdom. They take it as an insult to their religion. That is not an Arab rule; it is a Saudi rule. You must constantly be on guard to obey the rules of fasting in public. People have been pulled over by the police for smoking or chewing gum in their cars as they drive down the road!

The local participants fast during the day as required, but they stay up all night and eat and visit with friends and relatives. The souks (stores) are closed during the day and open at night. Well, they are sort of closed during the day and open at night. They all have different hours of doing each. The post office is closed all day and opens at night from 2200 to 0100 (10:00 p.m. to 1:00 a.m.). The workers are in a constant state of irritation due to the fasting, staying up all night, and sleeping during the day except for an hour or so when they may come to work. By the time the month is drawing to a close, everyone has gone crazy, participants and nonparticipants alike. I finally got to the point that I would not get involved in the nighttime traffic; the drivers were just too wild.

The Medevac hangar was completely screwed up. Our regular roster has six captains and six copilots. Four of the copilots left the country, one of the American captains left the country (he knew better than the rest of us), and the two Saudi captains were gone most of the month. That left five of us to do the job of twelve. Pretty soon, the two copilots refused the workload, so the captains ended up flying with each other. That wasn't as bad as it might sound because the workload slowed down with everything else.

One of the copilots explained what his twenty-four-hour period was like. At 1830 in the evening, they break their fast. They have a big meal, and afterward, the men go outside and visit until midnight when they eat again. Then they visit again until 0400 or *fajr* (dawn), the first prayer of the day. They have a big meal after the prayer and just before sunup. After the meal, they go to bed. Between the meals at night, they do whatever shopping they may have to do. The daytime is for sleeping, and if they must go to work, then it is just for an hour or so.

During the month, one of the Western captains and a copilot had a cuss fight and vowed never to speak or fly together again. A Western captain and a Saudi captain had a cuss fight in the airplane on the ground, and they have now taken vows to never fly together again. The water fountains are all closed for the month, and those nonbelievers are required to drink water, eat their meals, and smoke cigarettes out of sight. There is a little coffee room on the second floor of hangar-office complex. It is awful busy during Ramadan. The smoke is so thick you can hardly breathe while you are drinking your coffee. It's like the high school boys that had to smoke in the restrooms. A couple of times, I forgot and almost took my coffee with me to leave the room. Fortunately, someone reminded me before I got out the door.

Ramadan is followed by Eid, several days of *feasting*. During Eid, everything closes down, and the participants break their fast. The first morning of Eid is like Easter or Christmas—it is the one day of the year that everybody goes to church. The biggest of all services at the mosque are on that morning. The service lasts until noon, and after that, it's several days of a big blowout. The local television shows nothing but services at the mosque. The expats are having their own Eid parties. We were invited to several, but declined to go. We were ready for a rest. Fifteen days after Eid, we were still unable to buy stamps at the local post office; they had run out and just didn't have any.

"Do you have any stamps?"

"No, they are finish, finish."

"Will you have some soon?"

"Maybe next week, they are finish."

That exchange means, they have no stamps at the present time, and next week they may or may not have them. Maybe so. I think.

There are reports of traffic accidents that were caused by drivers passing out from fasting. Well, maybe they just went to sleep from staying up all night. The Western drivers agree that they only get out into traffic when it is absolutely necessary. The local drivers are just too much to deal with during this time.

For the enforcement of the rules, there are many extra police hired just for the month of Ramadan. Most of them are Bedouins, fresh out of the desert and do not speak English. In many cases, they are not even literate. So, if you have any kind of problem, you go to jail. They'll sort it out later when someone comes in that speaks English—maybe.

My friend Phil Hardy was out jogging the other night. He was running around the outside of the perimeter of the compound. It's about the same as around a city block. On the back side, he was nearly run down by two men in a Toyota patrol vehicle, a sort of enclosed, four-wheel-drive vehicle. He dodged the first pass, but when he saw them turn around and come back for a second pass, he really put on the speed trying to get out of their way first, and second maybe he could make it back to the main gate of the compound. He did make the corner, but they caught him on the straightaway.

They could not speak English, so while they poked and punched, they took him to jail. Resistance comes slowly here because when you don't speak the same language, it's easy to misunderstand just what is going on until it is too late to resist.

After arriving at the police station, they found someone who spoke a little English. It was at this time that he found that he had been arrested for drunkenness. The guy is a Mormon. He wouldn't smell of an empty bottle. He doesn't drink coffee or tea, and they arrested him for being drunk. During the interrogation, the English speaker asked who he worked for. When he replied Prince Sultan (the second in line for the throne and head of the Royal Air Force), they all got the message and came to attention and started saluting with both hands. They bowed and apologized, offered him Arabic coffee and tea. They don't know about Mormons, but they do know about Prince Sultan. He said they took him back to the compound, speaking Arabic and smiling all the way. It was an honest mistake. Why else would a grown man be out running down the road in his underwear at 10:00 at night? He had to be drunk. I've never been able to prove it, but always knew that jogging was bad for you.

Texans whipped the Mexicans at San Jacinto, even though the Mexicans outnumbered them many times over. The Texans attacked during the Mexicans siesta (afternoon nap). Well, that's dirty. It's as bad as the Yankee's licking the British. The Yankees just hid behind trees. It wasn't their fault the British insisted on wearing red coats and walking in straight lines! If a foreign power ever wanted to overthrow this Kingdom, then all they have to do is attack during Ramadan. You read of the Iraqi attack of the US naval vessel *Stark*? Hey, it was during Ramadan. The guy had been fasting all day, and they had him flying all night. What do you expect? He was about to pass out when he attacked the *Stark*.

JDF Letter :
Riyadh, Saudi Arabia
May 7, 1987

To my sons, daughters-in-law, and grandchildren of all sorts,

Well, guess what? We're coming back for a visit. You probably think we just left from the last visit. Even so, here we come again. This time, we will spend a little more time with you than we had time to spend the last time we were in Houston. The basic plan is to arrive in Houston in time to go to the Fox reunion in Wichita Falls on the third weekend in September. That should be the nineteenth and twentieth; however, it is not official yet.

I just talked to Richard Fox, my cousin in Fort Worth, and he said the date had not been made official yet, but would notify me if it was set otherwise. I will include phone numbers and addresses with this letter so you can make your own inquiries. It is about time that you assumed a little more active role in the Fox family reunion on your own, perhaps.

Do you remember the reunion has happened every year without interruption for over a hundred years? It may take some effort from the Houston branch to keep it going. I'll have to give my uncle Roy credit for a great deal of the effort during my generation. Who knows who will push for your generation?

Our arrival date is not certain yet, but hopefully, it will be around the seventeenth of September. There are a lot of arrangements to be made here before we can leave. I put our passports in yesterday for update, and Saturday, the first day of the week here, I will put in my leave request. There is a real shortage of pilots here at the present time, but I expect to leave anyway. My contract is up the last of August; however, it is our expectation to sign another contract to continue until January 1989. I'll be sixty years old then, and time to start a new adventure.

We are still negotiating on El Zoro's Retreat, a Neat Place to Eat. In fact, our potential partner and chef is in Barcelona at this time looking for a good location. Don't be surprised if it happens. If it does, we will rent a house large enough for you all to visit. Perhaps not all at the same time, but wouldn't that be great fun?

Another scenario is for us to go to Washington DC to live while I attend the Naval War College at the Pentagon. Hadn't heard about that? Well, it seems that the army is considering promoting me to colonel again, and if they do, then I would have to complete the Naval War College before I could be considered for the next promotion to brigadier general. No, of course not, they would never do anything like that, would they? Who knows? Stranger things have happened. The army really can't figure out what I'm doing over here in the first place. Perhaps they will think that I'm on a secret mission for Lieutentant Colonel. North.

I've been doing some writing, and Charlotte has been doing some cooking. I think she is getting better faster than I am. We have met a lot of new acquaintances, and one couple is here on a diplomatic passport. The wife is the daughter of a US congressman (democrat.) and has done some writing of her own. She has a brother that is a writer by profession, and she has promised to help me with my efforts. The help would be to judge whether my material is of interest and worthy of publishing. If it never gets published, then I wouldn't be surprised, but if I could get any of it published, then I will feel that I accomplished something of real value and have something else to leave for those to follow that might care.

Have you ever thought what a waste it is to spend a lifetime learning life's lessons and small bits of wisdom and then not be able to pass it on to you descendants? What a shame that each of us must learn all the lessons again. Well, you boys never met my father, and that is a real loss; you would have loved him. In the first place, he really loved children, and they all loved him. He was not a clown, but he was an entertainer as far as the children were concerned. You probably remember some of his quotes that I have repeated, and I wish that I remembered more. When my father spoke, I listened, and not because I was afraid of him; he never ever laid a hand on me. No, I listened because I respected him and recognized his wisdom. Yes, wisdom from a man with a third-grade education. I would have been wiser to have followed more of his suggestions than I did. The point is that there is very little left of him now. An old leather wallet, a few bits and scraps of paper, even the photographs are scarce.

Through all that has happened to me in the last year, I don't even have a photo of my own father, but I'll never forget him. When he thought I was old enough, he began the father-son talks. It was not exactly the way you may have seen it portrayed in the movies, but his talks had a lasting impression on me. Now my sons and their children will never know about my father, except perhaps if I could pass along a little of what I know about him.

That's the real reason we go to reunions. The chain of knowledge of our ancestors should continue, and this is a great way to do it. All of this is said just to invite you to go. If you can, make plans now because we are. It would be great fun for us all. Besides, I'll probably win a prize for the Fox coming the longest distance to the reunion. Hang in there!

> Love from the old couple, James and Charlotte
> Enclosures: Fox family phone numbers—personal

Dear Greg, Mary, David, Sandy, John, and Gail,

Just a little note to add a couple of items to the main letter. Number one is transportation. It would be good, Greg, if you were able to finish with the little Lincoln prior to our arrival. I don't mean for you to do the work, but to see that it is done. You know, tags, safety, etc. It will be more economical for me to spend the money on that car than to spend it on renting a car. I don't want to have to borrow one again; besides if it needs an exhaust system, carburetor, and front-end work, then do it, and maybe Mary would gain enough confidence to drive it. It will be better driven than sitting. We would expect to drive it to Wichita Falls to the reunion.

Perhaps you could share your van with your brothers; however, that's up to you. I understand the problem with the children. I was just thinking about saving expenses. We need to be in a separate vehicle because we will not be leaving directly after the reunion. There are some people there that I would like to see that won't be at the reunion.

In the meantime, I would still like to get that Jaguar out of your driveway. How are you progressing on that project? I know you are busy, but that is your way of life. Would you want it any different? If so, then now is the time to start changing. I don't think that you, Greg, are that much different than myself. You'll always have more projects than you can handle. Well, why not? Just see if you can slip mine in the queue when you can. The sooner you do, then the sooner it will be gone from sight. See you soon.

Dear Jimmy, Colleen, Ryan, Jamie,

Just a little note to add to the main one. Sure hope you can attend the reunion. It should be fun for the kids too. I don't get to talk to you as much as I would like. Perhaps I could make a deal. You can call me for about a third of what it costs me to call you; therefore, it's a practical idea for you to call me and then let me reimburse you. Please feel free to call, and I'll pay for it, how's that?

Dear Chuck,

Hope that you can get off for the weekend mentioned in the above letter. Perhaps you could ride with your big brother in his van. I'm trying to get Greg to finish up the Lincoln so that it will make the trip to Wichita Falls. I'm hoping that Margreetand Louise will be there, but they may come to Houston and then I would be obligated to give them a ride. Also, we may not be coming directly back to Houston. Otherwise, I would invite you and Lisa to ride with us. See you soon.

CAF'S Journal:
Riyadh, Saudi Arabia
July 9, 1987

FROM CHARLOTTE'S JOURNAL

Wednesday, July 9, 1987:

Our friends Joe and Renati had a baby girl born at 7:00 a.m. today, weighed 7 pounds and named Sylvia. She was born in Barcelona, Spain, and Joe (Joe Yashinski) is leaving Riyadh tomorrow morning to join his family.

Oh, didn't I tell you about Joe Yashinski? Well, Joe is the head (chief) chef at the Marriot in Riyadh. We met Joe there at the Marriot one day when he was visiting patrons in the dining room. Joe was wearing his tall white chef's hat and white chef's uniform. When he stopped at our table, I had to ask, "What is a nice guy like you doing here?" It was a comical question, but Joe answered seriously,

"I'm just working here until I can open my own restaurant somewhere."

"Well, where would that be, Joe?"

"I'd like to open one in Barcelona, Spain," Joe replied.

"Why Barcelona?"

"Well, you see, my wife's home is in Barcelona."

"Well, Joe, what are you waiting for?"

"Money is what I'm waiting for," Joe stated.

"How much do you figure you will need to open a restaurant?"

"I think that $100,000 would probably be enough for what I have in mind."

"Joe, this may sound personal, but how much do you have saved?"

"Oh, I don't mind telling you. I have $50,000 saved up, but it is coming slowly, and now we are going to have a baby. That will probably slow things up a bit."

This conversation was beginning to sound interesting to me. Joe had told me that he was twenty-eight years old. For a young man just twenty-eight and already with $50,000 in the bank was nothing like average to my thinking.

This conversation was extended by my telling Joe that I might consider being a partner with him if we could agree on the details. The next step was for Charlotte to invite Joe out to our apartment in Nasseem for dinner! That's right, my wife the great sport had just invited the chief chef of the Marriot out to dinner. Think about that.

Joe told us that his wife was returning to Spain in two days to have her baby there with her folks, and he was going to stay behind; therefore, he would be glad to accept the invitation.

Subsequently, I told Joe that I would match his investment with my own, and we would be fifty-fifty partners. He would handle the cooking, and Charlotte and

I would handle the front. He thought it was a great idea and would find us location when he joined his wife in Spain in a few weeks.

We talked some more about the type of restaurant that we would have. Joe said we could have a "white tablecloth type" shop in downtown Barcelona or a quick-food type on the beach. I told him that I would leave the choice up to him.

Joe had talked of his background earlier and told us that he had been raised in a restaurant in Boston. His father and his uncle owned one there. Further, Joe had always wanted to be a cook, and the results were easily judged at the Marriot, our favorite place to eat in Riyadh.

So the deal was set. We waited anxiously for Joe's return from Spain to see what our next adventure might be. Joe's return was with disappointing news. He found that in the two years since he first had the idea of a restaurant in Barcelona, the Japanese had moved in, and the price for a location like he wanted had doubled! It would cost at least $200,000 to get started. Well, that killed the deal for both of us. Joe didn't have that much money, and neither did I. Neither of us ever mentioned borrowing the needed amount. I had figured that our original deal would be workable, i.e., each contributed an equal amount in cash and an equal amount in talent. I knew better than to be a partner with someone that had nothing to lose but his time. I had been down that road before, and it is a road with an unhappy ending.

So we didn't get into that adventure, and looking back from a distance, we are both glad that it never happened. However, we were seriously committed for the original deal, and fate alone stepped in to kill the deal.

"Joe Yashinski at Charlotte's dinner"

Dispatch:
Riyadh, Saudi Arabia
July 15, 1987

THE DESERT FOX UNCOVERS THE CORPORATION

The name of the company is General Arab Medical and Allied Services Ltd. It is a wholly owned company by Saudi Arabians. They are the contracting agent for the Ministry of Defense and Aviation. The acronyms for the above are GAMA and MODA. Medevac is the program operated by MODA through GAMA for the medical evacuation of patients. The patients are all connected, i.e., they are connected to the royal family, or they are connected to the military. The royal family alone runs into the tens of thousands.

The ruler of Saudi Arabia is His Royal Highness King Fahd ibn Abdul Aziz Al Saud, custodian of the two holy mosques. He has a younger brother, His Royal Highness Abdullah ibn Abdul Aziz Saud, crown prince, leader of the national guard, who is first in line for the crown. Another younger brother, His Royal Highness Prince Sultan ibn Abdul Aziz Al Saud, second deputy prime minister, leader of the air force, inspector general, and the head of MODA. Therefore, the real head of Medevac is Prince Sultan.

These three men hold the reins of power in this country. The political sides of the country, that is the *Mataween* (fundamentalist enforcers), still have the religious side in strict control. The country was first consolidated under one crown in 1932 by King Saud, hence the name Saudi Arabia. The crown then passed from the first king, Saud, through his sons, in turn by their age, oldest first. All of the sons of King Saud were called princes, and all of the princes' sons are called princes. So there are princes that are in line for the throne, and there are princes that are not in line for the throne. It is all very confusing. I read somewhere that King Saud had thirty-eight sons at the time of his death in 1958. In 1978, there were over five thousand princes and an untold number of princesses. They don't bother counting the girls. I haven't heard what they plan to do when the last son of the original King Saud dies. They will survive, *Insha'Allah.*

Please don't consider that last statement as an idle comment. Much of what is done here is with the attitude of "It will happen Insha'AllahInsha'Allah." In other words, "It will happen if Allah wills it." The copilots report the ETA (estimated time of arrival) with an ending of Insha'Allah. They file flight plans that end with Insha'Allah. They drive their cars in such a fashion that everyone knows that the greater the danger they survive, then the greater their faith. Perhaps they will survive, Insha'Allah.

A great deal of what they do is on the spur of the moment, very little prior planning. You may call it what you like, laid-back, the *mañana* syndrome, or just lazy. Whatever, it is the custom here. It is not necessary to be here very long to see that the Saudis are accustomed to being in charge and having their work done by servants. When they graduate from college, they expect and insist on beginning as managers. This is commonly known and discussed by them in front of the Westerners. The problems generated by this thinking are discussed in the *Arab News*, the local newspaper. Years of tradition, augmented by the recent accumulation of wealth over the last few decades, is a hard combination to beat. Many don't even try to beat it. One of the biggest problems with the copilots here is that they expect to be captains too soon. They are willing to trust in Allah that they can handle anything that happens while they are in command of the aircraft. The Arab insurance companies don't share their faith.

Medevac operates from the local air force base. The whole complex of hangars, two-story office buildings, and single-story training buildings were built, and additions are now being constructed without the first construction plan. No, not one drawing. The Koreans doing the construction come out of the new building to measure something in the old building and then go back to the new building to start building again. They are doing the whole thing one panel at a time. No plan. Just four days ago, they poured the slab foundation for about three thousand square feet of additional floor space to the corporate office here on the compound. Today they were tearing it all out with jack hammers. It is 140°F, and they are tearing it all out. They had no plan, and they forgot to put the plumbing in first. Perhaps it will all work out, Insha'Allah.

GAMA operates through contracts with MODA. They are the agent or sponsor for people like me, doctors, nurses, technicians, and perhaps consultants in the medical field. The name implies interest in anything having to do with medical services, and that is the case. Their primary effort is to obtain contracts with the Saudi government through MODA for furnishing personnel to work in hospitals, etc. In the States, they might be called head hunters, but over here, there is quite a difference. The agent or sponsor is completely responsible for those that they hire and bring into the country. They must provide them a place to live, transportation to and from work, their medical, dental, and life insurance, transportation back to their place of hire each year, and finally their retirement.

If the individual gets in trouble while here or is able to leave the country owing debts, the agent is responsible. Because of this responsibility, the agent by law can keep the worker's passport. That is the reason that when you travel to some of the countries of the world without a proper visa, the hotel may become the agent of responsibility and therefore is allowed to keep your passport until you are departing the country with all bills paid. In Saudi Arabia, you are not going to get into the country on a hotel-sponsored visa. Only the government can approve visas, and you cannot leave until they have approved your exit visa. Exit and reentry visas are issued through the agent with the proviso that they be activated within sixty days;

if not, the visas are void. They are only good for six months. If you apply for one, receive it, then don't use it, then you are fined SR1,000 ($266.67).

All of this is just background for your understanding of a worker's situation here. The rules are the same regardless of your native country or your station in society. The doctor from the USA, the day laborer from Sri Lanka, or the pilot from anywhere—same, same, all same.

The GAMA hierarchy consists of the owner (sheikh). *Sheikh* is pronounced as the word *shake*. At one time, they tell me it had a dual meaning. One meaning was used to indicate a very religious person, one that spent much of his time in religious activities. The second meaning was used to indicate a person of power and respect. The second meaning has been officially removed. Friends and associates still use the term regardless of the official position. Fahad Mohammed Al-Athel and his two cousins that actually run the companies Sheikh Hussein Al-Athel and Sheikh Homad Al-Assaf. It is my understanding that Sheikh Fahad is the owner of several or many other businesses, so it's not strange that he is never seen, and his cousins actually run the company. Neither is it strange that they have an American, Terry Johnson, in a position as vice president, personnel.

There are four American captains here flying Gulfstreams. Two have been here over two years and are presently on ninety-day extension. The other two are in the eleventh month of their first twelve-month contract. I am one of the latter. The contract we signed gives the agent the option of holding us here ninety days past the term of the contract. We are promised a bonus at the end of the contract, but getting it at the end seems to become tricky if there is any disagreement on anything. No one seems to recall an instance where the bonus was actually paid.

The director in charge of Medevac for the army is Maj. Mohammed Al-Shablan, his assistant is Mohammed Hanno, a civilian. Major Al-Shablan is in Jeddah, taking training on the C-130, a four-engine turboprop. He has been gone five months and is not due back until the first of August. Mohammed Hanno is on leave for six weeks in Long Beach, California. There are four of the six copilots here that are in mutiny. The director is gone, his assistant is gone, and three of the four American captains will be gone before the first of August. If it sounds like the place is without management or direction, then you're just beginning to get the message. There is enough going on right now to fill several chapters of the book entitled *Believe It or Not, in the Sand*.

Last Wednesday, I was called out on a mission at 0800 and was gone all day. While I was gone, Charlotte received two phone calls for me. One was from Mohammed Hanno, and the other was from Eric Newbigin. My first thought was that Hanno was going to fire me and that Newbigin wanted to hire me. Well, neither one was correct. Newbigin wanted to pick my brain for information on a couple of new aircraft types that might be added to the fleet that he manages. Hanno wanted to tell me that all the expatriates were requested to be at Sheikh Hussein Al-Athel's office the next morning at 1000. I had my own ideas about why we were being called down to the owners' office, so I thought it would be a good idea for all the expatriates to meet the night before and cover the questions and answers that might be exchanged the next morning. We had the meeting and felt that probably nothing would come of it, but well, why not?

The two American captains on extension are Odie Pond and Walt Schmitz. The other two American captains are me and Phil Hardy. Phil has already signed his resignation and received his letter of release; he is definitely gone. I want to stay if they will settle down and leave me alone.

Odie Pond was away on leave for a few days, so he couldn't be included. It may very well have been his letter of over a month before that was the reason for this meeting being called. He had written a letter to General Hammed, the military leader in MODA, with responsibility for Medevac. The letter listed several complaints and requests, and so far Odie has never received an answer. As it turned out, Phil Hardy was called out on a mission later that evening and was gone all night, arriving home at 0730 the next morning. So it was Schmitz and I that had to make the meeting for all four of us.

VP Terry Johnson met us at the reception desk, and before I could say more than hello, he apologized for his inaction on my part, referring to the fact that he didn't realize that I had not been moved into my new villa months ago. He was referring to my letter in January of this year requesting that I be moved from this B10 unit into something more satisfactory because of several problems with the sewer. He did all this before I had a chance to even mention it—a dead giveaway of his guilt. His next approach was to try and find out why we had asked for the meeting with the sheik. He was speechless when Schmitz told him that we didn't request the meeting; the sheikh did. "Well, I was asked to be present," he informed us but told us to go ahead, and he would join us in a few minutes. The sheikh's office was on the fourth floor. Was it a coincidence that Terry had to make a phone call real quick, and we had to wait in front of the sheikh's office until Terry arrived? Once Terry arrived, then we were immediately ushered into the meeting. Ah, the silly games that grown men play.

The first five minutes of the meeting was to thank Schmitz for his extra effort at Medevac. It was never mentioned what the extra effort was, but the assumption was made that we all knew what he was talking about. This was followed immediately by the request. "What can we do to convince you to sign another one year contract?" Schmitz was quick to give the same answer that he had given the other pilots the night before when I posed the same question. The question was my effort to guess what the sheikh might ask. In my mind, it was apparent that the reason to call us down there was to try and get us all to sign new contracts. They waited until the last minute of the contracts and the sheikh's eminent departure from the Kingdom (he was leaving the next day) to try any negotiations. Anything he agreed to would have to wait until his return (mid-September) for his personal attention. The minor details could be handled (or delayed) by Terry Johnson. Schmitz listed three points: more money, an A villa, and a change in management at Medevac. Without a moment's hesitation, the sheikh promised to take his request to the highest level. He promised to let Schmitz know the results of his request very soon. Schmitz failed to mention just how much more money was needed and just what sort of change was going to be required in the management at Medevac. The only concrete request he made was for an A villa. The sheikh's answer was even less definite than the question. Ah, what silly games grown men play.

He asked me if I had any problem with working in the Kingdom. I told him that I liked the country and I liked the people. My wife liked the country and the people and wanted to stay. The only problems that I had experienced since arriving was one with the housing, and Terry had promised to take care of that. The second was a problem that I had with one of the copilots. "Ah yes, Eid, we know about him." I never mentioned his name. "You know, legally we can fire him, but in this country, we really don't like to do that," he said. I told him that I understood perfectly. "In our country, we have the same sort of thing. We call it civil service!" He looked directly at me for a few moments then laughed. I continued, "The main difference is that in my country, if you are going to have brain surgery, you don't ask for a civil service surgeon." This time he smiled. "And further," I added, "if you are riding in the back of an airplane, who do you want up front, a civil service captain and copilot or the best you can get?" He nodded affirmatively and smiled. I asked him if he knew about Jeppesen. Jeppesen refers to the charts, maps, and approach plates used by the flight crew. They are a necessary part of navigation equipment that is required by law to be aboard every aircraft involved in cross-country flight of any kind and any flight conducted in instrument flying conditions whether it is cross-country or local. Jeppesen is the trademark of a company in Colorado that produces these charts for the use of flight crews all over the world and was derived from the name of the founder. Many year ago, as a pioneer in airline flying, Captain Jeppesen kept notes on the airways, airports, beacons, etc., that he used to navigate by. His notes became very popular with the other pilots, and soon he was kept busy making copies for them. It wasn't long before the requests were outdistancing Captain Jeppesen's ability to keep up and continue his flying. A new business was born. He formed a company to publish these aids to navigation, and today they furnish them all over the world. He indicated that he did not. Terry said that he knew about them. "Well, Terry, maybe you do, and then maybe you don't. Do you realize that if the Jeppesen is not up-to-date and correct, then the aircraft is illegal to fly, and if it is flown and is damaged, then the insurance is no good?" Both Terry and the sheikh sat up in their chairs. The sheikh had to make a phone call.

It was obvious to me that the sheikh thought that I was one of the contract holdouts. It's less than sixty days to the end of my contract. They usually offer the new contract ninety days prior to the end of the old one. I can imagine that when he was briefed on the problems at Medevac, he was told that there were four of us that had not yet signed our contracts. He wasn't told that mine had not yet been offered to me. So he offered to guarantee, in front of witnesses, that if I would go ahead and sign my contract, then after his return, if I was still unhappy, he would be glad to release me. Just as long as I would give them enough time to hire my replacement. How long that might be was not defined.

The coffee was fine, but the rest of the meeting was about as productive as an extra set of tits on a boar hog. Later developments proved that last remark to be overstated.

Today is Saturday, the first day of their week. I called Terry Johnson to ask when I could expect a letter to the Nasseem compound manager regarding my move into an A unit. The story had changed completely. He said that he had talked to the second in command and was told that Schmitz and I would be moved into a nice B unit, and after the details were sorted out, we would be moved into A units in the fall! I told him that I wasn't interested in a nice B, and besides they were all full. I reminded him that he told me that I was eligible for an A villa due to my rank and position, and as of now, I was not interested in anything less. I added that I didn't intend to move twice on the way. He stated that he was leaving town in just a few minutes and would not be back until Wednesday. He asked for that much extra time to sort it out. The whole thing was a ruse to get me to sign the contract. It is obvious that he intends to hold the A villa as bait until I sign the new contract—the one that has not been offered yet! He's got another thing coming! It was my intention to stay. Now it's a matter of another corporate jerk trying to play silly games with me, and I've had enough of that already. A man should be able to determine at least the direction of the force when he is being "jerked" around. It is imperative that he knows whether it is the initiative and purpose of an individual or the overall design of the corporation. There are so many little people in high places that maneuver people around for their own purposes, all the while blaming others as company policy. A man needs to know which is which.

Several times in the thirty-eight-plus years that I worked for the Exxon Corporation, I saw things that were just not right and wondered why management couldn't see the same things that I saw. The first seventeen years, I was considered a member of the labor force, and the last twenty-one-plus years, I was a part of management. As a member of management, there were many times I had the fantasy that one day, one of the vice presidents or maybe even the number-one man might ask me for my opinion as to the nature of the problem of the group that I was associated with. In my fantasy, I would list the problems and an assortment of ideas for their correction. After listening closely and intently to my remarks, then he would thank me and go straight away to correct the problems. It never happened. What made it so real was that it did happen to me once upon a time while I was still in the army. It happened just as described above, except the man asking for my advice was a brigadier general, and I was a first lieutenant. The matter he asked about included removing an individual from a place of command and replacing him with the person I suggested. The conversation between me and the general was on a hill under the whirling blades of a helicopter, which interrupted my breakfast. The corrections I suggested were completed before sundown that same day. It spoiled me.

It never happened in civilian life, not in the "real" world, but I thought about it many times. As the years passed, the problems remained, and I had to reason why no one of influence ever seemed to care. That was the part that was so difficult to fathom. They didn't even seem to care. It is most frustrating to watch lazy, incompetent, unqualified, inadequate, unfit, insufficient, ignorant, inept people promoted and carried by their underlings for years, and those above them seem unable to see what is so easily seen by those involved.

Many years ago, while trying to make a living for my family and before I could find a full-time job in aviation, I was elected to the position of representative by my fellow workers to the Federation. The Federation was the company union. The company was the old Humble Oil & Refining Company. It was organized in Humble, Texas, about twenty-five miles north and east of Houston. The men that originated the company were oilmen, entrepreneurs, wildcatters. I never knew them, but I'll wager they were smart, hardworking, and a lot more. Their efforts developed into the oil company with the largest domestic reserves of any oil company large or small. This same little oil company has now become Exxon Company USA or EUSA.

During the 1930s, the labor unions were gaining much strength. The old Humble Company, as it was known, developed an idea to do the following:

-1—Handle the popular demands for a union to handle the employees' demands on management.
-2—Keep the outside union organizers out of their hair and their oil business.
-3—Fulfill the requirements for recognizing unions that was developing in the federal government. Their idea was to have an in-house union. They set up the in-house union by encouraging the formation of such a thing in a small department known as the crude oil department. The crude oil department disappeared long before my employment in 1948. The Federation remained, however, and is alive and well until this day.

The Humble Company was very careful to abide by all laws regarding their contact with the Federation. There was a lot that they could do legally, and they did everything that the law would allow. Management supported the Federation as best it could without violating any laws. In fact, it was my supervisor, a member of management that first pushed me into running for representative. I won easily on my first effort. No one else was even running.

My involvement with the Federation began in Wichita Falls, Texas, and ended in Tyler, Texas, some seventeen years later. The representatives met with members of management once each ninety days in the division office and twice a year in

Houston. A division office in Texas covered a lot of geography. Five divisions covered the entire state. They were North Texas, East Texas, Gulf Coast, West Texas, and Southwest Texas. Later, West Texas was expanded to cover California. These divisions were for exploration and production. They had nothing to do with marketing. My connection with the Federation continued until I was elected by the other representatives to the executive committee. I didn't have time to enjoy my new position of power and influence for very long, however. I was promoted quickly and therefore unable to continue as a member of the Federation. I had become a member of management. The company was very smart and very smooth, I hardly felt a thing.

It is my intention here to let the reader understand that I was not without experience when negotiating with management either in my own interest or for the interests of others. The management representatives that I dealt with as a member of the Federation were very good in their jobs. I suspect they were some of the best. The members of the Federation were certainly not the bumbling dummies that they sometimes appeared to be either. Those people will teach you about the real world of politics in hurry. I'll have to add that in my experience in dealing with the management representatives of the old Humble Company was, they never lied to me. They would try to mediate, negotiate, intimidate, and even meditate, but they never lied to me. These GAMA people will climb a tree to lie when they can stand on the ground to tell the truth. It is unbelievable.

This story is not over, and the way it looks now, it never will be. Will the copilots succeed in their mutiny? Will Major Al-Shablan really learn to fly an airplane? Will Mohammed Hanno really go to school in Long Beach? Will the Americans get their bonuses? Will the Desert Fox get his A villa? Stay tuned for the next episode.

Dispatch:
Riyadh, Saudi Arabia
August 4, 1987

A New Guy

Well, they come, and they go. The newest guy is a temporary stand-in for Major Shablan. His name is Captain Baghdadi. He may be new here, but I've known his type before. He's in love—with himself!

No announcement was made that he was going to replace Major Shablan as head of the aviation group. The captain just appeared one day and proclaimed himself as our leader. We were not told for how long this condition would exist, and we assumed it would be temporary. There was nothing official like a letter or a memo with a stamp was ever put out.

The rumor was circulated that the major was going to flight training—on the C-130! It surely could not be true, but that was the rumor. For whatever reason, we had a new CO, and he was anxious to show his authority. He called a meeting of all the flight captains. Its purpose was to make sure all the flight captains were setting the proper example for the copilots. This is from a Saudi National Guard (army) captain that didn't know anything about airplanes or what it took to fly them. Remember, in the Saudi National Guard (army), there was no aircraft other than Medevac. So whatever experience the new captain may have had, it was not in aviation.

Now he's going to tell us how we should set an example. The meeting had hardly begun before I brought up the fact that the two captains that were known to be the worst examples were not even present. Captains Schmitz and Yaghmour were well known for doing things in the air that was not approved by any authority. Examples were given of Captain Yaghmour taking off in MS3 on August 4, 1987, with two nurses sitting on the floor because there were not enough seat belts!

Captain Baghdadi was incensed! He would launch an immediate investigation into this allegation. First, he must have facts, not just secondhand innuendoes. (My words, not his.) I was asked to get each of the nurses involved, Kiel and Durham, to write letters describing the situation in their own words.

This exchange pretty well broke up the meeting, and I was free to provide the evidence to support my charges. After arriving back at the compound and talking to the nurses, I was told that there were many other examples of misbehavior by the same two captains. It was a common occurrence with Yaghmour. Just recently, nurse Baud had to sit on the floor leaving Cairo because Captain Schmitz allowed relatives to board until there was no seat left for her.

Other examples abound. Captain Schmitz rolls the Gulfstream with nurse Kiel in lavatory. Schmitz lands at an airport that had no lights and scared the doctor

Prabo and nurse Qviste. Copilot Kaka reported that Schmitz missed the runway and landed with two wheels in the dirt, and after landing, Captain Schmitz remarked on what a good landing he had made. Nurse Kiel reports that two nights later, she was riding in the jump seat when Captain Yaghmour and copilot Eid landed at Khamis on an unlighted runway against the instructions from the tower. Nurse Kiel said the tower was very upset with them.

The show goes on.

Captain Baghdadi got his evidence but held no more meetings. Someone must have told him that we were very short of flight captains, and perhaps he should use a little more consideration and understanding when dealing with them.

The captain refrained from calling anymore meetings, but he never failed to use a crowd of his "inferiors" to make statements. One morning with a large group of pilots and copilots gathered in operations, I approached Captain Baghdadi about paying me for an expense report that I had turned in for 300 riyals (almost a $100) and was overdue. Baghdadi made a show of looking at my copy of the expense reports and with a sweeping gesture of his arms stated, "Oh, for just 300 riyals why, that is such small amount for a person of your wealth. Why don't *we* just forget it?"

"Well, if that's the way you feel about it, then consider this. I won't fly anymore trips until the expense account is paid."

"Ha ha, you must be kidding."

"Try me."

I was paid the 300 riyals, and the captain did not try me anymore.

Captain Baghdadi was a temporary replacement for Major Shablan. The major returned in a few weeks without learning to fly the C-130, and what passed for normal returned to Medevac.

JDF Letter:
Riyadh, Saudi Arabia
August 5, 1987

TO: Tariq A. Baghdadi, Captain Engineer, Director of Medevac
REF: Medevac Mission to Gassim on 1 Aug 87

It has come to my attention that you require a written explanation of why I took the above-mentioned trip.

On the day in question, I was an F1, and Captain Yaghmour was an F3. The first mission of the day was assigned to me, and the second mission was to Gassim and was assigned to Captain Yaghmour, apparently. I say apparently because it was done prior to my return from the first trip.

I was returning to Riyadh from the first mission, and approximately ten to fifteen minutes prior to landing in MS3, we received a radio call on VHF 135 in Arabic. Even in Arabic, I can recognize "Captain Fox" when it's mentioned. The call was taken by copilot Kaka and was relayed to me. He said that Captain Yaghmour was requesting that I take the trip to Gassim in his place since he had family business to take care of. I believe he said something about taking them to the airport. I responded that I would take the trip.

It was my thought at the time that it would be myself and copilot Kaka that would be on the mission. After more Arabic conversation on the radio, copilot Kaka asked me if I had any objection to flying with copilot Eid. My answer was "whatever," meaning whatever the assignment is then, okay.

After arriving at the hangar, I found that MSD was already to go with copilot Eid and the flight nurse. In fact, they had been waiting on me to arrive. Captain Yaghmour thanked me for doing him a favor, and then he and copilot Kaka went toward the hangar. It was necessary for copilot Kaka to finish the paperwork from the first mission.

Those are the facts of what transpired in the aforementioned incident. Apparently, there was a lot more going on that I didn't know about.

1. All arrangements were made in Arabic, which I don't understand.
2. All arrangements were made by radio VHF 135, which is not private and is monitored there in the hangar and by Romeo base.
3. All arrangements were made while the F1 crew was out of town and out of touch.
4. All arrangements were made at the hangar in full view of interested parties.

It is interesting to me that by answering a call of distress from another crew member, it appears that I have done something wrong. What have I done wrong?

Captains of aircraft, such as we fly, are supposed to make decisions constantly based on their best judgment. Their decisions often mean life or death for those that have been entrusted to their care. If it is the intention of Medevac to reduce a captain to the task of simply administering policy, then I suggest that Medevac is paying far too much money for captains. Their pay should be more like that of a clerk.

In the past I have responded to emergency calls to fly when I was not on duty and was not in uniform. I have responded when the situation seemed to require it without going through channels. If I am to be criticized for these actions, then of course, in the future, I will refuse any action that does not have approval of the Medevac director, whoever it might be.

You may recognize, of course, that this action will take away my prerogative as captain. You may also recognize that as a captain without recourse, there will be many occasions that I will not be able to move the aircraft until I'm assured that I have approval of the Medevac director.

These situations are not always simple, so the other side of the coin is a different picture. The other way to look at this situation is as follows:

If you have a captain that is not able to be trusted with small things, then how can you entrust him with the things that concern life and death. If you have a captain that will not follow proper safety procedures in normal times, then what trust can you have that he will do the proper things in an emergency? It seems to be the judgment of the captain that is being questioned here.

Further, in this period of training and transition for the copilots, it would seem that you need examples from the captains in the most proper way to fly these aircraft and also the most proper way to make decisions regarding the operation of these aircraft.

The answer you may be looking for in this incident may not lie in writing new directives that clerks can follow, but instead, you surround yourself with those people that can be counted on to do the right thing without first being issued a memos or directive.

In over forty years in aviation, I have never crashed an airplane or hurt a passenger. I have never been disciplined for actions inappropriate to the situation that I found myself.

If this letter does not satisfy your needs, then be advised that I will discuss it with you further or resign my duties, whatever is your choice.

James D. Fox, Captain Medevac

JDF Letter:
Riyadh, Saudi Arabia
August 15, 1987

THE A VILLA
FROM THE DESK of JAMES D. FOX

TO: Mr. William A. Earl, Director of Operations

cc: Mr. Hussein Al-Athel, Chief Executive Officer
Mr. Homound Al-Athel, Director of Personal
Mr. Robert Braden, Project Administrator
Capt. Tariq A. Baghdadi, Medevac Project Director

Reference: GAMA Contract Renewal of James D. Fox, Captain, Gulfstream

Attached is the original of your letter of intent that was hand-delivered to me during the last week of July. It is unsigned. A wise man is very careful what he signs and what he gives his word to.

It is apparent that GAMA has no intention of moving me from this apartment as was promised. It is also apparent that the end of my contract is the thirty-first of August. With thirteen days of leave accumulated, I expect the eighteenth of August to be my last day of duty.

On or before the eighteenth of August, I expect the following:

1. Final pay
2. End of contract bonus
3. One-way air tickets to the place of hire
4. A letter of release
5. Exit-only visas for my wife and me

For your information, the point of hire for me was Houston, Texas; my wife's ticket was from Los Angles, California.

Men of honor do as they say or as they agree. I have stated to all that if GAMA failed to do as they agreed, then I would have to leave the Medevac flight staff. I intend to do exactly as I stated.

James D. Fox,
Captain G2 and G3

Author's Note: After this letter, I was asked to make several meetings with Bob Braden, the local GAMA contact man, to one of the Athel brothers. They all acted like I was upset about not getting something I wanted that had nothing to do with a change in apartments. Sheikh Athel insinuated that if it was booze or something else, it was readily available. Did he not get it? Had no one told him that all I wanted was to move into an A villa that because of rank and position I was due in the first place?

Bob Braden was the low man on the totem pole. Bob was a retired US Air Force colonel, I was told, and each time we talked, I got the impression he was very uncomfortable talking to me. It was one of those situations where he knew I was right, and he was on the wrong side of the argument. It was like listening to the fellow who handles the press briefings at the White House. He knows he's on the wrong side of the question but has to somehow make it sound like he's giving the right information when it's obvious that he is not.

This argument went on for a couple of months until the last day before my contract was to end. Bob called me over to his office there in the compound.

"Jim, I wanted to talk to you and see if we can't straighten out your problem."

"Sure, Bob, it's easy. Just give me permission to move into an A villa."

"Well, now, Jim, let's get serious, you know it's not just that easy."

I love it when the other side gets down to the point of saying, "Let's get serious." They are completely out of ammunition.

The real story is that the A villas were in short supply, and they were used as bargaining chips to use on those new hires that were being a little reluctant to sign their papers. It was as simple as that. Bob had at first tried to tell me that there were none available when it was easy to see there were vacant units.

The evening of that same last day, Bob knocked on my back door of the B unit next to the cesspool. He was in his skivvies.

"Hello, Bob, what do you want at this time of night? It's bedtime."

"Okay, Jim, you win. You can have the A unit."

"Oh yeah, when?"

"Anytime you can get ready. It will be the one next to the front gate."

"Okay, Bob, you mean no more jacking me around like waiting until I come back?"

It was all over, and we moved into our new apartment next door to my friend Hakim Al-Alaway. Hakim was a new hire and had been placed in an A when he arrived. Hakim was a Saudi, and he knew the tricks.

JDF Letter:
Riyadh, Saudi Arabia
August 8, 1987

Hello again from the Desert Foxes,

Please excuse this form letter, but it is the best way I know to tell the most number of people what our plans are. This is assuming, of course, that this letter is found by someone that is interested in our plans!

We are coming back to the US in a couple of weeks and would like very much to see as many of our friends as possible while we are there. There is a schedule enclosed. Hopefully, it will remain unchanged at this late date. We have been trying to leave since the first week of August but have been requested to delay several times. There is a serious shortage of pilots that are willing and able to assume the duties of this job, evidently; therefore, we are constantly short of bodies.

My first year in the Kingdom of Saudi Arabia and I have seen much. Too bad no one will believe it except someone that has been here. Peyton Place, Dynasty, Dallas, etc., can't hold a candle to the intrigue that we see here daily. I'm not just talking about the hes and shes, but also the job. You can miss a week of this serial, and you won't even recognize the players. Since I've been here, we have lost four pilots. One was fired for smuggling, two quit, and one became a runner. We've hired one pilot in the same time frame. Last night, I heard that one of the Saudi captains and two of the Saudi copilots are quitting to fly for someone else. That leaves me and one Saudi captain to fly two Gulfstream IIs and one Gulfstream III. It is mischief like this that has been screwing up my vacation schedule.

I'm sorry if this sounds selfish for a person that is involved in a profession of saving lives. Well, it turns out that so far I haven't had a real ASAP mission since I've been here. We fly patients from one hospital to another. That can't be regarded as all that life threatening. We are supposed to be in the air within forty minutes of the callout. Well, that's a little ridiculous, seeing that the compound is twenty minutes from the air base. It is always the same. Aviation managers are always overstating and overcommitting their staff. The management is told anything necessary to justify the real cost of men and equipment necessary to operate an aviation department.

The aviation managers are usually so overgrateful for just having their job, they just can't play it straight with those that approve the budget. If they would just stop and think, then they would realize that the last thing that upper management wants to lose is the aviation department. The corporation's jet is a very important *bennie* (benefit) and will be one of the last things removed in any austerity program. Aviation managers will be a chapter heading in my book, so there is no use going into that now.

The book is coming along pretty good. I haven't had time for any finished writing; the schedule is just too busy. The last year has been very busy. I've flown 365 hours, with 365 legs, and 365 takeoffs and landings. I couldn't average fifty a year of any of those categories in the States.

Flying with copilots is a new experience for me, and I'll have to say I'd rather fly with these guys than a few of the captains I've known in the past. It was not easy, but now we have a good time, and they are even telling Aggie jokes. We had a mission last week to pick up a hundred-year-old woman at Al Abaha and transfer her to Khamis. She was unconscious and partially paralyzed from a stroke. It seemed useless to make the trip. The flight nurse made the comment, "I wonder why they even bother to move her to Riyadh?" The copilot said, "Maybe she has never been there before!" He turned to me and said, "I am stealing your sentences." He had heard me make the same statement a week before with another patient. He thought it was funny before, so he used it himself. He was careful to give me the credit.

A few weeks ago, as we were leaving the cockpit, the copilot Whaled Zahed put his right hand to his chest and observed that he had lost his name tag. The tags have our names printed in English and Arabic. I said, "Oh yeah, well, I found a name tag yesterday but didn't know who it belonged to." He looked at me for a couple of seconds and then grinned broadly, started poking me on the shoulder with his finger and said, "Aggie, Aggie, Aggie."

Back to our trip. We are trying to visit around a few dates that are solid. The Fox family reunion in Wichita Falls, Texas, is on the twenty-sixth and twenty-seventh of September. I have training scheduled with FlightSafety International in Houston on the nineteenth through twenty-third of October and in Savannah from the twenty-sixth through twenty-ninth of October. After Savannah, we will leave for a few days in Madrid, Barcelona, and Rome before returning to Riyadh. We hope to visit with you if at all possible while we are in the States time permitting.

Keep your nose up in the turn, and we'll see you soon. Sincerely, James D. and Charlotte

Dispatch:
Riyadh, Saudi Arabia
August 20, 1987

THE TCNs

The Kingdom is well organized in the use of foreigners to fill the local need for labor both skilled and unskilled. The skilled workers are considered professionals and can be from most anywhere. There are many doctors from Asian countries. The unskilled workers are from any part of the world where labor is cheap. *Cheap* is the operative word here. Skilled or unskilled, the Saudis are going for the cheapest they can find.

Workers from the Western world are commonly called expats, which is a short term for expatriates. The unskilled workers from a third world country are called just TCNs.

There are stories of foreigners from these third world countries that have been here many years and are not allowed to leave. Does that sound like slavery? Well, of course, it is, and to add credibility, I must say that I believe the stories. How could this happen? Well, if a person was brought here without someone on the outside making inquiries about their whereabouts, then who would even know? Some countries don't protect their countrymen very well, and even if they do, someone must complain to start the process. Young women are still sold by their families for work in foreign countries. They are used as house servants and or concubines.

In the Singapore paper, there are many advertisements, offering foreign nationals as servants. You can order them by nationality, sex, size, and shape. Of course, in Singapore, it is all legal and aboveboard, but here, who is to say? I have been told of women from Sri Lanka (Ceylon) and India that were brought here as servants and have been kept against their will for many years. They are released only after their employer releases them. If you think that is farfetched, then perhaps you should try reading newspapers printed in foreign countries.

The nurses that fly with me tell me of nurses from the Philippines that have just disappeared. No, they didn't go home. They just didn't show up for work one day. The nurses, as women, are a tight-knit group, and they keep up with each other. The nurses that fly with me are all from the Western world and come with advanced nursing credentials. The nurses that come from the third world countries come with only the basic credentials. The basic credentials are all that will be recognized by the Saudis. They will work below their station because the money is still much better than they could make back at home. These girls are subject to shabby treatment from their male employers.

Do I know this as a fact? No, but it comes from several sources.

The TCNs that I am most familiar with are those living in the same compound with me and Charlotte. They don't have individual apartments but instead live in bunkhouses. All men living together in a barracks type of building similar to the US Army in the old days. Not exactly the same, however, because the TCNs here are allowed to do their own cooking in the barracks.

Mohammed, our houseboy, wanted to do some ironing for Charlotte. He took some of my uniform shirts home with him to iron. When he returned them, they smelled of cooking grease and smoke so bad they had to be re-laundered.

Mohammed Whakel, the young man that cleans our apartment part-time, delivers our daily copy of the *Arab News* and is from Sri Lanka, the small island country just off the southeast coast of India. Your old school books probably called it Ceylon. He is a full-time employee for GAMA,[10] the same contractor that I work for. Little Mohammed is only a little over five feet tall and weighs maybe ninety pounds. He is a good worker and can be depended on to do what he says he will do. There is a small language problem, but his English is OK. "I am thinking" (Their favorite saying that precedes most of what they say).

"Mohammed Wakeel"

"Hello, Captain, it is Mohammed here," he calls on the phone.
I will answer something like, "Yes, Mohammed."

---

[10] GAMA - General Arab Medical and Allied Services. Seems like that should be GAMAS, but don't try to figure it out now, maybe later.

"Captain, I am coming now." He is probably smiling as he speaks to me from the other end of the phone. He is almost always smiling.

Their pay is minimal, something like $300 per month. That figure is not exact, only hearsay, but it is common knowledge. Mohamed told us that he was saving his money to open a luxury store in Sri Lanka his home.

Of course, I asked, "Mohamed, what is a luxury store?"

He said, "Oh, that is where they sell milk and bread and stuff like that."

"Can you make a good living that way?" I asked.

"Oh yes," he answered, "very good."

"And how much would that be?" I asked.

He answered in rupees, so I asked how much in American dollars? His answer was a $1 per day. Mohammed knew that he could support his family on $1 a day!

Mohammed was a good worker, reliable, and responsible. He was always on time, he never stole anything, he was courteous, and he did good work. We paid Mohammed to clean our apartment once a week and to bring a copy of the daily *Arab News*. In addition, he did odd jobs when we requested.

Charlotte still talks about his manner of speech. He could not speak without wagging his head back and forth. I think if you held his head steady, his body would wiggle.

He would call before coming and say, "Ah, Captain, I am coming now." At other times, it was, "Ah, Captain, I am thinking."

A couple of days after Christmas, I was sleeping in because of returning late from a flight the night before. Charlotte had given me a fancy smoking jacket for Christmas. I don't know why women like to give men smoking jackets. It has nothing to do with smoking, but perhaps it's an impression left over from a Hollywood movie about Ronald Colman or something. This jacket was maroon with lots of fancy dragons and other Chinese embroidery trim in gold and black on both sides, front and back. I hate to think what she paid for it. I wonder whatever became of that jacket.

Mohammed rang our doorbell to deliver our newspaper. When I answered the door wearing my new, gaudy smoking jacket, he said, "Ah, good morning, Captain." And as eyes looked me up and down, he smiled with huge bright eyes and added, "I'm thinking you are very handsome this morning!"

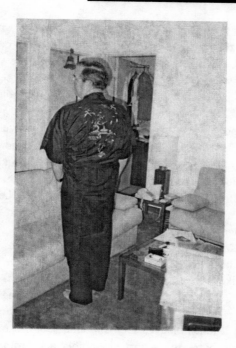

"JD and his new smoking jacket."

"Thank you, Mohammed, I guess. Ah, what can I do for you this morning?" You might say that I wasn't ready for the compliment.

Mohamed had to tiptoe to reach five feet, but what a nice man. He cried and hugged me around the waist—that's as high as he could reach—when we were leaving the Kingdom. He said he wanted to go with us, and he would be my *man*. But I had to explain that we didn't do things in America like they did in Saudi Arabia, so it would be best that he stay where he was.

Mohammed's father died a few years ago and left his wife and family with little chance to survive. Mohammed was the only son of age and was the only chance the family had. It was necessary for the family to gather all their savings together and "buy" a job for the young man of the family. Yes, in many third world countries, it is necessary to "buy" a job in a foreign country. Often, it is necessary to pay just for your name to be on the list of job applicants, even if you don't get the job. Labor contractors in the third world work under the rules set down by their own government for enlisting workers to be exported.

Many workers in these foreign labor markets become very frustrated and look for someone to vent their frustrations upon. While I was in the Kingdom, I made trips to Africa, Pakistan, and Thailand to pick up wounded Saudi diplomats whose job had to do with the procuring of local laborers. The suspected assassins were frustrated locals who were venting their frustrations!

Labor agreements are negotiated by a country that has workers, but not the work. The country that has excess workers seeks labor agreements from more affluent countries for more reasons than just to benefit the worker. The home country becomes involved in the workers' endeavor and receives a part of the workers' pay as taxes. The taxes are often extracted as withholding and are never seen by the worker.

Mohammed reported just before he went on annual leave that he was going to be married when he got home. Charlotte got all excited and gave him $300 for a wedding present! I said she got all excited. Well, she did, but as it turned out, he didn't get married; he got engaged. He explained when he returned that his intended had to come to his home and live with his mother for a year before they could be married. Well, that meant that he got another wedding gift next year. I wonder how that custom would work in our country?

One of the TCNs in the compound operated the mailroom, which was also the video library. He told Charlotte that his wife was having a baby. She loaded him up with baby gifts like she was back in California, and the gifts were for the boss's daughter. We had priority for mail delivery and videos after that.

The TCNs here are very serious about their work. They live frugally by desire and necessity. Mohammed's salary is around $300 per month, and he sends practically all of that home to support his mother and brothers and sisters. We usually pay him for the month on the last cleaning day of the month, which may be almost a week before the last day of the month. Yesterday was such a day. He politely refused the pay offered him, saying, "If you please, sir, I am thinking, if you pay me on payday at the compound (the last actual day of the month), then I will not spend but send all home, thank you."

These people are allowed by Saudi Labor Law to return home, the point of hire, once a year at the expense of the employer. They receive round-trip airline tickets and thirty days of paid leave. It is a time of great excitement, and each traveler has his arms filled with gifts for his family. The usual item is a boom box[11] of large size.

Mohammed is Moslem as most Sri Lankans are. The second largest religion there in Sri Lanka is Christian, I am told. Because of his color, which is very dark, he is cursed by some Americans as just another "damned sand nigger." My fellow Americans can be an embarrassment sometimes.

The Sri Lankans will deliver the paper to your door each day for the cost of the paper and any tip that you want to give them at the end of the month. It is necessary for the TCN to pay for the paper out of his own pocket. The normal tip is fifteen or

---

[11] Portable radio of large dimensions.

324

twenty Saudi riyals[12] ($4 to $5). They will clean your apartment once a week from top to bottom, vacuum the carpet, scrub the floors, do the windows, wash your dishes, and launder your clothes all for SR150 ($40) per month.

One American here, Capt. Walt Schmitz, from Washington State but claims to be from Texas, was one of Mohammed's newspaper customers.

One evening, Captain Schmitz was walking his dog through the swimming pool area. He had the only dog allowed to be in the compound and was proud of this distinction. There, he met Mohammed and several of his Sri Lankan friends. Mohammed noticed the captain had his fancy, expensive camera with him, so he asked, "Oh, Captain, will you take a picture of me and my friends please?" He probably wanted to send it home.

The American replied, "Certainly not, I didn't buy this camera to waste film on a bunch of monkeys!" Mohammed's friends asked, "Why you do work for such a man? Why do you call him your friend? He is without honor!" Mohammed had no answer.

Later, it was necessary for Mohammed to stop delivering the daily paper to the captain because of Schmitz's failure to pay at the end of the month.

It doesn't take much to treat your fellow man as a man, but it does take something, and I'm sorry to say there are many Americans that don't have that something. They give the rest of us a bad name.

Americans, like me, are almost the only source of pilots to fly the type of jet aircraft that the Saudis have here for their Medevac operations. When you spend $5-20 million for an airplane and your pilot must come from one source, then you have a situation, which may cause that pilot to become somewhat arrogant.

Such incidents are not isolated, not rare, but rather common I am ashamed to report. It is a bad face, fashioned by a few, that all Americans, all white faces, all Christians must wear.

What a miserable life these men of unfortunate birth must live. They leave their home, family, and country to work in a foreign country for money to support those loved ones left behind. They live in barracks with other unfortunates like themselves. They come from Thailand, Pakistan, Philippines, Sri Lanka, and any other place that will provide cheap labor. They are transported to and from work by their employers. They are not hired on a married contract, so that means they are not allowed to bring in a wife. No fraternization is allowed here, so that means no female companionship of any kind for eleven out of the twelve months. Despite their background and some are college graduates, they are treated by most as low class and unworthy.

---

[12] Saudi riyals - SRs have a value set by the government as 3.751 to each American dollar. This does not float as other foreign currencies, but only changes at the discretion of the Saudi government, which is not often.

We speak of discrimination here, but most of the people I know have no knowledge of how *real* discrimination looks.

While in a meeting with Captain Cox (a Brit), a pilot and administrator for GAMA, not Medevac, he asked if I would like some tea or coffee. I replied that I would, and he called for his clerk in the next room, "Jeffery, oh, Jeffery. Jeffery, Jeffery, oh, Jeffery. Here, Jeffery, coffee, Jeffery in here, coffee, Jeffery." Jeffery was a clerk typist from Pakistan. He had a college degree and did most of the office work, but he was not recognized for what he did but for his class. Jeffery could never be more than a TCN.

Bruce, the dispatcher for Medevac, was a nice-enough fellow to work with, and he was very competent in his job. He was a white man from South Africa, and I have never heard such raw hate in Texas for a black man as Bruce was willing to state in public. To him, the black man was no better than a dog!

That is part of what I saw in the Land of Sand and Sun.

I am continually reminded of Gunga Din (pronounced DEEN), the poor water boy in the writings of Rudyard Kipling. He was ridiculed and despised by many of the British as a being of low class, but at the end of the poem, he continued to bring water to the soldiers even after he was mortally wounded. A British soldier grievously wounded and thinking himself near death now saw life and man with a different set of values. He said,

> Though I've belted you and flayed you,
> By the living God that made you,
> You're a better man than I am Gunga Din.
>   (Rudyard Kipling, "Gunga Din")

326

JDF Letter:
Riyadh, Saudi Arabia
September 5, 1987

TO: Director of Operations
                   Medevac
FROM: James D. Fox, Captain
                   Gulfstream II & III
REFERENCE: Delay on HZ-MS4 while in London on 25-28 Aug '87

The aircraft in question was scheduled to leave at 1200 hours on Thursday, the twenty-seventh of August. The preflight was completed, and catering was being stored when it became noticeable that the cabin was getting very warm. I adjusted the cabin rheostat to cold and noticed that cold air was coming from the cockpit outlets.

The air continued to get warmer. It became obvious that the cabin rheostat was not controlling the cabin temperature. I switched the selector switch on the overhead panel from normal to cockpit because it was equally clear that the cockpit rheostat was working normally. The air continued to get warmer.

The passengers arrived approximately one hour early around 1100 hours. The cabin had just begun to fill with smoke. We were in the midst of trying to sort out just what the problem was, and it was too early to tell the passengers anymore than the simple fact that we had a problem and that there would be a delay of at least two hours. The handlers had already told me that it would take at least two hours to arrange for a new takeoff slot, maybe more.

I suggested that the passengers be moved to a place where they could wait with more comfort for the next two hours or until we could have a better understanding of what was going to be required before we would be ready to leave. I also suggested that the bags not be loaded because they would just be in the way while we were working in the baggage compartment.

The princess was there in an ambulance, and after my explanation, they all left with the British Airways handler. It was my understanding later that the handler had arranged for them to wait in a lounge there on the airport. I have no personal knowledge of this because I was busy with the aircraft all day.

A discussion was held with the flight engineer, after which we both thought the problem might be with the cabin temperature control valve. He started work on removing the valve, and I went back to the office to make the phone calls and send the necessary telexes.

When it was later discovered that the problem was not with the cabin temperature control valve, and after talking to the flight engineer about the length of time required for the repair, I advised the passengers that there would be at least a six-hour delay. The passengers asked British Airways to get them rooms at the Sheraton Skyline Hotel.

The entire crew spent the rest of the day at the airport. I suggested to the flight engineer that we could hire help if he needed help. He told me that it was pretty much a one-man job and that extra help would not be well used.

The time that I had given the passengers for the expected delay was up, and the aircraft was still not completed. I had no idea when to expect the job to be completed, so I made the decision to delay overnight. It was my decision. I set the takeoff time for exactly 24 hours late. My thinking was, that by that time the aircraft would surely be completed, the passengers and crew had been up all day and needed the rest, the catering could be reordered, and new airport takeoff slots could be arranged.

The aircraft was repaired and tested later that evening and proven ready to go once more. For the reasons stated above, I left the new plans unchanged.

The first officer, Daghistani, made all the contacts with the prince. Dahgistani told me that the prince expected me or British Airways to pay for his hotel rooms due to the delay. He may have been thinking about airline procedure, I don't know. I passed along the fact that I had no intention of paying his hotel bill. He would have to make his own arrangements.

The departure was made the following day without incident. The passengers were on time, and all was ready. No comment was made to me about anything. During the trip back, the prince came to the cockpit once and spoke to Daghistani in Arabic. When I looked around, he smiled and offered to shake my hand. That was the only contact that I had with the prince, personally.

As far as I'm concerned, the return trip was very uneventful. Except for the delay in London, all times were very close to estimated.

James D. Fox, Captain
Gulfstream II & III

Author's Note: This letter is in response from a Medevac request. It is another example of what may happen when you deal with a member of the royal family.

I am not the guy they need to deal with. I will show respect for their position, but I don't achieve results any better or sooner for one than another. I'll do my best, and that's the best I've got.

Several years before this incident, during the time that the air traffic controllers were fired by President Reagan, I was dressed down by the CEO of Exxon Company USA for a delay in departure from Houston. The rules for achieving a slot for a flight plan were almost impossible. We were only allowed six departures per hour from Houston Intercontinental Airport. You could apply for a flight plan no more than forty-eight hours prior to your departure time. This meant that there might be a large number of pilots trying to file a flight plan at the same time two days prior to the desired time they needed. It was critical to be within that first six callers at the exact time desired. If you missed your chance and chances are that you would, then you had to wait another hour and try again. If you wanted to leave on a Monday, then the forty-eight-hour rule was overpowered by the weekend rule. You may perceive that this situation could present a situation whereby the pilot trying to file a flight plan could in no way be sure of the outcome. Difficult was a word that didn't cover the condition.

I talked to a friend I had with the ATC, and he told me how to fool the system. He said that I could file a flight plan as if departing from a small airport in Texas that didn't have a slot restriction with an en route stop at IAH on the way to your final destination. That way, you wouldn't be affected by the IAH six slots per hour rule!

All these things had been accomplished on this particular day, but at the last minute, clearance delivery told me that I would have a one-hour delay! I got out of my seat and went to the rear to report to the CEO the delay we had just been given. He blew up in my face and screamed that he, yes, he would not stand for this kind of service. He would just sell all these airplanes and go on the airlines! Perhaps I should have just said, "Yes, sir" and left, but no, I said, "Well, it's your choice, sir, but as you can see, the airlines are having their delays as well."

There were several of the company vice presidents onboard, and they kept their council by saying nothing.

It never occurred to me that I might get fired for speaking back to the boss. I thought he was being unreasonable and told him so.

The royal family thinks you should be able to get nine women pregnant and have a baby in one month just for their benefit. Of all the so-called ASAP missions of mercy for the royal family while flying for Medevac, there were a couple of instances where the patient may have actually needed a medical flight. I flew from Riyadh to San Francisco on one flight to pick up a princess and return her to Riyadh. She boarded the airplane under her own power, took a seat in the back, and promptly asked her husband to "feed" her her lunch.

On this trip, I got a call from Daghistani after I had gone to bed, telling me that the prince had called and wanted me to pay for his hotel bill. He reasoned that the airline always paid when they had a delay. I told him to tell the prince that Medevac didn't pay me enough per diem to cover my own hotel bill and that I had no intention of paying his. Also, tell him that he was not riding on an airline and had not paid for an airline ticket, so he would have to pay his own bills. The prince had reserved a whole floor of the Sheraton for his royal group.

So when he got home, he complained to someone that complained to someone until it got down to me. If I answered the complaint or not, the result was the same—nothing. This whole thing of the royal family using Medevac when there was no medical need started a few years back when the princes started buying Gulfstreams by the case like eggs. They all wanted one each for themselves. After thirty-some-odd were bought and delivered to Jeddah, someone woke up and shut the process down. The Gulfstreams were taken away from each prince that had one and placed in a pool and operated out of Jeddah under the name of Saudi Special Flights. The princes pouted.

I was never tempted to ask for a job there with Saudi Special Flights even for more money. The grief would not be worth it.

JDF Letter:
Riyadh, Saudi Arabia
September 4, 1987

FROM THE RETREAT OF EL ZORRO

Dear Margaret, Louise, and Gerald,

This is just a quick note to accompany the enclosed stories. So much happens here and so fast that I can't get it all written down. It seems that brief logs and notes are all that I can do. The story on Daddy has been in my head for several months. It seems that what I know and feel for Daddy should be written down for all those that didn't have the chance to meet him. This is not an easy thing to do, but I am pleased with my effort so far.

I have a grandchild now that is named after him. The parents never knew Sandy, but from what I tell them, they think he must have been someone special. Don't you wish sometime that you could read about your ancestors? Well, perhaps my effort will provide that for our descendants.

It was noteworthy that Gerald had a difficult time when he first tried to talk about Sandy on the tape we received. Gerald, I know the feeling. Daddy was always very proud of you, and I'm sure you knew, even though he wasn't accustomed to passing out compliments. I enjoyed being with him because he could always manage for us to have a good time.

Sandy loved to play baseball, hunt, fish, and every now and then have a little drink. I could never fully share his enthusiasm for any of the above. That is not to say that I didn't enjoy being with him when we were hunting or fishing. Gerald, it's like when I go with you. It's not the hunting or fishing; it's just being out with someone that really loves to do what we're doing and can have fun doing it.

One of my wishes that can never be fulfilled is that I couldn't or didn't do more just to make him happy. Sometimes I think that parents are not wise enough for raising children until after they are fifty. Of course, children are past forty before they recognize the real attributes of their parents.

I never let Daddy know that I turned down an opportunity for a college athletic scholarship. I don't think that I ever told anyone, not my sisters or my mother. Charles Roby talked me into trying out for the baseball team at Midwestern one day. It was early in 1947. The redheaded left hander that was pitching for the tryouts was the star of the Wichita Falls Coyotes (high school) the year before. When it was my turn at bat, he was throwing them hard right down the middle. I knocked the first three in a row out of the park. The coach told the pitcher, "Hey, Red, bear down." That tall left hander threw me a curve ball that I had never seen before. I swung like I was going to knock it out of the park as well and missed it completely. The bat

331

came out of my hand and cleared the bench of those waiting to bat next. It didn't hit anyone, but I cleaned that bench out. The coach said, "Hey, boy, come over here." I thought he was going to chew me out for losing the bat. "What's your name, kid? You want to play baseball for me?" I told him I really didn't care for baseball that much. What I had wanted to do was play basketball. He told me to be back on the field Monday, and he'd get me a scholarship if I could keep hitting the ball like that. I told him that I had always hit the ball like that because I'd been taught by a pro. He said, "Well, you be back here Monday, and maybe you'll be teaching one of these days."

I never went back, and I never mentioned it to anyone. Sounds a little like Daddy's story, doesn't it? That's what dumb kids do. If I had been thinking at all, I would have done it just for my dad. (If I had played baseball for the college, then I would have missed my chance to become a pilot!)

No, it wasn't in my plans; after all, I was taking flying lessons at the time, and I was going to be a pilot. It never occurred to me to do both. Well, anyway, writing makes me think, and the more writing that I do, the easier it comes out. Maybe one of these days, I'll do something worthwhile. Remember, these stories are not complete; they are just an effort on my part to put it down on paper so it won't disappear. I want to thank you for the tape. I can use the story about Caswell and the coon hunt. I need some more and will get them at the reunion in Wichita Falls. The Sutton boys are always ready for me when I get there.

Hope to see you all soon,

Love,
James and Charlotte

PS How do you like this name for our restaurant in Spain, El Zorro's Retreat, Where the Elite Meet to Eat? I presume that you know that *fox* in Spanish is *zorro*!

Dispatch:
Riyadh, Saudi Arabia
September 19, 1987

TALK ABOUT YOUR BAD LUCK!

LEAVING RIYADH

Getting permission to go on leave (holiday, vacation) is not easy. Medevac is so short of captains the powers that be can easily find an excuse to plead for you to put off your departure just a few days longer. Then, of course, the days add into weeks, and the first thing you know it's the next month.

We have made plans in the US with schedules and tickets for the airlines. The airlines here are very flexible, thank goodness, but you can get tired of the endless changes. The Fox family reunion is scheduled for the twenty-sixth and twenty-seventh of September in Wichita Falls, Texas, and we wanted to get there a few days early for that, so it's finally set for us to leave on the twenty-second of September and *no later*.

Now that we know we are going, it's time to get Charlotte an exit and reenter visa. We have discussed the idea of spending just a few days in France on the way over, and to do that, Charlotte must also have a French visa. (In 1987, Americans had to have a visa to visit France.) So we had to send her passport to the French Consulate for the proper stamp.

Late on the sixteenth, I got a mission to Nashville, Tennessee! Oh no, you don't, I'm going on leave. Well, the negotiations began. When the smoke cleared—it never really clears in Medevac operations—I agreed to go to Nashville but wouldn't return on that flight. As it turned out, Mohammed Hanno was coming back from leave and would meet me in London. He would take the flight on to Nashville where I would get off and continue on leave. Hey, that would work out for Charlotte and me. She could go with me on the Gulfstream to Nashville, and we would save money on her tickets.

It didn't happen that way. Charlotte's passport was at the French Consulate, and they said it would not be ready until the twentieth. We couldn't get it back in time for my departure. This meant she would have to wait in Riyadh for her passport and then fly to Houston by her lonesome. Well, I knew she could do it, but it would really have been nice for us to be together.

As I said, I got the trip on the sixteenth, and we spent all day on the seventeenth getting the tickets rearranged. The quickest Charlotte can leave is on the twentieth, the day her passport will be returned, and she will have to change planes in Paris. Not only change planes, but change airports, from De Gaulle to Orly, that is. You know what that means—a big hassle and a chance to lose bags and or miss your connection.

Charlotte didn't lose her bags, but I did—hers and mine both. Charlotte's tale of what happened to her in Paris deserves a chapter on its own. I was so smart. I suggested that Charlotte didn't have to fool with her bags at all. She could send her bags with me, and then she could just travel with her purse! The French became very suspicious of a middle class or higher lady traveling from Riyadh, Saudi Arabia, to Houston, Texas, with *no bags.*

Her first problem was getting from De Gaulle airport to Orly airport. The taxi driver would not understand what she wanted, and they wouldn't take American dollars. She was losing precious time at the curb and worrying about missing her connecting flight to Houston, when a stranger approached and asked if he could help—in English. The stranger was a jewelry dealer from Riyadh! He not only translated her needs to the cab driver but paid the driver in French francs. He wouldn't take any money from Charlotte but gave her his business card. What a lucky break. You can imagine once we found his jewelry store in Riyadh, he was amply compensated for his friendly gesture.

But her troubles were not over. Once at Orly airport, the real hassle began. Charlotte arrived at the gate only after being passed off from one security agent to another. Someone had pasted a red note on her ticket. She had become a first-class security risk. The French were convinced that she was up to something, but they couldn't be sure of just what. The airline called for final boarding, and just before she was going to miss her last chance, she was once more held for a security screening. At the end of her patience, Charlotte demanded to know what was wrong. They didn't believe she was who she said she was, and they didn't believe she had come from Riyadh. Her passport and airline tickets were not enough proof. Why didn't she have any bags? They didn't believe her story about her husband being a pilot. She had a copy of an in-flight magazine from the Saudi flight she had arrived on, so they demanded she read the Arabic portion to them.

That was it. They had finally pushed my sweetheart too far. With a stiff back and tears forming in her eyes, she demanded they either arrest her or let her board her flight! They let her go, and she made the flight. It put a bad taste in her mouth for the French.

ARRIVING IN THE STATES

The trip for me across the Atlantic was uneventful. We landed in Bangor, Maine, to refuel, and Hanno surprised me by changing up the flight plane that I had prefilled from the UK. He filed for direct to Nashville, Tennessee, from Bangor. I told him that they would never approve a request for direct. He would have to file by the airways. He just shrugged off my suggestion and included medical emergency as part of his flight plan. We didn't have a medical emergency; he just threw that in to get what he wanted, and that was to fly direct without bothering with all that airways stuff.

We had left Heathrow at 05:30 and arrived in Nashville at 18:30. That's thirteen hours including six hours time zone changes. That's a long day, and I was ready to get on the airline and sleep all the way to Houston. I had forty minutes to make the connection, and I made it, and I did sleep all the way to Houston. But guess what? No bags in Houston. The airline had sent all the bags to Huntsville, Alabama, instead. Baggage tags for Houston and Huntsville are the same color and similar spelling. It's a good idea to check those baggage tags before you leave the bags.

My son Greg was there to meet me, and we spent that Saturday night visiting. Charlotte came in the next day, and we moved to a motel.

LONG TALK WITH MY YOUNGEST

I finally got in touch with my youngest son Chuck on Wednesday for lunch at the Dutch Kettle restaurant near Houston Intercontinental Airport. Chuck had dropped out of college and was driving a wrecker. I needed to talk to him about his future and find out what it was that he wanted. Chuck had finished a course in auto mechanics at the community college and had a natural talent for mechanical work. I couldn't help but think he was not living up to his potential. We had a long talk about his future and what he wanted.

Chuck went with me back to the Exxon hangar and spent at least an hour talking with my friend Jim Keegan. Jim was a very close friend of mine that had an A&P (airframe and powerplant) license, and Chuck respected his judgment.

I had made Chuck an offer for him to take a trip to London. I would give him a round-trip ticket and $500. The idea was to break the loop that he was in and maybe get him interested in the future. My Jaguar mechanic friend in England, David Groves, was ready to give Chuck a job and teach him to work on Jaguars. For you of the unknowing, the Jaguar engine either six or twelve cylinders are quite different from American-made engines and require a trained mechanic for just a simple tune-up. Trained Jaguar mechanics are few and hard to find in the USA.

We talked about how life is short and you never know what day is your last. The next afternoon, Chuck was hit broadside by a truck while just trying out a friend's motorcycle by just going around the block. They took him to the hospital, and he was put in ICU. I couldn't go see him because his mother was there, and I didn't want to stir up that hornet's nest.

Tomorrow is the Fox family reunion in Wichita Falls, which I had been attending on a regular basis all my life. It was a difficult decision whether to stay or go, and considering that Chuck's injuries were severe, but not critical or life threatening, I decided to go to the reunion.

Motorcycles Are for Losers

None of my three sons were allowed to have motorcycles when they were at home. Within a few weeks after leaving home, they each bought a motorcycle and promptly went to the hospital, at least once. None of the accidents included high speed or any circus acts. In most cases, it was at low speeds, and one was in a parking lot. My second son Greg broke his ankle that required pins because his cycle fell over on him when he was getting off.

Is this an indictment against parents restricting their children? I don't know and will not even venture a guess. Should I have let them have a motorcycle at a younger age and make certain they learned how to safely use one? I don't know, and I'm not even going to make a guess.

My father told me, "James, stay off them motorcycles. They'll kill you." I listened to my father and never ever even got on a motorcycle. In my opinion, motorcycles are for losers!

Charlotte arrived about the same time our lost bags were returned, so we had them just in time to put them on our flight out to Wichita Falls. Of course, you can't fly direct from Houston to Wichita Falls. You have to change planes in Dallas; another chance to lose bags.

Reunion in the Old Hometown

We made the trip to Dallas, then Wichita Falls, and guess what? They lost our bags! This is twice in a row. This trip is turning into a string of bad luck incidents. Little did I know what was in store. We got a rent car and found our way to the Holiday Inn.

We arrived just after lunch and found that Glen and Lavern Mitchell were waiting for us. They had driven in from Abilene just to see us. Glen and Lavern were old friends from way back and my sister Louise's very close friends. Glen was a navy pilot in WWII and wanted to know all about my new adventure in the Middle East. He was a PBY (flying boat) pilot and couldn't get over 200 miles per hour if he was going straight down. It was fascinating for him to discuss flying at over 500 miles per hour with me. We had a nice visit with them, and then they drove back to Abilene that same day.

My older sister Margret and her granddaughter-in-law arrived, and we picked them up and helped check them into our hotel. My son Greg and his wife Mary were already there, and we were visiting when my oldest son Jimmy and his wife Colleen arrived.

We were all checked into the same hotel, so it was easy to sit in the lobby and have a real get-together. We were all looking forward to the reunion tomorrow in the morning. The Fox family reunion had always taken all day Saturday and all day

Sunday. My sons wanted to spend the afternoon looking up their old homesteads. The homes where my sons had spent their early years from birth to second grade for Greg and the sixth grade for Jimmy looked much smaller than they remembered. I guess it's the same for all who try to return to the past.

DEPUTY SHERIFFS ARE FOR LOSERS

The Holiday Inn had a restaurant in the large atrium next to the swimming pool. We all met there for breakfast and continued our family get-together. As I paid the cashier and turned to walk away, a man and woman approached and said, "Are you James Fox?" Well, back in my hometown, and somebody recognizes me. "Why, yes, I am," I replied. He handed me a folded paper and said that I had been served. He was a deputy sheriff from Houston. My ex-wife was forcing me into court. I wished the deputy a nice day.

THE REUNION, WHAT HAPPENED?

We didn't go directly to the park where the reunion was to be held. The kids were so busy looking at the old homesteads. We didn't get to the park until about two o'clock in the afternoon. Nobody's home. The reunion always runs from Saturday through Sunday. Okay, back to the hotel. Get on the phone and try to call my cousins. No answer. Now I don't know what to do. I've come halfway around the world to a family reunion, and there's nobody at home.

Well, I wanted to buy a new pair of boots, so if we can't go to the reunion, then I might as well go to Henrietta, Texas, (nineteen miles east) and get me a pair of cowboy boots from Olsen-Steltzer. They were the premier saddle and boot shop for North Texas. That's the only place that I had ever bought cowboy boots, and they had made the saddle that my dad bought me when I was about fourteen years old. Bad luck again. Olsen-Steltzer was out of business.

Back to the Holiday Inn and more sitting around, drinking coffee and telling stories. We'll try for the reunion again on Sunday morning.

Sunday is the day, and the Foxes are gathering at the Girl Scout Park on the Seymour highway for the annual Fox family reunion. It was good to be there and visit with my cousins and my last surviving aunts and uncles. Aunt Velma, Aunt Melissa, Uncle Jessie, and Uncle Roy were the only ones left from a family of eleven. It was the smallest number ever gathered in my memory.

There was lots of good food there. There always was. I noted that none of Melissa's children were there. They came to see her for her surgery only a few weeks before.

Guy, my uncle Henry's son, was so drunk you could have arrested his brother. Well, he was having a good time, and no one was hurt. Plenty of homemade ice cream, and too soon it was over, and all started drifting away. Most had a distance to go and couldn't stay until dark. My sons all had to leave earlier for the eight-hour drive back to Houston.

We took our leave and went by to visit with Charles and Lola Sherfesee. Charles or Sherf as he was called had been my boss in the civil engineering department of the old Humble Oil & Refining Company. I had worked in the office next to his for twelve years, and we had grown very close. It seemed we grew closer after my departure from Wichita Falls.

It was nine o'clock Sunday when I called Roger Humphrey. Roger was a medical doctor that I had worked with at his clinic as a part-time helper (hypnosis technician) for a couple of years back in 1959 and 1960. That was before Charlotte and I got back together. Roger insisted on coming out to the hotel to see us even at the late hour. We talked until midnight, and Charlotte couldn't believe that Roger was still asking me to quit flying airplanes around and come back to work with him at the clinic. Roger and his partners used hypnosis with some of their patients, and I was the one that hypnotized the difficult ones. It was an extra job that paid $5 per hour, and that was good money in those days. Maybe I'll write that story someday.

Margret and her granddaughter were finally put on the airline. I thought we were going to have to render the young lady unconscious to get her aboard. She had decided that she was afraid of flying. Well, that's the way she came down here, wasn't it? I think Margret should have just left her at the terminal.

Our departure from Wichita Falls was delayed by a thunderstorm overhead the airport. So the pilot waited until it had passed, then he took off, and we flew through it on the way to Dallas.

On to California

The delay in Wichita Falls made out connecting flight for California very, very close. Too close when we arrived in California. Guess what? They lost our bags again! That's three times in a row. Does that sound like a conspiracy or just more bad luck?

Does this sound like we were spending a lot of money on airline tickets? Maybe I should explain, and when I do, then maybe you will also understand why we see so many foreigners riding around the country in the airlines. We learned that when you are living in a foreign country and buy a round-trip airline ticket to the USA, then you are able to buy what they call coupons for as little as $25 American. Each coupon is ticket to a new destination in the USA. That's right, you can fly from any place in the USA to any other place in the USA for $25. So for a couple of hundred dollars, you can do a lot of traveling. Our itinerary included a trip to California to see Charlotte's brother Jim and another trip to Oregon to see my other older sister Louise. The trip from Houston to Wichita Falls was only one coupon because stops to change planes for your destination only counted as one trip.

Our visit with Charlotte's brother Jim's family in San Luis Obispo was poorly planned. Jim was trying to leave on his annual hunting trip. I can't figure why we hadn't picked up on that sooner. Well, anyway, I had time to get a haircut. We had to stay an extra night anyway for our bags to catch up with us. That's right, they had been lost again. That was four times in a row. It looks like we are going for some sort of record, or maybe we'll get our names in the *Guinness World Records*. Or maybe it's just the baggage gods are angry.

THEN ON TO OREGON

More airline shenanigans. We flew the Metro III to San Francisco. They overbooked and offered us cash to sign up for the same flight tomorrow. We should have taken the offer of cash and a later flight. We had to wait four hours on connection in San Francisco for our flight to Portland. (Sorry about that. I meant Portland. Pilots think of cities as their three letter identifier. Overseas we use four letter identifiers.)

Louise picked us up at Portland and had a nice visit all the way back to North Bend, Oregon, down the coast from Portland. We stayed with my niece, Louise's daughter, Janell, her husband Carlton, and their son Craig. It was a nice visit with the Oregon branch of the family. Carlton is a pharmacist, Janell has a ladies dress shop, and Craig has video games in the mall where his dad's pharmacy is located. Craig makes $1,200 per week with the video machines. Not bad for a boy in high school.

My brother-in-law, Gerald, Louise's husband, can't get his breath if he doesn't get in a fishing or hunting trip every weekend. It's been that way since he was a teenager, and I was a subteenager. They were living in Albany, Oregon, a suburb of Portland, so after the visit down coast in North Bend, we went back to spend a little time in Albany. That meant a fishing trip. Well, it was less than a success. By that, I mean I caught more fish than Gerald did. In fact, I caught the only fish. Gerald was like an older brother to me. He was ten years older, a football star, and very close to my father. The three of us were either in the woods hunting, on the water fishing, or in between just waiting for the next adventure. And the trips were always that. I was neither the avid huntsman nor fisherman, but I always liked to be with my father because he was always a lot of fun, and he liked to have Gerald along because he was such a good hunter and fisherman. Margareet's husband Curtis was also an avid fisherman and taught Gerald fly-fishing. Curtis had passed away when he was only thirty-nine years old.

The funny part of this story is that I was a neophyte, amateur, beginner that didn't know what I was doing and always the one that caught the most or the biggest fish on these trips. Well, that's not quite right. Gerald was so competitive that the game could not be over until he won. A few years before on a trip to Oregon in the dead of winter, we had to—yes, we *had* to—go ice fishing on a frozen-over reservoir near Bend, Oregon.

"Hey, James, let's go ice fishing."

"Well, I don't know, Gerald, its only 8° out there."

"Yeah, well, that's what makes it great. Those trout will be hungry, and all you need for bait is little piece of Velveeta cheese. Why, we'll have to fight 'em off on a day like this."

The day was overcast and gray and just enough breeze to make you wonder what in the world are you doing here.

We got to the reservoir and found that another dozen or so intrepid souls were already there—fishing through a hole in the ice. Stumbling down the frozen bank of the reservoir, we got on the ice and didn't have to go more than one hundred feet to find a couple of unoccupied holes already cut in the ice.

"Hey, James, look we don't have to saw through the ice. We've got some ready holes."

"Oh yeah, maybe there is no one here because these holes are empty." My attempt at humor.

Gerald showed me how to do all that was needed to get started. You put a lead weight on the end of the line and a hook with cheese on it about eighteen inches up from the weight. Then all you had to do was lower the line through the ice until the lead weight touched the bottom and wait. I had barely got my sinker on the bottom when I felt the tug on my line. I knew enough to set the hook and pulled up a lake trout about eighteen inches long. It must have weighed a pound and a half. I'm not good on guessing about such things since I don't consider myself a real fisherman. But it was a nice catch, and Gerald hadn't even got his line in the water yet.

Now this may sound like good luck or great fishing or whatever, but once again, it was *bad luck*. I'm freezing, and we are not going to leave until Gerald catches a bigger fish! I caught a few more fish and quit because Gerald said that was my license limit. So, I just stood around shaking and shivering until Gerald caught his limit. I didn't understand why his limit was larger than mine but explained that it was because he had a resident license, and I only a temporary, or one-day license.

Since he caught more fish than I did, we finally left and went back to the cabin where it was warm. I'll have to add that my sister, Louise, can do a fine job on frying lake trout.

I almost forgot the trip that I made up to summer camp with the army reserve and spent the weekend with Louise and Gerald. This time, we had to go out into the Pacific and fish for salmon. To make a long story short, I caught the only fish that day, and it was the largest salmon caught and the prize catch of the season, or up until that time anyway. It weighed thirty-seven pounds and seven ounces, and Louise smoked it on her cooker all night, and we ate a big chunk of it just before I got on the airline back to Houston the next day. Unbelievable, right? It's all true.

BACK TO CALIFORNIA—BARELY

Our flight from Portland took us back to Los Angeles where we spent the night and visited some of Charlotte's friends. You know, she had lived in that area for forty years. Guess what? The airline didn't lose our bags! What I failed to mention was that Charlotte had taken a hard fall back in Riyadh that had left her with much pain in her left shoulder. She wanted to see her favorite doctor while in California. She really needed the relief. Charlotte had taken several falls while in Riyadh. I think it has something to do with her eyes. She misses steps or unevenness in the walkway. I try to watch out for her but can't be there all the time.

The doctor told her she would have to have an operation for a frozen shoulder. So I had to leave her there and hurry on back to Houston for my court date. We had relatives in Arizona and New Mexico, but they would have to wait until after my appointment with the court in Houston and Charlotte's operation.

Greg and Mary picked me up at the airport and put me up to save a little money, and it was a little closer to the court and lawyer.

To explain a little, my lawyer was green. It was his first divorce case. It may have been his first case for all I know, and we had been outwitted by the opposition. My savings account with Exxon I had given to my ex-wife, but I kept the company stock for myself. Of course I had given her the house, a new Lincoln Town Car, and all the furniture as well. But my lawyer overlooked the wording in the decree that stated I would continue to pay the temporary (contractual) alimony until she received the savings money from Exxon. Her lawyer saw a chance to really hit me a lick by not filling out the papers for the Exxon money! That meant that her money would continue to grow while waiting to be withdrawn, and I would have to pay her forever. After the divorce, I expected her to withdraw her money, so I quit sending the alimony (contractual since alimony is not required in Texas). Well, boom, she was cut off, and I was out of the country. So she filed a suit against me for failing to continue the alimony, and then since she had waited too long to move the money into another account, the IRS said that she owed them $25,000 in back taxes. Now she wanted not only the alimony that I had withheld, but she also wanted me to pay the $25,000.

The time in court didn't last long, and my ex-wife was not there. The judge said that I should pay the alimony that I had withheld, but I would not have to pay her IRS bill. After that was settled, it was not yet over. She, the judge, admonished my ex-wife's lawyer. She told him it was an underhanded trick that he had tried to pull on me, and she warned him to leave Mr. Fox alone from here on, and she didn't want to see him in her court again!

A little later, her lawyer, my lawyer, and I were standing in the hall for just a moment, and I asked her lawyer why did he think he could get away with such a crazy idea. He paused for a few seconds and said, "It's because I'm stupid." I said, "Shh, not so loud, there may be some folks around here that don't know that yet."

After all the running around, talking to CPA, Exxon, and the judge, all I had to do was pay the alimony, which I had intended to do in the first place; I knew if I didn't stop paying her she would just keep bleeding me. I had to do something to get her attention. The judge said I was to pay no court costs or lawyer fees. How about that?

A few minutes later, my ex-wife passed me in the hall. If looks could kill, then I wouldn't have needed my return ticket to Riyadh.

TAKE A BREAK AND SHIP THE JAGUAR TO THE UK

"The XKE after it arrived in England"

Since my Jaguar mechanic had left the States and was back home in England, I had an XKE that was giving me grief in Houston. When I left for Saudi Arabia, I left the XKE, a Chevy Beauville van, a Lincoln Versailles, and a Chevy Camero. Greg was supposed to have sold them and put the money in the bank. Greg had disposed of all but the Lincoln and the Jaguar XKE, and he didn't really want to keep it sitting in the street. While in England and talking to David Groves, my friend and factory-trained Jaguar mechanic, I decided to ship the Jag to England

and let him fix it up for sale. Now all I had to do was get it shipped. Sounds simple enough, but have you ever tried it?

After a lot of phone calls, we ended up with Gladys. Gladys should have worked for the government. She could talk for thirty minutes, and you still didn't understand what she had said. It was a long way to get the details straight, and as it turned out, the process was simple. It was getting the details straight the way they were presented by Gladys that made everything difficult.

Directions to the dock were vague and getting worse. I'm running out of time, and it's time for me to go. Greg said he would do his dad a favor and drive it down to the dock for me. Well, it was Columbus Day, and they are closed. Gladys didn't tell us they were going to be closed on Columbus Day. On the way back, the Jag overheated and quit on the side of the road. Had to call a wrecker and have it towed back to Greg's home on the outskirts of Houston in Spring, Texas. More *bad luck*. We have to leave, so I'll try again after we get back from New Mexico.

Oh, I forgot to tell you. Charlotte came in from her surgery with her arm in a sling. She said the operation on her shoulder was done without anesthetics and was the most painful she had ever experienced.

Take a Break and Go to New Mexico

There is a little fat girl in Albuquerque working for budget that I'll choke the first chance I get. The terminal is all tore up under construction. I'm talking all tore up. There were detours for the detours, and when we finally found budget, the fat girl was too busy talking on the phone to her boyfriend to wait on us. My patience was already worn thin from all the extra walking we had to do to find her in the first place. She finally decided to wait on us without hanging up on her friend. The paperwork was filled out, and directions were given for us to find the car. By now, it's dark and raining.

She gave me directions out the north side of the building instead of the east. Then it started to rain harder, and we were a quarter of a mile away and in the wrong lot. We found a parking man, and he drove us around until we found the car. Choking would be letting the fat girl off easy. Our luck was still running what you might call *not good*.

We drove to the Pounds' (Muriel Pounds is Charlotte's sister) ranch, which was a hundred miles southeast of Albuquerque near a little place called Cedarvale. We missed the turn off twice. Muriel was glad to see us and had a room ready for the weary travelers.

Muriel had her arm in a sling, which matched Charlotte's arm in a sling. Well, that was Muriel's *bad luck*.

OLD FRIENDS, FAMILY, DUST, AND MORE LAWYERS

One of the reasons we were in New Mexico was to try and wrap up the sale of the Fox Ranch. We called the lawyer about the ranch. He had good news and bad news. The good news was that one of the heirs wanted to buy the ranch from the rest of us. The bad news was she didn't have any money. So what's new?

Muriel's husband Tom was in a nursing home in Albuquerque suffering with dementia. We visited with Tom for a while, and he said he remembered me. Then on to Santa Fe and spent the night there. Visited with the Keelans, more kinfolks, and returned to the Pounds' ranch in Cedarvale. That evening Charlotte's brother Ben and wife with the other brother John came to dinner. The grandnephew, Marvin showed up with his arm in a sling. That was his *bad luck*. Marvin had played special music at our wedding. So there stood the three of them lined up in a row. Muriel, her grandson, Marvin, and Charlotte, all with their arm in a sling. There was plenty of *bad luck* to go around.

The next day, we visited with Dr. Dawson and his little brother. Robert Dawson graduated with Charlotte and me back in '46. That was forty-one years ago. Robert and I had kept up all the years with letters and phone calls. Neither of us had kept up with Charlotte. Robert is a doctor of agriculture and dean at New Mexico A&M University.

We all went to the Fox ranch about seven miles south of Cedarvale. It was depressing. The ranch house was falling apart and Eddie Sanchez was working on the windmill. The water level is at 380 feet, and the windmill seems to need constant work. Eddie is over a year behind in his rent for the ranch but promises to catch up this fall just as soon as he ships some more steers to market. Well, maybe.

One thing about the dusty trip down to see the ranch, it cured any thoughts we might have had about returning from overseas to live there. Come to think of it, we were vaccinated for that several years ago.

BACK TO HOUSTON FOR SCHOOL

Now it's time for me to attend the FlightSafety school on Atlantic procedures. FlightSafety is the factory-approved organization that offers schooling for Gulfstream and other crews. This school is four days long in the classroom, plus one day in the water for ditching procedures.

Charlotte and I drove the little Lincoln down to Hobby airport and checked into the Holiday Inn. My copilot Daghistani showed up about midnight, about par for him.

Daghistani is a Saudi and almost always in a jovial mood. How do you like that word? He has an infectious smile (another good word) and does a good job as a copilot. He wears a small Clark Gable moustache, a big smile, sparkling black eyes,

344

and weighs about 135 pounds. Daghi, as I call him, is a good copilot but would be no help in a fight.

We made it fine through the classroom periods for Atlantic procedures, but on the next to last day, we were told by the instructor to meet at the swimming pool in the Holiday Inn for the last class, and it would be on ditching procedures. We were also told to wear old clothes because we would all be going into the water! The class was mandatory to passing the course.

The next morning, all the class was present except Daghi. I wasn't too concerned because late was his natural state. Sure enough, after the rest of us were in the water trying to climb aboard the rubber raft, Daghi comes into pool area. He is dressed in a three-piece suit. Looks like he is ready for a night on the town.

"Hey, Daghi, you can't get in the water dressed like that."

"I don't intend to get in the water regardless of my dress."

"Daghi, it is mandatory to pass the course. You don't want to go home and have everyone know that you failed the course, do you?"

"I am not going to get in the water, and I'm not going to fail the course."

The instructor was there and heard the exchange and just lowered his chin and shook his head because he knew it was true. Medevac spent a lot of money; I'm talking a lot of money with FlightSafety and was not going to fail one of their crew members, especially a Saudi. (Saudis don't go into the water voluntarily!)

The week was not a failure in any respect. We both passed the course, and Daghi discovered Sam's Club. I let him in on my membership card, and he tried to buy out the store. I'm sure he had to pay extra baggage fees to get home.

Well, school's out, and Daghistani is loaded up and taken to IAH for his trip to Savannah. We still have our simulator training to do with FlightSafety over there.

TAKE A BREAK AND SHIP THE JAGUAR TO THE UK

More paperwork to do to get the XKE on the boat. Finally, the Jag is loaded, but there is still paperwork to do. How can that be? Never mind, just get it done so I can get out of town. I don't think I was cut out for this international exporting stuff.

TIME TO GO TO SAVANNAH

We had one more night to spend in Houston, so we had dinner at Papasita's with our friends Brent and Mary Crabe, and Riley and Jan Killian. It was a Saturday night, and the food and company were great. Remember, Brent was my best man at our wedding. Brent and Riley were great pilots and fun to be with. Their wives were fun as well. Do you know how rare it is to have couples that are compatible?

It seems that so often, if a man has a friend, then the wives can't get along. When you find couples that get along, then double fun.

Sunday morning, let's go to Savannah.

CHARLOTTE GETS TO RIDE IN THE GIII SIMULATOR
AND
A BAD NIGHT AT PALMER'S

We had a new instructor for ground school. He was boring, boring, boring. I won't mention his name, but we never had him again, and that was great. Studying the aircraft systems can be interesting or deadly dull. It's all in the instructor. This guy could make a class on sex dull—even with pictures.

"Mohammed Daghistani"

Daghi and I finished our time in simulator early with some time left, so the simulator instructor let Charlotte ride in the right seat of the GIII. She thought it was a great thrill. The simulator instructor asked me if I would like to fly the space shuttle. The GIII simulator was used by NASA for training the space shuttle pilots. By pulling a few tricks, the simulator instructor could deploy all the drag devices on the simulator, and it would fly just like the space shuttle! He placed us at twenty thousand feet of altitude and just a few miles short of the runway and gave me the controls. I just used the basic skill I learned from first flying a jet, i.e., point the nose at the runway and watch your speed. Since the simulator had become a glider, there was no power to add or subtract, and that made it more difficult. But the simulator instructor had made it easy for me by placing me at the right altitude and distance from the runway. All I had to do was keep the nose down, and when

346

I got down to what felt like the right place, then pull the nose up and flare until we touched down.

Charlotte and I made it, and no one was hurt.

One of the best places in Savannah for seafood, and there are a lot of them, is Palmer's out in the swampland. We took Daghistani to Palmer's. My halibut was so bad I had to send it back. They didn't even have any oysters. All in all, a bad night.

We finished up our school early and were gone by Thursday afternoon. The airline took us back to IAH (Houston) via DFW (Dallas). We had thought that we were leaving on Saturday, but an examination of our tickets showed that we didn't leave until Sunday. That would give me an extra day to try and get rid of that Jaguar.

BACK TO HOUSTON AND SHIP THE JAGUAR TO THE UK

All this time and the paperwork for getting that Jag out of the port of Houston is still not finished. What started as $600 ended up as $930 plus wrecker charges. Live a little and learn a lot.

SHOULD WE STILL GO TO GERMANY?

After all that has happened so far, we are seriously considering skipping our planned trip to Germany and going on back to Riyadh. Charlotte had never been to Germany, so we decided to go with our original plans and have a few days with the Krauts. Little did we know what was to happen next.

ARRIVING IN GERMANY WITH TIGHT BOOTS AND A LOCKED BRIEFCASE

Our nonstop trip from IAH (Houston) to Frankfurt had stops in DFW (Dallas) and Chicago O'Hare. I noted a funny sounding brake on the right side of the aircraft on taxi out of DFW. It broke down on the taxiway at Chicago, and we sat there an hour to be hauled in by the tug—another warning.

I failed to mention that I had spent some shopping money while in Texas. I didn't get my boots in Henrietta as planned, so looked for a pair in Houston. On Charlotte's insistence, I paid $400 for a pair of boots she thought were beautiful. I had never spent a quarter of that price for anything to go on my feet before. Oh well, we're rich now, so why not. I also bought a leather briefcase from Sam's. Well, Daghistani was buying all that stuff, and I had to buy something, and besides, I've always wanted a real leather briefcase.

This is going to be a long trip so once we were out of Chicago with our next stop Frankfurt, I pulled my new $400 boots off on the plane just to relax. We had the first seats behind the partition for coach, so we had plenty of room too (that was true back in those days). It was a good time to transfer all my important things into my new leather briefcase.

It was all a good plan, but after landing in Frankfurt, *bad luck* showed up again. My feet had swollen during the flight, and I couldn't get my boots on—that is, my new $400 boots. During the struggle, everyone is getting up to leave the plane. Charlotte can't stand to watch, so she tries to help by getting between me and what I'm doing. She does this all the time. I'm pulling on the straps of my right boot when my hand slips off, and my elbow hits Charlotte in the face. Result, a black eye, and the boot is still not on.

I was wishing for talcum powder or stronger arms when I finally got my boots on, and we got off the airplane. The relief didn't last long, however, because when we got to the first checkpoint, I found that my new briefcase was locked, and I couldn't get it open. Well, I could get one of the hasps open but not the second one. One lock worked, and one didn't. That doesn't mean it was half locked. We had to get help from someone with something to pry with, and we finally broke into my new leather briefcase where passports, money, declarations, etc., were kept safe. More *bad luck*.

We took a cab to the Kempinski Hotel Gravenbruch Frankfurt. It was a very nice hotel except the bed had a crack down the middle and a crack in the comforter. Well, it was a deluxe room with an advertised rate of 390 DM (US$245). Don't forget that's 1987 dollars, but with our discount from Universal Weather, it was only about $120. I think I've already explained that we use Universal for such things. Our dinner was $25 each, nothing special, and our breakfast was $13 each. We may be wearing tight boots and horsehair underwear, but we're right up there with the rich folks.

Kempinski Hotel Gravenbruch Frankfurt

Located in a sixteenth-century building, the Kempinski Hotel Gravenbruch Frankfurt provides air-conditioned rooms and suites with solid wood furniture. All rooms include slippers and bathrobes, etc., etc., etc.

First Rest Then

Tomorrow, I've got to find someone to fix the locks on my briefcase. We'll spend the rest of the day just looking around town. The following two days, we'll take tours and then an easy trip to Riyadh eh?

What Happens When You Try to Help a Stranger?

Okay, we found a shop that did locks, and they replaced the broken ones. After that, we took the hotel van to downtown Frankfurt. You know we can just stroll around a little. While looking in a bank window at a display of gold coins, two things happened. One was a midget from Yugoslavia that wanted to exchange German marks for American dollars; the second thing is all of a sudden, I needed to find a public facility really, really bad.

The midget gave me a story about not being able to get US dollars, and he needed them to give to his sister who was blah, blah, blah. I had been faced with this situation in South America a few years before. Locals are not allowed to have more than a small amount of US dollars. So I was inclined to help him out. Besides, I needed some German marks anyway, and I really needed to find that facility right away.

At the same time, Charlotte is pulling me away and generally having a fit. I'm trying to explain to her that I know what I'm doing and going for my money, and I really need to find that facility soon. Besides, I was going to make a little extra on the exchange rate the midget was offering. There is just too much going on for this ole country boy to handle. I made the exchange with the midget, got away from Charlotte, and rushed away for the public facility.

Once inside and relieved, I thought it might be wise to see what I had bought. The midget's con worked. I had bought with $400 about $60 worth of various foreign monies. Charlotte was right. I was wrong, and the *bad luck* was still with us. Charlotte wants to commit homicide on the midget. Too late he was long gone, and I told her he probably needed it for his sick family and a little daughter that needed an operation.

Well, that ruined the day and wasn't helping the overall average. We decided to cheer up things could be worse. We cheered up, and things got worse.

What Happens When You're Not Looking?

We're going to have our tour anyway. How about an all-day castle and Rhine River tour? Early the next morning, we're on our way down to the tour office. The hotel provides the transport. Big bus and twenty more or so folks to go with us to Heidelberg and the castle tour. It was a nice drive with the guide explaining landmarks, none of which I recall. Taking pictures has become a chore for me, so I give the camera to Charlotte. Good idea. My cheery attitude is suffering somewhat.

"Heidelberg Castle . . . home of a thief"

Off the bus at the castle with a few people already standing around like they had just finished an earlier tour. The guide takes us through the castle by unlocking doors in front of us and locking doors behind us. I thought that a little strange. Why not just raise the drawbridge? Charlotte taking pictures in large hall, she sat her purse down on the table, and I just sat down. As I said, my attitude was suffering.

We never saw the purse again. The guide ushered us out into the courtyard for a "break" he said, and then he disappeared. It was about this time that Charlotte quit taking pictures and missed her purse. We searched everywhere in sight—nothing. We couldn't find the guide as well. It at last dawned on us that the purse was last seen on the table in the large hall just before we went into the courtyard. That's it. Just get back into the large hall, and we'll have the purse. We can't, it's locked. Well, find someone with a key. It's not easy. When we finally find someone with a key, they reluctantly unlocked the large hall and no purse.

Nothing left to do but call the police. My call to the police in Heidelberg got no one excited at that station. It was more like ho hum on their end of the line. I tried to give an orderly account of what had happened, and they interrupted me to tell me to file a report with the police in Frankfurt. That's it, they weren't going to do anything. I have never fully understood why they could not do something, but that's what they said, and that's what I was going to have to do.

We had to finish our tour that day and try to find the Frankfurt police station in the morning. It was hard to enjoy what was left of the day. I got conned in the morning for $400 and Charlotte lost her purse in the afternoon. She had everything in that purse that she had accumulated since she was four years old.

The cab driver didn't want to take us to the police station and left us off around the corner. Now we have seen inside the British police station and also the German police station. We had to get the police report first. Everything else will not happen until you have the police report or several copies thereof in your hand.

WHAT HAPPENS WHEN YOU LOSE YOUR PASSPORT IN A FOREIGN COUNTRY

Well, nothing happens until you have the police report. The second step is to go to the consul general at the embassy of the country of your nationality. In our case, we had to use the American Embassy because they didn't have a New Mexico Embassy in West Germany. They have a Texas Embassy there, but they won't issue a passport to anyone that wasn't born in Texas. You can't just marry your way into a Texas passport. The photo machine takes four photos, so don't look down until the flash quits flashing. They will take US dollars, or they will exchange German marks. The entire operation can be finished in a couple of hours, including the search. The best you can hope for is a temporary passport, good for ninety days, unless you can produce a birth certificate. But the visas are gone. How Do You Get to Saudi Arabia without a Visa?

My first thought was that to get a Saudi visa for Charlotte make take several weeks. Better get her tickets to London so at least she can stay with friends while the several weeks go by that it takes to get her a Saudi visa. She got the temporary passport with the German police report, so then from the embassy to the airport and bought tickets on British Caledonian from Frankfurt to London. It's not very far, but expensive—490 marks ($300+ in 1987 dollars).

The night before, I had called Riyadh and left word with Jerry Padova, the mechanic. I told him to spread the word with Major Shablan that I wasn't coming back until I got my wife's problems straightened out. This was interpreted to mean that I wasn't coming back until she had her visa and could return with me to Riyadh. That didn't hurt. Got a call from Mohammed Hanno, and he said that they sent a telex to the military attaché in Bonn and for me to go there and get a letter from him early the next day to get the visa from the Saudi consulate. Sounds easy.

Arranged for rent car through the concierge of the hotel that night. Got a small Mercedes, new, 190, I think. Okay. Up up and away early the next morning. We planned for a 5:00 a.m. wake-up and a 6:00 a.m. departure, but we were up at 4:00 a.m. and away before 5:00 a.m. We were anxious. It was cold and foggy, and I knew when I left that I would never find my way back.

Interesting drive. Stopped for breakfast at a German truck stop. No English. Interesting. Arrived in Bonn before most everyone else. Before 7:00 a.m. saw some going to work traffic just like back home. Sat in front of a Mercedes place waiting for it to open so we could get instructions. That didn't work, so we drove around and finally found an Esso service station. Great, no English. Customer speaks a little English. He laughs and leaves. What are they all laughing about? It must be the question. "Vo is de Saudi Arabian Embassy?" Buy a map for 7 marks. Lieutenant colonel in the Luftwaffe asks if he can help and then said just follow me. He drove straight away to the Saudi Embassy and Consulate but no military attaché. We must get the visa from the military attaché.

With map and instructions, it takes an hour and thirty minutes to find, and it's not two miles away. Looks like a mausoleum. Behind a tall chain-link fence up on the side of a hill. The guard lets me in and points around the corner and up the stairs. Nobody's home. Finally, a middle-aged man shows up with a young helper—his copilot, I guess. Good thing the older man doesn't really know what's happening. They took me upstairs to a room with four men. One was sitting behind a desk with several phones on it. They claimed to know nothing of a telex from Riyadh. Okay, then looking at the red phone on the desk, I said that it must be a direct line to Riyadh. The man behind the desk admitted that it was. Well, then, I need to make a phone call to Riyadh and talk to General Hammed. They knew the general and reminded me that it was Thursday. Rats! I forgot about that. It's the weekend in Riyadh. Okay, then I'll talk to Major Shablan. They didn't know the major. I was adamant, and it took fifteen minutes to convince them to call, but they did. Nothing is easy here.

Major Shablan convinced them to issue the visa. Exactly what he said, I'll never know, but as soon as he was off the phone, the slowdown started again. The man behind the desk said, "Come back tomorrow for the paperwork."

"Why can't you do it now?" I asked, thinking there was no one doing anything within my view.

"Oh no, we can't do it today, you must come back."

"Well, I'm not leaving until I get the paperwork." With that, I had a final idea. They were all smoking cigarettes, so I just pulled out a cigar and lit it up, took a chair, crossed my legs, and was ready to wait. It must have been the cigar. The Saudis can't stand them. In five minutes, I had the paperwork in my hand and was out the front gate.

Okay, now back to the consulate, and it didn't take an hour and half to find it. Once there, everything was complete except they needed a fee for stamping the passport. Fine, how much? New problem, they wouldn't take German marks, American dollars, Saudi riyals because I had them. No, they must have a bank draft.

Now I have to go to the bank. We once again had to do a search, and when we found the bank, it was closed for lunch. That's right, closed for lunch. The *bad luck* bird is roosting on my shoulders. Okay, then we will go to lunch. Found a place, parked the car, and had a snack. Came out to find that I had a parking ticket. Back to the consulate, and the door is locked. They are closed for the day. I am reaching the knot on the end of the rope. While standing there fuming and considering kicking the door, it opens, and someone is leaving. I caught the door, forced it open, and went inside.

There is a ninety-eight-pound clerk behind the teller's window, and when I tried to give him the passport and paperwork and bank draft for the visa, he said he was closed.

"No, you're not closed yet, not until you stamp this passport."

"No, I can't do that, we are closed."

"Okay, then I'm just going to stand here and smoke a cigar until you do."

The cigar did the trick. That's an idea. Use cigars when questioning Saudis, I'll bet they would all confess right away.

I got the passport stamped, and we made it back to Frankfurt and bought Charlotte a new ticket for Riyadh. There was no refund for the ticket to London that she didn't use, and the new ticket to Riyadh cost more than her round-trip ticket to the USA had cost!

We made it back to Riyadh and needed a rest when we got there.

Talk about your *bad luck*.

JDF Letter:
Riyadh, Saudi Arabia
October 28, 1987

TO:　　GAMA Transportation Officer
From:　Capt. James D. Fox
Subject: Annual Travel Entitlement, Plus

This letter is to explain certain facts affecting my annual travel entitlement, plus other travel requirements associated with my annual leave.

During the latter part of 1986, Medevac made a training schedule for the flight crews to do their training with FlightSafety International at various parts of the United States. The location of training is dependent on aircraft crew assignments. The crews for the Gulfstream II and III must do their training at Savannah, Georgia. The Lear crews train in Arizona. Normal training periods for a crew member is approximately five days each six months. There are other special training sessions that are sometimes scheduled.

Medevac advised that we would attend one of the six-month training sessions while on our annual leave. The intent of that request was to reduce the cost of the two annual training sessions.

The first of my training sessions was in February of 1987. The second was scheduled for the second week of August of 1987. I took some leave with the February session and planned more during the August session.

During May and June, Medevac experienced a serious shortage of flight crews, especially captains. I was asked to delay my training and leave until some later date for the convenience and benefit of Medevac. I agreed to do this.

Time progressed, and the shortage of captains was getting worse not better. I informed Medevac that I had urgent business to take care of in the States and could not delay my leave later than the September 15 date. They agreed to September 15. Later, as the crew shortage was not relieved, I was asked to delay again at least until the first of October. We compromised with the twenty-second as absolutely the last day of work because it was imperative that I be in Texas by the twenty-fourth of September. We had an agreement, and Medevac arranged for my schedule with FlightSafety International to coincide with my leave. The Medevac flight schedule was also made to reflect my last day of work as September 22.

My lack of knowledge of how to get the airline tickets through GAMA and Medevac led me to be very late in obtaining the tickets. Before I had the tickets in hand, an emergency Medevac flight came up that was going to affect the scheduled departure for my leave. The trip required two captains to complete, and there were only two of us that had the necessary visas to make the trip. If I had not agreed to go, then the Medevac trip would be jeopardized. I agreed to the trip late on Wednesday, September 16. The trip was to leave at 0530 on Saturday, September 19.

This meant that I had to get the tickets for my leave on Thursday. I saw Mr. Brown at the GAMA office and signed some forms, then went to the STTD office to get the tickets. Mr. Brown told me to charge the tickets to GAMA, and we would sort out the details later. Now I am trying to sort out the details.

My understanding was that GAMA would provide two round-trip tickets to point of hire at excursion rates. I was also to be provided a single round-trip ticket from Houston to Savannah to Houston for training.

It is my understanding that GAMA has a special price from Saudi Airlines regarding the Riyadh-New York-Riyadh fare. Due to the constraints discussed above, my wife and I were not able to leave on the day the Saudi flight left for New York. The only flight that we could use on the twenty-second was a Saudi flight to Paris, which meant a change of airports in Paris, not a fun thing to do.

The development at this stage seems to suggest that no one wants to pay for the extra cost of routing through Paris or the trip to Savannah.

The agent at STTD tells me that GAMA usually buys a round-trip ticket only to New York and then gets VUSA tickets for the remainder of the flight to complete the total round-trip tickets. This does not seem to me to be the same as excursion round-trip tickets to point of hire.

This entire matter may be just a misunderstanding. It seems, however, that I am on the wrong end of the misunderstanding and will be the one that has to pay. If this is true, then be assured that in the future, I will not be so ready to adjust my plans for the convenience of someone else, especially if it's going to cost me extra to do so.

Could I suggest that GAMA and Medevac get together and sort this out? It is a great waste of my time to be running back and forth between GAMA, Medevac, and STTD because the result is that nothing is settled. It's just deducted from my pay.

I would like a response to this letter as soon as possible, please.

Sincerely,
Capt. James D. Fox
Fixed Wing, GII, GIII

Dispatch:
Riyadh, Saudi Arabia
October 29, 1987

MIDNIGHT RUNNERS

Leaving the country when you're in Saudi Arabia is not all that easy. Why not, you may ask? Well, the answer may seem to be complicated, but the real reason is that they won't to stay in absolute control of whatever they are involved in, particularly in their own country. They speak with fear of what happened in Iran when the "I told ya" took over. They don't want the religious fanatics to do the same thing here.

A parallel reason is a basic mistrust of those that are not Saudi. I didn't say Arab; I said Saudi. They are indiscriminate in those that they distrust. That is, Egyptians, Iranians, Jordanians, Iraqis, etc., are all looked on as substandard not to be trusted and worse. They will freely tell you that the Iranians are thieves, the Egyptians are stupid, the Syrians are treacherous, and on ad infinitum.

One of the first things that should make you suspicious is that the employer keeps your passport while you are here in his country. The stated reason is that he is responsible for your debts and actions, but that is a responsibility that has been passed down to the lowest echelon. "Besides," he will state, "you don't need it. Your Iqama will serve as your identification!"

Of course, the government does not want you to leave the country with debts, and the easiest way to control that is through the employers. The second clue is the travel limit place on foreigners here. We are allowed to be no more than 40 kilometers from the site of our employment without a special letter from our employer with seal, stating where we are going and when we must return. If you are caught without the letter, off to jail, or as the Brits say, "straight away."

The Westerners speak of "runners." These are people that leave without notice, i.e., they "run" away leaving the country, their job, their possessions, everything just to get out. If they don't have their passports, they can't run. To be a runner, you must have access to your passport with an exit visa. You don't know about an exit visa? Well, in the Kingdom of Saudi Arabia, when you apply for a work visa, you receive an entrance visa only. To leave the country, you must apply for an exit visa. The exit visa is only good for two months unless you activate it by leaving, then it is good for six months, i.e., you must use it in two months, or it's no good. The exit visa allows you to return based on your original entry visa. If you apply for an exit visa and do not use it within two months, then you are fined SR1,000 ($266.67).

Pilots like me are issued multiple entry/exit visas. These are not easy to get and are very closely controlled. The passports for all the Westerners in the company I work for are kept locked in a safe. When we are assigned an international flight, we are issued the passports. We are supposed to hand them back in when we return, but I do not, and they don't press me for it. The nurses are not treated quite so well. They have no slack whatsoever.

Just last night, one of the nurses told me that she was being allowed to go on a weekend visit to Jeddah, an hour fifteen by air on the Red Sea. Well, what is so special about that? She has been trying to go for two and a half years. She caught the regular boss out of the country, and his assistant gave her the letter.

Americans as a group know very little about the need for control of passports, work permits, identity papers, etc., because they never see them except in old war movies. They seem to be not a part of the real world. Well, let me tell you, foreigners here are a part of the real world, and once you leave the good old USA, then you better pay attention to the above.

Captain Schmitz became a runner! He had insulted one too many, and that one was not a TCN, but a Saudi! He and others had been overheard talking about the "rag heads," "dune coons," and "sand niggers." My friend Hakim Alaway met him on the sidewalk in our compound and told him he would be sorry for what he said.

Schmitz had already sent his wife home, and it was just before payday. He had just returned from an international trip, so he still had his passport. He collected his pay, and the same night he caught the midnight flight to London. He left everything behind that couldn't go in his suitcase! That's a runner.

Dispatch:
Riyadh, Saudi Arabia
November 15, 1987

JUST ANOTHER DAY

About 0930, Romeo called a mission to Khamis on MS4. Pick up a baby and return to Riyadh. It was my first trip with Hakim Al Alawy, a new copilot. I was an F1, and Eid was an F1, but Hakim volunteered to take his place because he had a mission the night before. Another new copilot, Hanee, wanted to go along, which I approved. I let Hakim fly the leg to Khamis, and he did a good enough job, but the third man was quite a distraction. Of course he wanted to ask a lot of questions, and he tried to read the checklist—all of which was a distraction.

On the approach into runway 14 at Khamis, the tower gave some garbled instruction that ended in ". . . four miles." I gave him a roger, and my mind went back to the cockpit because it was busy with watching and answering questions. A moment later, I asked if we were cleared to land, and he gave me some more garbled, then ". . . four miles." I rogered and assumed that we were cleared to land. It was absolutely clear and no other traffic in sight or on the radio. After landing, the tower called and angrily asked why we landed without a clearance. Hakim got on the mike after I took control of the airplane, and he made some pleadings in Arabic. It was rather lengthy, but after he finished, the tower was a little happier.

I asked him, "What did you tell him—that I was just a dumb Kawajee that didn't know any better?"

Hani said, "Yeah, that's just what he said. How did you know? He also told them that you were new and were very sorry and promised that you would never do that again."

It must have worked. Nobody shot at me.

On the return, Khalid departure fussed at us because we missed a radio call. On the climb out, I was flying, and Hakim was working the radio, but he got on the HF and was talking on the radio when Khalid departure called. I acknowledged the call but stood by until Hakim finished his call, which was only momentary. When he answered the call, he was told that we better pay attention. The day was started.

We arrived back in Riyadh and were still making out the paperwork when another mission was called to pick up a patient in Madinah. When I asked the condition of the patient, the nurse said that he had a cold that had developed into a bronchial condition. I said, "That's what I got."

Hani wanted to go again, but the politics got him. Hakim had been given charge of the three new hires and was supposed to see after all phases of the pre-training. Abdul Halawany, a helicopter captain, has been made in charge of all training, helicopter, and fixed wing. So his feathers were ruffled that he had not been asked about the first flight, therefore he would not approve the second flight. We left without Hani.

We got halfway to Madinah, and Rome base called for us to return to Riyadh. We needed to pick up a doctor for Madinah. We got halfway back to Riyadh, and Rome called and said never mind go on to Madinah. By this time, ATC knows we are all crazy. We arrived in Madinah, and the patient arrived with a friend or relative. The patient was healthier than I was.

As we were landing at Riyadh, MS3 was waiting at the hold short line for departure. They were just leaving for Madinah with a doctor. Surely the same one that we nearly had to come back to get. The passenger we brought back requested Hakim to carry his bag off the airplane. Hakim told him to get his own bag. We'll see later if something comes of that. Everyone asks, "Well, who carried the bag off?" The answer is I didn't, and Hakim didn't, so it had to be *Steffi* (nurse) or the passenger himself. Are you curious about who carried the bag? Well, you see, over here you never know for sure who has the stroke (power). This guy could have some very high connection or why so much to-do about picking him up and *all the doctor stuff.*

I got home in time to go to dinner with Jerry and Linda (Jerry's birthday). Italian night at the Marriott. Good food and we ate outdoors. Linda paid the check without my knowledge. I couldn't believe it. I usually get to do that. I was shocked. Later, we went to Jerry's apartment for cake. Had a nice visit until the drunks started showing up. A Brit, a Scott female, another male unknown, and Phil Thorpe, they were all so drunk, except Phil the Mormon. They couldn't hit the ground with their hats. We excused ourselves and went home.

Author's Note: I haven't explained about many of my associates, but it's time I did. Medevac had just taken delivery on five new copilots. By brand-new, I mean new to Medevac. Some had flying experience beyond flight school, and some did not. The ones just out of flight school with a commercial, multiengine rating had also been sent to FlightSafety for a copilot's training on the Gulfstream. They were very green and almost frightened to fly the Gulfstream. This group of about four took some very close watching. There were a couple of others that flying experience past flight school that included flying light twins solo in weather, either in the USA or Europe. Hanni had experience in the USA and Hakim had experience flying light twins in Europe. None of them had any time in the air in a jet.

As I found out later, Hakim had been the personal friend and pilot for Salem Bin Ladin. Hakim had met Bin Ladin while they were both stationed at Lackland AFB in San Antonio. It's a long story, but Bin Ladin was the son of the owner of the largest construction company in Saudi Arabia. As a result, Hakim became the personal pilot for Bin Ladin's family when they lived in Europe. He flew a light twin solo, and anyone that does that, and survives, has got to be a good pilot. More about Hakim and Bin Ladin later.

Jerry Padova was a Gulfstream mechanic from New York. His specialty was pancakes. Jerry couldn't buy the pancake mix he needed in Riyadh, so we had a standing order when we went back to the States. "Don't forget to get me some pancake mix."

JDF Letter:
Riyadh, Saudi Arabia
November 15, 1987

TO: Transportation Agent
              GAMA
FROM: James D. Fox
              Captain Fixed Wing
              Medevac
SUBJECT: Overcharges on Car Loan

     Please note the list of payments on my car loan as listed below. I believe you will agree that the last month payment was with held in error. This error has been reported three times verbally without action. I would appreciate the return of these monies as soon as possible.

Original car loan:		SR20,000.00
Deduction of car grant:		1,181.00
Remainder of loan for repayment:		18,819.00
Schedule of payments:	6 Oct 86	2,688.00
	31 Oct 86	2,688.00
	Nov 86	1,350.00
	Dec 86	1,350.00
	Jan 87	1,350.00
	Feb 87	1,350.00
	Mar 87	1,350.00
	Apr 87	1,350.00
	May 87	1,350.00
	Jun 87	1,350.00
	Jul 87	1,350.00
	Aug 87	1,350.00
	Sep 87	1,293.00
	Total:	20,169.00
Loan for repayment:		18,819.00
Overpayment:		SR1,350.00

Sincerely,
James D. Fox
Captain Fixed Wing
Medevac

Author's Note: Just another letter to keep the Saudis straight. Yes, I got the money, but only after this letter and more hard words. They just seem to hate to pay if they can keep from it. You have to remember that in this country, any interest charges are illegal! Even the bank does not pay interest on money kept there; neither can they charge interest. They have other ways of making a profit. You can be sure of that.

Dispatch:
Riyadh, Saudi Arabia
December 15, 1987

FLY ALL DAY THEN FLY ALL NIGHT

Still trying to recover from staying up till 0200 flying with Waleed and then agreeing to take his trip with Mohammed Hanno the next day. I didn't know that I'd be out until 0200 and then have to get up at 0545 the next morning. I flew six legs with Hanno that day. Now the following day, I had another full day of flying with Eid. A full day of flying with Eid is enough to make Samson want to grow hair.

At approximately 1900, I hear Alpha 30 being called and then Gulfstream I being called, and I made the remark, "That sounds like there is an international mission in the works." It was. It finally sifted down to a mission that if it left, it would leave about 0200. That departure time will make an arrival in London just after curfew (0630 on weekdays during the wintertime). Trouble is, if the doctors could leave now, they could take Saudi to Jeddah and then British Caledonian to London. But they would have to catch the 2200 flight to make the connection. No one would know until later.

It's my trip, and now it's time for the phone to start ringing. An international trip doesn't stay a secret for long, especially if it's a Western captain going. Hanno keeps his trips very secret. It sure would be nice to take a nap before flight time, but no chance. The phone rings about every fifteen minutes. The phone is interrupted by the doorbell. Mail is being delivered for transport to the UK. There are always special request for goods to be brought back. I wanted crackers and Miracle Whip dressing. Charlotte wanted Christmas cards and Christmas candy. Others have their own desires. No chance of sleep before the flight.

I checked with Romeo to see who my crew was going to be. They told me Eid, Cherene, and Phil Thorpe. Eid was the problem. I called Major Shablan and told him that I could not use Eid; he was just not ready for international flights. He agreed and said he would take care of it. He did. When they called the flight out, it included Eid *and* Waleed. That made Eid mad, and he refused to go. They hadn't checked with Waleed and found that his passport was in for update at the German Embassy. That left only one copilot—Daghistani. He would go. Daghi is okay as a copilot, always smiling, in a good humor, and always late.

While they were making assignments, they called for MS4 to make the mission. I don't know why. MS4 is the dog of the fleet, and a GII to London means an extra stop for fuel. Why not use the GIII? With its long legs, we could make London but without stopping. I checked with Romeo. He said that MS4 was just the next one up for a mission, any mission, so he assigned it. I decided that since there was not going to be any rest at home that I would go to the hangar. Once there, I talked to

Kevin Toshida, the mechanic on duty, and then made the decision to trade planes. I requested the GIII, MS3. This means the over flight permits will be for the wrong aircraft. The computerized flight plans will be for a GII instead of a GIII. Oh well, the flight plan was not filed yet, so no big deal. Bruce the dispatcher just crushed the paperwork into a ball and started over. I haven't decided what his problem is. He has been extremely quiet lately. Something less than vocal, yes.

Romeo calls and says that the doctors want to leave at 0100. I told him fine, they could leave anytime they wanted to, but that I wasn't leaving until 0200. It wouldn't do any good to get to London an hour before the airport was opened. The curfew, you know. Well, with head winds, we were not going to make it nonstop to London, and as it turned out, we could have left at 0030 and been okay. The fuel handlers in Athens delayed us. We were on the ground for one hour and forty-five minutes.

Pepe, our TCN gopher, picked up the catering at the main gate at midnight. There was plenty of food. Cherene had ordered it when it was thought that she and two copilots were going, and besides, she had to order for a couple extra, so we had plenty of food.

Didn't fill MS3 up with fuel since we were going to have to stop in Athens anyway. No use *tankering* (to carry more fuel than you need for the trip). It just made us burn more to carry it. One of my complaints with MS4 was the terrible configuration of the old 51 INS (inertial navigation system) and GNS (global navigation system). MS3 at least had the newer 72 INS and the later GNS. MS4 was the one that Hanno and I flew six legs with all day, and neither the INS nor the GNS was workings. I had just been flying MS3 that day and knew that it was a working airplane. Good decision. Besides, it's the long-range airplane, why not use it?

The fuel stop in Athens was terrible. The doctors and Mohamed went to the duty-free store. The handler took them, and we didn't get any fuel. I started on loading the next legs into the INS and GNS. After they got back, the fuel truck came. The handler took me inside to pay the landing charge. The landing charge is computed and received by man number 2 who has an office in the main building. We have to drive over there in the man number 1's little car. Man number 2, when we arrive, looks as if he is expecting trouble. Ever since the first time I came to this place, the charge has been almost exactly the same. It's $52 for the day and $72 for night, but it's still a big deal that has to be computed each time.

Man number 2 is over his head or in trouble with his wife or girlfriend or bank of loan sharks or something because he can't handle the strain. He is going through the tables of figures. He makes several phone calls and then decides the fee is $70. Fine, I gave him a fifty and two tens. Now he must make out the receipt. Halfway through, he announced a mistake. He must start all over. After much calculation and several more phone calls, he announces the new and correct figure is $78. I gave him another $10, and he tells me, "No no, too much. I don't have the change." He can't accept the wrong amount. I suggested that he keep the change or give me drachmas change or call his supervisor or write it on the receipt as a commission. He got so upset that he had to go to the employee's locker room for fifteen minutes.

He told me after his return that this was always happening to him. People would never have the correct change, and it would create problems for him because his boss would only accept the exact amount when he turned in his books. It seems so easy to figure out an easy solution for his job. I've been doing that all my life—figure out a better way to do a job. All he has to do is make a small investment in cash for making change—his own kind, drachmas—and keep them in his pocket. His customers would be happy, he would be richer, and his job would be much easier.

Just to think, we are talking about Athens, Greece, the seat of civilization, the birthplace of democracy, and I am dealing with a couple of guys that not only don't know anything, they don't even suspect anything! While I'm waiting, I ask man number 1 for my weather packet and a copy of the flight plan they prefiled. He knew nothing about it either. I asked, "Didn't you file a flight plan for me?" No, he doesn't know how. I told him to check with his supervisor. He came back and said no, I must file it myself. So I sent him back to the airplane for my briefcase, which has the flight plan from Universal that I had received in Riyadh. He left for that errand while man number 2 is deep into his new calculations. I didn't dare leave him. He might destroy himself, or there might even be the most dreaded word a pilot can hear when he is in the middle of a quick fuel turn around—*shift change*.

Man number 1 went to the airplane for my briefcase. Mohammed wouldn't let him take it. Impasse, finally, Daghi spun the combination lock on one side to set the lock. The other side was broken off last week when I broke my car. Man number 1 finally returns with my briefcase. Man number 2 is still calculating. I said, "Look, just make the receipt out for $80 and call $2 of it commission. You take the whole $80 your boss, gets $2 for Christmas, and I can leave, okay?" Yeah, that's a good idea, but then he starts to thinking, and it all comes unglued. He made the receipt out for $79 and kept the $80 with much crying for all the trouble. I was so tired by this time that it was not worth my trying to see the real problem. He wanted a tip! But the only way he could figure the tip was if I paid him the exact amount required by this paperwork and then give him the tip. If I could have given him $10 tip, there would have been no problem. Well, that's what I think now. Who knows? Maybe he was doing the best he could do. His act was convincing to me anyway.

Next, it was time to file the flight plan. I was escorted down the hall to the proper metro place, and I sat down at a table in the center of a large room with at least half-dozen pads of flight plan forms with carbons spread evenly around the table. About halfway through, abruptly a man number 3 arrives, takes charge, and tells me not to bother with the flight plan because it has been filed and is ready to take me back to the plane. Man number 1 has no objection until we leave the building and man number 3 wants me to ride with him. There are serious objections from man number 1. He wants me to ride with him. There is a pulling match. Man number 3 wins, but before he leaves, man number 1 tells me that he wants me to do him a favor. "No, I can't. I don't have time," I said. He wants me to buy something for him from the duty-free store. "No, no, I don't have any time. I got to go."

Man number 1 gets in the last word; however, after closing the aircraft door for taxi out, he comes running out on the ramp screaming and waving his hands with a piece of paper. I stopped, and Phil opened the door. He wanted to give me a copy of the general dec.'s(decliration) I don't have to make this up. Looking back, the whole problem was that I wasn't set up to give out tips. It was always a common thing back in the States, but the Saudis don't figure it into our per diem, so it's easy to forget about tipping. I soon got the idea it would save me a lot of grief, so tipping had to come out of my pocket.

The arrival into London Gatwick began as usual. We were cleared down from flight level 430 sooner than we wanted, but this time, there were a couple of new problems. They cleared us direct a few times without telling us our next point after the one we were cleared direct to. A couple of times, we were run through our cleared to point without being able to get the next way point out of the controller. They were busy, but they were driving me crazy. Daghistani miscopied a clearance to LSD and read it back (remember, Daghi is working in his second language). They had actually meant LYD. So we were going to LSD, which was on our original flight plan, therefore it seemed reasonable to me. This put us about 65 degrees off of the course that they wanted us to fly. So there was some gyrating around, but nothing dangerous, and we arrived at Gatwick okay and in plenty of time for the doctors to make their connection. We were on the ground by 0815, and their flight on Delta to Atlanta was not leaving until 1115, so they had three hours to make their flight.

Our lady handler was very courteous, but didn't quite put it all together. I told her we would need fuel, catering, and flight plans, permits, etc., for a 0900 takeoff the next day. She took care of fuel and catering but forgot the flight plans. She was busy trying to get the doctors gone, and when that was done, then she had to escort us through Customs. That's a new one. They inspected the plane, but we had to go through another checkpoint leaving the airport. She couldn't just drive us out with an ID card as at Heathrow.

I felt like a walking dead man by this time. It seems there are a lot of days lately that I have had that feeling. I'm getting old, and this flying day and night is not for the old men. The young men say it's not for them either. Regardless, there has to be a better way to play this game. I need to do for my job what I was so willing to do for the man number 2 back in Athens—figure out a better way and soon.

Called a message to Jag mechanic friend David's answering machine and fell asleep. It was 1030 by this time. David called at three and said he would be there by four thirty. I started to get up and didn't make it. David's call at 1630 from downstairs woke me up again.

David hadn't changed a bit since the last time we visited, neither had the drive back. It is always hair-raising. His mother was happy to see me when we arrived. I invited her and David out for dinner. She didn't have to check on anything before she accepted. First, however, David had to take me to his new favorite pub and show me off. He ordered a pint of nonalcoholic beer, and I agreed to try a half pint of the same. I must report that it was not bad. I have tasted the nonalcoholic beer they sell in Saudi Arabia—not good. David's brew was from Denmark and was okay.

My Jag from Houston was in David's front yard. Looked like it belonged there. He said he had a serious offer of buying from a local dealer that had seen it. He had been by a couple of times and called a couple of times. He offered £5000, but David told him I wanted a minimum of £10,000 as is where is. I'm sure he is interested in the Texas plates, which means that it is already accepted by the US. There would be no conversion, no EPA, no DOT, no Customs bond, no import duty, and it is already left-hand drive with air-conditioning. All of those things are extra in the UK.

David had a new place to eat that featured Mexican food. We went to the Vermont Exchange and found it to be very crowded in the pub, but we were taken in straight away to the dining room and seated. We had Tex Mex from their menu. David ordered for us all, and his mother enjoyed that I think. He ordered fajitas for each of us. Beef for himself and a combination beef and chicken for his mother and me. We also ordered a plate of salsa and chips. No, not chips. In England, that means french fries. The salsa and tostados comes as an appetizer there and is considered extra. David made up for the nonalcoholic beer at the pub earlier by ordering a margarita for himself and his mother. He ordered two more for himself before we left.

Mrs. Groves was very complimentary on the stories that I had left with them to read. Later, on the way back to the airport, David talked at length about the stories. He compared them to a couple of his favorite authors. I did not recognize either of them, but he discussed them at length. He has read quite a bit, or I am much mistaken. Such conversations help a lot to encourage me in my efforts at authorship. It is a lot of work, this transferring of thoughts to paper. It may also be enjoyable after completion, but it still represents a lot of work.

David took me back to the hotel, the Hilton Gatwick. The ride back there did not improve. I had promised to write him another check. He had just received a check for £600 from me, but parts, etc., for the Jag had to be paid for in advance, so he needed another four hundred. I wrote him one for five hundred.

I took off my shirt and then socks, and David got the idea that I wanted to go to bed. I finally got in bed at 0100. Thirty minutes later, Mohammed called and wanted to know when we were leaving. I had explained this to him and the girl at the airport when I arranged to be picked up at the hotel at 0700. I explained to him again at the hotel when we checked in. "Remember, Mohammed, be checked out and ready to go at 0700 here in the lobby. The driver will be here ready to go," I said. It didn't work.

The next morning, I was up showered, shaved, dressed, checked out, and waited in the lobby by 0650. Phil is there and checking out at 0655. The driver arrives while Phil is checking out. No Daghistani. I asked Phil if he had seen him. He said yeah, last night at about 0200, he was coming through the lobby with a girl on his arm. He stopped Phil and wanted to know what time we were leaving. This is less than an hour after he called me to find out the same thing.

At 0705, I tried to call him on the phone. No answer. At 0710, I told Phil I was going to try one more time, and if I got no answer, I was leaving him. I made the call, got no answer, and went to the desk to leave him a note. They told me that he had not checked out. In the middle of my note writing, Mohammed taps me on the shoulder. He is in a great mood. Wanted to introduce me to his girlfriend. She was sitting on the other side of the room. It was Susan, a dental technician that Charlotte and I had met at a pool party in Riyadh. Phil knew her from RKH (Royal Khalid Hospital) in Riyadh.

We arrived back at the GAT for British Airways Executive and no flight plans, no permits, nothing. The catering was going to be okay, but that was all. Well, it is a red alert. All had to be ordered from Universal in Houston. Waiting is hard. We were still waiting on a permit from Yugoslavia when I had to go and make sure the airplane was ready. We had made an estimated time of departure of 1100. Gatwick flow control gave a slot of 1110. I got to the airplane and found Phil had fired up the INS but did not put the position in before he turned it to align, so it's not ready and doesn't want to take a new position in align. I've got to turn it back to standby or forward to navigate before I can put a position in the machine. I checked my watch and figured we had enough time to start over.

It was about 1050. The INS was down to about seven minutes (fifteen minutes minimum for alignment) when the fire trucks started arriving. They surrounded us and the aircraft next to us. The police came up the stairs and said they had a bomb scare on the next aircraft. We had to move. Now I've got to go back to standby with the INS, no choice. We moved to another parking stand. I never heard a *boom* or *kaboom* before we left, so can't say what ever happened about the bomb.

I taxied out at the exact time I was supposed to be in the air, 1100. Joined a long taxi line and then a long line waiting for takeoff. We were about six back for takeoff when the guy behind us called ground control to say that MS3 had split flaps. Ground asked if we wanted to go back to a parking stand. I told him no, we would rather put the door down and look at the flaps first. He pulled us out of the line, and Phil had a look and came back to report that they look okay to him. We were directed back into the waiting line, but now we were two aircraft behind where we were. The guy that reported split flaps to the ground controller was now number 1 for takeoff. I wonder. Hmm.

1988

Dear Jean and Terry,

It was a pleasant surprise when I picked up my mail today, and there were letters from you two and the card with yours and Ron Baca's note. That started off my 1988 year just fine.

To realize that Michelle is seventeen years old and Brenda is married really makes me wonder where time has gone. It also shakes me up to know that my grandson will be ten years old in March. First thing I know, you two will be telling me you are going to be a grandmother, and then I will really faint.

Terry, now that Brenda has gone to Arizona, I am not surprised to find that you would be interested in living there. I had an opportunity to visit Austin in Tucson where he is now living and fell in love with that town. It was a relief to be there where it is quieter after visiting in Los Angeles, which seems to be more congested than when I left.

Ernesto's soccer games have crossed my mind several times, and I wonder if he was still playing. That game is over here what baseball and football is in the States big time. Jean, what time of the year were you in Hong Kong? It would be funny if we were there at the same time. James and I took a trip around the world in February/March, and we were in Hong Kong about the week of March 15. I think it is wonderful that you and Ernesto can travel with the team.

We have a beautiful lady next door from Honduras, who is married to a Saudi, and they have three lovely children—two girls, and the baby is a boy. Anyway, these two girls remind me so much of Michelle and Monique when they were small, six years and three years. We spent Christmas with them. The mother, Lilyanna, had never cooked a turkey, so I helped her make cornbread stuffing, and we cooked a twenty-three-pound turkey. We had another American family for dinner, making a total of twelve.

We can purchase almost everything in the market that you have in the States, but sometimes it will depend on when they get their supplies. We have the Al Azizia market, which is really A & P, and a large percentage of their products have Kroeger labels. There is a market called T & P that has Safeway labels, and it is arranged like a Safeway store. The problem we encounter is stale products. As nearly as we can ascertain, shipments come in about every six months. The product may be sitting in Customs, but by the time it is on our shelf, it is six months after the packing date.

You can pass the word on to American Popcorn Company that Jolly Time is on the shelf but won't pop. It is so dry here. There isn't enough moisture left in the popcorn to help it pop. The popcorn that is in a sealed jar does very well. There is a brand called Nutcracker packed by International Nut Corp., Lowell, Massachusetts

01853 and Orville Redenbacher (if and when you can find it). The reason I am so well versed on this is because I was trying to make popcorn balls for the children's stockings next door. I bought two cans of Jolly Time (they aren't really metal cans, just cardboard), thinking here is the best, but it wouldn't pop. It was thrilling to see a familiar brand on the shelf and so disappointing when it wouldn't pop.

Our dairy milk products are local and very fresh and good. Many of our cheeses and butters come from Denmark and Holland. Most of our jelly and jam come from Switzerland, fresh produce from Cypress, apples from France, avocados from Malaga, Spain, and believe it or not, there is a Monarch label being packaged in the Philippines. It is very interesting and exasperating at the same time to go shopping. Sometimes the product is there, but the name of it is different, and you really don't know the identification.

This has been a wonderful experience living in Saudi Arabia, and it continues to be interesting for us, enough that we signed a new contract that ends January 1989. We haven't made a decision what we will do when we leave here. That is too far in the future to plan now.

Thank you again for the correspondence and good wishes for 1988.

James and I wish you the very best also for 1988 and for your families. Tell them all hello and say hi to all my friends. Good to hear about Walt, and is his mother still with him?

Love

PS This is about the second time I have used James's computer. Most of my letters are handwritten, but today James is out flying, and I wondered if I could still operate the word processor as it is more legible than my handwriting. You know how I just *loooooovvvvvvveeeee* this thing (not).

CAF Letter:
Riyadh, Saudi Arabia
January 14, 1988

Dear Conners,

We received your beautiful card and enjoyed the letter part. It was good to hear from you and to know what you did for Christmas. Sounds like you had a hectic time but had fun. Greg certainly is a handsome lady killer. Thanks for the picture.

When I handwrite letters sometimes, I cannot remember what I wrote or who I wrote to, and I think it is called old age. Anyway, if I repeat myself this time, please overlook it. Now that James is out of the house, I can use his computer and keep a record of my letters.

Speaking of James, he is on his way back from San Francisco, I presume. They had a mission there to pick up a lady and bring her back to Riyadh. She is ambulatory, which should be a help. James has another captain, one copilot, an engineer, and one nurse with him. Since he does not have a relief crew, he will probably stay in London tonight for rest and come on in tomorrow.

Richard, my youngest son, called me yesterday morning early and told me that Anna was pregnant and that they will be expecting the baby around June 20. That makes number four. I talked to the children, and Melissa told me I had forgotten her birthday. I really feel bad about it. Richard said he had told her not to say anything to me about it, but she must have been hurt by it and rightfully so. Now to find out what to do for her to make it up is puzzling me. I did tell her I was sorry and that I would make it up to her. What I would really like to do is buy her one of the Pakistani dolls that are so elaborately dressed. They make beautiful costumes for their dolls, and I think she would be old enough to appreciate one. Maybe the next time there is a flight to Pakistan, I can have someone get one for me. Once I get it here, there is always the problem on how to get it mailed. I have to wait for someone leaving the country to get it mailed. Well, that is the way things are here in Saudi Arabia. No one said it would be easy.

The latest thing that happened was an announcement by the king that all the expatriates were going to be taxed on their income and any other thing like our housing. He rescinded the law the next day; however, I do not believe it is over because one of the nurses was telling me that the talk at the hospital was about a tax that would be placed on all people leaving the country at the airport. Well, they already have airport taxes in other countries such as Japan. We didn't know until our arrival there that it would cost us 2,000 yen to leave their country. That is a pretty good lump when the yen was worth 1.43 United States, and now I guess it is more since the dollar dropped against the yen. I think the king will come in through the back door with other things to get tax revenue to equal the 30 percent he wanted in the first place. There was such uproar when the announcement came out in the paper like people walking off the job, resigning their contracts, and making a general protest. I think that at that moment, if all the expats had collectively quit working, this country would have been paralyzed. You see, the Saudi wants to be in charge, but they do not work.

Much to my surprise, I had a Christmas card and letters from Terry Endlich and Jean Marquez from good old Bromar Food Service. They were nice letters, and not one word was mentioned of Bromar or anyone working there. The contents of the letter were about them in relationship to their families. Maybe I am not such a bad guy after all.

Christmas Day I was helping the lady next door cook a twenty-three-pound turkey. She had never cooked one before, and she wanted to have an American dinner; we were invited along with another American family of five, hence the twenty-three-pound turkey. I made up stockings for the three small children and stuffed them with toys, nuts, and made popcorn balls. We cannot buy Christmas candy over here, so I made fudge. When we came back from the States, I brought four pounds of Texas pecans, so the fudge came out pretty good. About six months ago, I found some marshmallow crème in one of the stores, so I had that to go in the fudge, which really makes it better.

James had his birthday on January 3, and I had some of his friends in for cake and coffee. I baked him his favorite chocolate/cherry cake, a lemon cake, a pineapple pie, and a mince pie. The bakery cakes here are terrible, so we just don't buy them. I don't know how they can make them look so pretty and taste so badly.

Hopefully, James will be able to bring me some walnuts from San Francisco. At least, I had it on my list with some other things that we either cannot buy, or they are always too stale when you do find the item. For instance, corn meal always has bugs or weevils as they are called, and the nuts invariably are stale. James likes Miracle Whip instead of mayonnaise, and when we first came over here, you could buy the eight-ounce size, and now that has disappeared, so he probably will bring some of that.

Janell, you probably wonder why I mentioned Bromar and the girls I worked with. Since you don't know who I am talking about, so I will tell you. I have taken a letter that I was writing to one of my friends in California and changed the salutation because my news would just be a repeat of what I wrote to her. That was a paragraph I could have deleted, and you wouldn't be the wiser, but I thought I would just leave it in anyway. Someday when we are lying on the beach in Hawaii and are bored, I will tell you about my old company where I spent eighteen years of my life and how I felt when I left there.

Doesn't that sound good, the part about lying on the beach with nothing to do but watch the clouds roll by and all the worry you have is in choosing where and what to eat? Your invitation sounds good to me to spend Christmas there this year, and if I can convince James, we will be there.

I had one Christmas in Hawaii, and it was *wonderful*! Our final departure from here should be near Christmas unless GAMA invokes the contract clause that entitles them to extend our time for ninety days. It seems to me that it would be just as easy to return to the States through Australia, New Zealand, and Hawaii as it would be to go west through Europe. We are about halfway from home either way east or west. Well, we will see how it turns out.

Greg called me yesterday to tell me that his dad made it to San Francisco okay, and by now, James has probably called your mother and dad and Margaret. James was only going to have two nights and one day there, and time goes so fast when there are return plans to arrange and shop a little. My only hope is that he got sufficient rest because he comes home so tired from these long trips, it takes about three days for him to get back to normal.

I took a break here and went for a walk around the compound. We have calculated that if you walk around the perimeter four times, it equals approximately one mile, so I did four laps. Exercise is the one thing that I miss the most over here. Actually, there is no excuse not to exercise, but walking around the compound inside four walls is not as pleasurable as walking the golf course or bowling. If you stop and think about it, we Americans are very spoiled, especially we Westerners with the wide-open spaces, beach, mountains, and just anything we want to do. It is there for everyone, and you don't have to be rich to take advantage of the benefits.

James gave me a wonderful Christmas present, a dishwasher. It is a portable Admiral made in Canada, has a butcher-block top, and does a wonderful job of washing everything. I am the only one on the compound that I know of that has such a luxury, and there probably will be no problem in selling it once we are ready to leave. At least I will have it to use for a whole year. It is a treat for me because I hate to waste my time doing dishes, never did like it, and there are some things better than gold.

We both send our love, and hope this will be a happy and prosperous new year for all of you.

CAF Letter:
Riyadh, Saudi Arabia
January 15, 1988

Dear John,

It was good to hear from you Christmas. Most people write Christmas letters, but I am different and am going to write an "after" Christmas letter.

When I handwrite letters, sometimes I cannot remember what I wrote or who I wrote to, and I think it is called old age" Anyway, if I repeat myself this time, please overlook it. Now that James is out of the house, I can use his computer and keep a record of my letters. Speaking of James, he is on his way back from San Francisco, I presume. Medevac had a mission there to pick up a lady and bring her back to Riyadh. She is ambulatory, which should be a help.

James has another expat captain, one Saudi captain, an engineer, and one nurse with him. Since he does not have a relief crew along, he will probably stay in London for rest last night and come on in today. At least that was the plan after he arrived in San Francisco. James called his son Greg in Houston, who in turn called me and said their estimated arrival time in Riyadh would be 6:00 p.m. today. Keeps me busy trying to figure out what is going to happen next.

We have a hideout radio that has Romeo's frequency, so I will hear him when he calls the hangar to be ready for the GIII arrival. It is called MS3, or as Romeo announces arrival, he will say, "Mike Sierra 3 ETA will be 1800 hours." We have one Brit named John whom we know, and he is very nice. When he is working in the radio room as Romeo, he will usually call me on the telephone after James contacts him from the air a few minutes out from Riyadh and tell me when James will touch down.

James always brings me a monthly schedule that shows daily what crew he will be flying with, and of course, there is no advantage to knowing except I can worry when he is flying with an incompetent copilot. We have a couple that probably should not be on an airplane much less in the cockpit of a jet.

My duties can vary quite a lot. Aside from worrying about James, which I do very little because I know how competent he is in the cockpit, I have a job maintaining utilities here in the villa. The plumber and I are getting to know each other very well because he has been here nearly every day since our return from vacation and has put in three new hot-water heaters in James's bathroom.

The last time he was here, he left to go to the warehouse to get some parts, and not more than two minutes after he left, the hot water broke loose at a joint in the pipe; the water was squirting straight out, hitting the wall opposite and falling on the table that had an electric razor, Q-tips, bathroom tissue, Kleenex, and many other things that were being soaked and would have to be thrown out. I couldn't get through the screen of hot water to reach the cutoff valve, so I went tearing out the door, running down the sidewalk (women don't run over here), and the plumber saw me coming. I started yelling at him and gave him one of Grandma Twyeffort's dirty looks, and he started running. He got to the bathroom before I did, so I don't know how he shut that hot water off. He was really in a swivet (tight spot) to fix the plumbing properly this time because he knew the fun and games were over. So far, knock on wood, it hasn't leaked yet, but the water isn't very hot.

James was complaining about his shower the day he left, but I told him he would need to talk to the plumber this time, because if I do, he will be afraid he will lose his job. Actually, it is more GAMA's fault than it is the plumber's because they give these TCNs so little to work with. I dried out the electric razor with my hair dryer, and so far, it still works. One of the latest things that happened over here to stir things up was an announcement by the king that all the expatriates were going to be taxed on their income and any other benefits like our housing, tickets for R & R, etc., which in our case would be at least 45 percent of James's salary, and most people would average at least 30 percent.

The law was to be effective January 20, but the king rescinded it the next day. People were walking off their jobs, resigning, and there was a general uproar of protests to the king. Suddenly, he realized he had been given bad information and probably didn't realize that the motion would stop if the expats left the country. You see, the Saudis like to be in charge, but they do not work. If the doctors and nurses would have left in mass, all the hospitals would have had to close, and that is just a small example of the workforce being expats.

There are a few people in this country probably that could not get jobs at home, especially in countries like Sri Lanka, India, Africa, Philippines, and Lebanon. However, most of the professionals are here because of the money they can make without paying taxes. No one would sacrifice green golf courses and supermarkets with fresh food just to be living in Saudi Arabia in the dry heat if there wasn't a good incentive. The king is probably not through with us yet because the latest rumor at the RKH (Royal Khalid Hospital is the military hospital), as repeated by a nurse, is that there would be an airport tax on all departures, and there already is a 12 percent tax placed on imports.

Airport taxes are popular in other countries as we found out traveling around the world. It cost us 2,000 yen to get out of Japan, and that was when the yen was about 158 to the US dollar. The king will still probably get the revenue he wants, but it won't be so obvious this time.

Living next door to us, we have a very nice couple. Lilyanna is from Honduras, and Hakim is Saudi. They have three lovely children, and they invited us to have Christmas dinner with them. Lilyanna is not Muslim, and she said she told Hakim when they married that he could not take Christmas away from her and the children. She decorated and had a Christmas tree (artificial), which she had to hide out in our villa once when her in-laws came over.

Anyway, Lilyanna had never cooked a turkey before, and she wanted to have a traditional American dinner, so I helped her. There was another American family invited (family of five), so they bought a twenty-three-pound turkey. It turned out to be one of the best turkeys I had ever eaten.

I brought back some felt stockings from the States when we returned from vacation and stuffed them for the three small children. I made them popcorn balls, which they had never seen before. Christmas was fun this year as James wasn't called out to fly that day. James had his birthday on January 3, and I had some of his friends in for cake and coffee. I baked his favorite chocolate/cherry cake, a lemon cake, a pineapple pie, and a mince pie. The bakery cakes here are terrible, so we just don't buy them. I have often wondered how they can make a cake look so pretty and taste so badly.

Hopefully, James will be able to bring me some walnuts from San Francisco. At least I had it on my list with other things that we either cannot buy or they are always too stale when you do find the item. For instance, cornmeal always has weevils, and the nuts invariably are stale. James likes Miracle Whip instead of mayonnaise, and when we first came over here, you could buy the eight-ounce size, and now that has disappeared, so he probably will bring some of that item. I feel like I have been long winded, but that is the best I can do for now.

We both send our love, and hope that 1988 will be a happy and prosperous year for you.

Dispatch:
Riyadh, Saudi Arabia
January 20, 1988

THE DESERT FOX GOES TO JAIL

Can you really know a country without visiting its jails? Just think about that for a minute. I've never been locked up in a jail, but I have visited them. I visited a prisoner in the Wichita Falls jail, but it was not very impressive. I mean there was nothing there that I would not have expected. You know, from what I'd seen in the movies.

Now, when a detective friend of mine took me on a tour of the city jail in Houston, it was another story. There are no pictures to record the scene, but if there were, I'm sure there would be several of me with my mouth open. That was an experience that is etched in my memory forever. I saw where the suspect was booked. I saw the white line on the floor where he/she stood to be photographed and the cage opening where the contents of their pockets were delivered to the man inside.

Then we went up a short flight of stairs to a small office where my friend left his sidearm before going into where the cells were. As we stepped inside the door, the first thing I saw was a large cell with several men in it. It was probably 20' x 20' with nothing inside like furniture, only a single drain in the center. The walkway alongside of the cells and the wall was only about three feet wide. It was not wide enough to walk through without the prisoners being able to reach out and grab you, which they did. I was walking a weak second to the detective, and when they put their hands on him, he said,

"Bless you, brother. I'll pray for you."

The prisoner said, "Are you a preacher?"

"Why, yes, I am," my friend said. Immediately, all the prisoners in the first cell fell back from the bars. It was evident that they didn't want to talk to a preacher.

Past the first holding cell, there were smaller cells with two concrete slabs protruding from the wall, one above the other. The concrete slabs had a lip around the outside that held a small mattress with white sheets and a pillow. The second cell was similar, but without the sheets and pillow. The next cell was similar except it didn't have a mattress. My friend explained that if a prisoner acted all right, he was put in the first cell. If he acted up, then he was moved to next cell, and then more of the wrong kind of attitude, he was moved to the last cell with no mattress. I got the picture.

As we were leaving the cells, the detective had one more cell to show me. That one had a steel door with a small barred window about the place where a man could look out and you could look in. It was empty, and my detective friend opened the door for me to see the inside. The cell was only about a foot deep and just wide enough for a man's shoulders. The cell was just large enough for a man to stand. There was a drain in the bottom of the floor.

"Hey, Fox, I want you to see this," said my friend, pointing to the inside of the steel door. It looked as if someone had been beating on it with a sledgehammer. Of course, this steel door was hollow, but you had to imagine the rage that it took for a man confined in such a small area could do such damage to a steel door with his bare hands!

I'll bet you never thought about that. Well, it wasn't the movies. It was the real thing. When you live in a city like Houston, you are living among the type of people that I saw that night in the Houston jail.

What has all this got to do with Riyadh? I guess I'll have to tell you.

I have been taught that a man ought to stand up for his rights. You know, what has an innocent man got to fear? If you're innocent, then no one is going to bother you, right? Wrong. You're going to be presumed innocent until proven guilty, right? Wrong. If the cops felt that way, then they would never arrest anyone. Think about that.

What does it take to go to jail when you're innocent? Just a little rain can do it. I should have known better Charlotte and I needed something from the market, and we left the security of compound late in the afternoon in the Pontiac borrowed from the GAMA motor pool. We had not much more than got on the freeway when it started to rain. That's right, it was raining in Riyadh.

As soon as the rain began, the traffic started bunching up. I didn't know why until later. It was because the locals started running into each other. The newspaper the next day said thirty-seven wrecks in the first fifteen minutes of the rain. That's about all the rain there was, fifteen minutes.

I had wrecked my Jaguar just a couple of weeks before. That's the reason that I was driving a borrowed car. Everyone agreed that I had been lucky—that is, being without an accident for over a year. Well, I had one back in December, and now it's my turn again.

All of a sudden, the car in front of me hit the rear of the car in front, and about the time I hit my brakes, I was hit in the rear by a minibus. *Wham*, and that Pontiac tried to fold in the middle. I wasn't completely disabled, but the rules are if you have an accident, then you must just stay where you are and not move. The cops will show up eventually, Insha'Allah, and all will be settled on the spot. That's right, no lawyers get involved. Everything is settled there on the highway. And the law is simple in the case of being hit in the rear: it is always the fault of the guy in the back that did the hitting. Seems fair, right? Well, how about if the guy that hits you makes you run into the guy in front of you? It wasn't my fault.

A long wait, and finally we get the word from another driver that the cops are completely overloaded and that everyone involved in an accident must go to the police station.

"What do you mean the police station? I don't know where the police station is."

"Well, there is going to be cop car along here pretty soon, and you have to follow him to the station, okay?"

I didn't see how a cop was going to get there for the traffic was three lanes wide and bumper-to-bumper as far as you could see. In the meantime, I got out and checked my front end for damage. Sure enough, the radiator had taken a hit and was losing all the fluid. Now what? Where do you get water in the desert? Guess what? There was a mosque just next to where we were stranded. I walked over there and went inside. Just inside the door was a big pan of water. Hey, that might work, so I looked around and found a bucket nearby. I guess that's what they used to fill the pan with.

I took the bucket and filled it with water from the pan and took it back for the Pontiac. Well, if it was holy water, then maybe it would stop the leak in the radiator. No sooner had I returned the bucket to the mosque than the cop car came by on the outside of the traffic with a string of cars following. I got on the end of the line, and we all went to the police station. We found a parking place to the station, but a new problem had arisen. Charlotte had been gone from home for over two hours, and it was time for a rest stop, and she didn't fancy inside the police station.

"Well, honey, there is not much I can do for you. I tell you what; there is the hospital right there. They surely have a restroom there. Why don't you try there? I've got to go into the police station."

"I can't just walk into the hospital and ask for the restroom. They may not even speak English."

"Never mind all that. Just across that drive is the entrance to the emergency entrance. So just walk in like you owned the place, and they probably have a restroom real handy. Okay?"

"Well, okay, I guess I don't have a choice."

"Look, I'm sorry, but there is not much I can do for you on this subject. Don't worry, you'll be okay."

Inside the police station, it was chaos.

"Does anybody speak English here?" No one even looked up. The room was full of people, and they were all trying to speak at the same time to the policeman behind the desk. Just like at any other place in this country, no one stood in line. They all ganged up and demanded to be taken care of first. I couldn't understand a word that was being said, but I suspect they were all pleading their innocence.

Well, I had my handheld radio, and this seemed like a good time to use it. I called Romeo base, and he told me to stand by. I stood by. After a short wait, Romeo called me back, and I told him to call my friend and neighbor Hakim Al-Alawy to come down and help me out with some translation. I heard Romeo make the call, but I couldn't hear anyone on my radio except Romeo, of course. Romeo called me back and said that Hakim was on the way. Another wait, and nothing changed in the police station. I couldn't tell if they were getting anywhere with all the Saudis talking at once.

Hakim arrived and joined in with the group at the desk. He got attention because he was in uniform.

"They say that you must pay for the damage to the car that you hit in front of you."

"But it wasn't my fault. The minibus that hit me knocked me into the car in front of me."

"It doesn't make any difference, you must pay anyway. That's the law."

"Well, it's not right, and I'm not going to pay."

"Okay, but if you don't pay here, then you'll have to go down town to the main police station. They can't do anything else here."

"Well then, can I ride with you? That Pontiac is not going to make the trip."

Hakim was obliging, and as soon as we picked up Charlotte, we went downtown to the main police station. Charlotte's trip into the hospital had been satisfactory, and soon enough, we arrived downtown. It was when we passed through the front doors I realized we were also in the main jail! We had been at a substation at the other police station. This was the real thing, and you had to pass through the jail to get to the desk to settle my affair. The trip by cells gave me a new attitude about the whole situation. Houston prisoners had it nice.

Arriving at the main desk, I was surprised to see the old Bedouin that drove the minibus already there. What was his problem?

After seeing the jail cells, I was told through translation that to settle the matter was simple. I could either pay for the damage to the Toyota driver that I had hit, or I could go to jail until I did pay. No lawyers, no judge, no jury, it was all simplified.

I called GAMA and gave them the story, and they said, "No problem, *mafi mesculah*, insurance would take care of it, so agree and give them the insurance information." Okay, I did all that, but then there was another problem.

The old Bedouin that hit me had no insurance, but he did have seven children. Hakim said he was begging for mercy from the Kawajee (that's me). Have mercy on this poor man with no insurance.

"He says he has 1,500 Saudi riyals on him, and that's all he's got."

"You mean he wants to settle for SR1,500? Why, that won't even begin to fix that Pontiac. I think the frame may be bent. It tried to fold in the middle."

"Well, if you don't accept his payment, then he has to go to jail."

I turned and looked back at the cells I had just passed, and with a big sigh, I agreed to the amount he offered.

For some reason, that didn't need translating. Instantly, I had a new best friend. There were hugs, kisses on both cheeks, and wishes for a long life for me and my sons. He didn't mention my wife or any daughters that I might have.

Then the police told me the rest of the story. The old Bedouin had just got of jail from an accident last week when he hit a Brit. Through Hakim the translator, I suggested that next time he might try for a Frenchman, you know, kind of spread it around.

Dispatch:
Riyadh, Saudi Arabia
January 21, 1988

NEWSLETTER

Well, I've got the tape of Tom T. Hall going on the right, and Romeo base is behind me calling out a mission to King Khalid Military City, Ta'if, then back to Riyadh (for someone else), and Charlotte is cooking supper, just right for writing a few lines to my friends.

I've got no idea what I'll do for excitement when this tour of duty is over. Yes, I think of it like an assignment in the military, just another TDY (temporary duty) station. A little play like this isn't too bad even when you're pushing sixty off the calendar. There is never a dull moment here. Even when nothing is happening, you can't help but wonder, *What are they up to now*?

It really started to get in high gear last April. Four of the six copilots mutinied over doing the Jeppesen revisions. Then came Ramadan, the Moslem holy month, and the resignation of three more of the expat captains. We had already lost one of the expat since I arrived in September of 1986. When they leave, it will leave only me and two Saudi captains. Two actually resigned in August, and the other did a midnight runner the first of September after he had received his monthly pay. He had just returned from annual training in the USA, which cost the Saudis $10,000. He is now blacklisted from ever working in Saudi Arabia again.

The midnight runner was Captain Schmitz. He was finally confronted for the way he talked about the Saudi copilots. My friend Hakim, who was a copilot at the time, braced him one day in the compound where we lived. Hakim told Schmitz that he was a no good liar and his mouth was going to be taken care of soon. Schmitz knew that Hakim was connected, and the threat went straight to his heart. He took his annual leave in conjunction with annual training at FlightSafety in Savannah. He was gone quite a while, and when he came back, it was payday again. Fresh from vacation and training, Schmitz kept his passport and did the runner the next night after getting paid.

Since that time, we lost one of the Saudi captains and two Saudi copilots and hired four more expats. Three of the expats are on the scene, and the fourth is coming. The last to arrive is from Canada and didn't pass the checkout, so he will be leaving in a few days. The fourth is due here around the first of March. It was found that he had *assumed* (forged) experience in the Gulfstream that was not his, so he may not ever get completely off the boat. And that is just the beginning.

After our great fiasco of a "bad luck" holiday in the United States and Europe, we arrived back home about November 7. Since our return here, I've had a trip to Osnabruck, Germany, several trips to London, UK, and three trips to the USA. I've been averaging seventy-five hours a month. All of these trips have some sort of a hidden hooker in the deal.

I've had double orders of copilots because the one that is due to go on the rotation schedule is not worth a spit in the ocean, so take two. The last trip to the United States was not my turn, but the captain that was due on the schedule had some mysterious reason preventing him from taking a trip to the States. Never did we find out what that was all about. The second in order didn't want to go because his wife was due to arrive here from Germany at any moment. She hasn't made it yet. The third in line couldn't take the trip because he hadn't been checked out yet, so I took the trip to San Francisco to check out the new expat captain. Guess what? I had to turn him down. He just didn't act like a captain. There was some kind of something he screwed up every leg. He was okay in the right seat as a copilot.

It is beyond my comprehension how the minds of some grown men function. They run out of or off from work in the United States and come over broke and in debt. A few even have to forge their credentials to get hired, and when they get here, they act casual and indifferent about keeping the job. I guess it must be the "easy come, easy go" syndrome.

Dispatch:
Riyadh, Saudi Arabia
January 24, 1988

JUST ANOTHER MAINTENANCE TRIP TO EUROPE
AND
A LITTLE CAR WRECK

I've just been notified that I'm taking old MS4 a GII to Basel, Switzerland, tomorrow at 0900. We'll leave it there for about three to four weeks of maintenance and interior work. We then go by commercial air to London to pick up another GII that has been in maintenance at Cambridge. With a little luck, I'll be back here by Sunday the twenty-fifth.

The partner is a Saudi captain, Khalid Al-Ghoraibi, who has not been released yet. He is a young man, twenty-seven years old, and competent as a pilot. He told the CO that we would be back probably Friday or Saturday. We leave on Thursday morning and arrive dark time in London. Friday, we test fly the airplane, if it's really ready. It'll be noon by the time we were ready to fly the test. A couple of hours of flying, and the squawks will have to be worked off on Saturday, if they work on Saturday. Well, you can see why I told the CO we would be back as soon as possible, but don't get in a strain watching the horizon until about Sunday or later.

This job comes with a lot of takeoffs and landings and a lot of engine starts. Many times, we have to reposition to or from the VIP gate at the air base here for pickup or delivery and always for international trips because we meet Customs and Immigration there. The flow in the cockpit becomes very comfortable.

I can tell the difference in my own flying because of the increased number of operations and also the continually changing of conditions. I think a couple of years of duty here doing the things that I have seen and been doing would make anyone a better pilot; it would have to.

It is a real pleasure to see the copilots improve in their skills and feel that I had something to do with it. I was told on my arrival here that the copilots were absolutely not to be trusted in an airplane and would never be able to check out as captains. Two have just checked out, and two more are in the final phases of checkout.

The expats have a selfish interest to serve in keeping the Saudis from checking out as captains. The only reason we expats are here is because of the shortage of Saudi captains. When the Saudis become captains, there are just that many less jobs for the expats.

I hadn't been here very long before my copilots were asking me, "Why did you do that?" They saw me doing things in a way that made more sense to them than they had seen before, and besides, I was willing to explain the things that I did. I can remember asking questions as a copilot that were never answered. Later, I was told it was for my own good. The senior captain told me, "I knew it would be better for you if you figured it out by yourself."

All of us in the aviation business have some very similar stories to tell; just the settings are different. The next phase of this job begins after the Saudis get enough confidence to scuttle the expats so they can be in complete charge. The harmonic ripple to that thought is that the head Saudi in this organization is not qualified in the Gulfstreams or anything else. The term used in describing Major Shablan usually is, "He doesn't know airplanes from tall buildings." He is not at all anxious for his underlings to gain the advantage of him. Who knows? They might end up being his boss. The drama and intrigue go on.

I can remember when a young man flying with me as a copilot for Exxon was maneuvering to get the boss's job. My thought at the time was let him have it. I didn't want to be boss anyway. Now in retrospect, I should have put grease on his skids. Think of all the folks that would have helped. He made it to the top, and two and a half years of my worst time was spent working for that guy. (Exxon recommended that he resign about a year after I retired. They finally discovered he was an alcoholic.)

We're still trying to get on the golf course but haven't been able to even think of golf for months. No days off. Lately, no car either. I called tonight, and they say they have finished my car and were just having the tires balanced. They promised to deliver it tomorrow for my approval. They had little to do besides replacing parts. That's the reason it took six weeks to repair—spare parts. They replaced the front left fender, front bumper, both left wheels and tires, the complete steering assembly, and the complete front sub-chassis. None of the other parts were even scratched, so it should be good as new or better.

Maybe I forgot to tell you about my car wreck. It was a one-car accident and all my fault. Charlotte and I were trying to find the Diplomatic Quarter on an errand. I was doing about sixty miles per hour as we crossed over an overpass, when surprise, surprise, the road made a sharp ninety-degree turn just on the downside of the overpass. No warning and hitting the brakes on the Jag helped little as I slid into the curbing on the turn. The Jag hit the curb hard and cratered both wheels on the driver's side. No one was hurt, but my feelings. That was my number-one accident, in my life, that could be judged my fault. No one over here was surprised. They said I was overdue. You have to have at least one wreck a year over here, and I have been here almost a year and a half.

Dispatch:
Riyadh, Saudi Arabia
January 25, 1988

NEW PILOTS

Wonder where they come from?

We keep getting a new pilot now and then, and I can't help but wonder where they all come from. They show up with some sort of resume that on the face of it looks phony, but they are hired anyway. We just got a new guy from Canada. He claims to be an ex-Canadian fighter pilot. Well, he may have been, and as it turned out, he acted like one. He was tall, handsome, arrogant, and full of tall tales.

It became my chore to check him out for international travel—that is, across the Atlantic. Our trip was to San Francisco to pick up a princess in MS3. We had a stop in London, and the new captain made it clear that he wanted to stop in Montreal on the way.

"No, I'm sorry, but Montreal is not on our route, and we won't need to stop that close to Bangor, Maine, anyway. We can make it nonstop to San Francisco from Banger without refueling."

"Yeah, but, I've got an old girlfriend in Montreal, and we could stop and spend the night there. I'll get you a knockout for a date, and we'll have a real party. What do you say?"

"Look, I've already told you, it's not on our route. We have no reason to stop there, and I'm not interested in any knockout date you might dig up. So forget it. Understand?"

In London, I left orders with the handler for an early-morning departure and requested the flight plans to be filed for Bangor and San Francisco, then went to the hotel and went to bed. The next morning at the airport, I was surprised to find that my co-captain had called the handler from the hotel that night and changed the order for flight plans to include an overnight stop in Montreal.

I had to change everything back to what I had originally ordered. We had to get a new departure slot. This caused a delay and put me hot. On the return trip, I had to interrupt his number-2 engine start. He was about to let the engine over-temp while he just sat there and watched it happen. In London, he was in the left seat, and I tried to show him the airport diagram so he would be familiar with the taxi route when ground control cleared him.

"Oh, I won't need that. I'll just follow the yellow strip." Well, there are a lot of yellow strips, and he got lost and caused another delay with ground control talking ugly to us. Needless to say, I gave him less than a satisfactory grade on our eventual return to Riyadh. He didn't last long after that. They didn't fire him right away, but he was soon replaced by another wannabe. You see, the Medevac people get their pay if they have a body over here they can refer to as a pilot. They don't even care if he can fly airplanes as long as he is present for roll call so to speak. They get paid. So no matter how bad the guy is, they will keep him here until they find his replacement.

The Captain Newbigin that flew for GAMA called me one day and asked me to come by his office there in the compound. GAMA had part of its corporate offices there in the same compound where we lived. He and his copilot Cox wanted to ask me what I thought about a new pilot they were considering hiring.

The new guy was named Bormann, and it struck me that he had the same name as the infamous German war criminal. Well, that was enough to make his name stick in my mind even though I'm terrible at remembering names. I looked over Bormann's resume and noticed that he was another simulator instructor from FlightSafety. He had the bare minimum required 3,000 hours of time in the Gulfstream. Was it a coincidence that his experience was the exact amount of minimum time required? I remarked out loud at my suspicions, and the unit clerk, Jeffery, spoke up, "I believe he is the same fellow that sent in a resume just a few months ago."

"Well, see if you can find it, Jeffery. I'd like to see it. I don't know what exactly I expected to find, but something was bothering me about this guy."

Sure enough, a comparison of the two resumes showed a glaring conflict. On the earlier resume, Bormann showed 3,000 hours in a Challenger (Canadian-built jet) but no time in a Gulfstream. That resume had been turned down due to no experience in a Gulfstream. Then in his second effort with GAMA, his resume showed 3,000 hours in a Gulfstream and no time in the Challenger! The fraudulent resume stood out like a neon sign. Newbigin and Cox examined the two resumes and said a collective "hmm." Guess what, they hired him anyway!

It was easy for me to see what had happened. Bormann wanted the job—no, needed the job badly—enough to lie and cheat to get it. He was working for FlightSafety and was able to get some time in the Gulfstream simulator and end up with a rating, but no time in the aircraft. GAMA needed to fill a slot at Medevac, so they hired him, and never mind if he could really fly the airplane or not.

Bormann showed up in operations a few weeks later where I met him for the first time. Of course, I remembered his name and introduced myself.

"Hi there, Captain Borman, I'm Jim Fox. Where are you from?"

"Oh hi, why, I'm from Texas."

"No, you're not. Now tell the truth. Where are you from?"

"Uh well, I'm from Illinois."

Another guy that thought his home state was not good enough and claimed Texas for his own. Sure enough, they paired him up with me for his checkout. On our first trip, he flew the empty leg to Jeddah. On the ground, while waiting for the ambulance to arrive, I thought it was time for me to get things straight with the new "captain."

"Bormann, that was a pretty poor example of flying for a captain with 3,000 hours on the Gulfstream."

"Well, I uh . . ."

"Never mind, I know about how you got your time in the simulator, and I'm here to tell you that I don't care as long as you can get it into the air and back on the ground without hurting anyone. Because you see, while you're here flying missions, I get to rest, so I want you to stay and keep on keeping on. Do you get it?"

"Uh, well, yeah, I uh . . ."

"Okay, I'm going to give you a little advice. You better start acting like a captain real quick or these Saudi copilots are going to chew you up and spit you out. They've been flying on the airplanes for seven years, and they have seen lots of captains come and go, so they sure know what a real captain looks like. So I'm telling you, better start acting like one real quick, or you're going to feel the door hit you in the back on your way out."

It didn't do any good. The guy was a loser. He wanted the job badly enough to lie and cheat to get it, but on his first trip with me out of the Kingdom, he came to me with a problem. We were sitting on the ramp in Frankfurt, getting ready to leave for Riyadh when he came and sat down next to me with his problem.

"Hey, Fox, where is a good place to hide a *Playboy* magazine on the airplane?"

I couldn't believe he would ask me such a question. In the first place, it showed so little respect for me and the job he held.

"Bormann, as far as a *Playboy* magazine is concerned, there is no place on this airplane to hide it. If I find out you have one board, I'll stop in Cyprus and leave you there. Do you get me?"

"Oh yeah, well see, I was just kidding. Don't get sore."

But guess what? About three days after our return, someone asked me if I'd seen the *Playboy* magazine that Bormann brought back from Germany. I never said anything to the authorities, but Bormann didn't last very much longer. He was involved in an incident over Madinah where the Gulfstream suddenly pitched over in a sharp nose down and wingover for no apparent reason according to Bormann and his copilot. They lost over fourteen thousand feet before they could recover. Hair-raising! Strangely, I was the only one that believed Bormann's story, and it took over two months before the same aircraft repeated the maneuver with Mohammed Hanno. Then they knew Bormann had told the truth, but by that time, Bormann was gone.

(A couple of years later, Bormann sent me his resume and asked for help in finding a job.)

Wonder what it would have been like if a check pilot really had the authority to turn down a new pilot picked out by the boss back in the old corporation. Interesting thought. I'd probably still be pushing a survey crew down a pipeline right of way. There would be some others doing something else also, I'm sure. Well, that's not exactly true in my case because I never failed a check ride.

Oh well, never mind what might have been. It's more reasonable to think of what really was and is.

Dispatch:
Riyadh, Saudi Arabia
January 26, 1988

A LITTLE SMUGGLING INCIDENT

I missed the mail, so am finishing this at a later date. I made the trip to Basel, Switzerland, and Cambridge, England. No serious incidents, but as usual, interesting. Arrived in Basel and was surprised to see no snow. Well, a little on the mountaintops, but none on the ground at the airport. It was a very mild day. We had the chief of maintenance and a biomed technician with us to get the work started on the aircraft. So we just hung around for a while until we got freebie baseball caps with the maintenance company's name, Jet Aviation, on them.

There was a three-hour wait for the only flight to London. We arrived in London about 2000 hours and were met by a driver for Marshall's Air Center in Cambridge. He was driving a 1985 Jaguar XJ6 just like mine in Riyadh. We were told that Cambridge was anywhere from thirty miles to two hundred miles north of London. None of our advisers were correct. It was an hour and a half by Jaguar. Cambridge was a very active place in World War II. Because of the very flat land about, it was desirable as a location for basing the bombers that were making raids in Europe. In fact, Cambridge was where they launched the bombers that made the raid on Libya a couple of years ago. The other side of the Cambridge coin shows twenty-six colleges. Hard to believe, eh?

We arrived on a British Airways flight into Heathrow, and it was a clear and lovely night. The temperature was moderate, and it looked as if we would have a beautiful day for our test flight the next day. Sometime during the night, it turned cold. I woke up during the night, too cold to lie there and too cold to get up. You know the feeling. I finally got up to look for another blanket. No luck. Tried to turn up the heat. No luck. Tried to call the office. No luck. The place of residence was the Barnwell Lodge. The desk clerk was the owner, and as soon as he checked us in at about 2300, he went to bed. I was on the north side of the building and would have no relief until I got up and dressed. A miserable night. The next morning, there was six inches of snow everywhere. The ceiling was on the ground, and the wind was out of the north at fifteen gusting to thirty knots. Chill city.

By three in the afternoon, the sun was out, the snow was melting, and we were in the air. Strange weather there. Well, that's not the story I wanted to tell anyway. It was on the return to Riyadh Saturday night when things started to turn foul. Slow Williams was the engineer that had been left with aircraft to oversee the work being done. Don't ask me where he got his nickname, but it was appropriate.

We departed Cambridge at 1300 after a two-hour delay for maintenance on a last squawk, and with a stop in Athens for fuel, we arrived in Riyadh at 2350 (ten minutes until midnight). The Customs made their usual mess of our luggage, but as soon as they finished with our bags, they ordered us off the airplane. One of the pair got in the jeep and left the scene. Soon, he returned with a large screwdriver. The Customs agents boarded the aircraft while we stood on the ramp and tried to stay warm. I was wearing a leather flight jacket, and I could feel the chill.

Khalid was allowed to go with the agents onto the aircraft, and they were gone for about fifteen minutes. That left me to stand there with Slow Williams, wondering what in the world was going on. When the agents and Khalid returned, they were holding up the evidence they had found: three bags of pornographic material, eight books, six devices, and three bottles of German Spanish Fly.

Okay, everybody goes to jail. There was no search in the aircraft. They knew where to look and what to look for. Khalid told me later that they had gone directly to the lavatory in the rear of the cabin, pulled up a section of carpet, and then removed a panel from floor with the screwdriver.

The only thing that saved the innocent was about two hours later, the guilty confessed to his crime. This was after the strip search. Slow Williams said all he wanted was to spice up his sex life a little. I should have guessed his guilt when we were standing together on the ramp while the agents were alone inside the aircraft with the screwdriver. He was overly anxious while I was just trying to figure out what was going on.

During the body search, they found out who had the money. They wouldn't let any of us go until I paid for his fine. They knew that he didn't have any money. He had spent it all on porno. Shades of Robicheaux. The first thing I thought of was all the previous years of crossing the border with Robicheaux, when he always smuggled something. Nothing that I ever knew about beforehand and nothing of any value as far as I knew, but always something. I always dodged the bullet then, but now they got me. The great injustice of it all. Why do the good guys always have to pay? Well, if you ever saw a Saudi jail, you probably would pay the other guy's fine just to quit watching.

The fine was SR1,700 or about $453.12. I made a big show of giving the money to Slow in front of witnesses. I didn't want it to look like I was actually giving the money to the Customs agents. I told him in no uncertain terms in front of the agents that I wanted my money back by nine the next morning. You never know later how it might sound. Perhaps I would be admitting complicity by paying the fine, or maybe it could be called a bribe. Who knows what it would sound like a few days later at another interrogation? Many things can get turned around when you are working against the language barrier. The Customs agents made a big show of the whole thing, but the result showed that all is not equal. The penalty is much more severe for booze than it is for porno. Don't ask me why. It was a little later that Slow confessed that what he was really afraid of was that the agents might want to search his apartment. He had stills there making wine and beer.

After a few days of meeting and investigations, it seemed that nothing else is going to happen to Slow, and he paid the fine back to me early the next morning. The overriding thought in all this is: How did they know which panel to pull on that aircraft? They didn't look in the aft equipment area, nor did they pull any other panels first. They knew exactly where to look for the forbidden loot. The popular thought is that all Customs agents are interconnected like through Interpol, the term for International Police cooperative effort. It is further thought that there are paid agents around the airports that collect fees for reporting such things as a crew member that loads a forbidden item destined for another country. The item is not forbidden in the country of departure but is not allowed in the country of destination. An interesting thought for all those that might be tempted. It occurred to me that the hangar where the aircraft was parked while the maintenance was going was open and facing the local Customs agents office. You don't suppose they were watching, do you?

Well, another mission has been called to Frankfurt and a second to London. I missed the time of departure for this letter to Frankfurt, but we have more British stamps anyway, so will put it on the boat going for London. Oh yes, my son Chuck has decided to take my offer of a trip to London to see the country and perhaps to learn to be a Jaguar mechanic. He'll be arriving around the first of March. The plan is for him to live temporarily with my friends David Groves and his mother. Mrs. Groves has agreed to this arrangement on a temporary basis, so it will give him a chance to get his feet on the ground. David has offered him a job working with Jaguars and American cars. It may be a good chance for him to learn a trade. If he can become proficient on Jaguars, then he will have no trouble finding a job in the States on his return. Perhaps it will be just a great adventure! I would have loved the opportunity when I was young and footloose. Besides, I'll be able to see him every few weeks if the trips to London continue as in the recent past.

Just a word about the mail over here. We are beginning to see postmarks from the States now and then that are only seven days old. That's great. Yesterday, we received a letter that was posted on November 17, 1987. That's over two months. So just about the time you think it's getting better, it's not. We try very hard to answer each letter we receive, but no system is perfect. There is evidence that a few letters coming and going didn't make it, but they are in the vast minority. We welcome your letters and hope to hear more.

They (censors) pass audiotapes with no problem as long as they are marked as audiotapes. Videotapes will be confiscated until they can be reviewed, and that takes maybe six weeks. Hang on it's got to get better.

JDF Letter:
Riyadh, Saudi Arabia
January 27, 1988

To: GAMA Transportation Department
Atten: Mr. Antoine Samara
From: James D. Fox
Subject: Insurance Repair of Jaguar Automobile

On or about the December 5, 1987, my automobile was damaged in an accident. The auto was damaged by hitting a curb on a sharp turn on the highway. It hit the curb on its left side with a great force. The obvious damage from the impact broke both left wheels with more serious damage to the steering and sub-chassis of the auto. Less obvious damage was jammed bonnet and boot. Apparently, there was further damage that was unnoticed at first glance. Only two days ago, the auto was returned to me as completed. The repairs have not been completed to my satisfaction. The discrepancies that I have noted are as follows:

— A very definite wobble from left to right. It is most noticeable at thirty to forty kilometers/hr.
— A roaring sound from the rear end most noticeable at slow speeds.
— A loud wind noise at highway speeds from the right side.
— The cigarette lighter is missing—the interior is filthy with paint dust.
— The headliner is soiled in front. The carpet in front is covered with mud.
— There is no freon in the air conditioner.
— The evidence of repaint is noted in the wheel wells and in the engine compartment.
— The red polishing compound is still evident in the wheels and engine compartment.
— The bonnet will not stay latched on the right side.
— The left rear window is inoperative.
— The left front seat belt is jammed.
— The paint is damaged on top of the right front fender or wing by buffing. This area was not damaged in the accident.
— The boot has not been painted properly.
— The automobile as returned to me is filthy inside and out. The repair people had this automobile in their possession for six and half weeks. Two weeks ago, I visited the garage where the repair work was in progress. The auto was covered in paint dust at that time. The bonnet and left front fender were removed, which allowed accumulation of paint dust inside the engine compartment. The agent for the insurance company by coincidence was present during my visit. I told him to convey to the garage owner that

393

I would not tolerate any sloppy work on the Jaguar. He said he understood and for me not to worry.

I should have worried.

I would like to point out that this automobile is a Jaguar, not a Chevrolet. The insurance premiums are paid to cover an expensive automobile. I fully expect the repair work to reflect the condition of the automobile before it was damaged. I can see no reason for accepting anything less. As a customer, you would expect the repair facility to at least deliver the automobile in a clean condition. The repair people told me that they would make discrepancies good for up to a year. I hope that doesn't mean they will take a year to make things right. I have been without my transportation for almost two months at considerable discomfort to myself and my wife. A final thought. I purchased this automobile from the local Jaguar dealer because I wanted a fine car with little chance of trouble. That is all I expect to be returned to me.

Sincerely,
James D. Fox
Captain, Medevac

CAF Letter:
Riyadh, Saudi Arabia
February 11, 1988

Dear Mary and Greg,

Mary, the large envelope came yesterday with the pictures, report card, letter from SSA, and your letter. Thank you for sending everything. I know when James gets home, he will be happy to see the excellent report cards of David and Sandy. Tell the boys I am very proud of their accomplishments also. The pictures indicate that you all had a very nice Christmas.

It is too bad that Gail and John had to suffer with the bad old flu, but I guess that is just part of growing up. They will have a better immunity in the future after building up the antibodies by this session. James has a theory that we should allow our bodies to build up their own natural immunities, and that is well and good, but sometimes there is a lot of suffering that goes along with it. I will say that he does have good resistance to germs, and he heals rapidly if that is good enough proof of his theory.

I tried to call you the other night and found out that I have your old number. James has gone to Cleveland, Ohio, which you probably already know by now as I am certain he had called to check in with you. Nothing ever comes out right since I lost my purse with my address books. I just had two, and they were in my purse. Anyway, because of this, we have been putting names and addresses in the computer (rather James has) with telephone numbers. Apparently, when you moved, he changed the street address in the computer but didn't change your telephone number.

Over here, we have to have the telephone number in advance to place the call. Forget trying to get a number through information from here, so I will have to wait until James comes home to get your correct number. James has been gone since last Friday. Apparently, the crew stayed overnight in Athens that night. They were on their way to Geneva, Switzerland, to pick up a forty-year-old man that had a heart attack and were to take him to Cleveland. Geneva has a curfew and they couldn't make the time before curfew, so they lost one night in Athens.

Now they are sitting in Cleveland with a broken part on the aircraft, and according to the newspaper here, the weather in England may cause them further delay on their return. They have been having winds the velocity of a hurricane in London, and the airports have been closed. Maybe by the time James leaves Cleveland, it will be settled down. I know he will not start out if the weather does not permit. We are without Gulfstreams here at Medevac until his return. One plane is in Switzerland for maintenance and repairs.

The chief mechanic left at 2:00 a.m. this morning to go to Switzerland. They requested he come and see the aircraft because the underneath structure is broken, and they claim a wing will have to be removed in order to repair it. He said it was caused from overweight or landings that were made too hard. The nurses tell me we had a captain that rolled the airplane three or four times every time there was a new nurse hired. I have heard James say that rolling if not done properly could cause damage to these airplanes. After hearing crew conversations for a year and half, I suspect all three things have happened to that airplane.

Did James tell you that the day before he left we got our car back? On second thought, I think I have already written you and told that story. If I am repetitious, please overlook it. Sometimes I forget what I have written to whom, and further than that, I forget who I have and haven't written to, but it is right down embarrassing when I forget to write at all. There was an article in a magazine the other day that I read, saying that now we have the computer that makes writing easier, people have a tendency to be too wordy.

I talked to Jeannie Shelton, and she had been in touch with California Motor Vehicle in response to a letter I had written to them to get my driver's license replaced. She said they would send me a temporary license, and when I returned to California, go in to DMV and have my picture made and they would reissue a new one with my picture on it. Little by little, maybe I can restore all my documents as they were. It certainly is a long drawn-out process from long distance.

I did laundry this morning, so I guess I had probably better go bring in my clothes and do the ironing. I let the houseboy do some of it, but my finer things, I do myself. Take care and thank you for the large envelope of things.

Love,
Charlotte

CAF Letter:
Riyadh, Saudi Arabia
February 11, 1988

Dear Thomasene and Milton,

Thomasene, your letter came yesterday, and I was very happy to hear from you. James isn't here, so he won't get to read your letter until he comes home. He had a trip to Switzerland to pick up a heart patient and take him to Cleveland, Ohio. James left here last Friday, and hopefully, he will be home tomorrow. He was supposed to have been home last night, but they have been in Cleveland with a broken part on the airplane, and they didn't get it fixed in time to get home last night; they were still sitting in Cleveland.

I talked with Jeanie Shelton this morning, and she is doing fine and said she talked to you recently. Hopefully, I will get to see Jean and Edna in England in the month of May. We are planning a tour together through the British Isles that month. I decided that when James goes to FlightSafety in Savannah, I will go on to England and meet Edna and Jean, then he can come back to London and join up with us. It is so far to the USA. I am not interested in beating myself to death making that trip again until we return for good. Fortunately, James is unselfish with my time, and we have a houseboy to do laundry and keep the house clean when I am not here, so he will make out okay the short time I might have to be away if our departures are not together.

Sounds like you have a good plan for the summer, and I can bet that you wish it would hurry up and get here.

Every one that sees Jo Jo's and Meghan's pictures think they are very cute and pretty girls. Suddenly, I realize that Jo Jo has a birthday, and I didn't get a card off to her. Please tell her that we wish her a happy birthday even if our wish may be late. We will be thinking about her on her special day anyway.

Richard called me not long ago (the first time over here), and he let me talk to the grandchildren. I felt terrible when the first thing Melissa said was, "Grandma, you forgot my birthday." I wanted to cry, and Richard was embarrassed as he had told her not to mention it to me. Her birthday was November 2, and that was our first day in Germany where we had the big theft fiasco. Our trip and my aching arm just made me forget, and I didn't know it until I talked to her.

Well, I try and sometime fall way short of the goal. I know how important birthdays are to children, and it is crushing to be forgotten.

I never heard from Diane and Von for Christmas, so I wonder about them. Both of my address books were lost in my purse that was stolen, so I don't have their address. I wrote to Bob and Jean and ask them to send it, but so far, I have not received it. Sometimes I think we do not get all of our mail, like I told Muriel. Just the other day, her letter of November 17 just came. That was over two months in coming. Better late than never, I guess.

How do you like your Lincoln? Would you buy the same car if you had to do it over? When I come home for good, I want to buy a new car, but right now, I don't know what kind. I was very pleased with my Ford Crown Victoria, and you know how much I like Lincolns also. James likes the new Oldsmobile 98. We rented one in Savannah, and the mileage was fantastically high on gasoline, which is something to think about when we get back to high gasoline prices.

Over here, you can fill up our Jaguar (two) tanks on less than ten US dollars. Speaking of the Jaguar, we finally got it back from the insurance repair company the day before James left on his trip.

It seems to be in good running order, and we are certainly happy to have wheels again. Two months without a car is almost like being in prison. Never in my life did I think it was a big thing to go grocery shopping. If you don't go anywhere, then after a while that becomes a big occasion, and you get dressed up, put on makeup, wash your hair, and curl it because you are going grocery shopping. Believe it or not, that is the highlight of my week. Good thing I had early training living in Cedarvale, or I couldn't fit in here.

The first year over here was new, exciting, and interesting, but now that the new has worn off, time drags because you know the routine. You find yourself marking time because this feels what it is, a temporary station. Being in the armed services must feel much the same way. When James is here, there is a lot of intrigue when he relates the happenings in Medevac.

Tonight, I am invited over to my friend's house for dinner as her husband left for Geneva, Switzerland, last night. People from here go to Europe like we travel from Los Angeles to Houston. One of our planes beside the one James is on is in Chicago. A pilot and copilot left today for Paris to rest up so they can meet the Chicago plane in Paris and fly it on in to Riyadh. It is a long flight from Chicago to Paris, and they need a fresh crew to bring the plane on in. Rosalind's (my friend) husband is the chief mechanic at Medevac, and he has gone to see about a plane that is being repaired in Switzerland. Seems that the underneath structure is damaged, and to repair it means removing a wing, so he got this urgent call yesterday to come.

There was a bad automobile accident last night at the military base north of here, and it seems that the king's camp was there. Well, one of the nurses was here at my house when she was called for the trip, and the radio room told her it was to pick up two bodies and three patients. With all the fast airplanes out of the country, what is left to fly in the Kingdom for Medevac is one Lear, C-130s, and helicopters. They called out one of the C-130s, which is manned by military crews, but they use our Medevac flight nurses. Well, one of the patients died before they arrived, and the king personally became involved and wanted to know why the response time was so long. I saw the nurse about 4:00 p.m. today, and she was just getting in from that trip. She was going home to rest, so I will see her tomorrow and will get the whole story then. I certainly am glad James was not on that trip.

One thing that made the response time so long, the C-130 airplane is slow. The Gulfstream that James flies cruises at 650 miles per hour, or maybe they call it knots per hour, and I don't know the speed of the C-130, but it must be about half the speed of the Gulfstream. Probably someone is going to be in deep trouble over this. Surely, am glad it was military (they are all Saudis) and not expats with Medevac.

This is definitely a different world over here, and we have had a wonderful experience by being here, but we are about ready for the next adventure. James keeps wondering what he can do to top this, and you know, Thomasene, I wouldn't be surprised if he doesn't find something much more interesting and exciting to do. One thing he wants more than anything is time to write his stories. He has made outlines and will fill in the details later, but he says things that make good stories happen so fast that he has a hard time just making the outline. Apparently, James never forgets events, and he can make an interesting story out of most of them.

You should talk your mother into getting one of these simple computers that she could use for a word processor and type her stories. It could serve her a dual purpose because she could log ranch activities, bills for Tom, other expenditures, and print out any kind of report she would need for her tax accountant. I would love for Muriel to write some of her stories that she knows whether they be about the family or whatever. It is so much easier to correct errors than typewriters, and you can store everything on a disk. It is just a thought.

Guess this is enough of this; I will give you a rest. Thank you for the nice letter; the stationery was really cute. Surely would like to see all of you.

We send our love,
Charlotte

Dispatch:
Riyadh, Saudi Arabia
February 15, 1988

LINDBERGH DID IT, DIDN'T HE?

It is February, and we are returning to the Middle East from a Medevac mission to the United States. We had picked up a "heart patient" in Geneva for transfer to a hospital in Cleveland. The "heart patient" was the personal doctor of Prince Knife of Saudi Arabia. I believe the patient was from Egypt but had been diagnosed there in Geneva as needing what was available in Cleveland. We were dispatched on the fifth to Geneva, spent the night there, and picked up the patient the following morning.

Now it's the eleventh, and after several days in Cleveland[13] with a mechanical trouble, we're returning to Riyadh. It's a four-hour trip from Gander to Shannon, so the captain, me, has little to do but look out the window and ruminate. (Good word for a country boy, eh?)

The winter night is very dark and very cold. Peering into it through the pilot's DV window is a constant reminder of the great expanse of nothing that is just outside the window. The Atlantic, seven miles below, is not visible in the dark. We know that it is so cold that survival in the water is measured in minutes. The thought of ditching in those icy waves is so bad that the thought won't stay in your mind for more than an instant. Even if you survived the ditching, how long could you last until someone found you? No one could be there before morning for sure. It's too bad to even consider. No, the North Atlantic would not be a choice of places to spend the night in February.

Sure, it's wintertime out there, but here inside we are warm and comfortable. We are eastbound at forty one thousand feet, crossing the North Atlantic in a Gulfstream II. The jet stream is helping us to maintain almost 550 knots (632 miles per hour). The air is smooth, and we expect to make it from Bangor, Maine, to Shannon, Ireland, in four hours and five minutes. No passengers in this trip, so we can get up and stretch our legs anytime. There is a forecast for some rain showers and snow showers in Shannon at the time of our arrival. It's going to be an easy trip.

We are monitoring 121.5 megahertz, the international emergency frequency, as a matter of procedure and habit. It is not uncommon to hear someone on the frequency that needs a relay to Gander or Shannon Oceanic Control. They may have lost their high-frequency signal for a while or just be having communication

---

[13] More about Cleveland in the story *Words to Die For.*

problems. Now and then, it's someone that does not even have the equipment installed and is riding "piggyback" on our equipment.

My crew is Khalid Al-Ghoraibi, a Saudi copilot, and Kevin Tschida, an American flight engineer. We hear some faint voices on the emergency frequency that sounds more than the normal routine. It is an airbus with a German registration calling another aircraft with a French registration. There is something about "returning to Gander." This sounds interesting. Let's turn up the volume and start paying attention.

At first, we can only hear the airbus; we must not be in range of the second aircraft. Gradually, as we come into range, we can tell the airbus is speaking with a German accent, and the second guy is an American. It's the American that's in trouble and returning to Gander. The airbus is asking for his location, true air speed, ground speed, and ETA (estimated time of arrival) at Gander. The American gives his coordinates quickly but then hesitates, and the frequency goes dead before he can give his ground speed and ETA.

We copied his location as 50:48 north and 44:26 west the time is 00:17 UTC (Universal Coordinated Time, you tell me why it's not UCT). By habit, I'm writing down the facts and time as they come over the radio. We do a quick plot and see that he is over 350 miles out of Gander. That doesn't sound too bad for a jet. If he has lost an engine, then his drift down should be adequate for that distance. The American reports his true air speed as 145 knots! Our friend is not in a jet. He must be in a little single-engine aircraft! That's right; it's another Lindbergh trying it again!

You can cross the North Atlantic today with all the comforts of home. Sit back, savor your complimentary peanuts and soft drink, read the paper, or take a nap. You can have your choice of schedules, carriers, nationalities, day, or night. Either way, it's all part of the grand vacation or just another day in the life of a businessman.

This may be true for the thousands that cross as passengers of the commercial carriers, but what about the crews? Well, they have all the comforts of home as well. Consider the flight crews that maneuver multiengine aircraft, the rulers of the sky, across vast expanses of ocean and ice. They sit in seats that cost more than $35,000 each with electric controls for up, down, fore, and aft plus several adjustments to fit the contour of their backsides. They have multiple forms of navigation with precision that will guide them safely to their destination thousands of miles away. Several forms of communications, high frequency, very high frequency, and even ultrahigh frequency radios are available. Aircraft with multiple and redundant systems are the common thing today. Their performance is in excess of the requirements for the trip by a comfortable margin.

The pilots of the so-called business jets have the same or similar systems and equipment. The equipment that I fly is a Gulfstream II or III. Crossing the Atlantic is well within its certified limits. Aircraft performance, navigation, communications are all set by common sense safety standards. Sure, it's easy. You can relax or have a cup of coffee with your hot meal or sandwich. Maybe you would rather just graze off the cheese tray and later have a piece of fruit. Coffee, tea, milk, or three different kinds of juices, they are all available any time you want.

Who would guess that the Lindberghs are still up there doing it? Of course, I'm referring to the pilots that ferry single-engine aircraft from the western hemisphere to Europe or beyond. Aircraft that ferry from the United States to Australia often take the long way around from west to east just to take advantage of the tailwinds and shorter distances between landmasses. They can cross the Atlantic by what we call the northern route with stops in Greenland and Iceland. That means that they will be able to use the navigation and communication equipment that is normal to the smaller aircraft. They don't need to have sophisticated long-range navigation and communication equipment required by the larger jets that fly the more direct courses known as the NAT tracks (North Atlantic tracks). These routes are so densely populated with traffic that your aircraft and equipment must be certified by the aviation authority of the country where the aircraft is registered.

The NAT tracks cover a block of altitude from twenty-seven to thirty-nine thousand feet. Their location is supposed to be the shortest distance between Canada and Europe. Actually, the location of the tracks is changed each day to take advantage of the jet stream. The Oceanic Control people are careful to be sure that there will be a minimum of problems with aircraft that can't maintain their flight plans for direction or altitude. They expect pilots to maintain very precise speeds, altitudes, and direction. Any errors accumulated will be quickly noted by the radar operators at the far end when your blip shows up on their screens. Violations and fines are filed against pilots who do not fly within the limits of their flight plan.

The fuel handler in Shannon, Ireland, tells me that there are three to five small single-engine aircraft a day that stop there for fuel after making the crossing. I would never have guessed it. Yes, the Lindberghs are still doing it for sure. The original Lindy flew solo across the Atlantic over fifty years ago. He made the crossing in a single-engine aircraft named the *Spirit of St. Louis*. His route was from New York to Paris, nonstop. He was the first man in history to accomplish this feat, and in my opinion, he is still one of America's great heroes. What he did gained him the recognition, praise, and respect of the literate world. Books are still being written about the man, the machine, and the long lonely hours it took for him to make history.

How much safer is it today under the similar conditions? Well, at this point, the arguments begin. You will never get two pilots to agree on anything, but those that make the trip in a single-engine aircraft will say that it is much safer.

"Oh really?" I say.

"Of course," they say. "The engines of today are much more reliable. We have much better forms of navigation and communications. Of course, it is much safer."

Well, consider this. Lindbergh's engine made the trip without a miss. You can't be any more reliable than that. He didn't have a radio because he couldn't stand the weight, but if he had one, it wouldn't have helped a bit in the crossing. Who would he talk to? His navigation was dead reckoning, but it was good enough, considering he had no worries of other traffic to miss.

All will concede that the trip today is much easier than it was for Lindy, but is it any safer? Not much! The one thing we do have today that Lindy did not have is good weather stations. That is a big plus. Even now, we sometimes arrive at our distant destination with a few surprises. The main difference is, we are better prepared with equipment in the air and on the ground to handle bad weather than was even dreamed of when the first solo crossing was made.

I have never had the opportunity or notion to cross any large body of water in a single-engine airplane. I am perfectly willing to leave that to those with greater desires and needs than mine. But it might be interesting to think of what you would need and how you would go about doing it—if you had to. First, let's consider the limits of the aircraft and equipment that needs to be ferried across.

An example, single-engine aircraft would probably burn around twelve to sixteen gallons of fuel per hour. The wing tanks might hold as much as sixty gallons of fuel. That would give you a flight time of about four or five hours. If you could maintain a ground speed of 150 knots, then your range would be something like 750 nautical miles. The shortest distance between Gander, Newfoundland, and Shannon, Ireland, is *almost two thousand* nautical miles. Some singles will do a little better than the example just given, but many will not do that well. These are just a few figures to think about. How about a little safety margin? What I described was takeoff to burnout. Our example pilot must remove the extra seats to make room for installation of extra fuel tanks in the cabin just for the crossing.

One of the better singles, as it comes from the factory, should be able to handle four adults at two hundred pounds each, perhaps another two hundred pounds of baggage, and with the wings full of fuel, and that is *it*. Fuel is figured at six pounds per gallon. One hundred gallons would be six hundred pounds. You'll have to allow some extra weight for a raft, surely.

If his aircraft could maintain 160 mile per hour and the distance to cover in two thousand miles, then the simple math would show that a pilot would need enough fuel for at least twelve and a half hours. That's from takeoff to burnout. No reserve. If he burns sixteen gallons per hour, then he will need at least two hundred gallons of fuel for the trip. No reserve. With this much fuel onboard, you can see he is just like Lindbergh—over maximum gross weight before takeoff!

That is the fuel consideration. If the pilot chooses to fly directly from landfall to landfall, then his normal communication equipment will be of use only about one hundred miles away from a ground station and perhaps two to three times that for any airborne stations. His navigation is much simpler. The normally installed navigation equipment will serve him if he takes the much longer northern route. If he chooses to fly the short route, he can buy an add-on LORAN-C. It is something of a new innovation for small aircraft. A LORAN unit that you can buy for less than a thousand dollars will constantly give you your latitude and longitude anywhere in the world. Some models will give you much more, but they cost more as well. (GPS navigation was not available in those early days.)

Well, that about covers it. Get the extra fuel tanks installed, buy yourself a small LORAN unit, a small life raft, add plenty of coffee and sandwiches, check the weather, and away you go—alone. There will be no extra space or weight available for a passenger.

Is that it? Sounds okay? What happens if you have an engine problem? "Oh, they are very reliable," you say. I'm sure that is true. As a matter-of-fact, their reliability has been a concern of mine since my first flight lesson in 1947. My first flight instructor would give me as many as three simulated forced landings in a thirty-minute ride. In the years that followed, his instruction has saved my life more than once. (Thanks to Lt. T. E. Kane wherever you are.)

In those days, federal aviation regulations made it mandatory to carry a flare pistol in the aircraft if you were flying passengers at night in a single-engine airplane. In forty years of flying, I have lost an engine three times when I was flying a single-engine aircraft. I have had some of my students that suffered engine failures in single engine aircraft, and to this date, I have never bent one nor have any of my students. The only way you can achieve such a record is to practice and teach:

1. You must be able to see the ground, to which, you are surely descending when the engine stops.
2. Find a suitable bare spot to make a safe landing *within your gliding range.*
3. Keep the aircraft at the proper *air speed* to achieve that glide.
4. Try *anything* to get the engine started before you touch down.

I have always been a strong believer in being ready when the only one you got quits. Some might say that my views are outdated. They may be right, but on the other hand, maybe that's how I got to be an *old pilot.*

The jet engine brought a whole new meaning to the word *reliability* in aviation. They just seem to run forever without a problem, we are told. I've had three jet engine failures in the last twenty years. Fortunately, they didn't all quit at the same time, and I had other spares that continued to work fine. No, if it's mechanical, electrical, or physical, it may quit at any time, so if you want to survive, you better be ready. Being prepared may mean prepared to pay for your latest bad decision. For all the young pilots, I recommend that sometime, if you have the chance, ask an *old* professional pilot what he thinks of flying a single-engine aircraft at night, cross-country, for any reason. Be prepared for a lengthy answer. If it's dark and cross-country, you have just violated rules 1 and 2.

We listen as best we can to hear the ground speed and ETA of our fellow countryman that is in trouble. Each time, he will only give those items that he can read directly—that is, indicated air speed, altitude, and coordinates. His signal is improving all the time, and we can hear that he has low oil pressure and his engine is running on the red line. He reports that he is level at eleven thousand. You don't have to be a pilot to know that the single-engine pilot may have only minutes before the engine freezes up and the prop stops.

Once the engine stops, if he maintains the best glide speed, he will descend at about 750 feet per minute. You can divide his altitude in thousands of feet by 750 to know how many minutes he will be in the air after the prop stops! Eleven thousand feet of altitude will give him about fourteen minutes and forty seconds to the water.

The airbus again asks for his ground speed and estimated time of arrival in Gander. His signal has been gaining in strength, but now there is no answer.

The airbus tries a couple of times more with no response. Maybe the poor guy has gone in. The airbus keeps trying. He needs to pass information to Gander control for possible search and rescue. I can stand the suspense no longer, so I give the pilot in distress a call. He answers! After my identification, I ask him his aircraft type. He replies, "A Mooney." Hey, I'm thinking, I did some instruction in Mooneys years ago; maybe there is something I can help him with.

We exchange a couple of transmissions, and he tells me he will be glad for any help. "What temperature is on the red line—oil or cylinder head?" I ask. "Oil," he replied. "Okay," I return, "start a gentle climb of about two hundred feet a minute and see if your oil pressure doesn't start to increase and your oil temperature starts to decrease."

In about two minutes, he calls to say, "It's not working"!

"Hey, man, give it a chance, hold the climb for ten or fifteen minutes, and then see what happens. Don't worry about gaining altitude, any extra you get will just be a bonus later," I add.

He said, "I don't need any more altitude, I've got plenty."

My answer to that didn't go over the radio. Nobody has plenty of altitude when they are three hundred miles from land in a single-engine airplane and the prop stops. There was no need to remind him of what should be so primary. Then I asked his ground speed again, and there was a long silence. For a few moments, it appeared that we had lost him. Then it hits me. He is not answering any questions that require calculations for an answer!

When you're alone in the cockpit and have problems like this young man has, time becomes all distorted. It can seem like hours since a moment ago, and at the same time, the minutes remaining for life itself are only an instant away.

My mind began to build a visual picture of this stranger in the Mooney. He is alone because of all the extra fuel he is carrying in cargo fashion inside the cabin. He needs the extra fuel because he is taking the short route under the NAT tracks. His flight plan will call for about twelve and a half hours in the air. I know that by chances of probability, he is a young man that needs the flying time to feed his career and maybe even to feed his family. Young pilots are worked hard and paid little. He probably doesn't have an autopilot because of the type of aircraft he is flying. His problem with calculations would suggest that he is hand flying the machine. He may have little experience in this particular aircraft.

There is no minimum experience required by model or brand of small aircraft, so it's "Take it around the pattern a couple of times, kid, and you'll be okay." "Nothing to worry about. She's brand-new, so what could go wrong?" I can hear the man saying the words. He's thinking, "So what? I'm covered by insurance. Besides, the kid needs the time and money. I'm doing him a big favor." If the kid raises too big a ruckus, then he loses the job. "There are plenty more that are willing to do it, kid, and probably for less money."

No wonder he is slow on the calculations. He is alone, in the dark, hand flying, and he knows that every second that passes may be the last one for his engine, and it's the only one he's got. This young man is in deep trouble.

I can visualize the perspiration on his face and hands. His mind is desperately trying to think of something that he has overlooked or left undone. Time is his enemy, and the enemy has him surrounded. Simple things take much too long, and complicated things are impossible. At first, he didn't believe what his instruments were telling him. Everyone knows those little plastic instruments for oil, fuel, alternator are Mickey Mouse K-Mart and should not be taken as the absolute truth. Every pilot worth his wings flies fuel burn by time and not those *el cheapo* gauges that never work right. So he waits too long in deciding that he really does have a problem. That's how he got 350 miles out over the ocean. How do I know that? Well, if he had a sudden loss of oil pressure and a sudden rise in temperature, it would have resulted from a sudden problem. Most likely, we would never have heard him on the frequency; it would have been all over in a matter of moments. No, he's had this problem for a while; it was just not that easy for him to detect.

In the midst of all this, he has to remember so many things. *How will I know which direction to head into the water for the ditching? It's so dark out there; will I even see the water before I impact? Will these extra fuel tanks stay put in the impact? Will there be time to get the raft out before the aircraft sinks? Oh yeah, surely there will be time, unless it flips over! Oh Lord, can I get out if it flips over? Should I have the door open when I hit, or should I let the cabin fill with water and then try to open the door? The flashlight, I'll need that. I wonder if it will float. What do the gauges say now? Oh, that's right, I just read them. Please, Lord, let it keep running! Maybe it will be okay.*

The voice of his first flight instructor floats through his mind. *The first rule in any emergency is, you must keep flying, whatever happens, keep your head and keep flying. You must never stop flying the aircraft.*

They are calling again on the radio, asking for ETA. What was it? First the ground speed, and then how many miles? Why can't I think? I've got to think. Stay cool, use your head, and settle down, you have to settle down.

If he has the LORAN-C navigation equipment, it may or may not be able to give him all the answers he needs. It depends on how much he paid for it! As I said, the LORAN—C is inexpensive and easy to carry in a small aircraft. You don't even have to install it. You can buy one and carry on several different trips. Ferrying aircraft leaves a pilot at the mercy of whatever equipment happens to be installed. Yeah, it's probably a LORAN-C, and right now, he's wondering how accurate it is. He even begins to doubt his ability to understand what it says. If the problem persists much longer, then all the self-doubt of his young life will begin to settle down around his shoulders. At some point, he will become cool, his mind will begin to work, his senses will begin to get sharper, and he will be the best pilot that he has ever been, or he won't make it.

He is wondering about his decision of making this trip at night or even making the trip at all. He even has time to think of his wife and kids. Will he ever see them again? Will they know he was thinking of them when it happened? Will he ever do this again? The questions come quickly now, but that's all there is, questions. There are no answers.

When he finally answers our radio call, I ask him his location again. Quickly then, I calculate his ground speed by comparing his earlier location to his present location. His ground speed is only 135 knots. His ground speed is needed, so Gander control can estimate where he might be when all contact is lost.

I tell him that his problem is low oil quantity. He is either losing it or burning it, and that keeping the nose high will help the oil pump pick up whatever oil is left. If that engine holds ten quarts of oil, then he may only have half of it left. We all feel his elation a few minutes later when he reports, "Working, working!"

He gives his location again. We plot it as 5037 north, 4512 west. The time is now 00:31 UTC. We figure his ETE (estimated time enroute) to be two hours and thirty-four minutes. Oh man, that is a long time to nurse a sick engine.

There are probably several aircraft that have been listening to our exchanges on the frequency, but it's the airbus that asks if we are going to handle the relay of information to Gander control. I tell him, "No, you go ahead, we were just trying to help." There is a couple of *rogers* on the frequency, and then we lose the Mooney for good. Because of the higher altitude of the airbus, we can hear him asking a few more questions, but we can hear no more replies from the Mooney.

There is more I wanted to say to my comrade in the dark, like when you get to fourteen or fifteen thousand, then pull the power back some and let the engine cool as you descend, then start the climb all over again. But it's too late. He is gone, out of range, I'm sure. Maybe he will think of it on his own. He'll have to think of it if he's going to make it. Survivors must become very resourceful to become survivors.

The airbus must be westbound (we never even asked) toward Gander the same as the Mooney. We are eastbound and only in range of the Mooney for a few minutes. We calculate the Mooney's ETA at Gander to be about 03:00 UTC, the same as our ETA for Shannon. Another coincidence in a line of coincidences.

There is little else on our minds as we continue in the dark. Will he make it? It'll be tough as he has a long way to go. It all started at 00:17 UTC, and now it's 00:31. Only fourteen minutes. It seems like much longer than that. Now we have two and half hours to Shannon. He has about the same amount to Gander. We can't stop talking about him. Even if we do stop talking, we can't stop thinking.

Flight crews that count their time in years instead of hours have a catalogue of incidents they remember where their safe outcome was not in view for what seemed like an eternity. We all have the memories, but some have difficulty voicing them, even to another pilot.

On landing at Shannon, we ask the tower to check the location of the Mooney pilot through Shannon control and Gander control. He calls back at 03:05 and says that the Mooney is on Gander radar and twenty miles out. My crew exclaimed in one voice, "All Riiiiiiight!"

What are the chances of a single-engine aircraft making it across the North Atlantic at night, in the winter, you say? Good I guess, a lot of them make it. But if you ever visit the Gander control center, look at the wall representing the North Atlantic. Way over to the right, you may see a wall full of red Xs that marks the spots for those that didn't make it. What are the chances of a fellow over the North Atlantic *anytime* finding someone on the frequency that has flown a single-engine aircraft like his and has had the same problem he is having? It takes a long line of lucky coincidences on top of his bad luck.

When Lindy did it, he used skill, daring, and a lot of luck. If he had to do it again today, he would need skill, daring, and a lot of luck. His old pilot buddies would still call him Lucky Lindy.

I never learned the pilot's name, but if fate ever brings us together again, then I'd like for him to pick the names of some stocks on Wall Street for me. They would have to be great ones!

JDF Letter:
Riyadh, Saudi Arabia
February 15, 1988

CONCERNING OVERNIGHT TRIPS

To: General Abdul Hameed Al-Faraidi, Director of Medevac
        Mr. Hussein Al Athel, Chief Executive Officer, GAMA
        Mr. Robert Braden, Project Administrator, GAMA
From: James D. Fox, Captain, Fixed Wing
Subject: Management of *Overnight Trips* for Medevac

This letter is in the form of a suggested checklist for the minimum requirements regarding the dispatch of aircraft and crews on Medevac overnight trips. The handling and selection of crews assigned to overnight trips needs your immediate attention. The method of dispatching these trips at the present time leaves much undone and in my opinion is very unsatisfactory. The salient points for you to consider are as follows:

1. Financing of the trip. There is no reason why a captain should have to spend his own money to finance any portion of a trip for Medevac. In the past, I have had to pay for landing costs, tips for line crews, and copilot expenses, etc. It sometime takes two or three months for repayment of these funds.

Some kind of financing must be arranged so that the crew does not feel that they are losing money on the trip. It is the popular conception now that every trip that is overnight out of the Kingdom is going to cost the members extra money. There are crew members that have declined to make trips because of the money they know they will lose.

A recent trip took us through Geneva, Switzerland. The hotel we were booked into by our handler gave us rates of SR870 per night. We had to scramble to find something more in line with what we could afford. Our final choice was the Ramada, and the rates were SR594 per night. A light snack for lunch for four was SR411 (that's SR104 for my part). The snack was two hamburgers, two bowls of soup, and two salads with soft drinks for four people. Do I need to remind you that our per diem for expenses is only SR300 per day, I think?

Transportation is also very expensive. Surely, it is not necessary to remind anyone of the losses suffered by the riyal and American dollar in Europe. The fluctuation of the dollar and riyal should not be at the expense of the flight crew. There are several ways to attack this problem, but so far none of them have been put in place. The management's vacillation around per diem is part of the problem, not the solution.

The per diem has changed several times in the last few months. At the present time, I have no idea what reimbursement to expect. Even if the captain is given cash for the trip, his guideline for its use makes it very unclear what it is to be spent for. Phone calls are difficult to justify after return, which makes me unwilling to call back reports. No collect calls can be made, and all other calls are suspected of being unrelated to business, regardless of amount. It is a well-known fact that tips to line crews at airports is a common requirement of aircrews, yet Medevac has no way of handling these payments.

The so-called per diem must pay for food, lodging, transportation to and from the airport or hospital or both, and all other costs that we cannot charge to the handler. In some instances, the handler will not accept any charges except fuel and catering. The captain has to pay for landing fees out of cash. In my opinion, traveling money should be advanced to each crew member before departure. In lieu of that, then arrangements for prior payment by Medevac should be made for lodging, food, transportation, etc., prior to departure.

The crew should not have a last-minute scramble for money when the preparation of the aircraft for departure should be the paramount thing on their minds.

2. Minimum equipment required for the assignment. The lack of spare parts in our hangar is jeopardizing the assignment of missions. My last trip to the United States should have been canceled at the VIP gate before the mission ever left the ground. One of MSD's inertial navigation systems failed. There are no spares, and it is a mandatory piece of equipment. We have three Gulfstreams with a requirement for two inertial navigation sets on each aircraft that crosses the Atlantic. There were only four inertial sets available instead of six plus spares. There was one aircraft already in London with two inertial sets installed. The other two were on MSD, and when one failed, the trip should have been canceled. I overruled my better judgment to try and accommodate those that called the mission.

We later got the inertial working prior to the Atlantic crossing, but it was in Shannon, Ireland, with the patient onboard. The trip was very nearly canceled there for lack of minimum equipment. That would have been not only embarrassing but perhaps dangerous for the patient.

3. A proper schedule for international crews. A schedule that is made without regard to personality and is strictly complied with makes it much simpler for the individual crew member to have his money, clothes, etc., ready when he knows that he is next up for an overnight trip.

At the present time, the schedule is adjusted almost every time an overnight mission is called. This only causes people to be upset and creates possible delays. The crew members should be scheduled to fit the needs and requirements of Medevac, not personalities.

Training requirements for upgrade should be considered when picking a copilot for overnight trip assignments. A crew member that chooses his trip is unfair to the other crew members.

If a crew member is unable to take a trip because of holiday or sickness, then he could be bypassed and would be first up for the next trip. A crew member that turns down a trip without an excellent reason should be put on the bottom of the list or removed from the list altogether. This would stop the procedure of choosing trips by turning them down because of knowledge of a better one that is coming in a few days.

4. The realistic use of the term ASAP when calling a mission. This last trip of MSD to Cleveland was launched on Friday afternoon as an ASAP mission. It was soon apparent that the patient could not be accepted in Cleveland until Wednesday and that the parties in Switzerland knew this before we ever left Riyadh.

This is not a criticism of those that authorized the mission. There is a question as to the nature of the mission as it was called. An ASAP it was not. We would have been in a much better position to launch the mission on Saturday or Sunday morning. There was no need to call a crew that had already been out flying all day. The term ASAP has lost its meaning. It is so overused that no one believes the radio when an ASAP mission is called. Prudent use of the term would help to restore the intended meaning.

Response times have been increased by several changes in the Medevac operation. New regulations for fueling have increased the time necessary for preparing the aircraft. No drivers at the compound when a mission is called require that a driver must be found at the hangar and called for a pickup at the compound. The round-trip from hangar to compound to hangar is a minimum of forty-five minutes. The call for a driver is initiated by the compound operator. There are many times that he is delayed in his call due to no lines available from the compound.

5. Guidelines for crew rest. Crew rest is a very necessary part of any long trip. Consideration should be made prior to a mission being called before the pressure of the mission begins to rest too heavily on the management's shoulders. Real rest for the crew is sleep time, not the time spent arranging the next leg, aircraft maintenance, or details pertaining to the flight. These points are offered as a checklist only.

There is much more thought needed before any real changes should be made. But changes should be made. In my opinion, these listed changes should make a better Medevac operation.

James D. Fox
Captain, Fixed Wing

Author's Note: *As a result of this letter, nothing was changed.*

Dispatch:
Riyadh, Saudi Arabia
February 20, 1988

WORDS TO DIE FOR

As I walked into operations, the smoke hung in the air like a cloud. The Saudis love their cigarettes, and they keep them going most of the time. There were seven copilots sitting around the table in the center of the room, all talking and laughing and burning their cigarettes into butts. They love their cigarettes, but they also love storytelling. When they are revising the approach manuals, they can do both.

Waleed Zahed is rather short, stocky, with black wavy hair, and the favorite storyteller of the copilot group. When all the other copilots are doing their revisions, Waleed can't do his because he must stand to tell his stories, and besides, he must use both his hands for gestures.

I love to walk into the room when Waleed is holding court. He knows that I'm going to help him in his storytelling, and it will be twice as much fun for us both. I tell him a joke in American, which all the copilots understand, and then Waleed repeats it in Arabic, which all the copilots also understand. They laugh at the joke when I tell it in American, and they laugh just as much when Waleed repeats the same story in Arabic. I get twice the mileage from a story, and Waleed gets full credit for my story when he translates it.

Waleed tells a joke of his own in Arabic. Every Saudi within earshot just falls down laughing. The joke is easily the funniest of the current batch. When the laughter dies down a little, I say, "Okay, Waleed, now tell me in American."

The joke teller was still laughing at his own joke, but he turned to me with a puzzled look on his face. He held both hands in front of him with the palms facing each other as if he were about to applaud or grab something. He still was puzzled. I could almost see the wheels turning in his head. Waleed was trying to translate the joke he had just told in Arabic into my language.

"Well, you see, this is an Egyptian joke, see, and I don't know . . ." His voice sort of trailed off.

"Don't tell me that, now just tell me the joke."

"Yeah, but I don't know . . . you might not understand it," Waleed tried to explain.

"Well, I don't know . . . maybe, but okay. Now let me see." He is still unsure of what to do with his hands as his mind tries to put the Egyptian joke told in Arabic into American.

As my friend draws his mental translation to completion, the room grows quiet. Every Saudi in the room knows the problem that Waleed has, and they want to hear how he handles it.

"Okay," Waleed begins. "You see, this Egyptian comes home from work and spits in the sink . . . and breaks it."

The room erupts into laughter again. Just as before, all those that had laughed themselves into a fit are doing the same again at the same joke. I waited for the punch line.

"Well, go on, Waleed, what's the rest of the joke?"

"That's it, Captain, that's the joke."

"But that can't be all of it, it's not even funny."

"Sure it's, it's real funny," Waleed insisted. "You see Egyptians are strong but stupid, see?" he continued.

The other copilots slowed their laughing down just a little to nod in agreement with the storyteller.

I had to retreat from the logic of my friend because I knew what the problem was. So much of what we laugh about in jokes is a play on words. To enjoy the humor, the listener must understand the different meanings of a word or a phrase. The purposeful misuse of some words is the sole basis for some jokes being funny. In our language, there are many words that can be used in several ways.

It's the joke telling that helped me come to a fuller understanding of the subtleties of dealing with people that speak my language very well, but without a full understanding of the different forms the meaning may take. What am I talking about?

That very thing was the basis for Khalid's anger with me. He had misunderstood an American word that almost led to a fatal mistake for us all!

It all started back on the February 5 with a trip assignment to pick up a patient in Geneva and transfer the same to Cleveland, USA. The patient was the personal physician of Prince Knife, one of the princes in line to the throne. It's a long line, and I don't know what his position was, but he was to be considered very important, therefore his physician was to be considered VIP as well.

The trip was assigned to me with Khalid Al-Ghoraibi as copilot and Kevin Tschida as engineer, two nurses, and a young doctor from Pakistan, all on MSD, the dog of the fleet. This Gulfstream was a constant headache in the avionics department. I found out later that it had been bought in Florida from a company that did not furnish a wiring diagram with the sale, a monumental mistake by the buyer, Medevac. The scuttlebutt was that there was a hefty *baksheesh* payment (under-the-table kickback) was made. True or not, whoever negotiated the purchase had to be incompetent, crooked, or both. I lean toward the latter.

Rules for crossing the Atlantic requires two working INS that had been calibrated and approved for the NAT. Also we were required to have two working VHF transceivers. MSD only had one of each, and they were intermittent. I complained to no avail because there was nothing else available. Of course, they wanted us to launch after a full day of flying. I had just flown MSD that day to Jeddah and back and knew what worked and didn't work; furthermore, they wanted me to launch ASAP, and all involved knew that we couldn't get into Geneva early enough to beat the curfew.

The pressure was too great. All the VIPs involved required that we get in the air immediately regardless of the condition of the aircraft or any curfew requirements. So we launched at 1355 and got into Athens 1820 just in time to spend the night. I hate to spend the night in Athens. The cab drivers are all crooks.

As I have already stated, the "heart patient" was the personal doctor of Prince Knife of Saudi Arabia. I believe the patient was from Egypt but had been diagnosed there in Geneva as needing what was available in Cleveland. We arrived in Geneva the morning of the sixth, and the patient couldn't be located. So much for all the hurry to get to Geneva!

I don't know anything about the doctor that was sent with me for the care of our lost patient. He was not a cardiologist, but an anesthesiologist, and on top that, a freshman from Pakistan. I felt sorry for the young doctor; he was scared to death because of his responsibility of caring for such a high-level person.

We arrived in Geneva early after lunch, and as soon as we learned that our patient was out of pocket, we went to the hotel. That night, I got a call from Riyadh, and they wanted me to find the missing patient.

"What do you mean you want me to find the lost doctor? Do you realize it's Friday night here, and everyone that is not in the hospital may be anywhere? Now look, I'm not going to run around like a chicken with its head rung off looking for a lost doctor in Geneva. You've got a hospital full of doctors there in Riyadh, plus the people that thought up this trip in the first place. Get them to find the doctor, or you have a doctor on the trip with me; get him to look for the patient." With that, I gave the phone to the young Pakistani doctor who was shaking his head no. But these people nod when they mean no and shake their head when they mean yes.

He got the job done, and we were all set to make a departure next morning at the crack of noon. We were expecting an ambulance, but the patient arrived in a limo and walked onboard without help. His heart trouble was not evident.

We left Geneva with a scheduled stop in Shannon for fuel. MSD was a GII and didn't have long enough legs to make it from Geneva to the East Coast of America or Canada, nonstop.

The patient had brought along a couple of doctor friends with him, and they got off the airplane in Shannon to visit the duty-free shop. They spent an hour there and delayed the flight until I almost missed my slot to cross the Atlantic.

We had arrived in Shannon with less avionics than required by regulation, but there was no way air traffic control would know as long as we were able to make the way points of NAT tracks as assigned. While on the ground, I reset the sick INS, and lo and behold, it started working. So we crossed the Atlantic to Gander with our finger crossed, then to Cleveland, arriving late in the afternoon. Immigration made us wait two hours in the airplane before they would make their check and clear us to leave. More frustration.

It was very cold with snow on the ground in Cleveland, so I had the aircraft stored in a hangar because I knew medical supplies didn't need freezing and the temperature was below freezing and would be colder that night. Also, I had decided to get our avionics fixed before we went back, and that would probably take a couple of days at least. It did.

Well, fast-forward to the day of our departure. I was not supposed to allow the Saudi copilots to fly from the left seat of the aircraft, but I let certain ones of them to do just that when we were in the United States. I felt that they needed the experience if they were ever going to become captains. Several of the young men had the potential to become good pilots, but after seven years of flying in the right seat, they had never been encouraged to fly as captains.

The treatment of Khalid and the other copilots by the Americans that preceded me may have contributed to his near-belligerent attitude. The young Saudis had been called dune coons, sand niggers, and worse by the American captains flying the Saudi aircraft which they crewed. The Saudis felt they had to tolerate the insults if they wanted to stay in aviation, but they didn't have to like it. I treated my copilots like I would want to be treated, but not all could accept me as being different.

Khalid was one that didn't see me any different from the other ugly Americans, and that was also a possible contributing factor to our near-fatal experience in Cleveland.

There was about six inches of old snow on the ground at Cleveland Hopkins International Airport that morning, and as we taxied out, it was difficult to tell taxiways from runways, from ramps, and open ground. Khalid was in the left seat, and knowing there might be a problem for him, I took the time to explain to Khalid with a chart our taxi route to the runway for takeoff.

As we came out of the ramp where we had been parked for four days, we needed to make about a forty-five-degree turn to the right, which would put us on a taxiway parallel to runway 23, which we were going to use for takeoff. We would be heading N53° east or, basically, northeast. All the necessary information for taxi was given to us by ground control before we left the parking area. Just to help, I explained to Khalid on the map the instructions we had just received. It's more than a courtesy for a crew to share information; it is a requirement.

As we moved away from the chocks, a Falcon 50 jet landed on runway 23, the same runway we were to use. The landing jet turned off and reversed his direction onto the taxiway. He was heading toward the main ramp under the control tower. The Falcon jet was abeam of our parking ramp as we approached the taxiway. Just for clarification, the ground control operator said, "Hotel Zulu Mike Sierra Delta (HZMSD, our Saudi tail number) pass behind the Falcon Jet." Since I was in the right seat, acting as copilot to Khalid, I replied, "Roger." The die was cast.

Khalid heard what I heard. The engineer, Kevin, heard what I heard, and we all thought we knew what the controller meant.

In a large aircraft, the steering is accomplished by the man in the left seat. Foot brakes are on both sides, but the steering is on the left side only. Khalid was steering the aircraft.

It was only a short distance from where we came out of our parking ramp onto the east-west taxiway to the turn into the main ramp under the tower. Khalid was following the Falcon Jet, and when the Falcon Jet turned right onto the main ramp, Khalid turned right behind him.

"No, no, Khalid, straight ahead, straight ahead!" I said with urgency.

"No, I must follow the Falcon Jet!" Khalid insisted with a frown.

"No, Khalid, straight ahead, that way." I pointed back to the taxiway, northeast of our position.

"Mike Sierra Delta, stay on the taxiway, turn back on the taxiway." The ground controller was watching our progress and saw us start into the main ramp. He verified what I had just told Khalid.

The temporary captain turned the aircraft back to the left with a frown. Quickly, we were back on the taxiway and heading northeast toward the end of runway 23, our departure runway. Nothing was said, and I assumed the little discrepancy was over, but it was far from over.

The departure end of runway 23 was bisected by runway 28 at an angle of fifty degree. From our taxiway to our departure runway, it would be necessary for us to make a 180-degree turn to the left. Since jets don't need a run-up like aircraft with reciprocal engines, they are often cleared for takeoff from the taxiway as they approach the end of the taxiway.

Approaching the end, I changed to the tower frequency and reported ready. The tower controller responded, "Mike Sierra Delta, you are cleared for takeoff runway 23."

With fifty feet of taxiway left, I started my last effort to stow maps, charts, pencils, and whatever. I don't like loose items in the cockpit for takeoff or landing. A single map fell to the floor, and I bent over in my seat to pick it up from the floor. Khalid started his turn on to the runway just as I bent over. It only took two seconds, but as I raised my head, Khalid was pushing the power levers (throttles) full forward for takeoff. He didn't wait to see if I was ready. He didn't say a word. He was still chaffing from his correction by the ground controller and me.

"No, Khalid, don't" was all I had time to say as I reached forward with my left hand and jerked the power levers from his right hand and brought them back to idle.

With a surprised and angry look on his face and with his mouth open to object, the Saudi was cut off by the tower. "Cancel takeoff, cancel takeoff, Mike Sierra Delta, cancel takeoff." The urgency in the controller's voice didn't fully conceal his disgust with us. He didn't know who was in the cockpit. All he knew was that they had a Saudi Arabian tail number, and they spoke with an American accent. What he did know for sure was that he didn't want them killing themselves on his airport.

Khalid found his voice. "What's the matter? What did I do?"

"You turned down runway 28 instead of 23, Khalid, it was the wrong runway," I spoke slowly and clearly, and without sarcasm, because suddenly he knew he had nearly killed us all. The midpoint of runway 28 is where it crosses the end of runway 23. Our weight required nearly six thousand feet of runway for takeoff. That figure is always calculated by the captain before each takeoff. Khalid had made the calculation himself. There was only a little more than three thousand feet of runway in front of us when Khalid started his takeoff roll. If I hadn't stopped him, he would not have had enough runway to get in the air, nor enough to stop the aircraft before he ran off the end.

The snow helped to obscure the obvious, but it was mostly attitude that interfered with the temporary captain's attention. He knew he was a good pilot—no, a great pilot—but now he had lost face in front of all these Americans. Somehow, it was my fault.

It had all started when he heard "pass behind the Falcon Jet," and he interpreted that as "follow the Falcon Jet." It was just that simple. It wasn't the proud Saudi's fault; it was that stupid language of theirs. If they were speaking his language, it would never have happened.

After a stop in Bangor, Maine, we refueled, cleared Customs and Immigration, and changed seats. I would assume my seat as captain for the Atlantic. It was normal for me to sit in the left seat even when I let the copilots fly. Company procedure required that they always fly from the right seat. It was another reason for Khalid to know that I wasn't going to tell anyone about his error.

Our route would include stops in Shannon to spend what was left of the night. Then the next evening, we would leave London and schedule another fuel stop in Athens. As I have already stated, MSD didn't have the long legs (range) of the GIII. From Athens, we could make it nonstop to Riyadh, Saudi Arabia, our home base.

The excitement of the Mooney over the Atlantic (see the chapter "Lindbergh Did It, Didn't He?") helped to thaw my Saudi copilot out just a little, and the cockpit was back to its usual quiet, almost formal atmosphere two nights later as we were en route from London to Athens.

Click. I felt the GII move slightly beneath me. My eyes passed the master caution panel in the center of instrument panel and saw nothing lit up. Then I glanced down at the center console and the autopilot. The master autopilot engagement lever was in the off position. Some sort of electrical glitch, I thought, so from habit, I put my left hand on the control yoke with both feet on the rudders, and with my right hand, I carefully reengaged the autopilot. It took hold and nothing happened. I thought, *Yeah, that's what was happening, just some stray electrical glitch.*

A few moments later, I noticed that Khalid had Kevin leaning over the console and whispering about something. Apparently, Khalid's cool mood didn't extend to the flight engineer. Then *click* again, and the autopilot disengaged.

"Hey, what are you guys doing over there? Can't you see you're knocking the autopilot offline?"

Kevin spoke from his bent-over position as he looked back at me from over his left shoulder. "Well, something has happened to the VOR on this side. We were just trying to see what it is" (navigation radio).

With the two of them bent over, the circuit breaker bulkhead on the right side was exposed to my view, and I could see a circuit breaker had popped.

With a casual voice, I said, "Well, why don't you just push that circuit breaker back in and see if that fixes it."

Four eyes turned as a single pair to see the white area of the circuit breaker in plain view. It was just a moment of astonishment, then Kevin laughed. Years of training always taught flight crews that with electrical problems, the first item you always check is the circuit breaker. It's not only the most likely problem; it is also the easiest and quickest thing you can do.

Kevin straightened up, pushed the CB back in, the VOR righted itself, and all was back to normal. All but Khalid. His anger came to the surface. He had lost face once again in front of the Americans. As he spoke Arabic words of anger, I tried to pass it off as the nothing thing that it actually was.

"Hey, Khalid, forget it. It was nothing. Everybody makes a little mistake now and then."

Khalid ignored my efforts to console. He continued to berate himself in Arabic and American. "I should have seen it. It is so primary. I should have checked the CB first, and then it would have all been okay." "Look, Khalid, don't make such a big thing of it, okay? It was just a little thing. No harm done, and like I said, it happens to everyone now and then."

"It doesn't happen to me, not me it doesn't," he continued.

"Well, Khalid, maybe that's part of the problem." My remark caused his face to jerk in my direction as he looked me square in the eyes.

"What do you mean, 'that may be the problem'?" He was barely controlling his anger.

I answered slowly and without rancor, "Because, Khalid, *no one* is as good as you think you are." If looks could kill, I would have been a dead man. I had meant to help the young man, but instead, I had just made an enemy for life. And I lived in his country.

CAF Letter:
Riyadh, Saudi Arabia
March 12, 1988

NEW ADDRESS

Dear Friends and Loved Ones,

We have some good news for you even though it is one and one half years' late. The Foxes have obtained an APO Box at the US Military Post Office in Riyadh. The box is restricted, which means that we are only allowed twelve ounces per letter, but that is quite a bit. All envelopes *must* be marked First-Class Mail, but your postage will be the same as it would be in the States.

The following items are strictly prohibited from mail entering and leaving Saudi Arabia. Items indicated by an asterisk require a special permit.

1. Posters, pictures, paintings, books, catalogs, or magazines depicting nude or seminude persons and pornographic or sexual items of any type (as determined by the Saudi Customs agent on site)
2. Religious items, to include but not limited to Bibles, crucifixes, instructional material, etc.
3. Pork or pork products
4. Narcotics
5. Alcoholic beverages or any foodstuff containing alcohol
6. Firearms of any type; this also includes air guns and toy guns
7. Fireworks
*8. Government symbols; to include, but not limited to, stickers, flags, etc.
*9. Military clothing or equipment, other than for personal use
*10. Radio and electronic items, to include but not limited to base stations, handheld transmitters, etc.
    Distillation equipment, candy, cigarettes and cigarette advertisements, chemicals, medications, and alcohol (medicinal or industrial)
11. Videotapes are prohibited, regardless of weight
12. The following items are subject to confiscation and/or censorship by the Ministry of Information or Ministry of communications:
    a. Films
    b. Records
    c. Printed matter, e.g., books, magazines, catalogs, newspapers, etc., not printed in Saudi Arabia

Our new address is:

LTC and Mrs. James D. Fox
USMTM PO Box 1463-R
APO NY 09038-5364

Maybe this will speed up our correspondence time, and it will not take so long for our mail to be delivered to you and vice versa. The other address is still good also but use of this new APO Box should give us better service and postage will be less.

Again, just remember to mark all letters First-Class Mai" when using the above address, or it will be returned to you.

We are both doing fine, and since we want to get a mailing out to everyone on this new address, we will have to write more later.

Love,
James D. Fox

Dispatch:
Riyadh, Saudi Arabia
March 14, 1988

Pilots and Mechanics

Well, the old story about the problem that some mechanics have with pilots has reared its head again. Recently, I have had a couple of run-ins with the chief of maintenance over here. Doug has a position that eliminates pilots as a source of any useful information concerning what may be wrong with the aircraft they have been flying. I've run into this before, and it creates situations ranging from mild irritation to life threatening.

I was flying MS3 at forty-one thousand feet over the Alps on the way to Frankfurt when I heard a *click*, and the autopilot dropped off the line. I tried to reset it, but it wouldn't come on line. I noticed also that the manual trim wheel was inoperative. The manual trim wheel wasn't just *inop*; it was turning freely in either direction. That's a new one, and it's a no-go item at such an altitude. We were nearly on top of Basel, Switzerland, so I made the decision to land there and see what was wrong.

As soon as I got on the ground, I called Riyadh and told them my problem. Doug, the M/C, said it was the *stab-aug* computer. He also told me to fly on to Duesseldorf, and he would ship the part to us, and the onboard mechanic could install it. I told him that I didn't think it was the stab aug computer because we had also lost the manual trim wheel. We didn't just lose the use of the manual trim wheel. It was turning free like it wasn't even attached to anything. The M/C insisted that he was right, but about that time, the local mechanics at Basel told me what the real problem was. It was *not* the stab-aug computer.

The manual trim wheel is attached to the *stab-aug* computer by a "bicycle chain." The chain was broken. Of course, it's not really a bicycle chain, but it looks just like one. No one had heard of such a thing happening before, and of course, they didn't have one in stock in Basel. They would have to order one in from Savannah, Georgia. It just so happened that MS4 was there on the ground for maintenance and wouldn't fly for another two or three months. It was the one with the bent box beam I've mentioned before.

"Hey, I've got an idea. If it will fit, why don't we take the chain from MS4?"

It did fit, and we were ready to go in a couple of hours. Another conflict between a pilot and the maintenance chief.

We also lost the number 2 VHF transmitter and the right engine nacelle heat on the way to Basle, all no-go items. When I got back, I talked to Jerry Padova about his and Acker's troubleshooting. Then I told him if he wanted to look real good, he should start getting MS3 ready for a hard failure in the aux pump area.

It's been warning us for some time. The Gulfstream rep John McGinnis at Jeddah had just been telling me about the same problem that we are about to have—three times with me on the ramp at Riyadh and once in Germany and once again with Daghistani in Germany. It's a warning. Can't talk to the M/C, too hardheaded.

One that really pulled my cork under was when they would release an aircraft to fly when they knew it had a serious problem. An intermittent problem is one that anyone that fixes things hates to deal with. Because since it is intermittent, then you can't fix it until you catch it in the broken state.

MS3 was dispatched to Khartoum, Africa, with an APU (auxiliary power unit) that intermittently would not start. Does that sound bad? No, not too bad. The APU doesn't even work while you're in the air. All it does is provide electrical power and air-conditioning for the aircraft when on the ground, and, oh yes, it is needed to make an engine start. The Gulfstream uses Rolls-Royce Spey engines, and they are started with an air motor. Most airports have a GPU (ground power unit) for aircraft to use if needed, but few have an air start unit. If the onboard APU on a Gulfstream doesn't work, then you can be stuck on the ground wherever you may be for some time.

Khartoum, Africa, sits at the junction of the Nile and White rivers. They had a flood, and the Saudis dispatched several C-130s to the rescue with supplies. A few days later, I was sent via MS3 with ten doctors to see if they could be of any help. On arrival, it looked like the runways themselves were the only things above water on the airport. As usual, we started the APU on the rollout down the runway. The doctors were unloaded, and we started the wait.

We waited eight hours, and when the doctors returned, they told us they never got past the first checkpoint. They had been all day trying to get past Immigration! Why should we be surprised? On arrival, we saw stacks of supplies all around the airport that had been brought in for the poor people that were without shelter or food. The relief supplies had not been inspected as yet, therefore could not be released. I told ya' the Sudanese *don't trust nobody*. More than likely, the local tribal chief had not yet figured out how he would be able to best profit from the distribution.

That is the problem with USA trying to help such nations, many examples of goods just sitting on the docks without distribution. I was taught that by the US Army in the Command and General Staff College.

Oh well, it doesn't have anything to do with the maintenance problem. We made the trip back to Riyadh, and a few days later, I drew the straw that sent me on a mission to New Haven, Connecticut, in MS3. Waleed and I were prepositioned in London to be ready to take the aircraft with a patient onboard on to New Haven without an overnight stop.

We were at the airport about a half hour after MS3 had landed. It was nighttime, and there was lots of activity going on when we were dropped off by the handler. The fueling trucks were there, but they were not refueling the aircraft.

"What's the matter here? Why aren't you fueling the aircraft? We need the tanks topped off, we're crossing the Atlantic."

"We can't fuel the airplane because one engine is still running."

"What do you mean? Didn't the captain shut the engines down when he got here?"

"No, Captain, he said he had to leave one running because the APU wouldn't start, and it's against the law to fuel an aircraft while the engine is running."

The "captain" had left the scene with his engineer in charge. The engineer was a Saudi and a nice fellow but a little short on experience and could not express his opinion to a captain.

I told the handler to get me a GPU so we could shut down the engine on MS3, and also we would need and air motor to make an engine start if the APU still wouldn't start. After a short delay, the GPU showed up; it was hooked up, and I shut down number 2 on MS3. While in the cockpit, I started setting up the navigation systems with Waleed's help. We had plenty of work for the both of us to do. Suddenly, I felt the lights in the cockpit starting to dim. What was happening? The GPU was hooked up, but when I checked the voltage, it was less than the aircraft battery voltage. The GPU wasn't charging; it was draining our batteries.

I got the handler on the stick for another GPU, and it showed up just before the aircraft went dark. Okay, now we got a GPU that's working, and we can finish getting the aircraft ready. Luckily, the air motor unit arrived, and we made the engine starts okay without a working APU. I made the decision to cross the Atlantic in that condition because we wouldn't need it again until on the ground in the States, and we could get help there. Also, we had a patient onboard and needed to be gone.

On the ground in New Haven, I called Gulfstream in Bethpage, New York, and told them of my APU problem. They sent a technician over in a light plane, and he had the problem fixed in about thirty minutes. One of the reasons that made troubleshooting the APU for not starting was because it was easy to see it was getting fuel and spark, and that's all you need to start a turbine engine. There is no timing or distributor to worry with. We could see fuel dripping from the tailpipe, and we could hear the *snap, snap, snap* of the igniter firing. So what could be wrong? The tech showed me the old spark plug that he had removed and replaced. It had a small crack in the porcelain insulation, so it was firing back to the base not out at the end of the plug like it's supposed to do.

I found out that the M/C back in Riyadh had known that the APU on MS3 was intermittent for almost two weeks. He had sent me to Khartoum with an aircraft that if the APU failed to start, we could have been stuck there for no telling how long. That's one of the reasons that we had developed the habit of starting the APU on the rollout. If it doesn't start, then you better leave an engine running. Of course, if you do that, then you can't get any fuel!

It goes on and on.

Dispatch:
Riyadh, Saudi Arabia
March 19, 1988

TERRORISTS SHOOT UP SAUDI DIPLOMATS

Talked to the biomed technician today at coffee table, and he told me all about his trip to Lagos, Nigeria, this last week. They were launched on the mission in a C-130 because there were no Gulfstreams available. That's how close I missed the trip. They stopped in Jeddah for information on the three patients they were to pick up and to fill up with fuel. They also needed to finalize the over flight permits through diplomatic channels. The patients in Lagos were part of the Saudi diplomatic community. They had been shot by terrorists. I'm not all that familiar with the C-130, but it's a four-engine turboprop, so it must flight plan around FL200 and 275 knots. They must have great range for a Medevac flight because they would be carrying very little weight. At any rate, their launch from Jeddah should take them to their destination.

Their point of entry was Port Sudan and then over Khartoum in the Sudan. I've been that way myself a couple of times. They were something like four hours into the flight and halfway across Chad when they were told they had no right to be flying in Chad's airspace. They were told to go back where they came from *immediately* as they would soon be dodging rockets. Chad is still at war with Libya. They *don't trust nobody*. So they went back to Khartoum. The Sudanese like to give you a hard time, but I think it's mostly bluff. They are so poor that they really want you there and bring money. The fuel bill alone will probably buy some general a new Mercedes. But they have shot down aircraft before with surface-launched missiles, so it's best to pay attention even if they may be bluffing.

The C-130 sat on the ground in Khartoum for three days while the diplomats and bureaucrats figured it out. I remember the trip to Mexico for the old Humble Company. The manager of the Baton Rouge refinery was injured in a car wreck in Mexico. What a mess! It took about ten days to extricate him and his wife from that bunch of money-hungry bureaucrats. On landing in Nigeria, they were immediately surrounded by soldiers armed with automatic weapons. The soldiers demanded to know who they were and what their reason was for being there! Oh boy, the left hand and the right hand. The flight crew was all Saudi; only the nurse was not Saudi. The captain finally made himself understood to someone in charge, and they were allowed to send for the ambulance with their three patients. They were also allowed to buy fuel.

After fueling the aircraft, the fuelers (plural) came aboard and asked the captain if he had something for them. The captain shrugged his shoulders and pretended to not understand—a gesture that is used often in this country. While he was feigning ignorance, he was speaking in Arab to others of his crew. He said, "Offer them a Pepsi, maybe they will be satisfied with that. Make that a Pepsi in a bottle; they will probably eat a can." The crew had a big laugh, and fuelers were happy to get a cold drink. The ambulance arrived in due time; the patients were loaded, and the departure was made.

En route the story was unfolded. Their three patients were leaving a hotel in downtown Lagos. As they entered the Mercedes with diplomatic plates, they were approached by an individual who knocked on the driver's window. He appeared to want to ask a question. The driver was not a regular driver, and the two fellows with him were just friends. None were considered important people. They were just employees of the diplomatic mission to Lagos. The man driving the car was alone in the front seat while his two friends were in the backseat. It looked like to the stranger that two important people had just left the hotel with their driver. The man in the front seat became excited when the stranger started knocking on his window. He nervously tried to start the car. At that time, the stranger exposed an automatic weapon and opened fire on the man sitting on the right in the rear. Three rounds hit the man. The first went through his shoulder while the second and third went through his left arm between the shoulder and elbow. *Dat, dat, dat*, just like stitches. He said he couldn't believe he had been shot, even with the noise of the gunfire. He said he didn't remember hearing any sound from the gun.

The driver could see that he was not that safe, and having failed to start the car in his nervous condition, he attempted to save the situation by opening the door of the car and slamming it into the gunman. The force of the door deflected the weapon upward and knocked the gunman off balance. The driver grabbed the barrel of the weapon pointed into the air. As they struggled for possession and control of the automatic weapon, the third occupant in the car decided to go for help. In other words, he lit a shuck. The driver lost the contest with the gunman, and as the barrel came down between them, the driver took a single round in the left shoulder. He went down to the ground. The gunman turned and fired a short burst at the fleeing third man. Would you believe it? He was shot through the left shoulder. The gunman disappeared in a flash. He had shot all three of the Saudis, and none of them were seriously injured. Lots of blood and no police. In a few minutes, the sidewalk and traffic had returned to normal. It was all a mistake, and no great harm done. All in a day's work in the southern part of Africa.

Dispatch:
Riyadh, Saudi Arabia
March 31, 1988

To: Mr. Hussein Al-Athel,
           Chief Executive Officer, GAMA
From: Capt. James D. Fox, Fixed Wing Medevac
Subject: Resignation

Dear Sir:

Due to personal reasons, I find that I can no longer fly for Medevac; therefore, I hereby request a release from my contract so that I may return to the United States.

During our last meeting, in July of 1987, you told me that if at any time during the next term of my contract I felt the need to leave for any reason, then all I had to do was let you know my wish to leave and give you a reasonable amount of time to find my replacement.

This letter is your notice. I would appreciate being allowed to leave just as soon as possible.

I would appreciate a letter of no objection so that I might return at some time in the future; however, the letter is of no great consequence.

I would like to be reimbursed for the airline tickets used in my last FlightSafety attendance. Your people have the details.

> Sincerely,
> James D. Fox
> Captain, Fixed Wing
> Medevac
> cc: Bob Braden, Project Administrator
> Maj. Al-Shablan, Project Director
> Maj. Hasoon, Assistant Project Director

Author's Note: Just another attempt at justice in a foreign land. GAMA always dragged their feet when paying expenses. It was just their natural way. I can't really come up with a reason for their attitude, but it was at least consistent. One day in operations with a roomful of witnesses, I confronted the then acting head of Medevac, a Captain Baghdadi.

"Captain, I would like to be paid for the expense account that I turned in more than a month ago."

"Oh that, it was only about 300 riyals, wasn't it?"

"Yes, that's right, and I see you are familiar with the document."

"Well, it's such a minor amount, why don't we just forget about it?" The captain delivered that line with a big smile and chuckle as he performed for the group of pilots and copilots there.

"Okay, Baghdadi, if that's the way you feel, then I won't be flying any more trips until I'm paid the full amount, which was 348 riyals."

The smile disappeared, and he glared at me. He had noticed that I didn't refer to his rank but just called him by his last name. It was a sign of disrespect. The silence lasted only a few seconds, then the captain turned and left the room.

I got the check the next day before I was called out for a mission. I don't make idle threats, and the captain believed me.

This was not the only offer I had made before leaving.

Dispatch:
Riyadh, Saudi Arabia
April 1, 1988

THE DUST LICENSE

You can't really appreciate a story about the "dust license" unless you understand about the Atlantic license, and you can't understand any of this unless you first understand about a character named Eid Al-Roudan. Well, maybe not understand him, but maybe just to know about him. I don't know if Eid is understandable.

Eid (pronounced EEd) was one of the Saudi copilots that kept all the captains flying for Medevac on their toes. He was a chubby little fellow, and he couldn't have been more than about five feet six inches tall. He usually wore a slight smile, not a big smile, but a little one, just a trace of one. It was a smile with a little mystery, just enough to make you wonder what he was thinking about. After you knew him for a while, you knew that he was up to something devious. In addition to the above, he was a supreme liar, cheat, and lazy (see separate chapter on Eid).

The guy had been working as a copilot for Medevac for six years when he made his first trip with me, and he couldn't fly a Gulfstream worth beans. Well, you say, he hadn't been trained properly, nobody liked him, or no one would give him a chance. Those descriptions could have all been true, but in my opinion, there was another reason more complex and more difficult to believe.

I'm quite sure that Eid was a person that chose to be a pilot because of the imagined prestige that accompanied the title. He learned two things early in his flying career. First, he wasn't any good at flying airplanes, and second, he had a talent for covering up his deficiencies with tall stories. The tall stories were not only about his accomplishments in aviation, but fantasies about what he did outside of aviation. The stories were used as a distraction from what he was supposed to be doing.

If Eid had picked almost any other job, then his ineptitude would soon have been noticed, and he would have had to move on to something else. In aviation, he had used political favors to get the job as a copilot, and once in aviation, he could count on his captain to do all the work. Since the captains were mostly foreigners, he could use the "poor me" defense for not doing any better if and when he might be called before the boss. Copilots were not pushed into being a captain, even though that was the stated policy of the government. In fact, most copilots were overanxious to be promoted even before they were ready. So Eid was often tolerated by those in power perhaps because he was never pestering for a promotion.

There must have been some fantasy floating around in his head at one time because he showed me his pilot's license, which had a Lear type rating on it. Eid wouldn't know how to fasten his seat belt in a Lear. He freely admitted that he "bought" the type rating without ever going near a Learjet. He claimed that he paid $5,000 American to a corrupt FAA check pilot in Arizona for the type rating. Eid was such a liar. Why would anyone believe that story? No one knew the truth of the source of the type rating, but there it was on his license. Other copilots confirmed that they knew of a FAA check pilot in Arizona that sold Lear type ratings. I never asked for his name or tried to go any further into that story. It could have been that on that one point, Eid had told the truth. One thing we all agreed on was that he didn't know how to fly an airplane, Lear or otherwise.

Eid's decision to fly for Medevac or the Saudi Armed Forces provides a good lesson for the reader to consider. First, he could get the job with no qualifications by utilizing his political contacts. Political contacts are a big thing in his country. Every story of success outside the royal family can usually be traced to some form of favoritism.

Now wait a minute. Some of you have already seen a hole in this story of Eid working as copilot but worthless at flying an airplane. It's not that hard to explain—money. Any flight school in the United States that gets a contract from Saudi Arabia to train Saudis to fly is not going to jeopardize that lucrative contract by rejecting anything that is sent to them in the form of a breathing body. They are going to get that breathing body through the system. Period. I've seen the system work firsthand.

Once I took an applicant for a type rating on a Lockheed JetStar to Atlanta, Georgia. He took his check ride with the local FAA check pilot and got his rating after the check pilot told me in private.

"The boy has a few problems and really is not ready for this rating, but I'm going to go ahead and give it to him because I know you guys over in Houston. You fly two captains in the cockpit, so I know he will have someone watching over him until he gets a little more experience, okay?"

The FAA check pilot mistakenly thought that I was his training captain, which I was not. The point is, he knew our operation, and he would like to be the one to give the next check ride for us when called on. A rejection reflects on the one that recommended the applicant, and that could mean a written report from all involved. Too much trouble. Just pass him. It's all about money, folks.

Once into the government job, Eid could play his games of deception, distraction, and deviation. In our country, it is called smoke and mirrors. You see, my friends, when a person works for a small—to medium-size business in any part of the world, his performance is closely monitored. If the same person works for a large corporation or the government, then his performance is not only monitored less, but incompetence is much harder to detect and to deal with.

A small businessman will merely get rid of a worker that doesn't produce.[14] In the government, a supervisor hesitates to chastise or recommend an employee for dismissal. It's easier to promote, transfer, or maybe hire a helper for him. The inept employee may be costing someone a fortune, but so far he is removed from the one that is paying for his poor work, the offender goes unnoticed or ignored. In the USA, we readily accept this situation and call it bureaucracy. Whether it's the government or a large corporation, the results are all the same.

In most of the world outside of the USA, all aircrew members wear uniforms with their rank shown on their shoulders or sleeves. One stripe denotes a hostess, two stripes for a flight engineer, three stripes for a first officer (copilot), and four stripes are for the captain or pilot in command. In the USA, most corporate pilots do not wear uniforms, but in other parts of the world, they all wear uniforms.

The uniform is known as a mark of authority and prestige and is universally respected. In Europe, almost every takeoff results in a landing in a foreign country. I once took off from Basel, Switzerland, for a short test flight around the airport, and as I circled the airport, I was handled by Swiss, French, German, and Italian air traffic controllers.

The uniform is also a quick ticket through the Customs gate at foreign airports. A crew member's uniform is admired by many, and with some, even held in awe. Eid loved the uniform part of his job.

Eid had found a perfect place for his talents, or condition, if you prefer. He could play the part of a copilot without much effort. All he had to do was talk on the radio, and talk was something that he was good at. He didn't have to do any paperwork and was so unreliable in any of the rest of his duties that most captains did their own preflight rather than trust him.

The only real responsibility he had as a copilot was to do the Jeppesen[15] revisions. I found out later that he didn't do them, but instead, he just threw his revisions in the trash! Any complaints would be somehow blamed on the cursed Kawajee[16] that he was assigned to, and he could expect no retribution.

---

[14]   A sign seen on the bulletin board of a small business in Texas: "Do you want to travel, visit strange places, meet new people, and have excitement in your life? Then just screw up one more time!"

[15]   Jeppesen: The name of revisions mailed out to aviators who subscribe to the services of the Jeppesen company. The service provides approach charts and en route maps for the entire world. These charts are a necessary part of a pilot's navigation requirement. Regulations require that a pilot in command is responsible for having up-to-date charts for every flight. If a pilot was ramp-checked by the aviation authority of whatever country the pilot might be in at the time and did not have up to date charts, that pilot could be in deep trouble. It is considered *very dangerous and foolish* to fly on instruments without current charts.

[16]   *Kawajee* (Kah-wah-gee): An Arabic slang word for the *foreigner*. Not a term of endearment.

430

It always amazed me how he could stay just a step ahead of his adversaries. He had an answer, and usually with some form of documentation, for whatever charge might be leveled against him. If he was questioned about why he wasn't willing to take a check ride, he would remind the department head that he hadn't been to the proper school in the States. He knew that we were all scheduled to go to schools that most of us never attended. So he would remind the department head that he had not gone and therefore should not be expected to perform well on a check ride.

He knew his detractors very well because he could always pick a point that he knew they were not well versed on, and they would have to back off until they checked on what he had just claimed. While they were checking, if they ever did, he would get his way. By the time they came back to him on the first item, he would have one or two new ones for them to check. Yes, Eid knew how to work the system, and he worked it very well.

You see, Eid, in addition to his other talents, was an accomplished liar. He would climb a tree to tell a lie when he could stand on the ground to tell the truth. The truth was just not in the man. A psychologist might describe him as a pathological liar. That type is usually a person that lies without realizing that he is lying. I am not qualified to judge that, but I think the psychologist would be wrong in that analysis of Eid. I had the feeling that he knew exactly what he was doing. Eid's string was finally played out while I was still flying for Medevac, but that was couple of years after the incident described here.

Eid's end in Medevac is worthy of a stand-alone story that I'll tell later. He had played his game in Medevac for about eight years before they caught on and finally terminated him.

When I was being checked out by Odie Pound, another expat from the States, he told me about Eid.

"You'll soon see that Eid is probably the smartest copilot we got. He's also the richest. Yeah, he builds shopping centers on the side. He's smart and rich, all right."

"Well, what is he doing working here?"

"Oh, I don't know, it's just something he wants to do, I guess."

Eid wasn't rich, but he was smart. Odie Pond bought his stories hook, line, and sinker. He was smart enough to stay ahead of the hounds. He was devious enough to arrange to work when he wanted and to take only the trips that he wanted. Odie, as it turned out, was completely fooled by Eid.

Most crew members wanted to take international trips. It gave them a chance to get out of the Kingdom, have something to drink, if they drank, and watch some up-to-date television.

Eid didn't want to go on all international trips, just the ones to the United States and Europe. He carried extra epaulets for his out-of-country trips. As a copilot or first officer, he was supposed to wear three stripes, but he carried four-stripe epaulets, which had a little loop (like the French wear) on the top stripe to denote something special. He would wear the false stripes when out of the country and tell people that he was an instructor captain.

He was so brash and so accomplished that most people were taken in by his stories. He must have known that sooner or later everyone would catch on, but it didn't seem to bother him. It only took me one trip to find that his self-stated flying accomplishments were just a figment of someone's imagination. No, it wasn't that I was a lot smarter than all the rest; it was because I gave my copilots a chance to fly the airplane. It was my intent to help them do better. It was easily noticed that Eid was not accustomed to flying at all and didn't really want to fly. To a captain that is paying attention, a young copilot that doesn't want to fly the airplane is a dead giveaway that something is wrong. Eid could handle the communications from the right seat for an in-Kingdom trip, but when we left the country and you needed more help from him in both communication and navigation, he was less than worthless. "A sack of sand" would be an overstatement of his qualifications. You couldn't trust him to do anything right. He would either never mind a requirement or screw it up, and you never knew which it was going to be next.

So when I got a call from Romeo[17] for an international trip and Eid was called as my copilot, I turned him down.

"Romeo, this is 68,[18] you're going to have to get me another copilot. I'm not going to make another international trip with no help, and Eid is no help. So you may just as well call the major and get me another copilot, or you can call out another captain because I'm not going with Eid!"

Oh no, now I'd done it. I was pushing the major, the manager, into a corner, and Romeo was in the middle. My friend, Hakim, another Saudi pilot, was visiting in my villa at the time, so he called Romeo and volunteered for the trip. Hakim was a good pilot with good experience even before he came with Medevac, perfectly acceptable by me, so I thought everything was settled. I found out differently the next morning.

Early the next day, I was in operations with Hakim getting details for the trip when our attention was distracted by the arrival of Eid in his traditional dress, not his flight uniform. All aircrew members came to the airfield in their uniforms. Saudis that wore uniforms as part of their jobs were the only Saudis that were allowed to wear any type of clothing other than their traditional dress. We always wore uniforms to fly at anytime we visited the military airport where we worked. Eid arrived in his thobe, igal, ghutra, etc., and he knew he was the center of our

---

[17]   Romeo was the call sign for the control operator for all the handheld radios in Medevac. All crew members had handheld transceivers for local control and all aircraft had HF (high frequency) transceivers for long distance. We could call Romeo base from the air over Europe or from anywhere in the Kingdom.

[18]   Each crew member had a radio call sign. Mine was Gulfstream 68. Informally, we might just be referred to as 68.

attention. Even the TCNs[19] knew that something unusual was happening. He gave us all a knowing smile and went to the major's office without delay.

"Well, I wonder what that's all about."

"No telling, Captain, you know Eid, he's probably going to cry to the major about your treatment of him."

"Well, he can cry all he wants. I'm not changing my mind."

The chubby copilot went into the major's office with a smile for everyone, and he came out of the office about a half hour later with a smile for everyone, including me. He announced quietly to the dispatcher that he would be going on my trip as a supernumerary pilot!

Hakim flashed to white heat. He announced to all that if Eid was going, then he was not going! On that pronouncement, Eid left operations and the air base. It was as if he had just tossed in a bomb, then strolled off, completely confident of its outcome.

The major's office was soon occupied by one mad Saudi, my friend Hakim. He couldn't believe that he, a good pilot, had been replaced by a bad one. The major wanted to make everyone happy. He told Hakim that he could go and that Eid was just an extra helper. Hakim restated his position of not going if Eid was even on the airplane. Now the major had to find another copilot.

In a matter of minutes, another copilot was chosen, and the trip was back on my schedule. Khalid Al Gharabi had been assigned to the trip. Khalid was a capable copilot and was not intimidated by Eid or any of his stories.

Khalid told me later while we were en route to the States that Eid had told the major that he *had* to be assigned to the trip because he, Eid, was the only copilot that had an Atlantic license! Khalid translated the conversation that Eid was having in Arabic with our passenger, the prince.

The prince was a brother to our primary passenger, which was his sister, a princess. There had been a natural gas explosion in their home, and the princess was badly burned. We were taking her to a hospital in Baltimore.

The prince had asked why Eid was dressed as a crew member, yet he never went near the cockpit. Eid explained that due to his holding the required Atlantic license, he was along merely to make sure the trip was operated according to international law.

I guess he figured if the story worked on a major, then it ought to work on a prince. His reasoning was based on the assumption that the higher the position, the

---

[19] TCNs: third country nationals, the working class from Third World countries. The Western world was considered First and Second World countries. Asia, Africa, and most of the rest of the world was considered as the Third World. It was not really a geographical thing. It was, instead, a reference to the type of worker that a country produced. In the Western world, workers were considered professionals. A country that provided Saudi Arabia with their peasants or working class was considered a Third World country. I don't know who started the description, but it wasn't me.

less the knowledge of everyday things. Come to think of it, that reasoning would make a lot of sense in some places I know.

The major had accepted the story because he didn't know airplanes from sailboats. I learned later that immediately after our departure, the major called all the copilots into his office and demanded to know which ones, if any, had an Atlantic license. My friend, Hakim, told me that the copilots just looked at each other because they didn't know what the major was talking about. Of course, there is no such license.

The copilots knew that, but their reaction to the question only convinced the major that he had caught them all off base. He told the group that they would not be able to go on any more international trips until all had attended the proper school and had the proper licenses in their hand. He told Bruce, the dispatcher, to call FlightSafety International in Savannah, Georgia, and to get the copilots on a schedule for training.

Bruce was confused because he had never heard of such a license. When he called the States, he was embarrassed.

"You want to send seven copilots to what kind of school?"

"Well, whatever it takes for them to get an Atlantic license."

"Sir, I'm sorry, but the FAA doesn't issue any such license, and I don't know anyone that does. Are you sure about this?"

Bruce knew then that he and the major had been had, Bruce had been embarrassed, and Eid was on his way to the USA. He had done it again!

FlightSafety International, a training facility for pilots from all over the world, offered a three-day course on international flying with a two-day course on survival appended to the end. Most everyone had attended this course. It was a nice-to-know kind of school, but not a requirement by any government regulation.

Eid knew this, and he also knew that I had been flying "certification" flights for the inertial navigation equipment installed on our aircraft. The equipment had to be certified as accurate enough to fly the NAT (North Atlantic Tracks). Eid knew the major knew of the certification flights that had been made, so he just added everything up and gave the major a new term, which sounded plausible to the major. The devious copilot had added two and two to get twenty-two, and the major bought the package.

By the time that I returned from the trip, even the TCNs were laughing about the Atlantic license. So now you know enough to appreciate what happened next.

I was called out for a patient pickup in Ta'if. Hatim Bashir was assigned as my copilot. The trip was about an hour each way, and as customary, I let the copilot fly the empty legs from the right seat. Somewhere in these stories, I have confessed to becoming less than diligent in checking the weather before a flight inside the Kingdom. I know it's a bad thing for a captain to confess too, but the weather is never (almost never) a factor, and therefore it is very easy to slip into such a bad habit.

Hatim was one of my favorites. He was a lot of fun to be with, and he was a much better pilot than he thought he was. The young man was a product of several years of being mishandled by the captains that he flew with. I had tried to let Hatim fly all the approaches when we were on international trips together because he lacked confidence in himself. He would fly a good approach but would have sweat dripping from both hands and his chin by the time he got us on the ground.

A captain must first gain the trust and respect of his copilot before he can be effective in his teaching. I had gained Hatim's respect, but his progress in gaining respect for himself had been slow. I knew it was just a matter of time and experience before Hatim became a good captain. Of the original seven copilots that I flew with in Saudi Arabia, later two quit or were allowed to resign, and four were pinned as a captain.

Halfway to Ta'if, the center called and told us that the weather was very bad at our destination. That was something that just never happened. Air traffic control *never* warns about the weather at your destination. A pilot is expected to know what the weather is at his destination before he takes off.

Hatim took the call from the right side, out of habit, and said, "Captain, we must turn back. The weather is very bad in Ta'if!"

"Well, wait a minute, what kind of bad weather? He didn't say what kind. Call him back and ask what kind of bad weather is he talking about."

The center came back in Arabic and told Hatim that it was sandstorm.

"Captain, we must turn back at once! It's a *sandstorm*."

"Wait a minute, did he say anything about the sandstorm besides that it was bad?"

"No, Captain, he just said it was very bad."

"Well, call him back and get a complete briefing and tell him to speak English like he's supposed to."

The man on the other end was getting a little hostile with all these questions, but he told us the sky was obscured, visibility was a quarter mile in blowing sand, and the wind was out of the east at forty knots!

I had Hatim to make one more call and try to find out the date and time of the observation just reported. My experience told me that we might be hearing about weather that had happened yesterday! It turned out to be current.

The weather reported was bad, but it was local. It was something that we could test and still have no trouble in returning to home base. Our problem for landing at Ta'if was double bad because the weather condition required a precision approach. The only precision approach to the airport was for runway 35 (north), and the wind was out of the east so strong that we couldn't land to the north. They had a non-precession approach for runway 7 (east), but it required a ceiling of four hundred feet and visibility of one mile for landing. We didn't have enough visibility or ceiling to land to the east.

Hatim wanted to return to base and just forget the whole thing. I told him that you could never know what the weather is for sure unless you take a look, and that meant to make an approach just as if you meant to land. I had a hunch that it could improve before we got there. Nothing stays the same forever. Besides, I knew a trick that might work.

"No, Hatim, we're not going to turn back. This will be good experience for you. You can make an instrument[20] approach at Ta'if just like it was snow or fog in the States. See, it'll be a good experience for you, and besides, if we go back without trying, then it will make the captain look bad for not checking the weather. Just keep flying the airplane, Hatim, *mafi mesculah* [no problem]."

It was nervous time for Hatim, and he started to sweat. I wasn't nervous because I knew we were in no danger. Hatim had heard stories of airplanes falling out of the sky in sandstorms because of the air intakes for the engine stopping up, which caused the engine to quit. This is true for reciprocal engines, but not necessarily true for jets. The sand in a sandstorm would only polish the turbine blades of our jet engines, so there wasn't much to worry about. Well, maybe a little sandblast effect if we stayed in it too long, but it didn't seem like a great concern to me.

I saw this as an opportunity for Hatim to build his confidence, and besides, I had never seen a real Arab sandstorm before. I've seen some bad ones in West Texas and New Mexico. It would be interesting to see what they were like in Saudi Arabia.

"You're doing fine, Hatim, just keep on flying the airplane."

We started our descent from flight level 390 (thirty-nine thousand feet) about hundred miles from destination.

"Hotel Zulu Mike Sierra Four, this is Ta'if approach, you are cleared for the approach to runway 35, descend and maintain 8,000 until crossing the VOR, over."

I returned the call from the left seat because Hatim was deep in his concentration for the approach.

"Roger, Ta'if approach control, Mike Sierra Four."

Then the rest was up to us. We were cleared for the approach, we had been given our limits, and the people on the ground were through with us. At least that's what they thought.

At ten thousand feet, we entered the sandstorm, and the visibility was almost nil. The visibility was so bad, I could hardly see the wing tips of the GII. The approach at Ta'if for runway 35 was a fifteen-mile teardrop beginning over the VOR at 8,000

---

[20]   Instrument approach. An aviation term for utilizing onboard aircraft instruments that can utilize ground-based signals to fly down a localizer beam that provides guidance along the horizontal and a glide slope beam that provides vertical guidance to the runway. The Saudi copilots had a minimum of real experience in flying approaches due to the lack of limiting weather in their home country.

feet and extending out to fifteen miles south of the airport. The elevation at Ta'if is 4,848 feet above sea level, so at 8,000 feet, we were just over 3,000 feet above the ground. As we crossed the four-mile mark leaving from the VOR on the field, we suddenly passed out of the storm and into the bright sunshine!

The sandstorm had a vertical wall from the surface of the desert to ten thousand feet, almost two miles straight up! It could have been mistaken for a cliff.

As we left the sandstorm, Hatim wanted to shorten the approach and turn back to the airport on the localizer just off to our right. He was in the clear sky and felt he could do anything with the sun shining.

"No, Hatim, just hold what ya' got. Just keep on keeping on. Don't fall into a trap and make things harder for yourself. Keep flying the approach just like you were still in the dirt."

"But, Captain, we're in the clear! We can just turn back now; there is no need to fly all the way out to the fifteen-mile mark!"

"Oh yes, there is, you just don't know it yet. Just play like you're in a simulator back at FlightSafety in Savannah. When you know it's just a simulator and not real, you have to fly the whole approach, right? Well, do the same thing here. Besides, if you turn now, you're real close to the localizer (inbound approach path), and you'll have to make a real steep angle of bank to keep from overshooting the course. That means that you'll probably still be crisscrossing and trying to get stabilized on the localizer about the time you go back into the dirt. Why give yourself all that grief? Just keep on keeping on, Hatim *mafi mesculah* [no problem], *Inshallah* [if it is God's will]."

It was good advice for anyone at anytime, but I wanted a little extra time for my trick to work. Several years before, I had flown a holding pattern[21] for two hours at an altitude of ten thousand feet above Abilene, Texas, waiting for a change in the sandstorm below. It was almost the exact same situation. Visibility was so poor that you had to use the precision approach, and the crosswind was so strong that we couldn't land. After two hours and no change, I had to make a decision. There were two choices. One was to land at San Angelo to the south, and my passengers would still have time to drive back to Abilene to their meeting. My second choice was to continue to hold for another hour to see if the weather would improve. If I could get

---

[21]   Holding pattern: The flight path of a holding pattern is in the shape of a horse racetrack. The straight legs are of a designated length with the ends a half circle to be flown at a standard rate. The purpose is to give the pilot a course to fly that he can hold with precision while he waits for his time to make the final approach to land. Sometimes he is holding for weather to improve, and sometimes he is holding while other aircraft make their approaches. Holding patterns have, in many places, been replaced with the controller's use of radar. With radar, the aircraft is just vectored around until the controller is ready to let the pilot land. In my opinion, it is not good to rely so heavily on the radar.

into Abilene at the end of the next hour, then my passenger would be able to make their meeting. My first priority was to get my passengers safely on the ground; my second priority was to get them to their destination on time.

OFFICIAL DUST LICENSE

HATIM BASHIR

IS ISSUED THIS LICENSE & WHEREAS IT BE RECOGNIZED BY THE ENTIRE ILLITERATE WORLD AND ALL CONTIGUAS PARTS THEREOF FOR EVER AND EVER. SO THERE!

James D Fox, CFII/D (DUST)

1 APRIL 1988

"Dust License"

I decided on a third choice that had just formed in my mind. I had detected a cycle to the wind velocity. It was reported as out of the east at forty knots (forty-six miles per hour), but sometimes it would drop to about twenty knots. The cycle was such that I thought that I might be able to get on a long final where I would have time to adjust my speed to be able to land at the lower cycle! It worked like a charm. I was the only aircraft that had been able to land or take off in a six-hour period! Well, maybe it would work again, twenty-five years later and on the other side of the world.

I called the tower controller and told him I wanted him to give me constant readings of the wind by direction and velocity until I reported that we were on the ground or that we had missed the approach and were leaving the area. The Saudi controller thought I was not only a Kawajee, but a crazy one as well. It took a couple of efforts on my part to convince him that I was serious, but he finally agreed to this strange request.

Hatim knew that I had just requested something from the tower that he had never even heard of before, and maybe, just maybe, it was a Westerner's trick that no one had ever told him about. It captured his imagination, and gradually he quit sweating. I could almost see his confidence grow. If he had a secret, then perhaps he could do this thing. It was like magic, a talisman, and it was working!

Hatim flew the best approach that I had ever seen him do, and I only helped by suggesting speed changes. He stayed on the gages (instruments) like a good boy until I called out the runway in sight. He looked up and made the landing. We had caught the wind at its lowest velocity, and Hatim couldn't believe what he had just done! He was so tickled with himself that he released the yoke before he had set the nose on the ground and literally began clapping his hands. He was laughing and giggling, absolutely proud of himself.

He had done what he didn't think anyone could do, and he would never ever be the same pilot that he thought he was before that approach and landing!

That evening, back in my villa, I got on the computer and made Hatim a dust license. I wrote the text to be awkward and silly on purpose and signed it with my correct CFII (certified flight instructor, instruments) endorsement, but added a *D* for *dust* at the end.

The next day, I made the award at the dispatchers' counter in operation with all the other copilots in attendance. We all had a great laugh, and Hatim got the bragging rights for some time to come.

Hatim became a captain later, and he still calls me from time to time. The last time I saw him, he showed me a billfold-size reproduction of his dust license that was sealed in plastic.

JDF Letter:
Riyadh, Saudi Arabia
April 8, 1988

Salute!

Well, Riley boy, how's it going? We received your letter containing the tax information for Charlotte. Thank you very much; it's always good to get news from home, even if it's a tax bill. You know, it's definitely United States. I was able to read between the lines when there was no note from you and was reminded that I hadn't answered your last letter. Let this be considered an answer.

Charlotte's mailing list has grown until it is completely out of hand. Her self-imposed register whereby she logs each correspondent in and then logs out her answer is kaput. She has tried to answer individual letters with individual answers. That can't be done. I told her, "Honey, they are writing one letter each, and that means you must write thirty in reply. Why don't you write just one big newsletter for them all? Well, she tried that, but it didn't seem personal enough. Ah well, the world has other problems that we must solve, so on with it.

The last few days have been hectic what with the Israelis threatening to blow up the Saudi missile bases, the Iranians hijacking the Kuwait airliner, and the regular run of international trips that seem to be on us without let up. Yesterday, they were getting crews ready to man a couple of C-130s in case there were casualties on the Kuwait airliner. That mission didn't happen, but if it had, it would have wiped out our compliment of nurses and biomeds.

I was called out last night for a trip to Paris. When I checked on the details, I found they wanted me to leave at midnight and return the next evening. At first blush, it sounds okay, but the radio room had already given me phone numbers to call the hospital, the prince, and the prince's son. I knew the trip would get me into Paris at Le Bourget around 0700, and before I could get away from the airport, it would be 0900 or 1000. It would be 1100 before I could get into my room, and with a lot of luck, I might get the phone calls made by noon. By that time, I would have been up for thirty hours. I would have to get up by 1800 to shower, dress, and get to the airport by 2000 for a 2200 takeoff. Then I would be up the rest of the night flying back to Riyadh. I might get six hours sleep in forty-eight hours if no one called in Paris, and they often do.

So I told the operation manager to get someone else for the mission. That's the first time I've turned a trip down, and it was overdue. I'm getting too old for that foolishness. Besides, I have had dealings with these princes before, and they are mostly rude and overbearing, especially when they are out of town. I have had them to insist that I make a quick turnaround and take them back to Riyadh. That's after flying all night to get there. I had one that insisted that I pay for his hotel bill because we had a mechanical delay, and he had to spend a night in London. I didn't pay his bill, and I didn't make the quick turnaround either, but I hate the hassle. Last night, I decided to settle the hassle before I left. I told the operations manager that I would take the trip if I could come back the following morning, or in other words, I wanted twenty-four hours' rest before returning. He couldn't accept that because of the pressure from Paris that had already been applied for an ASAP mission. Returning a patient from Paris to Riyadh is not an ASAP mission. If it were from Riyadh to Paris, maybe, but Paris to Riyadh, no way.

They found another captain to take the mission, but at 2200 when the copilot, a Saudi, arrived at the hangar and found that he was not going to spend the night in Paris, he turned the trip down. There was some fast juggling to find another victim at the last minute. I went to bed at 0130, and the mission still had not launched. Just like I thought, they were already eating into the crew rest at the other end. The prince in Paris was still going to expect the crew to leave the following night, regardless of the time they arrived.

Charlotte and I just returned from the Desert Inn for Friday brunch. It is a US Corps of Engineers' dining facility, and we like to go there for some US food. While we were having lunch, Romeo base was calling the dispatcher for the phone number for the crew in Paris. I knew it, I knew it, they were going to call the crew and wake them up from their short rest with some sort of urgent message. Good luck, boys. It's a mess, and this old man is getting difficult to deal with.

All of this is close on the heels of my letter of resignation last week. Yes, I resigned. The following day, I was called into Major Shablan's office for a chat. During the hour that I was in his office, I heard myself described in glowing terms. I should be getting my hero medals any day now. I found that I was the finest pilot and all-round best guy that had been on the scene so far. My letter stated that I wanted to leave for personal reasons. The major wanted to know more of my real reasons after the initial period of his adulation and praises. Reluctantly, I described several thorns that were in place and festering. He skipped the ones that he could not or would not address and made a great pretense of solving the one or two easy ones. When I reminded him that they had owed me for an airline ticket for FlightSafety training since last October, he called in the Sri Lankan clerk and demanded that Captain Fox should be paid and wanted an answer within twenty-four hours. That was over a week ago, and nothing has happened yet. You see, I work for Medevac, the Medical Evacuation Program that is sponsored by the Ministry of Defense and Aviation, or MODA. MODA is headed by His Royal Highness Abdul Aziz Abin Sultan, who is the number-three man in the Kingdom. His brother is head of SANG, or the Saudi Arabian National Guard, and is the number-two man in power. All of the military medical service is under the national guard, or army. They provide the medical service and facilities for the national guard, air force, navy, and the royal family. So Medevac is under the direct control of an army major, operating from an air force base with civilian employees. All of this is complicated by the fact that as foreigners, we cannot work directly for the government. We are therefore paid and administered by an agent, General Arab Medical and Allied Services, or GAMA. If you don't get GAMA out of that, then don't worry about it. Nobody said it had to make sense.

The trick over here is to have so many levels of responsibility that you can never track down who is screwing up, lying, or ignoring the problem. It works well. Sheikh Hussein Al-Athel who is the CEO of GAMA called for me to come to his office for a visit. He wanted to chat about my letter of resignation. I didn't get his message until over twenty-four hours after he sent it. When I called him back, he said he wanted to chat with me. I told him that I would be glad for the chat, but I didn't think it would do any good because it was apparent that no one in Medevac or GAMA wanted to pay me the SR3,092 ($800) that they owed me. He assured me that he wanted to pay me and that if I would come to see him, he would write me a check for the disputed amount. That was Tuesday, and this is Friday. I'll try to get in to see him tomorrow. It will be fun to watch the tap dance.

These people are champs when it comes to negotiations, haggling, and delaying. It is their natural way of life. The one thing that throws them is the fact that they can't intimidate me. I've already resigned, and they have nothing to threaten me with. They need me, I don't need them, and I remind them of this fact often. It is in an enviable position that I find myself. Besides, I spent fifteen years with the old Humble Company's Federation and have had more than just a little experience haggling with some pretty tough old birds.

It is common practice here to hold a man to his contract end, especially if he wants to leave, if for nothing else, just to give him a hard time. In some periods of grace, they will allow him to leave after sixty days or a reasonable period to find his replacement. In addition to that, they can cancel his end of contract bonus.

The last one is the real kicker; it amounts to almost $5,000, so far, in my case. So when Major Shablan told me that he would release me without a holding period if I was determined to go but that I should please "think about it for a while." I agreed to think about it. He started to tear up my letter, and I said, "Oh no, I said that I would think about it. I didn't say I would forget about it." He made a show of placing it in a conspicuous letter file on top of his desk and said with a large smile that we would discuss it again next year. I said, "Major, I'll be sixty years old next year, I can't stay here forever." "Ah yes, Captain Fox, but it is your mature wisdom and experience that we need for our young copilots," he stated with outstretched arms and a straight face.

So I'm thinking about it. Turning down the trip to Paris last night may take some of the glisten from my halo. We'll just have to wait and see. You know, it's not much different working here than for other places in the world. Considering my experiences with Humble, Exxon, the army, and now the Saudis, it is not difficult to see similarities. You may remember my old friend Sherfesee, the old artilleryman. It was he that taught me as a young man that there is some confusion in the minds of many regarding the definition of opinions and convictions. His teaching to me was that opinions are what men argue about, and convictions are what men are willing to die for. A man of wisdom should know the difference and plan his life accordingly.

Jim Keegan will remember from many of our late-night "high-level" meetings that the above sage sayings were repeated. My father added his wisdom with the instruction: "James, *there ain't nothin' free* in this world. Everything you want costs something, so be sure you count the costs before you make a decision, and you won't go through life crying about your bad luck."

Laying your job on the line is never easy, even for your so-called principles, but I'll have to confess. It's getting easier all the time.

Enough, enough, let's get back to what's happening to you and yours. Now that Jan is not answering the phone as Global Industries, what is she up to? How is college treating the offspring? What is the new Exxon Company like? It is not easy keeping up with the real stories by browsing though the Annuitant News.

I have tried my hand at some stories about aviation. Charlotte says they are each an improvement on the other. I am beginning to believe there is no truth in this woman, but she is by the far the best that I have ever met. I wrote one called the "Mystery Flight." It had to do with a flight I made in 1968 with Beck and Robicheaux. I tried to write it as fiction, you know, using fictitious names to protect the guilty. The innocent don't need protecting, but I found that I was unable to do a decent job without using real names. The story just wouldn't come out. It's a problem I haven't quite licked yet.

I'll send you a copy, but be careful who you show it to. I wouldn't want to hurt anyone's feelings. It's one thing to speak of someone's idiosyncrasies in a small group where all can laugh together, but I have come to find it is quite a different situation to write it down in hard copy where the affected parties don't have the ability to answer back and defend themselves. I would appreciate hearing your thoughts on this, and any suggestions would help.

One of my considerations is to write the story with real names so the story will come out, and then with the word processor make a global replacement of the names after the story is finished. Tell me what you think. I have sufficient material for a book now but have not decided what material should be included; therefore, the name has not developed in my mind. Charlotte has suggested that I use a name with the word *adventures* in it. How about *The Adventures of the Famous Flying Fox*? Not good, eh? Well, she has some definite ideas about its contents, and her comments are very important to me. Yours, Brent's, and Keegan's comments will be welcome. A few selected others like Jan would certainly be welcome as well.

I think you may realize that I am very serious in my endeavor, and even though all that is done is done in good humor, it is still easy to hurt someone's feelings. I would not like to hurt anyone's feelings, but I do want to write the stories. When I write about the antics that Brent and I have pulled on each other in the air, I am quite sure that he would not be offended. However, there are other stories that can't be told unless someone looks a little foolish. What do you think?

God is in his heaven, and all is good with us here. Hope that you and yours are enjoying the life that the Father has given us. Give my regards to all, and you have my permission to share this letter with those of your choice.

> Best Regards,
> James D. Fox,
> Captain, Fixed Wing,
> Saudi Armed Forces,
> Medical Evacuation Services
> Riyadh, Saudi Arabia

PS I sent in my request for retirement from the USAR a couple of weeks ago. If all goes well, we will be able to return to the States in January on a MATS flight out of Dhahran. If I last that long.

PPS Riley, I'm going to try and send in some change of address forms from here to have the mail there forwarded to the APO number. Surely, the PO will have them. If not, then I may ask you to send me a few. I hope you know that Charlotte and I certainly appreciate your efforts in this regard. Thanks again.

Dispatch:
Riyadh, Saudi Arabia
April 17, 1988

A JOB OFFER IN JEDDAH

Today is the big day. We are going to Jeddah for a four-day holiday. It is the first time that Charlotte and I will have visited a part of Saudi Arabia other than Riyadh, the city of our residence. Doesn't sound like much, but there is more to it than meets the eye.

There were several days spent in preparations for the trip. The first consideration is to receive a travel letter from Major Shablan, the operations director. As non-Saudis, we must have a letter from our employer in order to travel outside the limits of our place of employment. The actual distance has never been specified. The letter must be requested through the operations officer. The request for the request must be submitted to the Sri Lankan clerk, Jeffery. Once the operations manager has the request, then he has the letter composed in Arabic by Kabakibi (Cah-bah-key-bee), the translator that also does the requests for all our permits, visas, and other requests from the government.

Kabakibi is the bottleneck in the process. He always demands a black-and-white passport photo and a form that must be filled out. Later, he can never find his copy of anything. A request to trace the location of applications that have gone astray must be accompanied by, you guessed it, a black-and-white passport photo and a form to be filled out. When I first came here, I thought that he was just a little slow or dumb. Now that I've been here for almost two years, it is clear to me. He may or may not be dumb, but his big problem is being lazy. He is almost as lazy as a fellow I used to work for.

Therefore, you must work the chain of command from the bottom to the top, just to take your wife to Jeddah. I made several trips to the airport to pick up the letter before I finally received it the day before departure. I had also requested discount tickets through Medevac because I have learned that they have a discount agreement with British Caledonian that can be as much as 75 percent. This request must start with Philip, the switchboard operator. It's another form to fill out that must be typed and be signed by Major Shablan. The day before my departure, I finally received both forms. By this time, I was a little out of patience, so I just grabbed the forms and left to go to the BCal ticket office and get my tickets.

Arriving at the BCal office, I was more than just a little perturbed. They told me that the request for discounts was no good. "What's the matter with it?" I asked. "Well, it hasn't been signed, but that doesn't make any difference because the contract with Medevac ran out on the first of the month and has not been renewed. And besides that, BCal doesn't fly between Riyadh and Jeddah." Well, dad-gum.

445

The facts start to settle in place. All ticket prices within the Kingdom are absolutely controlled by the government-sponsored airline, Saudi, and they don't give any discounts to anyone inside the Kingdom. Neither do they allow foreign airlines to fly any of their domestic routes inside the Kingdom. Competition forces them to get with the program outside the Kingdom, but they don't allow competition within the Kingdom.

I moved down the line of travel agents to my favorite travel agent, Mr. Yoyoung. Mr. Yoyoung is from the Philippines and speaks excellent English. He represents American Airlines, but we like to use him because of his English. It is surprising what a difference that makes. Mr. Yoyoung was delayed by a phone call. The travel agents here are busier than a one-legged man at a soccer meet. By the time I got my request in for tickets on Saudi, it was prayer time, and we had to leave. We'll have to pick up the tickets on the morning of our departure. The frustration of trying to get something done here is absolutely devastating.

We returned to the villa just in time to receive a phone call from Hakim Al-Alaway (Haa-keem A-lah-wee) in Jeddah. He told us he was going to pick us up tomorrow in one of AMC's (Aviation Management Company, I think) corporate jets. AMC is a consortium of several Saudi businessmen. They are considered the richest men in the Arab world. One of them, Salem Bin Ladin[22], owns the National Commercial Bank, which keeps the Kingdom's money. He is the only stockholder. He is also the owner of several other businesses in the USA including Jim Bath and Associates. The same man (Salem Bin Ladin) treats Hakim as an adopted son. Now that's a real bonus. (See epilogue.)

I wasn't absolutely surprised to be picked up because Hakim has been trying to get me to bring Charlotte over to Jeddah for a visit for a couple of months. Hakim was a Saudi pilot here in Medevac that in 1987 was hired with a Lear type rating, but he was not allowed to fly as captain in the Lear until after ninety days' probation. Within his first nine months, he was released as captain on the Lear and went back to the States for initial training on the Gulfstream. While there, he got his type rating on the Gulfstream. That's not bad for this part of the world. When I started letting him fly the left seat of the Gulfstream, the political tap dancing started and didn't stop until the "insiders" moved through Major Shablan to require a minimum of seven hundred hours in the right seat before *anyone* would be allowed to fly from the left seat. All the other copilots had over two thousand hours in the right seat of the Gulfstream, even though they were nowhere near ready to get a type rating. Hakim had some good experience flying single-pilot IFR in Europe before he came to Medevac, but that was not counted. The effect was to force Hakim to move on to another job. His potential with AMC in Jeddah will be more fully realized anyway.

---

22   Salem Bin Ladin, the older brother of the infamous Osama Bin Ladin. There were approximately fifty siblings in that family.

We drove to the private terminal at King Khalid International Airport and parked the Jaguar in the covered parking. We parked next to another Jaguar that we recognized. It belongs to the executive secretary to the Minister of Oil, whom we met a few weeks ago, but that's another story. Once inside the terminal, our bags were X-rayed, and we were treated like important people. I'm talking VIP. We were escorted to a private lounge, but we preferred the more public lounge that was located adjacent to the ramp behind full glass walls. A TCN (third country national) appeared from behind a curtain to ask of our desires for food, drink, or newspapers. We took coffee, but I forgot to warn Charlotte that it would be strong. She had to order a cup of hot water to thin her coffee. They make it so strong that reflected sunlight could show particles and a green caste on the surface of your coffee. It makes Cajun chicory seem weak in comparison.

We were under constant supervision as long as we waited there. The handler, Arabasco (one of the companies owned by AMC), kept us informed on fifteen-minute intervals, the location and time of arrival of HZ-AM2, which was on the way to pick us up. Hakim had told me he was going to Dhahran first; he would pick us up on the return to Jeddah. Since Riyadh is between Dhahran and Jeddah, I assumed that we would be his only passengers. We were soon to find that was not the case.

The AMC agent told us when HZ-AM2 was on the ground. He added that it would take about five minutes to taxi in, and then they would take on fuel so we should expect to depart in about fifteen minutes. They were quite professional in their handling of us. Hakim came in during the refueling and greeted us. At that time, he said that we would be sharing the cabin with some cargo, so be prepared. I think Charlotte was a little apprehensive at this point. Things had been going too smooth.

We were escorted to the ramp after the AMC agent had me to sign our names on the manifest. A manifest is required of all passengers at any airport by any operator in the Kingdom for security reasons, you know. The aircraft was a Lear 55, which is one of latest models of Lear. It had seating for seven, but it would be best if they were very close friends. Charlotte and I took the two main seats—they are easy to locate—and settled in for the ride. Then the cargo arrived.

We saw a TCN pushing a shopping cart across the ramp with what looked like an old Bedouin by his side. There were five small boxes about the size of cigar boxes, and each was about all one man could carry. *It was gold bullion*! They sat the boxes down in the aisle between Charlotte and me. The old Saudi, got onboard and sat up front opposite the air stair door. My guess, he was to accompany the gold. The gold was in small boxes about the size of a small cigar box—that is, a cigar box for twenty-five cigars, not fifty. The box tops were marked with the contents and weight. Each of the small boxes was marked twenty-five kilos of 999.9 gold. That meant each weighed a little over fifty-five pounds. A quick calculation revealed that we had roughly $2,000,000 (1988 price) in gold setting on the floor between us.

Charlotte was convinced that we were going to be hijacked or something. Before long, it made her so nervous she had to go to the ladies' room, which was also the men's room and the toilet. The door to the toilet was jammed with the boxes of gold. It was necessary for me to move a couple of them forward about a foot to get the door open. I reached over the arm of my seat to move the boxes one at a time. It looked simple. Just pick up the back couple of boxes and leapfrog them to the front, easy. I swear they felt more like hundred pounds than they did fifty-five. The old Saudi didn't even appear to notice.

We were served breakfast by the copilot, Mohammed, and crossed over some thunderstorms, but otherwise, an uneventful one hour and twenty minutes was consumed by the trip to Jeddah. Hakim made a smooth landing on runway 16 center, and there were two vehicles waiting on the ramp when we taxied up. One was a long black Cadillac limousine, and the other was an old beat-up Datsun pickup with the tailgate down. My first thought was that the gold was going in the limo and that we were going to ride in the Datsun. We soon found that the limo was for us, and the Datsun was for the gold. They unloaded the gold first. It was placed, a box at a time, on the very back end of the Datsun truck bed, and then they threw what looked like an old saddle blanket over it (would you believe a camel blanket?). The tailgate wouldn't close, so they just drove off with the gate hanging down! I wanted to follow just on the possibility that a box might fall out. Each box was worth about $400,000. I have never cared about gold jewelry for myself, but that kind of jewelry I wouldn't mind too much.

Hakim drove us home after we left the limo at the Arabasco General Aviation Terminal. Hakim and Lilly were our next-door neighbors in the GAMA compound back in Riyadh, and we had become very close. Lilly is from Honduras and is a very sweet young lady. They have two daughters, Lena and Linda. They have one son, Sultan. Lena is six, Linda is four, and Sultan is a little over two. You must understand that it is very important for a Saudi to have a son. Young Sultan is just a little mess. His father is proud as proud can be. The little girls are cute, but Sultan is his father's son, and all others must take a backseat to him.

Lilly and the children were excited to see us, and there was much hugging and kissing going on—very unusual for *Kawagees* (cah-waa-gees) to be greeted in such a fashion. Charlotte had been thoughtful enough to buy gifts for all, including the host and hostess. We had to wait a few moments to clear the house of other guests. Other children of the compound used the Al-Alaway house for their afternoon meeting place.

The children were absolutely overcome with the gifts. They were totally unexpected. Charlotte always makes up for my inattention to such details. We had tried to insist that we stay in a hotel but were told if we did, they would be insulted. Well, the house was large enough for us to be out of the way, but I just didn't want to be a bother. I can see now that we would have made a mistake to stay in a hotel. They were very gracious hosts, and the children were delighted.

Lilly expected to cook us dinner the first evening, but I explained my rules. We were going to eat out each evening at a place of their choice, and it was to be my treat. I was not going to let our hostess stay in the kitchen all the time, and I was not going to let Hakim pay for anything. Those were my rules, or we would just go to the hotel straightaway. Okay, we had a deal.

The Al-Alawyas live in a two-story house, which is located inside a compound, of course. The compound is one that you can drive your car into. Haven't seen one like that in Riyadh. Maybe it sounds like a small thing, but it means a great convenience to be able to park the car next to the back door. A garage you say? Forget it, I have not seen one in this entire country.

The first night, Charlotte and I decided to order a different dish and share. We were in a restaurant on the Red Sea, situated in the middle of an amusement park. There were several such places along the coastal drive. I ordered a grilled whole Nijel fish for myself and a large order of grilled prawns for Charlotte. The service was terrible, but the food was worth writing about. No one in the place spoke English, so Hakim was constantly getting up and chastising everyone in the place. We were the only guests. We had arrived a little before sunset, and that is too early for Saudis. The Saudis like to eat around nine on ten o'clock or later during the month of Ramadan. Well, it was a big fight for service, but the food was great. The price was right as well. For four adults and three children with drinks and gratuity, the total was only SR300 or $80 US. The fish and shrimp were as good as I have ever eaten.

Jeddah is located on the west coast of Saudi Arabia. It is almost halfway between the Gulf of Aqaba on the north and South Yemen on the south. It is one of the three major cities. The other two are Dhahran and the capital, Riyadh. Jeddah is to the west coast what Dhahran is to the east coast, or as you know, the Persian Gulf. Jeddah is the only major port on the west coast and is very near Mecca, the Moslem holy city.

The city is modern by the standards of this part of the world.

It is a little more relaxed in the Moslem tradition than in Riyadh. The meaning of the last statement is simply in the manner of how the local people and their religious police, the Mataween, interpret and enforce the religious rules. It can make quite a difference in the day-to-day family activities. The Westerner gets the impression after residing here for a while that the enforcement of Moslem laws is mostly for show. Riyadh, the capital, has many foreign visitors, so the show is more necessary. This may not be the case, but it is the consensus of the Westerners that live here.

After telling all that, now I have to say that on our last night in Jeddah, we were dining with the Al-Alaways and the Ponds in an outdoor restaurant that was raided by the Mataween. We never saw it happen before, but they came into the dining area, herded out all the Arab types, and made them go pray. The Al-Alaways were not bothered because they were with Westerners, but all the rest were taken from their food. It was prayer time. Restaurants usually have a curtain to pull across the front when it is prayer time. This one was so large and most of the dining was outside near the water that it was impossible to conceal the fact that there were Moslems inside that were not praying, and that's a no-no. I presume they can return in forty-five minutes to finish if they desire. We didn't stay long enough to find out. Think about that sometime when you are trying to decide if you want to get up on Sunday morning and go to church—voluntarily.

There is a beautiful drive along the beach, which is covered with all sorts of interesting and unusual pieces of sculpture. One in particular that Charlotte and I noticed was a huge block of concrete that had half an automobile sticking out each of several sides. The autos weren't old wrecks but were late models and gave the appearance that they had hit the object at great speed and pierced it to half their depths. We noticed that there were autos on some sides that appeared to be departing the block rather than arriving. They were at different angles, so that the autos coming out didn't appear to be the other half of those going in. When we drove by at night, we noted that the protruding autos had headlights and taillights that were on and working.

The Red Sea is very blue in color except in a few spots near shoreline, where the water becomes a beautiful turquoise shade. They say there are rocks under the water that give it the turquoise hue. The waves are similar to what you might see along the Texas Gulf Coast. They are not very large, which would be no good for surfing. The fishing is great they tell me, but I doubt that I will have a chance to try that for myself. Some scuba diving might be fun because of the beautiful seafloor. The pictures I've seen are incredible. The locals say the Red Sea is well populated with sharks, so that lets me out.

I remember swimming in the Bahamas with my son Greg a few years back. We were only a couple of hundred yards off the beach snorkeling underwater with a camera when we saw a shark that was under the water with us. As a kid, I was impressed with Johnny Weissmuller's swimming as he played the part of Tarzan in the movies. He looked like he was doing sixty miles per hour when he was going after an alligator that was about to get Jane or boy, some good-looking guest star. If Johnny had been between us and the beach that day, he would have been run over and finished a poor third. I beat Greg to the beach by just a little, but it was because I was going for help. I'm quite a bit more cautious now. So those of you out there that remember how we did it forty years ago, well, it just doesn't happen that way anymore!

The second day of our visit, Hakim broke the news that I felt was coming, I just didn't know when. He wanted to know how I would feel if I were asked to take the job as aviation manager for AMC. I felt earlier that he might ask me to come over and fly a Gulfstream that they were thinking of buying, but I was not prepared for the manager's job.

I said, "What is the matter with the one you have now?"

"He is off sick and won't be coming back. He has cancer," Hakim said.

"Well, that's too bad Hakim," I said.

I didn't know the man, so there was not much else that could be said about that. This was a delicate situation. I have thought in my mind for years what I would say if ever approached with such an offer, so the conversation was completed in my mind many years before. I'm sure my old friend, Jim Keegan, could tell you right now without reading further what I said. I suggested to him that I would not be a good choice for the job. He assured me of his confidence that I could do the job.

"Hakim, it's not an issue in my mind whether I could do the job. The issue is if I would be allowed to do the job. I know that you have great influence with at least one of the principals of AMC, but I would have to please not one, but all the owners. I would likely have ten bosses, and there is no way that I could please them all without becoming their yes-man. If it were only one, then I might consider the position, but even then I would have to ask the one man if I were going to run the operation or if he was. The world is full of men that have been in a strain for years waiting for the chance to be boss at any price. Hakim, I've worked for that type of man, and there is no way I'll ever agree to become one of them. Sorry, but the answer will have to be no."

He was a little disappointed but not as much as I might have thought, considering that I had just turned down the offer to be his boss. I was to find out the next day that he had another card to play. The company had been trying to make a decision between a Gulfstream IIB, Falcon 900, Gulfstream III, or Gulfstream IV. The third day there, he came in from a short trip to find me deep in a paperback book on Yeager. Hakim was excited and started in with questions on the comparative merits of the Gulfstream IV and the Falcon 900. He wanted to know which I would prefer.

"The Gulfstream IV," I said without time to think.

"Yeah, but why." He wanted to know.

"Well, it's easy, I don't want anything that the Frogs make."

"Oh, be serious," he said.

"I am serious. No one can match the Gulfstream in service centers or range, and you know those bosses of yours will want to take that thing all over the world. When they decide to spend $21,000,000 for a bird, they are going to try to fly its feathers off, so you better get one with range and plenty of service centers."

My answer about the Frogs was true, but it was mostly a conversational device to give me some time to think. We old guys have to use a few tricks if we are going to keep looking sharp. Who said start looking? I added later that I didn't have any hard facts for him but suggested that he call the marketing vice president for the Gulfstream company. He jumped on that idea like a hen on a June bug. Within fifteen minutes, we had more facts than we could load into a new Gulfstream IV. Do you think that the vice president in charge of marketing for a company doesn't have all the information on his machines and that of the competition? Does a wild bear sleep in the woods? Happily, we were told that the IV was almost two million dollars cheaper than the 900, but three million dollars more than the III. The VP didn't recommend a IIB. Of course not, they had none to sell! They did have IIIs and IVs for sale. While Hakim was on the phone, I whispered "trade" to him.

The Saudis were traders a long time before Columbus discovered America. I was wasting my time, but he was way ahead of me.

"How about a trade in of a Lear 35 and 55 on a III or IV, uh-huh, well, okay, how about mailing that material to my home? I don't want the hired hands to know all my business. Okay, thank you very much, I'll be talking to you again. Good-bye."

Hakim had done very well and was winking at me all the while he was on the phone. His giant smile showed that he was very pleased. He could just as well have said, "I love it when a plan comes together." He waited for just a few seconds and then asked me if I would move to Jeddah to fly captain on a new GIV! That was his next ace. He hoped that I wouldn't want the bosses' job because he wanted me to fly with him on the new airplane while he gained the experience he wanted in the Gulfstream. He made sure that I wouldn't be disappointed by not being asked about the top job since it would soon be general knowledge. My answer also revealed that I would not be standing in his way when he was ready to take the top slot for himself. Once I had turned that slot down, then he was free to ask me about the one he really wanted me to take. Sharp young trader.

Are you surprised to find that a young man of twenty-seven years is plotting his career by planning who will be his next boss? You say only in Saudi Arabia? Well, maybe you better have a quick look around in the United States. I think they are a little more obvious here, that is all.

My young friend had just spent the morning with one of the principals of AMC and had been asked to work up some figures for buying a new airplane. They were tired of the BAC-111s that had to stop for fuel on the way to Europe. They wanted an airplane with some range! Well, I had them figured right, and when they want to buy something, they don't have to worry about what the stockholders might think for there aren't any.

I told Hakim that when he got permission to make the purchase, he should give me a call, and we would talk. We were both very pleased. He knew that I would give him a square deal in the cockpit and would be no political problem for his future. He also knew that I didn't want to work forever, and this would be a good way for me to go out in style. He was right. If the deal comes in and is anywhere close to my desires, then Riyadh and Medevac can color me gone.

The last night in Jeddah, we spent with the Al-Alaways and the Ponds a couple that left Medevac last summer. Odie Pond is flying for a one-airplane company (NATCO, I think) in Jeddah. He is the chief pilot. He is the only pilot, but it counts just the same. Odie's wife is named Geisel, a French-Canadian. They could not digest their food for trying to wrestle out of Hakim and me if I were going to come to work in Jeddah. All we would say was, "Well, we're working on it." We probably should have told them more. I would hate to think they might hurt themselves worrying about it. Oh well, it's all just a game anyway.

Charlotte got a new necklace to match her bracelet and earrings. They are made with two colors of gold rope. I told her that it was going to be difficult for me to be impressed by gold after my ride into Jeddah next to those five boxes of it.

It is the seventeenth today, and we are back in Riyadh. We had a bad trip back on Saudi Airlines. The 747 was packed like a cattle car, and the weather was bad, and I don't like anything about the way they do it over here. The terminal at Jeddah is a beautiful piece of architecture, but that is the end of it. We went to the terminal almost two hours prior to flight time, and we barely made the flight. First, you must wait in line to buy the tickets, and that is all you get at that window, just your tickets. Second, you must wait in line for seating and baggage check-in. The third phase only happens if you haven't missed the flight by this time. You go through a security check like you may have never seen, but they don't have any hijackers here, so we try to understand. Next, it is time to find the gate. It is never the one printed on your tickets. This can be the final trick that gets you. We were lucky and saw a lot of people moving through gate 4, which was only two gates away from the one marked on our ticket. That's close enough. Let's go for it.

Believe it or not, Mr. Ripley, we got on the right bus without asking anyone. That's right, I said the bus. You don't take a ramp to the plane; they use a lift bus like those at Dulles in the United States. As I said earlier, we barely made it. We had to take seats in row 63, just a few rows from the absolutely tail end of the plane. For those of you that don't consider yourself seasoned travelers, may I suggest that you not pay a lot of attention to those wags that tell you the tail is the safest place to be. It may be the safest place to be if the plane crashes, but you will have to admit that on most flights they don't crash. If I thought there was much of a chance of crashing, then I wouldn't get on the thing in the first place. No, the better advice is to take seats near the mean aerodynamic chord or somewhere near the center of the plane. That area will do the least amount of moving in turbulent weather.

The trip back to Riyadh was a rough ride. There were a lot of thunderstorms, and I am sure the captain was doing his best to miss the worst parts, but it was still a very rough ride. It was probably the roughest ride that I have ever had as a passenger. I was trying to read the copy of *Yeager* that Hakim had loaned me. The agitation around me was getting to the point I couldn't read anymore. The passengers on both sides were filling burp bags, and Charlotte and I were in the middle, passing extra bags in both directions. A young man one seat over from Charlotte was so scared he was trying to pray and so sick he couldn't. They need a little more room to pray than we do, you know, with bending over and all. He just couldn't get it going; he was rocking back and forth while chanting, and the motion only added to the sickness he was feeling. When we finally landed, let me tell you, there were some grateful people on that 747.

Our Jag was still parked next to our friend's car, so I guess his trip was longer than ours. The storm we had passed through on the way into Riyadh caught us as we left the airport. It's forty kilometers into town, and it rained on us very hard all the way. It slacked a little as we ran into the Panda store for some milk and held the slack while we unloaded at the compound. It continued to rain all night and the next day. It rained more in the next couple of days. Strange weather for this time of year here. Does that sound like we're locals? Well, all in all, we had a good trip to Jeddah, and we thought you might like to hear about it.

Epilogue: The individual referred to was Sheikh Salem Bin Ladin. He died on May 29, 1988, just north of San Antonio, Texas, in a crash of his ultralight aircraft. Salem Bin Ladin was a multibillionaire, probably the single richest Saudi. He was one of the principals of AMC and a very close friend of Hakim Al-Alaway and King Fahd. He was forty-one years of age. His ultralight hit power lines while he was attempting to take off downwind. For some reason, the Saudi newspapers said the accident happened in Houston, but Hakim told me it was San Antonio.

Salem Bin Ladin dies in air crash

By Farouk Luqman
Managing Editor

JEDDAH, May 30 —Salem Bin Ladin, chairman of the board of the Binladin Brothers for Contracting and Industry, died last night at the controls of a private aircraft he was piloting. The crash took place in Houston, Texas, in the United States. He was 41.

His father, the legendary construction pioneer of the Kingdom had also died tragically in a company plane crash in the desert near Jeddah in 1968.

A spokesman for Salem's brothers, who form the board members of the family's vast construction empire, said here yesterday that they were still awaiting details of the tragedy and would issue some information when they received it.

Salem, one of 54 brothers and sisters, was acknowledged as one of the most brilliant businessmen in the Kingdom, who, with his brothers, guided the company after the death of their father and developed it into the largest privately owned construction company in the world.

The company, according to informed sources, achieved dizzy heights of success in the 1970s and early 80s when it handled business valued at several billion riyals in any given year. In addition to construction projects in Makkah and Madinah, the company diversified into scores of other commercial pursuits from steel imports to telecommunications. Salem was said to be the single most successful company member in obtaining new businesses.

His hobbies including flying, at which he excelled, and this became his passion. In the last few years of his life he enrolled as a medical student in Egypt and commuted to classes in his plane, one of several owned by the ever-growing conglomerate that formed the Binladin group.

In an interview a few years ago, a brother revealed to me that the company owned the largest number of Caterpillar machines outside the United States. At one time the number soared to 1,000 and could be even higher today.

The late Sheikh Muhammad immigrated to Saudi Arabia from Hadramaut, now in South Yemen, as an ordinary laborer on simple con-

Salem Bin Ladin

struction sites and slept in the open air, according to my knowledge based on personal interviews.

He promptly showed a flair for building that was soon recognized by King Abdul Aziz, the founder of the Kingdom, who awarded him several contracts to herald the reconstruction of the country. He is said to have impressed the king sufficiently to ensure his continued patronage although he had no formal education of any kind. But he could read a blueprint in minutes and decide on changes on the spot which qualified architects had overlooked.

In just a few years he had become the principal contractor of the Kingdom and went on to establish the basis of the empire that was later to mushroom into one of the largest privately owned companies in the world. It was left to his sons to turn it into the world's premier family-owned construction firm.

Salem was an ebullient man, possessed incisive wit and profound business acumen. He was a great conversationalist and a delightful public speaker as I judged for myself at some of the functions he organized to launch his completed projects.

"Newspaper clipping on Salem Bin Ladin's death"

JDF Letter:
Riyadh, Saudi Arabia
May 8, 1988

Dear Robert and Marge,

I was just looking over my list of things to do immediately and saw the note that I made reminding me to write an answer to your Christmas letter. So here it comes. I bought a book a while back, titled, *Improve Your Memory and Beat Procrastination*, but I mislaid it before I got around to reading it. Perhaps, if I live long enough, the problem will cure itself.

We are wishing that we had a chance to talk with you more about your retirement. Once again, the specter of retirement is raising its ugly head, and we must once more face the dragon. You know, in my profession, when you stop for six months, then it's all over. You can't just try it out for a while for retirement is a firm commitment. Currency is lost in just ninety days, and no one wants a pilot that is not current. Even simulator time necessary for recurrency can cost ten thousand dollars, and that can make it all not worthwhile. It's all federal regulations, you understand, and has no bearing on a man's ability to fly a particular type of airplane. I haven't flown a Lockheed JetStar in nearly three years, but I could go out tomorrow morning and make a trip to London or Frankfurt with no problem. I flew one solid for sixteen years and then part time for two years more, and you're not going to forget all that in ninety days.

All this to say that we are thinking of retirement on my next birthday, January 3, 1989, but we are making no absolute commitment for the reasons just enumerated. The ability to make a little money by writing is attractive to me, but I feel that I'm a long way from being commercial in my efforts. Charlotte and my other critics tell me that the results are improving with each story, but that is not a commercial opinion, which is the only one that counts. I will enclose a couple of my latest efforts at story writing. So far, all my stories have been nonfiction, and sooner or later, I'm going to have to try some fiction. It will be necessary because no one has enough personal stories to keep an audience interested forever. Though, I'll have to admit, there are still more stories in my head than I have had time to write so far.

I have started keeping a record of who received what stories. It is necessary because I can't remember what has been sent out. For example, I can't remember if I gave you a copy of the Cedarvale Baseball Championship, so I'm going to send you a copy. If I've already given you one, then please don't be offended. Maybe you can send it on to a friend that likes baseball.

Charlotte and I have been talking lately about renting a house on the southwest coast of England for a year. It will be in the area of the county of Devon. We are not sure yet, but if we leave Saudi Arabia next January, then it would be a good time to rent the house. The Devon area is a summer resort and very popular at that time of year, but you can get an annual lease in the winter for very little. The landlords try to make a years' profit on rent in June, July, and August, so the rest of the year is practically a gift. We are going there for a twenty-one day tour of the UK, Scotland, and Wales on July 1 of this year, so we should be able to make up our mind at that time. My youngest son, Charles or Chuck, is in the UK now. He was supposed to be training for a job as a Jaguar mechanic, but it didn't work out. The owner of the business was an acquaintance of mine, but he turned out to have a drinking problem, and his business is going down the tubes. It looks like Chuck just got a nice visit to Europe out of the deal. Well, I wish the opportunity had come to me when I was his age. No telling what the difference would have made.

Considering that last thought, I could not have made a better decision when I decided to come over here to the Land of the Sand and Sun to fly the Saudi's airplanes and have some fun. Maybe I could try my hand at poetry, what do you think? The adventure has certainly been here, and I wouldn't trade the experience for two spotted dogs. On the other hand, I wouldn't give a three-legged cat for much more of it. The money is good, but we are both about ready to leave. Onward and upward. By the way, Robert, do you know what you call a one-eyed, three-legged cat with no ears and only half a tail? *Lucky*.

The flying here was very interesting in the beginning. But too soon, it becomes more of a chore than a challenge. I have flown into Abu-Dhabi and Qatar (near strait of Harmouz); Al-Ahba; Al-Baha; Al-Hasa; Al-Jouf; Amman, Jordon; Arar; Athens, Greece; Bahrain (Persian Gulf); Basel, Switzerland; Cairo, Egypt; Cambridge, UK; Dhahran, Doha (Persian Gulf); Dusseldorf, Germany; Frankfurt, Germany; Gassim, Geneva, Switzerland; Gizan, Hail, Istanbul, Turkey; Jeddah, Jubail (royal and navy), Khamis, Mushait; Khartoum, Africa; King Khalid Military City, Larnaka Cypress; London, UK; Madinah; Muenster, Germany; Munich, Germany; Najarin; Osnabruck, Germany; Quesumah; Rabat, Morocco; Sharurah; Sulayel; Tabuk; Ta'if; Turaif; Yenbo; and maybe a few that I have forgotten.

I have been into some of the most beautiful terminals in the world that are located here in Saudi Arabia, and I have been into strips in the middle of desert with nothing else there but a couple of Bedouin tents. I have flown through their thunderstorms, dust storms, and around their hailstorms. I have flown patterns around the rocket firing. I have flown through Iraq's airspace several times without ever being able to establish radio contact (I'll fly the airplane, and you watch for the fighters). I have been into Jordan at night when the direction of takeoff is always to the west, regardless of wind, so that we wouldn't violate Israeli airspace. I have flown across the Atlantic Ocean eight times, the Persian Gulf several times, the Red Sea and the Mediterranean umpteen times, and I haven't been here two years yet.

The problem becomes one of boredom and frustration. Frustration is accelerated by the boredom and vice versa. The two feed on each other, and soon they are no longer little parasites that gnaw at your insides but become monsters that can devour you completely. So when they talk to me of staying longer, I don't have to go back to the villa and check with Charlotte. She says that she has enjoyed it here, but she is ready to leave as well.

I will have to say that the desires that I had while attending Corona High to travel around the world and have a great adventure have, in many ways, come to be. Furthermore, I have found the woman that should have been my wife since 1946. Charlotte and I still have fun and laugh all the time. We have never had an argument. Come to think of it, she has never even made me sad. What a girl! I wish my mother had lived long enough to see it all happen.

You may note the new printer, Robert. It's an Epson LQ-850, one of the nicest gifts that I've bought for myself in sometime. It is a twenty-four-pin printer, so it is fast and also gives a good letter quality of print. There are several tricks that it does with the paper too, like pulling back paper so that none is wasted after tearing a sheet off. It comes standard with a single-sheet feeder as well. Well, I had to get it. My publishers insist on quality print, you know!

We send our regards for your health and that of your family's. We are both well. We would like to see more of you, but in lieu of that, write if you get the chance. We love to get the mail.

> Love to all,
> James D. Fox, LTC,
> USARUSMTM PSC BOX 1435-R
> APO NY 09038-5364

PS How about that? The government let me have an APO number, so you can mail just like domestic. Make sure it is first-class postage and marked as First-Class, twelve-ounce limit, and we'll let the ol' US Air Force deliver it!

CAF Letter:
Riyadh, Saudi Arabia
May 10, 1988

Dear Henryetta,

I spent three hours writing a long letter to you yesterday on James's computer, and when I was through, I lost it all when I went to print it. Oh, the frustrations of the computer! Here goes again, and hopefully this time it will work for me.

We were very surprised to hear that you were moving to Santa Fe, but we think you made a wise choice—that is, if you can endure the cold winters there. I think it is more endurable now with modern conveniences and better housing. The wind and snow won't come through the cracks as much as it did on our old houses of sixty years ago.

If you have a map, you can locate Corona down in the central part of the state, and that is where James and I graduated from high school, and he still has a ranch there. At least he owns part of it. The ranch belonged to James's mother, and he has bought one sister's interest. There are four sisters, and he would like to buy all their shares; however, like in most families, there is one that is giving him a hard time about it. They have been trying to settle between themselves and have made very little progress in eight years, so now James is going to court to clear the title and have them settle things. His mother didn't leave a will, so everybody loses in the end, and the lawyers get richer.

On the brighter side, we are planning a tour of the British Isles in July with my friend Jean Shelton and her friend Edna Weaver. Our tour starts on July 2 and goes for twenty-one days. We are ready for a diversion from the Land of the Sand and Sun.

This is the month of Ramadan, a religious month for Moslems. They fast all day, break their fast at sundown, and stay up all night eating and praying. The last prayer before sun up is 4:00 a.m. That would be okay, but they have their mosques about every two blocks, and they have a loud public address system in each mosque. Our compound is located between two mosques; therefore, we get stereo sound, which will awaken anyone that isn't deaf. These people get crazy during this month, so we do not go out much after dark until Ramadan is over, and that is followed by ten days of Eid. Eid is a big celebration, mostly family get-togethers and a lot of food.

Alcohol is banned in this country, and if you are caught with it, home brew or whatever, you can be put in jail or sent home, maybe both. Naturally, there always will be some that don't obey the rules, and they may not be caught, but it doesn't make sense to take the risk. Before you come over here, they spell out the rules, so a person has the option to accept or refuse the contract.

Our contract is up on January 31, 1989, and I think James will not renew. We both feel like we have learned all we want in Saudi Arabia, and now it is time to move on to the next phase of our life.

One purpose of the tour of the British Isles is to give us an idea of a place we would like to live for six months to a year after we leave here. James has been writing stories, which he wants to combine into a book, and we think that it will add to his writings to experience another part of the world. When we finally go back to the States, we may settle in Austin, Texas.

Our reasoning for choosing Austin to be our home is that it is situated near a military base, and this will help us living on a fixed income. James will be retiring from the army on his next birthday (sixth), and we will have full commissary and PX privileges. That is an advantage. Also, he will still be within driving distance of Houston if he needs to visit with his children. Texas has no state income tax, which is a definite plus.

In Austin, James will still be in touch with his pilot friends, and if he wants to fly a trip once in a while, he probably can pick up piecework when the mood strikes. He also wants to buy another small airplane for us to have fun with, and there are a lot of small airfields in that part of the country.

Since I have left California, I have found that being laid-back is suiting me just fine, and Texas is far more laid-back than Southern California. Another reason is that we will not be in the same town as James's ex-wife. I really don't trust her, and I told James it would not be comfortable for me if we lived in Houston. Besides, Houston has too much humidity for me. The mildew spore is in the air, and I am very allergic to it. Austin will have humidity but not as much as Houston, so I am told. I will just have to go there in their worst month and find out for myself.

You and I had the best years of Southern California, and even in 1970, it was still a wonderful place to live in. Strange what eighteen years can do to a city!

I doubt if we will ever live on the ranch in New Mexico, but we may go there in the summertime if we have an RV. There is a nothing type ranch house on it, and a single lady lives there. She works for the forest service and spends her time on the lookout tower on top of the Gallinas Mountains. James lets her live in the house rent-free just to look after it. The land has been leased until now, and he wants it to lie out for a year since it looks like it has been over grazed. The well has been giving trouble, and he may have to drill a new one or case up the old one so they can keep the sand out.

Tonight, James has gone to Jeddah to take two doctors and has been told to stand by there for them. Usually when there is a trip like this, the doctors are after kidneys or other organs for transplant. Jeddah is on the coast of the Red Sea, and just recently, James and I went over there and stayed four days with one of our Saudi friends. Actually, Lilyanna is not a Saudi, but her husband is, and the children are being trained in the Arabic schools. Lilyanna is from Honduras, and she met her husband who was in the States going to school. Hakim is a pilot, and they were our next-door neighbors here in the GAMA compound, and we became good friends. Lilli and I were in the backyard at the same time hanging up our clothes, and James was flying with Hakim, so we had mutual things to talk about. Also, they have three of the cutest children—Lena, Linda, and Sultan. Their son was named after the Saudi astronaut Sultan who is a good friend of theirs.

Henryetta, when James and I married and came over here, it was like I was a different person stepping into a new world. Sometimes I wonder if it is real. Probably the only regret I have is not being younger and having the energy of a young person. There is so much out there for me, it is scary that I may not get it all in a lifetime. Actually, in reality, it seems like I have lived about four lifetimes already, but interestingly enough, James says that I am still the same person he knew in high school.

I am so happy that you have left Shorb and have made a change for yourself. It just feels good sometimes to go for it.

Keep in touch and let us know how things go for you. Maybe we will see you in New Mexico sometime after we come back home.

Love,
Charlotte

CAF Letter:
Riyadh, Saudi Arabia
May 17, 1988

Dear Helen,

Your nice letter came a couple of days ago, and it was strange that the day before, I remarked to James, "I wonder what is going on with Helen because I had not heard from her some time." It is good to hear that you are in better health, and your business is coming along okay.

My heart aches for Sally and Jack both. They had so many good years. It is a shame that the bottom seems to be falling out. Somehow the final decisions always rest on the woman. If things don't work, she always gets the blame.

James has gone to Basel, Switzerland, to test-fly and pick up an airplane that has been there for repair for about six months. These airplanes get so abused because the military says the captains have to let the copilots fly at least one leg per trip so they can learn. The Gulfstream jet is too expensive to be used as a training airplane, but they do what they are told to do, and as the result, this one airplane had a split in the bottom of the fuselage. Gulfstream (from Savannah, Georgia) sent a representative over to Switzerland, and they said they had never seen another airplane with that problem. Anyway, they had to remove the wings in order to do the repair work. What gives me the creeps is that James delivered the plane to Switzerland and didn't know it was in such bad shape. It is a wonder it didn't split wide open when he landed. James left here Sunday, and I haven't heard yet when he will return. You can believe he won't accept delivery until all is correct. I don't have much confidence in the mechanics we have here in Riyadh either.

James and I both have had about all of Saudi Arabia we can stand. By the time his contract is up on January 31, 1989, we will be ready to say good-bye. About the time we feel like we are saving money and making progress, we have something like the IRS come along and hit us a lick, especially this year after I took out my profit sharing from Bromar and James had his severance pay from Exxon. It chokes me up, but we have to pay it anyway.

It is my intention to try to come home this fall, if James goes to FlightSafety School in Savannah, and look for a house to buy so I won't have to pay income tax on the sale of my home on Sharon Place. If you are past the age of fifty-five, there is a one-time allowance of $125,000, and I want to take advantage of that. There is a four-year allowance for reinvestment, but real estate is still going up most places, so I think the sooner I do it the better. Besides, we would like to have a house to go home to. I think that is bad grammar, but it says what I want.

James and I have discussed the fact that I don't like Houston, and we both agree it wouldn't be comfortable to live in the same town as his ex-wife, so we are going to be looking over Austin, Texas.

The things that prompt us to look there are the following:

1. Property is less expensive than anywhere else according to an article we read recently.
2. Texas has no state tax. (This year, I have to pay $1,000 California tax on top of my IRS.)
3. Austin has a military base. After James retires from the army, we will have all military privileges. When you are on a fixed salary, this is worth consideration.
4. There is a country club lake area that has a golf course, and we have talked to several people that say the homes are large and beautiful.
5. There isn't such bad traffic as Los Angeles and no smog.

The disadvantages are probably more heat and humidity than California, but everyone says it is better than Houston. Well, what do you think? If we get a place, you will have a place to come to for a long vacation, and we can do some golfing and maybe some side trips. Think about it anyway.

There hasn't been much of interest happening here except this is the end of the month of Ramadan, and that month of fasting and praying is ended with ten days of Eid celebration. Eid is much like our Christmas holidays where there is feasting and exchange of gifts. We learned last year to just stay off the streets until it is all over. The Saudis get a little crazy at this time.

We are looking forward to being gone the month of July to England. If you have talked to Jeanie Shelton lately, she probably has told you that we are meeting her and Edna in London and are taking a twenty-one-day tour of the British Isles together. We will cover Scotland and Wales but not Ireland. We don't have enough time for that. I have been trying to persuade James to let us return through Portugal and spend a few days there. Our tour will be over on July 21, and we would still have a few days left for Portugal. I have a brochure showing the *Algarve*, and it looks like my type of recreation. Anyway, we will have to wait and see what the boss does.

That is about all I know for now. Last night, I watched the video we took going around the world. I had forgotten that we ran into Chip in Hawaii, and we got a conversation with him on video. What is really bad, Helen, I couldn't remember Chip's last name until just now. It has been so easy for me to forget Bromar and the people there. That is a lifetime away from me now, and I still feel good about leaving there.

Incidentally, I was talking to Al Marino, and he said Nancy was coming to Cairo to cruise down the Nile. Her girlfriend and she would meet up with Nancy's parents, do the cruise together, and then her parents would go on to Kenya for a safari. I wish she would get a Saudi visa and stop off to see us. Cairo isn't more than two or three hours' flight from here.

I forgot to tell you about Greg Fox. He and Mary have bought a piece of property and are constructing a new house on it. Well, Greg was using a skill saw overhead, and it got loose, came down on his left shoulder/arm area, and cut him badly. He didn't sever the artery, which was very lucky, but it required a lot of stitches to put him back together. A little more and his arm would have been amputated. James says Greg is a potential self-destruct person anyway and has been all of his life.

Congratulations on your new forklift, but for crying out loud, be careful with it. We don't need any more casualties in this group.

How are JK and his new wife doing? Sounds like things are about the same for Jan. Do you think she will ever remarry? Next time you talk to them, be sure to give them my best.

Probably when we go to Texas, you will meet the man of your life.

Won't that be fun? There are definitely some nice people there, and I have good vibes about it.

We send our love, and thanks again for the nice letter.

CAF Letter:
Riyadh, Saudi Arabia
May 17, 1988

Dear Muriel,

Your letter came several days ago, and I started handwriting a letter to you, but James is out of town, and I can use his computer. He doesn't mind me using it, but when he is here, he is always working on it, so I don't interfere. It is so much easier than handwriting. Arthritis must be setting up in my right shoulder, and this is so much easier. Old age certainly has its penalties.

Sounds like you have dentures now. I knew you had a bridge or partial, but when did you get a full plate or plates? You certainly have my sympathy as I can remember how Papa used to whittle on his to make them more comfortable, and Ray was always going to the orthodontist for adjustments. You are right, I do take care of my teeth, and so far they are good, but if I ever lose them, it probably will be because of gingivitis of the gums. Papa or Mama told me one time that was the cause of Papa losing his teeth, so I hope it isn't inherent. The gum surgery I had was enough to make a believer out of me.

James has gone to Basel, Switzerland, to test-fly and bring back an airplane that has been in for repair about six months. These airplanes take a lot of abuse from the inexperienced copilots and maybe some captains that like to show off by rolling the airplane. We have heard that Walt Schmitz who used to be here rolled the airplane every time they had a new nurse onboard. That weakens the fuselage, and on this particular plane, the belly of the fuselage was split. No one here knew it, and James flew it to Switzerland for regular maintenance and routine checks. Well, when they found this problem, a representative from Gulfstream came from Savannah, and he couldn't believe what he saw. He said in all the history of Gulfstreams, he had never seen that particular damage. To repair it, it has required removal of the wings and major overhaul of the fuselage. When this type of thing happens, I lose faith in the other airplanes that are here in the hangar. Wonder what is wrong with them! Quite frankly, this wouldn't be a bad job if there was better maintenance of the airplanes. I will be happy when we are through here. I can't let myself worry too much about things I can't do anything about.

My reassurance is that James will not take risks knowingly, and he is a very good pilot. In this business, experience counts for a lot, and it is James's disposition to remain calm in a crisis.

We are looking forward to July when we go to England to meet Jeanie and Edna for our tour of the British Isles (except Ireland). We don't have the time it would take to see Ireland, and that isn't high on my priority list anyway. I have been trying to persuade James to let us return via Portugal. I have a brochure of the

Alcarve, and it looks like a great place to go if you like the beach and golf. So far James has not made a commitment, but I am working on him.

I had a letter from Helen, and she says she is in better health than she was when I saw her in October. She really looked bad then, so skinny, but she says that she has a good doctor she likes and he has done a lot for her.

Austin called on Mother's Day and said he was going to Minnesota this week for a week of training, and then in June, he will be certified as a counselor for alcoholics and addicts. He changed clinics there in Tucson, and he said he liked the new job better. He wants to get back into school. The last job took up so much of his time he had to give up his classes. When I was visiting with Austin, he took me to the college or a university (?) there in Tucson. We walked on the campus, and Austin showed me around. I hope he doesn't get discouraged. He tells me he misses San Francisco, but I hope he will make enough new friends to keep him in Tucson. I can understand why he misses San Francisco, and I would be lying if I told you I didn't miss California, but it has become so overcrowded and busy that it has lost most of its charm for me.

James and I have been talking about settling in Austin, Texas, but I have never been there and am eagerly looking forward to checking it out. Maybe it is my age, but I like the laid-back life that goes with Texas. Of course being married to James has something to do with that, but he would go with me anywhere I wanted to live. Neither of us wanted to live in Houston as long as his ex-wife lives there. I don't like the climate in Houston, and I don't like all the pine trees that keep you from seeing out. James says that Austin is more open and is hilly country.

The humidity there is less than Houston also. Well, maybe a little.

If Medevac keeps their schedule, James will be sent to Savannah in October to FlightSafety school, and if that happens, I may come with him and go to Austin to look at real estate. How about meeting me there? You and Maxine could hop in your new car, and with Maxine driving, you would be there in no time. Maxine could help me bargain for a house as she has dabbled in real estate. You could give it some thought anyway.

James is still trying to get things straightened out on the Fox ranch. He has written to Jim Hall and asked him what would be entailed to go to court and get things in order. Seems that Wanna Beth will not cooperate, and that seems to be the only recourse to get things settled. It is too bad, but James has tried to reason with her for eight years and has gotten nowhere.

James also requested Jim Hall to send Eddie Sanchez a letter to remove his livestock and pay the money he owes. He intends to talk to Steve about the well as soon as he hears back from hall on some of these things. If we settle in Texas, there is every possibility that we would spend the summers in Cedarvale if we can ever get things straightened out, so we can buy the rest of the ranch. James would like to have an RV, so if nothing else, we could stay in it for a short time in good weather.

Too bad we cannot make the reunion this year. The timing just isn't right, and we probably wouldn't have enough time anyway, considering what we have to do if we come to the States.

I am so far behind on letter writing. For some reason, I haven't been able to write like I did when I first came over here. Hot weather is here now, and there are days when I only leave the house to walk to the mail room and back. That isn't enough exercise, and lack of exercise probably contributes to my complacency.

We are at the end of the month of Ramadan, and this is the second day of the ten days of Eid that follows Ramadan. There will be eight more days of feasting and celebration, then things should return to normal. Maybe I can then go shopping. We learned last year just to hibernate and stay off the streets during this time when the Saudis go crazy. It is bad enough in normal times.

I don't think I told you about the Saudi family that lives on the compound, slaughtering a goat in their front yard. They strung it up over the sidewalk, and the Brits nearly had a fit. Most of them had never seen anything like it. The Brits are protective of animals and don't have much stomach for the realities of life.

The only objection I had was that it drew flies, but I guess there were a lot of complaints registered with the manager of the compound. James and I thought it was rather funny because it created such an uproar.

I guess this is all for now. Keep your letters coming, and by the way, the last two had far too much postage. When you use the APO Box address, the postage is the same as it is in the States. Twenty-five cents for the first ounce, etc.

We send our love, and say hello to Tom and the family.

Dispatch:
Riyadh, Saudi Arabia
May 20, 1988

TEST FLIGHT OVER FOUR COUNTRIES

F light instruments can be very important to pilots that need to keep a steady course and altitude even on the fairest of days. They are mandatory when flying without reference to the ground or horizon, sometimes referred to as flying in instrument conditions (IFR). The greater the speed of an aircraft, the greater the difficulty in maintaining a steady course and altitude. Pilots that fly jets are constantly referring to their instruments even when they are flying in visual conditions.

Some of my friends that flew in World War II, and very little since, have an idea that we present-day fliers spend too much time looking at instruments and not enough time looking out the windows. They have even added that there would be fewer midair collisions if the pilots spent less time looking at instruments. Their observations are only partly correct. The truth of the matter is that the modern jets can't be hand flown in a precise manner by looking out the window. A slight change of pitch can make quite a change in altitude and speed in seconds. The FAA gave me my type rating check rides in a jet on a clear day without a hood to simulate instrument conditions. In the faster aircraft, you must watch the instruments close, or you're not going to stay within the parameters needed to pass the check ride; therefore, they don't bother making you wear a hood for the check ride. In smaller and slower aircraft, the pilot is always given his instrument check ride wearing a hood.

Pilots love to argue. They will argue over most anything. They will argue over about why there is nothing to argue about. The Federal Aviation Authority stays up late at nights looking for new things to make sure that pilots don't run out of things to argue about. Here is a good one. What is your primary flight instrument? This is one of the FAA's favorites. Endless hours have been spent by pilots denying the FAA's current position on which of the aircraft's instruments should now be labeled as the primary flight instrument. Apparently, this is a problem for all the non-fliers that populate the offices of the FAA. They have spent so much time planning their rise via seniority within the confines of the bureaucracy, they become obsessed with the idea as it applies to aviation. Therefore, if an aircraft has two engines, they demand to know as to which is the most critical engine? It follows that if you are flying with more than one flight instrument, then as a pilot, you should know without hesitation, which is the primary one of the group. They cannot understand why the old pilots won't agree with the FAA's choices.

The FAA wants you to tell them that when flying a multiengine aircraft, the most critical engine is the one with the generator on it or the one that when lost gives the most asymmetrical yaw, or whatever. The young pilots are taught these things, and they believe them. The old pilot insists that the most critical engine is the last one left running. On the other hand, the most critical engine might be the first one that quits, if you can't maintain flight with the one that is left. The old pilot will tell you that the primary flight instrument is the one that will keep you from flying into something hard, like the ground before you're ready to land. Be serious, they say. Well, that's the bad part, I am serious. Of course, this line of thinking is suspected of being only a ploy by the old guys to keep the new guys in their places. You know, we got to keep these new guys with their college degrees in their place or they will pretty soon be running the whole show. Well guess what, it's too late. The guys with the college degrees have already taken over, and us old guys are way in the minority.

That doesn't mean our ideas are no good. That doesn't mean that all of a sudden we don't know how to fly an airplane, and that doesn't mean that we should all be relegated to the old folks' home. What it does mean is that the bureaucracy in charge is becoming less populated with pilots and more populated with people who have little or no experience in aviation. Whether or not they have a college degree is beside the point. The intellectuals have seen that it is possible to educate professional people and see them go directly from their schooling into their jobs and become a productive part of our society. How much experience must you have after law school and the bar exam before you are able to go to court and defend a man's life? None. We are living in an age that says that education is the answer to everything. Shouldn't we agree that it is only the entry requirement?

The educators have found it necessary to give way to certain professional societies' requirements, which make it mandatory that a graduate must suffer further training in the form of experience before they can be released into their profession. Doctors are a good example. Their education is only the beginning of their practice of Medicine. The American doctor is respected the world over. There are few places on this entire planet that do not have instant respect for the American doctor. There are many reasons for this, I'm sure, but let me suggest that the primary reason is that they are controlled by other professional doctors, the American Medical Association. Okay, I'm not a doctor, but just an observer, but if I'm wrong, let me know.

The next question is, if any of the above is true, then why does the American public continue to support the idea of filling the seats of almost *all* aviation authorities with people that have no experience, no background, and perhaps only a bureaucrat's interest in aviation? The FAA makes decisions based on the thinking of engineers, lawyers, and accountants. How can the voter allow the National Transportation Safety Board to be chaired by a woman that can't distinguish airplanes from a ski lodge? These people are installed by political favor. A background in flying is difficult or impossible to find in the bunch. The poor, dumb flying public doesn't know and doesn't care. They just want their plane to be on time and not lose their bags. Don't they know that broken schedules and lost bags are the results of poor management? If you trace it far enough, it will take you all the way back to the US Congress. Why not the president, well, who thinks that he is in charge? Because he is not the boss. He is not the manager; he is only the leader. If you think he is in control, then you have probably been voting Democratic for some time, and that's why we have a Republican president and a Democratic Congress.

Do you want to tell me that putting professionals in charge of a professional organization is not the final answer? Do you want to tell me that there are some rotten apples in the American Medical Association? Then I would have to agree to both of the above and more, but no one said that it was a simple problem with a simple solution. The proper solution starts with endowing control to people that know what they are doing. It is only meant to be the start.

On second thought, this whole idea is preposterous. I'm whistling in the dark, and no one is listening. The traveler says, "Well, it's still a lot better than a bus!"

My crew and I just returned from four days in Basel, Switzerland. Just like they say, "It's a pretty country, but take away the mountains and lakes, and what have you got?" We went to pick up an aircraft that has been in maintenance for the last four months. After four months of maintenance, men taking pieces off and putting them back meant that we would have to make a test flight. Taking an aircraft for a test flight after they have had both engines off, replaced the center box beams that form the heart of the aircraft "chassis," reworked the avionics in the cockpit, and completely removed and replaced the interior means there will probably be a lot to look for and probably a lot to find. If the test flight is made during local thunderstorms, through the mountains, the normally dense European traffic, in a strange location where you are unfamiliar with the names of any navigation aids, where a tight pattern of testing requires that you over fly Switzerland, France, Germany, and Italy, can fill up your day. This test flight was about to teach me new respect for an instrument that has always been a friend, but I never thought of it as a primary flight instrument.

The aircraft to be tested was a Gulfstream II. On the first test flight of HZ-MS4, I learned how important a little flight instrument can be when it doesn't work. The RMI is the instrument to which I refer. To those that don't know, that is a radio magnetic indicator. It is just a little needle that points to the radio station that you have tuned in. It is a handy indicator to have when you are not real sure where the navigation fix is located that you have tuned in. Most small planes don't even have one installed. It is hardly considered an instrument critical to flight. It is not even on the required list in the FAA regulations.

We made all the ground checks that we could make near the hangar of jet aviation. We were able to contact Stockholm, Sweden, and receive a strength 4 signal report on the high frequency radio, but the RMI needles would not point at anything. That is not uncommon on the ground, especially in Basel, because the only station nearby is blocked on the ground by hangars and other buildings.

It is usual for the RMI not to work on the ground anywhere. It is also not unusual for the RMIs not to be needed in the air. It was meant for the test flight to be very structured and disciplined. I had filed a flight plan specifically for a test flight and had requested a verification of our route prior to engine start. This was to make sure they didn't spring a surprise on us as we were taxing out for takeoff. I didn't want to be figuring out a new and strange route at the last second.

Sure enough, they changed the whole flight plan. Altitudes and routes were changed so that the whole plan was different and strange. The local air traffic control people have to respect the flow control of several different countries, you know. I had planned a triangular flight path that would be flown in a clockwise manner, which would bring us back to Basel in about an hour. Once I lifted off the runway into the clouds, there wasn't more than ten minutes of the next one hour and fifteen minutes that I felt like I knew where I was. The SID (standard instrument departure) required that after takeoff, we fly runway heading, 160° until 400 feet above ground and then turn right heading 250° and continue climb to 7,000 feet, on crossing the Basel 192° radial. Then we were to turn left around the non-directional beacon, to intercept the Hocwald 200°radial to Hocwald thence flight plan route. Piece of cake, right? Wrong. As soon as I had turned right to the heading of 250°, the controller liked my rate of climb he should have. We were only carrying fourteen thousand pounds of fuel and were climbing like a fighter, but limited to 7,000 feet. He liked our climb gradient because it cleared us from the noise abatement area, not the mountains, so he cleared us direct to another station that neither my copilot Hatim nor I recognized or had any idea where it was. The first thing to do is find it on the map, right? Well, good luck, we finally found it on the map for Germany. We hadn't planned on Germany, so the map had to be brought to the surface. Hatim found the station and tuned it in. The RMI should point straight to the station, then we would only need to fly that heading and no problem. That's a good plan, only the RMIs are swinging aimlessly as if there was no signal. A quick check for redundancy on the other side of the cockpit showed that the copilots are doing the same as mine. The RMIs are useless. I'm in a climbing turn, and I don't even know where the nondirectional beacon is, and that is what I need to make my turn around to miss the first mountain.

This is Switzerland, right? We are mostly in clouds, and the radar is almost solid red with mountains and thunderstorms.

Trying to talk to the female on the frequency impersonating an air controller is a waste of time, but Hatim is trying, and all I can do is to try and continue flying the original SID regardless of the way we are cleared. At least the SID's route will keep us at a safe altitude. Too late, Hatim has changed frequency to the new VOR that we are cleared to before we realize that the RMIs don't work. There is not enough time to manually center the needle to find the course to the VOR. And tuning a floating head VOR is not as easy to do as the old fixed card with a needle that only swings right and left. We were further disoriented by the mind-set of expecting to fly southeast and then being cleared direct to a station that was northeast. Where am I? And where are those mountains, especially the one that goes to eighteen thousand feet.

The route I had planned was changed prior to our engine start, and that's not too bad, but the second change was made after we were airborne and in a turn. A pilot would not do that to another pilot. Perhaps I should have waited until next month when I could have counted on visual conditions for the flight. Well, I am a stranger in Switzerland and have no idea of the weather patterns. You can keep learning if you can just keep living. The worst part is this: The bureaucrats never learn, and they are always in charge.

I found it to be especially difficult to accomplish the original mission of testing the aircraft for snags. We were so busy due to the constant changes in routes and altitudes issued by the four different countries that we were flying over. We were really a pain in their traffic area, even though we tried to stay around twenty thousand feet to keep out of the denser traffic. It was a test flight, certainly, but more for the crew than the aircraft. We got the job done the second day after the ground crews got it all working.

Excitement like this usually doesn't last very long, and all those in back of the bulkhead behind the pilot's head are unaware that there is anything happening of an unusual nature. It's just as well. They can't help anyway. As pilots, we make the ground checks, and the rest is a matter of trust and talent. You have to be able to trust those that work on the aircraft you're going to fly, and you have to have the talent to handle the problem that may come up.

Well, we only had to make two test flights, and by the time we made the third takeoff for our trip back to Riyadh, we had a lot better handle on where we were and what we were doing. We also had everything working except the coffeemaker. Well, you can't have everything, but I would rather have the RMIs than the coffeemaker for low-level test flights in Switzerland. On that day, I would have been ready to nominate the RMI as a primary flight instrument.

Author's Note: In my opinion, the most important flight instrument is the one which when lost will cause the pilot to lose his control of the aircraft.

JDF Letter:
Riyadh, Saudi Arabia
May 28, 1988

To: Medevac Director of Operations
From: James D. Fox, Captain, Fixed Wing, G2, G3,
Subject: Recommended Training Syllabus for Beginning Copilots Assigned to
         Gulfstreams

Sir:

The following is an outline to show my thinking for the training necessary for the new Medevac copilots that hope to transition into the Gulfstream. This letter is meant to be an outline only because of the time consideration needed for its preparation. The basic thought behind this outline is to take a young man that is proficient in fixed-wing aircraft but has little or no time in turbojet aircraft, which require a type rating to fly as pilot in command. It is presumed that the individual described here has already completed a jet transition course and an initial training course on the Gulfstream. The application of this training outline should provide the student with the knowledge and skills to become a competent copilot on the Gulfstream. The training course should be considered only as the beginning of the students' training career.

1. In the first increment, the students will be taught the basic method of normal takeoffs and landings. At least one training period will be devoted to air work to give the student confidence in his ability to control the aircraft in the air. This training will be conducted with all aircraft systems operating normally—that is, no simulated emergences. Emphasis is on the normal takeoff attitude, power setting, flap retraction, gear retraction, and climb-out procedure. They should be told the time and amount of each change of power coinciding with their flight configuration, airspeed, and altitude.

The first increment of landings should be taught in such a manner that will instill confidence in the student of his ability to land the aircraft in a normal and satisfactory manner from a *visual* approach. Emphasis should be on developing the individual's judgment and proper application of power and drag to make a smooth approach and normal landing. It is my opinion that a good *visual* approach displays considerable judgment on the students' part. Instrument approaches, single-engine approaches, and simulated landing emergencies are *not* to be demonstrated to the student at this time. The student will complete this initial training when he has demonstrated his *consistent* good judgment and landing techniques to anyone that flies with him.

The length of time needed for this first increment of training is determined by the frequency of the training periods and the aptitude of the student. Each training period will require approximately one hour in the air. At least twice that time will be spent on the ground in briefing and debriefing sessions. If each participant could receive an hour of training per day, then he could probably be completed in this first increment in two weeks or ten hours. The Medevac strength in captains is very short at the present time, therefore the flight periods will surely have to be spaced further apart. If they are spaced too far apart, then a certain amount of effectiveness will be lost and have to be repeated. If too much time is lost, then the whole program will be lost.

I suggest, therefore, that the flight instruction periods should be scheduled on the normal Medevac duty roster. The schedule will have to reflect certain days for training. It will not be satisfactory to just try and fit the training in when able. There is no value to be found in beginning a program of instruction that is so full of flaws that it has no chance of survival from the beginning. The students must have a *minimum* of one hour of flight training per week, or it is of no use to even begin the program.

2. The second increment begins when the first increment is completed to the satisfaction of the IP and director of operations. The second increment will consist of approximately ten hours of training in basic instrument approaches. This is not meant to be a course of instruction to teach instrument flight. It is meant to be a second step in the progression of training for a copilot. It should further instill confidence in the student and all that fly with him. There is no graduation day for the second increment. Ten hours is recommended, but it is not a hard number. Some students may well require more. They will be considered as completed in the second increment of this training when they have demonstrated their ability to understand and complete an approach of less than visual conditions at any type of approach aid in the Kingdom of Saudi Arabia. The student should not be expected to fly within the minimum requirements of a captain. After all, they are students and are still in the learning mode. At this point, they are flying in normal conditions, and they should not be expected to be competent in handling emergencies, real or simulated. If the student cannot hold his altitude or airspeed to FAA requirements in an instrument approach by the end of ten hours of practice, it does not mean that he has failed, but it does mean that he has not finished and needs more training.

3. The third increment of training will include ground school on other duties of the copilot in completing a Medevac mission. The subjects covered will be the proper communication procedures in the Kingdom of Saudi Arabia, the proper operation of the lift on MS3, the proper operation of invertors and converters needed for the medical equipment on the Gulfstreams, and finally, a complete briefing on the long-range navigation and HF communication sets installed on the Gulfstreams. Of course, some of this information is passed along during the normally assigned Medevac missions, but it should be reaffirmed in a proper ground school

classroom environment. The instruction of this third phase should be done by those most expert in the area of instruction. For example, operation of the long-range navigation equipment might be taught by one or more of the senior copilots on the Gulfstream. Hatim Bashir or Waleed Zahed could do an excellent job of this. The medical equipment class should be taught by a biomed technician. Operation of the lift and cargo door seals could be taught by a mechanic. All instruction should be attended by the IP and under his direct control. His participation is to insure that all subjects are covered and all students participate.

4. I would consider that five hours or less would be sufficient for the fourth phase, which would include single-engine procedures. This training will be repeated in the simulator, therefore there is no need to spend much time in the aircraft on this training. Single-engine procedures in the Gulfstream are important, but there is no need to press too much on this point at this time. All single-engine procedures should be simulated only; real engine cuts near the ground are definitely not recommended. Any real engine cuts should be done at altitude only and with an engineer present.

This training should be accomplished prior to the students' next participation in a flight safety course. The simulator training should augment the completion of these first four phases of training.

During the flight training periods described above, at the discretion of the IP, certain other persons should be allowed to go along on the training flights as observers. *No one* enjoys going along as an observer on a training flight, more than once, that is. But due to the shortage of time available to the IP, he should be allowed to combine the preflight briefing with all three participants and then fly all three on a single flight if possible. This may not always be an advantage, but it should be at the IP's discretion.

5. The fifth increment or phase of this training can be conducted at any time starting from this day. The fifth phase will include one trip to Europe or the USA as an observer only. The observer will be required to remain in the jump seat as a true observer, and not the rear of the aircraft as a passenger. One trip as observer should be sufficient training for the student to make the next trip in the right seat. The students' second trip to Europe should be accompanied by a second qualified copilot. The reason for this is because all captains will have to participate in the final checkout of the student for international travel. It would take too long for any one IP to conduct all the international instruction for all the students. The students' performance on international trips can be observed and augmented if necessary by observance of the second copilot.

The new copilot should attend a course on international procedures prior to being released from this fifth phase of training.

The purpose of this training outline is to organize a plan whereby the new employee of Medevac with a minimum of prior experience can be trained to function as copilot on normal Medevac missions both domestic and international. The individual that completes all five phases or increments of this training should be ready and able to fly anywhere in the world with a fully released captain on the Gulfstream. It is also the foundation of all future training of the individual as he continues a career in aviation. It is my feeling that all too many have found themselves deep into a career in Aviation without a good foundation. On completion of the above-described five phases of training, further training will be on the advice of the IP, at the discretion of the director of Medevac.

James D. Fox

CAF Letter:
Riyadh, Saudi Arabia
June 1, 1988

Dear Louise, Gerald, and Margareet,

Thought I would drop you a line while James is out of town and I have access to his computer. It is so much easier to write on it than it is to write by hand. James has his room set up with a nice stereo, so you can play music of your choice while writing on the computer. One thing that is a little much for me, and that is the air conditioner that he keeps at such a cold temperature. I have to put a sweater on, and it is 108 degrees outside.

James has gone to London. Yesterday, he flew to Jeddah to pick up a princess that had to be transferred to a hospital in London. From there, he was to take the aircraft to Cambridge for annual maintenance. From Cambridge, he was going back to London to meet Chuck and stay a couple of days with him. He will probably be home Thursday night or Friday. Chuck likes England, but his working relationship with David has not been working out. Chuck says that David drinks a lot and doesn't tend to business like he should, and they have had some strong disagreements. Seems that instead of David working on James's Jaguar like James thought he was doing, David was driving the car. One of the fellows told Chuck the reason it wasn't running was because David took it out on the freeway, drove it 165 miles per hour, and blew the engine.

When Chuck found out about this was about the time he and David had a blowup. Anyway, Chuck tore the engine down and with very little help from David has put it back together and may have it running by the time James gets there. This has been a good experience for Chuck, and he says that he feels a lot better about himself than he did when he went to England. That made James feel good, and he thinks this may be the event in Chuck's life to help him mature.

Jimmy called the day before James left and said that Colleen inherited some money from her father. (You did know that Harry passed away earlier this year, didn't you?) Anyway, they were all excited because now they are going to have a nice vacation in a few days. Their plan is to rent a motor home and drive to Washington DC, and when they return, they are going to look for property to build a new home.

Greg and Mary have just about finished their new house. Their move date (they hope) will be July 4. I don't remember if we wrote you about Greg almost losing him arm. He was working overhead with a skill saw. The saw got loose and came down on his left shoulder and almost amputated his arm. Fortunately, it didn't cut the artery or the main nerve. I can't remember how many stitches he had, but Mary said it was difficult for the doctor to remove all the sawdust and debris, and they were afraid of infection. He is almost healed now but doesn't have full use of the arm yet. Every time I think about it, my stomach gets queasy.

How are Janell and Carleton and family? I think a lot about Janell closing her lovely dress shop, and I won't be able to buy any more pretty clothes from her. James always notices when I wear one of her dresses, and that makes me feel good.

We leave June 30 for England where we will meet Jean Shelton and Edna Weaver in London for our twenty-one-day tour together. I am mentally ready to go but don't have the slightest idea what to take for clothes. Jean said it would probably be cool in Scotland and that I would need a sweater and raincoat. When we wrecked our car and left it to be repaired, my umbrella was taken from it, and I haven't found a replacement for it yet. It was one that folded up small enough, and I could carry it in my purse. I used it more for the sun than I did for rain over here.

Thomasene and Milton called the same night Jimmy did, so we had news from Cedarvale also. Well, not much news from there, but James told Milton that he had written to the attorney Jim Hall to have Eddie Sanchez remove his livestock and pay up his back debt. James sent you a copy of the letter. To date, he hasn't heard from anyone. Guess it will all just take time.

Last night, one of the nurses, Mary Logan (Irish) and I hired a limousine and went downtown to the Chinese restaurant (Gulf Royal) for dinner. Eating is about the only thing women can do over here, so we do plenty of that. There just isn't any place in the world that has as good food as in the good old USA. I don't believe the average American realizes what a privilege it is to be a US citizen and live in that great country. No wonder there has been so much immigration in the last ten years to America. Any tourist going there makes a mental note to come back there to live and be free to do anything they want to.

We are going to have a wedding here on June 25 (both bride and groom are Brits) between nurse Jenny Madill and John from the radio room. They are both nice people and probably will be very happy together. The wedding will take place at the British Embassy, and we are going to be invited to attend. Jenny called me this morning to tell me about it. Maybe I will need to buy a new dress appropriate for the occasion. I just don't have a thing to wear!

James says that he has just about had all of this fun he can stand and is certainly looking forward to the end of his contract. Don't let that fool you though; he just made a commitment to train the Saudi copilots and stayed up almost all night two nights before he left for London to write a training syllabus for the director of Medevac to approve. Seems that the copilots didn't like the training captain they had; they all got together and requested Captain Fox (James) to help persuade James to accept the additional work. James has not wanted to get this involved, but he likes these young men and says maybe that is what he needs to do to end his flying career. He says that if some of the old captains had not passed on the benefit of their flying experiences to him, he would not have been successful, so he feels that he should do the same. What will happen if Medevac begs James to stay on after the end of the contract? I don't think James knows that answer yet.

I don't know if you read in the paper about the airplane crash in Houston and killed in it was Salem Mohamed Bin Ladin. He was flying a glider, and being too low, he hit a pole. This man was a close friend of our friends Hakim and Lilyanna Al-Alaway. He was also one of the wealthiest men here in Saudi Arabia. I talked to Lilyanna yesterday in Jeddah, and she said they brought the body back to Madinah around 4:00 p.m. and that Hakim had gone to the burial.

This man supported Hakim through his flying school and has always treated him like a son. When Hakim left here (Medevac), he went back to work for Salem flying a Learjet, and that is the aircraft he picked us up in when we went for the visit in April. I think we wrote you about that. James being in London, I don't know if he has read about this tragedy. There was an article in our Saudi newspaper yesterday.

I guess this is about all I know to write about today.

I know James would join me in sending our love. Write soon and let us know what is happening.

Margaret, when is Toni planning her wedding? Be sure to let us know.

Love,
Charlotte

Dispatch:
Riyadh, KSA
June 10, 1988

JUST SOME JOURNAL ENTRIES

June 6, 1988

Finally got a trip to EGLL. Took MS3 to Cambridge for two weeks of maintenance. Waleed Zahed copilot did a good job. We picked up a princess (an old princess) in Jeddah and took her to London, then ferried the plane to Cambridge. Took seventeen minutes to Cambridge but took four hours to get back. The driver was lost most of the time. He swore he knew where he was going, but he kept stopping at gas stations without buying anything. He would come out muttering that these D—*Pakys* don't know anything, and then we would drive some more. The *Pakys* run the filling stations and 7-Elevens in England like the Vietnamese do in Houston. The Vietnamese do it in Houston because they expect to own the store soon, and they usually do. The *Pakys* do it in London because it is all they can find to do, and they are just holding on by their fingernails. Looks the same, but there is a big difference.

June 7, 1988

Spent the day at the hangar after going to the bank to collect my pay. Not much happening. The PCA licenses came in for Long and Bruno. Good for a year. That helps. They have been screwing around with Long's license for at least five months. Talked with one of the Filipino helicopter mechanics. We talked about Filipino history. He said they were under the Spanish flag for five hundred years, until the Americans. Their primary language is English or American. Spanish is an elective in school. He said his grandmother spoke Spanish, but now all is forgotten, only a few in the south still speak Spanish. The original Filipino language was derived from Southeast Asia, not the Orient. They write left to right, not right to left or in a column top to bottom. Hatim is making an effort to get operations straightened out. His first big effort is to get everyone to turn in their request for leave before the fifteenth of this month, for the rest of the year. It is a big job and one that has never been done. They usually just wait till it happens then try to make it work. That's the reason they have six fixed-wing captains of the Gulfstreams, and sometimes they only have two that can fly. Good luck. Pool party tonight for Cherene, her birthday I think. They will have Lebanese buffet, but I think we will eat out at the Desert Inn just in case.

479

June 29, 1988

We are leaving for the UK tour tonight. Just finished correcting the Jeddah story and the English teacher's story. Thought of a good story line. Pa Maxwell, feeding the hogs, twisting the knobs on the TV fifty miles a day, and can you get Waco on that thing? Also about when he was town marshal of Alvord, Texas. Remember my maternal grandfather was killed in a gunfight in Oklahoma Territory when my mother was only four years old.

"Toga Pool Party"

Author's Note: *The reader must remember there is little to do here in the form of social activities. There are no movie theaters or any other form of recreation for mixed company except eating out. We attended a secret meeting of a group of amateur actors that were going to put on a play. They were in the process of finding a place for their theater, and they were trying to recruit more actors and also get an idea of the audience they might expect. It never happened. The word got out, and once it became known to the Saudis, there was too big a risk to try and put on the show. We would have all been fined or deported or both.*

So you can take your lady to the Marriott for dinner and eat in the small family area, stay home and watch videos that have been copied so many times that the pictures have horizontal flagging at the top of the screen, and the audio is so distorted you can't understand what they are saying, or you can go to a pool party. Pool parties are very popular in our compound even though we have a mixed group here. By mixed, I mean the compound is populated with all kinds of religions. The Moslems are supposed to be offended by men and women together in a social atmosphere. However, inside the compound walls, we are not bothered by the Mataween or religious police.

"Let's have a pool party" is a common expression here when there is the slightest excuse. Birthday parties, anniversaries, national holidays (any nation will do), or just make up a reason.

The parties are not rowdy, but every now and then, something happens that is noteworthy like the night that Kevin Tschida threw Jerry Padova's cat in the swimming pool!

Jerry's cat was a tomcat and presumed to be the master of the compound. He roamed inside the walls with impunity and knew how to open the slide window into anyone's villa that wasn't locked. Most of us wondered how the cat survived those in the compound that came from countries that ate cats. But the old Tom did survive and continued to show himself at the pool parties.

I should mention there were about equal numbers cat lovers versus cat haters in the compound. The pool parties were held inside the walls around the huge swimming pool. As you can tell, it was well lighted and equipped with adequate lights, tables, and chairs for the get-togethers.

One night, old Tom decided to invite himself to the party and proceeded to stroll down behind the chairs of the participants that had their backs to the pool. Tom took his time and rubbed up against certain legs that happened to be there. Kevin Tschida did not like cats! That's probably an understatement because I don't really know that much about Kevin. We flew together often, but the subject of cats never came up.

"Please note the lady in the foreground wearing a head covering. It was not uncommon for some of our Saudi friends to bring their wives here because they knew they would not be bothered by the police."

When old Tom made it to Kevin's chair, he proceeded to rub his back up against Kevin's pant leg. Kevin didn't say anything, but with one motion, his right hand came down from the table, grabbed old Tom by the fur on his back, and slung the cat out into the pool. I was sitting across the table from Kevin when this happened and saw the cat land in the pool about twenty feet out from the bank. That cat made good time getting back to the bank, climbed out right there close to Kevin, and shook the water off. Then old Tom calmly wondered over to the building next to the pool, jumped up to window shelf, and began to clean himself in front of all to see.

There was murmuring from the crowd of cat lovers and laughing out loud from the cat haters. Kevin made no note of anything and just continued with what he had been doing. The murmurs and laughter soon died down, and everyone continued with the party. About fifteen minutes later, old Tom returned to the party and began to repeat his previous routine, and everyone noticed. Well, when he got down the line of chairs and finally came to Kevin's pant leg, he did the same thing that he had done before—started rubbing his back.

Old Tom repeated his act, and Kevin repeated his. *Whoosh* went Kevin's right arm, and once again, old Tom was flunk twenty feet out over the pool. But this time, there was something different. Just like in a movie cartoon, old Tom's feet were doing sixty miles an hour before he hit the water, and to those of us watching, it was as if he was suspended for a microsecond over the pool. When old Tom came down, he ran across the top of that pool and out on bank without getting wet! This time, there were no murmurs, no laughter because we all were sitting there with our mouths open. No one could believe what they had just seen.

When old Tom hit the bank, he did stop to shake himself because there was nothing to shake off, but instead, he left the pool area by hitting that ten-foot pool fence at full speed, and it was up and over. That was the end of old Tom for that night and that party. Kevin went back to his plate of barbecue.

"Jerry Padova holding court. That's Linda Baud sitting just in front of Jerry. They were married after leaving KSA. Jerry maybe announcing pancakes at his B unit the next morning."

"A birthday boy took an unexpected swim at his birthday party."

CAF Letter:
Riyadh, Saudi Arabia
June 13, 1988

Dear Muriel,

Time must be going rapidly as I didn't realize I had not written since May 17 until we received your letter yesterday. I don't count letters back and forth, knowing that the mail doesn't always go through.

Speaking about the mail being all fouled up, we got into a flap with American Express in about February this year. One day, they sent us a telegram saying that we owed them nearly $1,800. I checked back to our last statement and figured out that we had paid them in November with pound sterling, and they credited us for US dollars, which meant we came up short by $1,200 by their figures. They took that amount and added it to December charges, and we never received that statement. It took several months, telephone calls to the States, several nasty telegrams, and a visit several times to American Express here in Riyadh to finally figure out that American Express had sent us that December statement. We had two statements subsequently, but we never received that particular one. I was writing letters, trying to call their attention to the under credit for the pound sterling, which was paying about $1.82 US at that time.

In the meantime, Jeanie Shelton sent a check to them from our joint bank account so they would not close our account. We need the account for traveling, so we don't have to carry so much money. Anyway, American Express sent us a photocopy of the December statement, and we finally received the $1,200 credit due us; they received our check, so everybody was finally satisfied. Guess what, yesterday we received the original statement. There had been another apartment number written on the envelope and apparently placed in the wrong mailbox here. Probably the apartment was empty, and no one ever checked the box until this week when we finally received it. How is that for a story of aggravation and embarrassment? Many times our mail has been opened; it feels good to have an APO Box where we can pick up our mail from the good old USA post office. We do appreciate the US military being over here.

My shoulder does bother me quite a lot, but I have days it feels better, and I keep exercising it so it won't freeze up on me. Guess I will have to make a trip to my doctor if we come home in October. I was going to try to get out of a trip to California because it is so far, but it will be worth it to feel better. I thought I was through with the shoulder business when I had the surgery done on the left shoulder. Aren't we lucky that we never had these problems when we were young? Poor Papa suffered so much, and I often think that if we could have had the modern medicine of today, he wouldn't have had so much pain.

Do you hear from the rest of the family? Bud wrote to me and sent the pictures he took at your house when we were there. I answered him but have not received a reply. Jim and John write very sparingly.

I was in a big way cleaning up the house today when they shut my water off and had to stop. I got caught with Pine-Sol all over my hands and had to use some of our drinking water to wash them. We buy our drinking water in five-gallon drums. It is supposed to be delivered on Monday, and I try to keep a minimum of three drums on hand at all time. During Ramadan, our delivery service didn't come for two weeks, and naturally we ran out and had to buy some at the market. The nurses say that living here in the desert a person should consume at least four liters of liquid per day to keep from dehydrating.

We are looking forward to our trip with Jean and Edna, especially I because I haven't been out of the Kingdom for eight months. To stay on an even keel, it is almost necessary to get out of here every six months. That is probably why they give us R & R every six months. We have just been waiting for Jean and Edna to get their act together.

The last time Thomasene called, she told me about the cruise you and she are planning in November. Sounds wonderful, and I know how much fun you two will have. I have very fond memories of our cruise up the Mississippi, and I think it will be even more fun to go down the river and end up in New Orleans.

Did I tell you that James finally had a trip to England and was able to have a visit with Chuck? I think I wrote you that Chuck had gone to London in February to work with David, the Jaguar mechanic. Anyway, James had a trip to Cambridge to take a GIII aircraft for maintenance, and then he went on down to Cobham to see Chuck. They had an enjoyable visit for several days. Chuck says he likes England, but he doesn't think much of David. Apparently, David would rather drink than to take care of business, so Chuck is going to go back to Houston soon.

Is there anything you want us to purchase for you in England? If you think of anything, you can always call Jean before she leaves, and we can look for it for you. It will be easy to buy there because we can have things shipped back to the States whereas here, we can't ship anything. Jean and Edna leave for London on July 1.

I can't think of anything else of much interest. James is out flying today. He had a trip to Dhahran. That word looks misspelled, but it is correct according to the map.

We both send our love, and say hello to Tom and the family.

Love,
Charlotte

485

CAF Letter:
Riyadh, Saudi Arabia
June 16, 1988

Dear Al,

You have been on my mind all morning, so I decided the best way to spend the day is to write a long overdue letter. Your birthday was sometime this month, so best wishes for a happy birthday a little late.

James and I are looking forward to seeing Jean and Edna on July 2 in London where we are meeting for a tour of the British Isles. It will be more exciting for me, considering I have been in these four walls and a walled compound for nine months; however, James gets out a lot, otherwise he would find staying here most difficult. Like today, James is in Malaga, Spain. They left yesterday to pick up a patient to be returned to Riyadh. There was also a body to be brought back, but at the last minute, it was decided to ship it via commercial carrier. Just from the sound of it, there was probably an automobile accident involved. Recently, James had four days in London with his youngest son, Chuck, and while he was there, he bought another Jaguar.

We are now the owner of three Jaguars, and we found out that the two purchased outside of the United States cannot be shipped into the States after July 1, 1988. Only dealers can now import cars, and the cost of freight to and from London has doubled since we shipped the car from Houston in October 1987. That car can be shipped back into the United States because it already has a Texas registration.

Chuck thinks he has a buyer for the old car. Recently, James was in Basel, Switzerland, and ran into a fellow pilot from France who is a collector of Jaguars, and he was very interested in that particular model. This man's surname is Kahn, and aside from being a pilot, he owns jet aircraft and is a wealthy businessman. Well, anyway, his agent in London got in touch with Chuck, and they are going to look at the car. Hopefully, it will sell, and we can have that headache off our minds. There is a long story around that car, and I will tell you briefly about it.

James shipped it to his Jaguar mechanic friend, David, so he would work on it, as the expression goes fine-tune it. James kept sending David money to buy parts, etc., but he never seemed to have it running. James sent Chuck over to learn the mechanics of Jaguars from David. David had ten years' experience training at the factory and is a very good Jaguar mechanic. James knew him in Houston and saw evidence of David's skills. Making a long story short, Chuck found out from one of David's friend the real reason the car was not running was because David blew up the engine on the freeway doing 165 miles per hour. David has a drinking problem and was driving the car around and spending the money on everything except repairing the car. Chuck has overhauled the engine with a minimum of instruction or help from David and now has the car running in good shape. Maybe that was the best experience Chuck could have had in the learning of the Jaguar mechanics field, so James feels that his efforts have not been in vain with Chuck. The boy needs to build self-confidence and further develop the schooling he has already had in mechanics. He needs a means of supporting himself. Driving a wrecker in Houston is starvation wages and a dead-end street. That is the job he has had for some time. Chuck is young and has much potential, and maybe this little venture will add to his development. Just getting out of Houston for a while and traveling should help his perspective.

Al, I will be looking forward to your next letter and statement.

Dear Nancy,

Old ladies forget some time, and I cannot remember if I thanked you for sending the Bromar ink. It was most enjoyable reading and was fun to see some familiar faces. Looks like BFS better get off the stick and report news from their division. They were about the only division not reported. It would be interesting to know what is happening there, but maybe they don't want anyone to know for sure.

We have on our schedule this fall for James to be sent to FlightSafety school in Savannah, Georgia, again. By that time, I will be ready for another trip out of here, so I plan to come home with him. After school is over the end of October, we will have twenty-one days of vacation time. It is our intention to spend a couple of weeks in Texas looking for a house to buy or at least explore the town of Austin. Then James wants to attend a computer convention in Las Vegas starting on November 14. I will need to be in Los Angeles to see my doctor on either November 17 or 18, so maybe we can all get together while we are there. I swore that after our last trip, I would not try to cover so much traveling when we were in the States, but it cannot be avoided this time, and I would rather beat myself to death traveling than to stay here. James's contract is up on January 31, 1989, but that is not to say we will actually leave here then. There is a ninety-day clause on his contract that can be invoked if GAMA feels like enforcing it, and it is done quite often to other people, so it may be April before we can leave.

The other day, one of management approached James to see if he would be interested in a deal of being here six months and off for six months after our present contract is over. I know how badly he hates to hang it up because once he quits flying jets and does not go to FlightSafety school ($10,000 per year to stay current), he will be through. As long as he can pass the physical test, I guess, why not continue? Maybe being off for six months at a time would be a better way to ease out. Total retirement is not too appealing to James, so I can tell that he might be interested in their offer.

Looks like this letter is long enough, so before I bore you too badly, I will sign off.

Let us hear from you both soon. We send our love, and hope to see you over margaritas this fall. That certainly is a pleasant thought!

Love,
Charlotte

PS Since the rest of this page is blank, I will write some trivia.

There is a birthday party tonight for a couple of fellows, and our invitation read Black Tie. Since we have a different English language interpretation from the Brits, I asked as to what it meant. My answer was, everyone was to wear a black bow tie. Seems that the nurses have little outfits made much like the playboy bunnies wear only with stocking supporters, and they wear bow ties. Sounds cute, but there isn't a figure in the bunch qualified to wear such a costume. I definitely will have to take some pictures. James probably won't get home in time for the party, so I will have to go with Rosalind and Doug Acker, my friends from Savannah, Georgia.

Incidentally, we can buy roses in the market over here. They cost about $1.25 a piece, so once in a while, I treat myself to roses if someone else doesn't buy them for me. They have beautiful long stems and will last for three or four days if cared for properly. You can hardly beat the price either.

JDF Letter:
Riyadh, Saudi Arabia
June 26, 1988

To: Major Shablan, Project Director
Cc: Robert Braden, Project Administrator
Subject: Dispatching and Coordination of Medevac Missions
From: James D. Fox, Captain, Fixed Wing, Medevac

Dear Sir:

It is with regret that I write this letter. Yesterday, the patient that I was dispatched to pick up in Sharurah expired on the ground in Sharurah. The patient's doctor was upset with the Medevac operation and myself in particular.

The doctor had the mistaken idea that he had spoken to me on the telephone while coordinating the pickup of his patient. He told me that he was told on the phone that "he must have the patient on the airport ramp at exactly 1415Z because Medevac is very busy and has many other appointments and can't wait."

The patient was a baby, less than one day old, and was being kept alive with the hospital's ventilator. The doctor removed the baby from its life support system to take it to the airport so as to arrive at exactly 1415Z. My arrival at Sharurah according to my aircraft logbook was 1425Z. According to the doctor, his patient expired because it was off its life support system too long.

It has been my practice, for long before my arrival in Saudi Arabia, to give estimates regarding my arrival and departures as accurately as possible. Some aircrews give false estimates on purpose to insure that ground crews would be in place when they arrive or depart. This has never been my practice. The 1415Z time that the doctor used to defend his patient's expiration must have come from the time that I gave to Romeo Base (Riyadh) just prior to departing Riyadh Air Base. The time was based on my *estimate* for arriving in Sharurah. As you may be aware, a trip to Sharurah is not just another routine mission. Communication is far from routine, and continuous contact with air traffic control is impossible. Therefore, the cockpit is very busy with efforts at maintaining some sort of contact with ATC by relay or with other agencies, like Khalid Approach, Killer 1Radar, etc. This is further complicated by the fact that there is no contact at the airport of destination. Updating estimates is sometimes impossible.

The NOTAMS were examined prior to departure and indicated that the only landings permitted were from east to west. This added suspicion to my mind as to airport and runway condition. I felt obliged to make a low pass before landing. This was done and may have added an additional five minutes to our landing time.

After landing, I took the aircraft to the terminal, which was found to be deserted. There was noted some activity at the far east end of the airport near the fire department. I made contact with them on 121.9 megahertz, and they told me to follow a fire department vehicle to their ramp. This I did and found the ambulance there. This probably took another five minutes of time. With all factors considered, it was a good trip.

This letter is in no way an effort to explain away any guilt on my part because I have none, but it is an explanation of what happened in case you have any inquires. Furthermore, it is an appropriate time for me to make some observations that might improve the future operations of this kind for Medevac.

In the first place, the coordination with the patient's doctor was poor. The doctor should not have been told that we couldn't wait for his patient's arrival at the airport.

In the second place it seems to me, considering the critical needs of the patient that some effort could have been made to take the portable ventilator from the aircraft to the hospital to collect the patient. There would have been no need for the patient to remain off its support system in that case. We have done exactly this at other times.

In the third place, *estimates* are only that—*estimates*—and should never be used as hard times, especially in life-or-death situations. In a life-critical situation, I would give a time that was far enough in advance so that I could be assured that I would be sitting on the ramp and ready when that time arrived. In my past career, when I was dispatched to pick up VIPs, it was customary for me to arrive at least two hours before the assigned departure time because my passengers were too important to be kept waiting. In case of weather problems, it was common for me to leave the preceding day. It was as effort to make absolutely sure that the aircraft and crew were in place and ready at the predetermined departure time. Hard arrival and departure times take extreme measures.

In the fourth place, it seems to me that entirely too much responsibility is left in the hands of Romeo Base. Romeo Base either has been given too much responsibility or has assumed too much. I try not to get into areas of medical decisions. My area of decisions is in the aviation field. It seems to me that all too many aviation and medical decisions are being made by Romeo Base. There is a question in my mind of whether or not they are qualified to make such decisions.

I felt emotionally down from the experience. The baby may or may not have survived under the best conditions. I would like to have given it a better chance but was unable to do so for the reasons stated above.

Signed:
James D. Fox, Captain, Fixed Wing, Medevac

Dispatch:
Riyadh, Saudi Arabia
June 30, 1988

TO THE DESERT FOX FAN CLUB,

Well, Riley Boy, I've been trying to get this letter off for a couple of weeks, and every time I start, it turns into another article of philosophy. That's as good a description as any I guess. This time the effort will probably work because I don't have time for any foolishness. I've got to get right down to it because we leave tonight at 2300 for the UK. We are going to join a couple of Charlotte's girlfriends from California for a twenty-one-day tour of the UK, including Scotland and Wales.

This is a bone fide tour, so we can't be late, or it's a no-show. You know, if this Tuesday, we must be in Edinburgh or something like that. We received your letter just a week ago that had been mailed in March, I believe. We received a letter two days before that had been mailed in December. The censors must be getting caught up on their reading. One letter had coffee stains and looked like it had suffered a hard time on the way here.

Anyway, you never said who the check was from! The $2,000 one, that is. If it was from a Mr. Eddie Sanchez, then you'll get a laugh out of this. I called several times and never could get in touch with you to see if the check from Sanchez had arrived. It is for grazing privileges on the ranch in New Mexico. I called Mr. Sanchez in February and gave him a deadline to pay the money, which was over a year overdue. It was due in December of 1986. He assured me he would mail it. Of course, I've been in contact with him before on this matter, so it wasn't something new. Failing to receive the check or any information on its presence in Houston, I had a lawyer in Albuquerque to file on him for nonpayment of lease money and start eviction proceedings. What a laugh. He is going to swear that he paid the money, but his canceled check is not going to have my signature on it. Don't worry, I'll make it right, but the more I thought of it, the funnier it got. You couldn't ever plan a scam like that and make it work on purpose, but accidentally, it works fine.

I have a copy of Word Perfect 4.2 for you and the documentation. I got it for myself but decided to stay with good old Word Star 2000 + Version 3.0. They are all getting so big and complicated that learning a new procedure is a real pain. Besides, I don't have the inclination to keep learning the new ones. It cuts down on the time left for real productive writing. Speaking of that, I've had to settle lately for just outlines. I can't seem to get the time to do a finished article or story, so I do an outline, which will preserve the thoughts and facts, if any, and can be expanded later.

I never heard any more from Keegan on the job offer I called him about. It was a chance for him to check out as captain on a Gulfstream II, but I guess he felt it was too far down the path.

At any rate, he made the comment about my "mystery flight" story, "When are you gonna quit fooling around and get around to the real story of the old Humble aviation department?" Enclosed is a copy of the outline, which is my beginning. You may note that it doesn't go past 1986. Handle this carefully, but I would like some additional notes from Keegan or whoever is knowledgeable and willing in the area. The outline will reveal some of my thoughts and the general direction of the story. The final draft of course will be greatly expanded. Now is the time for input from any that wish to add their two cents.

As to the above, it would never be my intention to hurt anyone's feelings, but I know you can't tell a story without someone disagreeing with some part of it. The original participants didn't agree on what was going on when it was going on, so I'll have to be prepared for great disagreement.

I intend to make the story about a fictional flight department, but all will be able to read between the lines. There will be a note in the foreword or preface of the story to the effect that names and places have been changed to protect the guilty, the innocent don't need protection, but if the reader thinks this story is a fantasy, then they certainly don't know anything about *corporate aviation*.

One of the interesting things to me is the large number of aviation departments that will fit the same pattern as the old Humble Company's. It will be my effort not only to tell the story in an amusing fashion (hopefully), but I will try and explain why the aviation departments so often are managed by the wrong people. Surely, there must have been many like myself that spent many frustrating hours trying to figure it all out. Well, I think I know. We will just have to wait and see.

My son, Chuck, is doing well in London. I visited with him for a few days about three weeks ago. In fact, we bought another Jaguar. It is an XJS 1976 and a real beauty. The plan was for Chuck to bring it back with him and sell it in Houston. Twenty-four hours after buying the thing, I checked with Houston for final details, and they told me to forget it. The new US Custom regulations go into effect July 1, 1988, and the car would have to be cleared by US Customs prior to that for an exemption.

Oh well, just another of Fox's frustration in trying to own a twelve-cylinder auto. I can sell it in the UK, no problem. In the meantime, Chuck is having a nice time driving it around the UK. He is going to meet Charlotte and me in the morning at Heathrow. I have ridden with him around the English countryside and am impressed. The boy does a good job maneuvering around on the wrong side of the street.

Yes, Riley boy, I could teach a course on international procedures, although I would not intend to compete with the fellow that taught my course there in

Houston last year. His replacement taught one afternoon and was definitely third rate. Teaching is a lot more than knowing the facts, right?

Speaking of teaching, my flight instruction has finally been activated. I have three full-time students and a hangar full more waiting their turn. I got into it reluctantly, but the effort has been more than worthwhile. For the first time in a long time, I feel that I am able to pass something along to someone that needs what I know and appreciates me giving it. It was never my intention to come to the Land of the Sand and Sun (where the stars come out at night, and we all have fun) and teach Saudis to fly Gulfstreams. What an aircraft for primary flight instruction! It goes something like this:

"Okay, Daghi, this is going to be a crosswind takeoff. You know to hold the ailerons like a turn to right into the wind and be ready to hold left or the opposite direction rudder, don't you?"

"Yes, Captain."

"Okay, then here we go."

"It's pulling to the left, Daghi, give it more rudder. More rudder, Daghi, it's still pulling to the left. Ailerons right, Daghi, you're holding them the wrong way."

"Captain, you are confusing me."

"Never mind that. It's V6, so rotate."

"Okay, Daghi, we're out of the traffic pattern, so put it on autopilot and tell me about how I am confusing you."

"But, Captain, you were telling me the wrong ailerons and rudder to hold!"

"Daghi, we were taking off on 34 center, which way was the wind from?"

"I don't remember, Captain."

"Does 310 sound familiar to you?"

"Yes, yes, Captain, that is it!"

"No, Daghi, the wind was from 010, not 310. That's the reason the aircraft was trying to go to the left. If the wind had been from 310, we would have been trying to go to the right, okay?"

"Captain, those guys in the tower are very confusing, I can't understand what they are saying."

"Daghi, they are all Saudis today. You mean you can't understand your own people?"

"They don't speak good English. They should be run off and replaced with some Americans."

"No, Daghi, that's backward. The Americans were here doing it first, they were run off so your people could do it."

"Well, I don't care, they can't speak good English, and they all should be run off straightaway."

"Okay, Daghi, well, you got it into the air, and we didn't hurt anyone, so can you tell me what you learned today about crosswind takeoffs?"

"Yes, Captain. Never believe a Bedouin working in the tower."

That's a little of what it's like, but some of them are coming along very well. There have been two to check out as captains recently, and all were sure they would never make it when I first got here. Slow progress, but progress at any rate.

Time is getting on. Say hello to all who care and wave at the rest. Best regards to all. Perhaps we'll see you in September, October, or November, not sure about it yet, but it won't be all that long.

Sincerely,
James D. Fox
Note the address:
James D. Fox, LTC, USAR
USMTM BOX 1463-R
APO NY 09038-5364

Mark the letter First Class and no more than twelve ounce. Regular US postage. I thought I wrote you about that. Anyway, the USAF will probably do a better job of getting it here than the other guys.

Dispatch:
Riyadh, Saudi Arabia
June 6, 1988

TRAFALGAR TOUR OF THE UK
OR
TWENTY-ONE DAYS ON A BUS

You can't be of little faith or lacking in fortitude. You can't be indecisive or of little cash assets because you will need all of the above and perhaps more to make the Great United Kingdom Trafalgar tour!

There will be twenty-one days of travel, castles, abbeys, palaces, churches, medieval history, Scotch broth, and minestrone soup. Yes, it is a sizable chunk to bite off. The beginning is filled with energy and expectation. After about seventeen days, those feelings are replaced with sore backsides and the desire to see no more castles, abbeys, palaces, ancient churches, or hear anymore medieval history for some time to come. We felt we could do without Scotch broth and minestrone soup for a while as well.

If this is going to be considered a factual tale, then a little truth must be added from time to time. It was a great trip! I wouldn't take a million dollars for the experience or give a dime to do it all over again. Strange, but it seems that I said about the same thing for the time I spent in the army. How can I expect to explain what it was like to be in the army? How can I expect to explain what it was like to take a concentrated course in English history, travel over three thousand four hundred miles in a bus, stay in sixteen different hotels, all in twenty-one days? Both questions have the same answer, and that is, you can't. But what follows is my humble attempt to relate to you, my tolerant friends, a small portion of the second experience and none of the first. The experience that I refer to is the tour around the United Kingdom, of course.

I have made several previous trips to England and have spent as much as a week seeing the countryside, but my wife and I felt the need to see more of the country and its people. We have considered renting a cottage and living there for a year. The problem was that we didn't know where that year should be spent. Our solution was to take the UK tour and use it to find a place that we would like to spend more time. It was a good plan. We had been advised by the Brits that we work with to try the Devon area. Devon is a county on the southwest portion of England and is very busy in the summer months. We picked a place we would like to return to, but it wasn't Devon. I'm getting ahead of the story, but perhaps the results of our study should be left for the end, not the beginning.

How Do You Pick a Tour?

If you are expecting a scientific answer to the above question, then you got a free expecting coming. Charlotte's two girlfriends in California did all the research and took care of all the booking details. That may ruin the effect, but one of the primary reasons that I agreed to the plan was that it was going to cover just what I wanted to see. This was reinforced by the knowledge that Charlotte wanted to go, and I felt it would be especially good for us to share the experience with friends. So there you have it: if you want a perfect trip, let someone else do all the work, then just tag along with them. The secret's out. That is how to plan a tour.

Okay, Let's Get Started

We left Riyadh at 02:45 for London, SV Flight 033. The flight is forty-five minutes late in departing (Saudi Airlines Flight 033). Our arrival in London on Thursday morning was just right to coincide with the opening of the airport. Then we were greeted with one-hour long lines at Immigration, Saudis cutting the line just like back in Riyadh. Charlotte winked at the little Saudi boys.

Chuck, my youngest son, met us and found the hotel in almost two hours. He was driving "his" XJS (1976 twelve-cylinder Jaguar). Didn't tell you about the XJS? Well, it was an investment. I intended to ship it back to the States when we went home, but the import law changed the same week that I bought the can. They made it legal only for dealers to make the import. One step forward and two steps backward. Chuck said that he loved the car, made his Trans-Am back in Houston look and run like a piece of junk! Quite a statement from Chuck! Charlotte sat in the backseat with the bags and her chin between her knees.

Stopped for gas and bought a map.

The Ramada Hotel in Londonhad our reservations, but they didn't have any record of the Trafalgar tour or our friends from California, Edna, and Jeannie. That seemed strange since we knew they were staying at the same hotel. Their reservations were supposed to have been made by the tour group. Surely, the Ramada should know all about the tour since the tour was starting there. Well, that's what the brochures said.

Okay, so we are a little early. I spent Thursday, Friday, and Saturday selling the XKE, the one I had shipped in from Houston. My jaguar mechanic friend David had found a fellow that dealt in secondhand Jaguars, and he was interested in my Jag. It was unique because it had Texas license plates, a right-hand drive, and air-conditioning. The earlier deal with my acquaintance Khan didn't come to fruition (I love those kinds of words, don't you?).

I made the final deal to the used Jag dealer Charles Robinson for £4,800 (pounds). One more of my headaches gone.

Charles had an interesting collection of Jaguars. I took many photos. The way he got into the restoration business was interesting. He collected five old Jaguar XKEs and decided to give them all to a restoration company. In exchange, they were to restore two for him. They restored and sold his cars and then declared bankruptcy. All he ever received was half of one chassis. He still has it just the way he got it—a reminder of how he got into the business. I met Charles on Thursday afternoon. I went there to accept his offer of £5,000 that he had made to Chuck earlier. Before I left, I had agreed to let him have it for £4,800. I'm still not sure how that happened. Maybe I danced myself around the room on that one.

I had forgotten to bring the title with me, but he wasn't too interested in my Texas title. All he wanted was a bill of sale from me and a slip from the Customs people saying that the duty had been paid. That's the way they sell cars in the UK. It is very simple. We were supposed to bring the car over the next day, which we failed to do because of too many trips to London and going to bank.

I converted my British money to US money at 1.7045; by that evening, it had dropped to 1.6905. Sometimes moving fast can be a definite advantage. You can't get a bank draft on foreign currency. They have to be ordered, and it takes a couple of days. If you know where the main bank is and have an account in it or one of its branches, then they can issue the draft, but the branches cannot. So I was doing a lot of running around while Charlotte was shopping!

We started early and took almost all day on Saturday just to deliver the XKE. David had found some help to deliver my XKE to the dealer. The driver of the van pulling the trailer[23] with the Jag hadn't been to Charlie's place before. The directions there were as complicated as a lawyer's will, so we said that we would follow him to the first petrol station, then he would follow us to Charlie's place. Naturally, he lost us before we ever got to the petrol station. We knew that we would never see him again.

---

[23]   Peter, the driver, and Austin, a master mechanic for the McClarion racing team, who had volunteered to stay off the tour this year because most of the money comes from bonuses when they win. He thought they didn't have a good chance this year. They have been winning steady, and he's sorry he didn't go.

"My XKE. I loved that car. Just couldn't keep it running."

We drove around for fifteen minutes just looking for him. We finally gave up and went to Charlie's place. There was the van and the Jag. The driver had been there for about fifteen minutes. In the fifteen minutes that they had been there, they had volunteered the information on all the crappy work that David had done on the car. Well, what are friends for, eh? Anything to help a sale. Charles wanted to start the engine, but I said no because I wanted the money first. The deal had been for as is where is. The dealer insisted that the deal was set, and he just wanted to hear what it sounded like.

He started it up, and it sounded fine to me, but Charles noted the slow rise in oil pressure to sixty pounds. I stated it had always done that. All the instruments are slow, voltage, gas, etc. We went over and started another Jag up, and the pressure was immediately to eighty pounds, so at least the buyer is not unaware. Chuck figures that the dealer already has another engine to go in it. I remembered when David dropped that engine of mine on the driveway back in Houston on August 1984. The engine and transmission fell eighteen inches to the pavement due to a malfunction of the engine lift. It must have hit hard enough to warp the case without cracking it. That would have caused pressure on the crankshaft and all kinds of other problems.

We found that Customs had charged us too much on arrival, and we should have approximately £500 refunded. The check will have to come to David. The final paperwork will go to Charles.

"Chuck and "his" Jaguar"

Next, I need to sell the XJS that Chuck is driving before he leaves to go back to the States. Chuck is going to do a little work on the XJS and hope to get £3,000. I must be dreaming.

Charles, the dealer, offered me £2,000 on the XJS, admitting that it was worth £3,000, but just not enough slack for him to work with there. I couldn't agree with his math, so I turned down his offer. As a result, Chuck didn't sell the XJS until the first part of August; a month later, Chuck took £2,100 for it. The dealer knew what it was worth a month before.

Charles had a 1946 Jaguar convertible, chassis number 001. It was the first convertible that Jaguar ever built. The interior was all rotted out, but it was all original rot. He bought it for £10,000 and was putting in the Christie's auction around the middle of July. He hoped it would fetch £20,000. The motor still would start up and run. It belonged to someone in Hollywood until 1955. He didn't know the history after that. We read in the paper later that someone else had a 1936 Mercedes convertible entered in the Christie's auction. It was not the first one built by Mercedes, and the engine had not known to have run since 1955. According to the *London Times*, it was sold to a bidder by phone for £1,588,000 ($2,699,600 US). I did not hear what Charles got for the Jag convertible. Maybe there was not enough money left after the Mercedes sold.

"Jaguar convertible, chassis number 001, and my son Chuck"

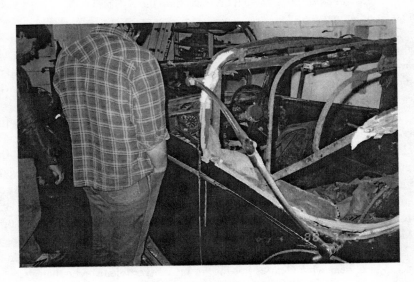

"The Jag convertible needs a little work."

While I'm doing all this trading, Charlotte found her way to Harrods. She had lunch there and bought a few things including a bow tie for me. I was impressed that she handled herself so well in London. She caught the cab at the hotel, went to Harrods, and returned all by herself—not bad.

"The engine looks ready to go."

Thursday night, Charlotte, Chuck, David, Beverly, and I went to Chi-Chi's in downtown London. It is a Mexican food place just off Piccadilly Circus. The food was good. David drove us down there in a small Mercedes, customer car.

Clothes once removed from a suitcase and put into a closet grow like mold; they never ever fit in the suitcase again.

The only thing worse than eating at Ramada is a Holiday Inn, anywhere. But it's all relative, I guess. I wish it had been a relative that ate that fish I had the other night at the Ramada. Charlotte had a tuna steak! I never heard of such a thing. My advice to you is don't ever try to eat something if it is called a tuna steak. It will be bad for you. It looks like a beef steak. Charlotte only had two or three bites, and she said that she couldn't eat anymore because it was blistering the top of her mouth. Well, she has allergies, so I tried a bite, and it blistered the top of my mouth. It wasn't hot like Mexican food. It just blistered the roof of my mouth. The tongue was okay.

Saturday night, we found the Chelsea Steak House. The food was great, even if the sidewalks were rolled up. The man at the off-license place (liquor store) was helpful in our locating this place. We told him were looking for a good restaurant. He asked if we were interested in ethnic food. We considered that we were not. We figured that we had eaten all the ethnics we cared for. He sent us directly to the Chelsea Steak House. It was excellent food and not expensive considering where we were. The steak was £7.40, plus veggies, plus, plus.

Sunday, we watched the tennis matches. We liked the Swede and hoped he would win. It took him several starts with the rain out. Our Swede finally won. The Swede doubles beat the Germans.

July 2, 1988

Saturday, Day 1: The tour starts from the United States. Jeanie and Edna leave LAX(Los Angeles) in the evening hours to arrive in London Heathrow around noon on Sunday. It's about an eight-hour flight, plus an eight-hour time loss in crossing time zones.

July 3, 1988

Sunday, Day 2: Jeannie and Edna arrived late in the evening at 7:30 p.m. Their trip from Los Angeles was delayed by one of the passengers who had a heart attack, and they diverted to Detroit. No one was allowed to leave the airplane. Then they had to make another stop in New York for a crew change. The first crew ran out of duty time. What a joke, but the girls were delayed about seven hours, and there was no one to meet them at the airport! They were a little hot.

July 4, 1988

Monday, Day 3: We went on a half-day tour of London. It was mostly boring, and we had to wait in the London traffic. You would have thought that they would have known a Monday morning in a large city is going to have traffic problems, especially if it rains. It rained.

My first thought was to skip the tour, and as it turned out, that was my best thought. We visited Westminster Abbey and noted that the largest monument and statue in the abbey was of a very popular politician. The statue was of a man in a half-reclining position on a lounge. There were two female and one male statue of slaves standing by his side. The man was *Charles James Fox, born January 24, 1749, NS, died September 13, 1806.*

About the time, it started to really pour down rain. The tour guide dumped us off the bus to see the Tower of London. We found out later that she had no intention for us to go inside; we were just to have a look from the outside in the rain. What a dumb idea that was! As soon as we got back on the bus, the rain quit. Jeannie and Edna got lost, so I had to go find them. They didn't get lost from each other.

Charlotte says she knows why our forefathers left the UK. They were the smart ones. Of course, her father came from Belgium. That didn't count. She was just speaking in general terms.

The tour just dropped us off downtown, a couple of blocks from Harrods. Never thought a tour would just drop you off without taking you back to where we were picked up from. We had lunch at a pub and caught a cab back to the hotel. The cab tab was £4.90, and I gave him £6.00. The wind was blowing hard.

Now we are all back at the Ramada Inn West in Fulham. We know it well and how to find it from several directions. Their restaurant was the pits, but then it's a Ramada, right? Even in London, we should know better.

The tour included the bed and breakfast, also dinner. The breakfasts at the Ramada were sort of like C rations and left on the hall on the floor in front of your door. Don't worry about anyone taking them. Are you kidding?

We were hoping the rest of the tour will be better than the first day. Well, so far, the hotel didn't know about the California girls' reservation on the tour. The first part of the tour was mostly riding on the bus and sitting stopped in traffic. When we finally got off the bus, we were soaked in the rain. The girls got lost because of poor instructions from the tour guide, and then they just dropped us off downtown for us to make our way home as best we could. Yes, let's hope for some better days to come.

July 5, 1988

Tuesday, Day 4: Wakeup call at 6:00 a.m., bags in the hall by 7:30 a.m., and on the bus by 8:15 a.m. It was to become a regular thing for the next three weeks—London, Oxford, Blenheim Palace, Stratford-upon-Avon, and Birmingham.

"Shakespeare's Home. We stopped by, but no one was home."

July 6, 1988

Wednesday, Day 5: Birmingham, Coventry, Bronte countryside, City of York with its Shambles and famous Minster, overnight inn (?), I've already forgotten. It was just one church after another until after just a few days, I was able to replace the tour guide with description of where we were and the dates that made this place famous. In fact, I started acting as I was the guide and was giving my own description of where we were and what we were seeing. It was just in fun, and I didn't think anyone was paying attention to what I was saying until we got off the bus in front of one more church and Edna asked, "James, what is this place famous for?"

"What are you asking me for? I just got here." That's about the time that she started calling me "Sir James."

"My first impression was something put up by McDonald's for the kids to play on."

"They do get to all looking the same."

"Charlotte and Jeanie did have fun . . . the bags."

"Some of the sights were intriguing. You can't see their bags."

Well, I can't go on with this. It was pack your bags, get on the bus, see more of the same things you saw yesterday, then get off the bus, go to the hotel, and unpack your bags. It was definitely not a trip I would choose to take again. There was learning associated with the experience. Edna, Jeannie, Charlotte, and I always shared a table and found that we could not get coffee served with our breakfast. It was always brought around after the meal, not before or during. One morning just

505

after we were seated, I got up and served the table with coffee. The result was that we didn't get any breakfast. The waitresses saw us drinking coffee and decided that we were through with breakfast.

We did see some pretty countryside, but twenty-one days was too much of packing and unpacking. I took thirteen rolls of 35mm color film with thirty-five pictures per roll. That's a lot of pictures. Back in Riyadh after they were developed and I started looking through them, I was struck with the fact that indeed they all looked alike. I never even opened all the folders of pictures. You couldn't hire anyone to look at them. Who wants to see someone else's vacation pictures, especially when they all look alike?

It was a relief when we were once more back in our A villa in Riyadh.

CAF Letter:
Riyadh, Saudi Arabia
July 30, 1988

Dear Arlin,

I know it has been a while since I wrote, and it is my turn to answer you last letter. As James would say, we have been out of pocket. We just returned from a three-week tour on the United Kingdom. We covered England, Scotland, and Wales. It was very interesting but very tiring. Sleeping in a different bed every night for three weeks and packing and repacking luggage every day becomes a tiresome chore. To top it all off, there were forty-three people on the tour bus passing colds around, and naturally toward the end when I began to tire, I caught a cold. At least James waited until he got home, but then he couldn't fly. Oh well, everything has passed, and James went to work today, and I am going to try to catch up on my correspondence.

James has had an offer for another job in Jeddah but has told them he doesn't want it. They called again this week and want him to submit a resume, which he has not done. I think he is mulling it over in his mind because the offer is a good one and pays more money. We are so ready to come back to the States to live, but there the money steadily goes out, and here we can save it or do anything we want to in traveling. As always, it will be a big decision to make. There are two strikes against living in Jeddah because it is hot and humid all year around. We were there visiting friends in April, and it was 104 degrees Fahrenheit and about 90 percent humidity. Your body felt sticky even in air-conditioned rooms.

We want to go to Austin, Texas, and look for a house to buy. Even if we stay in Saudi Arabia, we need a home, and real estate is steadily going up. It is either now or never for what we can afford. Texas has some pluses over California, but climate is not one of them. They do not have a state income tax, and real estate property is less expensive. We can probably buy a two thousand five hundred square feet home with a large lot and double garage for $120,000 in mint condition. That is in Austin and Houston is even cheaper. We, especially me, have chosen not to live in Houston so we can be away from James's ex-wife.

Did I tell you that last year the ex-wife served papers on James when we were at the Fox family reunion in Wichita Falls? He was very embarrassed. She wanted James to pay the income tax of about $25,000 on the lump sum annuity she got from him, which was part of the divorce settlement. We had to interrupt our vacation time so he could spend a week with the attorney preparing for court.

Not only did the judge decide in James's favor, he also allowed James to cancel the insurance policy he was carrying on her through Exxon. Sometimes it doesn't pay to be greedy. If she had not served papers on James, he would never have cancelled the insurance policy, which was a considerable amount. All the way

507

through his divorce, he had tried to be fair on their settlement, but she gave him a hard time, and that is why it dragged out for so long.

I am going to have to mail this through the Saudi post as I cannot get down to the US post office on the military base today.

Keep sending our mail to the APO Box as it is better service to here.

We send our love, and let us hear from you soon. Hope you are both well and that you are making it okay.

Love,
Charlotte

CAF Letter:
Riyadh, Saudi Arabia
July 30, 1988

Dear Edie,

Your letter of July 14 just came in the mail. After I read it, my heart ached for your mother being sick and you having all the responsibility.

My sister, the eldest in our family, is the same age as your mother, and the seventies have not been good to her either. She had open heart surgery with a triple bypass. There have been complications from that as one of the arteries didn't respond properly, and the doctor said she was not in good enough health and strength for a second surgery, so she has been making it on two good bypasses.

Shopping for your gold is no bother. Bartering at the gold souk is about the only type of shopping that I enjoy here in Saudi Arabia, especially if I can find what I am looking for. On my next shopping trip, I will look for the engraved bangle that you want. As a matter-of-fact, I think I will buy one for myself as well. This year, the cost will probably be more for that item, but not much. The cost on the tricolor flexible bracelet (like I was wearing last time) is $297 US. You wanted a mesh bracelet like Riley gave Jan for Christmas, but so far I haven't been able to find one like it. I have two that you may select from if the one you want doesn't show before we come home. One costs $133, and the other one costs $122. These two are narrower than Jan's. I will never be offended if you decide you do not want any of it because I will just keep it for myself. That is the beautiful part about investing in gold; it retains value. Besides, I like to look at it. I cannot remember what your bangle cost, but if you have it in your head, you can add it to two of the above bracelets and get an approximate idea of your costs. Anyway, if you think of anything else, let me know.

We had a most enjoyable vacation in the UK. We left here a few days early before our tour started so we could spend a few days in London. One day when James was busy with his son Chuck selling his Jaguar, I called a cab and went to Harrods on a shopping spree then had lunch downstairs in the pub by the men's department. I think it was called the Green Room. Ask James sometime about the tie I bought him at Harrods.

We must have retraced your steps when we took the city tour that took us by Hyde Park, and then on our extended tour, we stayed two nights in Edinburgh. We both agree with you that the Scottish people are warm and friendly. While in Edinburgh, I shopped for Waterford crystal, and later in the tour, we visited the Wedgwood factory, which was so very interesting. Since I already have a new china set unopened stored in California, I didn't purchase a set of china, but I did buy some coffee mugs in the Kutani Crane pattern and some ginger jars and condiment dishes in the Christmas pattern. Also, during our visits to the woolen mills, we purchased

509

sweaters, kilts, etc. We had everything shipped to the States, and the reduction of the VAT tax paid our freight. I could have probably bought my Waterford cheaper in the States if I could have caught a sale, but it has been my experience that it doesn't go on sale that often, and anyway it was fun to buy it there. I suspect there will be US Customs fees when this arrives in the States, but that is to be expected. That is just part of the trip.

Did I tell you that we are going to look for a home to buy in Austin, Texas, when we come back the next time? We already have real estate people sending us information on the Lakeview area. If we find a place there, you and your husband will have to come and spend a weekend with us sometime, especially when things begin to build up and you need a breather.

Well, Edie, I have a monstrous ironing to attack, and I promised James spaghetti for dinner, so I better close this down.

Incidentally, James will be writing up our trip, so we will send you a copy when he finishes.

We hope all is well with you and your family.

Love,
Charlotte

CAF Letter:
Riyadh, Saudi Arabia
August 1, 1988

Dear Muriel,

When we returned from our trip, your letter was waiting for us. We had an enjoyable trip, but we were glad to get home. It was good to see Jean and Edna. Edna and I picked up a cold, and we had several days of discomfort, then James got it as soon as we arrived here. At least James was able to wait to be miserable at home.

Yesterday, I received an announcement from Anna and Richard on the birth of their baby girl Sarah Elizabeth, born on May 30, seven pounds, nine and a half ounces, and twenty inches long. They didn't say if she was blonde or brunette. This was the sum total of the information they gave. Richard had moved and left no forwarding address back in March of April, and his telephone was disconnected, so I have had to wait all this time to hear about the baby. When he does this, I get so frustrated with him, but in all these years, I have not been able to change his ways. I am just grateful that finally he gets in touch.

We are having a classical Saudi sandstorm today. There have been more of these sandstorms this year than last, so I don't know if last year was an unusually good year or if this is an unusually bad year. Anyway, James is ready to come home. He has been for some time and is finding it hard to finish out his contract. It may all be decided for him if he didn't pass the hearing part of his physical this morning. He didn't pass it yesterday, and the doctor told him maybe because he was flying the day before and had the cold. He should rest overnight, take antihistamines, and then come back this morning for another test. He left here at 7:00 a.m., and it is now 11:00 a.m., and I haven't heard from him. The computer store is near the doctor's office, so maybe he stopped there. When he goes to the computer store, he gets involved in conversation with the owner and becomes unconscious of time. I can expect him when I see him.

I was so mad when I got home and found the enclosed cards in my purse and had not mailed them. I just wasted good stamps, and you never received the cards on schedule after all the effort it took to make sure I did it. I guess that day has arrived when I think I have done something and didn't. That must be what old folks are all about. Is Maxine ready to be sixty yet? How does it feel to have an almost sixty-year-old daughter? Austin was forty last month, and I find that hard to believe.

This letter will have to be shorter than usual as I have a million things to do. Thanks again for the nice letter.

Love,
Charlotte

511

Dispatch:
Riyadh, Saudi Arabia
August 22, 1988

NEW HAVEN, CONNECTICUT, USA

Got the call to tell me I had another trip to the United States. This time it was to be to New Haven, Connecticut. The last time I landed there was in 1968, I believe. It was with Morgan Hendrickson and Doug Brace. We took Vice President Vinn up on a Sunday afternoon. He was to investigate an oil spill. We spent almost a week there in subfreezing temperature, but that's another story.

Well, maybe it's worth telling here.

Monday morning papers in New Haven headlined the oil spill.

"Thousands of water fowl killed by massive oil spill." The headline was accompanied by a pitiful picture of a duck covered in heavy black oil.

Mr. Vinn called me on the phone and said he needed a helicopter to have a look at this massive oil spill. I hired one that would carry about twelve people. Mr. Vinn and I along with a bunch of newspaper and TV reporters boarded for the flight.

We flew up and down the coast of the suspected oil spill for a couple of hours. We found the slick, a small one, and one dead bird. The reporters couldn't believe what they saw. Someone must have exaggerated the facts. The facts were: An Exxon oil tanker was approaching the harbor and navigating by the harbor buoys. One of the critical buoys had come loose from its tether and floated in to the shallow water. The tanker ran aground and spilled some oil. A little. The oil that was spilled was light-yellow-colored heating oil, nothing like the picture shown in the newspaper. Surprise, surprise, another made-up story to embarrass the big oil company.

We sat on the ground for five days while Mr. Vinn dealt with the local officials trying to undo what the newspapers and TV had created. As I said, there were subfreezing temperatures all the time we sat there. Each day, Mr. Vinn thought that he was going to be leaving, so we would pack our bags, go to the airport, get the plane ready, and, with the APU running, spend the day. Late in the afternoon, we would get a call saying that we were not leaving. So we went back to the hotel to get our rooms and spend another night. This went on until Friday when we finally left, but not to Houston, just to Newark—our airport of choice when business was in New York.

The flight to Newark from New Haven, Connecticut, is only about twenty minutes in the GI that I was flying. We had used some fuel out of the right wing by running APU all week, but it wasn't enough to worry about since we were only going to Newark and we would need to top off the tanks when we got there.

ATC (air traffic control) would only clear us to eight thousand feet for the flight, and the air was so choppy, I chose to not use the autopilot, but hand-fly the short trip. Morgan was in the right seat doing his thing of whistling, waving his knees back and forth, and flipping the cover guards on switches—his normal self, the world's oldest teenager. I was busy flying with both hands when the left engine said, "Wow, Wow." I never know why, but as a natural reaction to an engine malfunction on my side, I always turn to look at that engine, especially on a turbo-prop. As I looked, the prop went into feather. When I turned back to the cockpit, I could see that Morgan had just done a manual feather on that engine!

There was no time to do anything else; we were just being cleared for the approach at Newark for a landing to the south. Newark had a ceiling three hundred feet in a hard blizzard of snow and limited visibility, and I'm making an approach on one engine. That's no problem, but when we got to minimum—no runway, no ground, go around! Now I'm making a go-around on one engine. The tower cleared me back to the outer marker for another try.

On the second try, I got it on the ground okay. As Mr. Vinn was leaving the plane, I apologized for the problem. He said, "What problem?"

While on the ground, I wanted to know what happened to that number 1 engine. Doug Brace then told me what happened. It seems that Morgan, the world's oldest teenager, decided on his own to level up the fuel between the left and right wings. The left wing had more fuel than the right because the APU had been using fuel out of the right wing all week in New Haven. So while flipping his switches, he opened the cross-feed valve that runs under the fuselage and connects the two wings. We were taught in school that when you select the switch to open the cross-feed valve, the little light comes on, but that only means that you have selected the switch to the open position, it *does not* mean that the valve actually opened!

The moisture in the jet fuel eventually settles by gravity to the bottom of its container. In this case, that was the lowest point in fuel system, which was the cross-feed valve. The valve was frozen shut and did not open when selected in the cockpit to the open position. Morgan selected the cross-feed switch to open and then turned off the left fuel pump for the left engine, expecting the right fuel pump to supply pressure for both engines through the cross-feed valve, which never opened. His action caused the left engine to begin to fail due to fuel starvation. All he needed to do was turn on the left fuel pump to restore the engine to normal. I didn't notice what he was doing, because he was just humming, whistling, and flipping cover guards like he always did.

I'll leave it to your imagination how I felt about my co-captain, the world's oldest teenager.

Well, that was my last trip to New Haven, and now I've got another one.

Waleed Zahed and I will be prepositioned in London to take the aircraft on to the US Gill, Daghistani, Mammon, Logan, and Qviste will leave here on Tuesday approximately 1700 hours to come to London with the patient. Gill and Daghistani will deplane in London and remain there to relieve myself and Waleed when we return. The engineer and nurses don't get relief.

I've all ready written about problems we had with the aircraft and its intermittent APU in another story, but I'd like to add just another little item.

The runway at New Haven is not half as long as the runways in Saudi Arabia, so for our return, we took a light fuel load and intended to make another stop in Banger, Maine, for the Atlantic crossing. I was letting Waleed fly the empty leg to Bangor, so he would be making the takeoff from what seemed like a very short runway to him.

Back in Riyadh, I had started a little joke one day when just before we launched, I pulled out a little pocket harmonica and played a little tune. My crew wanted to know why.

"Oh, that's just the custom in my country. Lots of captains do that just for good luck."

That's all that was said, no other comment, and from then on, I would often do the harmonica thing, and no one said anything.

That day in New Haven as we turned on to the runway for takeoff, and Waleed looked at that short runway that had buildings on the far end, he hesitated just a moment. When he hesitated, I said,

"Waleed, do you see those buildings down on the far end of the runway?"

"Yes, sir, I do."

"Well, when you get to them, you can kind of turn us up on the left wing and go right between if you can't make it over them, okay?"

After a little more hesitation, Waleed said, "Captain, would you mind playing a little tune on your harmonica?"

CAF Letter:
Riyadh, Saudi Arabia
August 24, 1988

Dear Josephine and Jim,

Your letter came today, Maxine's sixtieth birthday, and it was so welcome. We are sorry to hear about Jim's illness, but it sounds like you have a workable routine.

I will be the next one to be sixty years old, and James will reach it on January 3. Josephine, I cannot remember your birthday, but it seems to me that you were younger than the rest of us. Am I right?

We recently had a letter from Robert Dawson. He keeps in touch, and he said he has slowed down considerably since his retirement. Did I tell you that he had a brain tumor removed? I believe it was several years ago and recovered quite well. He had a few difficulties with memory, but to see him you would never know it. Robert and Lester came to see us at Muriel's home last November when we were there. Maybe I told you already. I am the one with the memory problem, and I haven't had brain surgery.

I thought it was interesting in your letter talking about the Civil War like it was only yesterday. Actually, it does seem that they are still fighting it in the South.

In June 1984, Muriel, Maxine and husband, Stanley James Brown, and I had the opportunity to ride in the paddleboat race from New Orleans to St. Louis for ten nights and eleven days. You probably know of this yearly race between the Mississippi Queen and Delta Queen as this has been a yearly event for some time. Anyway, we had the same feeling on this trip that the Civil War was still foremost in the Southerner's mind.

My paternal grandfather fought in the Civil War, and we stopped in Vicksburg to see him name in bronze in the Illinois Memorial. That was awesome, and my sister Muriel became very emotional. This grandfather was born in Brussels and came to the States as a child. Apparently, his parents settled in Chicago hence his joining the Illinois regiment. The list of names was of the participants of war from Illinois not a list of those that were killed as my grandfather survived and lived to have nine children. In the obituary of my grandfather nearly fifty years later, it mentions that his father was the first person in Brussels to have a printing press. All of this information was turned over to us when my parents died, and as a child in Cedarvale and Corona, the most I ever knew was that my father's mother was from Switzerland and his father was from Belgium. Papa was born in Brooklyn, and as a small child, his father was in business in Paris, so he lived there until he was thirteen, at which time he was sent back to Connecticut to go to school. He finished high and went on to Princeton class of 1904. Already you can see that I am half Yankee.

How did we ever get to Cedarvale? Well, one summer in the early 1900s, I don't know the exact year, my father and his brother decided the fun thing to do would be to go west. They caught the train in New York to ride it as far as it went into Texas. Where it stopped was in a little town called Valentine in or near the Fort Davis Mountains. Actually, it was very near the Mexican border. Probably Valentine was not much more than a railroad stop. Anyway, my father and brother stayed on my mother's uncle's ranch because that was the only accommodations available. My mother, grandmother, and the rest of her children were being provided for by her uncle as her father had disappeared into Old Mexico when she was eight years old and never was heard of again. Mama's family had migrated from the Deep South to West Texas, but I cannot recall which state they came from.

About the time my father arrived, Mama was eighteen years old, and he fell madly in love with her. His brother returned to New York, and Papa stayed to marry Mama. Eventually, when my sister Muriel was a child, they moved to New Mexico to homestead. Papa had fallen further in love with the West and talked about it until the day he died. He started teaching school in Cedarvale in a one-room schoolhouse that had the first through the eighth grade. He said Orville Fletcher was so big he could pick Papa up with one hand. Now you can see that the other half of me is Confederate. In our household, the Civil War was never settled when I lived there, but I heard it discussed many times.

I never was put to the test to see where my loyalties were until the trip up the Mississippi. Part of winning the boat race was the different contests we had onboard each day. One day, the riverboats docked side by side and had a Calliope contest to see which of their musicians were considered the best. During one of their numbers, we were given a choice of flags, Yankee or Confederate, and we were to carry them on a march around the promenade deck. I chose the Yankee flag, and my sister chose the Confederate flag. Funny what comes out at a time like this when there isn't much time for decision and no time to stop and analyze feelings on the subject.

It was so interesting to me that you mentioned you were doing a genealogy as we have just returned from an extensive tour of the United Kingdom where I was searching for some of my roots and James discovered his. We covered England, Scotland, and Wales. We knew that Twyeffort came to the States from Belgium, but one of my cousins in New York that has been working on our genealogy told me he had traced that side back to Wales. A few years ago, one of my friends in California found our name on a business in a little town in Wales. We selected this tour because it would take us to that little town. At the very last minute, the guide changed our route, and we missed it. I was so disappointed as that is not the kind of trip a person takes every day, but sometimes, we just have to swallow our lumps.

When we were going through Westminster Abbey in London, there was a huge bronze plaque in memory of Charles James Fox. James was so impressed because he named his youngest son Charles, and to see both of their given names and surname made him imagine his ancestry came from England. He doesn't have much history on the origin outside of the United States.

On this trip, we visited Plymouth and saw where our forefathers embarked for the United States. There were so many things of interest that we saw it would take more writing than this letter to cover, but I will tell you what interested me greatly. It was the tour through Lord Mountbatten's home. They had displayed a replica of all the crown jewels of the world. I thought the most beautiful were from Russia, Iran, and the diamond tiara that Napoleon gave Josephine. It dazzled me.

Well, Josephine and James, the reason that I have been so long-winded is because I am lonesome. James is flying a mission to New Haven, Connecticut, USA and has been gone for a few days. There is exactly zero that women can do here, so I pass my time by writing letters, reading, watching video movies, and having coffee with the nurses, needlepoint, cross-stitchery, embroidery, and a lot of daydreaming of our new home we plan to have when we come back to Texas.

This year, I had a new granddaughter, Sarah Elizabeth, born on May 30 to my youngest son Richard. She is number four child of his. My other son Austin is not married, so he has not given me any grandchildren, but I am still hoping. He was forty this year, so he is going to have to get going.

James has three boys—Jimmy, Greg, and Charles better known as Chuck. Jimmy has a boy and a girl. Greg has three boys and a girl, and Chuck is not married.

Our dream is to get the two clans together so they can become acquainted. My Richard lives in California, Austin lives in Arizona, and James's children live in Texas.

You two stay in good health and keep those nice letters coming. It is our intention to leave here when James's contract is over in January next year, so maybe we will be able to see you when we return to the United States. It certainly would be fun to have a nice visit.

Love,
Charlotte

Dispatch:
Riyadh, Saudi Arabia
September 6, 1988

NEWSLETTER FROM THE DESERT FOX!

HELLO AGAIN!

I've been trying to get this effort under way for some months now. Perhaps this will be the right time. There is never a lack of items to write about from here in the Land of the Sand and Sun, where the kawajees do the work and the Saudis have the fun. The shooting has stopped temporarily, most of it, that is, and perhaps the Middle East can return to its normal state. No pun intended, but the state of the Middle East is still a great mystery to most Americans, I'm sure.

No, the reason for taking so long to produce this letter is simply that I've been too busy to work on it. Oh, you say you've heard that before? Well, I've certainly used that excuse plenty of times in my life, but in this case, it's near the truth. My story writing has been reduced to making notes and outlines. I'll just have to fill them out later.

The absolute wonder of what happens around me every day has somewhat diminished, but not completely disappeared. There is plenty for me to report to you, but with the passing of time, I'm losing touch with you folks. Losing touch in the sense that it is no longer clear to me what it is you don't know and what it is that you may be willing to believe.

It seems that on each trip back to the States, I have less to say about living in the Middle East. The reason is due to the feeling I have of my audience not believing or just not understanding what I have to say. All here agree to what I have just stated. They agree that after a couple of years here, they have very little to say when they go home. Do you find all this confusing? Perhaps I'm proving my point. I'm sure that much of what I've reported is evaluated as "another one of Fox's windies." None of my friends that lived and worked in the Middle East in the past would voluntarily speak of their experiences without a lot of prompting. You can't prompt people for information unless you know what to ask because if you don't ask the right questions, then you can't expect to get the right answers. It's a catch-22.

Without reporting everyday goings-on here, there is little else happening in our lives. It is true that Charlotte and I went to England for about a month this summer. We took a twenty-one-day guided tour of England, Wales, and Scotland. The tour was by Trafalgar and was well worth the effort. We enjoyed Scotland most of all. The weather was excellent, after Saudi Arabia, and the people were very friendly. The Scottish countryside was also unique and interesting. But to describe the trip would require an extra chapter on its own, so I won't try to complete the description. To sum it up, Charlotte and I were completely satisfied with the trip and its results.

In the first place, it cured us of the notion to move there for a year. In the second place, it revealed the real reason that our forefathers came to America. We felt the time and expense were well worthwhile, and if we go back, it will most likely be to Scotland.

Family news follows: Jimmy, my oldest son, fell and broke his ankle while playing with his children this fall. (It runs in the family.) Chuck, my youngest son, went to England for about six months and is saving his money for a return trip. Ask Chuck, if you see him, how he liked working on Jaguars and Mercedes in England. That will get a rise from him, and if not, then ask him how he would compare driving a Trans-Am to driving an XJS V12 Jaguar. I sponsored Chuck to England for a part of his education. He tells me it was the best part.

Greg, my middle son, is building his own home. He almost severed his left arm at the shoulder with an electric handsaw (skill) while his family looked on. Fortunately, no permanent damage to Greg; however, Mary, his wife, says she may never be the same. Greg estimated that he could finish the house in three months last December. After a year of solid hard work, he now hopes he can finish in three months.

Two of my grandchildren are going to school and doing very well, it seems. The other four grandchildren are staying home and helping make their mother's day happy. Otherwise, no one is getting married or buried. No one is starting to or graduating from college. No one is going into or returning from the military. No one is even pregnant, that we know of. You see, we are a somewhat plain and average family.

Charlotte's children are enjoying good health, I believe. Austin, her oldest, is working in Tucson, Arizona, at a rehabilitation center. His fiancée is working at the same place. We have been told that they will be married soon. They are considering jobs here in Saudi Arabia, doing the same kind of work they are involved with in Tucson. I wonder where they got that idea.

Richard, Charlotte's youngest son, has a new daughter. She was born in May and is a cute little girl. Richard and his wife Anna have four children, one boy and three girls. They are all very nice children. The boy is named Daniel and is eleven, I believe. He and Greg's oldest son David would enjoy each other because they are both studious and well-mannered boys that like to have a good time at the same sort of things. Maybe I can arrange such a meeting sometime. It will take some doing, I guess, Greg and his family live in Houston while Richard and his family live in Los Angeles.

Well, that is it for the annual family letter. A man should never bore his friends with a long annual letter about what his children and grandchildren are doing.

The long annual letter of family doings is compared to the guy that insists on showing his latest "family pictures." His pictures can be produced at the least provocation. I knew a fellow once that carried a picture of his family in his billfold for just such occasions. Anytime that someone in the group produced family pictures, this guy would haul out his family picture and insist that all around agree with his assessment of "Aren't they a beautiful bunch? Have you ever seen such a lovely family?" The recipient always glanced at the photo as a moral and social obligation. What he saw was a toothless old woman and several ugly kids. His mouth would not form words. What he saw was so radically different from what he expected. He didn't dare say what he really thought of the group in the photo, and he needed time to compose an answer. During the period of time while he was thinking of an acceptable response, his face was closely studied by the man that had just produced the family picture. Some of us present could enjoy the discomfort of the new guy that fell for the joke. We had all been taken in before. The picture was not of the man's real family, but just a photo that he carried to show people when they were showing off their own family pictures. It's enough to make a man quit carrying pictures in his wallet.

Will wonders never cease? Technology has finally produced another new electronic device that I can no longer live without. Please note that my new toy, an optical scanner, has made it possible for me to illustrate my text. It is something that I have been dying to try out for a long time. The delay was just waiting for the technology to catch up to my dream. So, for the last few days, I've been perfecting my scanning technique. There are still plenty of cracks that I haven't looked into, but I'm pleased with the preliminary results.

For those that don't know, I did some illustrations in my youth and will be attempting to recapture the long dormant talent. *Recapture* and *dormant* may not be the right words. After some effort, the more proper words might be *death* and *resurrection*. The artist effort was a long time ago.

September 15, 1988

Well, two days have stretched into several days, and my optical scanner technique has not progressed beyond the initial effort. I won't bore you with all the computer technical details, but I'm very frustrated right now. The only thing to do is persevere and solve the problem of the scanned image later. If you're going to work with computers, then you better get accustomed to frustration and grief. It's a part of the game. I have given my final notice to the powers that be here. I told them that I would not be renewing my contract when it expires on the January 7, 1989. Of course they were heartbroken. I am hopeful that they will recover prior to my departure. They must realize that Saudi Arabia will have to press on and take care of its problems whether I remain here or not. A man cannot always expect such accolades at the time of departure from a job.

Sometimes it is enough to learn, at a later time, that upon your departure, it was necessary for the company to hire a couple of new guys to replace you. You may recall that when I retired from Exxon Co. USA, they retired four flight engineers as well. Perhaps that was just a coincidence.

Well, Fox, what was the best part of retiring from Exxon? It would have to be not having to go to Newark anymore. Well, Fox, what was the best part of your flying in the Middle East? It would have to be not having to go to Newark anymore. Can you believe that there are people living here in Saudi Arabia that have never been to Newark? Every real pilot should have his time in Newark listed in a separate part of his resume. There are some people living in Newark because they want to, I've been told. Someday I should write a paper on just that subject.

As for that matter, there are people living here in the Middle East because they want to. I don't fault them for that. I'm just glad that I still have a place to return to that is somewhere else. It's sort of like the monkey that had a date with a skunk. The next day his buddies asked, "Did you enjoy your date with the skunk?" The monkey stated, "Yes, but I think I have enjoyed about all of that I can stand."

The nights are beginning to be cool again, and it is amazing to me how quickly it happens. In a week's time, there is a noticeable decrease in the temperature. There is never a noticeable front or squall line that moves through, but once it changes, then you know that the next season is here. The study of weather patterns across the world's oceans and continents has to be fascinating subject, or don't you agree?

I have been using Version 3.0 of WordStar 2000 Plus for word processing on my computer. Soon after installing the new upgraded version, I noticed that I could no longer add footnotes to my text. No way to prove whether it was just a bug in the software or a bad copy from the Far East.

Last night, a friend of mine brought over fresh copies of some of my suspect software. My friend is Dr. Saleh from Egypt, and he is married to a girl that is Swedish and English. He doesn't trust the local software, so he buys his copies from the United States. There is an idea growing here that manufactures and others are intentionally bugging software. The term is *computer virus*, and so far, I haven't recognized the bad bug. However, Dr. Saleh's diskettes proved to be the cure for my footnote problems.

The doctor has made several international trips with me and loves to trade jokes. He has a quite a repertoire of Irish jokes. The Irish jokes, and others are the local replacement for Aggie jokes. "Hey, Pat, tell me how many ten pound notes I got in me pocket, and I'll give you both of them!" Pat finally gave up guessing and got nothing.

Dr. Saleh brought his little girl with him recently, and I couldn't help but take her picture as she sat in Charlotte's lap. The little girl's name is Hannah. The picture doesn't do her justice, I'm afraid, because she is a beautiful child.

Charlotte is planning a departure from here in a couple of weeks. That is, we have been planning for her to go early to Austin, Texas, to look for a place for us to live when we leave here. It is a strange feeling not to have a home somewhere. It is a unique experience for both of us.

We have selected Austin as a place to look for a house because of a number of reasons. It is close to a military base, and we have medical and travel privileges with the military. The housing is still a good buy there, it seems. The climate should be agreeable to both us. Also, Austin is widely acclaimed as a very nice place to live. I can never remember a time in my life when I could just make a choice and live anywhere. It is a lot easier to decide when you have a job that dictates where you must live.

Can't finish this now, so to be continued.

Author's Note: Sorry about the reference here to pictures that are not shown. The quality was so bad due to the type of software used to capture the photos. They could not be used. Sorry about it, but I didn't want to change the text, so I chose to just leave the text as is or was as the case may be.

CAF Letter:
Riyadh, Saudi Arabia
October 4, 1988

Dear Nancy and Al,

This will be a short letter, but I wanted to let you know that we plan to be passing though Los Angeles from November 6 to the 10, and hopefully, we can get together while at Jean's. Looks like Monday, November 7 or Wednesday, November 9 would be a night we could all get together for dinner. If you are free one of those nights, would you please call Jean and let her know and arrange a time with her? Tuesday night is her bowling night, and we will probably go with her to say hello to my old bowling team.

We are leaving here next week going direct to Austin, Texas. James will depart on October 12, and I will follow a couple of days later. We will be looking at houses to buy, and James is making plans to go into partnership with an old friend and retired pilot from Exxon. They will have an aviation company doing contract flying and whatever else it leads to. Nancy, tell DV that when he gets his jet, James will be able to furnish pilots for him. Ken has been doing this for five years since his retirement, and the load is getting too much for one man to handle. He has delivered eight jets to France this year and stayed long enough to train the crew, so most likely, James will still be doing international flying as well as domestic.

James will be going to Savannah, Georgia, to start FlightSafety school on October 24 through the twenty-seventh or twenty-eighth. We will meet up in Houston, visit his family, and go to Tucson on November 4 and 5 to visit with Austin, and on to Los Angeles on November 6. We only have thirty days to do all this, and considering traveling time, we will be pinched again for time to visit.

We have made definite plans to return to the States in January at end of contract, unless they offer James the king's fortune to stay. We definitely believe that they will be cutting wages on the new contracts as that seems to be the trend throughout the Kingdom with other companies.

Al, if we buy a house, I will be needing to withdraw some money, and it probably would be prudent to take as little as necessary to go into escrow and request a ninety-day escrow so I can take advantage of the last quarter this year. Does that make sense? I have already paid estimated taxes for 1988 to both the State of California and Internal Revenue, so I won't be needing a large amount like I had to pay for 1987. It was more beneficial for James and me to file separate taxes.

This is about all for now, and we will be looking forward to seeing you, and hopefully James will have a story or two for you.

Surely will be good to breathe some of Los Angeles' smog again and see my new granddaughter Sara Elizabeth. Yes, Richard did it again!

See you soon.

Love,
Charlotte

CAF Letter:
Riyadh, Saudi Arabia
October 4, 1988

Dear Jan and Riley,

Thank you for forwarding those horrible tax papers. Seems that IRS just does not want us to have the extension allowed without penalty to citizens living outside the country. We are legally allowed sixty days extension if we request it and our CPA did. It will probably take a long time for them to give us back our money, but we dared not pay the penalties and interest until it can all be resolved. Oh well, that is just another bump in the road and on to more pleasant things.

James will be in Savannah from October 24 until October 27 or 28 at which time we will meet up in Houston for a visit. We were wondering if we could get together and go to Poppa's for dinner one night with you and the gang. Maybe Saturday night on October 29 would be a good time. We will hold that night open and will be in touch with you before then to see if that is a good evening and check with you on the time. James and I are leaving next week and going straight to Austin to look for a house to buy. It will probably be necessary for me to stay in Austin the week James goes to Savannah. I will be wearing myself out house hunting, so I may need some margaritas at Poppa's to recuperate.

I know that Edie is on vacation about now, but if you happen to talk to her, tell her our plans because it will aid her gold fever. Hopefully, she will be back to work the week we are in Houston, and I can see her then.

James is wondering if anyone will remember him when he comes back to Houston. He has been so homesick this year I have felt sorry for him at times. I know that he has enjoyed these two years in Saudi Arabia and has no regrets coming here, but he dearly misses his family and friends.

This year will be more fun for me than the last one was because my shoulder is not in pain anymore. It is just about as good as it was before my injury. My trip to the United States last time was a nightmare.

We are looking forward to seeing you soon.

Give Mary and Brent our love and keep a little for yourselves.

Love,
Charlotte

Dispatch:
Riyadh, Saudi Arabia
November 14, 1988

November Newsletter

Where was I? Oh yeah, well, I couldn't get it all down before I had to leave the Kingdom, so I'll try to finish this letter now that we are back and beginning the recuperation that must occur after thirty days or more of leave and schooling.

Charlotte left for the States almost a week before I did. Never mind why because if I told you why, then you still wouldn't understand. Getting free airline tickets here for the return to the United States is a subject worthy of separate treatment. At any rate, she arrived in Austin late one Friday night and called me on Sunday night to say she had found a house. That girl don't mess around. The house is in Austin as planned and is on the side of a hill. It is a four-bedroom, single-story house, and is constructed of Austin stone or otherwise known as white limestone. The new home is actually between three and four years old. That is a just right figure for me because the yard is already landscaped and fences built, etc. Well, every little bit helps, right?

The time spent in the States was divided between buying a house, attending the NBAA (National Business Aircraft Association) convention, going to FlightSafety International for my annual PIC (pilot in command) check, visiting my kids and Charlotte's kids, looking for furniture, looking at new cars, and eating some good US food. The time passed quickly. It was over almost before it started.

Charlotte rode British Airways from Riyadh to London, changed planes and airports, and then continued on nonstop to Houston. After four hours in Houston, she went on to Austin and checked into the Hyatt Regency all alone. I left Riyadh about a week later on Saudi Airlines for New York. I had to make a stop in Jeddah. They promised me I wouldn't have to change planes. Of course, they always promise that, come to think of it. I changed planes in Jeddah, which caused an hour delay, and finally we were off to New York. From Jeddah to New York is a twelve-hour leg, and that is a long leg. I asked the ticket agent for a center section seat on the 747 and not too far back of the bulkhead. The idea was to fold the seat dividers up and get some sleep since this was an all-night run. Well, the ticket man got it almost right. My seat was in the center section okay, and it was not far back of the bulkhead; in fact, it was the first row back, and the seat dividers don't fold up on that row. So it was going to be a sit straight up leg.

The first thing you do on a long flight is locate the screaming and kicking kids. The screaming kids usually are about three rows in front of or behind your seat. The kicking kids are always sitting right behind you and intermittently kick the back of your seat.

In this case, the screamers were also doing the kicking. The fatigue associated with such a flight is often mistakenly attributed to jet lag. If all the screaming and kicking kids were stored in a sealed and separated compartment, then the traveling public might soon forget the overused term of jet lag.

Well, that trip is now history. It's time to get back on the job. We returned on the November 12, and my first workday was the night of the fifteenth. One of the Gulfstream captains got fired while I was gone. It appears that he engineered his own dismissal. He wanted to leave before his contract was up, so he just refused to sign his time sheet. After several attempts to force him to sign, which failed, he was fired. I'll have to admit that he knew how the system worked, and he had played it like a fiddle since the first day he arrived.

Now the agent (GAMA) is feeling me out to see if I might extend an extra ninety days. The first effort is to make the remaining people take up the slack. The last effort is to seek replacements. Come to think of it, what's so different about that? GAMA has since formally notified me that my contract will be extended up to ninety days.

Three of the expatriate Gulfstream captains have signed a letter of intent. That is the same as signing a new contract, so they will be only two pilots short at the end of the contract on January 7, 1989. They can live with that. Several of the nurses and mechanics have refused to sign, so that will be the real shortage. The new contracts are being offered for less money, so it is not a wonder they want to leave.

We were shocked to learn on our return that Dr. Saleh's youngest daughter died while they were in Cairo. It was a crib death, I heard. She was less than six months old. I haven't talked to him yet, but it must be an extra burden of grief for a doctor to lose a loved one under such circumstances.

Well, still can't get in all finished, so to be continued.

JDF Letter:
Riyadh, Saudi Arabia
December 1, 1988

To: Major Shablan
        Director of Medevac
        Saudi Armed Forces Medical Services
        Riyadh, Saudi Arabia
From: Capt. James D. Fox, GII/GIII
Subject: Offering the Sale of Three Matched Gulfstream IIs

Dear Sir:

The enclosed information describes three Gulfstream IIs that are being offered for sale by Exxon Company USA of Houston, Texas. They have been owned and operated by Exxon since they were new. At the present time, the aircraft are being brokered by Jim Bath & Associates Inc. for the price of $11,500,000 (US dollars) for all three. These aircraft are priced somewhat lower than other GIIs on the market at the present time.

I am very familiar with these particular aircraft, having been a captain for Exxon Company USA since the aircraft were purchased new. In addition to the competitive pricing, these aircraft have several other unique advantages:

1. They have matched cockpits, i.e., equipment and flight instruments have been matched for ease of crew's inter-use.
2. They have matched paint schemes.
3. They have been excellently maintained according to Gulfstream factory computer requirements.
4. Good records of installations are available which are invaluable for any changes that may be made at a later date.
5. They can be purchased as a group or as single units.
6. Single owner and operator since new.

Please note the individual prices:

    #79 . . . . $3,700,000
    #89 . . . . $3,900,000
    #94 . . . . $3,900,000

As a further inducement to purchase all three as a group, please consider the following. Exxon has a large supply of Gulfstream spare parts for these aircraft, which includes one spare Rolls-Royce engine. A spare engine is almost unheard of. Although the sale price does not include these spare parts, it is certain that after these aircraft have been sold, Exxon will have no further need for the spare parts. I believe that some arrangement could be made so that the spares could be procured with the purchase of all three aircraft.

Please let me know of your interest as soon as possible.

Sincerely,
James D. Fox

Author's Note: *It never happened, and I couldn't understand why. Medevac needed the GIIs, the ones they had were wearing out, and maintenance was becoming a real problem. I may never know the reason or full set of reasons why the Saudis were not interested, but my friend Hakim told me later it was because I had made the deal too open and public. He told me that the deal should have been made in secret with General Hamid, and therefore some room would have been left for the baksheesh or kickback. Too many people knew the sale price! The more time passes makes me think that was good reasoning on Hakim's part.*

Dispatch:
Riyadh, Saudi Arabia
December 27, 1988

DECEMBER NEWSLETTER

Here I sit in the nude because they have been flying my britches off. As stated earlier, after returning from the States, I started back to work on the November 14, and on the sixteenth, I had a mission to New Haven, Connecticut. Never mind if you don't happen to know just exactly where New Haven is. The point is, it's a long way from Riyadh. We had airplane problems in the States, as usual, and returned in the wee hours of the twenty-first. Then on the twenty-fourth, I had a mission to pick up an RTA (road traffic accident) victim in Bangkok. This mission was at the special request of the king, so "theees eees no kidding, you guys" as my Mexican friends would say. We flew nonstop from Riyadh to Bangkok in eight hours and ten minutes.

That is a long flight for me. It was planned for six hours and fifty-four minutes, but just before we got to Burma, they decided against letting us fly through their airspace. Their airspace extends south over the ocean for quite a distance, and we had to fly around it. That exercise took about an hour and fifteen minutes. We landed in Bangkok at 0500 hours and were able to get a room just before 0800 hours at the Shangri-La Hotel. We returned to Riyadh on the twenty-sixth via Muscat on the Persian Gulf. If you're wondering, yes, we flew around Iran also.

On the twenty-seventh, I went to Kuwait for the day and returned. On the twenty-ninth, I went to Bahrain for a patient pickup. To that point, every trip had been an international, and then we got busy. It's no hill for a stepper, right, guys?

I've got to show you a facsimile of what I have been issuing to the "special" copilots that have negotiated the Gulfstream to the ground safely in one of the local sandstorms. They are produced in copies, which are suitable for framing and then reduced to wallet size. I sign them as a CFII/D. The CFII is the abbreviation for commercial flight instructor and instruments. The *D* is my own idea and stands for *dust*.

Well, I'll have to admit it's not a bad way to end a career. After all the dull trips that I have made in the past, these last two and a half years have been interesting. Too bad I couldn't have done it thirty years ago when I didn't need the sleep so bad. That's always the way with pilots though. When you are young and want the time and need the experience so bad, then you can't seem to get it. You scrounge every ride in every kind of aircraft that lands. You have lots of want to, but no money and no experience and no chance of getting any. Years later, when somehow by chance and the will of the Almighty, you find yourself loaded with time and experience but a lot less want to, then everyone is willing to give you more time and experience than you are willing to handle. Justice is not of this world.

Charlotte found some jewels from Thailand under the Christmas tree. There were also several kinds and colors of silk mixed in with some fancy embroidered slipcovers for chair cushions. She's gonna miss that kind of stuff when we get to Austin. Maybe not so much; however, we do have plans for keeping busy on the golf course, and we will travel to see our friends.

I don't know how this picture of one of the nurses that I fly with got in here, but maybe you would like to see some of the things that a fellow has to put up with on this job.

Our latest plans include stopping off in North Carolina on the way to Austin and picking out our furniture at the factory. We have never had to buy a complete set of furniture before. There is not a single stick of furniture for the house in Austin, so it's start from scratch.

I can hear the sounds now. The women are all giggling with glee, the men are all moaning with pain, and both are thinking of the prospect of what I just said. Don't forget, we also have to buy our transportation. We have no wheels.

On Christmas Day, I was told that GAMA (the corporation) has found a replacement for me. As soon as he arrives, then I will be released. Oh yeah? They say it will take a month or six weeks for him to get here. That means we may be on the way home by middle of February. Don't anyone hold your breath. Sometimes it doesn't happen as easy as that. There is so much politics and double-dealing going on, it's impossible to keep up with what is going to happen next. I've started rumor control here several times, but the locals don't know how to keep it going.

Well, a happy 1989 to everyone, and I hope it finds you well and leaves you the same way. Say hello to any of my friends you see and just ignore the rest. We'll see you soon.

December 29, 1988

Just when you think it's safe to go back into the water!

Before I could get this in the mail, guess what, another international mission. The night of the December 27, I was called out to go to Karachi, Pakistan. It seems that the deputy consul of Saudi Arabia for Pakistan was shot by an assassin when leaving the embassy after work this same day. Some photos clipped from the local newspaper are included here. Apparently, the victim was in charge of issuing work visas for the locals that wanted to work in Saudi Arabia. They think he was shot by some irate worker that had been turned down. The bullet passed through his neck from his left to right and cut the carotid artery and windpipe, but just missed the larynx. He drove for help with one finger in the bullet hole and described his assailant before passing out from loss of blood.

By special direction of the king, I left at 2200 hours (10:00 p.m.) on the way to Karachi. When first called, I couldn't think what country Karachi was in. You know, six months ago, I couldn't spell *expert*, and now I am one.

Riyadh to Karachi at forty-one thousand feet, and with 130 knots of tailwind, we made it in two hours and thirty minutes. We flew over Dhahran, Bahrain, Muscat, the Gulf of Oman, turned left as soon as we cleared the south tip of Iran, and with a straight shot across the Indian Ocean, there we were.

My copilot was Abid Khammash, one of the new ones, and he got some good experience in handling the radios that night. High frequency is the only thing available over the water, and every flight within a radius of a thousand nautical miles was on the same frequency. We were supposed to contact Karachi control fifteen minutes prior to entering their airspace. I called for thirty minutes, and they finally answered me five minutes after we crossed their FIR (airspace boundary). Abid said what are you going to do if they don't answer your call and give us permission to cross their FIR? I said, "Well, Abid, if they can't hear us coming, then maybe they can't hit us either." Abid slid a little deeper in his seat.

We lost two hours to crossing time zones, so it was 0230 hours (2:30 a.m.) when we landed. We had made the entire trip across several countries without a single piece of evidence to show we had prior permission. We left Riyadh with verbal assurances that it would be okay. My reaction was to fill the GIII up with 28,300 pounds of JetA1 and told the dispatcher that I would go as far as I could, and when anyone gave me any lip, then I'd hold for a radio call or return to Riyadh, depending on where I was and what the fuel supply was doing. He agreed and sent the king's blessing. The psychology here is that as soon as he gets me into the air, then the pressure is off him. It's just that simple.

On that particular night, the tracks were greased and we left as Saudi Airlines Flight 7977 (SV7977), an unscheduled airline flight. I once wanted to fly for the airlines, and I finally got to do it just a week before my sixtieth birthday. I wonder if anyone would believe that I went to work for an airline just a week before my sixtieth birthday with no previous airline experience.

We were prepared to pick up the patient and return. I had a crew of a copilot, an engineer, a flight nurse (picture above), and two doctors, but the decision had been made by the locals. He was not stable enough to leave. We spent the night, or what was left of it, in the Karachi Sheraton. It was very nice and very inexpensive. The airline paid for our rooms. A big breakfast for myself, with extra coffee for my copilot and a doctor, cost me only $4 US. It was really a little over $5, but airline captains get a 25 percent discount! I knew all the time those guys were making out.

We had a 1430 hours (2:30 p.m.) departure, but I had time to go shopping at the mall next to the hotel. I found matching leather jackets for Charlotte and me. Also found a leather flight bag like I've always wanted and a leather briefcase.

Leather products are cheap in the Middle East countries, but they are the cheapest in Pakistan.

We loaded the patient about fifteen minutes after 1500 hours (3:15 p.m.) without difficulty. It took the doctors and nurse about twenty-five minutes to prepare the patient for flight, so we taxied out at 1540 hours (3:40 p.m.). The doctors had requested that we keep the patient at sea level pressure because of his oxygen needs. So we really messed up everyone's minds when we repeatedly requested Flight Level 220 (twenty-two thousand feet) from ATC (air traffic control). That is just too low for a jet, but we insisted. They let us climb to FL220 but quickly changed their minds and said the minimum altitude would be twenty-four thousand feet due to restrictions. That gave us a cabin altitude of one thousand feet; the doctors agreed, so we flew across the Indian Ocean at twenty-four thousand feet. I had refueled purposely for the low-altitude flight fellows, so don't be second-guessing me. We had over a hundred knots on the nose even at the low altitude. I might say especially at the low altitude because it was greater there than at the higher flight levels, and I still landed in Riyadh after three hours and fifteen minutes with 13,000 pounds of fuel. I had averaged just about 5,000 pounds per hour at .78 Mach if you ever have to try that sort of a flight.

The rest is history. My flight engineer said he witnessed some serious baksheesh (a tip is an honorable translation) being handed over to the doctors while they were in the hospital in Karachi. The rest of the crew got nothing. My last trip to United States was at the bequest of the king, and the doctor on that trip got a gold Rolex watch. I got what the little colored boy left of the watermelon!

Oh well, we don't do it for the money anyway, do we, fellows? It's the glory. That's the reason for it all. Well, I missed that as well.

1989

The Beginning of the End

JDF Letter:
Riyadh, Saudi Arabia
January 3, 1989

To   Whom it May Concern
From: James D. Fox, Captain, GII, GIII
Subject: Recommendation for Khalid Al-Ghoraibi

Gentlemen:

It has been my experience to ride as both a captain and cocaptain with the above-named individual. He has demonstrated his abilities as pilot in command of the Gulfstream II and III to my satisfaction. Therefore, considering that he is in possession of a valid ATP rating in the Gulfstream II and III, I recommend that he be released to fly the Gulfstream II and III as pilot in command with selected copilots within the Kingdom of Saudi Arabia.

James D. Fox
Captain, Fixed Wing
Medevac

JDF Letter:
Riyadh, Saudi Arabia
January 3, 1989

To: Director of Medevac
        Manager of Flight Operations
From: Captain J. D. Fox, GII, GIII
        Medevac
Subject: Release of Captain Waleed Zahed for Domestic Flights

It is my pleasure to recommend that Captain Zahed be released for domestic flights with Medevac in the GII and GIII aircraft.

In my opinion, Captain Zahed is well trained and ready for his assignments within the Medevac flight operations.

Captain Zahed has continually shown an excellent attitude and aptitude for his profession. His knowledge of the aircraft and calm disposition in stressful situations has been demonstrated to me in the two and one half years (2 1/2) years of our association.

I believe that Captain Zahed will become recognized as one of the better captains in Medevac.

_____
Captain James D. Fox

CAF Letter:
Riyadh, Saudi Arabia
January 5, 1989

Dear Muriel,

Before I get busy at other things, I will write you a few lines of update.

Last Sunday, James got out of bed and was dizzy headed and felt woozy all day. That evening, one of the GAMA fellows dropped by, and James was telling him about it. In the meanwhile, James had called one of his doctor (Medevac) friend and left word on his answering machine to call him at his convenience. The doctor's call came through while the GAMA fellow was here and advised James to come to the hospital so he could check him out. The result was that they kept James all week until today to run tests to rule out the possibility of a slight stroke. The next day, he was feeling fine and has ever since. Today being Thursday and the Saudi weekend, they gave James a pass to come home and want him back Saturday morning at 7:00 a.m. to do another test then I think they will release him. So far, all tests have come back negative, but they have a lot of equipment and doctors, so they are doing a thorough job.

To back up and tell you about the notice we received about our departure. The decision was to invoke the ninety-day extension to April 7 or until they could find James's replacement. We have heard that they are signing up a captain back in the United States, and he should be here within thirty to forty-five days. Now, even though all of James's tests have come back negative, Medevac may not want him to fly for them anymore. We will just have to wait and see what happens in the next few days.

That is the trouble over here. We cannot plan anything and expect it to happen until the last minute. Austin is looking better every day.

James had made up his mind that to stay another ninety days would have been just that much more money and wasn't going to fight it.

We have a buyer for the car who wants it on January 15, so we will be without wheels for a while. I have sold my dishwasher and exercise bicycle. James has decided to sell his computer if he can make a deal with the one fellow that wants to buy it. The more we can get rid of, the less freight we will have to pay.

James received his retirement notice from the army, and they sent him a beautiful certificate and lapel button done in gold and green, so I got together with the sergeant that runs the US military dining room and planned a dinner party for him on his birthday to celebrate his retirement. When James went to the hospital, I had to call it all off. We may still have it later, but it won't be as much fun as the surprise would have been. I told James on his birthday what we had planned to do for him, and he was pleased anyway.

539

The enclosed clipping was one of the international trips James went on recently to Karachi, Pakistan. Yesterday, one of the Saudi captains was telling us that in the *Arab News* written in Arabic they showed James in the picture. James said he was in all of the pictures taken, but when they published our English Arab newspaper, probably they didn't want the airplane identified, so they cut the picture down, which blocked him out. I asked the Saudi captain for his newspaper, and he said he would give it to me, but you know, they will promise anything and not always keep their promise.

Like James has always said, things happen faster here than we can write it down, so after a while, we don't try to keep up.

James is home now and says he feels fine. We do not think there is anything seriously wrong, and if you don't hear from us, you will know that everything is okay. The doctor wants James on a weight loss diet, and I go along with that!

That is about all the news for now. We both send our love and hope you have a happy, healthy, and prosperous New Year.

Dispatch:
Riyadh, Saudi Arabia
January 15, 1989

JANUARY NEWSLETTER

JANUARY 15, 1989

I just might as well quit calling this my 1988 newsletter and call it an early release for 1989. On January 1, 1989, I got up feeling a little funny. I don't know what it feels like to be drunk, but I felt like other people look when they are drunk. You might say, my equilibrium was slightly disturbed. That was the second morning in a row that I had awakened with this strange feeling, and on the previous morning, the feeling had disappeared within the first couple of minutes after getting up and going to the bathroom. However, on the second morning, i.e., Sunday the first, the feeling didn't disappear but lingered all day. I called one of my doctor friends at the RKH hospital, and he advised me to come on down while the symptom was still active. Of course, by the time I got to the hospital, all the symptoms were gone. Nevertheless, a new doctor from the States, a neurologist, only three days in the Kingdom, made a snap diagnosis from across the room that I had suffered a TCA or a ministroke. There were two other doctors present that disagreed with him, but they couldn't tell me of their disagreement until later.

You know the doctor's oath and all that. I think it's called Hippocratic Oath, which is why one doctor can't say something ugly about another doctor even if he knows it's true.

They wouldn't let me leave the hospital for eight days. They ran more tests than I can recall. They did a CAT Scan, an MRI scan, an electrocardiogram (several times), an echo electrocardiogram, an electroencephalogram, an audio encephalogram, a visual encephalogram, and a carotid angiogram (or as Charlotte observed, a corroded angiogram) and took my blood pressure, temperature, and pulse every two hours. It was an examination that I couldn't have afforded to miss. The test results were all excellent and negative. The doctor had spent a week and a lot of Saudi money to try and prove his original diagnosis of a *ministroke.*

The radiologist is a friend of mine, and he told me that he noted a restriction in the cervical spine, which may have been caused a year ago when the Saudi bus ran into the rear of the GAMA Corporation's Pontiac and gave Charlotte and myself whiplash injuries. All the doctors agreed that it could have been just a virus! They released me from the hospital but said I'd have to come back later for the report. When I called them back for the report, they said that my file was lost!

541

In the meantime, Medevac is still carrying me on the sick list, and I won't fly until the report is finished. I may have made my last flight here. At any rate, I feel fine and have since I checked into the hospital.

While I was in the hospital, another Saudi diplomat was shot and killed in Bangkok. That is the third Saudi diplomat that has been shot in the last four months. They were all in charge of issuing work visas for the country where they were stationed. One was in Turkey, one was in Bangkok, and one in Pakistan. The natives must be getting restless.

I've got to hurry this into the mail before something else happens.

James and Charlotte
9306 Ashton Ridge
Austin, TX 78750
USA
512-335-9880

Author's Note:Sorry about the fact that I mentioned pictures, but they just didn't make the cut.

Dispatch:
Riyadh, Saudi Arabia
February 25, 1989

WELL, FELLOWS, IT'S ABOUT OVER—OVER HERE

As you have probably noted, the writing has slowed way down. The reasons are several. My contract expired on my birthday, January 3. I went to the hospital for eight days with a misdiagnosed malady, I failed then passed my flight physical, then passed my flight physical, and finally, I refused to fly any more trips!

That's right. I said enough is enough with this bunch of administrators and put my foot down. I'll go back over the points of not flying here any longer.

First, as Charlotte has already noted, I had a dizzy spell one morning, which was new to me, and ended up in the hospital for an exam. The doctor was a brand-new applicant from Los Angeles—his third day in the Kingdom. He made his diagnosis from across the room before he even got close enough to take my pulse.

He called it TEA (transient ischemic anemia). He freely admitted later that this condition and *all* of its symptoms disappeared within twenty-four hours. In other words, at that time, I was free of the symptoms of the condition he diagnosed. Then how could he be so sure of his diagnosis? Well, just to be sure, he admitted me to the hospital for some tests.

I was in the hospital for eight days, and they did all the tests they knew how to do and two final ones that they didn't know how to do. I had electrocardiographs—that's plural—including a twenty-four-hour one and an ultrasonic of my heart. You know, like pregnant women get of their unborn child, X-rays front and back, dye inserted into the main carotid artery, and on and on for eight days. On the last day, they decided to give me a second electroencephalogram (brain scan). That's right, the first one didn't show anything. Wait a minute, that doesn't sound right. Oh yes, that is it didn't show any abnormality. So a second scan was scheduled. It was called a video electroencephalogram. Don't worry, if you haven't heard of such a test, neither has anyone else.

First, they clipped all those little clips to my head, then they started flashing large and bright strobe lights into my propped open eyes. They varied the frequency but not the brightness of the strobes as the test continued, while this big fat nurse attempted to make sense of what she was reading on the output. Results: inconclusive.

Next, they replaced the strobe lights with an audio amplifier, which was fed by wire to a set of headphones that they fitted on me. The same fat nurse then began to feed various noises through the amplifier into my headset. The fat nurse was not wearing a headset; therefore, she couldn't hear or know the volume that she was feeding into my head. After just a few moments of that, I stood up and started pulling the headset and electrical clips from my head. I wadded them up into a ball and dropped them on the machine the fat nurse was supposed to be monitoring. She had her back to me and couldn't see my anguish as she flooded my hearing canals with sound too loud to tolerate. Neither did she see me get up nor start tearing the machine's input leads from my head. She was shocked to realize that I was leaving. Of course, there was a language barrier, but she got the idea. I was through with the test and her.

After returning to my room, I called the desk and told them to check me out. I was leaving the hospital whether they were ready or not. The new neurologist from Los Angeles was in my room very shortly. He acted as if my leaving was all part of his grand plan. After eight days of testing, he had found nothing wrong with my arteries, my heart, or my head; therefore, he was standing by his original diagnosis—TEA because he found no evidence whatsoever! How does that sound to you? Since TEA leaves no trace of ever having happened and since he found nothing, then his diagnosis was proven to be correct.

During the week in the hospital, I had begun to wonder why this neurologist from Los Angeles was working in Saudi Arabia. He must have been like the two doctors that recommended the train ride from Bangkok to Singapore or maybe like the pilots that had lost their jobs in the USA and had to come over here to find work.

Author's Note: During that same week that they were giving all tests, there was one test they didn't give me—a blood test. It would have shown them that I had developed class 2 diabetes! That wasn't discovered until March when I went to another first-class flight physical from an FAA-approved doctor in Houston.

You see, a doctor's diagnosis TEA means a mandatory loss of a pilot's medical and therefore is through with flying—forever. I don't know nor am I accusing the LA neurologist of purposely trying to ruin my flying carrier, but that was exactly what would happen if the FAA ever found out about his diagnosis. Fortunately, the left hand and right hand most times don't communicate in the KSA, so the FAA did not learn of the doctors' silly diagnosis.

However, I did need a renewal of my medical certificate, so I went to the doctor from Pakistan that was approved by Medevac. He failed me for a hearing problem! I was incensed. The Exxon Company had given me an audiometer test every year since I started flying for them, and I had always passed without a problem. The test is performed through headphones in a soundproof booth to protect the subject from *any* outside noise. The *Paky* doctor didn't have a soundproof booth, so he seated me next to an open window facing the freeway! Of course, I failed the test, so would anyone else under those conditions.

The reader may not know, so let me explain. After this, I got out the FAA regulations regarding the hearing test for a first-class medical exam. The audiometer is not required, but a provision is made for its use if available. To pass the test, the applicant needs only to be able to repeat a whispered set of words or numbers from ten feet behind his back. Does that sound like something less than scientific? Well, it's supposed to be. The whole idea behind the described test is to leave the outcome up to the doctor giving the test.

All of the above leaves me in a foreign country without a current medical, which means my pilot's license is no good. The Saudis are still trying to get me to agree to stay on and fly for them. I still don't want to stay for several reasons, but I need to get my medical renewed regardless.

Someone mentioned that Lockheed had an American or British doctor that was a certified FAA doctor. Calling Lockheed and talking to the doctor, I told him of the hearing test that the *Paky* doctor had failed me for, and he just laughed.

"Come on over, Captain Fox, and I'll give you first-class physical." I did. He did an exam, and I passed but didn't get a new medical because he was out of forms. That meant that he would have put them on order from the USA, and that might mean a six-month delay. Well, shoot, that wouldn't do me much good. He charged me for the physical anyway. Are you believing all this? I am really fed up with trying to get the simplest things done.

Major Shablan suggested another doctor for me to try. He was unwilling to pay for this third trip to get a medical. I said that I wasn't going to dish out another $125 on his new doctor. No, it was time for me to leave.

"Sorry, Major, I'm not staying."

"But, Captain, we have already received permission from the king to waive the rule against you flying for us past your sixtieth birthday."

You notice he said "we" when speaking about getting permission from the king. That meant that not he but someone else had made the request. This meant to me that no one had spoken to the king, and he was just going to never mind the so-called sixty-year-old rule. For all I knew, there was no such rule. Everyone knew that was a USA FAA regulation for airlines, and the Saudis like to pretend that they used the same regulations as the USA. Medevac was not an airline, so the same rule in the USA would not apply to Medevac anyway.

What I haven't told you is the Ken Brace has written me a couple of times asking me to come back and go into business with him. He has an idea that he and I could start a training school for corporate pilots in competition with FlightSafety and Simuflight. We were qualified to give the same training those companies gave in the Gulfstreams I, II, III and the Lockheed JetStars. An initial rating in those types cost around $25,000 per pilot. Ken figured we could do it for half that, and instead of a simulator, we would use the customer's aircraft. I got my JetStar rating before they had a simulator, so it sounded like a good deal that would work. So that's what I decided to do. Go back to the USA and become a training captain. I could be well paid there for what I had been doing for free here.

Author's Note: Two things, first our first customer was in Kansas City, and I made a demonstration trip with them and thought we had a deal. They called me later and said their insurance company would not cover any pilot unless he had received training from a factory-approved training facility. That was the hooker in Ken's idea. The insurance companies and the aircraft factories were in cahoots with who could give training to the pilots that were going to crew their airplanes. There were only two factory-approved training facilities in the world—FlightSafety in Marietta, Georgia, for the JetStar; in Savannah, Georgia, for the all Gulfstreams; and Simuflight in Dallas, Texas, for the Gulfstreams II and III. We were out of business before we started. More on this later.

I must say that my tour in the Kingdom of Saudi Arabia has been an education, and parts have been fun. All the copilots except a couple have been very friendly and fun to fly with. I have already described Eid, so there is no use including him in this dialogue anyway. Oh, did I mention that Eid finally got fired? Well, he did, and I never found out the reason. He just didn't show up one day, and the report from Bruce, our dispatcher, just said he was fired. He didn't offer any reason why. Everyone was so glad to see him go they didn't push for why.

And Khalid Al Ghoraibi will hate me forever, and there is nothing I can do about that. The hate is his problem, not mine.

It was a custom of mine with the new copilots to sit down after a flight and discuss anything that they might be curious about. I often made the remark to the copilots that if they saw me doing something with aircraft that they didn't understand, then they should ask why I did it, and I would explain it for them. I added that if I couldn't explain why I had done something, then I probably shouldn't be doing it. That was something new for them.

I had come to realize that the Saudis were very family oriented, and that was a good way to start a conversation about our just completed flight while having a cup of coffee.

"Well, Ibid, how's your family doing?"

"Oh, just fine, except my father died this last week."

The remark was made without emotion. It was just something that had happened.

"Oh, I'm sorry to hear that. How old was your father?"

"He was 104." Again, without emotion.

I did the math in my head quickly, and since I knew that Ibid was twenty-four, so that meant his father was eighty years old when Ibid was born.

I kept up my side of the conversation on the same emotional level that Ibid was in.

"Well, then I guess that you don't have any younger brothers, do you?"

"Yes, I have one that is younger than me."

It was a struggle, but I kept my reaction contained. Ibid's father was beginning to sound like an interesting person.

"Where did your father live, Ibid?"

"He was living in Cairo when he died."

"What did your father do for a living?"

"Oh, he was retired."

"Well, yes, I thought that he would be. I meant what did he do when he worked for a living?"

"He was an assassin." It was just a simple statement of fact, like he might have said his father was a carpenter or plumber. I was determined to keep any sign of the incredulous feeling that was welling up inside me.

"Oh, an assassin, I see. How did he get started in that business?" I asked the question just as if he had told me that he was camel herder.

"Well, when he was just a young man, he was living in Syria, and he went to work for a sheikh for a year, but at the end of the year, the sheikh refused to pay him. He felt that working was not going to get him anywhere, so he decided to be a highway robber."

Ibid's story was beginning to unfold without any prompting from me.

"He was doing pretty good as a robber. He had a gang, and they were doing okay, but then my father fell in with some bad guys."

The story was coming to an end when he told me that his father was posted out of his home country, and that was when he retired and moved his family to Cairo. I wanted to know more about his father's career but just didn't know how to ask the right questions without offending my copilot. Ibid was such a gentle type, it just seemed impolite to ask any more questions.

That's the kind of people that I was associated with.

Epilogue

Back in the USA

Leaving the Kingdom is an experience all of its own. We had to sell much of our household goods plus the Jaguar. The Jaguar was easy to get rid of because it was in good condition (the wreck didn't show), and selling the household goods was a great adventure for Charlotte. I didn't participate in that part of the sales.

It is common to post Leaving the Kingdom notices on the bulletin boards of all the supermarkets. As I have explained before, some of the supermarkets here have been renamed by the Americans as Safeway, A&P, and etc. The notices were a great idea by whoever thought it up. Friends advised Charlotte to be sure to put a beginning time and an ending time for her sale of household goods. She was also advised to mark each item with its sale price. What she wasn't told was that the price marked on the item was not expected by the buyer to be the final price. Charlotte marked the items without a thought for the haggling that had to be a part of the sale. This created some heated arguments. The locals expected—no, demanded—that a lesser price should be accepted for the sale.

Some women came just for the social side of the event. They came in and seated themselves on the couch or whatever and expected to be served refreshments. Charlotte told me that there were ladies that came and never even looked for anything to buy. To them, a Leaving the Kingdom was a social gathering.

Charlotte's dishwasher went quickly and for almost what I had paid for it in the first place. All that was left was either boxed up and shipped or left with friends to sell after we left.

I should have let Charlotte tell of her experience as a sales clerk. They came early and demanded to be let in. Then stayed late and had to be forced to leave, even though they were not buying anything. I should have stayed around and made a video.

At almost the last minute before our date of departure, Medevac had a trip to Boston, USA. Hey, we decided to take our ticket money and just ride in the GIII for free! It was a free ride, but not without adventure.

As usual, MS3 the GIII had a few maintenance issues that the crew was not told about. Well, what's new? The crew was going to be Rich Walker and Tom Bormann as captains and Hatim Bashir and Kamal as copilots, with Andrea and Elizabeth as nurses. The double crew was to be split, sort of, in our stopover in London. Rich Walker and Kamal were going to stay in London while the rest of the crew went on to Boston. Since we were going to be spending the night in London, I couldn't see the reason for sending two captains and two copilots. The nurses and engineers never get relief anyway.

We launched on Saturday the February 25, and without strong headwinds, we made the trip in 7:20. Halfway across the Mediterranean, Kamal came to the back where Charlotte and I were seated and wanted to tell me what was going on in the cockpit. Kamal had been riding jump seat and watching the captain. He wanted to report to me that Captain Walker was not flying economy cruise of .78 Mach but was hauling it along at .82 Mach. Kamal wanted to know if I thought we could make it nonstop at that speed. I had to remind Kamal that I was no longer an employee of Medevac and had no authority. I didn't have any authority over any other captain anyway.

"But, Captain Fox, what if we run out of fuel?"

"Kamal, don't worry about it. The worst that can happen is we might have to land in France, and that will just cost us a delay, but no danger. You will learn that some of the captains that you are going to fly with have procedures and practices that you haven't seen before. For example, Captain Walker always flies at the higher Mach number. He doesn't seem to care if he had to change his flight plan and land short."

"But, Captain, we will lose our slot in the system and may have to wait on the ground for hours or another day!"

"No, Kamal, ATC knows that we are a Medevac plane, and some of the captains take advantage of that and claim to have a medical emergency to get special handling. I know that Captain Hanno does that all the time. Don't worry about it. It's not the same as if we were crossing the Atlantic. Okay?"

I guess the time I had spent explaining things to Kamal had given him confidence in me, so he returned to the jump seat for more watching the crew.

A little while later, he came back again, this time just to share a cup of coffee and chat. He told me that he was going to have to get off and stay in London, but he sure would like to go across the Atlantic.

"Well, Kamal, why don't you?"

"Why don't I do what?"

"Go on across the Atlantic?"

"Oh, that's because I haven't been released yet as copilot to cross the Atlantic."

"Well, how are you ever going learn if you don't do it? There is no such thing as studying a book for the experience. Look, you're not going to cost company any extra money. They'll have to pay your expenses whether you're in London or Boston. You'll just be riding in the jump seat anyway, so you'll be able to see what Hatim does as a copilot, and that will just get you ready to be checked out for the Atlantic crossings in the future."

"Oh, that would be great, Captain Fox, do you think it will be all right?"

"Sure, it will be all right. If anyone asks you about it when you get back, just tell that I authorized it." That's how Kamal ended up in Boston.

Our overnight in London was without incident except that Kamal had one more job of tattling on the captain before we landed.

"Captain Fox, Captain Walker changed the power settings twenty-three times after he left altitude [cruise altitude]."

"Yeah, Kamal, we noticed it back here. The passengers always notice it, and Charlotte has made her comment already."

Sunday morning, we were on our way across the big blue water. About three quarters into the trip, Kamal came back to report that we were burning a lot more fuel from the right tank than the left. It looked like the right tank was going to run dry before we got to Boston. Tom Bormann had flight planned for Bangor, Maine, for our destination and with Boston as an alternate. In pilot talk, all instrument flights must show an alternate airport in case you can't land at your primary destination. The rules say that you must have enough fuel to make it to your destination, descend, and make an approach; if you make a missed approach, then you must have enough fuel to climb back to altitude and make it to your alternate. I have kind of simplified that rule, but the idea is that you must have more than enough fuel just to get to your planned destination.

When Tom told me he had filed for Bangor with Boston as an alternate, I just asked him why.

"What do you mean why?" asked Tom.

"Well, Tom, you see if the weather is clear and you have enough fuel to make it to Boston as an alternate, then why didn't you just file for Boston in the first place? You could have used Providence, Rhode Island as an alternate. It's near enough to Boston that you wouldn't even need the required forty-five minutes of extra fuel."

"I guess that I just didn't think of it."

"Well, Tom, you can still call ATC and change your flight plan. They won't mind. That's less work for them."

So now we are on our way to Boston, and Kamal tells me that the captain is not sure if we will have enough fuel in right tank for the right engine. It's time for me to go to the cockpit.

"Tom, what's the matter, you got a problem?"

"Well, yeah, maybe. I'm not sure we're going to have enough fuel in the right tank to make it in to Boston."

"Tom, I flew this bird not too long ago, and it was having trouble with that fuel gauge for the right tank. Sometimes it would just go bonkers and give what you knew was a false reading. Maybe you're just getting a false reading."

"Well, maybe, but I'm not sure."

"Tom, you know you can open the cross-feed valve and pump fuel from the left tank into the right tank, don't you?"

"Yeah, I know that, but to make that left tank fuel go over to the right tank, I'll have to turn off the fuel pump on the right side, and I might lose the right engine, and I don't want to do that."

"Tom, you don't turn off the right fuel pump until you have opened the cross-feed valve."

"Well, yeah, but I'm not sure."

"Well, then leave it alone, and if you run out of fuel on the right side, you'll lose that engine anyway. So what's the difference? I tell you what, Tom, I'm going back and sitting down. If you need me, then just call."

I went to the back, and ol' HZMS3 kept moving toward Boston. It wasn't long before I felt the cabin air pressure change. That should not happen. Back to the cockpit.

"Tom, what's going on? I felt the cabin pressure changing."

Hatim, the copilot, said, "Captain Fox, it might be that cargo door. We've had a lot of problems with that seal getting rolled when it's not closed right. It might be that seal that's losing air."

"Well, there are only a couple of choices. We can descend below fifteen thousand feet to an altitude that we can breathe or stay at this altitude, and everyone go on oxygen."

Tom reasoned that it might quit leaking air, so he decided to just wait and see what happened. I went back to my seat, facing Charlotte, and decided not to say anything until I had to. No use in her worrying.

The leak was slow enough so that cabin pressure held long enough for us to start our descent down for our destination. I went back to the cockpit and found that we were descending for Boston and with a clear sky. I could see the Boston Logan International Airport.

I spoke to the cockpit, "It looks like you guys are going to land to the south."

Tom spoke, "Yeah, that's right."

"Is that what they said on the ATIS[24]?"

"Yeah, sure."

---

[24]   ATIS: *Automatic Terminal Information Service* is a recorded statement of the current airport conditions, which also tells of the current runway in use. This recording is updated when there is any change in the weather or conditions.

"Well, that's funny. Of all the times I've been to Boston, I've never landed to the south. It has always been to the north."

Hatim spoke up, "Hey, we can just turn the ATIS on again and make sure."

Now the ATIS said that the active runway was to the north. Just a little mistake, but it was just another nail in Tom's coffin. It would not be the last.

On short final, the red warning light came on for the right fuel tank! The right gauge was correct. Fuel had been transferring from the right tank to the left tank. The captain should have noticed not only the decrease in the right tank, but an abnormal condition in the left tank. Of course, this was exacerbated by the known problem with the right fuel gauge. Medevac maintenance goes on.

Once on the ground and the captain and two copilots wanted to have a conference with me about what they should do.

"Hey, guys, I'm not working for this outfit anymore. You're going to have to make your own decisions."

"Yes, but, Captain Fox, we need for you to tell us what would you do if you were in charge here."

Tom had nothing to say. The Medevac copilots had already written him off as a captain. He was just the guy flying the airplane. I couldn't help but feel a little sorry for Tom. I knew his career with Medevac was over. He just didn't know it yet. My mind went back to the day I told him he had better learn to act like a captain—quick.

"Well, fellows, if it were up to me, I wouldn't take that airplane back across the Atlantic until that cargo door seal is repaired. You know if that seal decides to let go when you are at the point of no return, then there is good chance you're not going to make it. The faulty fuel gauge you can live with if you monitor the fuel level shown by the known good indicator. You must time the fuel burn with what you know the expected burn rate to be because you're down to that one gauge."

"Yeah, but who can we get to do the maintenance here?" said Hatim. Tom was still silent.

"Hatim, I'd first call Major Shablan and tell him the aircraft must be serviced before you can return. I would tell him that I wouldn't bring it back until repaired. Then I'd suggest that he call Gulfstream in Savannah and see if they have slot for you."

"Captain Fox, will you stay with us until we see what's going to happen?" urged Hatim. Kamal said nothing but was listening intently.

"Hey, guys, we've got an airline to catch. We're going home."

"Please, Captain Fox, do this for me," Hatim pleaded in almost a whisper.

"Okay, you make the call to Shablan, and let's see what happens."

We spent the night while the telephoning was going on. This delayed our departure until after lunch the next day. Major Shablan tried for a maintenance slot in Savannah and was told that there would be three-week delay. They did find an approved maintenance facility in Chicago that would take them right away.

So that was it. HZMS3 was now going to Chicago for the cure, and Charlotte and I were leaving for Oklahoma City. Why Oklahoma City? Well, that's where we pick up a new 1989 Crown Victoria from her nephew-in-law, the Ford dealer there. We had bought a house in Austin, Texas, but had no wheels or furniture.

Charlotte and I often recall the last time we saw the flight crew there in Boston. Hatim and Kamal were showing tears in their eyes as they waved good-bye and watched us leave the hotel on the up escalator. It made me feel like I was deserting them, but I had done all I could do while I was there to do it. The mother bird must have similar feelings when she solos her little ones.

Author's Note: It was not the last that I heard from the crew. Now remember, there were three men and two women in Chicago with nothing to do but see the sights. They are sending me postcards almost every day, telling me of their adventures. One day, they decided to visit Canada; it wasn't that far. Going to Canada was easy, but they found that their visas would not allow them to enter the USA from Canada. Now they were locked out. Well, they finally convinced the border guards to let them back into the USA, but now they are out of money, and they are going to be in Chicago another week or ten days! It was nothing new for me. The Saudi copilots were always running out of money, and they found that Captain Fox was an easy touch.

The copilots often called me after that whenever they were in the USA, and once I flew over to meet them in Houston. Waleed Zahed was flying captain, and Linda Baud was his nurse. They were in HZMS3 again.

None of my Saudi friends have called me since 9/11.

CPSIA information can be obtained at www.ICGtesting.com
Printed in the USA
LVOW120413120213

319641LV00003BA/7/P